Old Money, New South

THE SPIRIT OF CHATTANOOGA

CHATTANOOGA
HISTORICAL
FOUNDATION

P.O. Box 2053, Chattanooga, TN 37409
www.historyofchattanooga.com

OLD MONEY
New South

THE SPIRIT OF CHATTANOOGA

Dean W. Arnold

Title: Old Money, New South: the Spirit of Chattanooga
Author: Dean W. Arnold
Copyright: Chattanooga Historical Foundation, 2006

ISBN: 0-9749076-3-4
Library of Congress Control Number: 2006900200

Cover Design: Rob Tipton, Hilton Head, SC
Cover Background Photo: Doug Barnette, Chattanooga, TN
Title Wording: Shaun LaRose
Typesetting: Dan Bockert
Copy editors: Jared Brewer, Dan Bockert

To purchase this book ($24.95 + $3.00 shipping), make check payable to Chattanooga Historical Foundation and send to:

Chattanooga Historical Foundation
P.O. Box 2053
Chattanooga, TN 37409

For online orders and further information:
www.OldMoneyNewSouth.com

To contact the author: dean@deanarnold.org

CONTENTS

Foreword

Note to Readers

FOREWORD

I remember well the day in 1969 when I gained a commission to paint President Richard Nixon. I was 31 years old, and the moment permanently shaped my career. For Dean Arnold, this extraordinary project is likely to do the same.

I know Dean well. We have worked together and been good friends for a decade. I was honored to be asked to join several of many fine artists in Chattanooga to provide artwork for his book.

Dean Arnold the journalist has been after the true story for as long as I have known him. He brings the vantage point of a neutral observer, born elsewhere. He says what he thinks but is willing to admit when he is wrong. He has marched for causes, muckraked, and generally stirred things up.

Over the years I have observed a profound evolution. Learning and experiences have made him more seasoned, deliberate and benevolent. A widely read historian, he made himself an authority on the Native Americans in this area. Intrigued that Chattanooga became one of the wealthiest communities and reached the top of the list in charitable giving, he resolved to interview fifty of its most prominent individuals and learn about their ancestors. He knew it would make a good story. Of great significance was their almost universal willingness to level with him. Largely because of this fact—and Dean's long established objectivity—the following pages have the unmistakable ring of truth. The resulting work has become a phenomenon, the definitive book that unravels the curious web of this city.

The narrative is enormously interesting, particularly to me. When I came here from Memphis to attend the University in 1962, I landed right in the middle of this local stage and its principal cast of characters. For five years I was one of the students who ministered to the youth at First Presbyterian Church, and my young parishioners were the scions of these high achievers. Several of them grew to become interviewees for this book. I wish there had been such a manual back then so I could have understood and appreciated the interesting, even historic, situation I had stumbled upon.

I have painted the portraits of a number of those interviewed, including prep school founder J. Park McCallie and Ambassador, Senator, and Labor Secretary Bill Brock. When painting these local legends or great names like Nixon, Princess Grace, or Norman Vincent Peale, one of my great privileges is to sit and converse with such people. My favorite question is, "Tell me how all this came to be?" In this way I appreciate how much Dean Arnold must have enjoyed his interviews. The answers are riveting. You will enjoy every page of his masterful storytelling.

Gordon Wetmore
Chairman
Portrait Society of America

This book provides a portrait rather than a chronology. Although all events cited are true and accurate, the writer employs the artist's brush more than the historian's fact sheet to create an illuminating image of the city.

For this reason, the reader should prepare for various jumps from past to present and from one time period to another. Also, this portrait may be a bit impressionistic. Every detail could not possibly be covered. Only a sampling of key characters and families were placed on the pallet, just enough to capture the image. Therefore, many worthy and deserving names are necessarily left for later treatments.

The first chapter is significantly longer than the others and serves as a summary for the rest of the book. Each chapter, including the first, is basically self-contained and can be enjoyed apart from the others. However, this is not recommended, as certain themes throughout the text build upon each other. But it is helpful to understand that each chapter serves as a fresh angle in exploring the uniqueness of Chattanooga, and they sometimes cover the same historical ground from different perspectives. In some places the same wording is used.

The author makes no attempt to conceal his own religious and philosophical perspective, but he does strive to represent other worldviews fairly, and also to admit—even laugh—at the weaknesses in his own. Generally, readers are left to draw their own conclusions. Likewise, they are encouraged to draw the author in sketch form. He is still on a journey.

Dean W. Arnold
Chattanooga, Tennessee

For my father,

Jack Arnold

1935–2005

Old Money, New South

THE SPIRIT OF CHATTANOOGA

Artist: Gordon Wetmore

CHAPTER ONE

The Spirit of the Fathers

Chattanooga has always been a mystery.

Some say it means "eagle's nest" or "mountains looking at each other." Perhaps it means "fish bringer" or "hawk's hole." Currently, the most oft-repeated definition for the ancient Native American word is "rock coming to a point." This would suggest the point of Lookout Mountain, an eminence rich with symbolism overlooking the city and the Tennessee River. But experts generally discount the theory. It is a mystery I have always wanted to unravel.

The Cherokees said they didn't know what the word *Chattanooga* meant. They got it from the people before them. Who they were and what they did on this soil is currently known by only a handful of people. Those facts were uncovered after the publishing of the most recent histories written 25 years ago. This book will let readers in on the secret.[1]*

Another mystery ripe for unveiling is the essence or spirit of the city. What makes it unique? What defines its special personality—or, as one local leader calls it, the spiritual DNA of the city?

We know a Southern city can be contrasted with a Northern town. But what distinguishes Chattanooga from its Southern counterparts and from its neighbors two hours away—Atlanta, Birmingham, Knoxville, and Nashville? What makes Chattanooga unique?

---

[1] An asterisk (*) indicates further commentary with the endnote at the back of the book. An endnote without an asterisk provides only the source or sources used in the previous section.

This quest applies for every city. For Chattanooga, there are a number of distinct characteristics to discuss regarding geographic realities, ethnic heritage, race relations, religious trends, Christian influence, Native American roots, Civil War fallout, and historical tragedies. But in trying to find the essence of this city, you soon learn that nothing defines Chattanooga quite like the phenomenon of its longtime leading families. Though active in the town's agenda, they remain quiet and private. Many are unusually wealthy. Most live on Lookout Mountain. They have a reputation for being generous and civic minded, yet elusive. They will tell you they care deeply about their community, but they are accused by some of wielding too powerful of an influence. Sometimes the indictments of "the power structure" from those in "the valley" are bitter.

It is a polite town where names are not usually named in the press. "It is not considered good taste to brag about one's ancestors," writes Helen McDonald Exum, but, thankfully, she does a little naming and bragging for her friends through an unlikely medium: her *Chattanooga Cook Book*. Featured in forty-five newspapers, thousands of folks bought it to learn the leading families' recipes along with Helen's historical tidbits and family anecdotes.

Right after explaining the secret to Mrs. Bill Brock's egg casserole (Mr. Brock was a U.S. Senator and later became Reagan's Secretary of Labor), Helen praises "the children and children's children down to six and seven generations" who could live anywhere but "choose the same pleasant hills and valleys of Chattanooga that their fathers loved."

She names the Luptons, Kruesis, Smartts, Brocks, Friersons, Keys, Longs, Williamses, Rawlingses, and Pattens "who have all given character, color, stability, and leadership to our city."[2]

To locals, the names are almost legend. John T. Lupton II—"Jack" for short— sold the world's largest Coca-Cola bottling company for $1.4 billion in 1986. He is "more of a symbol than a real person," writes *Chattanooga Times* publisher Paul Neely in, perhaps, the only article ever published that attempts to assess the man. "Depending on the view, he can be gentle, modest, courtly, and reflective. He can also be rude, domineering, profane, and impatient."

"I love Chattanooga. I desperately love Chattanooga," Lupton said in one of the few articles quoting him. He backed it up with a $25 million gift to the local university. Before that he raised nearly $50 million for an aquarium that is generally credited for reviving the city's prospects. His family has given hundreds of millions more to charities over the years.

Lupton has no time for critics. "If what I'm doing is good enough, I don't give a damn what they think," he said. And he has no time for class envy. "As long as there is an earth, there will be rich, medium, and poor people. There ain't anything that anyone can do about it."[3]

POWERFUL NAMES

>–+→–०–←+–<

Since I had resolved to discern the spirit of Chattanooga, I determined to interview as many of the leading families as possible.

The time had come to separate truth from myth. Lupton was an obvious choice for an interview since the newspaper back in 1988 had named him the most powerful man in the city. But maybe I needed to warm up first. I would approach Lupton later and start with number two on the list: Scott L. Probasco, Jr.[4]

Though his name is not cited in the 1969 cookbook, Probasco is distantly related to every family listed by Helen. (Yes, every single one.) He goes by Scotty. His trademark is a traditional bow tie, Honduran cigars, and the comment, "Great work!" Although his position as chairman of SunTrust Bank seemed intimidating, I felt a little better about my chances for a friendly interview.

However, my chances could diminish depending on Mr. Probasco's opinion of my journalistic enterprise over the past eight years (or did he even know about it?) A four-page news publication sent to 8,500 fax machines each week, the *Chattanooga Fax* reported on people and events sometimes left untouched by the rest of the media. Though I did not attack character, I did criticize actions and ideas of local leaders—like the mayor's attempt to take over the privately owned water company, backed by a financial report from high-profile accountant and civic booster, Joe Decosimo.

The sons of Joe Decosimo didn't like my reporting. "Have you ever considered that you must earn the right to be taken seriously in this community?" asked Tom Decosimo, in a terse letter-to-the-editor for the *Chattanooga Fax*.

Certain residents in the valley had warned me of the difficulty of breaking into the town's inner circle. Tom's brother, Fred Decosimo, sent me a letter the same day: "Now, I sincerely ask you to ask yourself, 'What have I given to this community?' From where I sit the answer will not be long. My father does not have the time to answer…you, but I have neither his patience nor his grace."[5]

I was hoping Scotty would have the patience and the grace. As it turns out, the second most powerful man in Chattanooga is also related to the Decosimos. Probasco accepted my request by letter for an interview. But I did not mention the *Chattanooga Fax*.

As I took the elevator to his office on the 16th floor of the SunTrust Bank building, I glanced at my notes. I had done my homework on Probasco and his background. His grandfather founded American National Bank, formerly called the Bank of Chattanooga. Harry Probasco hailed from Ohio, and his ancestors sailed to America from Holland. In all my interviews, I wanted to learn how much these leaders knew about their heritage. I love genealogy, and from my own experience, I knew that while one kid may know a lot, that may not be true for the others. Does it matter? Does one reach community leadership and success through the knowledge of your heritage? Can it trickle down even if you are not consciously aware of it? Does it really make a difference? And how much does Scott Probasco really know about his background?

The elevator doors opened, and I walked through the foyer toward his office. In my peripheral vision, I could see the stately boardroom of the Benwood Foundation. Directly in front of me stood a giant portrait of Benjamin Franklin Thomas, father of the Coca-Cola bottling empire and the man responsible for the Benwood Foundation.

In 1899, when Ben Thomas and his friend Joe Whitehead, both young, struggling attorneys, traveled to Atlanta to ask Asa Candler for the rights to bottle Coca-Cola, the soda fountain drink was already popular in the South. The successful Candler did not want to bother with the untested and unreliable bottling concept. However, he finally relented after much pestering. They must buy the syrup only from him, he said, and could keep the remaining profits. Candler thought nothing would come of it. Legend says he sold the rights for one token dollar. The contract does not mention it. The two Chattanoogans had a friend wire money for the train ride home.

Over time, more bottles were sold than fountain drinks. Due to Thomas's vision, Coca-Cola became the most widely distributed product in the world and the second most recognizable word on earth. The first is "okay."[6*]

Candler came to regret the offhand agreement and later sued to regain total ownership of the empire. He was unsuccessful. Dozens of fortunes were made, most by people living in Chattanooga or by Chattanoogans like Whitehead who moved to states across America with the rights granted by Thomas to "bottle gold." One historian called it "a license to print money." Chattanooga became a city with a lopsided percentage of millionaires. With the growth, philanthropy, and cultural development that resulted, the late Ben Thomas today makes a strong claim as a father to the city.

It is uncertain how many millions Harry Scott Probasco made as it remains uncertain how much his grandson is now worth, but the boardroom for his bank and for Thomas's Coca-Cola Bottling Company, the bank's single largest depositor, were one and the same for many years. Thomas

Ben Thomas

took a turn as bank president, and Thomas's nephew and heir, George Hunter, served as best man in Scott Probasco, Sr.'s wedding.[7]

So I was a bit more intimidated when I approached Scott Jr.'s door for the interview. A 1962 article in my notes described him as tall, handsome, friendly, gregarious, trim, athletic, and in excellent health. When he rose from his desk and dashed over to greet me, that is exactly what I saw. Only his gray hair betrayed the 40-year gap. He seemed like a really friendly guy.

He would have put my fears to rest immediately, but another article quoted a friend who warned not to let Probasco's wild enthusiasm fool you. "That's purposeful on his part. He's a good judge of character. He's very shrewd...always thinking, even when he's acting crazy."[8]

The office was not so intimidating. It could not have been much more than 250 square feet. Two humidors containing large cigars sat on the desk. The furniture was older, suggesting a legendary Scotch trait among Chattanooga's elite for ridiculous frugality mixed with an unusual generosity in the right situation.

"Would you like a cigar?" he asked.

"Yes, sir."

I have always loved cigars but generally cannot afford the really good ones. He handed me a long, fragrant stick of tobacco.

"Here. Live it up."

Then he brought out a special tool.

"Here, let me cut that in two for both of us."

Half as confident in the likelihood of a lengthy interview, I started with family history. The tape was rolling.

"You don't have to know everything," I assured him. "A lot of people don't know much about their ancestors."

"Yeah."

"Don't feel pressured."

"Hmmm. Well...the Probascos came from Madrid, Spain," he said, "and then they moved to Holland, and they stayed there and took on the Netherlands culture. It went from *Probasko* to *Probasco*. But then they left Holland, actually in the late, very late 16th century and landed in Maryland."

"Okay."

Not a bad start.

"Do you have Spanish blood?" I asked.

"I wish there was. I wouldn't have this terrible light skin. That's just where the Probasco name started."

I've always loved names and their meanings. However, according to the *Dictionary of American Family Names*, the etymology of *Probasco* is unclear.

"My grandparents on both sides were basically Scotch or English," he said. "We've got some old diaries and an old Bible where it was written in the front cover of the thing."

"Where was your grandfather from?"

He said Harry Probasco came down from Cincinnati, after a brief stint of banking in Indiana, following the Civil War. There is still a fountain in Cincinnati with Probasco written on it. "A lot of people from that area came down to Chattanooga in the early '80s. They were all carpetbaggers, really."

"How many generations back were the Probascos in banking?"

"According to the Bible, there were money-changers in Madrid."

It was an odd statement. Upon further questioning, he told me some of those non-Spanish Probascos in Spain were Jewish.

"I'm probably tenth generation in the banking business. I don't know. You want a Coke?"

We drank a Coke. He told me his desk and furniture belonged to his father, as did the Scott L. Probasco nameplate. His father served as a major in World War I and a colonel in World War II.

"He was skinny and tall like me, and he was a hell of a man. A natural leader, totally different from me. I'm like my mother—door's open, happy. He was . . . people were all scared of my dad."

When young Scotty returned from Dartmouth one Christmas his Dad sat him down.

"'Well, son, what are you thinking about doing?' Dad said. This is silly, but at the time I was thinking about becoming a preacher. But I kept going [along at the bank] and I said, 'Well, you know, Dad, I'd really like to work at the bank.'"

"He was at this desk looking at me. I'll never forget it. 'Good,' he said. 'Good,' he said."

Scotty had already worked a few years as a teller, and his father made sure he did not confuse a banker with a clerk.

"'But son, I want you to be more than a banker,' he said. 'I want you to be a businessman.'"

"Yes, sir."

"Now, do you know the definition of a businessman?"

"No, sir."

"Son, the definition of a businessman is a man who gets the business."

"Yes, sir."

So, he got the business, Scotty said. He told me he never knew his grandfather, who died a year before he was born. But Harry and Scott Sr., age 21, had a similar conversation over a beer in Germany.

Scott Probasco, Sr.

"What do you want to do, Scotty?"

"Well, Papa (he called him *Papa*), I'd like to start a trust company in Chattanooga."

Scott Sr. was young, but ten generations of banking experience allows you to quickly learn the difference between a banker—what his dad did—and a trust company, which manages estates and resulting fortunes that are inherited. It was a good business for the town that started Coke bottling.

"Well, fine son," said Harry. "I'll help you."[9]*

The Godfather of Chattanooga

Scotty and Scotty Sr. were both only sons. And Scotty's dad and granddad were both devout members of the First Presbyterian Church, a "new school" Presbyterian congregation that allowed for "enthusiasm" in worship, a way of saying they were a bit more serious. It was also the city's largest, most prestigious, and influential church. Harry was chairman of the Building Committee in 1904.

A page in the First Presbyterian history book displays a couple of large, old, black-and-white photos of the two men most responsible for the major Presbyterian edifice on McCallie Avenue. They were arguably the two most powerful men in the city at the time. Sitting side by side on the same page, they look almost alike—around the same age, both with thick mustaches, both in suits, and both looking slightly to their right. The only difference is that John T. Lupton wears a long tie. Harry Scott Probasco wears a bow tie.[10] Not much has changed in a hundred years.

"He is one of the most modest of men regarding his vast interests," writes Zella Armstrong regarding Jack Lupton's grandfather in her "Who's Who" history of Hamilton County. She credits Lupton with "almost literally obeying the Biblical injunction not to let the left hand know what the right hand doth."

These were devout and committed Christian families who were serious, like the church. They took their cues from the even more serious and luminary figure behind the First Presbyterian phenomenon, the man who offered the dedicatory prayer when the building was completed. The Reverend Thomas Hooke McCallie led such a faithful regimen of family devotions (which included his two sons who founded the McCallie School in 1905) that it stuck for over a century. His great-grandson, Allen McCallie, currently an attorney at the Miller & Martin firm, told me their morning family devotions growing up were non-negotiable. But those later generations had it easy. Thomas Hooke's dad required strict twice-a-day sessions in the 1850s.[11]

The original John T. Lupton caught Ben Thomas at just the right time in 1900, when he needed significant capital for his bottling opportunity. Lupton soon surpassed Thomas in wealth and became one of the richest men in the country. His Lyndhurst mansion in Riverview, 34,000 square feet, provided visual evidence for the gigantic fortune. Reputed to be the largest in the South, the showplace by the river boasted ten bedrooms, twelve baths, an indoor swimming pool and bowling alley, as well as a ballroom with a pipe organ.

If Thomas is the father, then J. T. Lupton is the godfather of Chattanooga millionaires. Downtown developer Tommy Lupton, Jack's cousin, explained to me how J. T. Lupton kept it in the family. "There were fourteen kids in my daddy's family: eight brothers and six sisters. J.T. almost hired every one of them, or their husbands, and then gave them different Coca-Cola territories to run. Uncle Charlie took over Texas. Uncle Fred was New Orleans, and Frank Harrison's daddy was North Carolina, and things of that sort."

Mr. and Mrs. J. T. Lupton's only child, Cartter Lupton, was eleven when they moved into the mansion. When he died in 1977, his $200 million estate was the largest ever probated in the South. By comparison, Howard Hughes's estate the same year was $168 million. Similar to Hughes, Cartter Lupton was considered a recluse.[12]

"He was very shy, very shy," Scott Probasco told me. "I mean, you'd never see him at the Mountain City Club or anything like that, but he was a devout, strong Christian. Very conservative. Very generous. I really loved him. He was a whale of a guy."

Probasco often approached Cartter for his various fundraising efforts. "If he said to me, 'Scotty, that's the biggest fool thing I ever heard,' then I knew he was hooked. One time he didn't raise cane, and I didn't get any money."

When Cartter came of age, he left Lyndhurst for another home in Riverview, right next door to Scott Probasco, Sr.'s columned mansion. Scotty's sister Alice was a childhood friend with little Jack. They corresponded when Jack went off to the South Pacific in World War II. Four years later, they were married.[13]

Scotty Probasco is Jack Lupton's brother-in-law. In a city where many families are intermarried, this particular merging of families is key. For the purposes of this book, I call it the Lupton-Probasco axis (see chart on next page). There are several other axes to discuss, but Lupton-Probasco is central and is connected to all the others.

The Obligation of Nobility

In her cookbook, Helen certainly did not overlook Alice Lupton, the glue for Lupton-Probasco. Alice provides Helen with a recipe for Sapphire Fish Chowder

LUPTON ~ PROBASCO

Coca-Cola Bottling's wealthiest owner since it began in 1899. In the 20th century, no family owned more Coke bottling assets than the Luptons.

JOHN T. LUPTON
1862–1933

Founder of American National Bank (now SunTrust), also called the "Coca-Cola Bank." His board comprised the city's most powerful men.

HARRY SCOTT PROBASCO
1858–1919

CARTTER LUPTON
1899–1977

SCOTT L. PROBASCO, SR.
b. 1890–1962

JOHN T. (JACK) LUPTON II
b. 1926

= *(MARRIAGE)*

ALICE PROBASCO LUPTON

⇨ *(BROTHER)*

SCOTT L. (SCOTTY) PROBASCO, JR.
b. 1928

served with either cornbread or crackers. "It depends on whether there was any fish left from the meal before, what is in the refrigerator and so on," writes Helen. That is because Jack likes to fish at their North Carolina getaway in the Blue Ridge Mountains and often experiments with trout on the grill. "He likes to use olive oil, butter, lemon juice and spiced Parisienne seasoning."[14]

He likes fish. "I remember when Jack dreamed the idea that we needed an aquarium here," said Judge Walter Williams, a high-profile African American who once publicly criticized Jack but now has close ties to Lupton-Probasco. "Everyone said this is just a rich man wanting a fish tank. I couldn't really see the rewards of an aquarium."

Williams also publicly criticized the metro government effort pushed by Lupton and chaired by Probasco to merge the city and county. "I said I'd meet this fellow who was trying to push this down our throat, and I'll debate him anytime, anywhere—on the mountain, in the valley. I was throwing things his way, I guess, but he just called me on the phone.

"We need to have lunch," said Lupton. "Why haven't we ever met?"

"Well, you never called me."

Jack took him to lunch at the Chattanooga Golf & Country Club, and a lifelong friendship ensued.

Lupton called him one day from somewhere in the Carolinas. "He just called me and started laughing on the phone and said, 'I bet you don't know who this is. This is Jack Lupton. Well, goodbye.' He does that kind of stuff."

In sharp contrast to families like the Luptons, Williams told me he never had any interaction with his father or grandfather and knows little to nothing about them. Many in the black community share this same disconnectedness with previous generations. The judge, however, found a way to overcome those obstacles. He was elected in a citywide race—twice—making him a leading African American in a city where blacks are not the majority. He has come to appreciate the differences between his and Lupton's backgrounds.

"People who don't have resources—we are sometimes limited in our thinking. I was dealing with the rent payment for my office and all that. People who have resources can sit back and dream 30 years and that kind of stuff."

The newspaper article that listed Lupton's name as most powerful said it another way: "Inherited with that aristocratic name was the notion of *noblesse oblige*, an altruistic idea." The French phrase means "obligation of the nobility," a sense of duty by the more fortunate to lead and provide for the community.

Tommy Lupton has his own way of articulating it. "I came in with some prestige and a good name, and I was always conscious of the responsibility to live up to that name." In high school they called him "Tommy Baylor of Lupton School," even

Walter Williams

though his side of the family doesn't share Jack's level of wealth. "You always live under the awning that someone in your family had some money, so that kind of rubs on you because you've got the same name. I told Jack one time, if I'm going to live up to his name, he better help me out a little bit."

Williams accepts the local nobility as neither good nor bad, or perhaps, both good and bad. He notes that blacks have gone places that poor whites could never go. He says the division is more about money than race. "Chattanooga is a money town, and it's about the haves and have-nots, and there's nothing negative...well, I say negative...it's, you know, Chattanooga has always been more of a controlled city. Unlike in Atlanta. Unlike Birmingham,...Montgomery, or Nashville. There are identifiable names that clearly run Chattanooga. Names run it now [and] clearly in the past ran Chattanooga. There's no question. The Luptons are clearly a powerful family in this community, and in a positive way."

"Chattanooga is fortunate to have people like Jack Lupton and the Scotty Probascos and the others...who have tried to move the city forward, because if we had not had them, we would still be just an old dirty city. But we are clearly the shining star, in my judgment, of the New South."

The Renaissance

Very few today disagree with Judge Williams's assessment of the renewal. In 1969, the federal government declared Chattanooga "the most polluted city in the United States." Walter Cronkite announced it on the evening news. But 30 years later, *U.S. News & World Report* listed Chattanooga as one of three North American cities with the ability to clean up their act and "make things work."

A *Parade Magazine* cover story agreed: "Once a prime example for everything wrong with America, Chattanooga (pop. 148,820) is turning itself around. The city's formerly decaying riverfront is now a thriving entertainment district that draws more than a million visitors a year. Electric buses, locally built and free to ride, ply downtown streets. A not-for-profit group is spending more than $30 million a year on housing. And the air, once so dirty you had to drive with your headlights on at noon, is clean again."[15]

Tommy Lupton

"Mother used to take her little white hankerchief out and wipe my nose and it would just be black from soot and stuff like that," said Scotty Probasco. "I mean, it really was pretty dirty. And we're in a bowl, so we really had to try to clean the place up."

He explained that after World War II, Chattanooga became the eighth largest manufacturing center in the country—and

14

number one in the South by some accounts. Over 80,000 manufacturing jobs were provided by textile companies and by foundries that worked with iron and metal castings. One book listed over 1,500 products manufactured in "The Dynamo of Dixie," the nickname for the powerful but dirty city.[16]

To fight the pollution, a group of private citizens met with the Chamber of Commerce and with government officials in 1969 to form the Air Pollution Control Board. A former chemistry professor at Harvard was chosen as chairman. Dr. Marion Barnes, president of Covenant College, had recently moved the fledgling school from St. Louis to a new Lookout Mountain campus at the old "Castle in the Clouds" hotel.

Now deceased, Dr. Barnes was 90 years old when I interviewed him. It took a while for him to open the door after I rang the bell. I heard him whistling loudly as he hobbled to the door with his walker. The small, cheery widower kept whistling as we moved to sit on the couch.

"I think after the polluters saw that we were going to handle them fairly and honestly, they began to get in line and cooperate," Dr. Barnes told me. He whistled a little while longer, delaying the interview.

He informed "the polluters" he was required to enforce the law. "I know that every one of you is in violation," he told them.

Barnes said the companies were accustomed to "playing politics" and skirting the law. The academician soon got a taste of the political game.

"One day I got a letter from Chicago. It was the president of Velsicol Chemical Company. Velsicol was one of our worst polluters."

The two knew each other. They both had held high positions at a major chemical company headquartered in St. Louis. "He says, 'Our company likes to support activities that are positive in a community where we are going to work,' and he says, 'We understand that you are doing a good job as chairman of the Air Pollution Control Board.'"

The Velsicol president's letter included a check—a large contribution to Dr. Barnes's college, which was struggling and in desperate need of funds.

Dr. Barnes called the chairman of his college. "Unless you overrule me, I'm returning this money right away."

After three days, the college chairman called back and agreed.

"So I returned the money and that's the last I heard of it. I even suggested to this guy that if he really wants to help the city, give the money to the Red Cross. And thank you so much for thinking of Covenant College."

He started whistling again. It suddenly occurred to me he was actually regaining his breath. Instead of forcing his guests to hear awkward and desperate gasps for air, he whistled while he breathed in and out.

"That information got out to the community, of course," he added, "And the polluters knew that I wasn't available for funds and therefore they'll have to get in line, I guess. After seven years, everybody towed the line, and we didn't have to run anybody off."

But if environmental regulations did not chase away manufacturers, then national and international economic trends did. During the 1970s, Chattanooga lost tens of thousands of manufacturing jobs, including those provided by its largest employer, Combustion Engineering, which made nuclear reactors.

This downturn helped inspire Jack Lupton to take action through his charitable foundation, which he named Lyndhurst, after his grandfather's mansion. The city "damned near died on us," said Lupton.[17]

Jack Murrah, who serves today as the Lyndhurst Foundation president, agreed. "When Chattanooga hit the skids really bad with the big recession in '82, I think Jack [Lupton] became even more committed to using the foundation to reinvigorate the city." Murrah was hired initially by Rick Montague in 1977, and the two worked together for a decade while Lupton demanded innovation and change for the city.

"Jack Lupton was able to impossibly, perversely cut against the grain," said Montague. "I was given a mandate, and I liked the mandate very much—to see how we could really have an impact on Chattanooga."

This mandate led to the creation of Chattanooga Venture, the entity behind the planning and visioning process involving large doses of public opinion that has now put Chattanooga on the map. (Later chapters cover in detail the chain of events, beginning with Lupton's change in mindset to the creation of Chattanooga

CHATTANOOGA
"The Dynamo of Dixie"

The smokestacks of the **Dynamo of Dixie** are proudly displayed
in this poster distributed by a local bank (c. 1950).

Venture.) This "Chattanooga Process," as some city planners around the country now call it, is what caused *U.S. News* to say Chattanooga can "make things work." Chattanooga Venture recruited a board from every sector of the community in 1984 and conducted a group planning process called Vision 2000, asking citizens to dream of what Chattanooga could become by the year 2000. Over 1,700 people attended a series of meetings during a twenty-week period. A "Commitment Portfolio" identified forty goals and 223 projects to improve life in the city. Ten years later, Chattanooga Venture boasted thirty-seven of the goals to be totally or partially fulfilled. In 1993, ReVision 2000, chaired by community college president Jim Catanzaro, gathered 2,600 people for a similar process. Many of those ideas can be seen on the downtown landscape today.[18]

Miles of parks and riverwalks now surround each side of the Tennessee River. The downtown saw major urban renewal. A world-class aquarium and the Children's Discovery Museum are in walking distance to a renovated bridge—said to be the world's largest pedestrian walkway—which connects foot travelers to another multimillion dollar open-spaced park across the river with public carousel and performance theater. Building on the momentum, Mayor Bob Corker launched another $120 million campaign to expand the Hunter Museum of Art and add riverfront parks and developments.

The accolades reached a rather extraordinary level when *National Public Radio* included Chattanooga in a month-long feature of five great cities. The other four were Paris, London, Amsterdam, and Chicago. *NPR* elaborated: "Chattanooga possesses a strong sense of community, a handsome natural landscape, and seems to have the ability to solve problems that are often daunting to bigger cities."[19]

Lupton is always a driving force behind the high standards of progress and even the push to include the public. "You can't do much better than what we've tried to do as far as representation is concerned," he said, in reference to the sixty-member board governing Chattanooga Venture. "We've put the representatives of . . . well . . . what haven't we put? Maybe the indigent or the lame."

However, his own personal involvement is more tricky. "I want to play my part properly so I don't overexpose myself and they say, 'This is Lupton's deal.'"

"And we have planned like hell. But if you don't plan it, you go down there and build catfish shacks on the river. So you did have to go through an ultra-long and an ultra-boring—as far as the community was concerned—session after session. And then, when you finally come up with the thing, everybody's saying, 'Well now, let's by God do something!'"

Lupton uses religious language for his decision to immerse himself in Chattanooga, calling it his "awakening." Others refer to the "reborn American city."[20] The most common term used is *renaissance*, meaning renewal. The Renaissance Commons sits

(Top) **Pollution** blocks the view of Lookout Mountain from Missionary Ridge. Today, the view is clear in the daytime and evening.

on one side of the river in the Bluff View Art District. The new Renaissance Park, part of Mayor Corker's major expansion, lies just across the wide stream.

The major guru for renaissance does not consider himself a religious man, but Stroud Watson, winner of the prestigious Thomas Jefferson Award for Public Architecture granted by the American Institute of Architects, speaks with all the zeal and idealism of a true believer.

"I want to see a diverse variety of people come to live together in close proximity—to live, work, and play at one place or in a series of connected places that builds a community spirit, a sharing spirit, and a sense of responsibility to each other."

Watson has plenty of personal experience with and without community. He lived in a commune in Arizona in the '60s, spent five years by himself on a boat in the Carribbean during the '70s, and later observed the positive and negative aspects of a socialized planning process he helped oversee in London. He is founder of the University of Tennessee's Urban Design Program and now Chattanooga's Design Studio. His fascinating story and interview are told in Chapter Three.

For the bespectacled Watson, who dresses casually in a suede vest and sports long gray hair and a stringy white beard, it is all about the common good. No individual, whether a builder or just a student, should be any better than the whole. This idea of common good, he says, goes back to the Constitution.

"The intent of life, liberty, and the pursuit of happiness was not the pursuit of happiness of you, individually. It was the pursuit of happiness of the community as a whole."

Watson's Urban Design Center was initially funded by the Coca-Cola–endowed Lyndhurst Foundation, as was Chattanooga Venture, Vision 2000, and ReVision 2000. The Benwood Foundation, created by original bottler Ben Thomas, also played a role. Jack Lupton himself, at one time the world's largest independent bottler, gave multiple millions of his personal funds to several of the projects, most notably the $45 million Tennessee Aquarium.

If any one person gets credit for Chattanooga's renaissance, Jack Lupton is the name usually mentioned. "He's the cornerstone of it all," says another multigenerational Chattanoogan, Albert Waterhouse, of Waterhouse Public Relations. He refers to him only as Mr. Lupton. "I want to be careful. To me, people like him are kind of godlike."

"It's hard to describe the impact of that one building on this city and its future," said Frank Brock, another multigenerational citizen, who admits he was initially skeptical of Lupton's aquarium. Even the *Tennessee Encyclopedia of History & Culture* assigns Lyndhurst and the Luptons with "much of the credit for this transformation."[21]

Chattanooga after the renaissance

About the only longtime Chattanoogan who chose to clarify the extent of Lupton's impact is his brother-in-law, Scotty, who chaired the Chamber of Commerce when air pollution cleanup and community turnaround efforts first started to gain momentum in the 1960s, a decade before Lupton found his stride.

"He should have started sooner," Scotty told me. "He was just slow getting there. When he got there, he came on the scene strong. So if he had started sooner, we'd have just been that much further ahead."

A City with Foundations . . .

Probasco is also willing to talk about his brother-in-law's religious leanings. "He's got a great heart. He really does. Surprisingly, he's not swell-headed or cocky, but he's never had to work for a board or anything. He owned all their businesses, so he has never reported to anybody, including God. I mean, I have a little problem there."

"I love him. He was the best man at my wedding. He's the closest thing I had to a brother, really, so I love him."

Eventually, it was indeed Jack Lupton and his affiliated foundations that ushered in the city's renewal. For a century, Chattanooga has enjoyed more foundation money than the rest of Tennessee combined, more than giant neighbor Atlanta, and more than most other major cities in the United States. (A foundation is a legal entity that allows someone's millions to be taxed less if set aside for strictly charitable purposes. The donor appoints a board of directors to oversee the giving.) The Lyndhurst Foundation's assets totaled $163 million in 1999, and Benwood's were $103 million. Chattanooga cannot be understood outside the context of the Coca-Cola bottling fortune.

However, in 1999, Lyndhurst was merely the third largest foundation in Chattanooga. Another fortune also defines Chattanooga: the Provident Insurance company, started a century ago by the devout Presbyterian Thomas Maclellan. On the list of foundations mentioned above, the Maclellan Foundation, with $607 million in assets, sits at the top. Its sister foundation, the R. J. Maclellan Charitable Trust, with $236 million in reserves, takes second place. (The two have since merged and the assets of all foundations on the list have fluctuated since 1999.) Maclellan money also launched the Dora Maclellan Brown Foundation, the Hugh and Charlotte Maclellan Foundation, and the Helen Tipton Trust, among others.[22]

While the Coke fortune is larger, it is spread out among a number of individuals and not placed primarily into tax-exempt foundations. The Maclellan family, however, has directed much of their fortune toward charitable giving, particularly toward nonprofit Christian and family-oriented ventures.

The Maclellan Foundation thinks globally. According to *Philanthropy* magazine, the foundation houses the world's largest searchable database of Christian funding opportunities, "an evangelical e-Bay for those looking for new ways to give." The database involves a cutting-edge "global mapping" procedure for 156 countries and lists statistics in each country regarding evangelism, church planting, pastoral training, leadership development, and giving trends.

The Maclellan Foundation was the primary funder for the "JESUS" film, lip-synched into 900 languages, which has been shown to over four billion people. Also, it has played a strategic role in 150 countries by helping with starting new churches, each led by indigenous pastors. The foundation cites 1.5 million new church starts in the last ten years—beyond the expected number of new churches—and projects 13 million more over the next decade.

This Chattanooga philanthropic entity is one of the largest Christian foundations in America and the largest foundation in the world for strategic giving to world missions. All of the major Christian organizations in the country beat a path to Chattanooga on a regular basis to visit this foundation. The country's five largest ministries have preset appointments every six months.[23]

However, the foundation's chairman, Hugh O. Maclellan, Jr., does not have the largest ego around. Usually he is the one in a meeting acting like a secretary by taking copious notes on scraps of paper. He is also known for driving used cars all his life—perhaps a minivan or an old Honda Accord.

"That was Bob Maclellan, Hugh Maclellan, Sr., their father. That's just the way they were," said Frank Brock. "And they were the big money."

"Hugh O. views everything in terms of churches planted and missionaries put into the field," said Sam Smartt, a colleague in Christian fundraising. "He is just unbelievably frugal." Like many, Smartt loves to give this descendent of wealthy Scots a fraternal ribbing. "Try to get Hugh O. to pick up a lunch."

Hugh O.'s son, Chris, tells the story of how his father called the kids over one day to show them his new car. "It was a used car with a new paint job."[24]

I interviewed Maclellan in his office at the four-story Market Center across from the Read House. The Lupton Company occupies the top floor. I took the elevator to the third floor where a large three-dimensional map of the world greets you on the wall next to the Maclellan coat of arms which says "Think On." Thomas Maclellan's relics—a plaid tie, eyeglasses, and a book to Thomas from a Scottish temperance society—sit below a sign which says "The Maclellan Family Foundations" and "Generous Giving: Experience the Joy." Clocks showing the time from various cities around the world grace the foyer and boardroom.

Hugh O. Maclellan, Jr. is of average height and weight, in his early 60s with a distinguished presence but with no airs. He talks about his personal struggles with pride and greed, but his surprising vulnerability suggests the opposite.

"What you tend to do when people come to you with hat in hand is get all puffed up," said Maclellan, when asked how a person deals with people always currying favor. "We don't deal with it very well," he said. He often refers to his ongoing struggle with the three P's of life: power, position, and prestige. "I think that businessmen are especially hung up on the three P's, and it keeps us from being effective."[25]

MACLELLAN

Founder of Provident Insurance Company and a zealous Presbyterian, Maclellan made a covenant with God in Scotland before moving to Chattanooga.

THOMAS MACLELLAN
1837–1916

ROBERT J. MACLELLAN

HUGH O. MACLELLAN, SR.

HUGH O. MACLELLAN, JR.
b. 1940

"Nancy and I started giving a minimum of 70 percent of our income. For us, that's not sacrificial in any way. Any middle-class Christian giving 10 percent to his church is more sacrificial than we are. Nevertheless, that 70 percent broke the power of money in our lives. It taught us to live on a semi-budget. We don't have airplanes, boats, and second homes."

Maclellan launched an international organization called Generous Giving, unique to the world, which encourages other Christians, particularly very wealthy ones, to give away their assets. This arm of the Maclellan vision is run by Hugh O's son-in-law, Daryl Heald, who told *Philanthropy* magazine that he and his wife, Cathy, started giving away 10 percent when they were married 17 years ago. They have now upped that to 55 percent of their gross income.

Hugh O. Maclellan talks about giving away more than just income. He says he believes there is such a thing as over-accumulation. "Five years ago, we gave away 14 percent of our assets, and there was such joy in that."

As a result, he decided to give 15 percent the next year. When his stock fell, he pulled back. "I became preoccupied with holding on to my money. When I'm in trouble, I always hold on to my money."

"I made a mistake of saying, 'Lord, I'll give it to you when the stock reaches sixty dollars per share.' It hit fifty-six and then went down to twelve...I should have been giving capital as the stock price increased."

Besides promoting generous giving, the copious note-taker also advocates keeping a written journal and rising early every morning to pray and read the Bible.

What drives Hugh O. Maclellan? He points to his early conversion at a Billy Graham Crusade, to being discipled in Christian living at age 30, and to the influence of Christian leaders and authors such as Bill Bright, Gordon McDonald, and Ron Blue. However, one should never omit from the list the fact that his great-grandfather, Thomas Maclellan, made a covenant with God at age 20 in the town of Blairgowrie, Scotland, before moving to Chattanooga and founding Provident Insurance Company.

"I now fall down before thy throne and prostrate myself at thy footstool," Chattanooga's first Maclellan vowed in 1857. "I renounce...my worldly possessions, my time, and my influence over others, all to be used entirely for thy glory." The written covenant goes on for two pages and says at the end: "And if this should fall into the hands of any of my friends when I am in the dust, may they make the engagement their own [and] partake in all the blessings of Thy covenant through Jesus, the great Mediator of it." He rededicated himself to his covenant, adding another paragraph, at age 50 and again at age 70.[26]

Five generations later, UnumProvident Corporation is the largest disability insurance company in the world. Hugh O. Maclellan, Jr. is joined on the Maclellan

Foundation board by his sons Chris and Dan and daughter Cathy. Thomas Maclellan has over ten progeny in Chattanooga age 40 and below, most of them minors. The name is safe for now.

The etymology of *Maclellan* is "son of Gille Faolan," an Irish missionary to the Scots in 630 A.D. Faolan's icon depicts him refusing the cup at table to show his disdain for worldly things. St. Faolan and three companions were murdered along the side of the road by bandits on Halloween, 655 A.D.[27]

Two Giving Strategies

The giving patterns of Jack Lupton and Hugh O. Maclellan differ significantly. Scotty Probasco, a devout Presbyterian and a member of UnumProvident's Board of Directors, serves as a bridge to the two fortunes.

"Jack is not as religious," said Judge Walter Williams. "I mean, he's a Presbyterian, but Scotty is truly religious."

Actually, Jack Lupton is not Presbyterian. In 1967, he ended several generations of Lupton tradition and left First Presbyterian Church. Later in the book, several pages will detail the events and ramifications surrounding that move.

The Lyndhurst Foundation gives its millions largely to local efforts such as Chattanooga Neighborhood Enterprises and the downtown development group RiverCity Company. They also were key funders for the strategic planning group Chattanooga Venture, which spawned Vision 2000.

While the Maclellan Foundation emphasizes world missions, nearly 30 percent of its giving is allocated to ventures in Chattanooga, including $1 million to the waterfront expansion. It also funds abstinence education, efforts against drugs and hardcore pornography, and the Chattanooga Resource Foundation, which networks the hundreds of churches and ministries in the area.

In 1997, the Maclellan Foundation helped birth First Things First which networks 235 public and private agencies to battle divorce rates and illegitimacy through educating couples. "We realized that the city's biggest problem was the breakdown of the family and that every part of Chattanooga was being affected by it," said Maclellan.

According to one Health and Human Services official, this Chattanooga public-private partnership now serves as a model for the country, providing technical assistance to hundreds of communities as part of President George W. Bush's Healthy Marriage Initiative. *Crisis Magazine* reported a 17 percent drop in the divorce rate in Hamilton County, Tennessee, from 1996 to 2000, as well as a 21 percent drop in unmarried teenagers having babies.[28]

"If you want to change behavior, and ultimately society, you must change the heart," said Maclellan. (The name *Hugh* means "heart" or "spirit.")

In support of education, the Luptons have funded the Baylor School and Girls Preparatory School (GPS), and the Lupton-endowed Lyndhurst Foundation also generously funds the Public Education Foundation. Historically, the Maclellans have funded the McCallie School and later the Chattanooga Christian School. They have also funded character education in the public schools.

Of course, no book on Chattanooga would be complete without lengthy commentary on the city's three nationally prominent prep schools—Baylor, McCallie and GPS—or its forty-five or more private parochial schools, and its largest private institution, the Chattanooga Christian School. Chattanooga has one of the country's highest, if not the very highest, percentages of students attending private schools as well as the highest percentage of dollars invested in those institutions. Later chapters will cover in detail this unique characteristic along with its complex relationship to the ongoing challenge to reform and improve public education.

Unified Fortunes

Although the two primary forces influencing Chattanooga now chart somewhat different courses, the two visions coexisted in harmony through the first half of the 20th century. The credit goes to the phenomenon of First Presbyterian Church.

Former Covenant College President Frank Brock is a multigenerational Presbyterian and also heir to the Brock Candy legacy, the South's largest candy manufacturer. He told me in his interview that most of Chattanooga's CEOs in the days of manufacturing grandeur were Presbyterian.

"I'll bet you anything 75 percent of the big money in Chattanooga has come out of the Presbyterian Church.... You'd be hardpressed to find a town where there's a stronger Presbyterian heritage than Chattanooga."

Chattanooga Resource Foundation President Doug Daugherty agrees. "You can't understand the early history of Chattanooga without looking at First Presbyterian Church. You just can't do it."

Brock points to the unusual leadership of Dr. James Fowle, the pastor from 1929 to 1967, as the key reason for Chattanooga's unusual philanthropy.

"Dr. Fowle was well-known for saying, 'All the money is right here in this room,'" said Brock. "And he was not ashamed to hit on the big ones in his church—the Benwood Foundation, which was Scotty Probasco, and the Maclellan Foundation, which was Bob Maclellan. They were the two big foundations, and Dr. Fowle had huge impact with both of them, and with every moneyed person in town...Cartter Lupton...You know, all the moneyed people."

"And he was very ecumenical in a sense. He would see benefit for raising money for the Hunter Museum or for the YMCA. He didn't think that Christians

Dr. James Fowle

gave only to Christian things. He looked at everything as being part of the responsibility we have to build a better community."

The seventh baby Dr. Fowle baptized was Scotty Probasco.

"His famous thing was when he would get ten or fifteen of us in a room," Probasco told me. Scotty gave an example of a $4 million effort to expand the YMCA headed by Fowle. "'Well, now, the money is right here in this room,' Dr. Fowle would say. 'Now, Scotty, what are you going to give me, boy?'"

"'Well, Dr. Fowle, I guess, you know, $10,000?' Sometimes it would be more." (According to one account, Fowle gave back a $20,000 check, saying, "You can do better than that.")

Scotty continued. "'Now Joe, what are you going to give me?' he'd say. You know, we about had it raised before we'd get started."

Dr. Fowle served on the board of trustees for Princeton Theological Seminary. He was also a benefactor for Chattanooga's university, for which he raised over $18 million during his lifetime. That figure in today's dollars is closer to $150 million.[29]

Most of Chattanooga's leaders and leading families have a rich Presbyterian heritage. Once again, Scott Probasco leads the way. According to an old pre–Civil War diary, both sides of his family were Presbyterian as far as he can trace. He tells a story about an ancestor named Gillespie, a Presbyterian father who drafted the denomination's founding documents.

"They were praying in Scotland, writing the Shorter Catechism, and they were arguing on the first question of who is God. They called on him to lead a prayer, to help them, you know. He started off, 'Oh God, our God infinite, eternal' and right on. They stopped the prayer and said, 'That's the answer to our prayer!' And that's the answer to the second catechism. . . It's just these little things you hear."

I researched it. The surrounding facts are true. George Gillespie, who was Probasco's fifth great-grandfather, actually moderated the 1648 General Assembly and is credited with drafting Chapter One of the denomination's constitution, the *Westminster Confession of Faith*, which contains the same words as the fourth answer in the *Shorter Catechism*: "God is a spirit: infinite, eternal and unchangeable in his being, wisdom, power, holiness, justice, goodness and truth."[30]

The history of First Presbyterian Church in Chattanooga is almost the same as the history of the city itself. With little exception since the city's founding, the majority of leaders in the community have been leaders at "First Pres." Chattanooga's first Mayor, James Berry, was an elder at First Presbyterian Church, as was nearly every succeeding mayor for the next 26 years.

It can even be argued that First Pres is the oldest institution in the area, older than either the city or county governments. Two missionaries from the Brainerd Mission to the Cherokees, founded in 1817 at what is today Eastgate Mall, joined the rest of the Brainerd missionaries on the Trail of Tears with their fellow Cherokee Christian brothers in 1838, but Ainsworth Blunt and John Vail got sick along the way and returned to Chattanooga. The two established the First Presbyterian Church the same year. Chattanooga's first church is an imperfect but valid continuation of the Brainerd Mission and a continuation of the first white-governed community in the area.

History has not always been kind to missionaries of the 19th century, and sometimes the criticism is valid when the missionaries' Good News included not just the Gospel but the message of European culture as well. Nevertheless, most of the Cherokees received these missionaries with great joy and gratitude. Also, the missionaries provided farming tools, housing, education, and much training in agriculture, animal husbandry, and many other practical skills. A large majority of the Cherokee nation converted to Christianity, drafting a Constitution in 1827 requiring belief in God by elected officials and acknowledging "with humility and gratitude the Goodness of the Sovereign Ruler of the universe."[31]

Life was difficult for the missionaries. John and Julia Vail buried several young children in the Brainerd cemetery. The day Julia arrived at the mission she was sick and remained so much of the time. She survived the events of the Trail of Tears in 1838 but became an invalid during the years her husband founded First Presbyterian.

A member of the Cherokee Supreme Court in Tulsa, Oklahoma, says tribal members today owe a great debt to the missionaries. "This debt is recognized by . . . reflecting on the hardships which these men and women of God faced—and overcame," writes Justice Philip H. Viles, a descendent of missionaries and Cherokees.

The Brainerd missionaries were idealists of the highest sort. The initial church membership was composed of one-third whites, one-third Cherokees, and one-third African Americans. On September 28, 1817, these members entered into a "Covenant of the Brainerd Church," vowing to "associate to each other as brethren" and "promising to watch over each other in Christian love." The missionaries despised slavery and all racism. "O when will this highly favored land, called the land of freedom, cease to traffic in human blood!" wrote one missionary in 1819. They believed their work on Chattanooga soil would affect later generations, referring to "this ground which is consecrated to God by the prayers, tears and charities of his people."[32]

The Missionary Spirit

In a real sense, the idealistic spirit of these missionaries to Chattanooga remains with the city to this day. The Maclellan-funded Chattanooga Resource Foundation advances an idealistic mission: "Chattanooga, a city for God." When this group commissioned the nation's leading religious pollster, the Barna Group in Seattle, they learned that Chattanooga had the highest percentage of people, in medium to large cities, who claim to be "born again" Christians. Another poll showed that 98 percent of the population believed in God. An outside marketing firm asked a question regarding favorite pastimes, and the activity of "reading the Bible" received the most votes.[33]

The Lyndhurst Foundation strives for another idealistic vision more secular or Jeffersonian. "If you believe diverse neighborhoods are a good thing, that means you hope to have a culture that will allow people who are conservative Christians, liberal Christians, Catholics, Protestants, Islamic, and Buddhist people all living in the same neighborhood," said Jack Murrah. "[You hope] they can be good neighbors with each other and actually have deep respect for each other's separate lives and separate ways of seeing the world."

That idealism shows in modern efforts to spur economic growth. Building on the accomplishment of cleaning up the air, Chattanooga dubbed itself "The Environmental City" in the 1990s and described itself as "sustainable," an environmental buzzword. "It has made a kind of secular religion of achieving sustainability," wrote the Leadership Academy at the University of Maryland. In 1995, Chattanooga hosted the President's Council on Sustainable Development. Vice President Al Gore pointed to Chattanooga as a model for the world; if a company wants to be sustainable, "Chattanooga is the place to come," Gore said. Chattanooga received a "Best Practices" award for its sustainable efforts from the United Nations at a ceremony in Istanbul, Turkey, in 1996.

One specific plan called for economic growth to result from companies locating to an "eco-industrial park" in the city's Southside. Jack Lupton espoused the idea along with building a nearby stadium. "I believe that stadium shows people we mean business. And if we can do that, I believe we'll take a big step towards an environmental-friendly industrial district and new places for people to live downtown, with grocery stores and little shops and the things we desperately need in our community," he said.

The Maryland Academy cheered Chattanooga's efforts to use zero-emission buses. "They found only one U.S. manufacturer. The solution? The community started its own company (Advanced Vehicle Systems). Now it has the largest electric bus fleet in the country, and it is the largest manufacturer."[34]

The vision for sustainability, however, did not help Chattanooga's struggle for economic stimulus and population growth. By 2002, manufacturing jobs continued to free-fall while the median pay of workers fell below 20 percent of the national average, worse than every neighboring city: Atlanta, Knoxville, Nashville, Birmingham, and Huntsville, Alabama. The population of the city actually dropped twelve percent from 1980 to 2000 while surrounding cities grew steadily.

The moniker of Environmental City eventually was dropped, and a new strategy of identifying strategic business "clusters" was adopted. The company manufacturing electric buses filed for bankruptcy.

The Chairman of the Hamilton County Commission, economics professor Richard Casavant, criticized the national award-winning efforts for urban design. "Everything that works downtown has been subsidized." The planners are "well intentioned," he said, but "planned economies don't work. Neither do planned societies. We're trying to plan the development of real estate." City Councilwoman Marti Rutherford blasted community leaders for treating Chattanooga like "an old woman who we keep putting more and more makeup on." She identified "agents of the power structure" whose various public-private partnerships failed to stimulate growth.

"The same people have for years developed one plan after another, and we are still waiting for a plan that will work," she said.[35]

Soon, the Chamber-sponsored efforts of Harvard Professor Michael Porter to identify strategic economic clusters—the Chattanooga Regional Growth Initiative—also lost steam. Chamber leaders were replaced just after Bob Corker was elected the new mayor in 2000. An emphasis on specific recruitment of industry followed.

"Bob Corker got it moving," said George Elder, a commercial real estate broker. "The reason heads rolled is that Corker understands land development. . . . The Chamber doesn't have a clue about land development."

Corker almost landed the big fish he was seeking near the end of 2002. He said he could hardly sleep the night before he got word that Toyota would not be choosing Chattanooga's 1,200-acre Enterprise South Industrial Park for a major automotive plant.[36] Chattanooga remains, in the minds of many, just one step away from the boom it desperately seeks.

"A company that will hire about a thousand people at a decent wage—that's all we need," said Tommy Lupton. "That would set the attitude of this town straight up."

Frank Brock says Chattanooga is experiencing the opposite of the perfect storm. "It's the perfect position for growth. We have almost no environmental problems. We've got very little congestion compared to most major cities. We've got very nice art in our museums and local tourist attractions," he said. "I just think Chattanooga is going to grow because its just got all the right things. It's got it all together."

Former mayor Bob Corker, who worked in the state capital as the Commissioner of Finance, believes the root challenge for Chattanooga is to change its business culture. He augmented traditional economic development strategies with an effort to recruit a number of venture capital firms, persuading them to locate in Chattanooga and help with small and minority businesses as well as new business ventures. "Nashville is about commerce and entrepreneurs and risk," he said. "We have not yet engendered that kind of culture."[37]

The culture prescribed by Corker—commerce, entrepreneurialism, and risk—perfectly describes the business climate in the late 19th century that produced Chattanooga's many manufacturing powers as well as the two major fortunes already discussed, Coca-Cola Bottling and Provident Insurance. If the past is prologue, Chattanoogans would do well to learn what events led to the enterprising and risk-taking culture that produced the great business successes spawned more than a century ago.

ECONOMIC DREAMS

When E. Y. Chapin arrived in the 1880s, Chattanooga was "a little city under an excitement that was as feverish as anything Florida developed a generation later." Risk was in the culture. "Earlier results had stimulated every man to outdo his neighbor in daring," said Chapin regarding the growing real estate boom. "Fabulous winnings tempted each man to out-bid his neighbor on the next turn of the cards."

Chapin's friend at Cincinnati Law School, Fred Ferger, convinced him to move to Chattanooga. Ferger was persuaded to move by the vivid accounts of Harry Scott Probasco, who had known Ferger in Indiana.[38]

"All the Chapins are kind of like family to the Probascos," said Scotty, who describes the original E. Y. Chapin as a "brilliant, fine man."

"What did they call him?" I asked.

"They called him Ed. Now there's an Ed Chapin the fourth."

"What do they call him?"

"They call him Chape. His wife is a very superior girl."

Scotty went on to list the other brothers—Garnet Chapin, Jimmy, and Bill Chapin, now the President of Rock City, who I also interviewed.

Bill Chapin, described as a "gnome-like man with an impish grin" by *Southern Living Magazine*, spoke with me from his office, which has large glass windows overlooking Rock City Gardens. He explained to me early in the interview how his great-grandfather went into the banking business with the Probascos and they took turns as president. That was a few years after E. Y. Chapin recruited another law school buddy to come to Chattanooga.

"He left Chicago and came to Chattanooga, met a guy named Ben Thomas, and became his law partner."

Close enough. The history books say Chapin and Coke Bottling founder Ben Thomas met at the University of Cincinnati.[39]

"He went bankrupt in Chicago. I'm not sure how he got to be Thomas's law partner."

Chapin and Thomas likely came up with the idea at the boarding house of Hettie and Lottie Williams at 302 5th Street. A number of young bachelors chose to reside at the Williams sisters' place after moving to Chattanooga to seek their fortune. Boarders included Coke bottling pioneer Joe Whitehead and another chum, Sam Erwin, who managed the phone company. The house was a hotbed for entrepreneurs, an early forerunner of the business incubator.

Ben "used to come in every few days with a new scheme to make a million dollars," said Erwin. "We would listen to his schemes and laugh."[40]

E. Y. Chapin

No one is laughing a hundred years later. Scotty Probasco's father and E. Y. Chapin II served on the original three-person board of the Benwood Foundation that resulted from Thomas's fortune. Scotty followed his father on the foundation, and Bill Chapin replaced his father, E. Y. Chapin III, on the foundation board that gives away millions each year.[41]

Bill also replaced his father as owner of Rock City through a creative investment venture orchestrated by Bryan Patten of Patten & Patten Investment Company. "Don't talk to anybody else," Bryan told Bill. "I've got all the people we need and all the money."

"It was a creative way to get it down to the next generation," said Bill.

Bill Chapin also owns the Battles for Chattanooga museum (the old Confederama). He told me another story about Bryan's great-grandfather, Zeboim Cartter Patten, who also happens to be the brother of Bill's Uncle's grandfather.

Z. C. Patten and his brother, George Washington Patten, were Union soldiers from New York who fought in Chattanooga.

"Z. C. Patten got wounded at Chickamauga." Later, he served under Ulysses S. Grant as his payroll chief. "He was the guy in charge of all the money."

"When Sherman left, he stayed in Chattanooga...and invited his brother to come down. And they started Chattanooga Drug and Chemical Company."

The business was later called Chattanooga Medicine Company, the well-spring for much of Chattanooga's later industry. Now it is known as Chattem, manufacturer of world-famous products like Gold Bond Medicated Powder, Icy Hot, Pamprin, and Bull Frog suntan lotion, but in the early days it created potions and elixirs such as Black Draught and Wine of Cardui, forerunners to Coca-Cola.

Z. C. Patten's daughter married another attorney who had moved to Chattanooga from Virginia to join the entrepreneurial crowd—John T. Lupton.

"They loaned Lupton money...to go to Atlanta to buy the Coca-Cola thing," said Bill. "[Thomas and Whitehead] got it from Lupton, who got it from the Pattens. They loaned him the money, and he never let them buy into the business. I think it has created some family tensions ever since."

The official Patten family history does not say it quite that way, but also does not refute it.[42*] Regardless, Chapin's story points to a major component of Chattanooga's economic history: the pouring in of the "Northern elite," mainly ex-Union soldiers, who sought their fortune in Chattanooga after the Civil War.

Chattanooga's strategic valleys, which led to her strategic railroads, caused Lincoln to plead with his generals in 1862 to take the town which he considered "more important than Richmond." Lincoln's obsession led to the second largest battle on American soil with 84,000 casualties in two days. Though smaller than the three-day Gettysburg battle, the Battle of Chickamauga resulted in the greater of the two in per-capita casualties. By 1864, over 100,000 soldiers, more than fifteen times the population, had seen the area with its beautiful mountains and Tennessee River.[43] More importantly, a number of them noticed its strategic iron and coal reserves.

General John T. Wilder was the first Union officer to shell the city in 1862, directing missiles at the steeple of First Presbyterian Church from his rampart position across the river near Stringer's Ridge (the Red Bank tunnel). At age fourteen he had apprenticed in the iron industry, so he could identify the rich iron deposits when he came to Chattanooga as well as the underground island of "black diamond" stretches—some of the nation's richest deposits of bituminous coal.[44]

After the war, Chattanooga experienced an iron and manufacturing explosion, a coal rush, and, later, a real estate boom. Wilder founded the Roane Iron Works, a mighty industrial manufacturer, and later helped start the Chattanooga Manufacturer's Association along with Yale graduate Xenophon Wheeler, another Union officer.

"I thought a place so strategically important in war ought to become a large, important place in peace," said Wheeler.

The city ran an ad in the *Daily Republican*: "WANTED IMMEDIATELY ANY NUMBER OF CARPET-BAGGERS TO COME TO CHATTANOOGA AND SETTLE…Those having capital, brains, and muscle preferred."[45]

Such community efforts inspired countless northerners like Chapin to move to Chattanooga and prosper. He created enough wealth to later establish Chattanooga's symphony, opera, and public library. To honor his efforts, a statue of E. Y. Chapin stands by the stairs on the third floor of the downtown library.

Another statue rests a few feet away. Although Chapin was probably taller, his statue is several inches shorter than the bust of Adolph S. Ochs, another northerner whose family migrated to Chattanooga a few years after the War. Ochs bought the *Chattanooga Times* and later a struggling paper in New York. Today, he is universally acclaimed as the man who turned the *New York Times* into the world's greatest newspaper and revolutionized the world of publishing.

Before moving to New York in 1896, Ochs spent decades promoting Chattanooga's economy. "Go ring your bell and fire your gun, shout glory, for the 'Boom' has come," reported the *Chattanooga Times*. Ochs launched the audacious "Over the River" company that promised the building of three bridges over the stream that had only a ferry at the time. These bridges were scheduled to connect to the land being purchased in a flurry of speculation. Many lots changed hands several times in a single day.

"If you bought a full subscription to the paper for one dollar, you also got a plot of land," the great-grandson of Adolph Ochs told me. Michael Golden, born and raised in Chattanooga, now serves as vice-chairman and senior vice president of the *New York Times*. His first cousin is the chairman. At a meeting with Mayor Corker and the Chattanooga media in the *Times* boardroom in New York, Golden described how Ochs's parents had to sign the papers for him when the 21-year-old bought the *Chattanooga Times*, then under lien to Zeboim Patten. Young Ochs, Chapin, and many others certainly exercised the bravado and risk that Bob Corker claims is necessary for an economy to grow.[46]

This particular boom turned into a major bust, however, and Ochs found himself heading for bankruptcy. Nonetheless, the wheels of progress were in motion, and the mountain of indebtedness inspired Ochs to travel to New York and devise an income scheme to dig himself out of the hole. His story, and the legacy of news and publishing he left with Chattanooga, is told in Chapter Six.

Africa Meets Appalachia

Another wave of settlers migrated to Chattanooga for reasons similar to the Yankees. Former slaves across the Southeast found great opportunities for higher paying jobs in factories and foundries that had little to no education requirements.

"My father and uncles tell the story that Chattanooga was a place that was growing and [had] jobs where there was opportunity…and foundries," said Lurone Jennings, a local black pastor, whose forebearers from past generations all moved from farms in Alabama. Judge Williams told me his ancestors moved up from Georgia plantations.

Today, Knoxville, two hours away, has less than half the number of blacks per capita as Chattanooga, according to Pete Drew, a former Knox County Commissioner who now resides in Chattanooga. "There were jobs, and they had some work to do here," he said.

But he also points to geography. "Knoxville and East Tennessee, for all practical purposes, are surrounded by mountains. Knoxville is blocked in. In Chattanooga, you have an opening to Georgia and Alabama, so if you check the family history of black people in Chattanooga, you'll find the overwhelming majority of them came from way down south, like Mississippi up through Arkansas and Georgia.

Such a migration was not typical nationwide until half a century later when blacks traveled north for factory jobs. Until then, former slaves typically stayed on the flatlands of the South.

"Chattanooga in many ways prefigured the great migration of African Americans to the industrial Great Lakes region," said Jack Murrah. "In fact, there's no urban area in southern Appalachia, to my knowledge, that has anything like the African American population of Chattanooga, so it stands out as a unique city in a unique region, a region that is not quite like the rest of the South."

"If you looked at the counties of southern Appalachia, I think probably the vast majority of them are 90+ percent white, many of them 95 percent," said Murrah. "It was not a region that was home to the large slave population in the South."

Before the Civil War, slaves in the South composed approximately 30 percent of the total population. In Memphis and West Tennessee, slaves comprised 60 percent. In East Tennessee, the ratio was significantly smaller. Chattanooga's population was 17 percent and in Hamilton County slaves comprised as little as 10 percent of the total population. In 1861, Hamilton County was the governmental body furthest south in America to vote with the Union against the slave-holding secessionists. A decade later, this pro-Union populace did not oppose an influx of blacks to the area.[47]

Former Chattanooga Venture Chairman Mai Bell Hurley agrees with Murrah. "When you look at it, we are an unusual community in that we probably have as high a percentage of African Americans and as high a percentage of Appalachians in one place as you'll find anywhere," she said. "By Appalachian, [I mean] people who were non-slaveholding families here and kind of came off the mountains and were very practical, independent people."

Frank Brock describes the Appalachians as the spine of a book. "If you look at the states of North Carolina and Tennessee, think of them as the two pages of a book with the center being in the Appalachian Mountains." Brock is referring to the Smokies, the mountain range on the border of East Tennessee and western North Carolina. "West Tennessee and eastern North Carolina were founded originally by landed property people. When their oldest son got the property, their second and third sons moved into the central part of the state—the Piedmont area of North Carolina and the Cumberland Plateau area in Tennessee."

Brock said these sons were less agricultural and built financial and banking industries in cities like Charlotte and Nashville. If there was no room for the third son in the family business or if the sons couldn't get along, they moved closer to the spine of the book.

"They all moved into mountains and holed up where they could be an isolated, ornery people in the mountains," said Brock. "And the mountains have always tended to be the refuge of the most independent [people], the guys who couldn't fit in anywhere else."

John T. Lupton and **Harry Scott Probasco** are pictured side by side in the most recent book on the history of First Presbyterian Church. (Top) A faded advertisement for **Wine of Cardui**, a Chattanooga forerunner of Coca-Cola, can still be seen when driving on Broad Street toward Lookout Moutain.

"When the war broke out, all up and down the Appalachian area there was a sense of independence," he said. "They certainly didn't feel attached to the landed slave South, and yet they weren't really that keen on Yankees...either. So it was more of an independent cuss contrariness than it was a Yankee love that made this region not really Southern and more open to Northern people, I suspect."

Although these people accepted Yankees, voted against the Confederacy, and were not particularly pro-slavery, they were not without racism. "Let the people who own niggers, protect 'em," said one East Tennessee editor and pro-Union political leader. Nevertheless, the mixing of Yankees and Appalachian folk created an atmosphere tolerant enough to encourage blacks to migrate along with Northerners. The same ad soliciting carpetbaggers also boasted that "the Ku Klux and other vermin do not extend over these parts."[48]

Lincoln's Republican party dominated for decades in Chattanooga after the Confederacy collapsed. These Yankees and Republicans were able to forge an effective coalition with new black voters, some of whom held positions as alderman in city government or as members of the state legislature. Blacks held more appointments and government jobs than anywhere else in Tennessee. In 1881, over half the Chattanooga city police force was black. By 1890, African Americans had mushroomed to 43 percent of the population. Before the war, only one in six were black.[49]

A journalist visiting Chattanooga just before the influx of Yankees and blacks described the people. "The occupants are sometimes negroes, but the majority are whites...Their delight is in the woods and the mountains," he said. "Their needs are a gun, a dog, a horse, a cottage, a wife, and a cow—and pretty much in the order enumerated."[50]

There is another reason these independent frontiersman were drawn to the mountains. Most of them were Scottish. They are sometimes called "Scotch-Irish" because they resided as refugees in Ulster, Ireland, for a few years on the way from Scotland to America.

"No one but the Scotch Irish who were used to rugged hills and mountains would have settled in East Tennessee," Martha McCoy explains to Helen in the cookbook. "East Tennesseans are different than Georgia people, we are not like Nashville or Memphis, we are just ourselves." Helen provides a recipe for Martha's ham using blackstrap molasses and gives another recipe for boiling ham in Coca-Cola.

Helen also comments on the Scotch-Irish theme. "East Tennesseans have a reputation for being shrewd traders, having solid-rock convictions politically and religiously, and demanding the right to do things their own way. Martha has the reputation for serving as delicious a country ham as you will ever eat," Helen adds without breaking stride. "She buys two pigs every year...butchers them and cures her own hams."[51]

These Scots brought with them the religious tradition that originated in Scotland—Presbyterianism. The great impact of the Scotch-Irish settlers and their form of Christianity on Chattanooga merits further discussion in a later chapter. They came to take part in the big economic boom and land rush that preceded the one involving Chapin and Ochs. That later boom does not cause potential issues of conscience for descendents today like Chattanooga's original land grab where settlers rushed in to claim property from the Cherokees who were forced from their homes. These Native Americans were then marched to Oklahoma in the 1838 Trail of Tears. The Cherokees and their predecessors also merit a separate chapter.

Cheap, Cherokee Land

These mostly Scottish families—the McCallies, Crutchfields, Gillespies, Keys, Kennedys, Williamses, Divines, Whitesides, and others—all have descendents today still living in Chattanooga. Some of them actually served as soldiers pointing bayonets at the nonviolent Indians in the confrontation oddly referred to in its day as the "Cherokee War" or "Cherokee Disturbance." Over 7,000 Federal soldiers traveled to Ross's Landing for the Removal, several times more men than lived in the small village. Business opportunities arose when bids were placed in the paper for supplying food to the people and feed to the animals in preparation for the journey.[52]

But the real chance for prosperity lay in obtaining land at basement prices. An acre sold for $7.50[†] but might be resold for ten times that price or more. The key was obtaining "occupancy rights." State and federal law rewarded settlers who squatted on Cherokee lands, a technically illegal practice, by allowing them the first chance to purchase the property when the Indians left.[53]

While 2,500 Indians were locked inside the "Camp Cherokee" stockade a half mile east of the river landing, Federal soldiers used axes and saws to clear trees for the new roads. Of the estimated 14,000 rounded up for the Trail of Tears, at least 2,000 reportedly died of dysentery, exposure, and other diseases in concentration camps like Camp Cherokee.[54*]

Early manuscripts portray a paradox during this transition time between good and bad soldiers and sympathetic versus opportunistic settlers. Mary Frist, a direct ancestor of today's Senate Majority Leader Bill Frist, complained about a sergeant with a scratchy beard who would kiss her against her will, but another soldier named Moses Wells, one of hundreds who later moved to Chattanooga, fell in love with an Indian girl in the camp who was "pretty and accomplished" and "played the piano and violin with proficiency."[55]

Wells described how they found Indians hidden in treetops, bushes, and hollow logs. It was raining the day a large number of Cherokees were marched down the

---

[†] $1700 (2006)

Rossville Road, now Market Street. They were not allowed to keep even their pets. "Want dog?" they would ask their white friends who had squatted on their land. "Good dog! Good watchdog. Take and keep dog." The wife of commissioner John P. Long—who later proposed the name "Chattanooga" for the town—said many of the Indian women were her friends and went to bid her goodbye. She said she could not stand it and would cry as if her heart would break, but she also admitted that she feared possible retaliation by the Indians and was comforted to have soldiers nearby. Plus, they "looked very fine."[56]

One old Indian asked a settler friend if he would do him a favor. "It was nothing more or less than that his friend should shoot him. He considered himself no longer of use to his family, tribe, or friends. . . The friend objected, but the old man insisted. They were sitting on a log. At last the friend yielded, took out his powder horn...and with it formed a rim in the center of the old man's forehead. Telling him to sit still, and doubtless bidding him a final goodbye, [he] shot the old man through the head."

Another Federal cavalry man, William Jones, snuck out from the stockade at night and played his fiddle while the Indians danced. He was punished when he was caught dancing with the girls and also for falling asleep on guard duty the mornings after the dances.[57]

One of the soldiers in the stockade with Jones was George Gillespie III, the great-great-great-grandfather of Scotty Probasco. When the Cherokees left, he moved into Daniel Ross's double log cabin at Ross's Towhead.[58] I wanted to learn more about Gillespie and more about how descendents of removal agents like Gillespie felt about such a heritage. However, I discovered that the expert on Gillespie history in town is none other than Tom Decosimo, the critic of my *Chattanooga Fax*, along with his brother, Fred. The Decosimos are related to Scotty through the "Gillespie-Sharp" axis. Scotty's grandmother and Tom and Fred's grandfather—both Sharps—were brother and sister (see chart on next page).

I did call Tom Decosimo. I was not sure exactly how he would respond, so I interviewed some others first. Allen McCallie, the Miller & Martin attorney who grew up with daily devotions, also has Federal removal agents in his lineage. Allen's great-great-grandfather, Thomas McCallie, had two brothers-in-law who marched off the Indians to Oklahoma—Robert and John Hooke. The son, Thomas Hooke McCallie, clearly remembered when his father took possession of the Cherokee property and built a house on what is today Centenary Methodist Church and the Memorial Auditorium.

"I was only three and a half years old, but I remember the trip well," he wrote. "We came in a flat bottomed boat covered over."[59]

GILLESPIE ~ SHARP

A founding father of Presbyterianism, Gillespie was a leader in authoring the *Westminster Confession* and *Shorter Catechism*, and chief apologist for Scotland's National Covenant.

GEORGE GILLESPIE
b. 1613–1648

GEORGE GILLESPIE II

GEORGE GILLESPIE III

CORNELIA GILLESPIE = **L. J. SHARP** 1845–1917

R. H. WILLIAMS 1862–1944 = **MARGARET GILLESPIE SHARP** 1876–1949

JOHN CESSNA SHARP 1882–1955

SCOTT L. PROBASCO, SR. 1890–1962 = **MARGARET WILLIAMS** 1904–1964

JOSEPH DECOSIMO b. 1925 = **RACHEL DIVINE SHARP**

SCOTT L. (SCOTTY) PROBASCO, JR. b. 1928

TOM DECOSIMO b. 1956

FRED DECOSIMO b. 1951

(Charts are partial, not exhaustive, highlighting key links or characters in the book.)

They were moving from Cherokee lands as well, which Thomas McCallie had acquired in Rhea County. The deed from that property was brandished by Allen McCallie's cousin at a dinner 150 years later.

"Gladys showed up with the original grant deed for the McCallie family farm on Grasshopper Creek, and I think the deed had an 1838 date on it," said Allen. "So, literally, they claimed the land upon the Cherokee removal."

"You think what a terrible thing the Cherokee removal is—and there's my family taking a farm out of property from which Cherokees had been removed. Apparently, my forefathers lived on both sides of the river before eventually moving to downtown Chattanooga. So Tennessee's history with the Trail of Tears directly impacts upon my family."

In 1835, Samuel Williams worked as a tailor in Greenville, Tennessee, with future President Andrew Johnson. Both left that trade. Williams headed for the Cherokee territory and squatted on Moccasin Bend and the nearby island, now called Williams Island. At that time, the area across the river was known as Ross's Landing. John Ross, the Principal Chief of the Cherokee Nation, and his brother, Lewis Ross, owned a store, warehouse, and ferry located at what is today the Tennessee Aquarium and Walnut Street Bridge. Their father, Daniel Ross, was pure Scottish and built a house closer to the foot of Lookout Mountain after marrying a woman who was one quarter Cherokee. The ferry was originally near Daniel's house which sat on the land currently used by the Chattanooga Christian School for a track—behind the offices of WDEF-TV. In the 1800s, it was called "Ross's Towhead."[60]

Samuel Williams started the area's second store. He had grain milled at Ross's Towhead by Andrew Ross, another brother of John's. Williams also built the area's first plank house. The wood was cut by the mill at the Brainerd Mission, floated down Chickamauga Creek and then down the river past Williams Island to a landing near the "Suck part," the dangerous whirlpool later called, simply, the "Suck."[61]

In 1838, John Divine spent a night at the Henderson's Inn on First Street but could not continue his journey. He had lost his wallet. He eventually had to sell his horse, but then Samuel Williams hired him to work his store. Divine became a partner in the business and married Samuel Williams's daughter, Elizabeth. (Widowed years later, Divine married the daughter of the town's biggest developer, Charles James. "He came into town and married the richest man's daughter," I was told by local attorney Robert Divine, his direct descendent. "When she died, he married the richest girl in town again."[62])

Samuel Williams was called the "Father of Chattanooga" for his early land development and business activities and for promoting the area. "He first seemed to have grasped the idea that there was a grand future to this city on the Tennessee River," wrote one business associate. Another businesss associate, attorney James

Whiteside, partnered with Williams in an 1838 land syndica-
tion venture. Whiteside bought thousands of acres and owned
all of Lookout Mountain and Cameron Hill. The 35-year-old
attorney from Pikeville, who had served in the state legislature
since age 24, was eventually called "Old Man Chattanooga,"
and sometimes "Old Man Lookout Mountain."[63] He owned
the area's first brick home at the foot of Cameron Hill (near
the Lookouts' stadium today) and built a mansion on the
tip of Lookout Mountain. A portrait of Whiteside and his
family on the back porch of their mansion still hangs in the
Hunter Museum. The scene behind them, with Moccasin

John Divine

Bend below, is the first image in existence of the area's famous view.

Whiteside introduced a bill in 1845 to bring the railroad to Chattanooga.
Though many local leaders took a part in bringing this strategic economic force
to the city, Whiteside played the biggest role. "[He] almost singlehandedly made
Chattanooga a railroad center," wrote historian John Wilson.[64]

Whiteside had several children. His oldest son married a Hooke and his oldest
daughter married a Gillespie. His son Charles married Emma Crutchfield. Emma's
sister married a McCallie, and Emma's granddad, Thomas Crutchfield, built the
city's first brick home at Cameron Hill for James Whiteside.[65]

The Famous Crutchfield House

The Crutchfields are another prominent founding family whose descendents
continue to mark the landscape today. A book of this nature would not be complete
without an interview with state senator Ward Crutchfield, a direct descendent of
the brick builder. Ward's great-grandfather is also the key character in the only event
in Chattanooga that shows up in *A History of the American People*, a 1999 national
bestseller by prominent British historian Paul Johnson.

Ward Crutchfield was serving as majority leader for the
Tennessee Senate at the time I needed to interview him,
but, like other prominent figures in town, I worried that my
past investigative reporting would nix the opportunity. His
son-in-law is former Chattanooga mayor Jon Kinsey, whose
water company takeover I had opposed. Ward's daughter
Missy also graced the pages of *Chattanooga Fax*. Twice, I
had printed comments by state education administrators
denying a charge that one of their vice presidents at Chattanooga State Technical Community College had starred in
a pornographic movie. The first administrator had used the

James Whiteside

name "Missy Crutchfield" in his written quotes, but I chose to leave out the name of the senator's daughter and refer to her as a "staffer." He said the 1984 movie in which she costarred with a Penthouse Pet of the Year was rated "R," not "X." In fairness to the other side, I noted that the movie did include an abundance of nudity. When the second administrator, the head of the Tennessee Board of Regents, provided another round of written quotes and used her name again, I called Missy Crutchfield.

"Just print my name and get it over with," she told me, adding that if she knew then what she knows now, she would not have done it. She was 21 at the time. "I wasn't thrilled about it. But we all make choices. We all try to be strategic in pursuing an acting career," said Missy, who later served as president of the high-profile Chattanooga Venture planning group.

At her request, I printed some of her prouder moments: she auditioned with Robert DeNiro, had a supporting role in a Brian DePalma film with John Travolta, and performed in a number of plays in New York as well as creating and playing the lead in an off-Broadway production.[66]

I guess the article came off well. Missy and I forged a friendship. Ironically, I finally got my entrée into Ward Crutchfield's office when his daughter called and encouraged him to give me a chance. It was a very Crutchfield-like thing to do, as later stories will show. It was also in line with the "Spirit of Chattanooga," a theme championed by the generation after the Civil War and led largely by William Crutchfield.

When I arrived at Senator Crutchfield's office, I was enthusiastically greeted by Linda, his longtime assistant. She gleefully chatted about her great admiration for Senator Crutchfield, offering little anecdotes such as the way he used to drive around poor neighborhoods in cold weather offering bags of coal from his trunk back in the days of coal-fueled fireplaces.

Ward Crutchfield is an old-time Democratic politician with a stereotypical Boss Hogg appearance. It is rare to see him without a cigar, including on the senate floor. (Tennessee legislators outlawed smoking in all public buildings except one—the state capitol.) He received dirty looks on the senate floor in the days before black legislators when he sat his African American friend C. B. Robinson next to him in the senate chamber.[67] Judge Williams calls Crutchfield a "master politician."

"If you look at Ward's district, without black support, he would not be in office. So Ward is a survivor. He does whatever favors he needs to do to keep his interests within the black community, and there's a lot of support—old-time support. There are some blacks who, if Ward said it was raining outside—even if they could see that it's not—they would go out with their umbrellas. Ward's a survivor."

Crutchfield was first elected to the legislature in 1956.

Linda pointed me down the long hall to Senator Crutchfield's office. Framed pictures of Senate Majority Leader Crutchfield with Governors and presidential candidates lined the walls, and a very large box of cigars sat just behind his desk. He kept his cigar in his mouth when he shook my hand, then he handed one to me.

"Did you have any ancestors who were elected officials?" I asked.

"My dad served in the legislature."

"When?"

"1917."

"Was he the first Crutchfield to serve in an elected office?"

"I don't know . . ." Ward paused. "His great-uncle, Tom Crutchfield, was mayor of Chattanooga."

Then he remembered another Crutchfield politician.

"William went to Congress."

"When did the first Crutchfield come to Chattanooga?" I asked.

"I need to find out. I'd guess 1830-something." (Actually, he is pretty close. The history books are vague on the date of the Crutchfield family's arrival, but Whiteside's house was built in 1841.) "They went through Athens—built and laid out and named the city of Athens. Came down through Virginia. They were largely builders. I don't know exactly where they lived at the time, but they came in here I'd say, well before 1840."

Originally, the Crutchfields came from Worcester County, England. Old family documents say "Cruch" or "Crutch" was a much-traveled district in the county and was laid out in the shape of a cross. Large crosses bearing lighted torches were said to light the highway, which became known as "the way of the cross," or "Crutchfield."

The Crutchfields were granted coat-armor in 1510 by Henry VIII, with a motto reading: "Worthy to bear the cross."

Thomas Crutchfield, the first recorded name in 1515, kept an ordinary tavern or inn in Worcester County. The Thomas Crutchfield who moved to Chattanooga

three centuries later also built a tavern and inn in the 1850s at the strategic point where the two new railroads met at the corner of Mulberry and Ninth Streets (Mulberry was changed to Railroad Avenue and finally to Broad Street). The three-story Crutchfield House soon became the "political, social and economic center of the town." It was replaced years later by the Read House, which remains on the same spot to this day.[68]

Ward Crutchfield on the senate floor

"When you come by the Read House," said Ward, "if you'll just look up just below the railing on the mezzanine, the Crutchfield coat of arms alternates with the Read coat of arms all the way around—and nobody pays any attention to it."

Citizens are paying more attention now to the House of Crutchfield. The longtime legislator was arrested on the senate floor on May 26, 2005, and handed a federal indictment for taking bribes.

Charles Love, a well-known African American school board member for Hamilton County, was described as the "bagman" for the fed's sting operation, code-named "Tennessee Waltz." Love pled guilty to a conspiracy to bribe Crutchfield. The indictment stated that Linda, Ward's assistant, received $2,000 cash in an envelope with the initials "W.C." from the organization that was asking for political favors. She then said to Ward, "He was mighty nice to us today." Ward's response became the cover story that week for the *Pulse*, Chattanooga's alternative weekly paper. "WE WILL DO WHATEVER YOU WANT US TO DO," the headline screamed, with the subheading, "The Fall of the House of Crutchfield?"

The feds will need strong evidence to bring down several generations of Crutchfield political power. Ward does political favors for a lot of folks. Why? "He's my friend," he usually says. Likewise, the indictment says Crutchfield met with the undercover agent, indicated he would sponsor legislation for him, and thanked him for "being my friend."

After the arrest, Crutchfield was immediately released and told reporters, "I haven't done anything wrong. I'll make a statement at the appropriate time." The time has not yet arrived, as legal proceedings were still in motion when this book hit the press.[69]

In 1861, the Crutchfields and the Crutchfield House were etched into the history books of America, thanks to the two sons of Chattanooga's first Crutchfield, Thomas and William. There is still a Thomas and a William Crutchfield in Chattanooga today, along with Ward. All three are attorneys.

"William was a Union sympathizer, and Tom was a Confederate," said Ward. "So they got into a big fight at the Crutchfield House." He pointed to a picture on his wall of Thomas and William, his great-grandfather, and a picture of the Hotel that made national news in 1861. Jefferson Davis stayed there on his way from Washington to Mississippi, where he planned to accept the presidency of the Confederate States of America.

Tom Crutchfield operated the hotel and was a former mayor. William ran a farm near the hotel, was an alderman in city government, and was described not only as highly intelligent, kind, and popular but also as "a man of many and pronounced eccentricities" and "peculiar beyond description." Both brothers were present when Jefferson Davis arrived.[70]

CRUTCHFIELD

THOMAS CRUTCHFIELD
1801–1850

William made national headlines after publicly confronting Jefferson Davis during his stay at the Crutchfield House in 1861. Tom quelled a brewing riot by persuading his brother to leave the hotel built by their father.

WILLIAM CRUTCHFIELD
b. 1824

TOM CRUTCHFIELD
b. 1830

THOMAS WILLIAMS CRUTCHFIELD, SR.

THOMAS WILLIAMS CRUTCHFIELD, JR.

WARD CRUTCHFIELD

(Charts are partial, not exhaustive, highlighting key links or characters in the book.)

Rising political star David Key, a figure in later Chattanooga history, escorted Davis to his room before persuading him to speak to the gathering crowd. Judge Lewis Shepherd provided a credible eyewitness account.

"Key...urged him to make a speech, which he reluctantly consented to do. He was fatigued from his journey and his heart was sorely depressed because of his failure...to bring about a peaceful solution."

"The speech was a calm, dispassionate review of the matters...It was not a fiery appeal to the passions and prejudices of the southern people against northern men...It was an invitation to the people to intelligently consider the merits of the controversy."

"William Crutchfield...an uncompromising Union man... climbed on the counter of the hotel and began a reply....Pointing toward him, [he] said to the people, 'Behold your future military despot!'"

Tempers flared and pistols were drawn on both sides. The screams of some ladies, including those of Mrs. Davis and Mrs. Thomas Crutchfield, added to the confusion.[71]

In his *History of the American People*, Paul Johnson says William Crutchfield called Davis "a renegade and traitor...We are not to be hoodwinked and bamboozled and dragged into your Southern, codfish, aristocratic, Tory-blooded South Carolina mobocracy."[72*]

Judge Lewis said "the incident would have led to bloodshed had not Mr. Thomas Crutchfield compelled his brother to cease speaking."

Davis, who was in another room when the accusations were made, said he had been insulted and asked if Crutchfield was "responsible and reputable." If so, Jefferson Davis was ready to challenge William Crutchfield to a duel, but a fight never ensued. Davis left the tense scene of armed and angry men and returned with David Key to his room. "Perhaps it gave Davis a foretaste," wrote one historian, "of the problems that the new Southern nation would have with the widespread Union sentiment in its back country and mountain regions."[73]

The showdown made headlines across the country. Jefferson Davis left on a train the next day for Mississippi. The incident provided a glimpse of the divide in Chattanooga over secession. Tennessee was the last state to vote to leave the Union, and Hamilton County was the southernmost local government voting to remain with the federal government—1260 votes for the Union, 854 for the Confederacy. The town of Chattanooga within Hamilton County voted against the Union, 421 to 51. Explanations vary. Perhaps those in the county migrated primarily from the North, while many Chattanoogans hailed from Georgia and Alabama. Chattanooga did have more slaves per capita—one in six compared to one in ten in the county. A more intriguing explanation is that the city had acquired a large debt in building its railroads and hoped secession would erase it. William Crutchfield, in his tirade, also lectured Davis "to teach the people of Mississippi to pay their state debt rather than to be talking secession in Tennessee."[74]

Eyes of the World on Chattanooga

Lincoln was aware of the railways in Chattanooga. In fact, he was obsessed with them, showing more insight than his less enthusiastic generals on the enormous strategic value in war of the new mode of transportation. The railroad also housed a new communications tool: the telegraph. The war secretary telegraphed General Halleck expressing Lincoln's displeasure "with the tardiness of the movement toward Chattanooga." Later that day in 1862, Lincoln himself sent a telegraph urging that nothing be done to "weaken or delay the expedition against Chattanooga" and insisting that holding the railroad in the region is, "I think, fully as important as the taking and holding of Richmond," the capital of the Confederacy.

The Union army took possession of Nashville on March 6, 1862. Lincoln named Andrew Johnson, the U.S. Senator from Tennessee, the new military governor. The former governor was forced to follow the retreating Confederate army into Murfreesboro and on to Chattanooga.[75]

Ex-Governor Neil S. Brown asked Thomas Hooke McCallie if he planned to remain in Chattanooga if the federal army entered the city. McCallie had been named pastor of "the First Church of Chattanooga" (First Presbyterian) on January 1, 1862, the same day he married Ellen Jarnagin.

McCallie assured Brown he would stay. "He asked me if I did not know that when the army entered Nashville, the preachers were among the very first persons sent to

The **Crutchfield House** with Cameron Hill behind

prison. I replied that I [did]. He then stated that he thought it very unwise for me to remain and that I had better go South. I replied that the Lord had called me to the work in Chattanooga—that I had more right there than the Federal Army and that if the Lord wanted me there, he could take care of me, protect me and sustain me and that I did not intend to go one foot away from my home." Soon, McCallie was the only pastor left in Chattanooga and remained so for several war-torn years.

The McCallie's first year of marriage was no honeymoon. "After the battle of Murfreesboro, this city became a veritable storm center," he wrote in his journal. "Our house during the winter of 1862 and 1863 was not only a hotel, but a hospital…The poor fellows on a cold night [would] begin to knock on our door…asking to be allowed only to lie on the floor rather than out-of-doors. We never turned any away as long as there was room." Every bed was occupied and every room and hall covered with bodies.[76]

Soldiers and civilians poured into Chattanooga on railcars, among them First Lady Mary Todd Lincoln's sister, whose husband was a Confederate general. Also arriving by rail were Colonel J. W. Gillespie and Colonel David Key, many of whose men were untested soldiers wearing country hats and suspenders. Key led an artillery unit on Cameron Hill against Federals bombing the hill from across the river. McCallie headed to the Crutchfield House, which had been turned into a hospital full of sick and wounded soldiers, to find the doctor, but he was dead. "In cutting off a limb, his knife went into his own hand, gangrene set in, and he fell a victim."[77]

As many as nine ministers stayed as guests at one time or another at the McCallie home, among them Dr. B. M Palmer of New Orleans who led a prayer service at First Presbyterian for the absent Dr. McCallie on a day of fasting called by President Jefferson Davis.

"Scarcely had he begun to pray till the screams of a shell flying over the church was heard and the distant boom of cannon from the opposite side of the Tennessee River," McCallie reports in his journal. General John T. Wilder was directing his men to bomb the most prominent landmark in town, the steeple of the church on Market Street. The leg of a young girl in the Higginbotham family was broken by the first shell. "The soldiers began to quietly withdraw, then the citizens, till presently the church was empty and still the preacher prayed." In fact, he never flinched from beginning to end. "When he closed his eyes, the church was full of people. When he opened them, it was on empty pews."

McCallie himself was in Cleveland, Tennessee, visiting his wife and his "emaciated" six-month-old daughter, Mary. "I pleaded with my Father to spare my child," he said. "While the case was pending and the child still lingering at death's door, I was called home by the very awfulness of the situation. The storm

Samuel Williams

was about to burst in a fury. The Federal Army was gathering in great force," kicking up "clouds of dust...that from any eminence was discernible for miles away."[78]

However, the Confederate commander, Braxton Bragg, ordered a retreat south into the woods of Chickamauga, Georgia, to the disgust of many Southerners. The Union army marched down Market Street playing "Yankee Doodle" and flew the American flag from the third floor of the Crutchfield House.[79]

By then, Tom Crutchfield had moved five miles upriver to a farm he named "Amnicola," in order to escape from the chaos of war. His brother, William Crutchfield, was arrested in 1861 on the charge that he was a "boisterous Union man." However, just before the evacuation, he was ordered out of town. His brother helped him slip through Confederate lines and across the river. There, he joined General Wilder and was given the rank of captain. He served as Wilder's scout since he knew "every road in the valley, every hog path on the mountain side."[80]

Samuel Williams, who started Chattanooga's second store and built the first plank house, gained national fame for his part in the Andrews' Raiders saga. Before the occupation of Chattanooga, the nation's attention was fixed on the runaway train story of James Andrews and his fellow Union spies who hijacked a train behind enemy lines in Georgia. Two of them initially stayed at the Crutchfield House, and circumstances forced them to attend a Confederate soldier's burial conducted by Rev. McCallie before they were able to sneak away to Kennesaw, Georgia. Once there, they stole a train called "The General" and began destroying bridges and rail lines in order to cut off the South's key communication links, but as they traveled north through Dalton and Ringgold toward Chattanooga, they found themselves hotly pursued by the civilian conductor of The General, William Fuller. Fuller pursued on foot, by pole car, and finally with another engine he obtained before successfully taking back his stolen train. The legendary chase was later dramatized in books and movies.

Andrews was captured. He received news from his Chattanooga prison that President Davis had ordered his execution. He escaped that night and swam the river to Williams Island, losing his pants and shoes en route. Andrews was a national news story by the time Samuel Williams came across a man at his spring house dressed only in a coat with feet badly scratched and bleeding. He offered to bring the grateful man some clothes but came back with two armed friends. Williams let Andrews, while under guard, eat dinner with his family and recount the interesting saga. The family felt sorry for him, but Williams delivered him to the authorities, who executed him. Andrews and his men later became America's first recipients of the Medal of Honor and are buried in Chattanooga's National Cemetery.[81]

Sunday morning, September 20, 1863, was a beautiful day for Rev. T. H. McCallie until he looked up Market Street from his church and saw a long line of ambulances. Casualties were pouring in from Chickamauga where the two great armies had collided into what became (and still is) the nation's worst two days of war. "The churches and large warehouses and old stores were filled with sick and wounded men," he wrote. "I saw a pile of legs and arms lying on the porch, the very sight of which was appalling."

Panic continued that night. Lincoln was awakened from his sleep with the terrible news. "The Federals had been defeated and driven back into the city," wrote McCallie. "They expected every hour to see the triumphant Confederates come pouring into the city." They built defensive works all night. "The next morning I walked out on McCallie Avenue and did not know the place. Hundreds of acres of fine timbered land lay naked."

But Bragg never attacked, even though his generals begged him to advance. Cavalry commander Nathan Bedford Forrest even rode in under white flag to negotiate a surrender without Bragg's permission but did not succeed. "Bragg had lost his great opportunity," said McCallie. "[He] had won a needless battle at a tremendous loss." The casualties included General Ben Helm, the brother-in-law of Mary Todd Lincoln.[82]

James Whiteside died while attempting to bring home his son, a sick soldier. His widow, Harriet Whiteside, refused to leave her Lookout Mountain home when ordered so by Federal soldiers. When the lieutenant returned to confiscate the family's rosewood piano, Harriett calmly informed the officer that she had stationed her daughter Helen at one end of the piano with a hatchet, and that Helen's sister, Flora, stood at the other end with an axe with orders to chop every single key to pieces if he set foot inside the house.[83]

Samuel Williams was being hunted by the Yankees for turning over Andrews for execution. General Thomas promised to hang Williams if he were caught. Federal soldiers swarmed the Williamses' home. Samuel fled, and the family was quarantined in an upstairs room. One night Mrs. Williams was frightened by a tapping on the window: Samuel had piled rocks against the house and climbed up. Mrs. Williams immediately instructed her daughter Allie to bang loudly on the piano to divert the soldiers' attention before he slipped away. He was forced to hide near the river under a rock. Occasionally, he would venture out to see his wife. He later hid south of Chickamauga at McLemore's Cove. Three weeks after the battle, Samuel's wife, along with his daughter, Mary Divine, traveled through the battlefield on the way to see Williams. "The awful evidences of that terrible struggle were still fresh," wrote Mary Divine, "…great forests twisted and shattered, the swollen bodies of dead horses and often bodies of unburied men."[84]

Surviving letters capture the sadness. "Dear Father," wrote Union soldier Merritt Simonds, "My leg is now mortifying above the knee, and the Dr's say I cannot live more than two days at the longest…I hope to meet you all in a better world. I would like to have my body taken home and buried beside my mother. I am comparatively comfortable at present. There is no pain in my leg."

An officer then wrote to the parents. "I am sorry to inform you of the sad intelligence that your much beloved son Merritt is no more. He died last night…We will bury his remains tomorrow and mark his grave distinctly so that they could be found if wanted."[85]

The Power of Forgiveness

For the next month, the eyes of the nation watched Chattanooga as the two great armies of the Civil War occupied their respective territories—Bragg hovered on Lookout Mountain and Missionary Ridge and up into Chattanooga Valley to Chattanooga Creek. The Union, which brought in Ulysses S. Grant to replace William Rosecrans as commander, set pickets from Chattanooga Creek across the Valley to Citico Creek and then to the river. During this awkward wait, the soldiers on each side of the picket line provided glimpses of the Spirit of Chattanooga.

"The pickets, divided by a narrow creek in some places and by a few feet of earth in others, formed close friendships. They exchanged coffee and tobacco and newspapers," writes historian Zella Armstrong. "Relations were in fact so intimate that orders were issued by the Federal officers forbidding friendliness across the lines. There is evidence, however, that the commands were not severely enforced."[86]

General Grant recounts in his memoirs a peculiar event when he visited the picket line one evening. "Turn out the guard for the commanding general," he heard called out as expected, but then he heard the same cry across the creek, only to observe several Confederates saluting him. Amused, he returned the salute.

Union General George Thomas assured Grant, "We will hold the town until we starve." The siege by Bragg was intended to starve them. But Lincoln urged Grant to persevere. "If we can hold Chattanooga and East Tennessee, I think the rebellion will dwindle and die," he told his commanders.

While Grant considered a way to break the siege and supply his army, the multitude of army bands on both sides dualed each other musically. One might play "Dixie" or "Bonnie Blue Flag," and the other side respond with "Yankee Doodle Dandy" or the "Star-Spangled Banner." One evening, according to Armstrong, "one of the bands on Missionary Ridge began to play 'Home Sweet Home.' One after another the Confederate bands took up the air and then the Federal bands joined in the heartbreaking melody. In a few minutes every band in the two great camps was playing, and the white palisades of Lookout and Walden's Ridge were echoing the soft strains, a mighty harmony. Men were singing, too, though some were sobbing."[87]

That same spirit was evident during a wedding on Signal Mountain a few miles away during the heart of the war. The well-attended ceremony led to an all-night dance. An eyewitness said soldiers from both sides attended, as well as deserters from both sides, and even spies from the respective armies. "Scarcely a harsh word was uttered during the whole night; all danced together as if nothing was wrong, and parted mutually the next morning....it is marvelous that bloodshed was not the immediate result."[88]

Grant's solution to the dilemma of no direct supply line for his army was a sneak attack in the night against soldiers at Brown's Ferry and Tavern just past Lookout Mountain on the river. (Brown's Tavern, built by mixed-blood Cherokee John Brown in 1803, still stands today, the oldest structure in city limits.) Officer Timothy Stanley commanded soldiers in 200 pontoon boats, which floated down the river around Moccasin Bend under protection of darkness. They opened fire on the few Confederate soldiers guarding the ferry landing and quickly occupied it.

Bragg, by now extremely unpopular with his officers and troops, was informed by one of his staff on Lookout Mountain that the "Cracker Line" had been broken. Bragg denounced the young man for believing fantastic reports. "Come here, General, and I will show you!" the young man replied, barely concealing his contempt. The view from Sunset Rock showed Federal wagons hauling supplies back and forth.

"Crush them!" Bragg ordered, but his forces were unable to recover the ground. Grant then held a strategic meeting at the Richardson home with his top commanders—considered the greatest gathering of Union generals in the war. Among them were George Thomas, Thomas Hooker, and William Tecumseh Sherman, soon to be famous for burning the South on his march through Georgia from Chattanooga.

At the meeting, Sherman asked a boy in the house, Joe Richardson, for a match to light his cigar. The boy proudly handed the general his hidden clump of matches so rare and valuable during the siege. Sherman lit his cigar and pocketed the rest of the matches. Sam Divine recounts the story: "Standing around for some time, thinking the general would hand them back to him, [young Joe] finally became desperate and mustered up the courage to ask the general to "gim me back dem matches." Gen. Sherman smilingly said, "Young man, you just charge those matches up to Jeff Davis. I need them in my business. I confiscate them as a military necessity."[89]

Within several days, Grant seized Orchard Knob, and the next day took Lookout Mountain in "The Battle Above the Clouds." The following day, Grant ordered Sherman to cross the river just up from the river landing of Chattanooga at the mouth of Chickamauga Creek. They camped at Amnicola farm, just a mile below the Confederate-held Missionary Ridge. Thousands of Federal troops were soon swarming the farmhouse and property of Tom Crutchfield, who had left Chattanooga to avoid the chaos of war. When soldiers began digging breastworks in his mother's flower garden, she berated the men until they quit. Later that night, the two Crutchfields dug up jars of gold coins that they had earlier buried there.

Crutchfield eventually sold the farm to the Montagues, who later sold it to Anne Lupton, the aunt of Tommy Lupton. "She bought that farm called the Montague Farm," Lupton told me in his interview. "It was a wonderful place to duck hunt on. . . . A black man—he must have been 90-years-old—would help me."

He would get the ducks for Tommy and also tell him stories. "But anyway, he says, 'I was on this farm when the Yankees crossed the river.'"

"Sherman's army crossed behind the hill," said Tommy. "The Southerners were on Missionary Ridge and they couldn't see them . . . and they eventually, from that point, attacked Missionary Ridge. Now this black man says, 'Tommy, there were dead Yankees as far as the eye could see. I laid under a big blowed down oak tree' is what he said, 'for four days and four nights. I was scared to death.'"

"The Confederates couldn't adjust their artillery," Tommy continued, "so the Yankees took Missionary Ridge and drove the Rebels back out of Chattanooga."

Sherman then began his famous March to the Sea. The night before the fateful battle of Missionary Ridge, soldiers viewed a six-hour lunar eclipse, deemed by many as a bad omen. "Chattanooga sealed the fate of the Confederacy," said Southern General D. H. Hill.[90] Within months, Robert E. Lee surrendered to Grant at Appomattox.

More Crucial than the War

The next few years were the most critical in all of Chattanooga's history. Chattanooga is often cited as a place with an extremely rich heritage. Ironically, the compliment is misleading. The city's three great events, the Trail of Tears, the Civil War battle, and to a degree the future establishment of TVA, are all indeed major historical chapters for the country. But their origins were not local, nor were their contestants. It is as if the city unwittingly provided the federal government with a stage called Chattanooga for three major sagas in American history, all bitterly divisive in a city that avoids strife. "Unknown men had written large pages of history there," claims one author.[91]

After the Civil War, Chattanoogans themselves wrote pages of history. Few of its citizens returned after the war, but the ones who did made choices of such noble character to cause the rest of the nation to observe and emulate them. Two of the families, the Crutchfields and McCallies, remain by that name in the city today.

David Key

It is also ironic that the fiery confrontation with Jefferson Davis by William Crutchfield appears as the lone Chattanooga event recorded in some American histories. Crutchfield's actions are arguably the opposite of the "Spirit of Chattanooga" that later emerged (although he was, in fact, acting to preserve unity). The rest of his life, however, was an unending display of peace rather than confrontation, unity instead of strife, and forgiveness over vengeance.

During the war itself, William Crutchfield received a letter begging for help from John Divine, Samuel Williams's son-in-law, who found himself imprisoned in Chattanooga after serving as a Confederate scout. Crutchfield, likewise a scout for Union Generals Wilder and Forrest, chose to forget the harsh treatment he received from Southerners after the Davis saga. He entreated General Thomas on Divine's behalf.

"General Thomas, you have a friend of mine down here in prison, and I want you to turn him out and I'll be responsible for him," Crutchfield said. Thomas agreed, on condition that Divine report to his friend every morning. Crutchfield later bought Divine's farm at the foot of Lookout Mountain for $90,000.[†]

Crutchfield offered similar support to attorney and Southern officer David Key, none other than the escort of Jefferson Davis at the Crutchfield House. Key sent Crutchfield a letter asking if he should return to Chattanooga. His concerns were valid. Radical Reconstructionists were making life more difficult for Southerners after the war than they did during it.

Lincoln, who pushed for lenient treatment for the South, had died from an assassin's bullet and was replaced by Vice President Andrew Johnson, the only Southerner to remain in the Senate after secession. That did not impress the radicals, and Johnson felt pressure to prove his Northern loyalties. He put Jefferson Davis in leg irons and imprisoned him for 720 days—mostly in solitary confinement. The South's ex-President had bugs in his mattress and only a horse bucket to drink from.[92]

For Key, a recent court decision was even more troubling. Debts already paid with Confederate money were declared invalid. In another case, Confederate soldiers, though acting under orders, could be held responsible for their actions. David Key asked his brother, Summerfield Key, to send Crutchfield a letter asking if he should return to Chattanooga with his family.

Crutchfield responded: "I presume he is aware of the various proclamations and the many difficulties on the path of a prominent Rebel." But he promised nothing bad would come from a Crutchfield. "I can assure you, Maj. Key would be kindly

---

[†] $10 million (2006). All currency equivalents are based on the Unskilled Wage comparison (see <www.eh.net/hmit/compare>). Although all comparisons have weaknesses, the Unskilled Wage appears more helpful than other common measurements such as Consumer Price Index, Gross Domestic Product (GDP) Inflator, GDP per capita, and Relative Share of GDP.

treated and such help as can be rendered by me and mine and all his old friends shall be freely, frankly, & cheerfully given."

Key did receive such help from his old friends. Though his health "was wretched" and he had no money, he and his family were given a house, rent free. Other friends brought them bread and a cow.

By 1872, Key recovered well enough to run for Congress, but he was soundly defeated by his friend, William Crutchfield. The election was notable. Tennessee was the first state to reenter the Union, but also the first to return to the Democratic party in 1869. The rest of the South soon followed. However, Crutchfield's victory in the congressional race helped lead Chattanooga into several decades of Republican dominance, defying the rest of the South and leading to the strategic coalition that welcomed Yankee industrialists and African Americans to Chattanooga. The ad inviting carpetbaggers to the area and denouncing the Ku Klux Klan also assured that those who arrived in the city "will not be required to renounce their political and religious tenants."[93] After losing to Crutchfield, Key held no grudges against Republicans or Yankees. He even invited General Sherman to his home years later.

Just after the war, Samuel Williams could not return to his home for fear of retribution for capturing the leader of Andrews' Raiders. His wife traveled to Washington to ask help from Andrew Johnson, with whom Williams had once worked as a tailor in Greenville, Tennessee. The President agreed to see Mrs. Williams immediately. He granted her husband a pardon. He also wrote a letter for her saying anyone who stole the Williamses' land must answer to the President personally.[94]

The man elected mayor of Chattanooga in 1871 was none other John T. Wilder, the Union general who first bombed the city eight years before, using the steeple of First Presbyterian Church as his target. "It was deemed appropriate," wrote a man in the paper calling himself *Rebel,* "to show that no bitterness engendered by the war remains in our hearts." Another man wrote that Wilder "once fought with all his dash and vim, and has not yet received one uncivil or unkind word . . ."[95]

William Crutchfield's wife met with General Thomas regarding the nearly destroyed state of First Presbyterian. Through her influence, Pastor Thomas Hooke McCallie's church received a federal grant so its building could be restored.

McCallie fought for unity in the community from the opposite angle of Crutchfield, urging moderation from the radical Republicans. He spoke from a position of authority, having faithfully preached without compromise to both armies during the war. One Sunday, the church was full of gray coats, and the following Sunday, he saw nothing but blue uniforms. "I must confess I went into the pulpit with trepidation," he wrote. "[They] expected me to pray for the President of the

United States and for the success of the Union army." Instead, he preached the verse, "Who is on the Lord's side?" and made sure "there was no politics in it."

At age 15, McCallie, at the behest of his mother, taught slaves how to read in the basement of First Pres, despite the fact that it was illegal to do so in Tennessee. Decades later, McCallie faced down a lynch mob of hundreds of white, racist vigilantes, but immediately after the war, he faced down a mob of radicals and blacks targeting ex-Confederates. "Some were driven away, some were killed, and a reign of terror prevailed in some neighborhoods," he wrote.

Radicals were demanding that McCallie change the church from its Southern Presbyterian ties to the Northern denomination. One leader offered him $1,000 to do so. When T. H. McCallie declined, the man threatened him. On a Sunday morning, a mob of nearly 100 men, armed with clubs, threatened the Presbyterian pastor with violence if he preached. He stepped outside, talked with their leader, David Nelson, and convinced them to leave. Later, Nelson was arrested. "Nothing but divine intervention had saved me...from a speedy and awful death," McCallie wrote later.

The editor of the only paper in town vilified McCallie for his moderate stance. "But I had my revenge," McCallie wrote. The editor's brother-in-law lay dying with smallpox and several pastors refused to minister to the contagious man. The editor finally relented and asked for help from McCallie, who led the man in a prayer of salvation. The pastor then rushed home and changed out of his contaminated clothes. The next day, the editor wrote: "May Heaven, whose minister he is, bless him for his kindness to the dying man." McCallie recalled to himself the verse that says, "If a man's ways please the Lord, he maketh even his enemies to be at peace with him." He wrote in his journal, "This was my revenge."

By 1873, McCallie considered himself too ill to continue as pastor of the church. In an unusual move of humility, he allowed his best friend, former Confederate Colonel Jonathan Bachman, to replace him as head of the city's most powerful and influential institution. It was "one of the most painful events of my life," McCallie said, but the office "demanded a stronger man, and I must give way." Nevertheless, he continued to preach in new churches nearly every week, and the two men worked side by side for exactly 50 years. "No other community in the world claims such a church history," claims Zella Armstrong. (She provides no proof, betraying her church membership. However, the arrangement was indeed extraordinary.)[96]

Later, the City Council named Bachman the "Pastor of Chattanooga." He had served under Robert E. Lee and as chaplain to Stonewall Jackson. He was well known as a veteran who had his horse shot under him in battle and ultimately was captured. But very few people knew that he carried a little sheet of paper in his vest pocket every day after the war for the rest of his life. When he changed suits, he would transfer the piece of paper. On it was written the oath of allegiance to the United States of America, which the Confederate officer had taken at the end of the war.[97]

A Light for the Nation

By 1874, the rest of the country was noticing the Spirit of Chattanooga. *The Daily Graphic* in New York spoke of Chattanooga's "mutual forbearance of others' opinions and a broadness and liberality that are very rare in any country. In no other Southern city but Chattanooga would you know a man intimately in business for years and never think of questioning his politics or in which army he served. The people [there] have but one idea, and that is Chattanooga."[98]

"Chattanooga knows no North, no South, no East, no West," boasted the *Chattanooga Times*. This reputation led to Chattanooga being chosen for the first reunion of Federal soldiers held below the Ohio River. The leadership of the event included ex-Confederates like David Key and Tom Crutchfield, and former Confederate Colonel Bachman, the First Presbyterian minister, who moderated a ceremony later that evening during which veterans from both armies eulogized the recently assassinated President, James Garfield.

The United Confederate Veterans also chose Chattanooga for its first meeting place. Over time, both groups of veterans began discussing plans to build a park at the site of the battlefield to commemorate the bloodiest two days in American history. On September 19, 1889, a great gathering of Blue and Gray was held to plan the memorial. Bachman led in prayer. *Chattanooga Times* publisher Adolph Ochs was elected chairman and welcomed the visitors. Yankee General John Wilder, who shelled the city before becoming its mayor, was chosen president of the event. The keynote address was given by the governor of Georgia, John B. Gordon, a valiant commander in the battle. Plans emerged to purchase the fifteen-square mile, 7,600 acre site as well as other strategic areas of the battles: Orchard Knob, strips along Missionary Ridge, and portions of Lookout Mountain.

Tents, barracks, and special housing arrangements were prepared for the thousands attending the great outdoor event. Afterwards, a colossal barbecue ensued. They cooked 104 hogs, 195 sheep, 122 goats, and served 12,000 loaves of bread. To end the festivities, 14,000 pipes were made from wood acquired on the battlefield and 85 pounds of Durham tobacco was handed out so all could smoke the pipe of peace. The *Veterans Report* described the historic gathering: "There they were seated together, side by side, all intent on one great purpose, and the heart of each one swelling with love and good feeling for the other."

The plans led to significant federal funding. President Benjamin Harrison approved the establishment of the Chickamauga and Chattanooga National Military

Park, the first military park in the history of the country and currently the largest. On September 18–20, 1895, an estimated 50,000 people—almost twice the population of the city—arrived again at Chattanooga and Chickamauga from all parts of the country. Ochs's paper in Chattanooga called it "the greatest dedication in the history of the world." In attendance were Vice President Adlai Stevenson, governors from 15 states, and a host of senators and congressmen.[99]

The downtown streets were swarming with enthusiastic vistors—the first major launching of Chattanooga's longtime tourist industry. A prominent opera company performed *The Pirates of Penzance*. Lectures were held in the city by H. H. Bancroft, the historian, Sir Henry Morton Stanley, the African explorer, and socialist Eugene Debs. Popular generals such as James Longstreet and Governor William McKinley of Ohio spoke to the crowds. The *Chattanooga Times* distributed a special edition containing 100 pages of details on the war saga. Over 100,000 copies were printed, making it "one of the biggest things in journalism," according to a New Orleans paper.

Captain William Fuller, whose train had been stolen by Andrews' Raiders, was an avid participant. He could be seen "mingling and shaking hands with Blue and Gray in like cordiality," wrote one historian, "gracefully demonstrating that insofar as he was concerned, the war was over." The man who led the nighttime flotilla of 200 boats around Moccasin Bend to attack Brown's Ferry, Colonel Timothy Stanley, was also committed to reconciliation. He chaired a committee to improve the river near the Suck.

During one of the major reunion events, General Rosecrans, supreme commander of the Union troops at Chickamauga, remarked that it is "difficult to find in history an instance where contending parties in after years meet together in perfect amity. It took great men to win that battle," he added, "but it takes greater men still—I will say morally great—to wipe away all the ill feeling which naturally grows out of such a contest."[100]

A Unity Destroyed

It was not the first time great efforts toward unity were exhibited on Chattanooga's soil despite horrible acts of terror and slaughter. The biographer of John Ross, Principal Chief of the Cherokee Nation for decades, says Ross's entire life can be described by "an overwhelming desire for Cherokee unity."[101] Ross's passion led to his uniting the progressive and traditional wings of the tribe, and their adopting the Cherokee Constitution in 1827, a document based on the United States' charter with three branches of government containing checks and balances within each.

John Ross

The Cherokees were considered the most "civilized" of all the tribes. The average Cherokee family in 1830 owned a log house, a small farm, a cow, various tools for agriculture and commerce, spectacles for reading, and a Bible in the Cherokee syllabary. They successfully developed their own written language, and a majority converted to Christianity. Many sent their children to be educated at the mission schools. Their best and brightest studied classical languages in New England and later represented the tribe as legally trained delegates in Washington, D.C.

Article Seven of the Cherokees' treaty with President Washington said, "The United States solemnly guarantee to the Cherokee Nation, all their lands not hereby ceded." The Cherokees kept their part of the agreement which called for them to "be led to a greater degree of civilization, and to become herdsmen and cultivators, instead of remaining in a state of hunters."

American settlers had grown used to the idea of taking Indian land. They held on to the Puritan rationale that God was bringing men from Europe to carry out the biblical mandate in Genesis to till the soil, which the Indians left alone as wilderness and hunting grounds. "The whole earth...hath been given to the sons of Adam to be tilled and improved by them," wrote Massachusetts Bay Governor John Winthrop in 1629. "Why then should we stand starving here for the places of habitation...and in the mean time suffer whole countries, as profitable for the use of man, to lie waste without any improvement?"

This philosophy met no real argument as long as the tribes being pushed west were "uncivilized." But the Cherokees created a serious problem for President Andrew Jackson and his settler constituency who hoped to make their fortune through Manifest Destiny. Jackson allowed Georgia to pass laws stripping Cherokees of their property rights. The President told the Cherokees they must remove to Oklahoma or lose all their land. America found itself bitterly divided on the "Indian Question."

A man who spent several years at the Brainerd Mission in Chattanooga and translated the New Testament into Cherokee was thrust suddenly on the nation's center stage. Missionary Samuel Worcester refused to take the newly required oath of allegiance to the State of Georgia, insisting he was called instead to the Cherokees, a sovereign nation by federal treaty. The Georgia Guard arrested him and he was sentenced to four years hard labor in the penitentiary. In what became the great civil rights case of the 1800s, all the nation watched as Worcester's case was heard by the Supreme Court. In a 5-4 decision, Chief Justice John Marshall ruled that the missionary be released—the Cherokee Nation was sovereign and not under the jurisdiction of Georgia.

Georgia refused. President Jackson defied the Supreme Court, failing to enforce its decision and creating the greatest constitutional crisis since the founding of the

United States. With relentless behind-the-scenes intrigue, Jackson threatened the funding of the missionary societies and convinced the incarcerated Worcester that he would bring civil war to America. At the insistence of the mission board in Boston, which reversed its longtime opposition to Indian removal, Worcester finally agreed to drop his case.

Principal Chief John Ross then watched his decades-long efforts at solidarity among the chiefs disintegrate as Georgia settlers burned properties and encroached on the land. A handful of desperate chiefs, sincerely attempting to save their people from annihilation, signed a treaty with Jackson agreeing to removal. Though the agreement represented less than a tenth of the Cherokee people, Jackson somehow convinced the Senate to ratify this Treaty of New Echota by one vote. John Quincy Adams called the treaty fraudulent and an "eternal disgrace upon the country."

In 1838, federal troops marched into the Cherokee Nation, seized the Cherokees, and placed them in eleven concentration camps around the region of Ross's Landing. Two thousand Cherokees were held next to Citico Creek (the current site of Chattanooga School for the Arts and Sciences near Erlanger Hospital and McKenzie Arena). Ross's Landing served as the epicenter for the removal. Of the 16,000 Cherokees removed, over 4,000 were lost, some dying on the march and many others from sickness in the concentration camps. The Cherokees were sent by boat and also by foot all the way to Oklahoma in the Long March now known as the Trail of Tears.[†]

Interviewing Today's Cherokee Chief

When I interviewed Chad "Corn Tassel" Smith, the current Principal Chief of the Cherokee Nation at his Tahlequah, Oklahoma, office, he shied away from emphasizing old wounds. He said he is more concerned with present-day injustices against the Cherokees.

"To some degree, these are things of the past," he said. "We see them as stories of inspiration rather than desperation. Instead of trying to right the wrongs of the past, or many times trying to fight the oppressive ignorance of the country, we focus on trying to improve our own quality of life."

In their current fights against big oil and big tobacco or for casinos on their land, he said they hear the same arguments they heard before removal: How can there be a sovereign nation within a sovereign state?

One-half Cherokee, Chad Smith is a graduate of the University of Georgia and has an M.B.A. and law degree. He did not provide any visible giveaways regarding his Indian heritage. (He did tell me they were quite comfortable with the word "Indian.")

[†] For citations and full treatment of this major saga in American history, see *America's Trail of Tears: a Story of Love and Betrayal* by Dean W. Arnold (Chattanooga Historical Foundation, 2005: www.TrailofTearsBook.com).

His modern office and sharp dress were upstaged by his articulate responses to questions about the 1830s, a decade I had been studying for two years.

"The 1830 Treaty gave the United States the authority to exchange lands," he told me, but instead the Cherokees became victims of simple racism. Their land was "basically taken by official extortion. Our institutions were more sophisticated than Georgia and Tennessee. We were 90 percent literate, which was probably ten times the rate of whites in those surrounding states. We passed a Constitution—that's what galled Georgia, that we had a constitutional government within its borders."

He said 80 percent of the settlers who took over their land left within 15 years. "They weren't of the quality or quantity to sustain themselves," he said. "Basically, the economics of North Georgia was not farming. The Cherokees used it very well in a subsistence economy—hunting and fishing and such, but if you go now to North Georgia, it's sparsely populated. Western North Carolina is sparsely populated. It's only now with the urban sprawl of Atlanta and maybe Chattanooga that there's been any significant population, so there was sufficient territory for 14,000 folks to have survived. It just wasn't politically popular."

"So what should we do now?" I asked him. "Should white America apologize or should there be reparations for past injustices?"

"If you'd live up to the original agreements, we'd be happy," he said.

Atoning for Sins of the Past?

Back in Chattanooga, the controversy remains after several generations. Does the question of past injustices linger with descendents of the soldiers who removed the Cherokees? It was time to ask for an interview with Tom Decosimo, Scotty Probasco's relative. They both are related to removal agent George Gillespie, Scotty's direct ancestor and Tom's great-uncle. Tom agreed to meet me in the boardroom of the Decosimo accounting firm in the Tallan Building, which overlooks downtown.

Tom said his ancestors on both sides ended up with the major prize—land. He is related not only to the Gillespies but also is a direct descendent of another removal agent, Elisha Sharp. Tom is also a descendent of John Cessna Sharp, the grandson of John L. Divine. Divine, of course, is the traveler who lost his wallet and married the daughter of Samuel Williams, the man who arrested the leader of Andrews' Raiders. Tom descends from Divine's second marriage with Rachel James, making Tom Decosimo the great-great-grandson of John L. Divine (see chart on next page).

Tom showed me an old wrinkled document—an ancient deed for Moccasin Bend. "John L. Divine ended up with Cherokee land," he said. "Not directly—he got it from Ephraim Hixson who got it from John Brown."

"The John Brown of Brown's Ferry and Tavern?" I asked.

SHARP ~ DIVINE

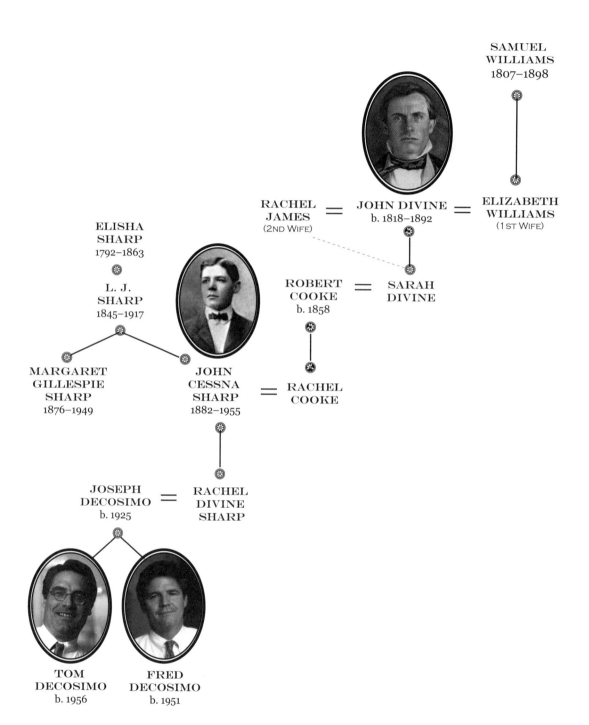

SAMUEL
WILLIAMS
1807–1898

RACHEL
JAMES — JOHN DIVINE — ELIZABETH
(2ND WIFE) b. 1818–1892 WILLIAMS
(1ST WIFE)

ELISHA
SHARP
1792–1863

L. J.
SHARP
1845–1917

ROBERT
COOKE — SARAH
b. 1858 DIVINE

MARGARET
GILLESPIE
SHARP
1876–1949

JOHN
CESSNA
SHARP — RACHEL
1882–1955 COOKE

JOSEPH
DECOSIMO — RACHEL
b. 1925 DIVINE
SHARP

TOM
DECOSIMO
b. 1956

FRED
DECOSIMO
b. 1951

(Charts are partial, not exhaustive, highlighting key links or characters in the book.)

"Right."

"That's the original deed?

"Yeah. My aunt carried this around in her damn wallet forever."

Just as things were warming up between Tom and me, another fellow walked in.

"Hi, how are you?"

"Hey, Dean."

"What's your name?" I asked.

"Fred."

"Fred. Oh…Fred! I've just heard your name, Fred," I replied, awkwardly. "Gotten a couple of letters from you."

"Well, that's all right," Tom interjected. "We've had a few bumps in the road." Everybody laughed. (I guess the spirit of Chattanooga lives on, even today.) Tom showed his brother Fred the deed to Moccasin Bend.

"We tried to lay claim to it, but to no avail," Fred joked.

I asked Fred how he felt about obtaining lands his forebearers moved onto after the Cherokees left.

"It's worse than that," he said. "Our ancestors helped usher them off."

"That's what Tom told me."

"It's one of those facts," Fred said. "I don't think I can pay anybody back for it. I don't think I should have to. I don't feel a great need to atone for the sins of four generations back."

Tom and Fred quickly pointed out that the 900 acres their ancestors owned was lost generations ago. "If I was still sitting on the land my great-great-grandfather got from the Cherokees, I might be a little sensitive to your questions," said Tom.

They also explained that ancestors on the other side of their family tree were kind to the Cherokees. One of their aunts was chair of the Chief John Ross Chapter of the National Society of the Daughters of the American Revolution, which now keeps up the Brainerd Mission cemetery, located between Kinko's and Eastgate Mall, the only remnant that remains of the effort to minister to the Cherokees. Their aunt and grandmother used to take them there.

"So when you were a kid, you got taken out to the Brainerd Mission cemetery? Is that right?"

"Yeah," said Fred.

"What did you do out there?"

"We planted a tree."

"How old were you?"

"Six or seven."

"What did you think?"

"That we were there to plant a tree."

I kept asking questions.

"You know, Dean...I didn't realize until I was much older...I just remembered being dragged out there by my grandmother. You're thinking, 'What the heck am I doing out here? It's cold.'"

But Fred and Tom's point was that the odd actions of some elderly ladies eventually made a real and lasting impact on them.

The whole saga was "ethnic cleansing," said Tom. "It's like what they wanted to do in Bosnia, but they got away with it."

He made the point that what happened was really not so very long ago. "It's not ancient history if your great-great-great grandparents were involved in that ancient history," he said.

Since there is still some kind of connection, however distant, many descendents, even today, must construct a rationale for the event or find some other way to find forgiveness or closure.

Of course, one helpful way to deal with the Removal is to embrace the concept that the Cherokees did the same thing that we did to them.

"The Cherokees displaced the Creeks," said Tom.

"The Creeks displaced the Mississippians," added Fred.

"You know, I'm on the board of the Friends of the Bend...," Tom began. But he was interrupted by his brother.

"Tom's trying to pay back."

"Trying to atone," Tom clarified with a half smile. "The fact of the matter is that the Cherokees...killed off their predecessors. Or, you know, that's what they think. This was a very valuable spot."

Tom got it right—according to the most recent histories, that is, written 25 years ago. However, groundbreaking discoveries in the past 15 years by scholars studying the Spanish explorers during the 16th century provide strong evidence to the contrary—that the Cherokees did not remove their predecessors but only occupied a deserted territory. Some may think this does not matter, but, for those so inclined, a later chapter provides evidence that our actions against the Cherokees were not just another round in an endless cycle of forced removals. Instead, our actions are indeed what many perceive them to be: a terrible injustice and tragedy.

Blacks and the Spirit of Chattanooga

Injustice is a concept never far from the minds of the major ethnic group that remains in Chattanooga: African Americans. During the golden age of the Spirit of Chattanooga,

Hiram Tyree

when Republicans and blacks ruled the day through a strategic coalition, local African Americans held major posts in the community, were elected to many city offices, and were appointed to a significant part—sometimes the majority—of the police force. Later, a group of leading citizens lobbied the Democratic Tennessee legislature to change the structure of city government in Chattanooga. For 60 years, from 1911 to 1971, no blacks held elected office in Chattanooga.

One particular black leader, Hiram Tyree, was a major burr in the saddle that motivated Chattanooga's powerful leadership to take action. An ex-slave who lost his leg in a railroad accident, Tyree became a successful shoe salesman and later acquired a great amount of real estate. He held several offices, including justice of the peace, school commissioner, alderman in city government (the precursor to City Councilman), and chairman of the local Republican Party.[102]

White leaders and citizens began to tire of the significant influence of blacks such as Tyree. According to one editorial statement in the *Chattanooga Times*, "We have no prejudice against the Negroes, but dislike to be ruled and ruined by them." Another man lobbying the legislature said, "If any of you gentlemen will come over to Chattanooga…we will furnish a nigger to arrest you, a nigger to lock you up, and a nigger to take care of you after you get into jail."[103]

The handicapped Tyree was particularly powerful as an alderman elected by his inner-city district beneath Cameron Hill. A city tax collector lamented that the election again brought them "a crippled negro; what in hell is coming in November?" Another *Times* editorial complained that Tyree's district could not be "captured from the negroes by any means."

John Divine's son, Sam Divine, called for Tyree's ouster in his popular column in the *Chattanooga News*. "When one or two boss politicians, in combination with a couple of ignorant Negroes and a handful of weak white brothers, can defeat the will of the people, then it is time to stop and think." He later had a personal confrontation with Hiram Tyree after Divine fired his son Wesley. Divine said Tyree "jumped to his foot" and began hopping around like a kangaroo. "Hiram is no baboon by any means," Divine wrote, "[even] if he does ape his white brothers in picking up the crumbs that fall from his (political) master's table."

Over time, local leaders and editorialists at the *Chattanooga Times* began decrying the tactics of "machine politics" and other corruptions deemed irreparable. Ballots were allegedly removed from the polls, and some ballots were given creatively colored covers to help illiterate voters know which candidate to choose. The Citizens Civic League—a forerunner to the Good Government League—was formed in 1909. The list of names included Pattens, Probascos, Chamblisses, McCallies, Brocks, and many others. This elite group called for nondescript ballots that required voters to be literate. They also called for a more permanent solution—changing the form of government from individual districts (called "wards" at that time) to five at-large commissioners, all chosen by the entire voting population. Ochs's *Chattanooga Times* framed the choice as either "good government" or "machine politics."

The effort was successful. The *Times* reported on Tyree's demise: "...his glory has dimmed considerably of late, and if the movement for commission government succeeds, his light promises to go out forever."[104]

Recently retired UTC history professor Larry Ingle sharply criticizes the 1911 change in government. "The ancestors of Jac Chambliss and Scotty Probasco, the good government guys, the goo-goos, they went up to Nashville [and] botched the wards," said Ingle during our interview in his home in Brainerd. "And when they did, there wasn't another black man to serve on the city commission until 1971."

"[Should we] let everybody in the community vote for all five members than to just vote for one? Doesn't that sound nice and democratic? It does to me!" said Ingle. "Except that when you elect someone from a ward, you elect someone you know and has a personal relationship with you...you get school teachers, drugstore operators, grocers, handymen, and next-door neighbor types. [But] if you're elect-ing people way over in Hixson you don't even know [then you choose someone whose] name might show up in the paper once in a while. And how do you get your name in the paper...by having influence and power and money. Right? You elect citywide and you get industrialists, lawyers for industrialists, lawyers for railroads. See the difference?"

Ingle, who is white, earned his doctorate from Wisconsin University and also participated in a black studies fellowship at Yale. While we were talking, a young black man, 25, popped in the door and went to his room—an engineering grad from Georgia Tech who needed a place to stay. He's like an "adopted son," Ingle said.

The UTC professor wrote his doctoral thesis on a black North Carolina con-gressman, the last in the South until 1973. "In 1899, North Carolina approved a constitutional amendment which disenfranchised blacks," said Ingle. "The next election, he didn't run. As he left the state, he said, 'May God damn North Carolina, the state of my birth.'"

Black leaders in Chattanooga today have found a way to improve their lot without leaving or damning their fellow white citizens. Judge Williams worked in the 1971 campaign of Commissioner John Franklin, the first black city-elected official since 1911.

"I was here when the victory celebrations took place," said Williams. "It was an exciting time because it gave promise that maybe we had now moved to another era in Chattanooga."

In 1988, black leaders filed suit against the city for violation of the Voting Rights Act, claiming the at-large system "dilutes the voting strength of blacks." After an

11-day trial, the judge ruled against the city. In 1991, a new City Council was established, comprised of nine separate districts—similar to the ward system before 1911.[105]

Strife? Yes. But it was all done without violence. In a real sense, the Spirit of Chattanooga had its effect on race relations in the city. "We really never had any large skirmishes from a racial point of view," said Judge Williams. "I mean, we've had one or two, but I don't call them mega-skirmishes—like Birmingham had, like Atlanta had, like Memphis had."

"These cities that had these problems dealt with them, and I think it was good to deal with them, put the real issues on the table, deal with them and move on."

"To some extent, one would argue that maybe that's Chattanooga's problem: we never had that. It's always been a more accommodating city. . . . You know, if there's a problem let's just push it to the side. Let's just try not to think about it. So . . . more accommodating."

Fathers, Forgiveness, and the Future

While Chattanooga's black community faced the challenge of forgetting the past, progressing forward, and all the while remaining in relationship with the city fathers, the sons of the city's leaders faced the same challenge with their real fathers.

"All men are, in some way, at war with their father," said Rick Montague. I had asked him about the father-son relationship between Jack Lupton and Cartter Lupton—both the wealthiest men of their generation. When Montague directed Jack's Lyndhurst Foundation in the early '80s, he was also Jack's son-in-law (he has since remarried).

"My dad was a very modest man. My dad shared a lot of characteristics with Cartter Lupton," said Rick. "Not given to talk about many things, so he didn't talk much about his family." He said Jack may be more like his mother, a more talkative type. Jack once said his mom could have been a comedienne if given the opportunity.

Jack Lupton made no attempt to conceal the contest between father and son when he gave a rare and lengthy interview to the *Chattanooga Times* in 1986. He sat at a marble table in a small conference room at his seventh-floor office in the Krystal Building. Behind him on the wall were two photographs—one of his grandfather, Coca-Cola bottling legend John T. Lupton, and the other of his father, Cartter Lupton, who expanded the bottling empire.

"The biggest problem that Chattanooga has ever had—they all buttoned it up at night and went home to their little bitty conclaves and nobody ever communicated with anybody—including him and his cohorts."[106] Jack pointed back to the picture of his father.

Cartter Lupton, who was rarely photographed, stands next to a portrait of his father, J. T. Lupton.

A **seal** with this scene hangs in the chambers of both City Hall and the Hamilton County Commission.

"They wanted to keep this place a secret. They didn't want anybody knowing about what a nice little deal they had here."

Like any son, Lupton is left to decide which of his father's characteristics are a problem and which parts of the family legacy he wants to carry forward.

"You know, the man back here" (he points again at his father) "raised me to understand something about giving money away intelligently. I don't know if I've done it intelligently, but he taught me an awful lot."

Scotty Probasco talked about his father in similar ways. He also pointed to an old picture behind him several times during our interview. It shows the bank's early board of directors. "There's old man Maclellan up there on the far end. His father was the founder of Provident." He showed me Cartter Lupton, E. Y. Chapin, and a number of other power-structure luminaries. Scotty's father, Scott Probasco, Sr., stood in the very center.

Scotty tends to be more community focused than his father, he said, and has a more outgoing personality, like his mother. "Dad always had a good concern for people and that sort of thing, but the city per se—he was in the old guard with all those old buddies that were manufacturers," he said. "He made the comment, 'We'll grow, we'll grow, we're well located,' but not really trying to put a thrust on it and not bucking all his old guard buddies that didn't really want to see it grow all that much."

"They would say, 'Scotty, why are you trying to make Chattanooga grow?' Because if you got a new industry or new plant in here, it competes for the labor market. So they didn't want it."

Scotty said that was the case during the '30s, '40s and '50s. "They didn't really want growth for Chattanooga because it competed for labor. Run the costs up. I'm telling you things that people are not going to tell you that much."

However, several of the interviewees provided the same candid information, including Frank Brock. His father ran the South's largest candy manufacturering firm. "I do remember my father saying, 'I don't know why everybody wants to grow so much.' I can remember him saying that. And my brother and I used to say, 'Dad, if you don't grow, it's like a bicycle—you either go forward or you fall over. You've got to grow.' And he said, 'Well, you don't have to grow fast.' And we would always say, 'Well, it's better to grow fast than to grow slow.'"

"One of the values, if you will, that Chattanooga had, I think, is that we didn't want to grow up," said Brock. "There was a strong sense that growth would ... create a lot of competition for jobs [and not be] good for local business. That was a very bad notion, I think. Atlanta clearly had a growth philosophy, and Chattanooga had more of a slow-growth philosophy, I think."

Brock is also left to weigh the good and bad of the previous generation. "In some ways they were doing the greatest thing for Chattanooga—they were running good businesses and creating great job opportunities for thousands of people, but there was a sense [in which] they were not progressively looking to the next era."

Frank didn't have a picture to point to, but instead he pointed to a building—the Mountain City Club. Legend says the "Guinea Table" at the club was reserved for only eight men—the city's eight most powerful. They determined the course of events and whether or how the city would grow. Most had died out by the time Frank was a young man. "It was in the southwest corner of the Mountain City Club in the private 'members only' dining room." Brock named Cartter Lupton, Scott Probasco, Sr., Bob Maclellan, and a few others. "They were the Guineas. Dad never told me about them except they were all rich-rich and they were in a world to themselves."

As usual, Jack Lupton had the choicest words for this small group of men who held back growth, a group which included his own father.

"Well, they were full of shit, as far as I'm concerned. And I told him so, in just those words, a good while ago. And that, I think, is what Venture has begun to overcome."

Three Pictures

Chattanooga Venture indeed included thousands of local citizens in the planning process to bring growth and improvement to the city. For Jack Lupton and his peers, their efforts to improve the direction of the previous generation demonstrates the exact opposite of a few powerful men seeking a way to control the city.

However, the perception for many people in the valley, perhaps a majority, is that the legend of a small, self-serving power structure remains a strong reality to this day. A 1999 professional survey conducted by the *Chattanooga Times Free Press* and WTVC-TV revealed that nearly half of all Chattanoogans believe that the people who control the city live on Lookout Mountain.[107]

What picture could these critics in the valley point to on the wall? Perhaps no image is more appropriate than the seal of Chattanooga on the wall of City Hall. Chattanooga's official emblem depicts a faraway view of the city, a scene of the Tennessee River curving around Moccasin Bend with the town and its buildings barely visible just beyond. The city is viewed from the perspective of Lookout Mountain. A powerful cannon in the foreground points directly from the mountain to the city.

This great seal looms as a large backdrop to the weekly meetings of the Chattanooga City Council. The county uses the same image in its seal, which also serves as the backdrop for its Hamilton County Commission. The seal is engraved in the stone foyer floor of City Hall and forged on the surface of the manhole covers all over the city streets. Depending on the viewer, the seal might communicate the area's rich history or perhaps the impact of the Civil War. For others, it may suggest the protective power of Lookout Mountain or perhaps something more ominous.

The survey article by the paper and WTVC-TV was entitled, "Local residents split over Power Structure." It quoted longtime critic Edna Taylor. "The same people sit on all these committees in town," she said. "There's no doubt that the people on Lookout Mountain are in control."

Taylor and other advocates were picketing outside the Chattanooga Choo Choo hotel when 1200 Chattanoogans gathered for a fundraiser for the Aquarium in 1988. The critics complained that tax money would be used for the project. They also complained that the Aquarium was not a major part of Venture's planning process.

"The word 'Aquarium' cannot be found one time…in the general goals produced by the Vision 2000 process," claimed a picketer quoted by the paper.[108]

Lupton never veered from his goal. "The aquarium will fool the hell out of all the critics," he said. "Of course, you can't make everybody happy. Folks are going to shoot at this. They have to do that. That's part of human nature. You can't please 250,000 people."

Jack's brother-in-law, Scotty, calls them "professional aginners," or folks who are always against any proposed idea.

Jack was asked about the accusation that he wants people's tax money. "Oh, they love to hide behind that. They love it. 'You're going to tax us to death.'…They can't say that about me. They'd love to, but I've got 'em. I've got not one thing to gain out of this except a better place for you and your kids and their kids to live. They can't lay that on me. . . ."

"They've been led to believe that the rich people of this world are out to f— 'em, [that] they're going to up their taxes and they're going to kill 'em. That is not the purpose of this at all. They'll find out."

The controversy reached a crescendo when Lupton was publicly criticized by someone other than a routine picketer—state senator Ward Crutchfield. Ward's great-grandfather, William Crutchfield, had no problem confronting Jefferson Davis, so apparently Ward had no fear in telling Lupton his aquarium might be a burden on taxpayers.

According to Jack Lupton, Crutchfield suggested to the press that Lupton's offer to put $11 million on the table for the project was "blinky," so Jack wrote Ward a letter.

"Don't *ever* (Lupton's emphasis) suggest to anyone that *anything* (Lupton's emphasis) I promise is 'blinky.' We are *going* to build the Tennessee State Aquarium, Ward, with or without you, and we're not going to charge the taxpayer another red cent—*and you know it!* Now, you take that message back to the boys who put you up to this crap!"

Lupton told Crutchfield the process will be "tough" and "slow" to "make this city a better place to live," and "consequently, we don't need people trying to undermine the effort. You got two sides to choose from, Ward, one constructive, the other destructive. Think about it."

In his letter, Lupton said he put his thoughts in writing "so we can refer to it in the future."

Senator Crutchfield, who lives in the valley, also responded with a letter.

I am "neither intimidated by nor controlled by anyone. I've never been anyone's 'boy' and I don't ever intend to be," he began.

"I was shocked and amazed to read that 'we're not going to charge the taxpayers another red cent,'" Ward wrote. "In case you haven't heard, they are asking for $4.1 million of taxpayer's money from the state this year." He went on to detail other sales tax and hotel tax monies based on still-unestimated growth revenues that he claimed were being called upon for the project.

"If you don't want to publicly lay out the full financing plans for the aquarium in advance, I suggest you just build it yourself," he said.

Ward told Jack he also chose to put his response in writing "so you, I, and the public can refer to it from time to time."[109]

In our interview, Ward Crutchfield mentioned to me the flap with Lupton. "He wrote a letter to me that I didn't like, so I wrote a letter to him and took them both down to the *Free Press*. They printed them both on the front page of the paper. He did not like that."

"We had some words, but I have no problem now."

A year after Jack and Ward's front-page duel, the same paper's front page announced that the aquarium would use no tax money. "Private Funds Will Build…River Facility" the headline proclaimed. In a compromise, state officials agreed to fund the multimillion dollar landscaping of grounds surrounding the building.[110]

Three Building Projects

The Aquarium is one of three building projects that symbolize the relationship between Chattanooga's leadership and its people. The Aquarium represents the successes. A decade after the Tennessee Aquarium's opening, it is difficult to find a protesting voice anywhere. This building, through a creative public-private partnership, changed the face of the city, revived an entire tourism industry, led to nearly a billion dollars in downtown investment, and lifted the spirits and self-esteem of an entire city.

On this one, Jack was right when he said, "The aquarium will fool the hell out of all the critics."

The second building project that exemplifies the relationship between leadership and populace is Finley Stadium. It represents the failures. On this one, Jack got it wrong. The stadium "will do far more than you or I can ever realize," he said. "If you think what we did on the river was something, wait 'til you see this."[111]

By 1999 local officials were complaining about urgent requests to fund a $300,000 shortfall for Finley Stadium, which sits on one end of the city's Southside Development, once highly touted as a sustainable eco-park. Even today, the stadium sits largely unused and has struggled every year since it was built.

Still, Lupton refuses to be deterred. He believes in trial and error. "Mistakes? Let's make sure we make some. [But] let's don't sit here and make the biggest of all. I don't have to tell you what that is."

"Do nothing. Do nothing."

County Commissioner Curtis Adams risked being called an "aginner" for criticizing the stadium boondoggle. He complained that they had been given "a pretty rosy picture of what was going to happen." Four years before, the stadium's executive director told downtown leaders the facility would be "in the black from day one to year one." They were told to discount the "naysayers" who talk about the stadium sitting unused.[112]

Many citizens believe projects like the stadium are forced upon the public against their will. City Councilwoman Marti Rutherford distrusts the public brainstorming and planning sessions. "I feel like it's all a done deal before it gets to us," she said.[113]

But leaders of the "Chattanooga Process" discount such theories. Jack Murrah said the idea of a secretive, conspiratorial group "making decisions for everybody else" does not happen, "and I think I would have been in a position where I would have seen that."

He said he participated in not one phone conversation or letter exchange with other leaders of foundations during the critical years of Venture. "Now is that a good thing? I would say no."

Mai Bell Hurley, who chaired Venture in its heyday, agrees. "We knew they weren't in a small room someplace. We thought it would be kind of neat if they would get in a small room."

"We used to laugh and say that if there were ten men meeting some place in some wonderful skyscraper, we didn't know where they were meeting. They weren't."

Chattanooga Times Publisher Paul Neely said "power structure" is an "outdated, simplistic phrase that fails to match the complexity of modern civic affairs. It's time we found some different words."

"I despise the term," said Jack Lupton.

Tennessee Aquarium during a nighttime storm.

Bob Corker gives "State of the City" address.

Neely said the major businesses in town are not even run by the big families any more. "The Luptons, Probascos, Davenports, Brocks, and Maclellans no longer rule their local companies," he said.[114]

A prime example used to quench power structure conspiracy theories is the attempts by Lupton and others to improve the Aquarium and riverfront area by closing down Riverfront Parkway. Of only two letters-to-the-editor I could find written by Lupton, one of them calls for the closing of Riverfront Parkway.

"What Jack Lupton wants, Jack Lupton gets, right? Wrong!" wrote columnist Bill Anderson in the *East Tennessee Business Journal.* "The parkway is still open. The 'power structure' was behind closing the parkway, but that meant nothing to traffic engineers and thousands of people."[115]

Frank Brock shook his head when I told him about the large number of Chattanoogans who believe the power structure controls things. "I just can't even fathom where they would get that," he said.

Perhaps they had heard him talk about the Guinea Table. Brock does make clear no such group eats lunch together today. "Well, if you consider me part of the power structure—which I guess would be a fair thing—I've not had access to Jack Lupton for years and years and years. Few people have. I've had access to Scotty Probasco, who has access to Jack Lupton. But Scotty has been a real big influence in this town in many, many positive ways. But it's just a power of persuasion—it's not the power of money. It's mainly because Scotty is willing to work hard on lots of specific projects. I would put right up there, with Scotty, Joe Decosimo, who doesn't have any of those same financial resources. Before him, Joe Davenport had a huge impact."

Brock pointed to public-private partnerships like RiverCity Company. "My sense is that they leverage that money extraordinarily well. It's more about people who are smart and had good ideas. . . . But with Jack Lupton coming in and saying, 'This is what I want'—it doesn't work that way. . . . Leadership is just far more diffused today than it used to be."

 Scotty Probasco also talks about the dilution of leadership. "Now you can't go to ten places and raise yourself ten or twenty million for a good cause going on. It's much more splintered now," he said. "But you could move some things forward real easily because we had a pretty close-knit powerful power structure in the last 25 years that wanted to make Chattanooga grow."

Writing about Chattanooga can be great fun. Maybe that is because I enjoy mystery and paradox, for just when you learn all the arguments for why there is no actual power structure in Chattanooga, the same folks begin to lament the decline of the power structure and all the benefits it brings to the city. I suppose both can somehow be true.

Probasco talked about nonprofits "that are running real scared because they have a younger board.... It's a tougher thing today. They wring their hands. Like when Jack Lupton dies, well, all of a sudden [he names a charity here] will lose a $100,000 gift. There's nobody sitting there to make up for that $100,000."

Scotty's concerns are echoed by Summerfield K. Johnston, Jr., another area Coca-Cola bottler. "When Jack Lupton is not here anymore, there's not a Lupton here that's going to inherit that mantle," Johnston said. "When Scotty is gone ... [no one is] going to wield the power that he did at one time and have the influence that he did."

Judge Williams said Coke magnate and CEO Robert Woodruff, now descesased, was the only man in Atlanta who was able to compete with the level of giving demonstrated by several in Chattanooga. "They don't have the kind of people to give at the level we have—the Probascos, the Luptons, the Davenports. They just don't have that. It's so huge. It's so large."

Chattanooga's Greatest Challenge

Mayor Bob Corker can clearly articulate a major transition—perhaps *the* major trend—occurring in Chattanooga today. He discusses Chattanooga's heritage of phenomenal giving by foundations as well as the unusual "massive concentrations of wealth" enjoyed by a few individuals. However, "lots of things have occurred," he said. "The face of philanthropy is changing dramatically right now with deaths and disablements and changes."

Corker mentions the recent deaths of the near-billionaire, Frank Harrison, Jack's cousin, as well as Lupton's sister, Elizabeth Lupton Davenport. Corker notes that near the time of their deaths, Jack Lupton himself suffered a stroke that left him in a wheelchair.

"It's just a huge change that's happening," Corker said during our interview last year. "It's an unbelievable transition, and I feel, actually, that it's sort of a privilege to be mayor during this period of time, where I see us sort of transcending the old but very good."

So who does replace Jack Lupton? Corker explains that no one person can do so. Ironically, if any one person might be named to carry Lupton's mantle into the next generation, the name of Bob Corker would likely be at the top of the list. For the first time in Chattanooga history, the major fundraising effort in town was led, not by a legendary layman or a prominent Presbyterian pastor, but rather by the city's mayor. Corker oversaw the raising of $120 million for the 21st Century Waterfront Project. He raised $47 million of it himself in seventy-seven one-on-one meetings. During his first twenty presentations, everyone he pitched said yes. "Bob

Corker asked me and other people to give $250,000 for his Riverfront project," said Tommy Lupton. "I think everybody gave it."

Like Jack Lupton, Corker is a man of many millions, although his fortune is estimated somewhere under $100 million, while Lupton's is somewhere under $1 billion. Corker made his money constructing malls around the country, but his fortune is now invested in downtown Chattanooga, thanks to Tommy Lupton, whose business owned several buildings, including the Tallan and Krystal Buildings, which house a great many of the city's prominent businessmen.

Tommy Lupton recounted the story to me of when he planned to sell his Stone Fort Land Company to a Birmingham company. "Bob Corker had told me, 'If you ever sell that business, you give me a call.' I remembered that, so I called Bob up and I said, 'Bob, I'm talking and negotiating to sell Stone Fort Land' and he like to fell over backwards. He said, 'I'll be over there in a minute.' And, sure enough, he came over here and we talked and ended up making a deal for stock instead of buildings which ended up being a much better deal for me."

"He made me an offer, and I said, 'Bob, you're about a million dollars short.' And he says, 'Help me to finance that and I'll give it to you.' And I said okay. So for the last amount of money, I took a note and he's still paying on that. He's current on all his obligations. He's a wonderful man to deal with. He's honorable in every respect. He's smart as a whip."

After that transaction with Tommy Lupton, Bob Corker became the largest property owner in downtown Chattanooga. In October 2001, Mayor Corker announced from a stage on the Aquarium grounds that he had arranged that the road next to him be given to Chattanooga by Tennessee Governor Don Sundquist. The city and the street in question would no longer be constrained by state bureaucracy. He was speaking of Riverfront Parkway, the third building project that symbolizes the relationship between Chattanooga's leadership and its people. Of course, many assumed the road would be immediately closed, another goal inevitably secured for the power structure, for Jack Lupton, or for his successor of sorts.

That is not what happened. As the Aquarium represents the successes of the "Chattanooga Process" and the stadium represents the failures, the Riverfront Parkway represents the positive reality. Through suggestion, initiation, effort, communication, argument, time, and compromise, the people and their leaders in Chattanooga found a way to "make things work," just as *U.S. News & World Report* described in 1998.

Riverfront Parkway continues to be a thoroughfare for the public, but it has been transformed from a wide highway separating downtown and the river to a more narrow, two-lane, pedestrian-friendly street. Oak trees, on-street parking, and state-of-the-art lighting have been added. Pedestrians, motorists, and boaters have easier access to the new pier over the river and the new housing and retail developments along the parkway. A pedestrian bridge connects to the Aquarium and Hunter Museum and a passageway underneath the Parkway—displaying shell art from precontact Native Americans designed by Cherokees in Oklahoma—also connects the city's downtown to its place of origin on the Tennessee River.

But while Corker made a major impact as mayor, he now spends much of his time oustide the city campaigning for a seat in the U.S. Senate. If he succeeds, another potential successor to the likes of Jack and Scotty will be tapped for more national concerns. Corker acknowledges that neither he nor any other one person, or even a few persons, can marshal such accomplishments in Chattanooga any longer. "I see a tremendous broadening of the decision-making process of involvement," he said during our interview in his office at City Hall. "When you look at the waterfront plan and 300 people show up, you look at public art and 500 people show up—I get the sense that today people almost come to these meetings because they're afraid if they don't, 'Something's getting ready to happen and I could have given my two cents but I didn't.'"

"I think we're going through a really interesting transformation in our community where many of the good things that happened over the last 15 years were generated by some really civically oriented, wealthy people who just made them happen." But there has been a shift because of the times and circumstances. Now it is being done in a "different way by a broader group of citizens with less concentrated wealth."

The challenge increases each year. In 2002, the *Chattanooga Times Free Press* announced that Chattanooga no longer leads the State of Tennessee in foundation wealth. In 1980, seventy-five percent of the assets of all foundations were in Chattanooga. Twenty years later, it has declined to 25 percent, with Nashville taking Chattanooga's spot for the first time in top assets.[116]

"Chattanooga is a much more minor player from the standpoint of having concentrated philanthropy in one place," said Corker. "The economy of the '90s is dead."

It will not be the first time, or certainly the last, that the "Spirit of Chattanooga" is called upon to to solve the newest and most pressing issues of the community. The city's first historian, attorney Harry M. Wiltse, wrote about the city's historic resolve during its first seven decades in the 19th century. He called it "The Chattanooga Spirit."

"*The Chattanooga Spirit* has been a verbal stimulant to civic pride for many years and has wrought at times marvelous triumphs over difficulties and disasters," wrote Wiltse. "Just as the *Spirit of Seventy-six* has been a slogan of patriotism, the Chattanooga spirit has been our watchword of municipal progress."[117]

Rev. T. H. McCallie

The *Knoxville Dispatch* described that same spirit in 1880. "Chattanooga has more backbone for its size and advantages than any small village we know of. She has as many lives as a cat. As to killing her, even the floods have failed. You may knock the breath out of her—that's all. She will refill her lungs and draw a longer breath than ever."[118]

Today's major question for Chattanooga, according to longtime *Chattanooga Free Press* editor Lee Anderson, is whether the next generation can step up. "The greatest challenge is to have the next generation as dedicated to the community personally as the last generation was because so many things now are not locally owned," he told me. Then, he named families like the Luptons, Brocks and Guerrys and others who are left with the challenge. "We need to be sure that the next generation carries on that tradition of personal involvement—unselfish, constructive contribution to the community for what's good for everybody."

It is left for the entire community to answer this call, but Anderson's challenge to those bearing recognizable last names in the community brings emphasis once again to that very defining characteristic of Chattanooga, Tennessee—the ongoing, multigenerational families that historically provide leadership to the city.

Will they even be here a generation from now? Names like Brock, Probasco, Maclellan, and Chapin seem to be safely continuing to the next generation. But it appears the Lupton name will die out with the passing of Tommy and Jack's generation. The name and DNA of the Crutchfield House owners will also continue in Chattanooga, but not by the same people. Ward's grandchildren, such as Missy's son "James Ward Crutchfield Corn," live here under a different last name. And two adopted Crutchfield sons carry on the name but not the genes of the man who confronted Jefferson Davis.

One Father's Powerful Legacy

There is one family, however, whose name remains prominent on the Chattanooga landscape and whose influence is more pervasive than all the others. This family unifies the city in a most extraordinary way and provides a great hope to the other families that the "Spirit of Chattanooga" will continue to prevail.

The progeny of Rev. Thomas Hooke McCallie have influenced nearly every key institution, church, nonprofit, and fortune in the town. This Presbyterian pastor, who remained when all the other pastors left during the Civil War, fathered sixteen children. Two of his sons went on to establish the McCallie School. The Chattanooga council named another son "Chaplain of the City." A daughter helped establish Girls Preparatory School, another the Bright School. McCallie himself founded numerous local churches, including Lookout Mountain Presbyterian, and he established a score of local charities that continue today.

(Right) **"Reconciliation,"** the top of the New York Monument

(Below) The **New York Monument** on Lookout Mountain overlooks Moccasin Bend and all of Chattanooga.

Allen McCallie is the current chairman of the Lyndhurst Foundation. Thomas Hooke McCallie III (Tom) has been the longtime executive director of the Maclellan Foundation. Franklin McCallie, an assistant principal of Howard School years ago, is credited by Judge Walter Williams as a key player in electing Chattanooga's first black elected official in 1971. Dr. David McCallie founded the modern Erlanger Hospital era as a separate legal authority of the state. Another great-granddaughter, Eleanor Cooper, served as president of Chattanooga Venture.

Direct descendents of T. H. McCallie have participated in nearly every conceivable aspect of the community. A large share of Chattanooga's leaders have been trained by McCallie headmasters, and Dr. McCallie's legendary church has trained and inspired the city's greatest developers and philanthropists. If ever there were one man worthy to be called the Father of Chattanooga, T. H. McCallie, both literally and spiritually, takes the honor.

He was a slight man. He suffered from a respiratory illness most of his life, which caused him to leave the pastorate of First Presbyterian prematurely. He was never a man of great wealth, but he passed on a legacy of faith, vision, excellence, and perseverance. The verse he preached from for his first sermon in Chattanooga on January 1, 1862, provides evidence. He preached from the same verse, First Peter 1:7, during his last sermon exactly 50 years later. The passage explains that his Christian faith "is more precious than gold." Even today, Rev. McCallie reminds the leading families of Chattanooga that money is not the ultimate answer to their problems. If the "Spirit of Chattanooga" is to prevail, then something, or Someone, greater than money must take the highest priority.

It was Dr. McCallie who served faithfully each Sunday whether the audience wore gray uniforms or blue. His example of love, unity, and tolerance—between North and South, white and black, and other barriers—models a prominent symbol on Lookout Mountain, a towering object resting on the mountain's very highest point. This symbol better exemplifies the true Spirit of Chattanooga than the symbol of a cannon and faraway view of Moccasin Bend used today for the city's official seal.

Just behind the cannons at Point Park stands the monument built by the state of New York—with the help and encouragement of another city father, Adolph Ochs. It is the largest monument in the Chickamauga and Chattanooga National Military Park and cost over $100,000, an enormous sum in 1910. It stands eighty-five feet high and rests on a base fifty feet in diameter. The sculptor entitled the monument, "Reconciliation." A Federal soldier clasps the hand of a Confederate soldier as they stand beside the stars and stripes of the American flag. Underneath are the words: "Reunited—One Country Again and Forever."

At the pinnacle—the highest point in the region—rests the image of an American Eagle sitting on the tip of the flag held by the two soldiers. With quiet strength, it peers past the men and across the valley like a sentry.

This statue, this symbol, reminds us that certain principles must be maintained. They are worth fighting for. More importantly, it actively instructs us to believe that unity, love, and forgiveness are supreme. The statue does not reflect a city exempt from past sins or current wounds. Neither does it reflect a community without current challenges nor numerous failed efforts to renew, revive, and reconcile.

But it does reflect the Spirit of Chattanooga.

———◆———

As I drove over Missionary Ridge in the late evening for the first time as a teenager, I felt a surge of adrenaline as we crested the hill and encountered the lights of Chattanooga below and Lookout Mountain above. It is a moment I will never forget.

Although the view is certainly lovely and picturesque, it is also a bit more humble than many more grandiose scenes in the country. With grandparents in California, I had already driven across the country several times before I came to Chattanooga. To this day, I cannot articulate exactly why my first encounter with the city was so powerful. Like many things associated with Chattanooga, it remains a mystery.

The process of interviewing Chattanooga's leaders and members of its longtime, multigenerational families was already helping to unravel some of the enigma. The newspaper clippings with quotes from Jack Lupton were also a great help, but I was looking forward to my own interview with him to dig deeper with questions about him and his family. However, next up on the list was a lesser-known name, a man who, surprisingly, has been named by leading magazines as the richest man in the area, more wealthy than even Jack Lupton.

I was certainly happy with the outcome of my interview with Chattanooga's second-most powerful person. After three and a half hours spent with Scott L. Probasco, Jr., I knew I already had enough information for the foundation of an interesting book. If ever a man could be called "Mr. Chattanooga," it is Scotty Probasco. While his brother-in-law Jack might be more influential—precisely because he goes slightly against the grain with his controversial leadership—Probasco more closely incarnates that nonconfrontational Spirit of Chattanooga that always seeks the greatest point of unity. He also embodies each unique quality of Chattanooga detailed in the remaining chapters of this book.

The Probasco name is also secure for now, as witnessed by an article in *Cityscope* magazine entitled "Great Work!" (Scotty's legendary compliment). The cover shows Probasco and his wife, Betty, with their four children—Scott, Zane, Ellen, and

Ben—and twelve grandchildren posing on the deck of their Lookout Mountain home. Scotty noted: "How often can you have four children with all of them living within a mile and a half of you?"[119]

As I stood to leave, Scotty walked over from his desk to shake my hand. Then he gave me an uncut, expensive, full-length cigar to take with me.

"This may be a Dominican...or a Honduran. Let me see if you got a good one."

"Oh yeah," he said, after the inspection. "Can you handle a whole one?"

I told him I certainly could. It was time to go.

"Great work," he said.

Artist: Cessna Decosimo

CHAPTER TWO

The Spirit of the Mountain

Coke, Cliffs, Keys, and the Carter Boys

"Chattanooga, Tennessee, is a pleasant city, nestled in the valley and protected by beautiful mountains and ridges," writes Helen McDonald Exum in the *Chattanooga Cook Book* introduction from her Lookout Mountain residence. "We are just at the foothills of the Appalachian Mountains, which begin just south of us and stretch all the way up to Maine."

"From almost any spot in town, you can look up and see the surrounding mountains, standing restfully and watchfully. They are always with us, and to those of us born here, they are a part of us."[1]

Longtime local historian Zella Armstrong, who had a penchant for hyperbole, insisted that "the panorama which can be viewed from Lookout Point is one of the most magnificent in the world." For Zella, it was a settled truth: "No place in America is more famous than Lookout Mountain."[2]

I guess you cannot blame Zella for rooting for the home team. She buttresses the argument in her 1940 history with a couple of stories from European royalty. For example, Prince Henry of Prussia, when admiring the view at Lookout Point, said nothing in Europe could compare. He also said every ten-year-old boy in Europe could pass an exam on the battles of Chattanooga. Zella backs up this latter claim with an anecdote from a friend in Chattanooga who was visiting Italy's royal family for dinner. The family's 17-year-old prince, who later became King Victor Emmanuel, gravely asked the guest from Chattanooga, "How many officers were killed in the battle of Chattanooga?"[3]

Helen discusses the extraordinary nature of Lookout Mountain from another perspective. "The mountains here are among the oldest in the world. They were once under water, consist of limestone in the lower parts and sandstone on the upper parts, and hardened some 300,000,000 years ago, which makes the Alps young by comparison." Zella tells us the fossil of a prehistoric shark was found on the mountain, a monster specimen larger than any shark now known.[4]

It turns out that these two clearly partisan ladies are not the only ones who think something special happens around Chattanooga's mountains. A young caricature artist who travels the country told me Chattanooga is one of his regular stopping points. "It's a vortex. It's got a certain amount of magic to it," said Andrew Wilkie of Minnesota. "The mountains here are the oldest in the world. The energy of the earth here is different. There may be something magic in the earth here."

He explained that, by "magic," he means something that we cannot yet explain. He named a few other magical cities, like New Orleans, Austin, and Boulder, where the mountain rock covers metals. In Chattanooga, the mountains cover clay, he said. He did not remember where he learned about the ancient status of the mountains in Chattanooga. I am certain it was not from Helen's cookbook, which was written before he was born.[5]

Bob Corker thinks the magic of the mountains contributes to the strong community spirit in Chattanooga. "If you really look at the geography of the executives and where they live—Lookout Mountain, Signal Mountain, Missionary Ridge, Riverview—it has caused us to have a real healthy and compact central business district," he said. "Executives are typically going to be in offices near their homes. In our community, the civic, business, and cultural center is downtown. In Nashville, it's very linear. You've got Downtown, Midtown, Brentwood. The center of the world now is Cool Springs Mall, which is a long way from the downtown community."

Bill Brock said the leadership in Memphis left downtown in past decades, following a centripetal versus a centrifugal force. "Memphis is spinning out to the extremes," he said, and noted the same is true for Washington, D.C.

"People still live in Chattanooga. They may live on Lookout Mountain, but it's so close they feel part of the town. Signal Mountain—same thing. Missionary Ridge, East Ridge, Red Bank. In Nashville, they live in Donelson or Franklin. Maybe the mountains kept us together."

Signal Mountain emerged as a town when developer Charles E. James needed a railroad spur at the tip of the summit for trains hauling coal and iron from Walden's Ridge down to Chattanooga. He chose a spot where a Federal signal station stood during the Civil War. Economic recessions slowed the project, but 30 years after James's first efforts, "Signal Point City" finally gained access by streetcar. Residents flocked to the "other" mountain.

Elder Mountain took its name after George S. Elder purchased a large portion of Raccoon Mountain in 1920. According to George Elder II, his grandfather got the inspiration during his honeymoon on Lookout Point. "He remarked to his bride that someday he intended to buy 'that mountain,' which was clearly visible to the west."

Another family story had it that Elder's wife was at her sister's on Missionary Ridge and said to George, "Wouldn't it be wonderful to own that mountain?" A third story appeared in the paper in 1923, ensuring that all the bases were covered. In this version, Elder was vacationing on Signal Mountain "and conceived the idea of buying Raccoon Mountain while sitting on the front porch of the Signal Mountain Inn."[6]

Cliffs, Bluffs, and Mountains

An eminence with cliffs or bluffs has been a part of Chattanooga from the very beginning. Originally, however, the mountains were uninhabited. Before the Civil War, prominent residents gravitated to the smaller version of the Lookout Mountain bluffs, the cliffs on the river next to Ross's Landing at what is now called the Bluff View Art District.

"The Cherokee sometimes call the city 'Atlanuwa' (Hawk hole), that being their ancient name for a bluff on the south side of the river," wrote 19th century Cherokee ethnologist James Mooney. The Tlanuwa were mythical hawk-like birds of immense strength. Legend said they built their nests in the cliffs at Bluff View and could carry off small children and animals. Mooney said this may be why some claim Chattanooga means "the crow's nest."

In the *History of the Army of the Cumberland*, Captain Thomas Van Horne said Chattanooga comes from a similar word "applied by the Cherokees to the cliffs rising boldy from the river above the town, which was derived from 'Clanwoowah,' the name of a warlike but diminutive hawk, which was supposed to embody the spirit of the tribe. Those cliffs were the primitive resting place of the bird [explaining] the myth that Chattanooga means "eagle's nest."[7]

Before Lookout Mountain became a popular place to live, the Bluff View served as home for several prominent families, among them the Maclellans of Provident, whose home now serves as a bed and breakfast. Next door were the Chamblisses, a prominent attorney family, and also on the street were the families of E. Y. Chapin, the entrepreneur, and James Inman Carter, a cigar wholesaler. Next to the Chamblisses stood the mansion that eventually became the Hunter Museum.

Attorney Jac Chambliss was born on Bluff View in 1910. The nonagenarian still arrives to work every day at the Chambliss, Bahner & Stophel law firm. Both of his grandfathers were attorneys—J. B. Sizer and Alexander W. Chambliss, who was mayor of Chattanooga in 1901. Alexander Chambliss served as key counsel for several prominent Chattanoogans. "He also, about that time, went to New York City with Mr. Adolph Ochs when he bought the *New York Times*. I have a copy of the letter that Adolph Ochs wrote him when he . . . was elected mayor. He was

The **Bluff View** served as an early identifier for Chattanooga. The first prominent families chose to live above its cliffs.

instrumental in organizing the Provident [which] was started by the original Mr. Maclellan who came down here. My grandfather Chambliss lived next door to him on Bluff View."

These two Bluff View families eventually moved to Lookout Mountain as did the Chapins and the Carters.

Mankind is typically drawn to higher ground, but these families may have also been drawn to the similarities between Lookout Mountain and Bluff View. Both have been named "Eagle's Nest" and have inspired theories for defining Chattanooga as a resting place for a great bird. At the meeting where the town chose *Chattanooga* for its name, one citizen proposed "Albion," since the white cliffs at Ross's Landing resembled those in Britain. (The Romans called England "Albion.") Similarly, the current most accepted definition of *Chattanooga*—proposed by Joshua Ross—is "Rock coming to a point; a cliff or bluff; or overhanging rocks."[8]

Mountain Money, Bluff Billionaires

As improvements in transportation progressed, the prominent families of Chattanooga followed the Bluff View families. Many were families of great wealth or became so eventually. Summerfield K. Johnston, Jr. lived three blocks from Bluff View at 505 Walnut Street. At age ten, his family moved to Lookout Mountain, where he was raised.

In many ways, Johnston does not fit the Lookout Mountain stereotype. He spends time all over the country, has deep ties to Cleveland as well as Chattanooga, and, though raised at Lookout Mountain Presbyterian, is no longer an avid church attender. He does represent that quiet, more anonymous descendent of multi-generational Chattanoogans who also happens to possess an enormous amount of wealth. In 1999, Johnston was listed as number 291 on *Forbes* list of the 400 richest Americans. While most Chattanoogans consider Lupton the city's wealthiest person, Jack was listed lower that year with $750 million in assets. *Forbes* placed Johnston's net worth at $880 million. All the other years, Lupton was listed higher even though his annual amount remains static at $750 million, adding a bit of suspicion to the calculations.

During our interview at his office in the Krystal Building, I asked Summerfield K. Johnston, Jr. about his spot on the *Forbes* list.

"I don't think they know what they're talking about," he said. "One tries to stay out of that . . . I try to stay under the radar."[9]

He does a good job. The typical litany of power-structure families in Chattanooga generally does not include the name Johnston. His low-key, mild-mannered demeanor intrigued me. I was not threatened in the least bit. I tried again, asking the money question from a different angle.

"So . . . how does it *feel* to be on the *Forbes* list?"

"I don't know. I've been too busy to worry about it."

Indeed, he has. In 1991, Johnston was the largest independent bottler of Coca-Cola. He has served since as president, vice-chairman, chairman, and now Executive Committee chairman of Coca-Cola Enterprises, the world's largest bottler of Coke. Coca-Cola in Atlanta—the company that makes the syrup—owns 37 percent of the bottling operation. Johnston owns 8 percent, the largest holding by any one individual.[10]

I needed a confirmation on what he was telling me. I mean, I was talking to a regular kind of a guy on the sixth floor of a building in Chattanooga, Tennessee.

"So Coca-Cola Enterprises is the largest bottler of Coke in the world?"

"The largest bottler of any kind in the world. It does $18 billion in sales—80 percent of North America and all of Western Europe."

That was it. He just matter-of-factly explained to me that he ran an $18 billion company. He went on to explain their relationship with the Coca-Cola Company in Atlanta. "They don't own Coca-Cola bottling. They've been in the bottling business and never were very good at it, but they own 37 percent of the company that I put together. I finally became the largest independent bottler in the country [in 1991], about $1.5 billion in sales. I merged my company with Coca-Cola Enterprises, which they had started, but they weren't doing very well with it. I went to Atlanta and ran it for 12 years. Built it into a $17 billion company."

Again, just matter of fact—$1.5 billion to $17 billion. Not a bad decade's work. I asked him what basic principles he relies on.

"Well, basically I'm a manager. That's what I do," he said. "I'm an operator. I like operating businesses. I like finding the right people and getting the best out of them. That's what good managers do. I don't care what kind of business it is—it just happened to be the bottling business."

"I think in life it's very important to be lucky as well as kind of smart, but it's really important to know the difference. I was fortunate. I had an opportunity. I had a business that I liked and I was able to understand it and build upon it. It fit me. I fit it, and I say that's luck. It's nothing that I did that really prepared me for that. It happened to work that way."

The First Coca-Cola Plant

How did Summerfield break into Coke bottling? Keeping with his spirit of the understatement, I'll just say his grandfather, James F. Johnston, got into it early.

"He got into Coca-Cola bottling in 1899," Summerfield told me. "He was the first bottler in the world."

"Did you know him?"

"No. He died before I was born. Ben Thomas was his best friend, and neither Thomas nor Whitehead had any money, so when they came back up here and recruited Mr. Lupton first to put some money into their venture, Thomas got my grandfather to put the money up to start the first Coca-Cola plant here in Chattanooga. They did it in partnership, and then subsequently my grandfather purchased his interest in it."

James F. Johnston

He showed me a framed letter on the wall. It was signed by Ben Thomas in 1901. The note confirmed that James F. Johnston had purchased Thomas's interest in the Coke bottling plant for $2,400. Designed and built by a next-generation William Crutchfield,[11] the plant was located on what is today Patten Parkway, next to the Volunteer Building.

"Did your grandfather go by James or Jim?"

"Jim. Mr. Jim, they called him."

"How old were they around that time?"

"Oh gosh, I guess my grandfather must have been 30 years old or something like that. . . . I guess they knew each other at the Mountain City Club."

"But this was the first bottling plant," I asked, "not just the first one in Chattanooga?"

"This was the first one here, the first one anywhere."

Johnston went on to explain that this first plant served a 50-mile radius. They sold the Chattanooga location but kept the small outlying towns. "We had a bunch of little plants. One in South Pittsburgh, one in Fort Payne, Dayton, Cleveland (TN), Tracy City . . . and he kept some interests in Mississippi, Kentucky, and some other places."

The Key Connection

As Johnston sat behind his desk with the Read House clearly in view from the window behind him, I was reminded of why Summerfield is almost always referred to with his middle initial "K." In fact, more often than not, his name is printed in full—Summerfield Key Johnston. Another common version, which highlights his heritage, is S. Key Johnston—the reason Summerfield goes by the nickname "Skey," as did his father.

Summerfield's grandfather, James Francis Johnston, had already married Elizabeth Key by the time he built the first Coca-Cola plant. Elizabeth was the daughter of Summerfield Key, the brother of David Key, who on that fateful day escorted Jefferson Davis to the Crutchfield House, the hotel which became the Read House.

"Summerfield Key and David Key were both lawyers," said Johnston. "They formed a regiment during the Civil War. One of them was captured at Vicksburg—I can't remember which one it was—and was later released. But they served with distinction for the Confederacy. And yet, after the war, David Key served as a Democrat in a Republican administration."

It was David Key who asked his brother Summerfield to send a letter to William Crutchfield to see if ex-Confederates should return to Chattanooga. After William Crutchfield, a Republican, welcomed them back with open arms, he defeated David Key in the 1872 congressional race. Then, Key was appointed to fill Andrew Johnson's vacated U.S. Senate seat.

Perhaps due to the kind treatment he received from Yankees and Republicans upon his return to Chattanooga, David Key developed a national reputation as a moderate who could act as a conciliator between the hostile Northern and Southern factions. When Southern Democrats met with backers of Republican presidential candidate Rutherford B. Hayes for a secret compromise, David Key was named as the strategic figure to unite the coalition. Hayes agreed to appoint Key to a top position in his cabinet, which would make him the first Confederate officer to receive such an appointment since the war—as well as the first Democrat and the first Southerner.[12]

Hayes won the election in November of 1876. The Spirit of Chattanooga had done its work. When the new President and David Key stopped in Chattanooga during a Southern speaking tour, Key reiterated his belief that the Confederacy had been a mistake but he had served "heartily and honestly . . . to the utmost of [my] ability." The *Chattanooga Times* editorialized that President Hayes's administration and cabinet was "locked by a Southern Key."[13]

During the President's visit, he stayed at David Key's house. According to Helen's cookbook, he "was treated to a cuisine of Victorian elegance which included oysters." That is why Helen included Elizabeth (Bess) Key Johnston's recipe for escalloped oysters in the *Chattanooga Cook Book*. "She was such a noted cook that Chattanoogans still talk about her dinners," wrote Helen. "After her death, with the same cooks and the same recipes and the same kitchen, the food was never quite the same. Her daughter-in-law, Mrs. Summerfield Johnston, was also a noted hostess and used the following escalloped oyster recipe."[14]

That particular Mrs. Summerfield Johnston, the one that apparently wasn't nearly as good a cook, was the mother of the Skey that I interviewed and the daughter of the good cook, Elizabeth Key Johnston (Skey's grandmother), who was herself the daughter of Summerfield Key. I was looking for more information on Summerfield Key, so Skey offered to let me peruse the family manuscripts at his farm in McDonald, Tennessee, between Cleveland and Chattanooga.

Family Papers and Polo

Bendabout Farms, like its owner, is understated and flies below the radar. Apart from a small sign and a long fence in either direction, you would not know there was much going on to the right of the two-lane highway. There does happen to be a first-class polo facility on the 3,300-acre property, since polo is the hobby of choice for Summerfield K. Johnston, Jr. and many of his progeny. Discretion seems to be a pattern for old money Chattanooga folks. Just around the corner sits Jack Lupton's Honors Course—discussed later in this book— which lies beyond a small, unmarked gate. But the little driveway in Ooltewah actually leads to one of the most celebrated golf courses in the world, the site for the 1991 U.S. Amateur and the 1996 NCAA Championship won by Tiger Woods.

During our interview, Skey made a small mention of his and the Johnston family's involvement with polo. I later learned that he served for several years as chairman of the U.S. Polo Association. His son, Summerfield K. Johnston III, competed for several years in the U.S. Open, and his daughter Gillian's team has won the championship. A local news headline also informed me that Skey's grandson, Will, had recently competed head-to-head against Prince Charles during a tournament in England.[15]

Skey's father, Summerfield Sr., an avid horseman, built the polo facility at Bendabout just prior to World War II and regularly invited up the Sixth Cavalry stationed at Fort Oglethorpe for some competition. Since the turn of the century, over a thousand cavalrymen had been stationed next to the Chickamauga battlefield, where they rode their horses through the park and competed on their own polo grounds nearby.

When I reached Skey's home at Bendabout, a nice, large farmhouse, I was met in the side room containing scrapbooks and manuscripts by a smiling, elderly lady named Elizabeth Neil or "Bess," Skey's second cousin. I mentioned to her Will's great opportunity to play against Prince Charles. For her, that was not the point.

"He beat Prince Charles," she said.

This lady was kind enough to show me the family papers at Bendabout Farms and also at her farm in Cleveland, Tennessee. Her grandmother and Skey's grandmother were sisters, both daughters of Summerfield Key.

Bess showed me an old bed at the farm that belonged to Bob Jones the First, founder of the famous ultrafundamentalist Bible college. "They couldn't fit the bed in their apartment," she told me, so the Joneses passed it to her. Bob Jones University is now located in Greenville, South Carolina but was founded in Cleveland just outside of Chattanooga. Bess went there when she was 18. "Billy" was there too, she said, referring to Billy Graham.[16]

DIVINE ~ KEY

Called the "Father of Chattanooga," Williams was one of three original settlers in 1835 and owner of the first land syndicate. He settled Williams Island and built the first store at Ross's Landing after the Cherokee Removal.

SAMUEL WILLIAMS
1807–1898

JOHN DIVINE = **ELIZABETH WILLIAMS**
(1 ST WIFE)

MARY DIVINE KEY

=

Key escorted Jefferson Davis during the infamous confrontation at Chattanooga's Crutchfield House. As the first Confederate to serve in the Cabinet after the war, he was the "key" to President Rutherford B. Hayes's national coalition.

SUMMERFIELD KEY
1835–1891

⇨ **DAVID KEY**
BROTHER

JAMES F. JOHNSTON
1865–1930

=

ELIZABETH KEY
1873–1948

SUMMERFIELD K. JOHNSTON, SR.
1900–1985

SUMMERFIELD K. JOHNSTON, JR.
b. 1932

She showed me around Blythewood Farms, another spacious property with hundreds of acres and 115 show horses. Her horses have won world championships "many, many times," she told me. One horse alone has won the world title ten times. At the barn, I met one of her granddaughters, a tall blonde just out of college, who is a third-generation horse trainer. She introduced herself as "Key."

Back at the house, Bess and I rifled through some old files. Then we found an antique chest that had not been opened in a long time. It was full of various documents. Bess showed me a handwritten letter by Summerfield Key in 1870. According to other documents in the collection, Summerfield Key, like his brother, also was acquainted with Jefferson Davis. While David Key escorted the Confederate president just before the war began, Summerfield served as his escort when Davis surrendered.

The 1870 letter, which Summerfield Key wrote to Mary Divine, discusses Davis. "But I must gossip a little," he writes. "Ex-President Davis has been on Lookout Mountain most of this week. A pretty large party of gentlemen met last week and agreed to pay him a visit—but I don't think any person went."

"Mr. Davis—traitor as he is termed by his enemies—is a man of a noble nature. . . . He has shown more heroism in submitting to the malice of his enemies than all his foes ever exhibited upon [the] field of battle."

Summerfield eventually married the woman to whom he was writing. Mary Divine was the sister of columnist Sam Divine and daughter of John L. Divine, the early Chattanooga settler who lost his wallet while passing through town before being hired to run Samuel Williams's store (which replaced Ross's store). While the Decosimo brothers are descendents of Divine through his second wife, Skey and Bess are descended through his first wife, Elizabeth Williams, the store owner's daughter. That makes Summerfield Key Johnston, Jr. (and Bess) the 3rd great-grandchild of Samuel Williams of Williams Island, the man who captured James Andrews and was called the Father of Chattanooga for his early land development.

Divine Memories

A memoir by Mary Divine "as told to the grandchildren" was also in the family papers Bess Neil showed me. Mary described her grandfather Samuel Williams's home on the north end of Williams Island that "seemed like a castle to a little girl." This is the same home where Sam tapped on the window from the second floor to talk to his wife while hiding from the Yankees. Daughter Mary described a white, porticoed house with a wide hall and spiral staircase, and a "huge fireplace with a painting of the river and mountain built in above the tall mantel." The kitchen was in a separate building, "connected by a high raised run-way made of big logs." A slave named Sarah, "the black turbaned genius of the big open fireplace," cooked "the most delectable dishes and always the air smelt of spices and flavors, so entrancing to childish noses."

When her Baptist mother died in 1863, Mary Divine joined T. H. McCallie's Presbyterian Church, the only church still operating during the war. Soldiers from many states swarmed the area. Mary lived near the railroad tracks. Once a soldier threw her a red apple from the top of a boxcar with a note tied to it: "Though I go to death and danger, please remember the Texas Ranger."

Mary recounts another story in which she and her daughter were burying one of the slave babies that had died. They put the little body in the ground after a short, simple funeral service outside as soldiers passed by. A Union captain demanded the small box be exhumed before he would believe that it contained no silver or valuables.

Another time, some soldiers asked Mary, who was an accomplished horse rider, to join them for a ride on Lookout Mountain. Her father, John Divine, adamantly refused to allow it. "Her love of riding was so much stronger than her sense of obedience that she mounted one of the fiercest horses and rode off." At the top of the mountain, she was thrown off the horse while still caught in the stirrup, dragged a few feet, and injured, dislocating her shoulder. An ambulance took her home. "Her father refused to speak to her for weeks on account of her willful disobedience. All her life her shoulder troubled her, often getting out of place from any strained position."[17]

A 1927 news clipping in the Johnston family papers eulogizes Mary Divine Key as "probably the oldest resident of the city." She was 81. Her son John died of appendicitis at age 45. Another son died at age 15. Today, no Keys remain in Chattanooga.[18]

However, her grandson carried on the legacy with his name: Summerfield Key Johnston. The senior S. Key Johnston may have remembered the consequences of his grandmother's insolence when he dealt with his father, James F. Johnston, who built the first Coke bottling plant. Jim Johnston was on the first board of directors for the Baylor School in 1893. He sent his son to Baylor, to the University of Virginia in Charlottesville, and to Harvard Law School.

"Back in those days, you did what your father told you to do," said Skey Sr., in a 1984 interview.[19]

"He said, 'You've graduated from the University of Virginia. You can go up to Harvard Law School.'"

"I said, 'Yes, sir.'"

"He wasn't particularly anxious for me to go in the Coca-Cola business. He really wanted me to practice law. But, actually, I didn't want to practice law. . . . When I came out of Harvard Law School, he said, 'Now, you can start practicing law.'"

"'Who's firm?' Summerfield asked."

"Mr. J. B. Sizer. I've already made arrangements for you."

Summerfield said he worked at the Chambliss & Sizer firm as long as he was required. "I didn't want to be a lawyer, so when my father died, I just gave it up."

But he remembered his dad's old ways when it came time for his son, Summerfield Jr., to choose a college.

During our interview, Skey Jr. told me the story. "I didn't know where I was going to go until he took me down to the train and put me on."

"I said, 'Where am I going?'"

"Well, you're going up to Charlottesville."

"I said, 'Okay.' He was a gentleman of the old school."

The younger Summerfield spent little time in school and instead found himself immersed in Coke bottling. After a successful half century of work, the company produced a limited "2001 Summerfield K. Johnston Coke Bottle" for a special scholarship fundraising event. Skey's picture is on the bottle with 1954–2001 below, along with the words, "He walks softly, yet his footprints last forever." Only 1296 bottles were made. They currently sell for $149.99 on the Internet.[20]

"My experience has been in managing people, managing businesses, managing money," said Skey Jr. "It's something I like to do. Fortunately, the business that I was associated with is a good business. It's one you can be proud to be a part of. It's not a dirty business. We don't kill anybody. Oh, some people seem to think we do. . . .We don't make them sick. . . . We provide a little pleasure, a moment of pleasure, slake your thirst—something that people enjoy."

The Real Coke Thing

I did not disagree. In fact, I drank a Coke during our interview, showing no disrespect for Skey's grandfather, but I wasn't going to tell him about my own grandfather. One of the books Grandpa Howard owned sits on my shelf: *China, Communism, and Coca-Cola*. He was a social activist in California before there were hippies, before the forerunners of the hippies, and he preached health food, no nukes, and the glories of the United Nations. He despised capitalistic corporations, and I suppose Coke was included in that list. He told my teenage mother he would rather her drink a beer than a Coke.

While most of this century Coke has been free of any substance that might compete with beer, Jac Chambliss points to a time when the nation was not yet settled on the question.

"Back in 1910, 1915, the government impounded 24 barrels of Coca-Cola and some of the syrup to condemn it as being unhealthy," Chambliss said. "That would have put the Coca-Cola Company out of business."

Jac Chambliss, 94, stands in front of a portrait of his grandfather **Alexander A. Chambliss** at the Chambliss, Bahner & Stoephel law firm. Pictured at right is Jac's maternal grandfather **J. B. Sizer**.

"They were just saying it was unhealthy?" I asked.

"It was . . . well . . . cocaine—that it had cocaine in it. I think that's what it was."

The case made national news for a several months. The attorney hired to defend Coca-Cola was none other than Jac Chambliss's other attorney grandfather, J. B. Sizer. "He represented the company in federal court here, and the case went all the way to the Supreme Court, and after several years it was won."

Tour guides today at the Coca-Cola Museum in Atlanta assure its 3,000 daily visitors that Coke *never* had any cocaine in it, according to Mark Pendergrast, author of *God, Country and Coca-Cola*. This bestselling author spends several chapters detailing the opposite truth and explaining the very fascinating story behind the origin of America's favorite drink.[21*]

Company legend describes Coca-Cola inventor John Pemberton as a homespun root doctor who cooked over a three-legged pot in his backyard. "He took a long wooden spoon and captured a little of the thick brown bubbling contents . . . lifted the spoon to his lips and tasted," the story goes.[22]

In fact, Pemberton attended medical school and earned two degrees as a doctor and a pharmacist. He conducted 12,000 chemical tests during his lifetime. He was highly influenced by an article written in 1876 by Sir Robert Christison, president of the British Medical Association, who extolled the properties of a plant chewed by Peruvians and Bolivians for 2,000 years, which acted as a stimulant, an aphrodisiac, and a life-extender. The ancient Inca Indians called it their "Divine Plant." The elderly British doctor described how he climbed a 3,223-foot mountain eating no lunch but chewing the "coca" leaf. "At the bottom I was neither weary, nor hungry, nor thirsty, and felt as if I could easily walk home four miles," he said.[23]

The coca leaf and its by-product, cocaine, quickly gained popularity. One journal said a "veritable coca-mania" emerged due to the "crusade against the enormously increased use of alcohol and morphine." Even Sigmund Freud wrote "a song of praise to this magical substance," which he shared with his fiance. Medical literature was filled with commentary on coca and cocaine, which manufacturers began to produce in tablets, wines, soft drinks, powders, and cigarettes.[24]

The demand was largely related to the myriad of wounds nursed by Civil War veterans, a significant part of the male population. Advertisements for scores of patent medicines filled the newspapers and made fortunes for men like Zeb Patten, also a Civil War vet, and his son-in-law, J. T. Lupton. Their Chattanooga Medicine Company successfully promoted the tonics Black Draught (pronounced "draft") and Wine of Cardui. You can still see a large, faded sign for Wine of Cardui painted on the side of an old brick building when driving on Broad Street toward Lookout Mountain.

Many former soldiers were addicted to morphine, the drug derived from opium, including John Pemberton, who was cut by a saber while defending a bridge. Three different people associated with the inventor of Coke attested to his addiction. In 1885, Pemberton himself wrote that "I am convinced from actual experiments that [coca] is the very best substitute for opium . . . that has ever been discovered."[25]

Pemberton's product before Coca-Cola was called "French Wine Coca," a direct copy of the wildly popular cocaine drink, "Vin Mariani." Corsican inventor Angelo Mariani provided approximately 40 milligrams of coca in his drink, a slightly higher amount than a typical snort of cocaine today. By the 1880s, Mariani had gained endorsements from Thomas Edison, President McKinley, Queen Victoria, and Pope Leo XIII. "The Pope apparently bore out Mariani's claims that coca extended life, since he died at ninety-three in 1903," writes Pendergrast. "According to an 1887 biography of Pope Leo, he took 'the simplest food, a little wine and water.' Looking at the Pontiff's frail body, the author wondered 'how the lamp of life is fed,' particularly when his face was 'of alabaster whiteness,' his eyes 'all-radiant with the fire of piety and fatherly kindness.' In fact, the Pope's lamp of life was fed by Vin Mariani, and the 'all-radiant' eyes may have taken their fire as much from coca as from piety."[26]

Pemberton credited Vin Mariani for inspiring his French Wine Coca and claimed to have seen the formula. He also believed he improved on it by adding to his recipe the kola nut, a product from Ghana in West Africa that natives claimed held powers similar to coca. The kola nut by-product was caffeine, which he claimed provided greater strength than coffee or tea.

However, Pemberton's plans for his exciting drink were ended by a vote of the Fulton County Government. Thanks to the temperance movement, Atlanta had gone dry. No more alcohol meant no more French Wine Coca or Vin Mariani. Pemberton frantically experimented with alternate forms of his recipe, adding sugars, oils, and fruits. After experimenting heavily with citric acid, Pemberton perfected a recipe referred to as "cococola" by his nephew in early 1886. Pemberton called it "my temperance drink."[27]

That same year, Dr. Pemberton submitted a paper to the Georgia Pharmaceutical Society, since he was too busy to give the speech personally, where he lauded the kola nut's caffeine and gave particular praise to the coca leaf: "Never in the history of the medical world has a remedial agent, within so short a space of time, risen from a comparative obscurity to such practical . . . importance." His first ad for Coca-Cola in the *Atlanta Constitution* in 1887 made similar claims. "This Intellectual Beverage and Temperance Drink contains the valuable Tonic and Nerve Stimulant properties of the Coca plant and Cola (or Kola) nuts, and makes . . . a valuable Brain

John Pemberton

Tonic and cure for all nervous affections—Sick Head-Ache, Neuralgia, Hysteria, Melancholy, etc. The peculiar flavor of COCA-COLA delights every palate."[28]

In less than a decade, however, medical journals reversed their position on cocaine and proclaimed it a dangerous, addictive drug. By the time Asa Candler bought the company, he felt compelled to make the claim that Coca-Cola only contained a hundredth of a grain of the drug, although Pemberton's formula called for ten times that amount. Either the formula had been compromised or Candler had launched a creative public relations effort. But the results were clear: Candler was successfully building a very profitable and famous company. However, by 1899, rumors were still growing that Coca-Cola led to cocaine addictions. Temperance women, who ordinarily would have approved of the drink, were turning against Candler.

In Coca-Cola's December 28, 1899, meeting of company leaders, the cocaine problem made the agenda despite the dictatorial Candler's disgust with the issue.

"Can't we just take out the cocaine?" asked one brave employee. "Does it really make that much difference?"

"So you really want me to change the formula of the country's favorite beverage because of some hysterical women?" thundered Candler. "Do you really want us to change Coca-Cola, the purest, most healthful drink the world has ever seen?"

"Never! There is nothing wrong with Coca-Cola," he concluded. "No, Coca-Cola has been good to me, and I will not change it. That's the end of this discussion."[29]

At this same board meeting, one particular event did not seem important enough for Candler to include for discussion. He did not bother mentioning that he had granted two lawyers from Chattanooga permission to bottle his product.

Chattanooga's Unsung Economic Hero

As the gang of fellows at the Williams sisters' boarding house met regularly in Chattanooga and laughed at Ben Thomas's daily schemes to make a million dollars, Ben's friend Sam Erwin finally was willing to give him some help after hearing the idea about bottling Coca-Cola. Thomas, back from the war in Cuba in 1898, had observed a successful carbonated pineapple drink there called Pina Frio.[30*] Thomas repeatedly told friends he needed a particular product for the fortune he was seeking, "something inexpensive that appealed strongly to the general public . . . something that could be used up quickly and then repurchased."[31]

Thomas then announced his desire to bottle Candler's successful Coca-Cola drink, but the Atlanta businessman was not one to be bothered since he had only encountered negative experiences with past offers to bottle Coke. The fate of Chattanooga turned when Thomas learned that his good friend Sam Erwin was Asa Candler's first cousin. Erwin agreed to make a trip to Atlanta in July of 1899 to provide the critical introduction needed by Thomas to access the no-nonsense Candler.

Erwin's name is rarely listed in the company of Chattanooga Coca-Cola luminaries such as Lupton, Thomas, and Whitehead, but the argument can be made that this good friend, who never profited from his key role, changed the course of local history as much as any Chattanoogan.

While it is easier to recount the story of Thomas and Whitehead gaining the contract from Candler in Atlanta as one, single visit, Candler later testified that there were actually several visits by Thomas from the time Erwin made the introduction to a year later when the contract was signed with Thomas and Whitehead.[32] Candler's chief concern was maintaining quality and high standards for his product. Though he liked the fact that both Thomas, 38, and the younger Whitehead were both lawyers, Candler did not have a good impression of Chattanooga. "I went up there once to bring back a fugitive nigger," he later said, "and I didn't think there was anything up there."

Candler told them "there are too many folks, who are not responsible—who care nothing about the reputation of what they put up, and I am afraid the name will be injured." He had reason to be concerned. An attempt at bottling the drink by Joe Biedenham in Vicksburg, Mississippi, in 1894 had run into problems.[†] The Hutchinson cap, which popped out by metal levers—thus the name "soda pop"—caused a bad odor in the drink if the rubber cork remained in the bottle for ten days. Understanding Candler's skepticism after previous bottling failures, the two Chattanooga men replied, "In all business we do in the bottling of Coca-Cola, we will make the name better every day we conduct the business." History proved them to be men of their word.

On the day the contract was signed, Candler wrote a letter to his son providing many details on a new idea for a fountain glass. He made no mention of the contract with the persistent Chattanooga lawyers, but he later said, "It's hard to knock a Chattanooga man down and discourage him."[33]

The next few months in Chattanooga would determine the rise and fall of many potential fortunes. Sam Erwin wanted no part of his friend's latest scheme. Several other friends also begged off, including one who said he could not reconcile his Presbyterian faith with the cocaine content.[34] Thomas and Whitehead,

Asa Candler

[†] Though, technically, Biedenham was the first to attempt to bottle Coke, he did not obtain a franchise agreement. James Johnston's plant in Chattanooga was indeed the first legitimate and *successful* bottling operation. (Interview with Summerfield K. Johnston, Jr.)

meanwhile, had difficulty agreeing on their national strategy and agreed to split the company. To make it fair, Whitehead was charged with dividing the two sections on a map. Thomas would make the choice. He selected the heavily populated Eastern seaboard and the growing West Coast and leaving Whitehead with the already fertile Southern market and most of the Midwest and West.

The two men caught another break. The problem of the bad-smelling rubber Hutchinson cap, which the Chattanooga bottlers initially used, was being solved just as they launched their new enterprise. The Crown Cork and Seal Company invented the crimped crown bottle cap, still widely used today, which solved all the former bottle cap problems.

At the time, a bottling operation required "a lot of hustle" and "a bit over $2000[†] to buy the necessary bottling equipment, which included a carbonator, bottling table, washing machine, settling tanks, washing tubs, bottles and cases . . . horse and wagon, as well as $2000 working capital." Whitehead had more difficulty than Thomas finding individuals to invest in companies. Once again, Sam Erwin played a pivotal role in Chattanooga history and in the destiny of Coke bottling's wealthiest family. He introduced Whitehead to John T. Lupton, who agreed to become an investor. Lupton paid Whitehead $2,500 for half his U.S. territory, which was quite a deal considering Johnston paid a similar price to Thomas for only a fifty-mile radius.[35]

The men with the territories became known as "parent bottlers"—Lupton, Thomas, and Whitehead (who died early and was soon absorbed by Lupton). The bottlers in various cities were dubbed "actual" or "first line" bottlers. All became rich, but the parent bottlers created some of the greatest fortunes in American history. These parent bottlers also helped start one of the very first franchising systems, "perhaps the most successful application of the franchising system ever produced"[36] and "one of the most innovative, dynamic franchising systems in the world." The parent bottlers built 400 franchises by 1909 and over 1,100 by the 1950s. According to Pendergrast, Chattanooga became "as much a Coca-Cola town as Atlanta."[37]*

The original incorporators of the Coca-Cola Bottling Company in December 1899 were Thomas, Whitehead, E. Y. Chapin, Hiram Pearce, and T. M. Carothers. Lupton replaced Pearce the following month, but a month before incorporating, the company had already placed its first ad in the *Chattanooga Times:* "Drink a *bottle* of Coca-Cola, five cents at all stands, grocers, and saloons."[38]

The Case of the Century in Chattanooga

But a year later, the growing cocaine controversy hit the *New York Tribune*, which quoted a white Georgian upset with a high number of "black cocaine fiends," saying

---

[†] $215,000 (2006)

Coca-Cola was producing in black patrons "similar effects to cocaine, morphine, and such like." The *Atlanta Constitution* reported that "use of the drug among negroes is growing to an alarming extent, . . . these drinks serve to unconsciously cultivate the habit."[39]

Around 1901, Candler was again compelled to explain how little cocaine was in his drink. He wrote a pamphlet called *What Is It? Coca-Cola, What It Is* in which he said "it would require about thirty glasses . . . to make an ordinary dose of the drug." He continued to praise the coca leaf, which makes a person "active, brilliant, vigorous and able to accomplish great tasks easily." However, by the next year, Candler had switched tactics and ordered his vendor to de-cocainize the coca leaves before shipping them to Atlanta. Once again, Coca-Cola barely escaped the fire because in December of that same year, the Georgia legislature declared all forms of cocaine illegal.[40]

Candler was able to avoid problems with the state government, but he eventually ran headlong into the wrath of the feds. In 1907, Coca-Cola officials saw the *Atlanta Constitution's* headline: "Dr. Wiley Will Take Up Soda Fountain Dope." Dr. Harvey Washington Wiley was the first head of the U.S. Bureau of Chemistry, a forerunner to the Food and Drug Administration. He became a household name after launching his "poison squad," a team of twelve young men who sampled various foods suspected to be dangerous. Popular demand for such investigations grew after Upton Sinclair dramatized the horrors of Chicago's meatpacking houses in his classic, *The Jungle*. Every reader remembered the anecdote of the laborers falling into vats and being turned into lard to be sold later. President Theodore Roosevelt also ushered in the progressive era, which included busting up the monopolies. Blowing the whistle on growing empires such as Coca-Cola was suddenly fashionable.

Candler, however, quickly countered the assault expected from Dr. Wiley by sending him a chemical analysis from an independent pharmacist showing no cocaine content. That did not prevent the federal authorities from seizing several barrels of Coca-Cola syrup at Chattanooga's main bottling plant and indicting the company. The famous case was officially named *The United States vs. Forty Barrels and Twenty Kegs of Coca-Cola*. The trial was held in Chattanooga over Wiley's strong objections. "It was equivalent . . . to trying the case in Atlanta," he said.[41]

Headlines on the trial continued across the country for weeks. The federal government sent agents to track jurors for suspicious activities and Candler hired private agents to follow the feds. Those federal spies noted their mistake in choosing for their accommodations the Hotel Patten, which was owned by J. T. Lupton. Wiley, a 66-year-old lifelong bachelor, made more headlines when he married Anna Kelton, a librarian less than half his age. Circumstances caused him to bring his new wife to the Chattanooga trial for their honeymoon. The celebrated federal official and his wife were treated like royalty by the locals even though most sided with Coca-Cola in the trial.

The federal indictment charged that Coca-Cola was "adulterated" and "misbranded." Realizing that cocaine was no longer in the drink, Wiley focused instead on the caffeine content as too strong, thus adulterating the drink. Ironically, the feds also charged that "Coca" in the name led to misbranding since cocaine was no longer in the drink.

The attorney defending Coca-Cola against Wiley was J. B. Sizer, the grandfather of Jac Chambliss, who works at his grandfather's law firm today. In a separate trial for Coke, Sizer had fought with such intensity that he fainted in the courtroom. During the *Forty Barrels* trial in Chattanooga, Sizer and the rest of the audience witnessed a number of entertaining charges against the soft drink, including a possible race-baiting accusation that a black cook's shirt was dripping with sweat while he stirred the syrup and spit on the floor. The judge was forced to reprimand Sizer's expert witnesses who laughed out loud after the prosecution claimed Coke had made one victim's heart so hard that after he died it was impossible to cut it with a knife.

After much testimony regarding the negative affects of Coca-Cola on various animals, Sizer complained that injecting frogs with Coke was hardly credible evidence. Harvard professor William Boos snapped back from the stand: "It is a difficult thing to feed a frog. Have you ever tried it?" Candler wrote to a friend that the "U.S. has almost exhausted its rat, rabbit & frog evidence."

The famous case ended in the spring of 1911. Chattanooga Judge Edward Terry Sanford (who was later appointed to the U.S. Supreme Court) decreed in favor of Coca-Cola.[42]

"My grandfather [J. B.] Sizer . . . saved the life of the Coca-Cola Company," said Jac Chambliss. "After it was won, he and my grandfather Chambliss were talking:

"Now, J.B, I've got to go to England. Don't you agree on a fee in that case until I come back."

"Okay."

When Chambliss returned, he asked Sizer, "What about the fee?"

"Well, they made me go and agree on one."

"Well, what'd you do?"

"Well, they offered me either $30,000[†] in cash or in stock," said Sizer. "I took the cash."

"Oh," Chambliss replied.

Jac Chambliss explained to me that the failure to choose payment in stock kept their family from possessing its own Coke fortune. "Probably saved me from being absolutely no good," he said.

[†] $2.7 million (2006)

CARTER ~ CHAPIN

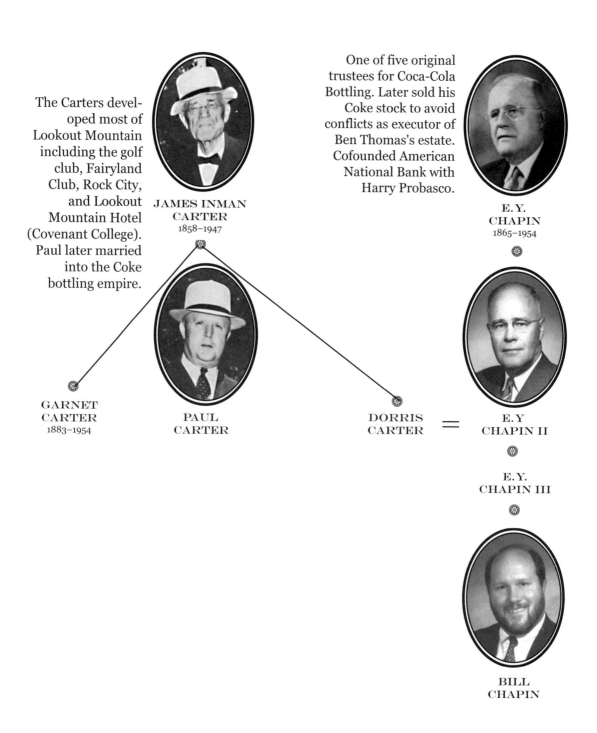

The Carters developed most of Lookout Mountain including the golf club, Fairyland Club, Rock City, and Lookout Mountain Hotel (Covenant College). Paul later married into the Coke bottling empire.

One of five original trustees for Coca-Cola Bottling. Later sold his Coke stock to avoid conflicts as executor of Ben Thomas's estate. Cofounded American National Bank with Harry Probasco.

JAMES INMAN
CARTER
1858–1947

E. Y.
CHAPIN
1865–1954

GARNET
CARTER
1883–1954

PAUL
CARTER

DORRIS
CARTER

E. Y
CHAPIN II

E. Y.
CHAPIN III

BILL
CHAPIN

(Charts are partial, not exhaustive, highlighting key links or characters in the book.)

A number of old Chattanooga families have similar stories of having just missed an opportunity with Coke. E. Y. Chapin, an original trustee for Coca-Cola Bottling, owed money to Ben Thomas when he died. "He was chairman of the board of all of Thomas's Coca-Cola bottling companies, which included Boston, Philadelphia, New York," said Bill Chapin. "And when Thomas died, my [great] grandfather was made executor of the estate, so he sold all his Coca-Cola stock to pay off the debt to Ben Thomas."

Bill explained to me that E. Y. Chapin wanted no appearance of a conflict of interest while serving as executor of Thomas's estate. But what if he hadn't sold the Coke stock? "He could have been the Cartter Lupton of the East Coast," said Bill.

Chapin's family did not completely miss an opportunity with Coke. The property where we conducted the interview was developed by Rock City founder Garnet Carter—Bill's great uncle. Between Garnet and his brother, Paul Carter, another great uncle, most of the Georgia side of Lookout Mountain was developed, all before Paul Carter married a Lupton and was appointed to run many of the Lupton family's bottling companies. He was the last surviving member of the Guinea Table.[43]

The story of Paul Carter (not to be confused with the first name, *Cartter*) is deeply entwined with the story of Chattanooga and Lookout Mountain in the 20th century. He was also a character. (Thanks to a memoir he wrote at age 89, he is heavily quoted in the following pages.) Like the Chamblisses and the Chapins, Paul Carter's family moved from Bluff View to Lookout Mountain in his youth. Along the way, E. Y. Chapin II married Paul's sister, Dorris Carter (see chart at left).

Before the Incline Railway was built, Carter describes the days of a steam engine that scaled the mountain gradually before skirting the bluff at the top. "This was a very spectacular experience and the ride was quite scary." Sometimes freight cars would get loose from the engine "running wild down the mountain." Automobiles were still not in general use. Later, businessmen would ride the Incline or the train down the mountain, "and others would walk down to St. Elmo by the Mountain path catching the streetcar at the foot of the Mountain near the old Sizer home."

"Sometimes he would walk down the mountain," said Jac Chambliss about his father. "Just walk straight on down the mountain and catch a street car in St. Elmo."

Soon Paul Carter began his lifelong career as a hustler-salesman. At age ten, he sold bottles of gun oil to soldiers at reunions and acted as tour guide for tips at an early mountain attraction, the Natural Bridge. In the summers, brother Garnet sold souvenirs while the younger Paul peddled lemonade at the train station. By age 15, Paul had given up on school and determined to help his father in the cigar wholesale industry. Many times, he would talk up his product around a potbelly stove while several men chewed tobacco.

"On many occasions I would smoke one of the cigars and . . . reach my hand into the smoke and, pretending to feel it, would say to the onlookers, "Feel it yourself, because you will find no grit therein!"

"This sometimes produced a laugh, but on other occasions, they thought I was really serious and would say, 'That thar is a fact. There ain't no grit in it.' Such remarks helped in my making many sales."

After a few years, Carter said the mountain began to grow "city folk" such as the Luptons, Davenports, Maclellans, Pattens, and Caldwells. A pre–Coca-Cola Joseph Whitehead lived next door to Paul's father, James Inman Carter. "He didn't visit with Mr. Whitehead as he would have liked to do. Whitehead had very little money and probably was jealous of Father's future outlook. But had Father only known what a fantastic fortune Whitehead would eventually amass, I 'kinda' think Father would have buddied up with him."

When Paul Carter was away traveling, he got caught up in a posse seeking vigilante justice for an Illinois sheriff who had been shot. But Paul got shot in the hip himself while chasing the villains on a horse. "On notifying Father about the accident, Dr. Walker had informed him that likely I would pass away and that if I had a black suit, Father should bring it along." Carter recovered two months later, and the nurse told him he may want to stop by the undertaker's before leaving to pick up the black suit his father had left there. "Also, I could look at the coffin that Father had picked out for me! On several occasions I was afforded the opportunity of telling Father what a cheap coffin he had picked out for me."

Reunion Inclinations

All his life, Carter had a love for the ladies. At age 11, his family moved off the mountain for a time, and he was compelled to list in his book "all his little sweethearts" that he must leave, namely Minnie Bell, Beulah, Nannie, Lorent, Conetta, and Edith. (At the end of his book, he includes his picture, at age 81 and a widower, with six giggling stewardesses he befriended on a trip to Spain.) When the Confederate soldiers picked Chattanooga for their 50-year reunion in 1913, it was only natural that event chairman, Bill Brock, Sr., would appoint Paul Carter the "Chairman of the Committee to Entertain Maids." A *Chattanooga Times* article reported that a problem emerged during the event. There were not enough men to escort all the women at the two official dances. "Mr. Carter has decided on an unusual arrangement. . . . He will have young ladies not assigned meet him at the Hotel Patten."[44]

Over 100,000 guests were in town for this major event, among them Paul's grandfather, John Garnet Carter, also a veteran at age 93. When Paul, Garnet, their father, the cigar wholesaler, and their grandfather met up at Market and Ninth Street, Paul suggested "that this great occasion 'demanded' that we all have a glass of beer."

"This was agreeable to all, and while drinking the beer, I asked Grandfather if he would also like to have a cigar. He said, 'No, Paul, I've never smoked in my life, am now 93 years old, and just think how much money I saved by not smoking!' That night Father told me that [Grandfather] hadn't saved so much because for the last twenty years he had been keeping him up."

Jac Chambliss told me he also attended a reunion of soldiers as a young man. "I remember they came to Lookout Mountain," he said. "They would have been in their 80s. As a matter of fact, I wrote a poem about it called 'Confederate Reunion.' I was impressed that they were coming together after 60 years, and it attracted me because of the brotherhood that existed between those who had been in the war."

It was the great reunion and park dedication in 1895 that inspired the widow of James Whiteside to build the Incline Railway that still runs today up the side of the mountain. Harriet Whiteside was reacting to another incline built to the tip of the mountain a few years earlier in order to steal money and business from her "Whiteside Turnpike." Another road had been built to compete with the turnpike and was named after Mr. Whiteside's son-in-law, A. M. Johnson, who married a daughter from James Whiteside's first marriage (not his second wife—the feisty and competitive Harriet). The paper referred to the saga as the "War of the Mountain Roads." The competing inclines were merely an extension of that contest.

Harriet Whiteside refused to allow the first Incline access to Lookout Point, which she owned. Adolph Ochs and Alexander Chambliss then led efforts to have the federal government purchase the famous point of Lookout Mountain to solve the problem. When it was announced that the purchase had been successfully accomplished, the *Times* proclaimed the long warfare over and said the point "would be open to all visitors and will remain so." In honor of his efforts, the observatory museum at Lookout Point is named after Ochs, as is the second road built up the mountain, originally named after A. M. Johnson

After James Whiteside's death in 1862, his widow Harriet controlled the land and fought the turnpike and incline wars until her death in 1903.[45]

Mountain Visions by Carter, Sr.

It was at the top of Harriet's incline that James Inman Carter lived with his two sons Paul and Garnet. Over time, the potential of Lookout Mountain seized the imagination of James Inman Carter, "who had visions of things others could not see," according to Paul. "He was sold on the beauties of Lookout Mountain and its future possibilities, and he was totally responsible for my getting interested. In fact, if the Carter Company ever had any loose money around, he would suggest that we buy some acreage 'back on Lookout Mountain,' and this is what we did and accumulated quite a sizeable tract." Before they developed these areas south of the Incline, Carter described them as nothing but "wild land."

There was a farm in the area owned by the Chamblisses. "Dad would hitch up a horse to one of the wagons, and we might go back to Lula Lake, or we might go back to the farm," said Jac Chambliss. "He had a little farm back on the mountain where the golf course is now. . . . He farmed it for several years until it was bought by the Carters when they developed Fairyland."

Jac pronounced it the way all the locals, those on the inside, know to pronounce it: "Fair-lund." The *y* is silent.

"When I was a boy of about ten, I went in a buggy . . . back to Jackson Hill—the Jackson family owned it—and it was pretty much an all-day trip," said Jac. "And the next thing I knew, the decision was made by the Carters to build that hotel back there."

Paul Carter explained how Covenant College was originally built. He and his father's plans "were to build a 200-room hotel out on Jackson Hill, which we owned and which was one of the highest points on the mountain. We owned about 2,000 acres of land and planned to secure at least another 2,000 acres, which [we planned to sell] to persons in different cities."

Meanwhile, Garnet was working on the area by the Chambliss farm. "Miss Frieda, his wife, wanted to save the area of the rock formations to develop a rock garden," writes Helen in the cookbook. "[She planted] moss and fern at the entrance of the caves, masses of rhododendron and laurel. Soon people began to ask to come through her garden, and as the numbers increased, Mr. Garnet decided to charge an admission of 10 cents a person."

Harriet Whiteside

"The most familiar part of Rock City to Chattanoogans is 'High Falls' or 'Lover's Leap,' which you can see from the Ochs Highway extension up the mountain. Indian legend is that an Indian Princess, Nacoochee, fell in love with a brave from an enemy tribe, Sautee. They married, much against the wishes of her father. In his rage, he threw the brave over the cliff only to see his daughter fling herself after him. It was an Indian 'Romeo and Juliet' story."

Helen adds that the Rock City Coffee Shop was for years the best place to eat lunch on the mountain. She provides the coffee shop's recipe for Rock City Chocolate Pie along with

Muffet Brock's directions for making Fudge Pie and a Lemon Tart recipe from Mrs. Hugh Maclellan.[46]

Garnet and Frieda had no children. The ownership of Rock City, which included their home, was passed along to their nephew E. Y Chapin, Jr. "Chapin" means light shoe, like what those elves at Rock City wear.

"In the mid-twenties, Garnet bought 300 acres up here," said Bill Chapin from his desk at Rock City. "And they hired a guy named Seth Rainer, who is the greatest golf course designer in America, to design Lookout Mountain Golf Course . . . and they developed Fairyland and built the Fairyland Club."

"You said Fair-ee-land," I noted. He was pronouncing the "y."

"Yeah."

"I mean, you didn't say 'Fair-lund.' You said 'Fair-ee-land.'"

"When you've got street names like Red Riding Hood and Cinderella and Gnome Trail and Wood Nymph Trail, it's a Fairy Land," said Chapin.

I let him continue. "The construction of the golf course was taking longer than the construction of Fair-y-land Club, so Fairyland Club opened and people were staying there. As entertainment for guests, he built a miniature golf course. He used cottonseed hulls and paint that were a by-product of Southern Cellulose and rolled this stuff out and made the surface of the putting areas and some hollow logs . . . and built some ramps, and everybody loved playing it."

They called it Tom Thumb Golf. It was the first miniature golf course in the world. "He got Babe Ruth to come up and play in a [miniature] golf tournament up here. He franchised it and started selling the franchise rights and ended up selling the company to a syndicate out of Philadelphia that took it national."

Three years after Garnet and Frieda invented miniature golf, 25,000 courses had been built worldwide with an estimated three million people playing the game each summer day.[47]

However, Garnet's successes were bittersweet for his brother, Paul, who was trying to buy land around Jackson Hill for cheap prices of around $100 per acre. Those prices shot up when Garnet's lots in Fairyland sold for $2,750 each. "He was a great salesman," said Paul, "indeed, the master of negative salesmanship and enjoyed with enthusiasm every opportunity to sell something to somebody."

Paul Carter directed his efforts to raising serious venture capital for his hotel project from prominent men in Pittsburgh. "As fate decreed, the night before we were to leave, on walking through the lobby of the William Penn Hotel, who should I bump into but my brother, Garnet." He was there to meet with the owner of the Tom Thumb territory in Pennsylvania. Paul invited Garnet to join him and his associates for dinner.

Garnet Chapin aims for the hole at the world's first miniature golf course, his **Tom Thumb Golf** experiment on the front lawn of the Fairyland Club.

Paul Carter and his first wife, **Mary Craig Carter**, are dressed for a visit to Paul's copper mine. She died in childbirth a year after their marriage.

"Well, bless Patty, before dinner was over, Garnet, in his negative talking way of salesmanship, after telling these people what he had done with Tom Thumb—which was now a dead issue—the associates seemed more interested in golf than they were in my hotel. . . . Even though they were 'sold' on the hotel and wanted to buy it, their opinion was—for quick money—Garnet's Tom Thumb Golf would be the most attractive of the two."

"Garnet agreed to sell them the patent rights, and everything he had in connection, but he told them they would be foolish to buy because the market had been saturated and that he didn't think any more golf courses would be sold. It seemed the more negative talking Garnet did, the more interested these people became—so Garnet agreed to sell all his rights for $200,000."[†]

Paul found a way to get him back, using a fake nose disguise and exploiting his brother's poor eyesight. "Uncle Garnet was running Rock City, and Uncle Paul came in with glasses and a fake nose," said Bill Chapin. "and told Uncle Garnet he was from the IRS . . . and he's got to have an audit . . . and to get his books ready and all this stuff."

Paul identified himself as "Mr. Solomon" and asked for the bookkeeper, and Garnet said she was on vacation. The next in charge was playing golf. "I understand you have these revolving gates or turnstiles which make a permanent record of the number of people entering Rock City," Mr. Solomon said. "Mr. Carter, this is a very serious situation and accurate records must be kept—hence with one of your main employees being in Florida and the other one out playing golf, this demands further investigation." Garnet, upset, started making phone calls to track down the two employees.

Bill finished the story. "It was a half hour later that Uncle Paul finally said, 'Garnet, it's your brother.'"[48]

———◆———

Paul Carter's life also had seasons of grief. His book includes pictures of a beautiful young woman named Mary Craig from Sweetwater, Tennessee. Paul fell "desperately in love." "Wooing her was my main interest, and this had been going on for several years. I finally won out."

But just less than a year after their marriage, a pregnant Mary Carter fell ill, and the doctor warned her against leaving her bed. "It was her desire to spend Christmas in Sweetwater," wrote Paul, "and so that is what we did. On the afternoon of December 31st, she became much worse and was brought to Chattanooga by ambulance."

[†] $7.2 million (2006)

"Mary Craig was expecting a child and she died in childbirth that night, and the child did not survive. I did not think I could recover from this blow, for she was the finest of the fine, and a most gracious lady." The usually verbose Paul Carter makes no other mention of this love and loss.

Carter Meets Coke

After many difficulties with raising capital, Paul Carter finally obtained financing for his grand hotel project on Lookout Mountain. The Board of Directors was comprised of Bill Brock, Sam Read, E. Y. Chapin, Paul Kruesi, and J. B. Pound. Construction began, and the laborers included 16-year-old Jac Chambliss, who earned one dollar a day. The opening ceremony on June 23, 1928, "was a grand occasion, attended by over 500 guests." Carter's enthusiasms led to broader plans—an air field, polo grounds, lake—making the area "one big playground."

But the next year, America's worst stock market crash forced Carter's dream into bankruptcy. After several owners and several names—including "The Castle in the Clouds"—the entire complex was deeded to Covenant College, a Presbyterian school looking to move from St. Louis. John Chambliss was among those brokering the deal. The building's name was changed to Carter Hall. Harvard chemist Dr. Marion Barnes, who led the Air Pollution Control Board efforts, assumed the leadership of the school. Two decades later, he was followed as college President by Frank Brock, grandson of two original hotel trustees—Bill Brock and Paul Kruesi.

Seven years after his first wife's death, Paul met and married Anne Lupton Harrison, a plain-featured matron, twice widowed. She was a half-niece to J. T. Lupton and owned several bottling plants. "Needless to say, Anne knew I was broke 'as flat as a flounder,'" said Carter.

Soon, Paul Carter found himself president of Anne's nine Coke bottling companies. Shortly thereafter, Cartter Lupton added several more to Paul's quiver, including plants in Macon and Dublin, Georgia, and in Houston, Texas. "Naturally, I did not know a thing in the world about the Coca-Cola business, but . . . I began to learn a smattering of the business. [However,] each and every year we were making gains in business and profits, which brought me much satisfaction and happiness when compared with [past] businesses."

After Anne Lupton Carter died in 1967, Paul Carter told his stepson Frank Harrison, Jr. that he wanted him to take over their Riverview home so he could move back to Lookout Mountain. He had fulfilled his "wanderlust" by taking cruises as an 80-something bachelor to Mexico, Norway, Spain, Russia, Thailand, and the Galapagos Islands, to name a few. "By this time, I decided that I had seen about enough, and that I would stay 'parked' in my home on Lookout Mountain."

He moved back into a house one block from the house at the top of the Incline purchased at the turn of the century by his father James Inman Carter.

A James Inman Carter athletic field was dedicated near Fairyland School by Rock City President Bill Chapin and town councilman Bill Glascock in September 2003—an idea they worked on for seven years. Plans included a large five-sided flagpole base showing the names of J. I. Carter's five children: Garnet, Paul, Lucille Glascock, Mary Lynn Stites, and Dorris Chapin. His last name did not continue beyond his two sons.

"Paul didn't have any kids," said Bill Chapin. "Garnet didn't have any kids, but they've had tremendous impact on kids and on people coming to Lookout Mountain with Covenant College and Rock City Gardens. And the others have progeny that are impacting the community and the world."

As Paul Carter reached age 90, he had no desire to be any other place than his early home atop Lookout Mountain. "I don't see how it is possible for anyone to be more happily situated than I am," he wrote at the end of his memoir. Paradise for Paul Carter was "being able to sit in a rocking chair on my porch overlooking the City of Chattanooga, which is the grandest view on earth."

Artist: Brent Sanders

CHAPTER THREE

The Spirit of the River

The Renaissance and the Recognition

A priest for the ancient Orthodox Church threw a bowl of holy water into Chattanooga's Tennessee River as depicted by a *Times Free Press* photographer on the front page of the "Faith & Community" section on January 8th, 2005. Wearing a long white robe with a gold cross stitched to the back, the bearded Father Jonas Worsham told the paper that the early Christian tradition starts the New Year. It is called the Feast of Theophany and includes the "Great Blessing of the Waters."

"We sanctify the waters as a vehicle through which we, too, can be cleansed," he said. He then threw a cross into the river. Three members of his Chattanooga congregation swam out to retrieve it. The one returning with the prize was sprinkled with holy water mixed with river water. "It's a symbolic and literal blessing of the waters so that they would be pure and clean in a particular area," Father Jonas said.[1]

The priest serves as an appropriate symbol for the origins of the river and the people in this place. The first European to set eyes on the river here, Father Domingo de la Anunciacion, who traveled with the Spanish explorers in 1559, called the great stream "The River of the Holy Spirit."[2]

But the Orthodox priest serves as a double symbol. He is also a Cherokee Indian. Born in eastern Oklahoma, Father Jonas Worsham retains his citizenship in the Cherokee Nation. His great-great-great-grandparents were removed from this area to Oklahoma and his great-great-grandmother was born on the Trail of Tears. His ancestors likely performed similar rites in these same waters.

For the Cherokees, in the beginning there was only water. They called the river Yunwi Gunahita, the "Long Man," a giant whose head rests in the foothills of the mountains and whose feet extend to the lowlands. His arms are the many streams that extend from the river throughout the valley. Traditionally, Cherokee men and women plunged into the cold water every day before eating any food, believing the literal and ceremonial cleanliness led to a long life.[3]

"When the new-born child is four days old, the mother brings it to the priest, who carries it in his arms to the river, and there, standing close to the water's edge and facing the rising sun, bends seven times toward the water," wrote Cherokee ethnologist James Mooney, who conducted hundreds of interviews with Cherokees in the late 1800s regarding their rituals and traditions. "He is careful, however, not to let the infant's body touch the cold water. . . . The prayer finisht, he hands the infant back to his mother, who then lightly rubs its face and breast with water dipt up from the stream."

The murmurs of the Long Man can only be interepreted by the priest. "In the words of sacred formulas, he holds all things in his hands and bears down all before him. His aid is invoked with prayer and fasting on every important occasion of life. . . . Purification in the running stream is a part of every tribal function, for which reason the town-house, in the old days, was always erected close to the river bank."[4]

Going Back to the River

"Going to the River" was the name for this ancient Cherokee practice. Many years later, Chattanooga leaders also felt the urge to return to the river, the city's place of origin. Indeed, "Returning to the River" has become almost a battle cry for the renaissance of Chattanooga, a process that began when purification of air and water became a critical necessity for the city. Whearas the Cherokees built a town house by the water, Chattanooga aspired to build a much larger civic structure on the river to provide meaning and hope to the community.

The first step toward renewal involved cleaning up the air. "Thirty years ago, it was still an old, dirty coal mining town," said Tommy Lupton. Most days, you could not see more than a block or two, and Lookout Mountain was rarely visible. By some accounts, darkness fell and the birds stopped singing by 2:00 p.m. Ann Coulter, a RiverCity executive, remembers her mother taking sooty clothes off the clothesline in disgust. "They were dirtier than when she put them in the washing machine." Businessmen's shirts turned dark around the collar, forcing some to change midday. "Even around your nose you could see black circles you had to wipe off," said Mai Bell Hurley.

In Chattanooga, tuberculosis rates were three times higher than the U.S. average. "George West had emphysema and actually died from it," said Frank Brock. "[His wife said] they could wipe the dust off their banister on their back porch in the evening, and in the morning it would be back there again." Brock also described picking up marshmallows off the candy company's conveyor belt as a child and making dirty thumbprints. Ron Littlefield watched "the TNT Plant pouring out just billows of yellow and red smoke which was oxides of nitrogen. You would have smog that would make Los Angeles look light in comparison."

Gene Roberts left the FBI in Los Angeles in the late '60s, and he and his wife and new baby returned to Chattanooga with excitement in a new Ford Mustang. But when they drove around Moccasin Bend, they were unable to see the city. "The pollution was just awful," Roberts said.

Walter Cronkite's announcement on the evening news coincided with a March 4, 1969, announcement by the U.S. Department of Health identifying Chattanooga as "the most polluted city in the United States."[5]

"Chattanoogans only put up with some things for so long," said Gene Roberts. The four-term mayor occupied a fifty-square-foot cubbyhole office at the Walldorf realty company when I interviewed him. He explained how a coalition of citizen activists and doctors formed to beat the smog. "And for the first time in my life, both papers took an active role and campaigned against the pollution problem. They assigned J. B. Collins and Springer Gibson to write stories every week. Typically they were front page. They didn't pull any punches. And that really got everybody going and, I think, pulled everybody together."

A year before the Federal Clean Air Act was passed, the Chamber of Commerce spearheaded the launching of the Air Pollution Control Board. Early on, Chairman Marion Barnes, the Harvard chemist, refused to take a check from Velsicol, a major polluter. Candidate Gene Roberts also developed a thick skin. "I introduced myself to a major manufacturer—the first ordinance on air pollution control was coming up. He asked what I was going to do on the ordinance, and I was honest with him and said I was going to support it. I never heard from him again."

Officials enforced filters on smokestacks and urged citizens to replace soft coal furnaces with gas and electric heaters. Soon, the city and its mountains became visible again. By 1988, the air in Chattanooga met all federal standards.

Littlefield described similar changes in the water. "About that same time, the Tennessee River was off-limits. There were signs telling you [not to] swim or have any kind of skiing or any kind of body contact with the water below Chattanooga because the sewage treatment plant was inefficient," he said. "There was just a lot of pollution in the water and a lot of industrial pollution." The riverfront itself "was nothing but two tire stores, a radiator shop, and a car wash," recalled RiverCity official Jim Bowen. Former Councilman Dave Crockett called it "an absolute dump—it was a good place to train public works officials on picking up garbage, wine bottles, and tires."

Smokestacks from the Dynamo of Dixie contributed to smoggy skies and the federal government declaring Chattanooga **the most polluted city in America**.

"Ya'll Oughta Build an Aquarium"

All that has changed. "The breakthrough, in my opinion, would be the Aquarium," said Frank Brock, who admits he did not initially embrace the idea. "When Jack Lupton put in the Aquarium . . . it completely changed people's image about Chattanooga and brought downtown alive," he said. "People in Chattanooga began to feel good about themselves. It's just hard to describe the impact that one building had on this city and its future."

Brock, like many, is quick to give credit to Jack Lupton for the Aquarium. Lupton, however, does not take the credit. He credits the inspiration of the Aquarium to former Tennessee Governor and presidential candidate Lamar Alexander, now a U.S. Senator. According to Lupton, when he and a delegation of leaders visited Governor Alexander in the mid-80s, Lamar told them, "What ya'll ought to do is build an aquarium on the river!"

"I thought it was a silly thing to do," said Lupton, "but then I also knew that Lamar is not a silly man. He had given it much thought." Jack then visited the aquarium in Monterey, California. "I came back saying we had to go ahead with it, so that's pretty much how it happened."[6]

Like the supposed one-time meeting between Asa Candler and the Coke bottlers, Lupton's story of a one-time meeting for the Aquarium may be a bit apocryphal. Perhaps it is Lupton's way of diverting the credit.

I had the chance to ask Lamar Alexander about it during a meeting in Washington between media and elected officials at the office of the United States Senate, the greatest deliberative body in the Free World. (This was the main office for the entire Senate, not just Lamar's office. On the wall hangs a portrait of Pocahontas and Andrew Jackson, and a painting of some prominent folks in the 1890s heading up Lookout Mountain in a horse and carriage. I got to wondering: Is it just the people around Chattanooga who get worked up over their heritage, or is it just that the world really does revolve around Lookout Mountain?)

Lamar was happy to answer my questions about Lupton's story of the Aquarium. "Jack remembers it a little differently than I do," he said. "He gives me more credit for it than I would give myself, which is odd for a politician, but here's how it happened. A delegation from Chattanooga came to see me about 1981 or so and said, 'The legislature just gave Memphis twenty million. Where's ours?'"[7]

Mayor Gene Roberts told me the same thing. Roberts had just finished serving as Governor Alexander's Commissioner of Safety in Nashville. He had seen the governor give big money to cities like Knoxville for the World's Fair and Memphis for the Beale Street renovation. "I told him when I left I was coming back to ask him for some money," said Roberts. "Not too long after I became mayor, I went to see him about that money. Pat Brock and Jim Kennedy, Jr. (at that time the President of Kenco) went with me. We laid out our request for money—just a few million dollars."

But Lamar told them Memphis only got their money "after a broad-based consensus-building discussion about the future." He told Roberts it would be easier to sell the legislature if Chattanooga could show some community involvement.

"I told him it would cost a lot more if we did it that way," said Roberts, "and he said, 'Okay.' We went back and talked with Mai Bell and the folks at Chattanooga Venture . . . and this idea of an aquarium came up. We took this and packaged it all together."

According to Roberts, the package included a $7 million aquarium. Another delegation of leaders traveled with the mayor to Nashville to accept the money. Lupton was one of a small group of people who listened to Lamar from behind his desk.

Roberts remembers Lamar's words vividly. "'I really like the idea of an aquarium,' Lamar said to us. 'I really do. It's unusual, but I really like it. I think you can pull it off but not if you're gonna build a $7 million aquarium. It has to be on a grand scale. . . . If you do that, I think you'll have an aquarium that will be there for a long time, [one] that you'll be proud of, and people from all around will come and visit.'"

Lamar related to me basically the same conversation. He told them their proposal was too narrow. "I said, 'Why would you build a small aquarium that only a few people would come to see? Why aren't you thinking bigger? Why don't you come back with an aquarium [proposal] that'll be the most interesting one between Baltimore and Miami, that everybody will want to stop and see?'"

"About all I was able to contribute was just to say, 'I don't think you're thinking big enough,'" said Lamar.

Jack Lupton

Gene Roberts

Lamar Alexander

Very soon afterwards, Lupton made his annual trek to see friends in Monterey, California, home of the world-famous Pebble Beach Golf Course. He was urged to visit the aquarium there. "Jack, like everybody else, I think, was thinking that an aquarium is a big fishbowl with four sides, like you see in dental offices," said Bill Sudderth, a business colleague. "'What's the big deal about that? So we build a bigger one, so what?' So he goes out to Monterey and has an incredible time, and sees school buses full of kids and people coming to the aquarium from everywhere."[8]

Not long after their meeting with Lamar, Gene Roberts got a call from Jack Lupton. "We'll raise the money for the large aquarium," he said.

It was Lupton's son-in-law who suggested he swing by the aquarium in California. At the time, Rick Montague was also serving as executive director for his father-in-law's Lyndhurst Foundation. Montague and several others provided leadership for a groundswell of activity, brainstorming, and planning over several years. This was the soil from which sprang, years later, the plans for a grand aquarium. When assessing credit for the renaissance of the city, one actually must study what happened long before that pivotal meeting with Jack Lupton and Lamar Alexander in Nashville.

Rick and Mai Bell

Deaderick C. Montague now spends his time as a writer. He no longer has an office, so I interviewed him in a side room at the Firestone store, Market Street Auto, just across from St. John's Restaurant, 1271 Market Street to be exact. He told me he is some kind of cousin to the owner, Krue Brock, Frank's son. I did not quite catch the exact connection, but by now, I had no doubt it was true.

Rick wore casual clothes and sunglasses around his neck. He sports long hair and looks late-fortyish, but he is more like late late-fiftyish. Hired by Lupton in 1977, he was in a position to see what happened and who was involved in the transformation of Chattanooga. I asked him about the role he played, and he quickly reframed the question.

"The downtown renaissance is a hard thing to talk about because there's not a clear beginning and clear end," he said. The first name he usually gives is Mai Bell (pronounced "May-bell") Hurley, the founding chairman of Chattanooga Venture. She is a former head of junior league, the symphony, the library, and the Arts Commission and the current leader of a host of other groups. She later became a member of the City Council. "Mai Bell was a power broker who really understood how a lot of things worked and how a lot of personalities worked," said Rick.

I never found out what Mai Bell means. I did learn that there was a steamship in Chattanooga in the 1890s called the *May Bell.*[9]

Hurley loosely led a series of meetings that both she and Montague point to as the time of critical mass, the "moment" for Chattanooga's leaders. These meetings led to the formation of Chattanooga Venture and to the now nationally recognized "Chattanooga Process." But Mai Bell is also quick to divert credit to others.

"None of us ever thought it was important to claim credit. What was important to us was getting things done."[10]

Lessons Learned in Indianapolis

The story behind those key meetings held in a storefront on Vine Street begins with a trip taken by fifty city leaders to Indianapolis in the fall of 1983. The trip, organized under the auspices of the Chamber of Commerce, which is also given some credit, was funded partially by Lyndhurst. The idea was to learn what another city had done. Specifically, Indianapolis had revamped their 19th century Central Canal and built a popular Canal Walk. "We went up there to get some ideas from that city," said Gene Roberts, who was mayor. "They had conflicts that seemed unsolvable. Some foundations put extraordinary amounts of money into the city. We were shown what the Eli Lilly money had done to help Indianapolis—built a huge zoo, a small aquarium."

During the trip, Indianapolis Mayor Bill Hudnut explained to the Chattanooga delegation the successful work of the Greater Indianapolis Progress Committee (GIPC), referred to as "Gypsy." Described as a blue-ribbon committee or a think-tank, the mayor explained this entity involving private citizens and local foundations akin to the public-private partnership that the listeners would later bring to prominence. Those in the room included Hurley, Montague, Ron Littlefield, Stroud Watson, Mayor Roberts, and many others with decades of work ahead of them in Chattanooga.

While Rick and Mai Bell point to the meetings on Vine Street in Chattanooga as the city's "moment," the two of them pinpoint the setting of their personal moment at the final dinner during the Indianapolis trip. After the group finished

Rick Montague   **Mai Bell Hurley**   **Stroud Watson**

their meal at an upscale seafood restaurant in downtown Indianapolis, Montague, Hurley, and Stroud Watson started talking. Mai Bell calls it one of those "critical little moments."

She told me about it during our interview where she now works at the United Way offices in the old Central Block Building, 630 Market Street to be exact. "It was a big moment for me," she said. "We were upstairs in the restaurant with a lot of people, and everybody just sort of broke up at the tables. And we happened to end up at Stroud's table. . . . We thought up the idea that we should find some way to perpetuate the things that we learned there [and] not to just have another episode with nothing accomplished—nice thing to know, nice trip to have, but nothing going on. So we created Venture."

Montague remembers the conversation. "We said, if anything is going to get done in Chattanooga, we need to have something that institutionalizes [the planning process]. So we decided we were going to start Chattanooga Venture."

Initially, it was not called Venture. Immediately upon return, the group announced a series of meetings to be held every Thursday afternoon. This "moment" lasted for several months and was called "Lessons Learned in Indianapolis." Numbers fluctuated—sometimes thirty, sometimes sixty, and other times fifteen. They met in the small storefront on Vine Street, eighteen-by-thirty. The smell of a healthy fire emanated from the woodstove heating system. (The space later became Divine's Pizza and is now a pottery shop. It sits next to Chad's Records & Tapes.)

Hurley named several very creative people involved in those meetings. "The more I think about that, the reason it was so much fun and the reason we accomplished what I think we probably did accomplish was the energy in that room."

They met around a long table. There was no dominant leader. "Who was sustaining it? We were sustaining it ourselves. We did not have a staff person that was convening us," said Hurley. "It was as genuinely creative a group of people . . . as dynamic a group—that's what made it work. Different people drove different parts of the ideas."

The Guru

Among the cast of creative, freethinking characters in the room submitting strong ideas and opinions was planning guru Stroud Watson. In fact, the Vine Street storefront served as the initial office for his Urban Design Studio, which still operates today. The bespectacled, bearded, bohemian professor eagerly shared mantras on the philosophy of form and urban life during those key "Lessons Learned" meetings.

"You design your city. You don't just let it happen!" Watson said. "Just like you design your day. You may not think about that, but you do."

"The building is subservient! The street, the neighborhood, the community, and the city—those are the four issues you think of first."

"The river belongs to everybody!"

Always smiling and enthusiastic, Watson wore a hearing aid, and usually spoke a little louder than everyone else, another quirk of his infectious personality.

"What does the whole river mean to us? Do we have enough willpower in our community to create access along that river?"

"We should thoroughly investigate the past, the present, and start the predictive future for the structure of the whole downtown, not just one building at a time!"[11]

Watson insisted that a community must discover "its inherited footprint" and determine the "heart" and the "center" of the city. "This is my grandfather's clock. I've inherited this footprint and I want to cherish that and continue to have it work. Maybe I'll add an atomic cell so it works better, but I wouldn't tear the guts out of it. I wouldn't take the faceplate off. . . . That's what we need to do with our city."

"The city's downtown is our living room. The riverfront is our front porch."

Watson was pushing his idealistic maxims at perhaps the lowest point in the history of Chattanooga's inner city. The last downtown department store had just closed. The front porch was inaccessible. After 5:00 p.m., the living room was a ghost town. "You could get [to the river] if you were a pole fisherman, probably under Veteran's Bridge," said Mai Bell Hurley. "You could roll a bowling ball down Market or Broad Street on a Saturday or Sunday and not hit anybody. It was white flight, although everybody had flown."

"Chattanooga used to be dead as hell," said Tommy Lupton. "I could take a rifle and, in midday, fire it down to the river and not hit a living soul."

With the help of a few students, Stroud Watson wrote a seminal piece on Chattanooga in 1982, "Images of the City," which identified the critical footprint. They proposed the northern focal point to be the river landing and the southern focal point as the intersection by Main Street where the Chattanooga Choo Choo Hotel stands. The two anchors are appropriately connected by Market Street, the former "Rossville Road," which earlier documents sometimes referred to simply as "The Road."[12] After much study and analysis, Stroud and the students concluded that the center of the city is, or should be, Miller Park, built just a few years before between the post office and library. It rests quietly along The Road and intersects another major artery, Martin Luther King Boulevard, which used to be called Ninth Street. The black community has deep, historic ties to this controversial street, a phenomenon discussed in a later chapter.

The City's Center: Miller Park

Miller Park needed strengthening. "What the city center needed was a clarity of urban structure that produced a memorable place," said Stroud. The result was the creation of Miller Plaza, a space for festivals and concerts highlighted by a glass, public-use building, the Waterhouse Pavilion, on the corner of the two streets.

The Pavilion was named after James F. Waterhouse, a partner in the Miller & Martin law firm and father of another interviewee, Albert Waterhouse. A portrait of the deceased Waterhouse hung over the head of Miller & Martin attorney Allen McCallie during our interview in the firm's boardroom, which provided a view of the Pavilion below. McCallie explained to me how the Tonya Foundation, another of Chattanooga's many philanthropic arms, was launched by Burkett Miller and used to build Miller Park and Plaza. A portrait of Burkett Miller hung just outside the boardroom.

Stroud Watson calls the Waterhouse Pavilion a central icon. "It is an incredibly fine piece of architecture. The Pavilion was meant to be a symbol for the community. It was placed in a position that looked down MLK Boulevard to the black community as clearly as it looked down Market to what was white. I mean, it was pretty clearly a black street and a white street at that time. It is almost a quintessential gazebo in the park. The edge of the building is like a Greek stoa, very simple. But we chose very urban materials."

Finished in 1990, Miller Plaza is used for public events, weddings, car shows, and political rallies. The Nightfall concert series features professional musical acts for several months during the year, drawing as many as 2,000 people downtown on Friday evenings. The city donated the land, and the private foundations funded the building, making the project one of the first successful public-private partnerships. Watson received the Jefferson Award from the American Institute of Architects for his years of vision, and the Miller Plaza design received the Outstanding Urban Design Award from *Progressive Architecture* magazine. "[It's] been a great social success," said Stroud. "It did create a center."

If Miller Plaza spiffed up the living room, the Aquarium certainly renovated the front porch. In fact, it was one of Watson's students who first suggested the idea of an aquarium during the creation of the "Images of the City" document. The idea was considered a little nutty and did not gain much steam. "Back then, it was 'those crazy students and the funny guy with the beard,'" said Stroud.

The original Urban Design Studio on Vine Street, led by Stroud and his band of students, resulted from Watson and Montague meeting after a lecture at the University of Tennessee in Knoxville. Stroud and his British wife had traveled from London to America for a twenty-city lecture tour on urban planning with stopping points that included UCLA, Texas A & M, University of Virginia, and Georgia Tech, before hitting UT. Watson had served as Coordinator of City Design, Planning, and Implementation for the City of Milton Keynes in England, a new town built from scratch and located between Oxford and London. Watson acknowledged the problems involved with the "socialist situation," but he said it verified important values for him. "It was a great experience."

He was looking for an opportunity to teach at a school of architecture in the states, asking each university if they had an understanding of the connection of urban design to city development as well as a vehicle for doing real development in the community. "From 1979 to 1980, I probably had twenty lectures clear across the country, and this is the only place that came up with the correct answer to both," he said.

Although the architecture school "didn't even know what I was talking about," Watson said "the dean got it." Eventually, the dean connected Watson with Rick Montague. Through a partnership with the Lyndhurst Foundation, Chattanooga was chosen as a "living laboratory" for UT's School of Architecture. Fourth-year students from Knoxville traveled to Chattanooga and began a fervent study of the history of the area. The design studio at the Vine Street storefront was born.

The Unusual Makings of a Guru

I interviewed Stroud Watson from his studio, part of the "Planning and Design Center," an official arm of the Regional Planning Agency, located at 1250 Market Street. The office overlooks The Road. More appropriate for Watson, the very first sketch of Ross's Landing in the courthouse records calls it "The Public Road."[13*]

His spot on the old thoroughfare between Ross's Landing and the Chief John Ross House sits nicely between the two spots on Market Street where I interviewed Rick and Mai Bell.

I asked Stroud about his early socialist proclivities, and he acknowledged that they have lessened since he moved to America. He cites Teddy Roosevelt and Ben Franklin as role models. "No individual, whether it's a builder or just a student, [should] be any better than the whole." He criticizes gated communities, and calls for individuals to come together for the "common good," an idea he says goes back to the Constitution. "The intent of life, liberty, and the pursuit of happiness was not the pursuit of happiness of you, individually. It was the pursuit of happiness of the community as a whole."

His concepts of the individual and the community were forged in a fascinating way. First, he joined a commune; then, he spent several years alone on a sailboat.

I asked him many questions about those experiences. He answered with much enthusiasm, always smiling, always with plenty of volume.

He moved to the University of Arizona for a teaching job. "I went in with eight of the faculty of the art school. We bought a dude ranch—this is 1967—and formed a community. We were written up in the *L.A. Times* magazine section, Rancho Lindavista. And it was great."

"And we did some wild things. I mean, Andy Warhol came out and filmed *Lonesome Cowboy* on our ranch, and we had FBI agents all over. I mean, it was wild. But the dean didn't like it, so I got fired."

"How big was the ranch?"

"Eighty acres. About twenty buildings. In fact, I was just talking to one [of them] the other night." Stroud's wife still visits every year. "I don't get out there as much."

"How many people were there?"

"About thirty."

"And how many people are there now?"

"About forty."

"What's sort of the mission statement or the religious statement?" I asked.

"Kind of a *Walden Pond* Two. Do you remember *Walden Pond?*"

"Yeah."

"And that's an interesting book. We started a shared kitchen, all that stuff. That fell apart in six weeks."

"Okay."

"And so what we did is we each had an individual place. We shared the community building, shared the artist studios, and we shared the responsibility. And the people became very close. It was a balance of public and private space, which, I think, all things have to be."

I continued with the questions. "Okay, you're in this community. It's working okay. Why do you leave? Why do you leave utopia?"

"Well, I got fired."

I thought about that for a second. "Why didn't you stay?"

Stroud thought for a second. "I could have stayed." Then he elaborated on some problems with the commune.

"I don't know if you were as conscious, but in '67 or so, a lot of not-so-nice things were going on in America."

"I was three years old."

"Yeah."

He continued. "We were doing some pretty dumb-ass things. And I wasn't very happy with that. Arizona had a [very big] drug culture . . . and one of the very best students I had got busted for bringing drugs in from Mexico. He's too young [18 years old]. Thrown in jail for ten years. This is absolutely absurd. So there were just a lot of things happening that just didn't feel good."

Stroud Watson lays out a vision for Chattanooga.

THE MILLER PARK

IN RECOGNITION OF THE UNTIRING EFFORT
OF BURKETT MILLER THROUGH WHOM
THAT THE PARK BECAME A REALITY. IT IS FITTING
THAT THE PARK BE A MEMORIAL TO HIS
FATHER AND MOTHER, WHITE B. AND MARY
MILLER. AND IT HAS BEEN NAMED
THE MILLER PARK
IN THE YEAR OF OUR BICENTENNIAL
1976

Dedication of Miller Park. From left: Scotty Probasco, Pat Rose, and Robert Kirk Walker. Dr. Marion Barnes is in background at center.

He named another problem with the commune. "It is somewhat in isolation from the rest. It starts to become its own form of a gated community."

Just when he lost his job and his passion for the dude ranch, he got lucky. "There are a few people who can always fall into a rug," he said. "I received a very, very large traveling grant from the University of Illinois to do whatever I wanted to do."

So he bought a boat in New York and sailed to the Caribbean. All he took for entertainment was a bag of books.

"How big was the boat?"

"Thirty-four feet."

"What kind of boat?"

"A Shuman single hander. Built in 1939."

"A sailboat?"

"Yes. Too beautiful to pass up. It was absolutely gorgeous. . . . It had a galley and forecastle, and there was a toilet between."

Sometimes he slept on the deck, sometimes in the cabin. Stroud lived on the sailboat for four years, traveling as far as Trinidad, Venezuela, and Aruba. "I almost went to Cuba but got chased off by a gunboat."

While docked in the West Indies, he made contacts that led to his planning job for the socialist experiment in England. As I considered the irony, I had to ask Stroud a question.

"Isn't it odd that someone who is so passionate about living together in harmony was able to be out four years by himself in that boat?"

"Oh, of course," he said. Then, he stumbled a bit. "And I can't answer. And I'm not a loner. I'm not—I mean . . . I'm not very social, but I certainly like interacting with people . . . Probably, my hearing makes it a little hard for me to do a lot of things. But, no."

Then he added a rather insightful comment. "The best community people are people who are secure in themselves first."

The Original Guru: That Crazy Italian

Stroud Watson provided more than his fair share of personality during those crucial meetings on Vine Street in 1983. But another flamboyant personality attended those "Lessons Learned in Indianapolis" sessions. He is credited by Rick Montague with providing the original impetus for the Renaissance. This New York Italian created the concept for "Five Nights in Chattanooga," a precursor to the Riverbend Festival in 1981, and was the driving force behind Vision 2000, the citizen planning movement named by *NPR, U.S. News & World Report,* and *Parade Magazine* as the key to Chattanooga's transformation.

Gianni Longo (sounds almost like "Johnny") was fortyish but looked older. Educated at an architectural school in Venice and born on the heel of Italy's boot, he had dark skin and frizzy hair that was balding on top. He lived in New York and dressed in high fashion—casual clothes but always a certain high-quality Italian sport coat, dark green and brown herringbone, made from Cheviot wool.

"It's hard to say, even to this day, what his profession is," said Rick Montague. "He spoke with an accent. Jack Lupton always referred to him as 'That crazy Italian.'"

Montague learned about Gianni Longo during a trip to Seattle to attend a dinner for the Council on Foundations. At the time, as head of the new Lyndhurst Foundation, Montague was searching for direction and ideas. "On everybody's plate is this little book called 'Learning from Seattle.' So I took this book back and read it."

"It's hard for us to believe today, but Seattle had gotten to the point that people were leaving it so fast it was considered a dead-end town. This little book talked about what had gone on to make Seattle successful." It was written by Gianni Longo and Partners for Livable Places. "So I called them up. And I said, you know, this is where we are. Of course, people's ears pick up as soon as you say, 'I run a foundation.' Aha, you know. So then began what I would argue was the central early relationship [for Lyndhurst]. Stroud would be the central late relationship, in my opinion, but the early relationship was with Gianni Longo."

"So, it's hard to say what it is they do. But there was something about him that made you think that something might happen. He and Roberto, who was kind of more professionally settled, invited us up to their place in New York, and it was a classic example of somebody trying to make a foundation think they were more substantial than they were."

"They invited their lawyer. They invited their neighbor and somebody else to pack the crowd. And they invited us for lunch at Gianni's loft in Soho. Well, we didn't know what Soho was. We didn't know what a loft was, and we certainly didn't know what the Institute for Environmental Action was."

"What's Soho?" I asked.

"Soho is 'South of Houston Street.' It's very trendy."

He continued. "So here's Johnny's loft on Wooster Street, which looks like a war zone . . . and they invited us for lunch. This is me and my wife, Alice, Jack Lupton and his wife, Alice, and Jack Murrah, who are all in New York together. So we go into this dark loft building that's about twelve stories tall. Their oven has gone out, so they're ferrying—I remember it vividly—ravioli, homemade Italian, up on this elevator that looks like Al Capone could pop out of the floor at any time."

"And here we are, and they're giving us this presentation. A lot of the content is very hard for somebody who is results oriented to get a fix on. It's 'neighborhood participation.' It's 'public participation.' It's things that to a businessman sound soft and stupid and waste your time. But Gianni was so seductive and fun. And we thought, 'What the heck,' you know. 'Please send Lyndhurst Foundation a proposal.'"

"Oh, God, this is great. So they send us this proposal . . . But what it proposed to do was very hard to determine. And Jack Murrah and I sold it really hard to the board. . . . We just decided, 'Okay, we're just going to kind of wade in. We don't really know where this is going to lead or what it is, but something about it we like. And these guys have seen things happen in other cities and, you know, they know something we don't know. Let's do it.'"

"So then Roberto and Gianni said, 'Okay, we're going to come down. We need to meet with the City Commission, and we're going to talk about what we're going to do.' It was at the Walden Club [at the top of Republic Centre], and in come all the members of the City Commission."

"This is important. This is very important. Prior to Lyndhurst's reorganization, the private sector basically looked after private institutions. . . . private people didn't seem to care much about things that happened in the city. In general, they were interested in things like the Hunter Museum, Baylor, McCallie, [etc.]. So this was an unusual kind of meeting because not only are we having out-of-towners come in to make this presentation, which we know is going to be kind of amorphous, but this is probably the first time some of these people have been in a room privately with [Lyndhurst board members] Rody Davenport, Burton Frierson, or Summerfield Johnston. I think they were still around."

"So, there is this presentation about what they're going to do. And we want to make sure that the city fathers know we're not doing anything behind their back, and that we have their tacit approval. . . . A lot of the things we're going to do are going to be kind of public, so we want them to understand what we're doing at least as much as we understand it, which is not a whole lot. So we have this meeting, and they kind of agree."

Five Nights in Chattanooga

Then, Gianni formed two major initiatives for the campaign: a publication and an outdoor concert. A large-format magazine would be placed in every Sunday paper. "It was going to be called *Chattanooga in Motion*," said Rick. "Of course, there hadn't been much motion, but, nevertheless, it was called *Chattanooga in Motion*. It had interviews with people who ran bars and businesspeople and this, that, and the other. It basically created some common history. . . . Then it announced that there will be a public concert series downtown. This was Five Nights in Chattanooga . . . five consecutive Tuesdays, and we were going to try to have something for everybody."

The five acts were B. B. King, Bill Monroe, Sarah Vaughn, Don McLean, and Hank Williams, Jr. "People were encouraged to bring a picnic basket and have dinner and all that kind of stuff. Well, this set off all kinds of alarm bells, because it was downtown and it was in the evening." One elected official grabbed Rick by the collar just before the B. B. King event and accused him of troublemaking. "Chattanooga is going to blow up tonight!" he yelled.

Mai Bell remembers the tension. "Gianni's idea was that you would have these five superstar nights and bring people to town," she said. "There were all these dire predictions about what would happen. This was the time when people didn't come back to town. There was clearly a fear."

Thousands attended every night, and 12,000 attended the final event. "People are all over the office buildings and down on the ground," said Montague. "It's a great crowd—the same a week later and a week later." According to Hurley, the mixing of people racially and economically worked very well.

"It was enormously important," said Stroud. "People from all kinds of different backgrounds came together to celebrate the *communitas* of the downtown." Montague said people tell him, "'I date the renaissance of Chattanooga to Five Nights in Chattanooga,' because it was a continuing place where people could come back to downtown and establish some physical relationship to it.' Nightfall now takes place within one block of the site."

Longo's third initiative was a masterstroke. Vision 2000 was just the initiative desired by the brainstormers at the Vine Street storefront who had determined to "turn talk into action." "That was a biggee because we had done a lot of talking," said Mai Bell, "and we needed to do something." That something was the creation of Chattanooga Venture, and its first initiative was the Vision 2000 campaign. "I wouldn't say we just thought up a visioning process all by ourselves. No, it was happening other places. But . . . when Gianni got to the table with his professional guidance of how to do nominal groups, how to design the plan, we named Venture," said Mai Bell, who was elected chairman. "Then, we together collectively created this thing called Vision 2000."

"We decided we were going to get people to sign up for the strands that they thought would build . . . the best sort of community, the ideal community. We said we weren't going to do an academic thing. We weren't going to do a professional planners thing. We were going to do a people thing."

Gianni was hired to formally run the Vision 2000 process. "He was a real animator and came up with lots of ideas to make the process fun," said Ron Littlefield, the first executive director of Venture. Vision 2000 was kicked off with a big event at UTC in September of 1984. The group was divided into task forces with particular questions: "What gives Chattanooga a unique sense of place?" or "What do we want Chattanooga to look like in 2000?" Small groups met under the titles: Future Alternatives, People, Places, Work, Play, and Government. Trained facilitators wrote down every idea submitted during what is often called a "visioning process," but is sometimes referred to as the nominal group process or "charrettes," an architectural word.[14]

"We told people we would write down every single thing they said, and we did," said Mai Bell. "The group would weed out ideas [and] we printed up this portfolio, which was very nonacademic. . . . The aquarium wasn't even in capital letters. I mean, it was just an aquarium. You know, just one of a long shopping list of things."

After 1,700 people participated over six months and identified 40 goals and 223 projects, the process conceived by Gianni Longo was complete. "It was a marathon and was both exhausting and exhilarating," said Littlefield.

Chattanooga Times editorialist Pat Wilcox praised the massive public involvement. "For years in Chattanooga, there was this idea that the people with money and power controlled everything. We needed to break out of that shell, and did."[15]

Of the forty goals, thirty-seven were claimed to be at least partially completed by 1994, including a renovated Tivoli Theatre, a massive riverfront development and new aquarium, an explosion in downtown housing through Chattanooga Neighborhood Enterprises, an electric shuttle, a pedestrian bridge, and the Children's Discovery Museum.

Leaders like Hurley and Littlefield admitted some of the projects had been discussed before Venture. It would be impossible to determine which initiatives were a direct result of Vision 2000, they said, but they cited Venture's ultimate purpose: to energize the community and to implement good ideas, regardless of their origin.

"Gianni was the one who masterminded Vision 2000," said Montague. "Other people will say, 'This was where the renaissance in Chattanooga began.'"

The Task Force Behind the Renaissance

The story does not end there. Another major idea and planning process was taking place around the same time as Stroud Watson's fledgling Urban Design Studio and Rick Montague's early meetings with Gianni Longo. The Moccasin Bend Task Force conducted sixty-five public meetings at which thousands of people discussed new plans for the famous "foot" below Lookout Mountain. Various complex entities owned or occupied the area, but most of the land was "mosquito breeding grounds," according to one official.

The vision of the Moccasin Bend Task Force started many years before when a kid named Dalton lived by Chickamauga Creek. "We'd build boats, and we would ride those boats down the creek to the Tennessee River and go down there and fish and camp and put out trout lines," said Dalton Roberts. He later was elected as county executive, the top post in Hamilton County. "Somebody mentioned to me about Moccasin Bend, and I remembered how much I enjoyed that river bank—fishing it, swimming and playing. I asked the county engineer to pull out all those maps and show me what we owned out there. To my amazement, we had 600 acres."

"So I talked to Pat Rose, who was mayor, and I said, 'Why don't we appoint a task force to see what we can do for that.' He said, 'That's a good idea.' We did it. . . . And we envisioned some kind of a park, maybe an Indian, Cherokee park. We didn't know what."

According to Rick Montague, Roberts and Rose were impressed with some early land planning done by Lyndhurst for the area around Miller Park, and they approached the foundation for help. "'We'd like to do that with Moccasin Bend,' they said. 'Would you pay for that?' We said, 'Yeah, that sounds great—a wonderful use of our money.'"

But the experts brought in by Lyndhurst found serious challenges and shared them during a key gathering. "They basically said, 'This is a great site, but we don't know anybody in the real estate business that would touch it. You've got sixteen different easements, a sewage treatment plant, a mental health institute, a radio station, and this, that, and the other, and it's a mess. There's unclear title,'" said Montague.

"So that night, Dalton says to me, 'Would you be the chairman of the Moccasin Bend Task thing?'"

"I'd love to."

"Great. I'll talk to Pat Rose."

"So Dalton was probably smart enough to know that, in getting me, he was probably going to get some Lyndhurst money—again, an example of how smart I am when I'm giving away money."

Dalton Roberts   **Jack Murrah**   **Ron Littlefield**

Stroud Watson also consulted for the Task Force. Predictably, Stroud called for a bigger vision. He identified a 22-mile stretch of the river that the Moccasin Bend Task Force should develop, connecting the ancient "foot" to the entire city. Roberts commended the efforts. "The city and the county government told them, 'That's great, give us some ideas, and we'll do something.' And they did."

Montague credits the task force's consulting firm Carr Lynch Associates with some of the earliest visioning work, which included sixty-five meetings over three years. "No Carr Lynch, no riverfront plan," Montague said. "No effort at public participation by the Mocassin Bend Task Force, no Venture following it."

Montague vividly remembers the unveiling of the 22-mile master plan at the new Trade Center. They expected 800, but had an overflow crowd. "It was a great moment from my perspective because there was a big curtain closing off the wall, and as the crowd continued to get bigger, they had to open this curtain and bring in more chairs. And it was a great presentation. I remember Pat Wilcox comparing it to an evangelical event. It was a real call to the altar of Chattanooga."

Giving Credit Anyplace It's Due

Montague gives credit to the Moccasin Bend Task Force. During that key after-dinner meeting in Indianapolis—the casual conversation with Stroud and Mai Bell that led to Venture—he told them, "We need to have something that institutionalizes what the Moccasin Bend Task Force has been doing."[16*]

Dalton Roberts also credits this effort. "I think the most under-credited group to [the renaissance] is county government," Roberts said. "The place where all this river stuff started, all of it, was on the Moccasin Bend Task Force. That's where the Tennessee Riverpark concept came from. And then out of that sprung Coolidge Park and all the other things."

Mai Bell Hurley provides her own diplomatic interpretation. "Some people tell the story that the riverwalk and all came out of the vision process. Other people would tell the story that it came out of the Moccasin Bend Task Force, and it was both."

Credit for the renaissance can be found in even earlier efforts. A 1967 "Better Environment Plan," led by *Chattanooga Times* publisher Ruth Holmberg and regional planner T. D Hardens, called for similar riverfront revitalization and planted seeds for later successes. Businessman Jack McDonald, a member of the Moccasin Bend Task Force, was the first to actively promote the idea of an aquarium, which was just one of many items on the task force's wish list. According to Bill Sudderth, McDonald "went around giving talks, telling everyone how great an aquarium would be . . ." Then, he pitched the RiverCity board. "The story I've been told," said Sudderth, "is that Jack Lupton, who was on the RiverCity board and at the meeting, said, 'That's the dumbest idea I've ever heard of!'" This was before Rick Montague encouraged Lupton to visit Monterey's aquarium.[17*]

Rick Montague credits Tommy Lupton's decision to invest in downtown. He said the Krystal and Tallan Buildings were "radical" and "groundbreaking" in their day. "[It seems] like a normal kind of thing people would do. Only, if you look back at it, no one was doing it."

Montague also credits an even earlier downtown renewal effort, when Mayor Robert Kirk Walker approached Scotty Probasco to clean out a derelict section in front of the post office, which became Miller Park, the "center" of the city. "That was a major psychological boost in downtown Chattanooga," Rick said.

During our interview, Rick Montague first credited Mai Bell Hurley for the renaissance of Chattanooga. He also credited Stroud Watson, Gianni Longo, Jack Murrah, Tommy Lupton, Scotty Probasco, Robert Kirk Walker, Dalton Roberts, the Moccasin Bend Task Force, Vision 2000, and Five Nights in Chattanooga, to name a few.

The only person he did not credit was himself, but Jack Murrah takes care of that omission. "Rick Montague was the key figure," he said. "Lyndhurst Foundation was a primary institution."

Watson also places the credit with Montague. "I give it to Rick. . . . when Rick came in and took over as executive director, they started questioning the role of a philanthropic organization," said Stroud. "I would give Rick almost as much credit as a mentor."

"A great deal of the vocabulary that you hear from Stroud you also heard from Rick," said Mai Bell. "You know, 'The downtown is all of our living rooms—the river is our front porch.' I give him really high marks and great credit for the energy behind the whole movement, really. He was kind of empowered to do it because of the role he had at Lyndhurst, but he was not directed to do it because of that. But he was very interested, as Jack Murrah still is, in the dynamics of what it took to build a fine city."

Montague-Moon-Chapin-Lupton

There are some who attribute Montague's involvement to the fact that he was related to Jack Lupton. This may be true, but not just because he married Jack's daughter. Rick was already related to Jack through the Montague-Moon axis. His full name is Deaderick Chapin Montague. His grandfather, Deaderick Moon, married E. Y. Chapin's daughter, Elise. Through the Chapin-Carter axis, which includes Paul Carter's marriage to Anne Lupton, Rick can eventually find his way to the Lupton-Probasco axis. Since the Chapins are related to the Pattens, that provides yet another connection from Montague to Lupton (see chart on next page).

"I knew both of my great-grandparents," Rick told me. "I knew E. Y. Chapin, and I knew his wife. He died when I was in the third grade. She died when I was in the sixth or seventh grade." He explained how they supported artists, writers, and playwrights, and he also explained their association with Harry Scott Probasco's bank. "They were all very civically involved."

Theodore Giles Montague, Rick's great-grandfather, moved to Chattanooga after serving in the 140th Ohio Regiment during the Civil War battles of Chattanooga. Five of his brothers and sisters followed him. He attempted to start a bank in Pomeroy, Ohio, but the federal government would not issue a charter there. They suggested Chattanooga as a growing city in need of a bank. A few years later, T. G. Montague was listed as one of the seven millionaires in Chattanooga by the *New York Tribune*. The others included Harriet Whiteside and John Divine.

Columnist Sam Divine wrote about Montague's sagacity in real estate. A row house development by W. G. McAdoo (who later became the U.S. Treasury secretary) ultimately turned into a boondoggle. He "got it in the neck," wrote Divine, while "our old but lamented friend T. G. Montague got it by the tail at the psychological moment and swung it into success and gathered himself a fortune therefrom."[18]

Rick said T. G. Montague's son, Norton Thayer, was "a capitalist—whatever that meant," but he lost his fortune. "The story in my family was that all the other Montague families had money, but my grandfather had died when all his irons were in the fire. I guess I heard my dad use that expression a hundred times: 'He died when all his irons were in the fire.' So his mother had to sell investments that would have been great long term."

Today, Rick Montague is no longer Jack Lupton's son-in-law. He is remarried to his second wife, Cannon Wann, and once again has no direct connection to a giant fortune. Although *Montague* means "pointed mountain," he no longer lives on Lookout and instead resides in a condo just off the Walnut Street Bridge on the north shore, where he can admire past efforts. He no longer plays a visible, high-profile role. "He's kind of taken himself out of all this," said Mai Bell. "He's moved on to a different place, although I think he probably still thinks about it."

A Public-Private Partnership Moment

When Rick Montague does think about it, the "moment" for him personally was also during that final dinner in Indianapolis. While Mai Bell's moment was just afterwards, Rick was impressed by the symbolism of the speeches made by both himself and Mayor Gene Roberts during that historic gathering.

"I got up to make some comments, and this was from naivete, because I'm also the host. Lyndhurst Foundation had paid for it. Gene got up to make some comments [first]. And, I'm sure, to the surprise of many people, I also got up and

A Union officer from Ohio who became a Chattanooga industrialist and one of the city's first millionaires, Montague built a Spanish-style mansion that was razed during renovation of Cameron Hill.

THEODORE GILES MONTAGUE
1836–1910

ELISE CHAPIN = **DEADERICK MOON**

NORTON THAYER MONTAGUE

MILDRED MOON = **WILLIAM L. MONTAGUE**
b. 1800

CANNON WANN = **RICK MONTAGUE** = **ALICE LUPTON**
(2ND WIFE)   (1ST WIFE)

(Charts are partial, not exhaustive, highlighting key links or characters in the book.)

made comments. . . . I look back on that and I think, you know, the political side of Chattanooga and the private side of Chattanooga were, during that era, trying to figure out how to work cooperatively together."

It was much easier for later mayors such as Jon Kinsey and Bob Corker, he said. "Gene's situation required more attention, I think, than we gave to that. We felt everything good that happens will reflect positively on Gene. And I think Gene frequently couldn't figure out where we were coming from or why we couldn't leave things alone or, you know, how much did he have to worry that we were going to undercut him, or that something negative was going to come out of this."

"And blithely, out of our naivete, we were just thinking, 'Hey, things are great, things are going to be great. We need to move faster, not slower. We don't need to have any sense of base. We need to push the momentum as hard as we can.' And I think Gene, through his years in government, was sometimes standoffish and skeptical and very much responsible for getting Lamar to put the state package together, which put bricks and mortar behind [the renaissance]."

Such early successful relationships of trust between political leaders and prominent citizens led to a distinguishing characteristic of the city that now gets national attention, as the last chapter of the most recently published book on Chattanooga reads: "The Chattanooga Process: A City of Private and Public Partnerships."

So, it becomes clear that many people and many initiatives deserve recognition for the transformation of Chattanooga, although a number of folks assess the credit simply to the efforts of Jack Lupton in building an aquarium. However, it is always a circle in Chattanooga. At the end of the day, Rick Montague points again to Jack Lupton as the single, most influential force behind these same efforts and initiatives that gave rise to the Chattanooga Process, the renaissance, and the Aquarium.

Ultimately, it was Jack Lupton who gave Rick Montague his marching orders. "I was given a mandate," said Montague. "And I liked the mandate very much—to try to think about how we could really have an impact on Chattanooga. [But] it started with Jack Lupton taking over for his father."

Since that generational transition led to, arguably, the key driving force in Chattanooga's future, it is discussed in significant detail in Chapter Eight.

———◆———

A description of the "Long Man," the Cherokees' river myth, was the topic for the lecture at the Aquarium theater in the fall of 2003. Dr. Michael Abram, head of the Cherokee Heritage Museum in North Carolina, discussed the rituals, purification ceremonies, and religious beliefs associated with the Long Man.

He said the river was also known as the "Long Snake." The myth of the "Haunted Whirlpool" described two men capsizing in a small boat. One was eaten by a great fish. The other escaped the swirling waters but only after witnessing "fearsome things in the depths."[19] Other Cherokee legends described river monsters, great reptiles, and sea serpents, which caused many people to disappear and vessels on the river to capsize.

As the white man arrived, the legends were soon corroborated. Thomas Jefferson described a whirlpool just below Moccasin Bend as early as 1788 in his "Notes on Virginia." This "Sucking-Pot," as Jefferson called it, "takes in trunks of trees or boats, and throws them out again half a mile below."[20]

Early Chattanooga historian Henry Wiltse quotes an old citizen of Chattanooga who corroborates the more eerie legends of a river monster. "It has been frequently seen by the Cherokee Indians, and by them was held in great terror, and the sight of it by any individual was said to be a precursor of early death. It was generally described as the length of an ordinary canoe. It has a head something like a dog's . . . a black fin, which was from 18 inches to 2 feet long . . . and it swam with incredible velocity. Many of those who saw it succumbed to the evil influence and shortly after gave up the ghost."

"The first witness . . . was fishing on the south side of the river near Vann's place. His estimate was that it was about 25 feet long. That summer he died. The next was Billy Barns. . . . He said it was yellow on the belly and blue on the back, was from 20 to 25 feet long. That summer he died. Jim Windon, in 1829, was sitting on a point of rocks below Dallas fishing. The monster slowly passed him not more than 10 feet distant. . . . That summer he died. The elder Mr. Puckett saw it in 1836, and I suppose the power of the serpent had begun to wane, as the witness escaped with his life . . ."

"The last witness that I introduce is J. C. Wilson, known by the Indians as 'Teese, or the hanging bird.' He saw it in 1839. . . . He says when he first saw it, it was in a playful mood and had just started for the north shore. When it turned and came back to the south shore he could see the ripple made in the water by its head, and its back fin was at least a foot and a half out of the water. It darted with incredible speed. He does not think it took more than two minutes to cross the river and back."

"After this it was seen no more. . . . probably it followed the Cherokees west."[21]

Artist: Andrew Wilkie

CHAPTER FOUR

The Spirit of the Valley

Ancient Crossroads and Classes

"The owners live on Lookout Mountain, the managers live on Signal, and the workers live down in the valley," said Larry Ingle, a retired UTC history professor. It was a phrase echoed by several people during my series of interviews, but not everyone views Chattanooga's geography the same way.

"If you look at a map, it will spook you," said Jack Lupton. "You couldn't put a pin on the map that was more strategically located than Chattanooga. You couldn't do it."

Indeed, a perusal of a three-dimensional, topographical map of the area reveals a particularly striking phenomenon: the spirit of the river meets the spirit of the mountain to form an extraordinary valley. The southern-flowing Tennessee River makes an abrupt right turn straight into the high Cumberland Plateau, forming the Tennessee River Gorge.

It is an "illogical river" says one geological scholar. This puzzling and illogical turn in the river is the ultimate reason for the existence of Chattanooga.[1]

The Great Valley, stretching from Philadelphia into southern Georgia, sometimes called the "Great Wagon Road," provided a passageway for America's early pioneers from the Northeast to wedge through the difficult Appalachian Mountains. Again, a topographical map shows a wide rut or groove—anywhere from several miles to fifty or more miles wide—which follows Virginia's Shenandoah Valley into Bristol and the Cumberland Gap. It provided a natural funnel for daring frontiersmen like Daniel Boone and Davy Crockett.

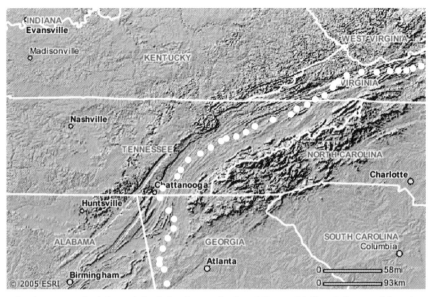

Settlers traveled from Virginia through the **"Great Valley,"** formed by the Smokies to the east and the Cumberland Plateau to the west.

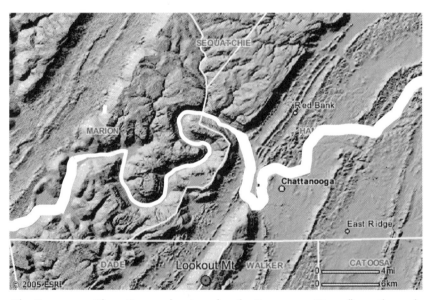

The **Tennessee River George** begins after the Tennessee River flows through the Great Valley, takes a sharp right at Chattanooga, and cuts through the Cumberland Plateau.

The Tennessee River and its initial tributaries flow naturally and logically for several hundred miles in the same southwesterly direction, surrounded by the Appalachian Smokies on one side and the Cumberland Plateau on the other. All reason suggests the waters will continue on to the seacoast of Georgia, but the river then takes its bold and unnatural course and cuts into a mountain range. Near the river's path is a similar groove for land travel to Nashville and Birmingham, undoubtedly caused by the same body of water when it ran higher ages ago.[2]

The First Travelers

Thanks to this strategic intersection in the middle of the southeastern United States, traffic since the earliest times has passed through the area now known as Chattanooga. The first traveler was the buffalo, laying down a path now followed by Interstate 24 to Nashville and Interstate 59 to Birmingham. The buffalo also paved the way through Virginia for Interstate 81 and to the Florida border on Interstate 75. "It is very wonderful that the buffalo's instinct should have found the very best courses across a continent," writes the author of *Historic Highways of America*. "Yet it did, as the tripod of the white man has proved."[3]

Chattanooga, actually, is out of the way if traveling in the middle of the Great Valley down the Great Wagon Road. It is much quicker to travel south straight from Cleveland, Tennessee, to Dalton, Georgia, and on to Savannah. Such a track also avoids the very inconvenient Missionary Ridge. But the interstate takes the long route over to the right by the Cumberlands and back, as did the buffalo, to gain access to the Southwest. A railroad company once attempted the shortcut by skipping Chattanooga but inevitably acquiesced to the more powerful geological forces.

The Native Americans merely followed the buffalo trails—whether Archaic Indians, Woodlands, or Mississippians. By the time of the Cherokees, the area of the "Great Bend" around the river served as an axis for the Cisca and St. Augustine Trail, the Tennessee and Great Lakes Trail, and the Great Indian Warpath. The first European explorers, Spaniards in search of "God, gold, and glory," were by necessity traversing the area as early as 1559, perhaps two decades earlier. The French came next. A 1715 British map confirms that a spot at or just south of the Bend was "Since ye Warre a French Fort." The competitive British also lusted for the strategic area, pinpointing a spot on a 1733 map at what looks like the Chattanooga area. It is marked as "A fit place for an English Factory." The river is oddly called "Hogohegee," but it does appropriately form below the Pelissippi, or today's Holston River, near Knoxville. A mark for rapids corresponds to the Suck.

In 1754, the young surveyor George Washington identifies the same spot that was eyed for a factory somewhere near Chattanooga. He calls it a "Fit Place for a Fort." Historian Zella Armstrong proclaims Washington's potential fort site as none

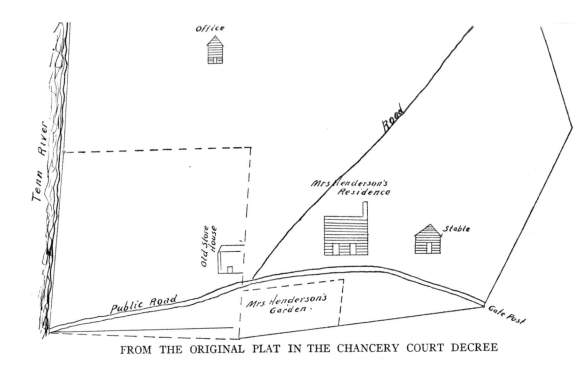

Office

Tenn River

Road

Mrs. Henderson's
Residence

Old Store
House

Stable

Public Road

Mrs. Henderson's
Garden.

Gate Post

FROM THE ORIGINAL PLAT IN THE CHANCERY COURT DECREE

The first known rendering of **Ross's Landing**, contained in legal papers disputing the ownership of Mrs. Henderson's Inn. The "Public Road" is in the general area of Market Street. The "Road" going northeast may have been the road to the mission, the Harrison Road, or may have connected to both.

other than Chattanooga. Of course, she offers no evidence, but it is worth noting the first attempt at a factory in the region. Elias Earle planned to build an ironworks in 1807 at the mouth of Chickamauga Creek, today's site for Stein Construction on Amnicola Highway.[4] I was shown the ancient site by Doug Stein, whose great-grandfather Gilbert started laying stones in Chattanooga in 1889. *Stein* means stone.

But the first documented fort in the region was not the Stein site. Fort Loudoun, just south of Knoxville, was built along the Tellico River, a tributary of the Tennessee. It was the most far-reaching British settlement in the West in 1756. The fort helped ally England with the Cherokees during the fight to extend competing empires in the New World, the French and Indian War. However, the Indians broke their alliance and joined the French in 1760 and captured Fort Loudoun.

The Cherokees immediately notified New Orleans, and vast provisions were sent up the river. But the party of Frenchmen could not get past the rapids at the Suck area. This likely explains early maps showing an "Old French Store." Goodspeed's map seems to indicate the Ross's Landing area for the store. The early drawing of Ross's Landing with "The Road" also shows a storehouse by the river. According to Zella Armstrong, it was much older than Ross's store, and many believed it to be the Old French Store. But Adair's history mentions the "Great Mortar," an Indian Chief headquartered, possibly, on the island later called Williams, who served as guide to the Frenchmen. Perhaps the store was located there, below the Suck, as seems more likely.[5]

At this point in the 18th century, no one inhabited the area now circled by the city limits of Chattanooga. The Cherokees lived to the north, the Creeks to the south. Hunters like Elisha Walden, the namesake of Walden's Ridge, traveled the region but did not settle there. Reports indicate the Native Americans may have avoided the area due to its reputation for causing sickness.

In 1770, the first person in a great while and certainly the first European settled permanently on the land of the future city. Scotsman John McDonald served as Indian agent for the British at Fort Loudon and moved south to increase his opportunities to trade with the Native Americans. For his residence, he chose an open, uninhabited spot where the Great Indian Warpath crossed Chickamauga Creek, today the site of Wal-Mart and Eastgate Mall. McDonald was soon joined by Dragging Canoe and the warring Cherokees, called "Chickamaugas," who later moved further south.

McDonald eventually built another house in a nearby strategic location, the lone gap in the ridge that allowed those following the warpath to reach Moccasin Bend and go further into the Southwest. (Today's "Ridge Cut" for Interstate 24 did not exist.) Later known as Rossville Gap, this convenient passage was also used for the historic Federal Road, known as the Georgia Road, the Augusta-Nashville Road, and the Federal Turnpike. This groundbreaking route for wagons and cargo was bitterly opposed by the Cherokees for many years before its completion in 1804. The Cherokee Nation was, in effect, blocking white America's access from the Southern states to Nashville, Knoxville, and beyond. President John Adams pushed to build a road through Cherokee territory but failed. Thomas Jefferson pushed with even greater determination, but the chiefs complained that opening up wagon roads would only add to murder, theft, and other problems already occurring with the settlers. The chiefs preferred to keep them as ancient paths. "We have no disposition to encourage they Travellers [sic] should pass through our lands as there is roads enough among the whites to go around," the chiefs said. But McDonald persuaded the chiefs to relent, and he was joined by James Vann.[6]

The Richest Man in the Valley

Vann and his son, known as "Rich Joe Vann," were perhaps the two most significant early residents of the Greater Chattanooga area, at least of those not related to John McDonald. Rich Joe Vann, part Scottish and part Cherokee, was a leading horse racing enthusiast. He attracted distinguished men from surrounding states who brought their horses to Vann's plantation to compete on his three race tracks south of the river, at what is now called Harrison, near the present Central High School along Highway 58. His tracks were a quarter mile, a half mile, and a full mile in length, respectively. The mixed-blood Cherokee was not only the richest man in the Cherokee Nation but also the wealthiest man in the entire region. (He owned 110 slaves, compared to Hamilton County's largest slaveholder who had 13.) He owned 800 acres, forty-two cabins, orchards, mills, and blacksmith shops. Jack and Tom Wisdom attended to his large stable of stud horses, and William Dugger served as his jockey. Fellow Indians also traveled many miles to see the races.

Vann enjoyed three wives at the same time, two Cherokee and one white. The

Joseph Vann

area, or someplace near it, was called Van's Town when destroyed in 1782 by colonial forces, which forced Vann's father James to move near Dalton, Georgia, where he built a magnificent brick home in 1804 along the Federal Road. Helen describes the house, still standing today, in the cookbook: "With its Federal style, its elaborately carved cantilevered stairway, and the latest elegant furnishings . . . it takes its place among the finest restorations in America for beauty, elegance, authenticity, and interest, and is the only mansion in America built by an American Indian." She describes a ceremony for the restored house in 1958 that included Will Rogers, Jr, a great-great-grandson of James Vann. She also includes a recipe for Indian Corn Pudding.[7]

Like his son, James Vann complicated his life by marrying two women—sisters, in fact. He was responsible for bringing the first missionaries into the Cherokee Nation in 1801, German Baptists from North Carolina, but was interested in schools, not religion. "White traders who married Cherokee women were seldom noted for their piety," said Cherokee scholar William McLoughlin, "and neither were their children." Vann shot his brother-in-law in a duel, inflicted 70 lashes on a man living with his sister, and forced a confession out of a white woman he suspected had stolen from him by stringing her up by her thumbs. He traded enormous amounts of whiskey and drank nearly as much. His cruelty and intemperance finally caught up to him when he was assassinated in 1809 by a disgruntled subordinate. "The bottle was in one hand, and he was lifting a cup of whiskey to his lips with the other," according to a report of the murder. "The door . . . was silently pressed open by the point of a rifle. In an instant, James Vann was dead."[8]

He rebuffed a chance to prepare for his Maker four years earlier when he lay critically ill for a time. "The missionaries came to his bedroom and tried to reprove him for his drunkenness, fornication, and wife-beating, hoping for a deathbed conversion," wrote McLoughlin. "After hearing them out, he rose up, 'jumped from his bed, seized a bottle and drank as much as he could in one gulp and said in anger that it was his house and he could drink as much as he pleased, dance, fornicate and what not and that it was none of [their] business.' When they said they would nevertheless pray for Jesus to save his soul, 'Vann left the room saying that he did not believe there was a Jesus Christ.' The missionaries concluded that 'the Devil has so possessed and bound Vann' that he was beyond human help."[9]

He did have his more redeeming, or at least patriotic, moments. Along with Chief Ridge, he led an armed effort to turn away a caravan of whites headed to build Earle's ironworks factory at the mouth of Chickamauga Creek. The federal government had agreed to cede six square miles to Earle without getting permission from the full Cherokee council. One hundred families were planning to move to the area, a significant community that would have greatly altered the early history of the Chattanooga area. However, Vann and Ridge believed the effort to be unlawful according to previous treaties and moved against the caravan headed up from southern Georgia. One federal agent said he had heard Vann "said some time ago that he intended to turn Bonaparte and now he has turned Bonaparte." Chief Ridge snatched the caravan leader's gun from him and fired it into the air. Another Cherokee soldier brandished a tomahawk and hit a man's face with the dull side of the blade. The ironworks party relented and headed home.

Rich as he was, Joe Vann was not exempt from the federal edict, and he moved out to Oklahoma with the rest of his tribe. However, he was able to transport his several-hundred-person entourage of wives, children, employees, and slaves in simple flatboats. They left early, unaccompanied by soldiers. A steamship was reserved for Vann and his immediate advisors, along with the prized horses. But only a few miles into the trip, the ship's boilers exploded, killing Joseph Vann and several others.[10]

Eying that Property Across the River

Around the time Vann was loading up for Oklahoma, white settlers on the opposite side of the river were greedily eyeing his property. The courthouse for Hamilton County at that time was located just across the river at a community called Dallas, named after U.S. Treasury Secretary Alexander Dallas whose son, a Vice President, became popular in Texas. (The old Dallas site is now underwater.) Before the Dallas site, the Hamilton County Courthouse was located in a number of homes, the first being at Poe's Crossing, now Soddy Daisy, where Hasten Poe operated a tavern. These early proceedings took place just after the county was created in 1819, the eventual fallout of Andrew Jackson's treaty in 1817, when he acquired millions of Cherokee acres.

The name "Hamilton" was chosen for the first secretary of the treasury, Alexander Hamilton, who had died a decade before in a dual with Aaron Burr. He was from New York, was against slavery, and favored the federal government over states rights, all views that would prevail when the Hamiltonians voted 40 years later to remain with the Union.

These early settlers were not allowed to reside across the river into Ross's Landing and Vanville, although many began technically breaking the law when the New Echota Treaty was signed in 1835. The land in Vanville looked more fertile than Dallas, and rumors began to spread that Georgia would build a railroad from the coast to Vann's former plantation. Dallas fell out of favor. In 1840, the people voted to make "Vann" the new capital of Hamilton County. The name was immediately changed to Harrison in honor of the famous Indian fighter at Tippecanoe,

First courthouse for Hamilton County: Hasten Poe's Tavern in Soddy.

William Henry Harrison, who had just been elected President in the "log and hard cider" campaign. Tom Crutchfield, Sr. built the new brick courthouse, and the developers of the new area included James Whiteside, Samuel Williams, and William Gardenhire.

William Gardenhire crossed the river early and settled in Chattanooga about 1832 with his wife Esther, daughter Susan, and a slave

156

named Ginny. Like the Vanns', William Gardenhire had a few family problems. After one year at the new farm, Esther went back to Roane County. Later, their daughter Susan said her parents "fell out about a colored woman." It was Ginny. She ended up bearing two bi-racial children, Mary and Martha.

Gardenhire built a farm almost exactly where Chattanooga School for the Arts and Sciences (CSAS) now stands, the site of the original City High School, later Riverside High. He let the cabin of an Indian named "Old Water Lizard" remain standing next to his house at the mouth of Citico Creek, now a facility for the Tennessee-American Water Company. Gardenhire operated a ferry across the river and walked fifty feet to a separate building for his office. His property was used for the Camp Cherokee stockade in 1836. To get to his house at Citico Creek from the new courthouse at Vann's old property, the traveler took the "Harrison Road," today Highway 58 and Amnicola Highway. At that time there were basically four roads in Chattanooga: the Harrison Road, the Rossville Road, the Brainerd (or Shallow Ford) Road to the mission, and the "Valley Road," now Main Street.[11]

Perhaps the Oldest Family Name in Chattanooga

Gardenhire is another prominent early family preceding Whiteside, Williams, and Crutchfield and is arguably the longest standing family name in Chattanooga. I interviewed Todd Gardenhire from his office in the Republic Centre, a few floors down from the Walden Club, where Gianni Longo entertained dubious city commissioners two decades before. Gardenhire deals in investments and made a run for Congress in 1992 against Zach Wamp in the Republican primary. Zach won, but lost the family-tree skirmishes.

"You know, I was always told they were one of the first families down here," said Todd Gardenhire. "They came down here with some land grants, and one of the original guys married Chief Pathkiller's daughter up in Roane County."

It was this marriage of a Gardenhire to a Cherokee chief's daughter that enabled them to cross the river early and live a mile up from Ross's Landing as citizens of the Cherokee Nation.

Todd talked about his ancestor Francis Marion Gardenhire who fought in the "War of Northern Aggression." Francis's grandfather, George, continued the Gardenhire name at age 84 when his 33-year-old wife Liza Ann bore him a son. Todd also talked about another colorful Gardenhire, also a Confederate, who laid out the city of Dayton and built its principal buildings. William "Lum" Gardenhire was a merchant in Harrison who brought four natives back from the Fiji Islands. He paraded the exotic humans around the country to curious crowds before selling them to P. T. Barnum for $20,000.[†]

[†] $2.2 million (2006)

Todd remembered how Lum died. "My grandmother always kept that old clipping. He was evidently partaking of a noontime activity at somebody else's spouse's house. And the guy, a doctor, came home and hit him with a can of cherries, so the headline read, "Lum Gardenhire killed with can of cherries."

Todd also talked about another Gardenhire legacy. "The Citizens Cemetery was started by our family back in 1832 or '33 when old man Montgomery died, the first mayor of Chattanooga. There was no basic cemetery, as such, in town. They were good friends, and so [Gardenhire] buried his good friend in the front yard. And when he died a couple of years later, he was buried next to him. And next to him was the original Bill Crutchfield who had bought his brickyard from my great-great-grandfather's property."

The cemetery is located between UTC and Chattanooga School for the Arts and Sciences, just below Erlanger and above UTC's McKenzie Arena. "So that became Citizens Cemetery," said Gardenhire. "He just said, 'Okay, my front yard—ten acres—I'm going to make a cemetery. Anybody who wants to be buried here can be buried here.'"

"Somewhere, I've got the actual handwritten sheets of when people were first buried over there," said Todd. "It's somewhere in my attic, but I've got it. It's just a little flip pad with the names."

The Early Chamber of Commerce

Recognizable names buried there include McCallie, Hooke, Frist, Kennedy, Long, and Mrs. Berry, wife of the first mayor. Todd Gardenhire did not quite get it right in saying his ancestor's friend, Rush Montgomery, was the first mayor, but he was close. Rush Montgomery was a very early promoter of Chattanooga, along with John P. Long. One might say they were the first two leaders of the Chamber of Commerce.

Historian Harry Wiltse passes along a story about Montgomery that he said "graphically illustrated the Chattanooga Spirit in its pristine days." A group of men that included early pioneers Williams and Whiteside gathered with some schoolboys by a pond on The Road by Ninth Street. "The question was asked where the center of the world was. Some of the boys said Baltimore, some said New York, some Washington." But as they began to walk away, Rush Montgomery "sprang to his feet, brought his cane down on the ground with a vengeance, and declared that if he was driving that stick for the center of the world, he would drive it in the pond we had just

Todd Gardenhire

left." The pond was located at the current site of Miller Plaza, today the "center" of the city.[12]

At another early meeting of settlers urging the recruitment of rail to Chattanooga, Montgomery proclaimed the day would come when "persons present would live to see two carloads of freight shipped to Ross's Landing daily." Egged on by applause, the lawyer from Pikeville added that "the town would eventually spread out over an area of ten miles, reaching to Lookout Mountain on the southwest and above the mouth of Citico on the Northeast."[13]

Montgomery "talked the loudest and longest" of anyone in town. He would often hop on a stump at Ross's Landing and proclaim his economic prophecies to friend and stranger alike. "Why, don't you see? The buffalo worked out the line; the Indian followed it; the white man followed the Indian; the wagon road and railroad take the same route; the mountains shut in here; the valleys stop here; Tennessee River must pass through here; fact is, don't you see, this is the funnel of the universe!"[14*]

This "Funnel of the Universe" phrase served as Chattanooga's key descriptor until it was replaced almost a century later with "Dynamo of Dixie."[15] Montgomery's fellow booster and cheerleader was John P. Long, the man famous in local history for suggesting the name "Chattanooga" for the town. Long made similar sweeping statements of an international nature. "Here is the gate through which the history of nations must pass," he said. These bold predictions were made at a time when the area was almost completely wooded. Nevertheless, Long built a log cabin next to the river for him and his wife. "I found all the requirements necessary to build a future city," he said.

Not all of Montgomery's prophecies have been fulfilled. His belief that Chattanooga would one day boast a population of one million left "people to shake their heads wondering how anyone could believe such predictions." Of course, he may yet be proven right. His more conservative prediction of 200,000 was eventually fulfilled yet was met with the same silent ridicule. The Valley Road was named "Montgomery Avenue" before changing again to Main Street, a decision Wiltse says has proven to be inaccurate and was made "by some petty meddlers with affairs of which they knew little."[16]

———◆———

Todd Gardenhire gained opportunity as a young, politically active college student with an historic last name to serve on the Board of Trustees for the University of Tennessee in Knoxville. Only one student in the state got the honor, and officials drew straws. Chattanooga was selected to send a student.

"In 1971, there was a movement on all the campuses nationwide—a very liberal element—to have students on the board of trustees of all these universities," he said.

Citizens Cemetery. (Bottom) A broken headstone against a tree with Chattanooga School for the Arts and Sciences (CSAS) in the background. (Top) Above-ground crypt of pioneer Thomas Crutchfield. (Right) A Gardenhire marker.

"Some businessmen in town knew of my conservative politics . . . and I was the first student on the Board of Trustees as a non-voting member."

"The first meeting—I've never forgotten it," said Gardenhire. The trustees had two big issues to discuss that day, the first one regarding higher academic standards. "And then the other issue they were going to talk about was Chattanooga. They were landlocked down there, and they knew there was this old cemetery down there that hadn't been used in 30, 40 years, and nobody really knew anything about it. And they were just going to quietly confiscate it a piece at a time."

"And I'm sitting there, and I kept raising my hand, and I said, 'You know, you really can't do that. You can't take that property down there.' They assumed I was taking the stand of a preservationist, somebody that didn't want progress and all this stuff."

"Is this UTC or UT?" I asked.

"UT Knoxville. Big daddy."

"The whole shebang?"

"The whole deal," he said. "The president finally turned and looked at me: "Boy, you need to understand something. We didn't want you on here to start with. You're here to be seen and not heard."

"Well, I appreciate that," I said, "and I understand my place in life. But that's not why I'm objecting. You can either listen to me today or you can listen to me on the six o'clock news, but it doesn't matter because I'm going to say what I'm going to say."

"Well, what are you telling us? Okay, say it."

"My family has the deed to that property and we aren't going to let you take it."

The trustees didn't believe him.

"I later showed them a copy of the deed. That kind of startled them. They were given assurances that no deed existed." The family gave the cemetery to the city as part of a deal that it would always be used as a cemetery or it reverts back to the family. "I said, 'Let's see, you have an archeological school, you have an engineering school that teaches surveys, and yet you can't find out this stuff? You know, you don't have an excuse for breaking the law.'" According to Gardenhire, the UT trustees never mentioned the subject again.

Fifteen years later, Gardenhire was in his office with a man promoting the vision for the UTC Roundhouse, the future McKenzie Arena. The man said things were progressing just fine, "But there's this lady that lives up here on High Street that's always stopping us."

"Well, what's her name?" Todd asked.

"Mamie Tucker—always a pain in our side."

"That wouldn't be Mamie G. Tucker, would it?" Todd asked again.

"Well, yeah. It would."

"That 'G' doesn't stand for Gardenhire, does it?"

"I don't know."

"Well, that's my great aunt."

"That started the cemetery fight in 1987 that we eventually won in Chancery Court," said Todd. "It caused them to put a fence up and those rock pillars up at the corners to mark it."

Kicking A City Father While He's Down

It was certainly time for Chattanooga to pay more attention to its historic Citizens Cemetery. A hundred years after John Long named the city, his grave had been nearly lost to neglect. As conservationist Robert Sparks Walker was labeling trees in the area, he stumbled when his foot hit a rock of some sort. He found a monument buried under the sod. Digging away the grass and dirt, he wiped moss off the inscription. It said, "John P. Long."[17] That same year of 1946, Walker and E. Y. Chapin, Jr. led an effort to restore the memorial of this key city founder.

Several men buried in that cemetery—Long, Montgomery, Allen Kennedy— acted on the vision to take advantage of the area's strategic valleys by obtaining the ultimate economic engine, the railroad. City fathers James Whiteside and Samuel Williams participated with Long, Kennedy, and others. The Lookout Railroad Company was formed in 1837, the community's first public-private partnership. A year before, the Georgia legislature had announced its intention to build the world's longest railroad, stretching from southern Georgia to some place "at or near Rossville." South Carolina had previously built a 136-mile track from Charleston to just outside Augusta in 1833, the world's longest to date. Georgia feared the competition, which is why it acted quickly.

The leaders of Ross's Landing in 1837 were troubled by Georgia's desire to locate "at or near Rossville." It was not long before communities at both Harrison and Hiawassee were making strong appeals to be named the northern terminus of the railroad. The Lookout Railway Company wrote to Governor William Schley and his response was not encouraging. "If the nature and face of the country be such as to permit the road to start from Rossville, it will assuredly do so—and if not, from the nearest practicable point on the line east of the place."

Georgia's rush to finish a thoroughfare beyond the Appalachians greatly added to the motivation to remove the Cherokees. Even before the railroad emerged, attempts were made by Wilson Lumpkin to solve the problem by building

John P. Long

a 12-mile canal to connect smaller tributaries that could take travelers to a place on the river beyond the rapids problem at the Suck, and at Muscle Shoals, Alabama. But the Cherokees refused to allow the canal. Lumpkin was later elected Governor of Georgia and eagerly pushed for railroads. Not coincidently, he was arguably the strongest advocate for Cherokee removal.[18]

Which Town Gets the Railroad?

The southern terminus for Georgia's railroad had already been decided upon as an uninhabited spot eight miles from the Chattahoochee River that could conveniently connect five other Georgia towns. The new town was simply called "Terminus," and later changed to "Marthasville" in honor of Governor Lumpkin's youngest daughter. By 1845, it was called Atlanta.

Clearly, whichever town gained the nod from Georgia would explode as a transportation center. Hiawassee fought intensely in the legislature, using "every device to which ingenuity could resort" to defeat the bill favoring Chattanooga. Announcements were made in 1839 that Chattanooga would indeed be chosen, but an economic depression hit the country and all construction on the railroad stopped in 1842. According to a Major McCullum quoted by Wiltse, the railroad tracks had been built all the way to Graysville with the intention of connecting at Harrison before the construction stopped.[19] For several more years, the monumental decision remained in limbo.

To understand the stakes at the time, one must understand the phenomenal growth of the cotton industry. Through its river traffic, Chattanooga was already moving 45,000 bales of cotton a year, second only to New Orleans as a provision market.[20] Britain was the major customer, consuming 79 million pounds of raw cotton in 1810. With new technologies and modes of transportation, Britain alone imported over one billion pounds of cotton by 1860. Historian Paul Johnson explains why cotton was so important. "Until the end of the 18th century, the human race had always been unsuitably clothed in garments that were difficult to wash and therefore filthy. Cotton offered an escape from this misery, worn next to the skin in cold countries, as a complete garment in hot ones . . . hundreds of millions of people, all over the world, were able to dress comfortably and cleanly at last." The land of the early colonies was more suited to tobacco, but in the new states seized by Andrew Jackson,—Alabama, Mississippi, and Louisiana—cotton was king. They were perfectly suited for growing it on a large scale.[21]

Chattanooga was already known as the doorway to the Deep South and through its river traffic became known as the site "where cotton meets corn." But losing the rail terminal to a nearby town would mean losing much of that status. The town fathers would also fail to land the single greatest economic opportunity in the area's history. "If Georgia fails to finish the road, all is flat in Chattanooga," said a frustrated Allen Kennedy. "But the general belief is that she will do it, and then we expect a rush to this place. . . . It seems we have had so many disappointments about the matter that I hardly expect much from the road, for as soon as one difficulty is done with, another is ready for poor Chattanooga."[22]

Hope for "poor Chattanooga" arrived when the Tennessee legislature determined to build its own railroad. James Whiteside, a member of the legislature, introduced the bill, and through his influence, Chattanooga was chosen for the southern terminus from Nashville. That decision erased any doubt regarding Georgia's choice for a northern terminus. By 1847, the final leg from Dalton to Chattanooga was under construction.

However, the Chattanoogans still had some waiting to do. Just beyond Ringgold, the project was stopped by a ridge tough enough to earn the name "Tunnel Hill." Digging through the ridge took a long time. Until then, train cars were transported over the hill with horses and oxen. On December 1, 1849, the first engine entered Chattanooga, "a little thing, with ball drivers, no flanges, and carrying the water tank on top of the boilers." "It was a great day in the little berg when we heard the engine puff and the whistle blow for the first time in our little village," said early citizen Thomas McCallie, the Presbyterian preacher's father. He said a bottle of seawater was brought to the celebration and poured into the Tennessee River, "marrying the ocean and the river."[23]

James Whiteside spoke at the ceremony, promising that one day iron rails would stretch all the way to San Francisco. A few months after that ceremony, the Tunnel Hill project was finally completed. The trains made their trip entirely by rail. A similar but more grandiose ritual was performed at the Tunnel Hill site using water from the Jordan River.

Whiteside had already invested a great deal in the area, betting on a successful outcome with the state legislatures. He became president of the most significant venture in the region, the Chattanooga Iron and Manufacturing Company, whose owners included Ker Boyce of South Carolina and Farish Carter of Georgia, both considered the wealthiest men in their state. Other board members included a U.S. senator, a former Georgia governor, and a U.S. cabinet member.

The Chattanooga Iron and Manufacturing Co. bought up 18,000 acres for mining on Raccoon Mountain and pushed for the mining of more coal fields along the railroad tracks. Foundries were also built, but the highlight of this company's several projects was a new coke-fired furnace just below Bluff View next to Ross's Landing. The ironclad furnace with cupola on top was one of the first of its kind in the country and the only one in the South. Iron ore, charcoal fuel, and limestone flux were brought in by riverboat. The Bluff View furnace produced 500 tons of pig iron before the pending war shut it down permanently in 1860.

The railroad industry, now stretching to California as Whiteside predicted, created an enormous demand for iron and coal, two resources that Chattanooga possessed in abundance. After several decades, these megatrends shifted the entire economy of the region. Three floats in a July 4, 1878, parade celebrating the god Vulcan summarized the great paradigm shift. The first float said, "Cotton Was King," the second said, "Iron is King Now," and the third, "Coal is Prime Minister."[24]

———◆———

During my research, I generally found words like coke, pig-iron, bituminous coal, and other technical terms rather confusing. The best explanation I received came from a very likely source, Hamilton County's longtime historian James Livingood. He was 93 when he invited me up to his Alexian Village retirement apartment on Signal Mountain. "Bring a friend or two," he said.

It was snowing that day. My friends, Nancy and Jana, and I were an hour late. As we walked around the complex looking for the right door, I saw an elderly gentleman sitting patiently outside in the cold weather, apparently hoping some guests would arrive. That turned out to be Dr. Livingood. We had a wonderful visit. The former Princeton instructor and longtime UTC professor displayed several books he had authored on one shelf in his small kitchen/living room.

I asked him to compare Chattanooga to Atlanta, but he did not care to talk about Atlanta. He wanted to discuss Chattanooga and the Cherokees. Since he's an expert in both subjects, I was happy to let him steer the interview in that direction. His broad, scholarly grasp of several centuries helped me better understand the big-picture factors surrounding the emergence of the iron and coal industries.

"When Columbus came to this country, all through North America . . . the Indians were working gold and silver, weren't they?" he asked. (Like a good professor, he conducted the interview with a lot of questions for us, his students for the day.)

"The American Indian, and this would include the Cherokee, did not work in iron, and there is a very easy explanation for this," he said. "Gold and silver are found in almost a perfectly pure state in the earth. Iron ore is filled with pollutants that have to be worked out of it."

"Now the American . . . [knew] how to use iron. And the early iron was absolutely essential for frontier life," he said. "What did the frontiersman need iron for?" (He answered the question himself before we were able to think up something.) "Horseshoes, for one thing. He needed iron to make hinges for his doors for a cabin. He needed iron for his fireplace tools. He needed iron for his kettles, his cooking utensils. There was only one thing that he couldn't make and still had to buy and that was crocheting needles and sewing needles. They had to come out of Europe."

He also discussed how iron grew in demand to build rails for the railroad, train cars, and wheels for the locomotives. "The locomotive was really a moving fire bed, wasn't it? And the fire bed was where you burned wood, and you burned wood in order to make steam for the water that you carried in the engine. The steam turned the wheels and made it go. Very simple, except a few things. They soon discovered that they couldn't make that engine go any faster than it went. They couldn't pull more cars than they were pulling."

James Livingood

"Somebody with a sharp mind, who possibly didn't have any education at all, found out what the trouble was. They were beginning to change the fuel in the locomotive from wood to bituminous coal, but bituminous coal didn't work any better than wood until somebody discovered that if you ground it up and made it as fine as granulated sugar and put that into the fire bed of the engine, you would make twice as many BTUs."

He was describing coke. Bituminous coal was simply coal with certain carbons in it. When coal is burned while deprived of oxygen, it becomes coke, similar to wood turning to charcoal. Coke was burned to make the iron for the trains and also powered the engines that pulled the trains. It is little wonder that Chattanooga became a major railroad center with her uncanny valleys and strategic coal and iron reserves.

The first railway reached Chattanooga before St. Louis saw a train and before a train connected Philadelphia and Pittsburgh. Soon, Chattanooga became the critical junction to all points south and west. Eight decades later, this phenomenal railway center received perhaps the nation's greatest popular attention when the Glen Miller Orchestra released "Chattanooga Choo Choo" in 1941. It became the first gold record in history and is considered the song that launched the big band era. Even today, Irving Berlin's song is the first association in the minds of Americans when they hear the word *Chattanooga*.

Similarly, one's first thought may be a singer and songwriter instead of a politician when the name Dalton Roberts is brought up in conversation. Roberts means "bright fame," and this Roberts was elected four times to the highest office in Hamilton County. The former county executive hardly missed a beat after leaving office to focus again on his music and writing. He was born in Watering Trough, a neighborhood in East Chattanooga. As well as anyone in the last half-century, Dalton Roberts embodies the Spirit of the Valley. In fact, *Dalton* means "valley."

Some give him the lion's share of the credit for Chattanooga's renaissance, but those political activities only capture a slice of his life. As one local writer said, "Dalton Roberts is equal parts politician, humorist, poet, songwriter, musician, author, and columnist." He writes a weekly column for the paper and has published a book of quotes and wise sayings from "the Downhome Philosopher," an eclectic mix of Christianity, Buddhism, points on meditation, bird-watching tips, and ancient Indian wisdom passed on from his Cherokee great-grandmother. Roberts has played at the Grand Ole Opry, and he has among his credits a song that topped the charts and another chosen as a theme song for an NBC-TV show.[25]

I interviewed him at a local greasy spoon that he picked out. For years, he has met weekly at such a joint with some old-time friends, a group they call the International Blue Tick Society. He was wearing a watch with some kind of little guitar on the face and wore yellow sunglasses. He used to wear red ones to keep out the ultraviolet rays, he said, but they also distorted his vision of the world. The amber glasses "add a slight tinge to your vision."

"I've never aspired to be a mountain guy," he told me. "I mean, that's a culture that I don't prefer." When he first ran for office, he gained popularity with his wry promise to "bulldoze Lookout Mountain for a better view of Georgia and Alabama." He failed to get an endorsement from either paper. He did win his first election, but he got only sixty votes from Lookout Mountain. Ironically, he married a gal from the mountain, a GPS graduate.

"We went somewhere to eat in the early days when we were just dating," Dalton said. "I got a biscuit and started sopping something out of my plate. She looked around like a hunted animal, you know, to see if anybody was watching me."

"Somebody might see you doing that," she whispered.

"Well, good. Maybe they'll learn to sop."

Her father took them up to the swanky Fairyland Club for dinner just after Dalton became county executive. When he walked in, the place "got real quiet . . . It was like, 'My God, what's he doing in here?' And I could hear people saying, 'There he is! Look over there.'"

"So in a few minutes I got up and saw one of the black waiters—they're all black waiters, you know—and one of the black waiters was a schoolteacher I used to teach with named Napoleon. He took me around and introduced me to all the waiters and bartenders and cooks back in the kitchen and all."

"What happened to you?" her father asked when I returned.

"Well, I saw I wasn't going to get no votes out here, so I was going around seeing my people."

He told another story about going with his wife to Lookout Mountain Presbyterian Church. "We was going up the mountain, and I saw these black people walking down the road with their Bibles."

"Good God, Betty. Do these people go to church with you all? I didn't know black people lived up here on the mountain."

"Oh yeah, they've lived up here ever since slave days. They've got their own church right down there."

"Well, doggone; that accounts for those sixty votes I got up here."

Dalton Roberts had an early penchant for bucking the establishment. "I hated school, just hated it. I went through all kinds of stuff—smoking, skipping class, oh hell, fighting. You name it and I was doing it. . . . I got kicked out of high school—permanently expelled from the county school system in the tenth grade."

"For what?"

"I turned a cow loose in the hall."

"In the hall?"

"Yeah. You oughta seen that cow bouncing around trying to get up on those slick waxed floors."

His father, a preacher, pulled some strings to get Dalton into Kirkman Technical High School. He was called into the principal's office again. "I thought, well, I can just tell you exactly what he's going to say. So I go into his office, and he leans back and props his feet up on the desk. He's looking at my record."

"I see here where you play a guitar."

"Yes, sir."

"Would you be interested in playing for some of the school functions?"

"Yes, sir," Dalton replied. "I'd be glad to."

He treated the delinquent like a good friend. Dalton Roberts walked out of the office a new man. "It's amazing how much a little love and understanding and support—just friendliness—can change a person."

Jeff's Favorite Valley-ites

This common man, musician, and elected official has gained a lot of fans in the valley. Among them is WGOW Talk Radio host Jeff Styles. "Dalton Roberts picks his guitar and doles out homespun, backwoods wisdom gloated with a gilded tongue and a honey-coated voice—all the while playing games of hardball and smashface politics like a chessmaster. . . . And underneath the faded fedora, overalls, and rose colored glasses, he's a Zen

Singer-songwriter Dalton Roberts (right)

Buddhist who proudly preaches the positive aspects of daily meditation and bird watching. I love this man."

Styles describes other valley-ites who represent the interests of flatlanders, such as the Minnie Pearl-esque City Councilwoman, Marti Rutherford. "Hats are inherently funny," says Styles. "Her sweet little-ol' Aunt Bee voice and personal demeanor combined with a deep populist streak added to a fearless antagonism toward the 'power structure' around here is a wonderful thing to watch."

Then, there are the longest-standing critics in the valley, "Edna Taylor and the Breathless Ladies," as Styles calls them. "Proudly standing against the Aquarium, Riverbend, the Greenway, and every other 'quality-of-life' improvement made in our city, these wise, seasoned citizens walk the fine line between good-old-fashioned pragmatism and feminine curmudgeonry."

"You can't argue with their personal knowledge of local history, and you can barely argue with their facts and figures. But their dire predictions of eventual, future financial disaster are designed in such a way that only our grandchildren will know if they have the right to say, 'I told you so' from the grave."

The Graft Will Always Be With You

While many area residents praise Chattanooga's championing of the public-private partnership, some in the valley criticize it. "What used to be called graft, cronyism, and conflict of interest is now known as the public-private partnership," said one local businessman.[26] Indeed, the age-old suspicion of self-interest creeping toward unfair competition has always been with us. In the 1850s, certain manufacturers were given a tax exemption for five years. "It would be mighty interesting if we could know how much that liberal encouragement contributed to the fact that Chattanooga is in the forefront of Southern manufacturing centers," noted historian Wiltse, seven decades later.[27]

Even earlier, the building of the Harrison brick courthouse in 1840 had the strong appearance of cronyism. James Whiteside was appointed along with six others by the legislature to determine a good site for the courthouse if voters approved of the move from Dallas to Harrison. Before the election took place, Whiteside, Crutchfield, William Gardenhire, and several others formed a land speculation company around Vanville, what became Harrison. Ultimately, Crutchfield was appointed to build the brick courthouse in that same approximate area.

Suspicions existed from the very beginning of the railroad. "It has been hinted more than once that what we call graft had crept into the railroad building . . . and mileage was unnecessarily stretched," wrote Wiltse. Specifically, he cited the fact that 14 bridges were built over Chickamauga Creek, from Graysville, Georgia, to Rossville, when only two were necessary if routed from Ringgold to Rossville.

However, others explained that the early plans to locate the terminus at Harrison accounted for the massive bridge-building contract.

When Chattanooga was initially named as the terminus in 1839, the Georgia legislature launched an investigation to see if any of the engineers involved in the surveying had bought up land by the newly determined route. When Whiteside successfully convinced the state of Alabama to build a railroad to Chattanooga in 1853, his son-in-law, A. M. Johnson, was the one paid to oversee the construction. Many in Chattanooga complained when Thomas Crutchfield somehow convinced Georgia to locate their terminal on Ninth Street, a full mile from the strategic riverfront. Crutchfield's home and property were at Ninth and Mulberry streets. When he built the Crutchfield House there and the depot was completed, Mulberry was changed to Railroad Avenue before becoming Broad Street.[28]

It was right around that area, a half century later, that Paul Carter confesses to some favoritism that helped him and his friends. Our friend from Chapter Two, who developed Lookout Mountain with his brother, Garnet Carter, provides a wonderful resource in his memoirs. He is the only person willing to state in print what many believe goes on behind the scenes on a regular basis.

"Joe Caldwell, Mark Morrison and I decided that a glass of beer before going home was exactly what we needed," wrote Carter. "But evidently we had more than one glass, for in coming out of the saloon and walking toward Ninth Street we were feeling pretty good. Who should we meet but Billy Smith, the policeman."

Carter then describes a shouting match in which the three make fun of the policeman, who promptly throws them in the paddy wagon before a growing crowd. "On getting booked at the jail, we asked for Chief Hackett, a good friend of us all. . . . The Chief finally showed up, wanting to know 'what you boys have been up to.'"

They promised to return to the courthouse Monday morning for a trial, so the chief released them. "The next morning, the three of us met," said Carter, "all

The Crutchfield House was built just across from the rail depot located at Ninth and Mulberry (Broad Street).

having looked through the Sunday morning paper most carefully, for we felt sure there would be a big story about us and our reputations would be ruined forever. But nothing was in the paper."

That same Sunday afternoon, they went to see Judge Martin Fleming at his house on Oak Street. "He answered his door, seemed glad to see us, and we told him our story and that we had to appear before him in court on Monday morning."

The judge described a situation in New Orleans where he had been arrested as a young man, and said, "I expect, too, you saw in the paper last week a report of a fight in the Greek restaurant between the Greek waiters and the customers." He told them the names of the customers, which included a McCallie. "Their names were not in the paper, nor will yours be," the judge said. "So just forget coming to see me at court tomorrow morning. And, furthermore, try to forget the entire incident."[29]

Needed: New Money for a New Economy

Such incidents only contribute to the strong belief of many in the valley that higher powers play by different rules and advance their agenda unfairly. "How Come the Big Dogs Get All the Bones?" asks the flyer for mayoral candidate Karl Epperson, pictured in a wheelchair with his faithful guide, a miniature collie. He got less than 300 votes in the election, but the paper still printed his bitter assessment of Chattanooga and his complaint that the political winners have all the same families for contributors.

"They say there is no political machine in Chattanooga, but if you believe that, then you aren't from around here," said Epperson. "There are probably 15 families in the greater Chattanooga area that control the city's politics. They think Chattanooga is their little Lego set."[30]

A columnist for *Chattanooga Fax*, who gave himself the pen name "Wilt Chamberlain," added similar but more sophisticated commentary: "Deep down in the bowels of our city are people who still think they can do it the old-fashioned way—inherit it, marry it, or package another public-private partnership around it."

"Big new money is not coming into Chattanooga. The same money that made this town is still making this town. New money comes to town and leaves after it finds our soft underbelly characterized by statements like, 'We built this town and we will decide how it grows.' When are we going to wean ourselves from the tit of public-private partnerships? Good as they are, they are about the only way we can finance anything these days."[31]

In the mayoral race that included Epperson and his dog, a particular public-private partnership took center stage in the discussion. The RiverCity Company was the subject of several articles, graphs, and a full-page spread on the cover of the

March 13, 2005, Sunday paper. The land development nonprofit corporation, first organized as the "Coordinating Council," was established in 1986 through the efforts of Chattanooga Venture and a meeting between the two Roberts—Mayor Gene and County Executive Dalton. In the article, the two leading candidates in the 2004 mayoral race disagreed over RiverCity's current activities. The article mentioned accusations of possible "self-dealing" and a perception of conflicts of interest.

"In my opinion, RiverCity has gone beyond the limits of what I think is appropriate as a nonprofit agency," said Ron Littlefield, who, ironically, served at one time as executive director of Chattanooga Venture, one of RiverCity's creators. "RiverCity has done a lot of good, but I think it has strayed from its original purpose."

Littlefield, who won the election, felt the same way about Stroud Watson, who then stepped down from his position after leading the design studio for 20 years. "The design studio was created to give broad conceptual plans and ideas to the future of Chattanooga," Littlefield said, "and they have fallen into the mode of being a regulatory agency." This micromanagement was discouraging development, he said, citing an example where a gas station was told to put their pumps in back. Instead, the mayor has moved Watson to the background. "Everyone reaches a certain point when you kind of run out of gas," Littlefield said. "I just think Stroud is very unrealistic, and that's part of his problem. Stroud is the kind of guy you'd like to have spinning out ideas, but not actually holding a hammer to force developers to do exactly what he wants."

Littlefield's opponent in the mayor's race, former RiverCity executive Ann Coulter, suggested he "was running against progress" with his criticism of RiverCity.

RiverCity officials dismissed Littlefield's comments as typical political gamesmanship. Jim Bowen, the group's first director, said over 500 communities around the world have sent delegations to study Chattanooga's downtown story. A Brookings Institute scholar said Chattanooga has become a national "poster child" for using public-private partnerships to revive a downtown.[32]

Marti Rutherford

Karl Epperson

Jeff Styles

Others are critical. A scholar with the Competitive Enterprise Institute admits that the city has gotten attention. "Foreign officials come calling from Shanghai, Stockholm, Prague. Praise descends from the United Nations," wrote Jesse Walker in a 1998 *Reason Magazine* article. "[But] Chattanooga is to urban planners what Cuba was to the '60s left: a junket, a model, and something likely to embarrass them 20 years later." Citing in particular the proposed eco-industrial park on the Southside, Walker calls it a demonstration project, not a living economy. "Government planners dreamed it up, and it will be financed, in large part, by federal dollars."[33]

It Always Comes Back to Jack

As usual, anything generally associated with favoritism, control, or a power structure conspiracy is connected immediately to Jack Lupton by certain valley-ites, rightly or wrongly. As Paul Neeley once wrote, Lupton is more a symbol than a real person.

Naman Crowe criticized Lupton in 1986 for pushing through his aquarium idea which "never made it through the Vision 2000 process as a high priority item." He said Lupton "holds the highest seat of authority . . . in the Chattanooga Venture hierarchy [but did not participate] in an active sense in the Vision 2000 process from which we were to obtain our consensus."

"We are not condemning this man for being rich," said Crowe, speaking on behalf of the Alliance Against the Aquarium. "But we are saying that great wealth too often translates into great power, sometimes even to the point of negating the will of the public."[34]

Marti Rutherford concurred. "I am concerned that citizen participation is only for show," said the councilwoman, 15 years after Crowe's criticism. "I feel like it's all a done deal before it gets to us."

Edna Taylor has similar concerns for Mai Bell Hurley, who oversaw the visioning process. "Mai Bell has always been nice to me, but she's nothing but a mouthpiece for Jack Lupton."[35]

Young attorney Bob Barnes added more strident comments. "It's all about power. Jack has it and you don't," he said in his "Fly on the Wall at City Hall" column. "Who said one vote counts more than one man—Lupton ain't even got a city vote. But his consent is the only one that matters."

Barnes names as his mentor UTC Professor Larry Ingle, who described the owners on the mountain and the workers in the valley. "That was true 25 years ago. I think it's true pretty much today," said Ingle. "There is just not much of a middle class." Barnes grew up in the poor part of the valley with Dalton Roberts, in East Chattanooga. Intellectually gifted, he attended McCallie through a scholarship and then Yale for two years. Tiring of the blue bloods in Connecticut, he headed back to UTC to graduate and led various political campaigns against the "power structure."

There is always great potential for a bitter divide between mountain and valley in Chattanooga. At various points, leaders rise up to providentially bridge the gap. Sometimes they come from unlikely places, like Watering Trough.

"I'm real glad I got elected because I think it gave me a different perspective on it than I had ever had," Dalton Roberts told me in our interview over biscuits and gravy. "I think I had always felt that there was this great division between the mountain and the valley. But as I watched it through a long number of years, I found that most of the people on the mountain wanted the same thing. They wanted Chattanooga to prosper. And that was a good revelation for me."

"The old manufacturing town power structure was pretty much entrenched and didn't welcome change and didn't welcome a whole lot of participation," Dalton said. "But I believe the current leadership has moved away from that. Big factors are people like Decosimo and Lupton getting involved in civic work, getting involved in building Chattanooga. Both of these men have contributed immensely [and] a lot of other men and women now, too."

In fact, Dalton's growth along such lines reached the point where his newspaper column in the year 2000 clearly admonished those who held his earlier views. "Once again we're hearing the old story that a tiny group of people—'the power structure'—have taken over our town," he wrote. "Don't think for a moment that I deny the existence of people bent on power. They're everywhere. In marriages, PTAs, companies, unions, elementary school playgrounds, even churches. There's one high-level report of a power-hungry angel trying to take over affairs inside the pearly gates. He got booted out, but he's been a devil to deal with ever since."

"I know about power. I ran against power when I had less money than it would take to throw a big wiener roast for the Watering Trough Chapter of the Harvard Alumni Association. The thing that empowered me was knowing that ultimate power belongs to people who vote."

"There is no organized tiny group calling the shots. If there was, they'd be fighting among themselves like mad dogs over who had the most power to decide what shots to call. We only believe in the existence of such a group because we don't want to get up off our big fat lazy excuses and exercise our own power."

So Dalton Roberts was willing to lead the people, the majority of the electorate who placed their confidence in him, to a place of less hostility and more trust toward the leaders on the mountain and toward the many multigenerational families who comprise that leadership. But don't think everyone in the valley was willing to join him—especially, the "Fly on the Wall," Bob Barnes, who called him a "Redneck Elitist." Barnes said he "used to like Dalton Roberts" for his taste in food, music, and dress. But not any longer, with Dalton's claims "that the power structure is a figment of the imagination."

"His populist rhetoric hides an elitist agenda," said Barnes, adding that Dalton should "quit pretending and come out of the Lupton-lovin' closet. Put on the turtleneck, head down to the Mud Pie, and strike up a sixties folk song about peace and love. . . . And Dalton, don't forget the cappuccino."[36]

Dalton and Bubba Square Off

One of Dalton's buddies in the Blue Tick Society warned him not to respond. "Never feud with a Flyspeck," wrote columnist Bill Casteel in a later summary of the exchange. Roberts is not one to back down. His opponent is also steeped in ancestral "bright fame," but Dalton renamed him "Bubba."

"With heavy heart I have learned that Bubba Bob Barnes no longer likes me. It kept me awake last night. I tossed and turned for at least two or three minutes."

"Bubba is really teed off because I won't come out of the 'Lupton-lovin' closet. You see, all real rednecks, according to Bubba Bob's *Field Guide for Identification of Real Christians and Rednecks*, must either hate Jack Lupton or hide in a closet ashamed to know him. . . . I have neither hemmed nor hawed about my friendship and appreciation for Jack. A man doesn't have to be broke to be my friend."

"I haven't met many rednecks so constricted in the cranial encasement to not appreciate a man who gave their city a $50 million gift that dramatically revitalized the downtown. All rednecks are not afflicted with knee-jerk envy and/or hatred for the wealthy. If I have to choose between Bubba Bob and Jack to keep my redneck credentials, Bubba Bob bites the dust."

Roberts is not the only valley-ite who has been bitten by his own kind for "growing" toward the vision of a harmonious Chattanooga. Talk show host Jeff Styles, a resident of Harrison, attended various charrettes and visioning sessions and articulated his positive assessment of the process, but his buddies made fun of him for it. "You used to damn the man. Now you are the damn man," they taunted. Nonetheless, he continued to defend the riverfront planning process.

The sometimes liberal, sometimes conservative talk show host, who sometimes sports long hair, sometimes short, was understandably hurt when Mayor Corker joined him in his studio for an interview and criticized Styles for calling the riverfront charrette "rigged" by the power structure. Styles was merely making the point that economic nirvana has not yet come to Chattanooga, but Corker, gun-shy from critical valley-ites that frequent talk radio airwaves, interpreted Styles's observations as unhelpful and ungrateful.

The next day, they conducted a second interview and worked through much of the miscommunication. It was a palpable example of the ever-challenging, ever-sensitive relationship between mountain and valley.[37]

After Dalton Roberts's first campaign, he never had a problem with the mountain folks again and carried Lookout Mountain the following three elections. "I just think they support whoever they think is for Chattanooga. I think that's what people in the valley do. You go into office and prove that you're trying to do something for this town, and you'll find plenty of support."

"You know, there's one word that I think tells you why Chattanooga is really experiencing a great deal of change, and that's *balance*. You talk about the mountain and the valley—I think you've finally got a balance there now. Even when you look at the ethnicity of the region, you've got a good balance. I like the balance we have ethnically in this town. There's just a better atmosphere, in my opinion, better than there used to be when I was growing up, for damn sure."

"It's balanced. It's economic balance. It's cultural balance between the mountain and the valley, between black and whites and other ethnic groups that are growing in this area. . . . It's just the right mix."

———

In a 1986 book entitled *Lookout Mountain: A Place and its People*, the beginning pages explain the geological forces that created the mountains in this region: the ancient oceans that covered the land made of limestone underneath and sandstone above. This all eroded and shifted to form our current topography.

According to the book, the area was at one time generally level. The sandstone in some places was hard and in other places soft, but every place was many times higher than the highest point today. The softer sandstone eroded completely to become our present valleys. The harder sandstone eroded as well, perhaps even more than halfway, but not completely. That remaining sandstone formed the mountains of today.

The book reveals the paradox: In the beginning, there were no distinctions: "Lookout Mountain, and the others in the range, are the skeletons of ancient valleys."[38]

MCDONALD

ROSS

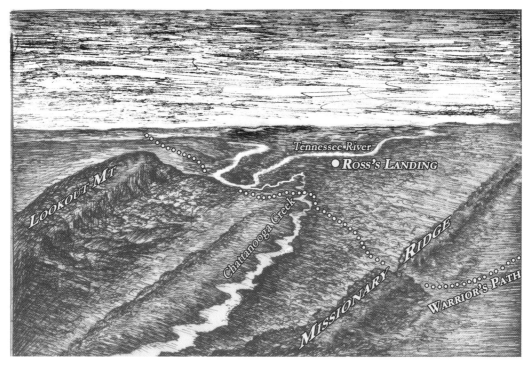

Tennessee River

Ross's Landing

LOOKOUT MT

Chattanooga Creek

MISSIONARY RIDGE

WARRIOR'S PATH

MACPHAIL

KENNEDY

Artist: Shaun LaRose

CHAPTER FIVE

The Spirit of Scotland

Earliest Settlers and Ruling Elders

Wisps of fog grace the sides of Lookout Mountain on any given day, perhaps most mornings, as Chattanoogans drive along the interstate towards downtown. It is nearly as common to see the entire top of the dark green mountain covered in clouds—as soldiers experienced in the famous "Battle Above the Clouds" in 1863.

Such scenery, reminiscent of Scotland's highest mountains in Inverness, likely served as a backdrop to one of the most important meetings in all of Chattanooga history. John McDonald, a native of Inverness, shook hands on an extremely cold day in January 1817 with missionary Cyrus Kingsbury.

The missionary purchased McDonald's crude farm and trading post, a small clearing with a few log buildings at the spot where the Great Indian Warpath crossed Chickamauga Creek, today the site for Eastgate Mall. The area was basically uninhabited when McDonald moved from Fort Loudoun in 1770 to this place so reminiscent of his Scottish Highland home.

The Highlander was paid $500 for the property by the Presbyterian elder Kingsbury, a leader of the religious group spawned by Scottish Lowlanders. The ink in the missionary's pen froze as he wrote of the event by the wooden fireplace. The door was open; there were no windows.

The missionary made the purchase on behalf of the American Board for Foreign Missions in Boston. The first thing he did was place a window in the rude cabin. He would soon be joined by several colleagues anxious to bring the gospel to the

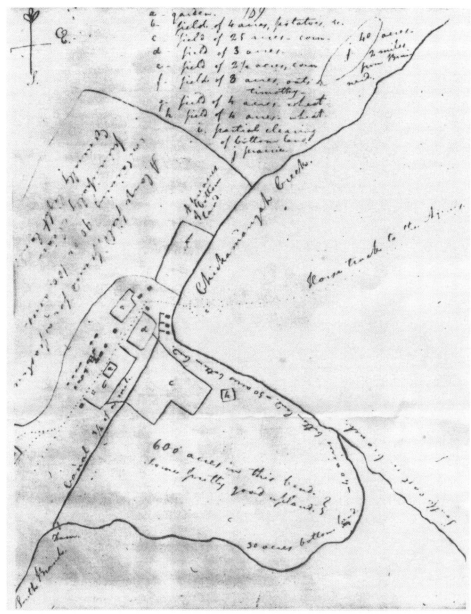

First Map. The first rendering of any kind of the greater Chattanooga area. This map was drawn by a missionary from Boston after visiting the Brainerd mission complex in 1822. "Chickamaugah Creek" is labeled just above center. A canal is shown starting with a dam at lower left.

Cherokees and also to the mixed-bloods in the area, most of them McDonald's relatives. But he was not successful with his first prospect.

"The old gentleman thinks he never did anything wrong," wrote Kingsbury after offering McDonald a solution for mankind's problem of sin.[1]

While Lowlanders in southern Scotland were some of the most zealous Protestants in history, Highlanders in the north were better known for their fighting prowess and, if at all religious, tended to remain Catholic. Their memory survives primarily through their costumes, especially the kilts, or skirts, made of tartan plaid and worn by soldiers who marched to the tune of bagpipes.

Only traces of this Highlander legacy remain today, such as the picture of Summerfield Johnston, Sr. wearing a tartan kilt and presenting a bagpipe-accompanied salute to Scottish friends like Roy McDonald and Paul Carter, who included the picture in his memoirs.[2] But such tributes remain few and distant, and the images themselves are more legend than reality. The kilt was simply a loin-cloth, and most soldiers wore trousers, according to Chapel Hill historian James Leyburn. Whearas the leader may have been decked out in kilt and full regalia, "only the romantic imagination can conceive that in these earlier days there were trim regiments of Highlanders in 'uniform,' marching behind the wailing pipes through the glen."[3]

The Highlanders are also credited by many with providing the seeds for the music of Appalachia, a phenomenon fueled by the guitar replacing the fiddle as the best instrument to accompany the old Scottish ballads. In this way, Scotland has greatly influenced not so much Chattanooga but the nearby city of Nashville, the center of country music.

Golf, the famous sport birthed in Scotland, has certainly made its mark in Chattanooga. The Chattanooga Golf and Country Club was one of the nation's first, constructed only eight years after New York's St. Andrew's Club blazed the golfing trail in America.[4]

Scotty Probasco met his wife Betty at the Chattanooga Golf and Country Club. "He went home and told his mother he had met the girl he was going to marry," said Betty. "His mother came rushing over to the club, . . . she mainly wanted to know where I went to church." Like his father, Scott L. Probasco, Jr. is an elder at First Presbyterian Church. (*Scott* means . . . well . . . a "Scot.") A one handicapper, he was captain of the golf team at Dartmouth.

Betty Probasco won the collegiate golf championship and went on to claim twelve state golf championships (four in Kentucky). She crowned her career as captain of the U.S. Curtis Cup team in 1982.[5]

Paul Carter, who ran several bottling plants, writes about how legendary golfer Bobby Jones was "a good friend of mine." An attorney for Coke bottling, Jones was a businessman and amateur golfer who won all four major championships in one summer before retiring at age 28. Not even Tiger Woods has accomplished that feat since Jones's Grand Slam in 1930. Bobby Jones later founded Augusta National, the most exclusive golf club in the world and home to "The Masters," the greatest tournament in golf.

I asked Scotty Probasco if he knew Bobby Jones. No big deal for Scotty, it seemed. It turns out his dad played golf with Bobby Jones pretty regularly.

"Did he play with him at Augusta?" I asked.

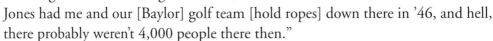

Dr. Cyrus Kingsbury

"Augusta wasn't that big a deal then," Probasco said. "Mr. Jones had me and our [Baylor] golf team [hold ropes] down there in '46, and hell, there probably weren't 4,000 people there then."

Bobby Jones's son was on the Baylor golf team with Scotty. "I used to go down and spend nights with him in Atlanta."

"But you did know Mr. Jones?"

"Yeah. Pretty well. Great guy."

Today, the country's greatest golfers visit Chattanooga's Honors Course, as do some of the world's greatest leaders who are avid golfers. The game born on Scottish links has certainly made its impact on Chattanooga, but it is, after all, just a game.

Previous chapters have discussed the legendary frugality of the Scots, and this national trait has indeed contributed to the character of Chattanooga today. Again, multimillionaire Summerfield Johnston provides the anecdote. His bigger multimillionaire buddy Cartter Lupton offered him $25 to jump into the ocean during a Florida boating trip. Despite the concern for sharks, Summerfield plunged into the water, but the frugal Lupton did not deliver. "Anybody silly enough to jump overboard with their clothes on wouldn't know what to do with $25," he said.[6]

"East Tennessee tends to be very Scottish and very frugal," says Tom McCallie, an elder with Scotty at First Presbyterian Church. He makes the point that UT Knoxville's orange colors derive from devotion to William of Orange, the great Protestant hero who saved Scotland from Catholicism. The same is true for the Orangemen of Syracuse. Others say the term "hillbilly" describes an avid Orangeman in the mountains.

"Presbyterians, historically, are known to be tight with their money," said Frank Brock, an elder at Lookout Mountain Presbyterian. "But I think the frugality in terms of spending kind of goes hand in hand with generosity. That sort of mentality [has] been around a while."

That aspect of the Presbyterian legacy is not the primary means by which Scotland has made its unmistakable imprint on Chattanooga. The key influence is that

Chattanooga's first settlers were from Scotland. As historian Paul Johnson writes, "It is almost a law of colonization that the first group, however small, to set up an effective settlement has more effect on the political and social character of the colony than later arrivals, however numerous."[7]

According to geologist Kevin Dunn in *Traces on the Appalachians: A History of Serpentine in America*, geological samples below the Appalachians, from northern Alabama through West Virginia, Syracuse (New York) to Maine and Nova Scotia, turn up a green mineral called serpentine. Similar mineral samples cannot be found on the eastern seaboard or under the Atlantic Ocean. Geologists found a similar vein of the green mineral once again under the mountain range stretching from Ireland through Scotland toward the Arctic.[8]

Dunn says in ancient times the two mountains fit together like a jigsaw puzzle before the continental drift pulled them apart to form the Atlantic Ocean. He believes the first journey from Scotland to Appalachia was made by the mountains themselves. Inspired by this research, best-selling novelist Sharyn McCrumb snapped a picture of a Scottish landscape and a month later showed it to several neighbors in Southwest Virginia. They all said it looked like nearby Bland County.

That is what happened when the Scotch-Irish came to America, says McCrumb. "They come to this country, look around, and hate the crowded, flat eastern seaboard. They get in covered wagons, and they keep going west until they hit the mountains, and then they follow the valleys south-southwest down through Pennsylvania. And finally, they get to a place where the ridges rise, where you can see the mountains and the trees in the distance, and it looks right, and it feels right. Like home. Like the place they left. And they were right back in the same mountains they had left behind in Britain."[9]

One Man versus Three Empires

Few if any Native Americans lived in the area when John McDonald, the first man of European descent, took up residence in the future city of Chattanooga in 1770. He was Scottish, having left Inverness only four years before at age 19. He descends from the MacDonald clan, the largest in Scotland, but only a minority of them live in the highlands of Inverness. The patronymic name means "world ruler."[10]

John McDonald left his homeland to make money, not to exercise religious freedoms. During a trip to London in 1766, he met a fellow Scot heading to America, and John was persuaded to join him. He landed in Charleston but took a trading job in Augusta that sent him to Fort Loudoun, south of what later became Knoxville, to trade with the Indians. He stayed there four years. Just before leaving the fort and moving to Chickamauga Creek, he married Anna Shorey, daughter of a

First four landmarks of Chattanooga. Clockwise from bottom: 1. The Brainerd Mission 2. John McDonald's home at Rossville Gap (later the Chief John Ross House) 3. Daniel Ross's home 4. Ross's Ferry (or Ross's Landing).

British officer and a Cherokee woman named Ghigoeie, of the Bird Clan. Scotsman William Shorey, interpreter during the French and Indian War, held the distinction of being one of the only whites to ever reach fluency in the Cherokee language. His son-in-law John McDonald followed in his footsteps.

McDonald's fluency changed his family's destiny when the boat of a fur trader from Baltimore was captured just above the Suck in 1785 by Cherokee Chief Bloody Fellow. Bloody Fellow decided to postpone the massacre of young Daniel Ross and his colleagues and get an opinion from McDonald, who lived about six miles away.

Bloody Fellow was a leader of the "Chickamaugas," militant Cherokees so named for moving south to the area around Chickamauga. McDonald, a Loyalist and Tory, welcomed the militant Indians. The Chickamaugas' great leader was Dragging Canoe, considered perhaps the most dangerous of all Indian leaders. (The exploits of Dragging Canoe are explained in more detail in a later chapter.)

At Bloody Fellow's request regarding his captives, McDonald traveled to the spot on the river just below the mountain at Lookout Valley and questioned the fellow Scotsman. Daniel Ross had set sail for America in 1770 with his widowed mother. She died during the journey, leaving Ross an orphan at age ten. He later joined the firm Mayberry's Trading Expedition, which commissioned him to take a boat down the Tennessee River. McDonald also learned that Ross's entourage included Chickasaw Chief Piomingo, who wanted Ross's firm to locate their trading post in his territory. McDonald warned Bloody Fellow that killing the men and taking their valuable goods would lead ultimately to war with the Chickasaws. Ross and the others were spared.

McDonald invited Ross to remain in the area as a trader. A year later, he married McDonald's 16-year-old daughter Mollie. A quarter Cherokee, Mollie's status established Daniel Ross as a legitimate member of the Cherokee Nation through marriage, just like McDonald, allowing him to settle in the area for life.[11]

During this same time, three European nations were battling for control of the Cherokees, and John McDonald served as the great advisor and strategist for Dragging Canoe. Apparently, he successfully played off all three powers. "In case of war with any foreign power, he may be very serviceable, or very dangerous," wrote one American official. Indeed, McDonald convinced the Chickamaugas to ignore American treaty proposals and carry on clandestine meetings with Spanish Governor Baron de Carondelet. McDonald began receiving an annual salary from Spain as the secret broker in 1792. A year later he assured a British officer he had not accepted any appointments from the Spanish, and told an American officer, "Believe me Sir, I shall never turn Spaniard."

Later, he accepted Tennessee Governor William Blount's appointment as agent to the Lower Cherokees in 1793. Blount knew nothing of the salary McDonald was still collecting from the Spanish, which continued until 1798. Blount enthusiastically informed the Secretary of War regarding the new American ally. "He has as much or more influence with the Lower Cherokees than any other man who resides among them."[12]

The First Family

After Britain and Spain backed away from the New World and President George Washington signed a peace treaty with the Chickamaugas, McDonald and Ross turned their focus to building a business and a family. McDonald's son George died,[13] but his two daughters remained in the area. His daughter Mollie Ross provided nine grandchildren for the area's first resident. Daniel and Mollie built a home around the year 1800 along the Federal Road, which appears on early maps as "Ross"—today the track of the Chattanooga Christian School just below Lookout Mountain.[14*] Apparently, Daniel Ross followed his instincts since the region called Ross in Northern Scotland is in the highlands, like Inverness. *Ross* derives from the Gaelic *ros* or Welsh *rhos*, indicating an upland or promontory.

A visitor described Ross's home. Containing a mill and deerskin tannery, it was "one of the best, well-framed houses, one and one-half stories high with good useful buildings such as negro cabins, stables, corn-cribs, etc." Another traveler observed the plethora of books, maps, and English and American newspapers and periodicals lining the walls, noting that he may as well have been in Scotland as the Cherokee wilds.[15]

McDonald, meanwhile, began building a spacious log house at the gap in the ridge where the Federal Road crossed into Georgia, next to a gushing rock and stream called Poplar Spring. Travelers reached the gap and spring after riding around Moccasin Bend and past Daniel Ross's trading post and ferry (near the former Wheland Foundry site at the mouth of Chattanooga Creek). Daniel Ross's first son, John, moved into his grandfather's house, probably in 1808 when his mother Mollie died. He established the area's first post office there. What was known as "McDonald's Store" became Ross's Gap or "Rossville."

John's sister, Susannah Ross, married Scotsman Henry Nave, and they built a home nearby (possibly near Bonny Oaks and Highway 153 today, or the intersection of Chickamauga Creek and the Harrison Road). Another sister, Jane Ross, married Scotsman Joseph Coody. They built a home two miles up from John's place in the Gap, somewhere in the heart of East Ridge along today's "John Ross Road," which apparently led from Rossville to the mission.

Daniel Ross

By the time John McDonald met with missionary Cyrus Kingsbury in 1817, almost every resident in the area was McDonald's descendent or his Scottish in-law.[16*] In fact, the missionaries chose the site in large part for this reason. "Those who will be first educated will be the children of the half breeds and the leading men of the nation," wrote Kingsbury. "On their education and influence the character of the nation will very much depend."[17]

Kingsbury may have felt like he got a real bargain paying $500[†] to the "old Scotch gentleman." But the wily veteran who outmaneuvered three empires likely got the better of the deal. Twenty-five barely improved acres in the middle of nowhere could easily have been worth far less than what the missionary paid. The day the deal was made, McDonald moved four miles away to live with his grandson, John Ross, in a far superior structure that remains standing today.[18*] Meanwhile, Kingsbury wrote to New England regarding articles and goods he ordered by river transport which "had arrived at a Ware house about 6 miles distant." It is the missionaries' first recorded mention of Ross's Landing, the heart of the future Chattanooga.[19]

This river landing below the bluff was not used by Daniel Ross, who used a landing by his home and operated a ferry there. It was sometimes referred to as "Ross's Towhead." One local historian speculates that problems with flooding led John Ross, around 1815, to move the family's landing upriver a few miles, where higher ground near the bluff was accessible.[20*] Also from that point, a straight shot to Rossville avoided Chattanooga Creek altogether. Thus, the "Rossville Road," the future Market Street, came into existence.

Ross owned the landing, but he neither lived at the landing nor worked there. He was not the first citizen of Ross's Landing. His ferryman gains that honor. "Old Billy Gentry," or "Uncle" Billy Gentry, is cited by historian Wiltse as the first resident of the future downtown Chattanooga. His small hut was located near Broad and Second Street today. The accounts are vague. It is unclear if Chattanooga's first resident was black, Cherokee, white, or mixed.[21]

By 1826, a decade before the Trail of Tears, Ross had moved to Head of Coosa (Rome, Georgia) and sold his house in Rossville and his business at the Landing to his niece and her husband, Nicholas Scales.[22] Whereas John Ross left a tremendous legacy in Oklahoma as the Principal Chief of the Cherokee Nation for four decades, his tenure in Rossville and at Ross's Landing was short-lived. His legacy for Chattanooga is restricted mainly to nomenclature.

The Very First Church

Unlike McDonald, the missionaries continually struggled with the Cherokee language and had few to no full-blood converts in the early days of their ministry.

[†] $81,000 (2006)

Neither did they make much progress converting John McDonald, or Daniel and John Ross. But the rest of the family became avid church members.

Kingsbury preached his first sermon at the Naves' home. Four whites, four blacks, and seven mixed-blood Cherokees attended. He preached at the Coodys' home next, and the racial profile was exactly one-third for each racial group. Early church members included the Naves, the Coodys, slaves named Juno and Ned owned by John Ross, a free black man, and McDonald's wife Anna. At age 73, the missionaries said she was "perhaps as universally respected and beloved as any woman of the nation. She has been a constant attendant to the means of grace since the commencement of this mission."[23]

One of the first Cherokee members, Charles Reese, caused an early dilemma for the missionaries. He arrived on the scene immediately to help with the construction work and was eager to join the church. He was also a hero in the War of 1812, swimming the river and stealing canoes from the Creek Indians. Unfortunately, he had three sisters for wives, all at the same time. One had died, however, and the other two he sent away "on account of the insolence of their mother." He lived with his fourth wife, and apparently had no problems with his current mother-in-law. The missionaries scratched their heads with such issues, and ultimately determined polygamists must live with the first wife only. However, Reese was made an exception and was baptized on February 1, 1818.

The first sermon topic named in the *Brainerd Journal* was on "Total Depravity," the foundational Calvinistic teaching that all men are sinners with no ability to do good apart from God. Kingsbury also preached a sermon at the "Ware house" two months after arriving, though few people were likely to be within earshot. He

Early sketch of the Brainerd Mission

also met with Assistant Principal Chief Charles Hicks, a prized early convert from the Springplace Mission, which was funded by the very rich but totally depraved James Vann. Hicks gave himself the name *Renatus* upon conversion, which means "Renewed." His son married Daniel Ross's daughter, Margaret.

It was not uncommon for several packages to arrive in one day at the mission from the post office in Rossville. Though John Ross avoided the religious excitement, he did appreciate a good business opportunity, and he loaned the mission money when times were tough. Like many other chiefs, he also greatly encouraged the educational efforts of the mission. Early on, the chiefs were suspicious of mere proselytizing, but they desired to see their children in schools. While a church did comprise part of the mission effort, the mission complex was primarily a boarding school that taught agrarian principles and practical life skills.[24]

"It was a unique outreach that got back to the Presbyterian concept that all of life was important," Tom McCallie told me. "So it was the first home economics school in the country, the first agricultural school."

Lydia Lowery, a 16-year-old relative of Anna McDonald's sister, finally got the nod from the missionary elders for church membership after twelve months of schooling. "For several months she has been under particular instruction as a candidate for baptism," wrote Kingsbury. This kind of rigor was typical for the Presbyterian elders. After one year, they had added only eleven adults and twenty-four children to their church. "The Lord has done great things for us, whereof we are glad," they wrote, adding that "Black, Red & White surrounded the table of one common Lord."[25]

Life was difficult for the missionaries. Consider just one couple, John and Julia Vail. She did the ironing while her husband oversaw the work of the farm. Julia was sick the first day they arrived after the six-week trip. While at the Brainerd Mission, at least five of their children died.[26]

"Unless one reads the records of Brainerd one cannot realize the hardships and privations these women had to go through," writes Zella Armstrong.[27]

The Lingering Impact of the Mission

On June 5, 1822, Elder Vail and Elder Ainsworth Blunt conducted a typical, very dry, very Presbyterian business meeting. (The *Brainerd Journal* is full of them.) The issue of the day was sent to a committee. "Resolved, that Brs. Vail, Ellis & Blunt be a Com. to select such oxen and steers to work this summer as they shall think best and make their report at the next meeting."[28] While anything but flashy, such routine meetings by elders, or "session meetings," played a significant role in Chattanooga's later development.

On any particular Sunday or at the special events like the Hicks-Ross wedding or the funeral of George McDonald, many of the same faces could be seen: the

Vails, the Blunts, Anna McDonald, Henry Nave, and Susannah Ross. Of those just mentioned, the Vails and Anna McDonald are buried in the mission cemetery, and each of the others buried several children there. The Brainerd Mission cemetery is the only surviving remnant of this first community in Chattanooga and rests beneath the only group of trees in sight amid the parking lots of Eastgate Mall and the businesses along Brainerd Road such as Kinko's and Office Depot. The John Ross Chapter of the Daughters of the American Revolution holds the deed to the historic property. The care for the grounds is donated by the Corker Group, which owns several buildings nearby.

On March 30, 2003, the bulletin of the Lookout Mountain Presbyterian Church included an insert reprinting a solemn oath made 185 years earlier by these same families buried in the cemetery. The missionaries, the family members of the McDonalds and Rosses, the free blacks, the slaves, and the mixed bloods each personally swore the lengthy oath. This "Covenant of the Brainerd Church," originally called the "Church of Christ at Chickamaugah," was made on September 18, 1817. It said in part:

"We do now in the presence of the heart searching God and before Angels and Men solemnly avouch the Lord Jehovah, the Father, the Son, and the Holy Ghost, to be our God . . . and we cheerfully give up ourselves, our children and all that we have to Him to be His forever. . . . We renounce forever, as objects of chief pursuit, the World, its pleasures, its riches, its honors, and our own private interests as infinitely inferior . . . to the worth, the excellence, and the glory of the ever-blessed God."

Since every one of these missionaries eventually joined the Cherokees on the Trail of Tears to Oklahoma, many today consider this covenant the only oath or treaty with the Indians ever kept by the white man. The covenant continues by vowing to do "the sacred work of building up the Kingdom, to associate ourselves with each other as brethren; promising to watch over each other in Christian love . . ."[29]

It was not the pastor, but a Presbyterian layman, appropriately, who suggested the 185-year-old Covenant be distributed in the bulletin. "He brought it to me and I said, 'Bingo! What consecration to the King,'" Pastor Joe Novenson told me. "I wonder if some of the blessings of the city came from the fumes of these forefathers. I bet we're running on the fumes of their prayers."[30]

Very few of the missionaries at Brainerd were ordained preachers. Most of them were Presbyterian "ruling elders,"

Brainerd Mission cemetery with Eastgate Mall behind *(Sketch by John Hooper)*

a concept that not only defines Presbyterian polity, but also has had vast impact on the structure of the United States government, and perhaps on the nationally unique "Chattanooga Process" of today.

John Vail and Ainsworth Blunt were also ruling elders. They, too, accompanied the Cherokee people on the 1838 Trail of Tears, but because of illness along the way, they were the only two to return. When they did, they founded the city's first church, "First Presbyterian of Chattanooga," to minister to the sudden migration of Scotch-Irish settlers, nearly all Presbyterian, who rushed across the river to claim the land vacated by the Cherokees.[31]

John McDonald and Daniel Ross had died, and all their descendents departed on the Trail of Tears. It was an unusual, abrupt, and unnatural halt to Chattanooga's history. The process would have to start over again, completely. The ever-important impact of the first settlers was made not by the Highlanders of northern Scotland but by the Presbyterian Lowlanders of southern Scotland. *Vail* comes from *MacPhail,* a clan in the Lowlands. Along with Ainsworth Blunt, John Vail provided the only link connecting Chattanooga's early history to its official founding in 1838.

When John McDonald and the missionary Cyrus Kingsbury shook hands on that historic day in 1817, the power symbolically shifted from the merchants and fighters of the Highlands to the religious elders of the Lowlands. McDonald was no doubt a fascinating and remarkable character, as was his grandson John Ross, but their legacy for Chattanooga resembles the kilt and bagpipe legend of the Highlanders: more romance than reality.

"The invasion of the Scots and Scotch-Irish is, I think, a very important part of our heritage," said Dr. David McCallie, an elder at First Presbyterian Church. "Just as the invasion of the Germans is an important part of Milwaukee's heritage. The invasion of the Swedes is a part of the Dakotas. The Italians are a part of San Francisco and Boston."

"Whatever came into the community, first put its stamp on that community. And it lasts."

UTC Professor Larry Ingle, an unbiased Quaker, echos McCallie's insights. "It's clear that the power is represented by the Presbyterian church in this town . . . " he said. "Maybe they just arrived on the scene first. There's an old truth in history: 'The law is always made by those who get there first.'"

Not Bored by Boards

The key to Chattanooga today, the unique quality that brings the city national and international attention, is its uncanny enthusiasm and ability in bringing together key leaders for projects. Leaders of the private and public sectors, trained professionals, and civically motivated layman all join together on a multifaceted board to discuss, brainstorm, strategize, and then execute a plan.

The final chapter of Chattanooga's most recently published history of yesterday and today is entitled, "'The Chattanooga Process, A City of Private and Public Partnerships." Native son Jim Frierson, who writes the foreword to the book, told the *Chattanooga Fax*, "We have to be careful to keep that public and private partnership equilibrium and balance in operation."[32]

Over 500 delegations from communities across the world have visited Chattanooga in the last two decades to learn more about the Chattanooga Process, that unique collection of public-private partnerships overseen by hundreds of civic-minded board members. This distinctive quality led the Brookings Institute to call Chattanooga a national model and led National Public Radio to feature Chattanooga as one of five great cities in the world.[33]

Other cities depend more on elected officials for leadership, and some prefer that style. "With all of the boards in this city, it makes you wonder who is really running the town," writes "Flyspeck" Bob Barnes in his column on city hall. "Wouldn't it be nice if elected officials actually managed the government they were elected to lead? Maybe I'm confused. I thought democratic government was actually supposed to be democratic."[34]

What is it about Chattanooga that inspires civic leaders and hundreds and hundreds of citizens to participate in its future? A number of factors could be cited, including bold ideas and extraordinary modern leadership as detailed in past chapters. This chapter proposes another key factor, a more historic quality, something so ingrained in Chattanooga's culture that those inside the community might take it for granted.

"Do you have any idea why Chattanooga has more boards or a board mentality?" I asked Frank Brock, who, as mentioned before, is a Presbyterian elder. (The word *presbyter*, in Greek, means "elder.")

"I don't have any idea. It's the only thing I've ever known," Brock replied.

Brock has lived in Chattanooga all his life. In fact, he has never lived, except for college, more than 200 yards from his childhood home on Lookout Mountain. His three children and eighteen grandchildren each live within a quarter of a mile of each other on the mountain. Brock was raised at Lookout Mountain Presbyterian Church, has also been the moderator of the board of elders at Lookout Pres, and served one term as moderator for the entire denomination, the Presbyterian Church in America.[†]

Despite his plea of ignorance, he did in fact provide some good commentary on how his faith tradition might have influenced the city.

[†] With over 300,000 members, the conservative Presbyterian Church in America (PCA) is the country's second largest Presbyterian denomination, behind the mainline PCUSA, which has over two million members.

"Presbyterianism lends itself to board participation," he said, contrasting the board-of-elders authority structure with the more centralized authority of a bishop in the Episcopal and Methodist denominations. "Board participation to me is almost a mark of a good organization. You rarely find a good organization that doesn't have a good board."

"When you look at the City Council or the school board or the Erlanger Hospital board or the Electric Power Board or the Allied Arts board, the United Way board, there is a sense in which the major entities that share the community are governed by boards, and people who are accustomed to sitting on boards—most people learn that in their church, not in their civic organizations, in my opinion."

Brock is also the former president of the Presbyterian-owned college on Lookout Mountain. He downplayed his executive role. "I would say one of the greatest things I did at Covenant College was build a board," he said. "If Covenant College had been located in Knoxville, Tennessee, it would have dried up and gone away. Memphis is a big Baptist town. Nashville is a big town that way . . . Atlanta is not as proportionally strong as Chattanooga. You'd be hard-pressed to find a town where there's a stronger Presbyterian heritage than Chattanooga."

In Frank Brock's denomination, the defining characteristic is not rule by bishop (Episcopal), by a pope (Catholic), or by a pastor (Independent). The congregation does not have the final authority (Baptist). The Presbyterian government has an uncanny resemblance to our constitutional framework with Congress (elders) balancing the powers of the people (congregation) and the President (pastor). Those same Presbyterian-influenced framers inspired King George to call the American Revolution "a Presbyterian Rebellion."[35]

Elders Rule

In Presbyterianism, a local church is governed by a group or "board" of elders, also called a "session." Usually, a church will have only one "teaching elder" (ordained preacher) and perhaps ten or more "ruling elders." The larger denomination is legislated by an annual General Assembly, a body comprised of usually one pastor and several ruling elders from each congregation in the country.

It may not be too far-fetched to view the Chattanooga Process as an unwitting reflection of that Presbyterian structure. The critical "visioning process" does not include the entire voting population but rather a few hundred active, concerned, responsible citizens who are considered good representatives of the larger whole, similar to a General Assembly. The resulting public-private partnerships are governed by boards that look like a session, comprised of mostly prominent citizens (ruling elders) along with one or two elected officials (teaching elders).

Chattanooga Resource Foundation President Doug Daugherty sees the impact of the presbyter. His foundation serves as a networking and umbrella group for area churches and Christian nonprofit organizations.

"If you look at the board of directors for so many organizations, the Presbyterians are over represented by an enormous amount. It's just—it's staggering. I remember Hugh O. Maclellan telling me that he was [at one time] on thirty-something different boards. That's just amazing."

"When people come to this community, one of the things they run into very quickly is the strength of the laity, or the lay people, of the lay leadership." (A *layman* is one who is not ordained or not a professional.) "In other communities, this is what they'll always say: 'We've got to get the pastors on board, we've got to get the pastors on board.' And I've heard that thousands, literally thousands of times. And if you think about it, that really does come out of a Baptist polity. In the Baptist community, the executive function is very much carried by the pastor. He is the executive even though he can be voted in or out [by the congregation]. In a Presbyterian polity, the executive function, while you do have a pastor, is invested in the session to a much larger degree than you would see in a Baptist church. There are Presbyterian churches that can function for years without a pastor in a very healthy, growing way. And in most Baptist, Church of God, and Pentecostal churches—if that were to happen, the church would just grind to a halt after a certain period of time."

"And if you're in a session in the church, you're learning a certain way of governing and leading, you know, that you're probably going to take to other places," Daugherty said. "I mean, I was talking to somebody the other day, and they were telling me that there are 1,500 nonprofits chartered in Hamilton County. That's just the ones chartered here, not the ones that have offices here and are chartered somewhere else. When you think about what that represents—put eight people in every one of those organizations for a board. That's an enormous amount of people."

Daugherty then told me about a new initiative called the Nehemiah Project, spearheaded by David Parker, CEO of Covenant Transport. "What did David think when he had this idea? His first thought was to call his pastor and some other pastors in town and get them involved. And he's Church of God, you know. If you would go to Hugh O. Maclellan and tell him you wanted to get something done, his first thought would be to call other businessmen in Chattanooga. I mean, very, very different. The way they think about the leadership function flowing through the community—very, very different."

"Now, in the Baptist church, somebody would say he was a businessman, and then he'd say he got saved from business to come to the church. Somebody running a church—if they came from business, they would think it was a real virtue."

Daugherty then contrasted this idea with the quintessential Presbyterian layman or elder, the figure uniquely linked to Chattanooga's early history. "They are probably in leadership in their business. There's probably inherited money. They're probably in leadership in their church. They're probably serving on any number of things. It's been expected that they will serve in any number of things since they were very young. They have probably seen this kind of leadership demonstrated by their parents' [and] their grandparents' involvement in things. Probably from an early age they went to testimonial dinners where their parents or grandparents were praised for something, and there is probably stuff named for them."

Frank Brock describes the negative side of the phenomenon. "It was so much according to wisdom, the way things were. You really didn't think a lot about it. John Wright [former president of American National Bank] acknowledged that he joined Lookout Mountain Presbyterian Church to make business contacts. He would volunteer to be treasurer of the church, and he would sit there and look at the membership and think of prospective customers for the bank. Then, when he went through a true conversion experience in 1975, that was part of his testimony."

"That's the way it was, the normal way of looking at things. It could also be put on the other side that the churches were in some ways more like boards of trustees than they were true elders and deacons. And people were sometimes selected because of their business acumen and their leadership more than their godliness."

Two "Quintessential" Elders

Be that as it may, Frank Brock represents that quintessential elder described by the President of the Chattanooga Resource Foundation. While he is certainly his own individual—he built himself a special desk at which he stands to work all day, and he buys green coffee beans direct from Greyfriar's coffee shop so he can roast them himself—he also conforms to the mold of his peers in Presbyterian leadership. "Stuff," as Daugherty said, is named after Frank's parents and grandparents, including various buildings on local campuses as well as the "Brock Sunday School Class" that started in 1942 at Lookout Presbyterian. He serves on boards outside the church, including the Maclellan Foundation, an honor for a non–family member, and Rotary, which he recently served as president. He comes from inherited wealth and held the position of executive vice president under his brother Pat Brock until the Brock Candy Company was sold in 1993.

Frank's brother, Bill Brock III, served as U. S. Senator from Tennessee in the '70s, as did Bill and Frank's grandfather, William E. Brock, Sr. He was one of those grandfathers in whose honor dinners were held while the grandchildren squirmed and fidgeted. With only a fourth-grade education, the senior Bill Brock chaired the University of Chattanooga, started a bank, and founded the candy company.

"An interesting story that we've always told in the family was that my grandfather was hired by Mr. Reynolds of R. J. Reynolds," said Frank. "They tried to convince Mr. Reynolds to sell tobacco to these stores around the country, and they knew that would require a traveling salesman and nobody would be foolish enough to spend all their time away from home. So finally they said, 'Well, Mr. Reynolds, we just got to find somebody.' And he said, 'Well, find the greenest, ugliest country boy you can find. Maybe he'll be dumb enough to do it.' And he traveled all the way from North Carolina over here to Chattanooga, Tennessee. He was gone for weeks at a time. It was really dirt roads and backbreaking work."

Bill Brock III told me Mr. Reynolds offered his grandfather a partnership. "He said no. He wanted to be on his own. He came to Chattanooga, went to work for a candy wholesaler, and kept trying to talk the wholesaler into making candy. The wholesaler said, 'No. I'll sell out to you if you want to make it.'"

"They made candy in the back room of a wholesaler," according to Frank's story. "In those days, they would literally cook it up in a copper kettle, pour it out on a marble slab, cut it by hand, and wrap it in wax paper."

The Brock boys also attended dinners honoring their other grandfather, Paul Kruesi. Owner of the American Lava Company and a Chamber chairman (as well as a founder of the national Chamber of Commerce), he was one of Chattanooga's biggest promoters and manufacturers, but Kruesi's father had a bigger claim to fame. He served as Thomas Edison's right-hand man. The Swiss-born John Kruesi actually built the first phonograph in 1877 after Edison provided the blueprints. He was the principal mechanic for countless other Edison inventions, including the incandescent light bulb. Today, Kruesi's great-great-great-grandchildren squirm at the table during the "Kruesi Spirit of Innovation Award" breakfast held each year by the Chattanooga Chamber of Commerce,[36] the most recent keynote speaker being Bill Ford, Henry Ford's great-grandson.

Sam Smartt

Bill Brock III

Frank Brock

Another daughter of Paul Kruesi married Burton Frierson, whose family runs the Dixie Group (Dixie Yarns). That makes the Brocks first cousins with the Friersons. Since Frank Brock's first cousin, Cartter Frierson, married the sister of Hugh O. Maclellan, Jr.'s wife . . . well . . . it turns out Frank Brock is actually a distant family member on the Maclellan Foundation board (see chart on next page).

After Frank Brock's tenure of running elders meetings at Lookout Presbyterian, he was replaced by Sam Read Smartt, Jr. "Frank was the one who talked me into doing it," said Smartt. "I'm not convinced I'm a good chairman. I think I get elected chairman because I'm a loudmouth or something."

It may also be related to the fact that his grandfather, Edmondson Smartt, was also chairman. Sam's great-grandfather, Polk Smartt, was a Presbyterian elder for 50 years. Also, his maternal great-grandfather, Sam Read, donated the land for the church.[37] Sam Smartt may not even be aware of all these facts, but the reality flows in his veins, despite his attempts to go astray in Athens, Georgia.

In those oat-sowing days at the University of Georgia, he ran the Georgia Theater, a live-music venue. After Sam hit the wall in his personal life, his uncle offered him a job back in Chattanooga. A few years and a conversion experience later, he found himself in church leadership.

One day he was passed on the street by a man headed to the Mountain City Club. It was Jack Lupton, a longtime family friend and the father of Cartter Lupton II, Sam's best buddy growing up.

"Smartt, you still a Jesus freak?"

"Yes, sir."

"Well, okay," Lupton said and kept walking.

Sam Smartt's father died when he was only nine years old. One day Jack Lupton told Sam to call him *Uncle Jack*. "I never could do it, and I always wished I had," said Sam. "A comment like that means the world to a kid without a dad."

Like Frank Brock, Sam Smartt is his own individual. He is also the quintessential elder. Stuff is named after his great-grandfather, like the Read House. (Sam Read's second marriage was to Katherine Key, David Key's daughter and Summerfield Key's niece. This connects the Read-Smartt axis to the Johnston-Key axis.)

Sam Smartt serves on various boards, including those of Child Evangelism Fellowship and the Chattanooga Christian School, which he has chaired for nearly two decades. He comes from inherited wealth. He is vice chairman of Kenco, a warehousing business founded by his uncle of Scottish descent, Jim Kennedy II, and Jim II's brother-in-law, Sam Read Smartt, Sr., who died in his forties in 1954. Kenco is now run by Jim Kennedy III and his first cousin, Sam Jr.

They picked a good industry. While Chattanooga continues to search for its economic identity, the Kennedys and Smartts have stuck with the warehousing

KRUESI ~ BROCK

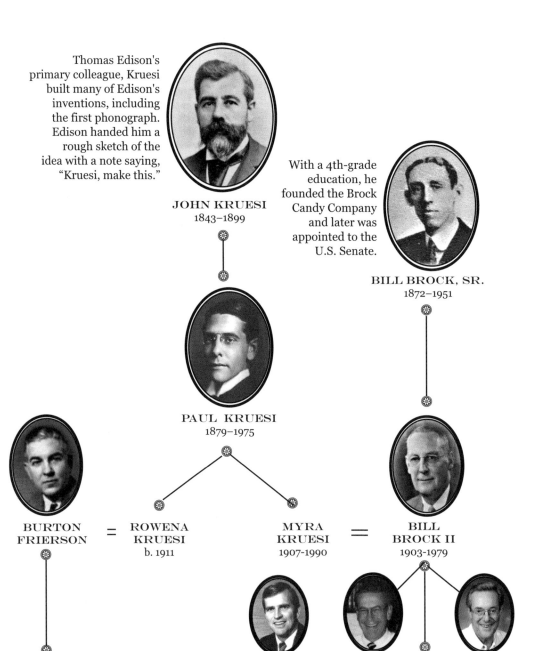

Thomas Edison's primary colleague, Kruesi built many of Edison's inventions, including the first phonograph. Edison handed him a rough sketch of the idea with a note saying, "Kruesi, make this."

JOHN KRUESI
1843–1899

With a 4th-grade education, he founded the Brock Candy Company and later was appointed to the U.S. Senate.

BILL BROCK, SR.
1872–1951

PAUL KRUESI
1879–1975

BURTON FRIERSON = **ROWENA KRUESI** b. 1911

MYRA KRUESI 1907-1990 = **BILL BROCK II** 1903-1979

CARTTER FRIERSON b. 1939 = **PATRICIA BROWN** ⇨ *SISTER* **NANCY BROWN** = **HUGH O. MACLELLAN, JR** b. 1940

FRANK BROCK b. 1942 **PAT BROCK** b. 1932 **BILL BROCK III** b. 1930

(Charts are partial, not exhaustive, highlighting key links or characters in the book.)

and logistics business. It has always worked for this area of strategic valleys and passageways, ever since John Ross built his first "Ware house" in 1815. Chattanooga was ranked the nation's fourth-best city for logistics in 2001 and continues to share top ten honors with places like Toledo, Minneapolis, Houston, and Anchorage, Alaska.[38]

"He's a very wealthy man," says Sam Smartt about his uncle, "and he is as frugal and as good a steward as I've ever met." Sam said he remembers his uncle never driving a new car and that he never had a company car. He just recently put air conditioning in his house, "but he hardly ever runs it."

"My grandfather was that way. . . . He was funny. He would travel all over the world, first class, and he would write letters and postcards to all the Rotarians while he was out traveling. But then he would wait until he got back in the States to mail them, because the postage was too expensive overseas."

Wet and Dry

I interviewed Smartt from his spacious deck on Lookout Mountain, which overlooks the house where Jack Lupton raised his family. We smoked a cigar. Unlike those Baptists with their strong executives, Presbyterians generally are okay with the moderate use of tobacco and alcohol.

The rest of Presbyterianism is pretty dry. I wanted to learn a little more about these dry elders' meetings that have shaped so much of Chattanooga's leadership.

"What happens in a session meeting?" I asked Sam enthusiastically. "How are they different from what happens with Baptists or Methodists?"

"You're gonna have to help me with that one. I've never been a Baptist or a Methodist."

"'I'm looking for details. How long do they last?"

"A couple of hours. Maybe three."

"Once a month?"

"Once a month, and we attend to the business of the church," he replied.

He then felt a warning was in order. "Generally speaking—I don't mean to throw water on this thing—but the session meeting itself oftentimes is a business meeting."

"That's what I'm looking for," I said.

He paused for a second, took a puff, and gave me a "whatever" kind of look. He then described the typical agenda: open with prayer, read the minutes of the previous meeting, then take committee reports. "You've got the music committee; you've got the worship committee. You've got these various committees, and they make reports, and rarely is it earth-shattering. You have a report on the budget, go over the numbers. Leroy the Methodist wants to get married in our sanctuary. Is there any Presbyterian that wants to get married that Saturday? You'll have the pastor give a report. He may report on sensitive subjects, not in a specific way, but he'll talk about marriages struggling or people that are having financial hardships."

"Is there a board table?"

"Yeah. The vice moderator—who is a ruling elder, not a teaching elder—runs the meeting. The pastor does not run the meeting. The floor can be given to the pastor, and the pastor will have his time for his report like a committee chairman would, but the vice moderator actually moderates the meeting."

"Is there the sense in those meetings that the pastor is one of several and not the big man in charge?"

"I would say most people solicit his opinion . . . but he is open to being questioned, and he will be questioned. He will be challenged. I've never been on any other sessions, so I don't know what it is like. But what I understand is [that in other churches] usually the pastor runs the show. Unless he is really off base, he gets his way. In our church, the agenda is being presented by the vice moderator, not the pastor. The pastor's opinion is sought on virtually every issue, but he's challenged freely. I think that's a real healthy thing, myself."

Those Smartt Brocks

Smartt feels a strong affinity toward his vice-moderating predecessor. "Frank Brock was right before me," said Sam. "I thought he was awesome."

Smartt does not mean "smart" so much as "that smarts," as in a stinging sensation. Just ask the pastor. *Brock* means badger, an animal regarded as disagreeable or contrarian in the Middle Ages, according to the *Dictionary of American Family Names*.

The affinity between Brock and Smartt may be also be explained by the fact that Polk Smartt and Bill Brock, Sr. were close colleagues. Frank's grandfather chaired the big 50-year Confederate reunion held in Chattanooga in 1913, and Sam's great-grandfather, Captain Polk Smartt, gave the keynote address to the veterans from across the country. Paul Kruesi served as publicity chairman.

News clippings from the event couldn't resist calling the chairman "plain Mr. Brock, with an emphasis on the adjective." The flashier Captain Smartt, leader of the army from Alabama, was quoted from his address: "[The Alabama brigade] was not the first to withdraw and did not retire from its position until the line was hopelessly broken at two or more points . . . by the Shallow Ford Road." The veteran of Missionary Ridge and the Battle of Atlanta was wounded nine times but never missed a day of action.[39]

"There were quite a few Smartts here that had an impact in this town," said Sam Smartt. His secretary keeps a list of all the Smartts—a couple hundred of them—on the computer. "We settled over in Smartt Station next to McMinnville, Tennessee, in 1805," Sam told me. "In fact, we just had our 200th family reunion. We have a reunion every year. It's the last Sunday in July, the Smartt Reunion. And it's a hoot, buddy. We've had it at Grandview at Rock City. We've had it at Bill Chapin's house at Rock City before. We've had it at Lookout Mountain Presbyterian Church three or four times. Mainly, it's over there where we all settled in 1805."

"Smartt Station?"

"Smartt Station. It's got its own post office."

"What do you do when you get together?"

"We have a good time. We have a meal, obviously—country ham, fried chicken, deviled eggs, you know, the whole scene. We socialize, and then we usually have some of the older folks in the group tell a story."

"How many come from Chattanooga?"

"This year we had about ten from Chattanooga. There are a lot more of them here, you know, 'cause all the Killebrews, Friersons, and Brocks are Smartts. They are all descendents of Myra Smartt, who was my grandfather's sister. When Bill Brock was running for Congress, he always came to McMinnville for the reunion."

Yes, that camaraderie between Sam Smartt and Frank Brock is thicker than just baptismal water. They are also second cousins. Polk Smartt's daughter Myra married the inventor's son, Paul Kruesi. So, just like Sam, Frank Brock's great-grandfather is Captain Polk Smartt, the Presbyterian elder of 50 years (see chart on next page).

Sam Smartt tries to explain these connections to his children at home, not just at reunions. "In my family, it happens around the dinner table—around Thanksgiving or Christmas dinner or birthdays—when you've got a lot of generations present at the table. My wife Donna will often comment about how amazed she is about all this genealogy that goes on—not only about our family but about other close friends' families here on Lookout Mountain and in Chattanooga—but, primarily, probably based on Lookout Mountain."

Sam knows the lingo and the definitions. "Cartter Frierson and his siblings are my second cousins. David Bennett is my first cousin once removed. There are so many connections between these various families. The Probasco and the Lupton families are intertwined. The Brock, Killebrew, and Frierson families are all intertwined. The Maclellan family is involved in all that, through marriages. So, I think that's interesting."

Smartt contrasts the phenomenon with other communities. "I also think there is an extremely strong Christian heritage—conservative Presbyterian heritage—in this community that is, I think, unique.[40*] It may not be totally unique. Columbus, Georgia, has got some stuff like that going on. But I don't know if they've got all the family connections like we do."

Because of the shift of influential families early in the 20th century from the valley to Lookout Mountain, the shift in Presbyterian influence is now shared in

READ ~ SMARTT

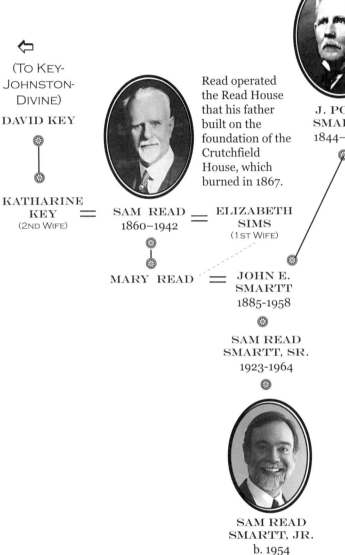

⇐

(TO KEY-
JOHNSTON-
DIVINE)

DAVID KEY

Read operated
the Read House
that his father
built on the
foundation of the
Crutchfield
House, which
burned in 1867.

J. POLK
SMARTT
1844–1914

KATHARINE
KEY
(2ND WIFE) = SAM READ
1860–1942 = ELIZABETH
SIMS
(1ST WIFE)

MARY READ = JOHN E.
SMARTT
1885-1958

MYRA
KENNEDY
SMARTT
1880–1941 = PAUL
KRUESI
1879–1975

(TO KRUESI-
BROCK)
AXIS)

SAM READ
SMARTT, SR.
1923-1964

SAM READ
SMARTT, JR.
b. 1954

(Charts are partial, not exhaustive, highlighting key links or characters in the book.)

large part by the church on the mountain. Smartt recognizes the influence of First Presbyterian. "It had a tremendous influence on a lot of those people," he said. "Cartter Lupton, specifically. I think the Maclellan family originally was a First Pres family. The Probascos didn't always live on Lookout Mountain. They lived in Riverview, and that's where Cartter Lupton lived, but Jack Lupton now lives up here . . . and Scotty Probasco now lives up here. His son Scott and his son Ben and both of his daughters live up here. First Presbyterian, I think, was the big influence on a lot of those families."

Doug Daugherty believes that the Presbyterian doctrine of infant baptism holds a key to its long-term influence. "It speaks of multigenerational families. It speaks of families that have a sense of cohesion from generation to generation in some way," he said. "I almost think that the institutions reinforce the families that are multigenerational, and the multigenerational families reinforce the institutions. I'm not sure I can make that case absolutely, but I think it's probably true."

"Now, I just want to say that I don't think that a few Presbyterians are responsible for all the good things that have happened in Chattanooga. You know, I don't want to overstate it. All the biggest churches in town now are Baptist. Chattanooga doesn't have a large Anglican community—just never has. And it doesn't have that big of a Presbyterian community, but its pretty significant in the sense of its history. It's got a very large presence. In fact, you can't understand the history of Chattanooga without looking at First Presbyterian Church. You just can't do it."

———◆———

When the founders of the first church in Chattanooga met on June 21, 1840, they called themselves "Presbyterians thrown together by the Providence of God," according to the handwritten minutes.[41] They met in a small log building on Fourth and Lookout Street (behind what is now the Provident Building). No one there was an ordained pastor. The handful of ruling elders included John Vail and Ainsworth Blunt from the Brainerd Mission, James Berry (who was inducted as the first mayor of Chattanooga that year in the same building), and another man named Allen Kennedy.

Allen Kennedy was his own individual, but, like Frank Brock and Sam Smartt, he also fit the description of that quintessential elder. Kennedy (no relation to Sam's uncle, Jim Kennedy) provides a nice bonus for readers since his picture stood the test of time. Zella includes the daguerreotype on the entire page four of her First Presbyterian history, saying it "no doubt exemplified the style for church." Kennedy also perfectly fits the firsthand description provided by a woman who observed Chattanooga's original elders when she was five years old:

"They were grave and dignified men, who wore long, black broadcloth coats and silk hats and carried gold-headed canes," wrote Ann Bachman Hyde. "[They] administered the spiritual affairs of the church and used discipline when necessary, a modus procedure which seems to have vanished."

"I do not recall any wives sitting with the elders. They always seemed to be with them . . . but in church I recall the elders sitting in solemn dignity with no female distractions, for it was then a man's world."[42]

We have no way of knowing if "stuff" was named after Kennedy's forebearers, but we do know that Colonel Daniel Kennedy III was a member of the North Carolina legislature and later a general for the lost State of Franklin. He fought a battle against Dragging Canoe's warriors on the slopes of Lookout Mountain in 1788.

It is also likely that Allen Kennedy came from inherited wealth. He was already a prominent businessman in Chattanooga by the time First Presbyterian was founded. He was one of the very first to cross the river to seek more opportunity at Ross's Landing. Family members recall waiting up all night for the day and hour to stake their claim the moment the New Echota Treaty was signed.[43]

A visitor from England visited Kennedy's Tavern in 1837. He described Ross's Landing as a "small village hastily built without regard to any order or streets. . . . Supposing, from the state in which the country was, that I should meet with all sorts of disorderly persons, I almost dreaded going to this tavern; but on reaching it, I was delighted to find it consisted of three new log huts, built upon a high piece of ground that commanded a beautiful view of the surrounding country. The landlord was very civil, and everything was tolerably clean." Despite the kind remarks, the traveler included some understated English humor: "On awakening I got a fine view of the surrounding country through the walls of my bedroom." Kennedy was later able to upgrade his tavern into the town's first hotel, the Kennedy House. It stood at 421 Market Street, a two-story square structure with a second-story veranda extending over the sidewalk.[44]

We know that this quintessential businessman-elder was quite involved in the community. He was a board member of the Lookout Railroad Company, formed in 1837 to bring the first train to Chattanooga. He was also one of six commissioners chosen by the early settlers—four were ruling elders—to ensure that the area's first residents obtained from the state legislature the "occupancy rights" they gained by crossing the river and squatting on the better pieces of property. The commissioners met in that same Little Log Cabin on Fourth and Lookout—sixteen by twenty feet with split logs for benches with no backs. Instead of a church bell, a large spice mortar hung from a stick-and-mud chimney that was struck by a

Allen Kennedy

pestle to announce church, school, government, and public-private partnership meetings.[45]

The floor was made from an old, abandoned flatboat, as were many structures in the new village. It was difficult to bring the large vessels back upstream after traveling downriver to the new settlement. They were usually torn apart for lumber. One observer noted that 200 used flatboats at any one time were stored along the landing from the bluff to the foot of Cameron Hill.[46]

Wolves and Wild Hogs

When George Rodenbaugh came to the area a decade earlier in 1828 for a hunting trip, he saw not a single resident in the heart of the valley. The McDonalds had died, the Rosses had moved to Rome, Georgia, and the missionaries still lived on the other side of the ridge. Only Uncle Billy Gentry resided in his small ferryman's hut by the river.

Early resident Andy Williams also says there were no people at that time in the vast wilderness. "The spies that Moses sent out to search the Land of Canaan could not have found a more beautiful valley, with everything to sustain life, except bread. Upon river and creek bottom grew as fine timber as ever grew on earth." He recalled one sycamore tree so large that a door had been cut through it large enough so a horse "could go in, turn around, and come out." He said it kept him dry on many a rainy day.[53]

Rodenbaugh said the valley contained an abundance of elk, bear, deer, turkey, wolves, partridges, beaver, and mink. Wild hogs were found in droves. A woman traveling to the mission from the river landing said she and her companions were "strangers in a dark forest."[48]

By 1837, 200 settlers had infiltrated the area, including Allen Kennedy and many soldiers involved with removing the Cherokees. One officer described the soldiers' houses as one room only, twelve to fifteen feet, made of poles six to ten inches in diameter. The business each day was conducted on the riverbank, but the homes were built on higher ground due to the abundance of fog and mosquitos. The landing was not gradual, but rather a steep cliff starting around today's Third Street. A handful of log stores were built on the higher, east side of Market Street. For some, it was easier to operate on the river. T. J. Lattner operated his store from a flatboat, and Ferdinand Parham, the first newspaperman, designed his newspaper on board and placed his printing press under a tree on the riverbank.[49]

The elder-commissioners met at the Little Log Cabin to bring order and structure to the chaotic village. They hired surveyors to plat the 240 acres bordered by the river and Ninth Street, and by Georgia Avenue and Cameron Hill. As in Philadelphia, the streets were named by trees from north to south and by numbers in the opposite direction. An historical marker on Ross's Landing today lists the first 53 citizens who obtained the land parceled by Kennedy and the other five commissioners.

No known direct descendents of these 53 names survive in Chattanooga today.[50*] However, one prominent descendent lives in Nashville. U.S. Senate Majority Leader Bill Frist is the 3rd-great-grandson of Isaac Baldwin, who is listed on the marker. The husband of Baldwin's daughter, Jacob Frist, is buried in the Citizens Cemetery next to Todd Gardenhire's ancestors. However, early records tell us this is not the first cemetery in the area. Isaac Baldwin himself was buried in Chattanooga's first graveyard in 1837, on the west slope of Cameron Hill, then called Reservoir Hill, near BellSouth Park today. Next to him was buried a negro who died from a spider bite. The markers of Baldwin and the others buried there are lost to history. Soldiers used them to build an arsenal during the Civil War. When it was torn down, one stone in the walls contained an incomplete inscription: "Sacred to the memory of _____, August 1837."[51]

After parceling out the land, Kennedy and the five commissioners rang the makeshift bell in 1838 at the Little Log Cabin to choose a name for the new town.[52] John P. Long, an elder at First Presbyterian Church, documented the discussion for posterity. Lookout City was proposed but called "too pretentious" for "a city in the woods," he said. Montevideo was ruled out for being too French.

John Long finally proposed "Chattanooga," saying it was "homelike, it was local and was the name of the valley and the creek in the neighborhood and . . . was the original name for Lookout Mountain."

Too difficult to pronounce, another man said. "[It is] too uncommon, too uncouth. Strangers would mispronounce it," he said. Then he offered the name Albion,

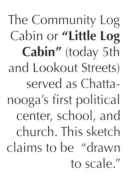

The Community Log Cabin or **"Little Log Cabin"** (today 5th and Lookout Streets) served as Chattanooga's first political center, school, and church. This sketch claims to be "drawn to scale."

after the white cliffs of the bluff overlooking the river. Another man immediately seconded the proposal. "Oh yes. Let's call it Albun. That would be splendid."

This mispronunciation brought the discussion back to Chattanooga. "The name might sound outlandish and strange to some ears," said Long. "But if our city was a success, it would become familiar and pleasant, and there would not be another name like it in the world." His argument carried the day.[53]

A few months later, seven alderman (councilmen) were elected for the new town of Chattanooga. They met in the Little Log Cabin to choose the first mayor from among their ranks. The honor went to James Berry, an elder for the church that met in the same building. Chattanooga's second, third, and fourth mayors were also members of First Presbyterian. For the next 26 years, nearly every mayor in Chattanooga was also a leader at First Presbyterian, including Dr. Milo Smith, who was elected seven times. He was the mayor when Federal troops overtook the town in 1863.[54]

At that point, Dr. T. H. McCallie was the pastor at First Presbyterian. When he resigned a decade later, he directed his efforts toward planting new churches in the community. As head of the Presbytery's home mission board, he met with First Pres member Frank Caldwell and approved the proposal to launch a new Presbyterian Church on Lookout Mountain.[55] Over a century later, the spirit of quintessential ruling elders like Allen Kennedy had passed to new ruling elders several generations later, such as Frank Brock and Sam Smartt.

But the spirit also got a boost from the genetic. Whereas Smartt's uncle is not related to Allen Kennedy, Sam Smartt is, on the other side of his family, a direct descendent of this early pioneer, elder, and commissioner. Sam's great-grandfather, Polk Smartt, married Rowena Kennedy, the granddaughter of Allen Kennedy.[56*] Thanks to the Kruesi Smartt connection, Frank Brock joins Sam Smartt as a great-great-great-grandson of that prototypical elder who founded First Presbyterian Church in 1840.

———◆———

Daniel Kennedy, Allen Kennedy's ancestor, came to America in 1716 after being banished from Scotland as a "King's Rebel."[57] The power between the king and the presbytery in Scotland had bounced back and forth for centuries after the church's founder soundly defeated the Scottish royalty in a revolution unique to the world in the 1560s.

After a young follower of Martin Luther was burned at the stake in Scotland, a Cambridge-trained Greek scholar named George Wishart conspired with unsuccessful assassins to overthrow the Scottish hierarchy. Then he began preaching throughout the country. "The only difference between the barons and bishops," he said, "is that one of these nobles has legitimate heirs, the other does not." Great crowds turned out to hear him. On one occasion, the pressing throng forced him to preach from a boat.[58]

Officials determined to have Wishart seized and executed. On the night he was captured, Wishart's chief disciple thrust his two-handed sword toward the soldiers. Wishart ordered him to stop and was led to the stake. He continued to preach from the fire until a soldier choked him to death with a rope.[59]

It was the year 1546. Earlier that night, Wishart, who believed he had the gift of prophecy,[60*] spoke words of comfort to his men. "Not many shall suffer after me," he said. "God will send you comfort. This realm shall be illuminated with the light of Christ's gospel, as clearly as any realm since the time of the apostles." The inspired reformer was helping to fulfill his own prophecy. Listening to him was the bearer of the two-handed sword, John Knox, the founder of Presbyterianism.[61]

Knox escaped to Geneva, Switzerland, where he studied under Reformation leader John Calvin. When he returned to Scotland, his reputation preceded him and the crowds shouted across the land, "John Knox is come! John Knox is come!" After one of his sermons, a priest with little sense came out with a richly ornamented image and proceeded to celebrate mass. A boy threw a rock, broke the image, and started a riot. Every convent in the city was sacked. The world's first democratic revolution was underway. Catholicism was banned and exchanged for Knox's new church of Presbyterianism—the theology of John Calvin with a unique form of church government based on "presbyters," or elders.[62]

Queen Elizabeth of England warned the prince of Scotland that a dangerous sect had arisen in both lands that would have no kings but a Presbytery.[63] Eventually, King Charles of England demanded that on a certain day the Scottish Presbyterians must switch from Knox's *Book of Disciplines* to the Church of England's *Book of Common Prayer*. Two of the King's councilors skipped the day's worship in apprehension of what might occur. In Knox's old church in Edinburgh, the service had

John Knox

barely started when Jenny Geddes, a working woman, hurled at the minister's head a stool she had been sitting on. Others began throwing their stools and various missiles. Similar riots took place around the country.[64]

Scotland's church leaders believed their choices were tyranny or war. They chose war and drew up the "National Covenant," which denounced autocracy and placed the seat of power with the people. (This document served as a model for the Declaration of Independence 150 years later.[65]) War ensued and many "Covenanters" fought and died for their beliefs, such as the ancestors of Thomas Maclellan, founder of Provident.[66*]

The drafters and first signers of the National Covenant, including George Gillespie, met in the Greyfriar's Church in Edinburgh and laid the document on a table for others to sign. A majority of the Scottish population lined up outside the church to sign the charter, an event unique to history. The Covenant's key theological defender was Gillespie, the seventh great-grandfather of Scotty Probasco.

The National Covenant helped lay the foundation for the British Revolution 50 years later,[67] when King William of Orange acknowledged that Parliament, not the king, would have primary control over government, with both submitting to a document inspired by the National Covenant called the Bill of Rights. It was nearly identical to the one embraced by America's Founding Fathers a century later.

Few today know about the National Covenant or the church where nearly an entire people signed over their country to God. One exception is the proprietor of Greyfriar's coffee shop in downtown Chattanooga, where Frank Brock buys his green coffee beans. Owner Ian Goodman, a McDougal on his mother's side, proudly promotes his Scottish heritage.

Scotty Probasco also voices a strong sentiment for this religious heritage from Scotland. "The only epitaph I want is one that says I was an elder in the Presbyterian Church."[68]

Artist: Andrew Wilkie

CHAPTER SIX

The Spirit of the *New York Times*

Adolph Ochs and the Competition

The only reason Adolph S. Ochs can be described as one of the most influential citizens in Chattanooga's history, and not simply the greatest, is that he left the city at the young age of thirty-eight. In New York, he became one of the most important world figures of the 20th century.

In 1896, the youthful *Chattanooga Times* publisher found a way to purchase a struggling newspaper with a hyphen, then called the *New-York Times*. With his genius and expertise, he transformed it into the most influential media organization in history. Through his only child, Iphigene, and his son-in-law, Arthur Sulzberger, Ochs created "arguably the most powerful blood-related dynasty in twentieth-century America," according to *The Trust*, a 1999 biography of the Ochs-Sulzberger axis written by Susan Tifft and Alex Jones.[1*]

Sulzberger's son, "Punch," continued as the *New York Times'* third-generation publisher, and two of his daughters remained in New York. Another daughter, Ruth Sulzberger, mentioned to a *Time* magazine reporter in 1950 as the father's favorite, carried on the family dynasty's tradition in Adolph Ochs's hometown as the longtime publisher of the *Chattanooga Times*.

Naturally, I had a bit of anxiety as I took the elevator to the office of Ruth Sulzberger Holmberg on Tenth Street, which overlooks Miller Park and Plaza. As I exited the elevator, a six-foot-tall bust of her grandfather, Adolph Ochs, greeted me in the foyer. It is the same statue that graces the New York paper's offices on Times Square. On the wall was a picture of my upcoming interviewee shaking hands with the Pope. Another picture, of John F. Kennedy, was scribbled with handwriting. "To Ruth with the warm regards of her friend," wrote JFK.

Like her namesake in the Old Testament, Ruth displayed the qualities of a loyal daughter growing up. She was the only sibling to express a desire to work in the family's newspaper tradition at an early age. She adored her grandfather Adolph, and they shared the same birthday, March 12. That quality of loyalty she learned from her mother, Iphigene, who described her Sunday outings with Ochs. "I used to follow him around at his heels," she said. "I was more faithful than my dog is to me."[2]

But Ruth Holmberg is no pushover. Early on, she shouldered difficult leadership assignments and agreed to be the first Jewish member of the Junior League. She has chaired the Chattanooga Chamber of Commerce, the Symphony, the Hunter Museum, the Public Education Foundation, and several other local organizations. Nationally, she serves on the board of directors of humble outfits like the *New York Times* and the Smithsonian Institute. She was the second woman to serve on the board of directors for the *Associated Press*, following *Washington Post* publisher Kathryn Graham.

Reporting in the Old Days

The first newspaper in the Chattanooga area did not survive history. A magazine quotes something called the *Hamilton Observer* in 1836, but no copy of this publication has ever been found.[3] Neither has the first edition of the *Hamilton Gazette*, started in 1838 and showing "Ross's Landing" on the masthead. It was composed on a flatboat and printed under a tree by the bluff.

The second issue was discovered, thankfully, among the archives of the Library of Congress. Times have changed in the newspaper business. One article on the front page provides advice to wives on how to be a "moral influence" on their husbands, citing the spouse of Jonathan Edwards as the prime example. Another article encourages study of the Bible.

Demonstrating the schizophrenia of Chattanooga's founding, two articles pay tribute to the "noble Indian," while two others list Ocoee land grant opportunities made available by the removal of those same Indians. The paper also published a sealed bid to provide provisions for the "emigrating" Cherokees. One advertisement recruits for the Temperance Society while another ad directly beside it lists the twelve different types of whiskey available at Ross's Landing.[4]

During the 1850s, two opposing papers championed the two great issues of the day, a tradition that has continued for most of Chattanooga's history. The *Advertiser* promoted secession while the *Chattanooga Gazette* preached the Union cause, another likely factor in why the county and the city voted differently on the issue in 1861.

Thomas Edison's primary colleague, Kruesi built many of Edison's inventions, including the first phonograph. Edison handed him a rough sketch of the idea with a note saying, "Kruesi, make this."

JOHN KRUESI
1843–1899

With a 4th-grade education, he founded the Brock Candy Company and later was appointed to the U.S. Senate.

BILL BROCK, SR.
1872–1951

PAUL KRUESI
1879–1975

⇨ (CONTINUED ON BACK)

BURTON FRIERSON = **ROWENA KRUESI**
b. 1911

MYRA KRUESI
1907–1990

= **BILL BROCK II**
1903–1979

CARTTER FRIERSON = **PATRICIA BROWN** ⇨ *SISTER* **NANCY BROWN** = **HUGH O. MACLELLAN, JR**
b. 1939   b. 1940

FRANK BROCK **PAT BROCK** **BILL BROCK III**
b. 1942   b. 1932   b. 1930

PATTEN ~ LUPTON

JOHN A.
PATTEN
1801–1847

Patten founded the Chattanooga Medicine Co. (Chattem) which produced Black Draught and Wine of Cardui (forerunners of Coca-Cola). He was the city's first millionaire and built the Ashland Farm mansion in Flintstone.

GEORGE
WASHINGTON
PATTEN
1836–1907

ZEBOIM CARTTER
PATTEN
1840–1925

CATHARINE
LEE
(2ND WIFE)
b. 1838

=

=

MARGARET
THOMAS
PATTEN
KRUESI
(PAUL KRUESI'S 2ND WIFE)
1891–1978

= GEORGE H.
PATTEN
(1ST HUSBAND)

ELIZABETH
PATTEN
1871–1941

= JOHN T.
LUPTON
1862–1933

(Charts are partial, not exhaustive, highlighting key links or characters in the book.)

LUPTON ~ HARRISON

JONAH J.
LUPTON
b. 1815

=

MARY
TAVENNER
(1ST WIFE)

The older brother of
John T. Lupton, Cornelius
Lupton's 14 children
inherited much of the
Lupton bottling and
land empire.

CORNELIUS
LUPTON
b. c. 1847

The Carters developed
most of Lookout Mountain,
including the golf club,
Fairyland Club, Rock City,
and Lookout Mountain Hotel
(Covenant College). Paul later
married into the Coke
bottling empire.

THOMAS A.
LUPTON
SR.

FRANK
HARRISON
(2ND HUSBAND)

=

ANNE
LUPTON
(WIDOWED TWICE.
FIRST HUSBAND
WAS JESSE EVANS.)

=

PAUL
CARTER
(3RD HUSBAND)

BETTY LOU
MADDIN
MCCALLIE

(TO MCCALLIE
AXIS)

THOMAS A.
(TOMMY)
LUPTON, JR.
b. 1929

FRANK
HARRISON
JR.
1930–2002

READ ~ SMARTT

Charter member of Lookout Railroad Company in 1837 and a founding elder of 1st Pres. Church. Before first train arrived in 1849, he worried that "poor Chattanooga" would never get an economic break.

ALLEN KENNEDY
1798–1857

WILLIAM KENNEDY

Read operated the Read House that his father built on the foundation of the Crutchfield House, which burned in 1867.

J. POLK SMARTT
1844–1914

ROWENA KENNEDY

SAM READ
1860–1942

ELIZABETH SIMS
(1ST WIFE)

MYRA KENNEDY SMARTT
(1ST WIFE)
1880–1941

MARY READ

JOHN E. SMARTT
1885–1958

SAM READ SMARTT, SR.
1923–1964

SAM READ SMARTT, JR.
b. 1954

DIVINE ~ KEY

Called the "Father of Chattanooga," Williams was one of three original settlers in 1835 and owner of the first land syndicate. He settled Williams Island and built the first store at Ross's Landing after the Cherokee Removal.

SAMUEL WILLIAMS
1807–1898

=

ELIZABETH WILLIAMS
(1ST WIFE)

MARY DIVINE KEY

=

Key escorted Jefferson Davis during the infamous confrontation at Chattanooga's Crutchfield House. As the first Confederate to serve in the Cabinet after the war, he was the "key" to President Rutherford B. Hayes's national coalition.

SUMMERFIELD KEY
1835-1891

⇨ *BROTHER*

DAVID KEY

KATHERINE KEY

ELIZABETH KEY
1873–1948

=

JAMES F. JOHNSTON
1865–1930

SUMMERFIELD K. JOHNSTON, SR.
1900–1985

SUMMERFIELD K. JOHNSTON, JR.
b. 1932

CONNECTING FAMILIES IN CHATTANOOGA

*

This chart appears as a fold-out insert in the book
Old Money, New South: The Spirit of Chattanooga
by Dean W. Arnold. For more information, see:
www.OldMoneyNewSouth.com
dean@DeanArnold.org
423-595-3621

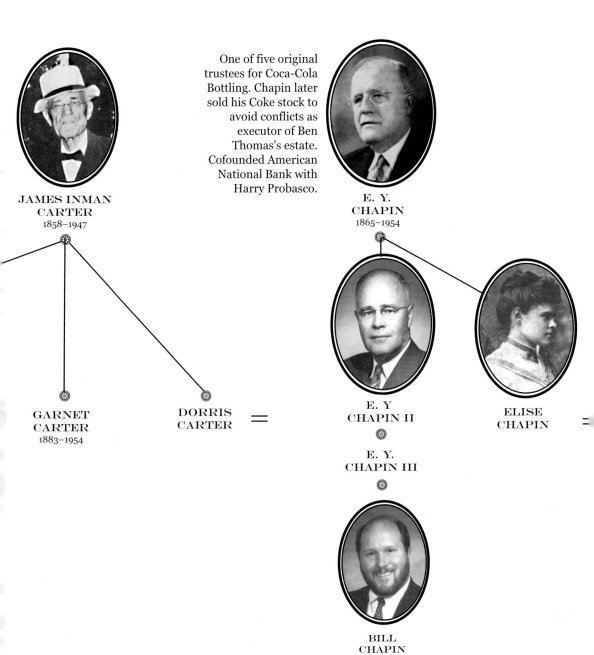

JAMES INMAN CARTER
1858–1947

One of five original trustees for Coca-Cola Bottling. Chapin later sold his Coke stock to avoid conflicts as executor of Ben Thomas's estate. Cofounded American National Bank with Harry Probasco.

E. Y. CHAPIN
1865–1954

GARNET CARTER
1883–1954

DORRIS CARTER =

E. Y CHAPIN II

E. Y. CHAPIN III

ELISE CHAPIN =

BILL CHAPIN

A Union officer from Ohio who became a Chattanooga industrialist and one of the city's first millionaires, Montague built a Spanish-style mansion that was razed during renovation of Cameron Hill.

THEODORE GILES MONTAGUE
1836–1910

NORTON THAYER MONTAGUE

DEADERICK MOON

MILDRED MOON = **WILLIAM L. MONTAGUE**

CANNON WANN
(2ND WIFE)
=
RICK MONTAGUE
=
ALICE LUPTON
(1ST WIFE)

GILLESPIE ~ SHARP

A founding father of Presbyterianism, Gillespie was a leader in authoring the *Westminster Confession* and *Shorter Catechism*, and chief apologist for Scotland's National Covenant.

GEORGE GILLESPIE
b. 1613–1648

GEORGE GILLESPIE II

GEORGE GILLESPIE III

CORNELIA GILLESPIE = **L. J. SHARP** 1845–1917

RACHEL JAMES (2ND WIFE) = **JOHN DIVINE** b. 1818–1892

ROBERT COOKE b. 1858 = **SARAH DIVINE**

JULIA DIVINE McCALLIE (TO McCALLIE-HOOKE-WHITESIDE-CRUTCHFIELD)

R. H. WILLIAMS 1862–1944 = **MARGARET GILLESPIE SHARP** 1876–1949

JOHN CESSNA SHARP 1882–1955 = **RACHEL COOKE**

MARGARET WILLIAMS 1904–1964

RACHEL DIVINE SHARP = **JOSEPH DECOSIMO** b. 1925

TOM DECOSIMO b. 1956

FRED DECOSIMO b. 1951

LUPTON ~ PROBASCO

Coca-Cola Bottling's wealthiest owner since it began in 1899. In the 20th century, no family owned more Coke bottling assets than the Luptons.

Founder of American National Bank (now SunTrust), also called the "Coca-Cola Bank." His board comprised the city's most powerful men.

JOHN T. LUPTON
1862–1933

HARRY SCOTT PROBASCO
1858–1919

CARTTER LUPTON
1899–1977

SCOTT L. PROBASCO, SR.
1890–1962

=   **ALICE PROBASCO LUPTON**   ⇨

(MARRIAGE)   *(BROTHER)*

JOHN T. (JACK) LUPTON II
b. 1926

SCOTT L. (SCOTTY) PROBASCO, JR.
b. 1928

(Charts are partial, not exhaustive, highlighting key links or characters in the book.)

LUPTON ~ PROBASCO

Coca-Cola Bottling's wealthiest owner since it began in 1899. In the 20th century, no family owned more Coke bottling assets than the Luptons.

JOHN T. LUPTON
1862–1933

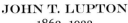

CARTTER LUPTON
1899–1977

JACK
LUPTON
b. 1926

Founder of American National Bank (now SunTrust), also called the "Coca-Cola Bank." His board comprised the city's most powerful men.

HARRY SCOTT
PROBASCO
1858–1919

SCOTT L.
PROBASCO, SR.
b. 1890–1962

SCOTTY
PROBASCO
b. 1928

=

(MARRIAGE)

ALICE
PROBASCO
LUPTON

⇨

(BROTHER)

As the war progressed, Chattanooga found itself with no newspaper. A Confederate legislator from Tennessee, who was commissioned to bring the state archives to Chattanooga as the Federals marched into Memphis and Nashville, saw the opportunity to start a paper in the strategic railroad town. Franc Paul immediately began the *Chattanooga Rebel,* which provided information on where to get food and supplies, but most importantly, it gave updates on the war. Sometimes Paul allowed his paper to be used to fool Union officers.

When the Federal army overtook Chattanooga, Paul moved two railcars behind his building in the night, loaded the presses, and moved them south. Two employees remained behind, using the vault of the Bank of Tennessee as a bomb shelter, and reported on the battle. An eight by ten, single-sheet edition of the *Rebel* bragged that it was the only institution left in town, but it had removed its printing operations to Marietta, Georgia.[5]

After the war, a myriad of papers came and went. Zella Armstrong counts over 150 in the city's history.[6]

The Rebel's Franc Paul left Chattanooga to manage the *Knoxville Tribune,* whose editor was the scholarly J. E. McGowan. The two men saw opportunity again in Chattanooga, and when they began to plan a new paper there, they decided to include a 17-year-old boy who worked for them. His "grim application to business" caught their attention.

Young Adolph Ochs began his newspaper career at age 11, folding and throwing fifty papers each morning at 5:00 a.m. for twenty-five cents a day.[†] Adolph walked four miles while delivering the papers, went back home for breakfast, and arrived at school by 7:00 a.m. His father, Julius Ochs, walked with him in the dark every morning to the newspaper's offices.

Julius was born in 1826 in Bavaria (southern Germany) to Lazarus Ochsenhorn, a prosperous diamond dealer and Talmudic scholar who excelled in languages and music while studying in Italy. When Julius encountered economic hard times and Jewish oppression in 1845, he contacted relatives in Louisville, Kentucky, and moved to America. (About that time, my great-great-grandfather made the same trek to America as a Bavarian Jew.)

Julius worked odd jobs around the South. In Mississippi, he observed slave auctions and declared the institution "a villainous relic of barbarism." His wife, however, was a Confederate. Bertha Levy, the mother of Adolph Ochs, militantly demonstrated her devotion to secessionist principles by getting arrested for smuggling quinine to Rebel forces. She hid it in her newborn baby's carriage. As a 15-year-old student at Heidelberg Seminary in war-torn Bavaria, she expressed sympathy with

---

[†] Approx. $25 a day (2006)

Hamilton Gazette.

VOTED TO COMMERCE, AGRICULTURE, MANUFACTURES,—LITERATURE, SCIENCE, AND THE FINE ARTS,—FOREIGN AND DOMESTIC NE

[E I.]   ROSS' LANDING, TEN. JULY 26, 1838.   NU

A. PARHAM,
& PUBLISHER.

zette is published weekly, at $2 50
receipt of the first number.—$2 50
50 after the expiration of the year
for six months.
s inserted at one dollar per square
, and fifty cents for each continu-

potency without having to gain it myself and had my library well supplied with choice gems of literature, and were surrounded by a few intelligent, confiding, trust-worthy friends, with whom I might spend a few hours when I became weary of reading,—I say if I were surrounded with these things, I have thought that I would be happy.

bove on the ground shook under our feet; the volcano blazed: the wind burst forth in irresistible blasts, and swept the living and the dead, in whirlwinds far into the desert. We heard the bellowing of the distant Mediterranean, as its waters were at our sides swelled by a new deluge. The lakes and rivers roared and inundated the land. The fiery sword shot tenfold fire. Showers of blood fell. Thunder pealed from every quarter of the heavens. Lightning.

empire, more extended than the empires of the east; and though they were the children of the forest, and though they left no monuments of sculpture, painting, and poecy, yet great were they in their fall, and sorrowful is the story of their wrongs. They once had cities, but where are they. They are swept from the face of the earth. They had their temple of the sun, but the sanctuary is broken down, and the beams of the deified luminary extinguished. It is

female public sh
ever will live.
applied to the
great and good m
ness consists. In
rather than in h
self. Or in othe
fluo to be seen an
make others seen
Spence felt.

10 Boxes Cordial, assorted,
10 " Prunes,
6 " Cod Fish,
10 Kegs Indigo,
3 " Madder,
3 " Cloves,
30 Bbls Flour,
Bacon and Lard, a large quantity,
40 kegs Nails, well assorted numbers.
Rolled Iron, Castings. &c.
Also, Molasses, a fine supply—delightful article for summer,
We also keep on hand a large and general assortment of

DRY GOODS,

And every thing that is usually kept in a store. We respectfully invite our friends and customers generally to call and examine for themselves, as we are disposed to sell upon reasonable terms.
G. & S. WILLIAMS.
July 23d, 1838---2---tf.

PROPOSALS.

SEALED proposals will be received until the 15th day of August, 1838, to supply the Cherokee Indians emigrating from this place and other parts of the nation, to the Cherokee Nation west of the Mississippi river, with rations to consist of one pound of fresh beef or three fourths of a pound of salt pork, or bacon, & three fourths of a quart of Corn or Corn Meal, or one pound of flour to each person, and four quarts of salt to every one hundred rations, the price per ration must be specified, bacon or beef to be furnished as required. The above articles to be of a good and wholesome quality. Also to furnish the teams and pack horses employed in the emigration with corn and fodder, the price per bushel for corn and per pound for hay or fodder. The above specified articles to be delivered at such times, and places, and in such quantities as may be directed by the conductors, on the following route, by the way of Gallatin, Tennessee, thence to Hopkinsville, Ky. to Golconda on the Ohio River, thence by Jonesborough, on the Mississippi river, to Caledonia, thence by Masses Iron Works to Springfield by Cane Hill to Fort Gibson.

LATELY RECEIVED,
AND IN STORE,

1500 Bbls Kings Salt,
25 hhds Sugar,
2 bbls Loaf do
60 " Tens Whiskey,
10 " Am Gin,
20 " Wine,
20 " Cog Brandy,
10 " N. O. Rum,
50 boxes Raisins,
10 baskets Champaigne & brand,
1 bbl & 20 doz Spts Turpentine,
3 " Brimstone,
2 " Copperas,
3 " S S Almonds,
15 " boxes Tobacco,
4 tons Bar Iron,
30 kegs Nails, ass'ed,
For sale on reasonable terms for Cash.
McCALLIE & LONG.
Chattanooga, July 18th, 1838---1---tf

PROSPECTUS
—OF THE—
Temperance Banner.

THE subscribers having been urgently solicited yb friends, and having given the subject mature deliberation, as they believe have consented to take the responsibility of editing and publishing the "Temperance Banner." This work, as the subscribers know, was commenced in May 1837, under the editorial superintendence of the Rev. D. Hoyt, who bid adieu to mortal scenes last August. Since that time the paper has been conducted by an association of gentlemen; one of whom will continue as co-editor. The Banner will advocate the doctrine of total abstinence from all intoxicating drinks;—except when rendered indispensible by the prescription of a regular physician, or necessary to the celebration of the Lord's Supper.

With party politics and sectarian differences and peculiarities it will not meddle.—Its appropriate sphere shall be an uncompromising and continual warfare against fermented and distilled liquors, under all their specious names and seducing garbs. We believe, the friends of the temperance cause, after having carefully examined the revolutionaries by dipping her handkerchief in the blood of an executed comrade. Decades after the Civil War, she insisted she be buried with the Confederate flag's stars and bars draped over her coffin.

That did not stop Julius from serving in the Union army. The two fought over the matter intensely their entire lives. "Mother [gave] father a lot of trouble," said Adolph, who learned early in life to distrust ideology and to work for a healthy compromise and seek harmony whenever possible, a trait he passed on to Chattanooga. Usually, "there [is] much to be said on both sides of most questions," the young man concluded.

Young Adolph Ochs

Adolph learned to work hard and stay out of trouble. He climbed his way up the ranks at the Knoxville paper—from delivery boy to floor sweeper to printer's apprentice to reporter—and gracefully tolerated nicknames like "Muley" Ochs, which derived from "ox," the literal meaning of his name. It also served as a backhanded compliment, since both animals are known for their prodigious output of labor.

It was that mulish work ethic that impressed Franc Paul, the former *Rebel* publisher, as well as *Knoxville Tribune* editor C. E. McGowan when they agreed to give 18-year-old Adolph one-third of the business in sweat equity for the new venture in Chattanooga.

"He came here as a very young man to start a newspaper, which they needed like a hole in the head," said Ruth Holmberg, his granddaughter. "He came here from Knoxville, and they started something called the *Chattanooga Dispatch*, and that failed."[7]

Mrs. Holmberg was perfectly gracious as we began the interview. I had no reason to be intimidated. "People are people," she later told me. "They're not much different if they're rich and famous."

The failure of Ochs's first venture with the *Chattanooga Dispatch* was related in large part to Franc Paul's addictions. Like many Civil War veterans, he was not only an alcoholic but also hooked on opium. The first issue of the *Dispatch* was nearly unreadable. Paul would not pay his employees unless they threatened to quit. When Adolph threatened to do so, he observed Paul in a pitiful state. "I just can't get along without you!" he cried. "No business can succeed without an Irishman or a Jew."

Drunk Frenchmen did not help. The business died. "He stayed here to clean up the debts," said Ruth. "He put out a city directory, which was the first city directory they ever had, and he met a lot of people as a result."

OCHS

Founder of the *New York Times* dynasty, Ochs coined the motto "All the news that's fit to print." He purchased the New York paper in 1896 as the 38-year-old publisher of the *Chattanooga Times*.

ADOLPH S. OCHS
1858–1935

IPHIGENE OCHS = **ARTHUR SULZBERGER**

RUTH SULZBERGER HOLMBERG
b. 1922

One of those people he met was S. A. Cunningham, owner of the *Chattanooga Daily Times,* which was in bad shape financially. Cunningham bought it from Thomas Payne and Zeboim Patten and still owed them money.[8] Adolph Ochs developed such trust with the creditors of the *Dispatch* that they appointed him as the receiver. Ironically, the man who owed the money was legally appointed to collect it. Cunningham so liked the honest and enterprising young man that he asked him to consider buying his paper, along with the remaining debt, for $800.[†] Ochs needed nearly half for a down payment.

"The *Chattanooga Times* was a struggling paper," said Ruth. "It was about nine years old [and] had very little circulation. He wanted to buy it and went to the bank to borrow $300."

"Do you have any collateral?" the banker asked him.

"No."

"Who could you get to cosign your note?" he asked.

"Nobody knows me better than you do," Adolph replied.

So the banker signed his note.

"I love that story," said Ruth.

"When he bought the *Chattanooga Times* he was 20 years old," she said. "His father had to come down [from Knoxville] to sign the papers because he wasn't old enough."

The deal involved a loan from a cousin in Louisville and a buyout of Cunningham's interest over a three-year period. Ochs persuaded McGowan to serve as editor for low wages early on, and four journeymen printers with the failed *Dispatch* agreed to do the same. They worked in a twenty-by-forty-foot, one-story brick shed at the corner of Eighth and Cherry, near the same spot where I interviewed Scotty Probasco at SunTrust Bank. The new publisher cranked out a revamped paper with several innovations. Most importantly, he proclaimed to Chattanooga, "We shall conduct our business on business principles."

Jon Meacham, today the managing editor of *Newsweek,* describes a century later how Ochs, starting with the *Chattanooga Times,* led the revolutionary change in journalism. "Until roughly the 1870s, American newspapers were essentially partisan, house organs for political parties or the whims of the publication's owner. There was no difference between the news and editorial columns: the entire paper was given over to provocative, necessarily unbalanced reporting. Ochs helped change that, deciding to keep the news columns evenhanded and confining overt political opinion to separate editorial pages."[9]

In his first issue as publisher, Ochs assured readers his paper would "move in line with the Conservative Democracy of the South." He also promised the paper

---

[†] $108,000 (2006)

would be "devoted to the material, educational, and moral growth of our progressive city and its surrounding territory."[10]

It was not long before Ochs's genius for management and promotion brought a healthy profit to the paper. In three years, he successfully bought out Cunningham, although the final price was three times higher than the original agreement.

Adolph Ochs was now in the position for which he had yearned: provider to his extended family and promoter for his new, adopted city. "I feel I am no longer a boy," he wrote confidentially to his cousin. "The mantle of fame and position rests on my shoulders; my parents, sisters and brothers around me sharing the fruits of my success." Several of them, including his parents, moved with him into a spacious home on Cameron Hill at Fifth and Cedar. Harry Adler, who married Ochs's sister Ada, was appointed head of the printing plant. His brother Milton Ochs took over as managing editor.

Milton married a "first-pew Presbyterian," raising eyebrows among some, but his wife, Fanny Van Dyke, rebuffed any hint at anti-Semitism. "These are my people," she insisted.

In fact, the sense of tolerance in Chattanooga was far greater than in most cities of the region. Adolph's brother, George Washington Ochs, was elected mayor twice. He did, however, change his name from Ochs to Oakes, some say to avoid German associations rather than Jewish. By 1878, only 773 of Chattanooga's 12,000 citizens were native-born, making the city an early version of New York's grand melting pot. "Chattanooga is not a Southern city nor a Northern city," said General Wilder, the postbellum mayor and manufacturing promoter. "One's politics, religion or section is not called into question here. This is the freest town on the map."[11] Such an attitude was welcomed by the Ochses, who had seen worse prejudice in Knoxville and other cities. Nevertheless, Adolph remained cautious. "We should live quietly, happily, unostentatiously," he told his fellow Jews at the Chattanooga Mizpah congregation, the city's first temple, which was dedicated by Adolph's father-in-law. "Don't be too smart. Don't know too much."

Ruth found it ironic that her grandfather helped establish the Mountain City Club, which later discriminated against Jews. She says discrimination still exists in Chattanooga and in New York. "It'll take another while . . . to make it gone," she said. "I see Jews appearing now in places where they certainly weren't when I was first here—clubs, Junior League, [etc.]. So, we are becoming more integrated in the community."

Scotty Probasco also sees improvement, but he agrees that problems still linger. "Yeah, you always have prejudice. There's no question about that."

George Washington Ochs (Oakes)

Scotty remembers vividly the time his father found out they had Jewish ancestry. "I'll never forget when my dad built this beautiful house back in 1929. It's still out there in Riverview, right on the river, thirteen acres. They were sitting in the den where they always sat before supper. I went in there and Dad was talking about the research he had done on the Probascos . . . how they left Spain due to religious persecution and then went to Holland."

"And Mother spoke. They were both having highballs. They would always have highballs before supper. Dad's was scotch and soda, and Mother's was bourbon and soda. And Mother said, 'Oh Scott, the Probascos were nothing but a bunch of Sephardic Jews.'"

"I thought Dad was going to die. I mean, in those days, prejudice ran a little higher. And I think, when you really look at it and analyze it, the Probascos were Jews. I'm proud of it."

"I love the Jewish people because, after all, they gave us God's word. Christ was a Jew. Of all those sixty-six people that gave us the Bible, only Luke wasn't a Jew."

"What was he?" I asked.

"He was . . . I don't know what he was. He was just a Christian."

"Okay."

"He was a Samaritan."

"Oh, okay."

"Or a something."

"All right."

"But I'm convinced I do have some chosen blood."

The Razzle-Dazzle Promoter

All things being equal, the relative tolerance of 19th century Chattanooga provided Adolph Ochs of German-Jewish ancestry with the freedom he needed to soar as a community promoter, perhaps his greatest gift. Circuses, amusement parks, fireworks, parades, and balls were all a part of his repertoire. He loved "the razzle-dazzle of the big show," as well as lavish Fourth of July celebrations or railcars filled with dignitaries and newsboys who distributed copies of the *Chattanooga Times* at every depot and farmhouse. He raised money to provide public access by incline to Lookout Mountain, and he raised even more money to keep the sides of the mountain covered in green trees. He was the major hand behind Chattanooga's Civil War reunion celebrations described in previous chapters. Before the grand reunion in 1895, he organized a promotion in 1886 for the iron and steel industry that included the largest gathering of U.S. congressmen and senators ever assembled outside of Washington, D.C.

Not all the promotions went as planned. He persuaded forty citizens to give $1,000 each to restore the old James Hall into a first-rate theater. When the debut for the new facility opened with the opera *The Princess of Trebizonde*, the rising curtain revealed a young lady wearing tights. Several in the audience got up and left.[12]

Some citizens in other cities tired of Ochs's boundless energy and enthusiasm for his hometown, a village that still suffered from muddy streets where cattle sometimes trod. "It is astounding how these Chattanooga fellows wade around in filth and blow and bellow," wrote one man from Morristown. "Probably it is because they have a good 'Ochs' to lead them. They 'hoop it up' as a major development every time a new peanut stand is opened."[13]

By and large, however, Ochs's reputation was growing steadily throughout the South. The *Augusta Chronicle* called him "one of the most enterprising men in the Southern press. He is ambitious for his city and tireless in his efforts to advance her interests and improve her connection."[14] While Scotty Probasco calls negative citizens "aginners," Ochs referred to anyone who opposed his municipal boosterism as "nay-saying croakers."

Perhaps his greatest publicity stunt, as a citizen of New York, evolved from a desire to add some sizzle to New Year's Eve celebrations. After fireworks were launched from his building on Times Square, Adolph concocted a scheme where a large illuminated globe was lowered down the flagpole and opened at the final tick of midnight to reveal the next number on the annual calendar. A century later, that New Year's Eve tradition at Times Square remains wildly popular.

Sam Divine called Ochs a "hustler."[15] The hustler's genius for promotion eventually caught up with him through his investments in Chattanooga real estate. He attracted investors on both sides of the Atlantic to purchase speculative lots on the north side of the river in today's Red Bank and Signal Mountain. As a partner in the Chattanooga Land, Coal, Iron and Railway Company, dubbed the Over-the-River Company, he persuaded everyone he could that the land filled with coal and iron reserves, which was about to be served by several bridges, was going to explode in value.

It did, thanks to Ochs's positive thinking. A tract for $800[†] bought in 1885 sold for $1,900 a year later and $30,000[§] the next year. Some deeds changed hands several times in a day. A Louisville relative criticized Adolph's "speculative tendencies," but the hustler was unfazed. "Gold-mine stock may be good, but I prefer Chattanooga real estate," he replied. Completely caught up in the euphoria, Adolph laid off one section of land and sold lots for "Timesville," with streets named after family and friends. "If you bought a full subscription to the paper for one dollar, you also got a

---

[†] $94,000 (2006)
[§] $3.5 million (2006)

plot of land," I was told by *New York Times* Vice Publisher Michael Golden, Ruth's son and the great-grandson of Adolph Ochs.[16]

Reality eventually hit the marketplace. Adolph unwisely secured one buyer's $103,000 note. A national economic panic arrived. Suddenly, the celebrated publisher and promoter found himself $500,000[†] in debt. Around this same time, Ochs was constructing the most extravagant structure in Chattanooga, the Dome Building. A six-story Italian Renaissance wonder with arched windows, cupola, and gold dome, it was Chattanooga's tallest edifice and still stands today. Adolph had already used the new facility for collateral on his real estate failures before issuing $300,000 in bonds from his Chattanooga Times company. When 10,000 people flocked to the dedication ceremony at Georgia and Eighth Street on December 8, 1892, most of them deduced from all appearances that Ochs was more successful than ever. As a plaque was handed to the publisher by Judge David Key, a few in the audience may have known better. This particular "razzle-dazzle" initiative was built by Ochs, some believed, precisely to conceal his wretched financial condition.

Over the years, the gold-domed cupola has captured the interest of various architectural scholars, but none of them knows exactly why Ochs added the unusual feature.[17]

Southern Rube Heads to New York

From 1891 to 1895, Ochs spent much of his time in New York seeking loans to solve his real estate woes. Nobody was interested. While staying in cheap hotels and walking to avoid carriage fare, he still refused to take small loans under $1,000.[§] "It looks bad," he told his brother.

Despite his severe financial problems, Adolph continued to flaunt a sense of prosperity and even voiced his desire to purchase another newspaper, especially one in New York. Thus, his reporter friend, Harry Alloway, felt it completely reasonable instead of absurd to inform him by telegram of an opportunity for a major purchase. The once credible but now bankrupting *New-York Times* was possibly available for sale.

Next to London, New York was the largest market in the world. The authors of *The Trust* write that it was "remarkable that as his situation became more and more desperate, Adolph decided to dig himself out of debt not only by acquiring another newspaper in order to generate income, but by acquiring a newspaper in New York . . . the biggest, most competitive and sophisticated market in the country."

"That he was drowning in debt and a southern rube . . . didn't faze him. On the contrary, it redoubled his resolve to 'overcome all difficulties and obstacles . . . at all hazard.' Like Houdini, Adolph delighted in making breathtaking

---

[†] $55 million (2006)
[§] $100,000 (2006)

The **Dome Bulding** still serves as one of Chattanooga's key icons.

escapes from seemingly doomed situations. 'I am of a queer make-up,' he told [his wife] in a rare moment of self-reflection. 'I am at my best in adversity.'"[18]

Alloway introduced Ochs to Charles Miller, president and editor of the *New-York Times*, just before Miller was to leave for a show at the theater. He quickly dismissed the idea of a small Southern publisher having the wherewithal for such a purchase. Adolph then offered his arguments. "Short and stocky, he was self-conscious speaking to large groups," according to *The Trust*, "but had a quietly commanding voice and a rare talent for seducing individuals on whom he focused his full attention. After years of extracting loans from skeptical bankers, he knew just what to say to convince his listener that he was honorable and trustworthy. So spellbinding was his power of persuasion that witnesses likened it to being hypnotized."

"Miller proved to be equally susceptible, and forgetting entirely about his theater engagement, he stayed up well past midnight listening to Adolph's plan to revive the *New-York Times* as an independent, Democratic paper."[19]

Miller then introduced Ochs to Charles Flint, the paper's most influential investor. Also mesmerized, he offered Adolph $50,000[†] a year to turn around the paper. Though privately Ochs admitted the massive salary was "most seductive," he turned Flint down, saying "he would not care to go into any property I did not control."

Flabbergasted but impressed, Flint introduced Ochs to the larger committee who demanded proof of his financial ability. For this trick, Adolph turned to his friends in Chattanooga. He asked a friendly creditor, Citizens' Savings Bank of Chattanooga, to temporarily place funds in his bank account. "I want some money to carry around with me so these people will think that I have it," he said. He would not use it, but he would have "the appearance of money behind him." It worked.[20]

Just as Ochs was reaching the goal, Flint made a move to retain his power at the paper and proposed a merger with *The New York Recorder*. The committee agreed, and Ochs was apparently defeated. However, editor Charles Miller, who stood to lose his job in a merger, teamed up with Ochs, and the two convinced three of the five members of the board of directors to put the paper in bankruptcy, making a merger impossible. Ochs met again with the committee, which then approved his previous proposal involving a conversion of stock, a bond issue, and a cash payment by Ochs of $75,000.[§] Adolph accomplished the stock conversion with the lead action of the *Times* top investor, the Gilded Age legend J. P. Morgan. Adolph met him at his 23 Wall Street office, and he promptly converted his $25,000 to Ochs's new arrangement in less than fifteen minutes of discussion. The others followed.

[†] $5.7 million (2006)
[§] 8.5 million (2006)

On August 13, 1896, the *Times* was sold at auction. Nearly penniless, Adolph needed $75,000 to complete his greatest scheme. *"I will win!"* he told his wife Effie. When the day arrived, Ochs purchased the paper for the starting price. There were no other bidders. "Adolph somehow managed to come up with $75,000. To the end of his life, he never revealed how he did so, and it remains a mystery," write the authors of *The Trust.* "The yokel from Tennessee had accomplished the impossible: he had bought the *New-York Times* using none of his own money. And if he kept his part of the agreement . . . he would effectively gain control of the *Times* for no personal stake except his hard work."[21]

Adolph immediately wired the news to his brother, George Ochs, who was running the *Chattanooga Times* in his absence. His brother broke down and wept. George wrote back, comparing his brother to "Napolean after Austerlitz . . . Washington after Yorktown, Wellington after Waterloo." His wife reminded him of where he had come from as "the little boy who tramped the streets of Knoxville . . . delivering papers."

Success and a Legacy

As with his Chattanooga paper, Adolph immediately made innovations to the *New York Times.* Pages of letters to the paper which disagreed with the editor were printed anyway, a radical concept. Book reviews became a popular feature. The appearance was overhauled for the better. Most importantly, he forged ahead with the professional journalistic philosophy that built credibility over the long haul. He created a slogan for the paper: "All the News That's Fit to Print." In his first issue as publisher, he promised to provide "a clean, dignified and trustworthy" paper. In a now-famous phrase, he said it was his earnest aim "to give the news impartially, without fear or favor, regardless of party, sect or interests involved." Newspapers across the country reprinted the high-minded aspiration. Other papers before promised to provide objective reporting apart from partisan sentiment. The difference, Adolph would later say, was that he actually believed what he said.[22]

Adolph Ochs

On the managerial side, Adolph slashed the number of employees at the paper. To avoid trouble, he showed the financials to the president of the printer's union, who agreed the massive layoffs were necessary. Firings included the foreman and the advertising manager, the latter so taken with Adolph's charm and warmth that he agreed to join him for dinner that evening. In a move that massively increased circulation, readership, and profits, Ochs dropped the price of the daily paper by two-thirds. Critics said it would ruin the *Times* to be associated with the sleazy penny press. Instead, it stole readers from Ochs's two main rivals, William Randolph Hearst and Joseph Pulitzer.

Four years later, Ochs had taken a debt-ridden company and earned a $1 million profit.[†] A few years later, he was one of the nation's richest men. All his early investors became wealthy.

Ochs tended to be conservative in dress and style, but his one extravagance was Hillendale, the sprawling mansion where he entertained the richest and most powerful people in the world. The 57-acre estate in White Plains boasted a 1,200-square foot-living room, 1,000-square-foot ballroom, and 1,000-square-foot library. The three-story, 32-room, colonial-style mansion also had marble floors, greenhouses, a private lake, a boathouse, tennis courts, a six-car garage, and a powder room larger than many bedrooms.

One of Adolph Ochs's most frequent visitors was his granddaughter, Ruth, who lived near Fifth Avenue with her three siblings, mother Iphigene, and father Arthur Sulzberger, who followed Adolph as publisher.

"Did you know your grandfather?" I asked Ruth Holmberg during our interview.

"Yes. I was thirteen when he died, so I knew him very well."

"Did you ever talk to your grandfather about the philosophy of journalism?"

"No. But we talked to him about what comics we wanted in the paper."

According to Ruth, Adolph spent a lot of time with his grandkids as he only had one child to spoil as a parent. "Oh, he loved children. He would come to see us every afternoon and bring us presents. So then, when my father came home, we weren't necessarily glad to see him. He told my mother to have her father stop bringing us presents every day or he was going to start competing. And there was a glorious period in our lifetime when [grandfather] would come around five o'clock with a present and my father would come at seven with another present."

"Tell me some more. I mean, not many people can talk about knowing Adolph Ochs personally."

"Well, he was very generous. The house was always full of relatives, hangers-on, people who claimed to be related. I have no idea if they were relatives or not. And we loved going to see him. We used to spend all summer up at their house."

Ruth and the Sulzbergers lived at 5 East Eightieth Street, half a block from Fifth Avenue and the Metropolitan Museum of Art. The five-story townhome, which included an elevator, was owned previously by the Rothschilds.

"Well, I grew up in New York and pretty much on a leash," said Ruth. "I wasn't allowed out of the house by myself under any circumstances."

"Because they were strict or because they were afraid of you getting stolen?"

[†] $108 million (2006)

"Well, both. And because New York is just not the right place for kids wandering around," said the woman who now chooses to reside in the more family-friendly Chattanooga. "We lived just a block from the park, but I wasn't allowed to go there by myself."

That problem was solved when Ruth turned 13, the year her grandfather died. The Sulzberger family packed up and moved to the country, to Adolph Ochs's mansion, called Hillendale. The Sulzbergers employed ten servants as well as a live-in cook and a chauffeur. In the evening, Iphigene would read Greek mythology aloud to her four children as her mother had done for her.

When she graduated from school, Ruth traveled to help soldiers in London during World War II and found herself in the midst of the Battle of Britain. After safely returning home and marrying Ben Golden, she returned to her grandfather's hometown, where her husband became the new publisher of the *Chattanooga Times*.

Several years earlier, in 1935, Adolph expressed a sudden desire to return to his hometown. "My grandfather always considered it home, and he died here on a return visit one day," said Ruth. "But when anybody asked him where he was from, he always said 'Chattanooga.' That was his home."

While eating breakfast with his brother at a cafe on Cherry Street, he suffered a stroke and died. The news was broadcast around the world. The international news wires agreed to remain silent for two minutes in honor of the great publisher. For decades, he had planned to be buried in Chattanooga but changed his final resting place to New York to be near his in-laws. He instructed the architects to use Tennessee marble for his crypt and to landscape with Tennessee flora.

Obstacles in Post-Ochs Chattanooga

Ruth and her husband entertained heartily at their Lookout Mountain home like the previous generations. But unlike her siblings in New York, and other contemporaries on Lookout Mountain who hired uniformed staff for their parties, Ruth served the guests herself and even asked them to help in the kitchen afterwards. Neither did she want hired help for her four children, Stephen, Michael, Lynn, and Arthur Golden. "My children are not going to be raised by nannies," she once told a cousin. "They are going to be raised by *me*."[23] That mentality made its impact on Stephen, the oldest. "There is a strong streak in Mother that the world doesn't owe you a living. The worst thing you can do is assume that there are things that are yours by right."

The children attended Lookout Mountain Elementary and private schools primarily, except when Stephen switched from Baylor to attend City High. The Sulzbergers had never been regular attenders at the synagogue, and the Goldens enjoyed celebrating Christian holidays by opening gifts under the tree at Christmas and hunting for eggs at Easter.

At their dinner parties, Ben Golden displayed a great knack for storytelling. "We'd laugh until we cried, he was that funny," said one acquaintance. Ben was Irish and sometimes took the kids to the Episcopal Church while Ruth hailed from a long line of leaders in Reformed Judaism, proudly Jewish but liberal and tolerant. In fact, Adolph's father-in-law Isaac Wise, Ruth's great-grandfather, founded Reformed Judaism in America.

The religious upbringing of Ruth's son, Michael Golden, was liberal enough to cause him surprise when some boys at Baylor made fun of him. "That I was Jewish was news to me," he said. His younger brother, Arthur, age seven, returned one day from a sleepover with a friend on Lookout Mountain. "Mom," he asked Ruth, "How come everybody in this family is Jewish but me, and I'm Presbyterian?"[†]

In fact, the religious tension in the Golden family was not the largest struggle. Like many fun-loving personalities, Ben Golden also struggled with substance abuse. He sought rehab for his alcoholism but continued to struggle. His wandering eye and abusive behavior finally led Ruth, the loyal one, to file for a divorce.[24*] Ben Golden died in Florida from emphysema five years later when Ruth's youngest child was 14. She paid for the funeral.

Overcoming the temptation toward bitterness a few years later, Ruth allowed a Golden in-law to interview her on camera along with her daughter, Lynn, and mother, Iphigene—three generations of the Ochs-Sulzberger clan. "What was the most significant event in your life?" they were each asked. For Mom, it was World War I. For Lynn, it was Vietnam. Even though Ruth suffered through the Battle of Britain, she courageously gave a more personal answer: "The most significant thing in my life," she said, "was my divorce."[25]

Ruth and Mr. Roy

There was a second reason that the word "divorce" summed up the 1960s for Ruth Sulzberger Golden. Not only did she find herself replacing her ex-husband as publisher of the *Chattanooga Times*, she also was faced with a major split in the publishing company. It drew national attention. "Divorce Chattanooga Style" ran the headline by *Newsweek* in its September 1966 article.[26]

Roy McDonald, a conservative Presbyterian, finally had enough of the "joint operating agreement" between his publication, the *Chattanooga Free Press*, and the *Chattanooga Times*. One of the first joint agreements of its kind in 1940, the two papers shared printing and advertising responsibilities, along with the profits, but maintained separate papers with their own reporters and editorialists.

"From the start, it was an unlikely match," wrote *Newsweek*, which called the story "man-bites-dog news" because the breakup was the first on record since the

---

[†] The grown-up Arthur Golden wrote the bestseller *Memoirs of a Geisha* (Alfed A. Knopf, 1997).

Justice Department began allowing such joint agreements. "The *Times*, taken over by patriarch Adolph S. Ochs in 1878, speaks in the well-modulated tones of enlightened, Eastern liberalism [while] the *News-Free Press* is caked in the Tennessee fundamentalism of owner Roy McDonald, 64 ('Mr. Roy' to the hired hands), an old-school champion of free enterprise who started the paper as a shopper's giveaway in his grocery chain 33 years ago."[27]

Roy McDonald

Ruth told me she had mixed feelings about Mr. Roy. "Well, personally, I thought he was very charming. But as a competitor, I couldn't bear him. Well, you know, there was a very narrow view."

Her assessment was more gracious than that of her older cousin, Julius Ochs, who once called McDonald "unspeakably unpalatable." *Newsweek* noted that McDonald considered TVA and FDR's New Deal unconstitutional, opposed Darwinism, and "once even characterized the Boston Tea Party as mob action by ruffians who destroyed private property." For his part, Mr. Roy seemed to enjoy fueling the stereotype, once quipping that he was "against progress in all its forms." His paper jabbed the Sulzberger's for sending *New York Times* executive Charles Puckette to help their sister paper. They were getting aid from "Communist-infested New York," the *Free Press* wrote. Others referred to the *Chattanooga Times* as "Pinky Puckette's Pravda."[28]

In the 1940 joint agreement, McDonald agreed to forgo a Sunday edition of the *Free Press,* and the *Times* agreed not to compete with McDonald's daily afternoon paper. Mr. Roy grew weary of the differing philosophies. "What disturbed McDonald was he thought the *Times* spent far too much space and money on national and international coverage while he concentrated on local events in a lighter fashion at less expense," wrote *Time* magazine. "Why should he pay half the cost of printing presidential speeches verbatim? Replied a *Times* man: 'We paid for half the Cub Scout pictures in the *Free Press.*'"[29]

At the end of the 1960s, the two major papers in Chattanooga were back to old-fashioned competition, parallel to the 1850s when the Union and the Confederacy each had a voice, or the days when Ruth's grandfather battled it out with Hearst and Pulitzer for primacy in New York. "I'm not worried," Ruth told *Newsweek*. "We've been in the newspaper business a long time, and we intend to stay."[30]

The McDonald Century

Roy McDonald's ancestors arrived in Sale Creek in 1821, two years after Hamilton County was established. They were not related to the area's first settler, John

McDonald of Inverness, but hailed from the more southern Glencoe, Scotland, at the foot of the Highlands. *McDonald* means "world ruler."

In 1923, Roy McDonald followed in his father's footsteps and started a grocery store. His father, Frank, operated a "Red Store" at the foot of Lookout Mountain near St. Elmo. He wore a red shirt while showing customers the day's specials, but later moved to Knoxville to start a chain of White Stores. Roy came back to Chattanooga to start a "Home Store" in 1923 at Fifth and Market Street, today's Jack's Alley and the former headquarters for the *Chattanooga Rebel*.[31] A few years later, there were seventy Home Stores in Chattanooga.

Traditional histories cite the origins of the *Chattanooga Free Press* as an advertising flyer printed by McDonald to promote his grocery chain. There was actually a more personal, particular reason for the business start, according to Lee Anderson, who delivered the *Free Press* starting at age nine in the Glendale neighborhood. Later, Anderson was named editor of the paper where he served for 50 years and also became Roy McDonald's son-in-law.

"In 1933, right at the depths of the Depression, Roy and Mrs. McDonald were scheduled to have a card game—a bridge game with a fellow who called on him from the *Chattanooga Times*," Anderson told me from his editor's office. The advertising salesman called to say he would be late and miss the card game. When he arrived, they asked what happened.

"Well, my problem was, I've just been fired."

"They can't do that to you."

"Roy, they've already done it. I'm fired."

"They can't do that to you," Roy repeated. "We'll start our own newspaper."

Lee Anderson said such behavior was typical of Mr. Roy. "He just decided to do something and did it . . . He adopted other people's problems. He was always trying to help somebody out. He was a strong, brusque personality that some people misunderstood, but he was big-hearted. He was trying to help that fellow out."

The ad salesman had two brothers in the publishing industry in Kansas. The plan was for them to finance the new paper with heavy advertising from Roy. That backfired, and the man backed away from the venture.

"By that time, Mr. Roy had gotten all excited and enthusiastic about it, and he started the *Free Press* anyhow, all by himself, in 1933," said Anderson. McDonald hired carriers to deliver around the area 65,000 papers full of nothing but advertising. About the same year that Adolph Ochs died, McDonald determined to make his weekly paper a daily and to add news articles and comics. He had a knack for what worked and for what people liked. They liked to see their picture in the paper. They liked to read about their local Kiwanis or Lion's Club or their children's ball teams and scout groups. Through dogged local coverage, conservative editorials, and a generous allotment of pictures, Roy McDonald found himself owning the largest daily newspaper in Chattanooga by 1942.

He had already bought out the *Chattanooga News* to form the *Chattanooga "News-Free" Press*, an ironic name that spawned decades of jokes.[†] The *News*'s owner, George Fort Milton, went down swinging. At one point, McDonald was found guilty by a jury for "restraining interstate commerce." In other words, Milton complained that a clause in the small print in McDonald's advertising contracts prohibited his clients from advertising elsewhere. Five of the six customers who testified said they did not know about the fine print when they signed up. Nevertheless, McDonald successfully eluded the legal problems (he was fined one cent) and bought out Milton's publication.[32]

To compete with the *Chattanooga Times*, McDonald sold his Home Stores, just as World War II began. "We were winning the war, but economically getting our brains beat out," said Anderson. By 1942, the McDonalds and the Ochses were both struggling. They agreed to join their papers and form one of the nation's first joint operating agreements. Over the years, the *Chattanooga News-Free Press* grew in popularity, exceeding its rival in subscriptions, and enjoying great financial success. But that was not his motivation, said Lee Anderson.

"Mr. Roy was never interested in wealth. He said that he realized he was a success the day he found out he owed $1 million. Money never meant anything to him. It was just a tool to do the things he wanted to do."

Mr. Roy drove an old Chevrolet. According to Anderson, Roy's grandson Roy Exum took the car one day to Newton Chevrolet to trade for a brand new one.

"I bought you a new car!" his grandson said.

"I want my old car back."

"Well . . . try it out."

Mr. Roy did not like the seat and did not think it felt right when he crossed a railroad track. He went back to the dealer.

"I want my old car back," he told them.

His wife would call Hardie & Caudle and have them send a new suit up to his office, but, according to Lee, he would keep wearing the old one until the seat wore out.

Mr. Roy did know how to use material things to motivate others, like the neighbor at his Sale Creek farm whose property he wanted to buy. "He pulled a red

---

[†] "News-Free" is now immortalized in Strunk and White's *Elements of Style*, one of the top-selling books of all time. After the entry "Hyphen" in the world-famous writing guide, they state, "The hyphen can play tricks on the unwary, as it did in Chattanooga when two papers merged—the *News* and the *Free Press*. Someone introduced a hyphen into the merger, and the paper became *The Chattanooga News-Free Press*, which sounds as though the paper were news-free, or devoid of news." (William Strunk, Jr. and E. B. White, *The Elements of Style*, Macmillian Publishing Company, New York, 1979, p. 35)

convertible up in front of this young girl's house and says, 'You can have this and so much for this plot here.' She hadn't wanted to sell but saw the red convertible. And so he expanded the farm to about 3,000 acres and lived there from 1950 to 1972."

Anderson recounted a conversation he had at a wedding reception with Mr. Roy and his banker.

"You know, I never mind paying interest, but I hate to pay principal," said Roy.

"Oh, Mr. Roy, you said that backwards," said Lee. "You mean you don't mind paying principal. It's the interest."

"No, I said it the way I meant it," replied Roy. Then he turned to his banker and introduced Lee Anderson. "This is my son-in-law, who doesn't believe in owing money."

Roy also believed in conservative principles. An avid member of First Presbyterian Church, he always hired editors with similar views, both politically and theologically. "He read a lot of history, biography," said Anderson. "He loved to read. That's where he got his real education. And he just developed conservative, constitutional economic principles and became quite adept at expressing himself that way." However, "in my many years of experience with him, he never told me what to write." But Anderson certainly wrote conservatively. The editorial page also included a daily Bible verse and extensive Christian commentary twice a year through detailed explanations of the Christmas and Easter stories.

The competing ideologies of the two newspapers clashed severely in the 1950s over segregation and civil rights. The *Free Press* editorialized against *Brown v. Board of Education,* which ordered the integrating of races in public schools. Meanwhile, the *Chattanooga Times* sent out John Popham of Virginia specifically to cover this major episode of the 20th century. Mr. Roy, however, said he was "almost ashamed" to share the same building as the *Times* after they supported the admission of the first black to the University of Mississippi.[33]

But such coverage may have been the *Chattanooga Times'* finest hour, according to Jon Meacham, who called the paper the "informal center of national coverage of the civil rights movement." Popham was the first full-time national reporter to cover the developments in the region, traveling 60,000 miles a year and mentoring the other national reporters who joined him.[34]

When the *Times,* after much internal disagreement, finally began running integrated obituaries, they quickly lost 3,000 subscribers to the *Free Press.*

"We were very strong supporters of the 1954 Supreme Court decision, which was a very unpopular position to take in this city," Ruth Holmberg told me. "And we lost a lot of circulation overnight over it. We pioneered for that, and we pioneered for liquor by the drink."

Maybe times had not changed so much since that first *Hamilton Gazette* newspaper in 1838. Then and now, the town argued over race, religion, and alcohol.

The *Free Press* refused to run liquor ads. Ironically, since they split all profits under the joint agreement, they made plenty of money off the liquor ads in the *Chattanooga Times*. But McDonald was willing to risk those benefits when he served notice to Ruth Holmberg in 1966 that he was ready to end the joint agreement. But he had a problem. The *Times* owned the building. Then, an "act of God" occurred, according to Mr. Roy, when the price of a building he had his eye on dropped from $1.5 million to $250,000.

Helen talks about it in her cookbook. "When *Time* and *Newsweek* came to report on our operation in 1966 . . . they printed in detail that my father felt his buying the old Davenport Hosiery Building for what he thought was a fraction of its worth, was an 'answer to prayer.'"

She calls her father, Roy McDonald, "Chattanooga's most unforgettable character."

"On this family newspaper, my father is publisher, my brother Frank McDonald is president, my brother-in-law Lee Anderson is editor, my husband Kinchen Exum is associate editor, my aunt Kitty McDonald writes a Sunday feature, I write a food feature and Sunday feature each week and there is a grandson in every department . . . This same story has been repeated over and over, with variations, as other Chattanooga families have built their businesses. It might be a store, a carpet factory, or a dry cleaners, but it gives a family a purpose."[35]

Competition by Roy

In the midst of his attempt to break the joint agreement in 1968, Roy McDonald was called to Washington D.C. to testify before a Senate Committee regarding a proposed law on joint newspaper operations. McDonald, with folksy chutzpah, seemed to enjoy his interaction with Tennessee Senator Albert Gore, Sr., a liberal Democrat:

SENATOR HART: The committee will be in order. Mr. McDonald?

MR. MCDONALD: My name is Roy McDonald . . . I am age 66 and reside in Sale Creek, Tennessee, near Chattanooga . . .

I think we are going to be successful. Why? Well, I have a local newspaper. I have that hillbilly touch, perhaps. Senator, I think I know what people in Chattanooga want in the way of a newspaper. I think I know the editorial position that will be largely supported by those people, and I think that over the years they have come around to our viewpoint—that of being a conservative newspaper.

SENATOR GORE: Mr. Chairman, this is the goal, it seems to me, toward which the

Committee or the Congress should strive: the preservation of editorial competition within communities . . .

SENATOR HART: Well, the case history, exhibit Chattanooga, establishes that competition and two independent papers is possible without this bill.

MR. McDONALD: Yes, sir. I think so. I plan to be there regardless of what you do about the bill. I plan to be there with my flag flying every day.

SENATOR GORE: Why do you not fly mine down there?

MR. McDONALD: I will, when you can get to where you can accept my viewpoint.

(Laughter)

MR. McDONALD: I think there will always be two papers in Chattanooga, regardless.

SENATOR GORE: Beg pardon?

MR. McDONALD: I think there will always be two papers in Chattanooga.

SENATOR GORE: And you think this would be desirable?

MR. McDONALD: I do, indeed.

SENATOR GORE: Then, we agree on this.[36]

So Roy McDonald once again published a Sunday paper. And, once again, the *Chattanooga Times* started an evening paper in direct competition with the *Free Press*. Mr. Roy did indeed have that hillbilly touch, and soon the *Chattanooga Times* was losing more than $1 million a year. To add to their problems, Mr. Roy won a $2.5 million antitrust suit from the Justice Department after the *Times* offered advertisers space in both papers for the price of one.

Competition was fierce. "We were constantly conniving all day long what to do," said Lee Anderson, "not only putting out the paper, but how to keep it afloat."

By the late '70s, McDonald's circulation was rising. Ruth Holmberg (who remarried a *Times* employee, William Holmberg) continued to watch millions pour into the paper from the Ochs family trust. She and Bill had dinner with their son and daughter-in-law each evening. "The topic was always the same: the worrisome state of the *Chattanooga Times* and the scurrilous tactics and shoddy journalism of the *Free Press*," the daughter-in-law told the authors of *The Trust*. Remembering their frustration, she said sardonically, "We'd wish for Mr. Roy to die; that was the daily prayer."[37]

Ironically, it may have been a living Roy McDonald, the one who testified that it was better to have two papers in town, that kept the *Chattanooga Times* alive for another two decades. *New York Times* publisher Punch Sulzberger sent his best executive, Sydney Gruson, to meet with Mr. Roy in 1980. Punch, Ruth's brother, had seen more than $6 million flow from the Ochs Trust to their paper in

Roy McDonald enjoys the power of his printing press.

Chattanooga. "My Vietnam," he called it. Punch decided he had done enough, but he told his emissary to start the discussions with a bluff. Gruson told McDonald that if he did not agree to a new joint operating agreement, "we will put all the resources of the *New York Times* behind saving the *Chattanooga Times*." Mr. Roy had heard this same threat in decades past and never blinked. This time, however, he agreed. But Roy said they must discontinue their Sunday paper and give him total control over the joint publishing company. *Time* magazine's correspondent called it a surrender. The reporter wrote to his editor, "Crusty, old Roy McDonald, the out-spoken, ultra-conservative publisher of the *Chattanooga News-Free Press*, has finally put to rest the ghost of Adolph Ochs."

Not quite. The *Chattanooga Times* and its journalistic tradition, thanks to Mr. Roy's agreement, continued to be distributed each morning in Adolph Ochs's hometown.

During those years of fierce competition, Roy and Lee received a phone call from a young man in Arkansas. Walter Hussman was facing a similar battle in Little Rock with another newspaper giant, the Gannett Company, owner of *USA Today*. Roy and Lee gave Walter some good tips, and Hussman's *Arkansas Democrat-Gazette* came out the winner. When Mr. Roy died in 1990, family members were ready to sell the paper. Rather than approach a national giant, they sold quietly to their friend in Arkansas. Hussman, however, had ambitions that, for some reason, Mr. Roy never held, or at least never acted upon. Hussman insisted he would have to buy that other paper in town as well. In 1998, the *Chattanooga Times* finally acquiesced.

"He is a nice fellow," said Ruth. "I think he is much more conservative than I am, but then so are a lot of other people."

The Ochs-Sulzbergers distributed their final issue of the *Chattanooga Times* after over 100 years of noted journalism in Chattanooga. The two papers were consolidated as the *Chattanooga Times Free Press* (the first joint issue was published January 5, 1999). The Ochs tradition deferred to the superior leverage of Walter Hussman, the man who had bought the *Free Press* after Mr. Roy died.

They laid McDonald plaid over Mr. Roy's coffin, said Lee Anderson. "He died at the age of 88 after putting in a twelve-hour day the day before. He carried a pair of scissors in his back pocket and would take those scissors, cut out tape that was being printed out, and set the type for the headlines. That's what he liked to do. Then he would go down to the mailroom and stand there with a bunch of black folks and stuff the inserts as it came off the line. And he put in a twelve-hour day, went home, got up the next morning and showered and shaved, dressed and sat down on a chair and went to sleep—which is the way he would have wanted to do it."

'The Lingering Spirit of Adolph Ochs

Postmortem, the Scottish son of the McDonald world rulers had taken away Ochs's prized possession in Chattanooga. But material things were never Adolph's chief concern. As he wrote at the early age of 17 in his handwritten autograph book: "Who steals my purse, steals trash," he said. "But he who steals my good name . . . makes me poor indeed."[38]

The Och's reputation and tradition continues in Chattanooga today. The Ochs-Sulzberger clan (affectionately dubbed "Oxen" by the matriarch, Iphigene) all meet together twice a year, once in New York and once elsewhere. Several times the group, considered by some as "the most powerful blood-related clan in 20th century America," has gathered in Chattanooga and will continue to do so.

"Where do you meet here?" I asked Ruth.

"At my house." (She now resides on Elder Mountain.)

"Did ya'll go out on the town anywhere?"

"Oh yeah. We went everywhere—the Aquarium, the park, the boat on the river."

"Where did you go to eat?"

"We went to the La Dolce Vita when it was still here. And, let's see . . . we had Sticky Fingers catered up to the house."

"We are a very close family," she said. "We meet all the time. We have a family reunion every fall."

While the Ochs tradition remains strong here, the name itself has expired. (Adolph once suggested to his brother's son, Adolph Shelby Ochs, to call himself Adolph Ochs, Jr.[39]) Of course, the original name was "Ochsenhorn."[40] While the plow attached to the Ochs family is with Chattanooga no longer, the horn or voice of Adolph continues with us, primarily through his greatest love: civic promotion. In fact, his granddaughter, who grew up a block from the Metropolitan Museum of Art, provided the largest gift by an individual to the $120 million 21st Century Waterfront Project, which includes a major expansion to the Hunter Museum of Art.[41] Mayor Bob Corker surprised Ruth and her husband, Bill Holmberg, during the unveiling of the glass pedestrian bridge over Riverfront Parkway. It now connects Walnut Street Bridge to the Hunter Museum, which historically struggled with being isolated from the rest of the downtown attractions.

"Ruth said the Hunter Museum needs to come off the hill and into the city," said Corker, so the city named it the Holmberg Bridge. "Surprised" is an underrated word," Ruth said, who used terms like "astounded" and "floored" to describe her reaction.[42]

The term was appropriate. According to the *Dictionary of American Family Names*, "Holmberg" means "island on a hill." Ruth Holmberg was merely carrying on the tradition of her ancestor, whose great love was building a city. Adolph Ochs himself, who had the blood of that original city-builder flowing through his veins, was carrying on a more ancient tradition. As Scripture tells us, Abraham "was looking forward to the city with foundations, whose architect and builder is God."[43]

Artist: Justin Cox

CHAPTER SEVEN

The Spirit of the Bible Belt

Family Values, Fundamentalists, and "Holy Fools"

In 1982, Chattanooga's Highland Park Baptist Church boasted 57,325 members. According to many accounts, it was at that time the largest church in the world.

Jerry Falwell dedicated his book, *The Fundamentalist Phenomenon*, to Highland Park's longtime pastor, Dr. Lee Roberson, who grew the gigantic church.

Highland Park's own history describes Roberson as "unashamed of his fundamentalist convictions" and one who "boldly preached separation from worldliness—defined as movies, dancing, smoking, drinking, etc., premillenialism, the inerrancy of Scripture, evangelism and a deep loyalty and faithfulness to the program of the local church."[1]

"We don't know what to do with Highland Park," said Doug Daugherty, president of the Chattanooga Resource Foundation. "How do you become the biggest church in the world in Chattanooga?"

A staff member explained it to him. "They had thirty-some chapels [in the Chattanooga region]," said Daugherty, "and some of them were whole churches, large churches . . . their students were members and missionaries were members. They have this focus on local church government, so everything that comes out of that church stays under the church. So that's the thinking."

"I later found out that during the period of time he was talking about, that it actually made it the largest church in the world . . . and I have no reason to disbelieve it."

"It was a reaction in one sense, but this can be said of all Protestant faiths. It was a reaction to Modernism in the 1930s. They had a spectacular guy, Dr. Roberson, who was an extremely focused individual. He was just focused with almost a military passion on a few things. And that's really how most churches get big, or most anything really gets big like that—usually there is one person focused on a few things. And he did that."

Over the years, the church and its school, Tennessee Temple, declined. "I think their church had gotten down below 500 members," said Daugherty. "At one time I think their student body was nearly 5,000. I think it got to less than 1,000. [But] they have gotten back to focus on their primary mission, which was soul winning. I mean, it's just a soul-winning machine. I don't know of a church that actually does it better."

Knocking on Every Door in Chattanooga

An interview with Lee Roberson was too important to miss. I met him in a small office across the street from Highland Park Baptist. Roberson was born in a two-room log cabin in Indiana in 1909 and came to Highland Park in 1942. He stood to greet me, a strong, healthy, and lucid 94-year-old.

Highland Park and Tennessee Temple, to the larger community, are often associated with conservative dress, suits for the men, dresses and long hair for the women. Many recall those same men in dark suits preaching in the streets or knocking on doors around the city. Dr. Roberson did not break the stereotype.

"You're wearing a suit," I said. "Do you always wear a suit?"

"Always. Always double breasted. Always the same color my whole lifetime."

"Is that more of a personal preference?" I asked.

"Personal preference, yes sir. I've always had it, just a part of my life. As a boy I started wearing double-breasted suits."

"There's a book I just read called *The World's Largest Church*. Now, is that true?"

"It was at one time. Yes. At one time it had the largest membership of any church in the world. That was done by inspection of certain men who knew churches, who knew denominations. And as a single church, it had the largest membership for a long, long time. For many years."

Roberson admits that he has always been concerned about numbers. But he says he also cares about individuals. "One is a number. One soul is a number, and I am interested in reaching as many souls for Jesus as possible."[2]

I asked him how his church grew so large.

"Every Thursday night about 200 of our people would go out visiting, door-to-door, and we covered much of the city. . . . We kept growing and took a survey of Chattanooga, all of it. I wrote letters to all the people who were unchurched, who did not belong to any church at all, and invited them to be with us. The letter paid off."

"How did you survey the whole community?"

"I hired a man. A man named Carlyle Brooks. A little fellow, very talented man who knew how to talk to people and went door-to-door."

"The whole city?" I asked.

"The whole city. Every bit of it. Didn't miss a soul."

"In person?"

"Yeah. One man."

"How long did it take him?"

"Oh, it took him a couple of years, and he didn't stop. He kept going every day. Very quiet little fellow. I can hear his voice, a very quiet, beautiful voice. He'd say, 'Friend, I'm doing some visiting. I'd like to ask you, where do you attend church?' They'd say, 'Well, we don't go anywhere.' He'd say, 'Oh, I see.'"

"And then he would get the name and address and write it on a card after he left the home. I began writing letters to the people, and most of the responses were good. I had a few that resented it some and said, 'We don't care for the letter. We're not interested in your church. We're not Baptist.' . . . But we sent a letter everywhere."

"We began with the old church on the corner, and it seats around 400. Then I built a sawdust-floor tabernacle across the street. It seated about 1,100 people. . . . I think that had a lot to do with helping us. It made us known. It was so unusual for a church to have a tabernacle, a sawdust floor-tabernacle in a city of this size, and I think that brought people to us. . . . We stayed there four or five years and then we moved into this building here, which seats up to 7,500."

"That guy went to every house in Chattanooga?"

"Oh, yes. We covered them all. We covered every home in the city."

Ecclesiastical Harmony: Fowle and the Fundamentalist

With such a broad grasp of the population, I asked him the next logical question. "So, what are Chattanooga people like?"

"That's a good question," Roberson said. "This city is above all others I know for Christian atmosphere, a love for churches of all denominations. Not just Baptist, but all denominations. It's different from any other. I've been in most of the major cities in America. I've preached in almost all of them. . . . there's a friendliness here toward the ministry that you do not find in many cities. I think it's exceptional, and that's to the credit of the people, of the gentility. A quiet acceptance of the denominations. There's not the rebellious fightings here among the denominations that you'll find in some places. I never found it here. A rather quiet acceptance. Every man would have his place and no one trying to overrun the other person, a very quiet acceptance."

Lee Roberson

"Do you have any idea why the people here are that way?"

"No, I do not. Except for my simple statement—I give it over and over again: Everything rises upon leadership. I think the leadership of the city has been the reason. Leadership in the churches, pastors. Leadership in the mayor's office."

And how did the world's largest church get along with the city's most prominent church, First Presbyterian? I wondered.

"Did you know Dr. Fowle?" I asked.

"Oh yeah. Knew him well."

"Tell me about him."

"Gracious man. Good man. And a good preacher. And loved people. That's the biggest thing about him, he loved people. A very quiet man. He wasn't noisy or vociferous. He was quiet and dignified. But people loved him everywhere and had great respect for him. He meant much to the city."

I noticed Dr. Roberson started to cry as he spoke about the First Presbyterian pastor. I could not resist asking, "Why do you tear up when you talk about Dr. Fowle?"

"Beg your pardon?"

"I think I saw you tear up a little bit. Why is that?"

"Well, he was a friend of mine. That's right. He'd come to see me and I'd go see him, and we had a good friendship together. Different denominations altogether. But his atmosphere and attitude toward people—you couldn't escape that. And they loved him. People loved him."

Dr. Roberson is also a gracious man, simple, and straightforward. Despite the stereotypes associated with Fundamentalists, he left a rather positive impression.

"I've had a great time in Chattanooga," he said. "I love this city."

The Facts on a Fundamentalist City

Doug Daugherty continues to admire the work of Highland Park. "We make fun of people knocking on doors and stuff. But I have friends, you know, where that's what changed their life. It's pretty remarkable when you think about it. I'm a Christian and I like to see people get saved and become Christians. I bet that 50 to 80 percent of the conversions in Chattanooga every year take place through the work and ministry of Highland Park."

He said Highland Park is the second highest spot in the area. "I actually found an old Civil War map. They called it something like Warrior's Hill. I'm the kind of person that sort of thinks, well, there was something invested in this place of fighting a fight and winning a fight. . . . And I think there's a blessing on this city. I think there's a grace on this city. Maybe some people would reduce it to sheer geography, but this city seems to have a capacity for starting things that go out. I think Highland Park is one of those things. The Highland Park model and the missionaries and everybody that went out—tremendous, tremendous influence for the good of the whole world."

According to the Barna Research Group in Ventura, California, the nation's most respected Christian polling organization, 94 percent of Chattanoogans call themselves Christians, and 86 percent said they had made a commitment to Jesus Christ that is still important in their life. Baptists make up more that 51 percent of the area Christians, followed by Methodists, Presbyterians, and Church of God, which are each at around 6 or 7 percent.

A poll by the Mason-Dixon Research firm, commissioned by the *Chattanooga Times* and WTVC-TV (New Channel 9) showed 43 percent of Chattanoogans believe wives should submit to their husbands, 66 percent believe it is wrong to have sexual intercourse before marriage; 97 percent believe in heaven, and 95 percent believe in hell. According to the Barna survey, Chattanooga has the highest number of "born-again" Christians per capita of any other city of comparable or larger size.

"It's like 64 percent," said Daugherty, whose organization hired the research firm to poll Chattanooga. "It's a huge number. The number of people who believe in God is like 98 percent." He said 79 percent told someone in the past year that Jesus Christ was their Savior.

Local news services also quoted the Glenmary Research Center, which showed that Chattanooga, with over 500 churches, boasts 50 percent more church attendance than the rest of the nation. This is not just a Southern thing. Hamilton Countians also attend church at a significantly higher rate than all the surrounding counties.[3]

"There was a marketing team that came here about ten years ago, and they were trying to figure out what people did around here for recreation," said Daugherty, "and the number one thing that came back was Bible reading. They didn't even know what to do with it."

Chattanooga: A City for God

Is Chattanooga a "Christian city"? Daugherty is comfortable using statistics to show Chattanooga is more particularly Christian than other cities, but he never used the term "Christian city" during our interview. He runs a foundation whose mission is "Chattanooga: A City for God." Board members include the likes of Hugh O. Maclellan, Frank Brock, Sam Smartt, and Senator David Fowler.

Tom McCallie, executive director of the Maclellan Foundation, avoids the "Christian city" moniker.

"I'm not sure you're a Christian city or a Christian foundation. I think you're a city of Christians that have a Christian ethos . . . that tries to do things in the way that would glorify Christ," he said. "I think there is a historical context to Chattanooga that has Christian underpinning roots. My concept is that if things can't be done here, they probably can't be done anywhere from a Christian perspective. This is a unique city."

Tennessee State Senator David Fowler, a Signal Mountain resident, also shies away from the term "Christian city" for Chattanooga.

"It's a town that I think is, by and large, family friendly. I mean, what other cities would have a Christian night at Riverbend and have 100,000 people show up? What other cities would have a National Day of Prayer event and get 20,000 people to show up at a football stadium under a pending lightning storm? Not to say we're a 'Christian city' or that we're all pure and innocent. We have our adult bookstores and other things. But, by and large, there's an appreciation and respect for families and, as trite as it sounds, more traditional values."

Fowler says the legislative delegation from Chattanooga is probably considered to be the most conservative in the state with Knoxville's a close second. Senator Fowler is a graduate of McCallie, UTC, and the University of Cincinnati Law School, thanks to the Chapin-Thomas Scholarship awarded each year to a UTC student. The media has quoted Fowler often where he takes a strong conservative position on moral issues such as same-sex marriages, the lottery, and the Ten Commandments. He gained international attention for his quotes related to a bill to advance creation vs. evolution in public schools. His position was more moderate than the bill sponsors, who called for removing those who teach evolution. Fowler advocated teaching both views. He was quoted in the *New York Times*, and the *BBC* interviewed him for their version of *60 Minutes* in Great Britain.[4]

David Fowler   **Doug Daugherty**   **Tom McCallie**

"My point wasn't so much to fire teachers for teaching evolution as a fact. It was to protect teachers who chose to let their students understand that there's a raging debate going on out there about the demise of Darwinism," he said.

The Monkey Trials

Fowler's position, in fact, was the same as that of William Jennings Bryan, the famous Creation advocate during the 1925 Scopes trials in nearby Dayton, Tennessee (forty miles away). Bryan actually disagreed with the Tennessee statute he defended. He backed resolutions in other states opposing evolution but disagreed with Tennessee's law, which made it criminal. Nevertheless, the high-profile nature of the trial led Bryan to travel to Dayton to participate in what became known as "the Trial of the Century."

It actually began as a strategy for economic growth by a few Dayton leaders at F. E. Robinson's drugstore. If they could find a local teacher violating the law, a big trial in their small town would boost revenue. Robinson, also the town's school superintendent, grabbed biology teacher John Scopes who was out playing tennis and asked if he'd play such a role.

"I said, 'Have at it,'" Scopes explained in an interview years later. "He just reached back across the counter in his drugstore and called the Chattanooga paper and says, 'I've arrested the fella who violated the Butler Act.'"[5]

When the famous criminal attorney, Clarence Darrow, a proud agnostic, agreed to represent Scopes, the media circus began. His opponent would be William Jennings Bryan, twice the runner-up for President and most recently the Secretary of State under Woodrow Wilson. He also taught the largest Sunday School class in America.[6*]

It would take a few months for the trial to occur. Chattanooga leaders recognized the enormous box office potential and tried to have the big show moved to Memorial Auditorium. When that failed, they tried to get a Chattanooga teacher to stand trial. The Dayton promoters successfully countered by conducting a special grand jury hearing to expedite the process in Dayton.[7]

The Dayton men were not disappointed. During the Scopes trials, visitors came from far and wide. Vendors sold food and trinkets outside the courthouse, and some even paraded monkeys along the sidewalk. The trial of the century was also known as the "Monkey Trials," and more words were transferred across the Atlantic about this event than any other, including the battles of World War I.

The trial reached its climax when Bryan and Darrow agreed to question each other on the courthouse lawn—the standard legal process giving way to everyone's demand for a public spectacle. As the agnostic Darrow tore into Bryan for his Fundamentalist views, the Attorney General finally arose to say, "What is the purpose of this examination?"

"The purpose is to cast ridicule on everybody who believes in the Bible!" Bryan exclaimed.

Darrow shot back. "We have the purpose of preventing bigots and ignoramuses from controlling the education of the United States!"

On the weekends, the media and major players of the trial retreated back to Chattanooga. Famous columnist H. L. Mencken, who constantly mocked the backward Tennesseans and said Dayton's water was unfit to drink, admitted that Chattanooga contained a "civilized minority."

In Chattanooga, Darrow lectured to large crowds on Tolstoy, one of his favorite subjects. He also read *The Significance of Existence* by I. Harris, according to a letter he wrote to my great-grandfather, Dr. Perceval Gerson, also a self-proclaimed atheist. Darrow and his wife Ruby were regular guests at the Hollywood, California, home of the medical doctor who sometimes urged Darrow to limit his alcohol intake. At the Gersons, the Darrows enjoyed lectures and lengthy visits from the likes of author Upton Sinclair, Planned Parenthood founder Margaret Sanger, and Emma Goldman, a promoter of anarchy and Bolshevism who was popularized in the movie *Reds*.

When the Scopes trial finally ended, the jury deliberated for only nine minutes. They pronounced the biology teacher guilty. The Tennessee Supreme Court, however, overturned his sentence on a technicality. The law itself stayed on the books but was left unenforced until it was finally repealed in 1967.

Five days after the trial, William Jennings Bryan died during an afternoon nap in Dayton. Bryan College, founded in his honor, began in the closed high school building where Scopes once taught. The conservative Bible college used his lab table for several years.

Years later, Darrow was indicted for jury tampering but eluded conviction. To his dismay, even his longtime friend, Dr. Gerson, believed he was guilty. "None of your friends blame you for what you did, Clarence," the doctor said before their group of artists and thinkers. "If you are guilty, what of it? You had to fight the devil with fire."[8]

While visiting business colleagues in the North, Scotty Probasco was often reminded of Chattanooga's Christian bent. "I used to get some ragging from those fellows," he said. "Of course, I was a Christian. I liked to have a blessing before supper. They didn't have much of that. 'Oh Scotty, you're down there in the heart of the Bible Belt,' they would say. My answer was, 'Chattanooga is the buckle of the Bible Belt,' and I mean that. We've had a tremendously strong Christian heritage and background in the community. . . . It's a giving community, a caring community."

Indeed, Chattanooga for many years has been among the nation's top cities for United Way giving and has actually been the number one city some of those years. Chattanooga's giving is almost double the national average, but it is not just those near-billionaires making it happen. Nearly three-fourths of the contributions come from individuals and small donors as opposed to corporations and foundations.[9]

"The secret of the United Way was the payroll deduction," said Daugherty. "You had a lot of manufacturers—everybody did payroll deductions. So, if you had the leadership, and you've got 5,000 manufacturing employees at Combustion or whatever, you're talking about a lot of money."

Probasco agrees. "That's the leadership of this community. How do you think they [became] one of the top three or four cities in the United States for the United Way?"

"Actually, at the top for a while," I said.

"We're still way up there."

"Right."

"That comes from the leadership of the power structure with a heart for people, for meeting needs."

"Where do you think that comes from?" I asked.

"It comes from the fact that we're the buckle of the Bible Belt. That's my opinion. That's my answer."

Christians and Politics

With so many people in Chattanooga calling themselves Christians, one would expect to see a good amount of charity and volunteer service here, said Daugherty. "The quantitative fact is that it's true," he said. He corroborated his belief by going through every single call taken for a year by the organization First Call for Help, a clearinghouse and referral center for people who need food, clothing, shelter, counseling, etc. "It's amazing. Three-fourths of all the organizations that respond to human need in Chattanooga are religious based. Most of them are Christian. We have a very high rate of civic virtue. If you could somehow measure that, we would have one of the highest percentages of civic virtue, I suspect, in the nation."

At this point Daugherty made some odd connections between the railroad and the city's essence. "This gets a little more far out, but I think there is a sense of sending. There's a sense of moving through. There are the train tracks that go through here, the river that goes through here, the interstates that go through here because we've got a break in the mountains. This is a transportation place, a place you pass through on the way to somewhere else. It's a sending place. I think that idea is even in the—it's the—sort of the DNA of the city . . . service and doing and helping."

Daugherty does explain that this Christian influence in Chattanooga is not a panacea. "There are some behaviors that it has affected a lot and some that it has not. It's not like the culture is saying, 'Okay, you think Jesus is God, now do this or act this way or be this way.' They're saying that sex is the number one thing or romance is the number one thing, or materialism . . . or friends . . . or music."

It has taken many years for this gigantic religious majority to flex its muscles politically. Years ago, Daugherty ran the congressional campaign for Jim Golden, who lost to Democrat incumbent Marilyn Lloyd in 1986. Golden was a member of the Church of God, which avoided hardball politics like most other denominations.

"This was one of the reasons he ran," said Daugherty. "There was this think-ing—a whole sense of separation and holiness and what is good and bad. And it was not good in the late 1900s and early 20th century to be involved in government and stuff like that. They supported a virtuous community, but they wouldn't have been involved in the leadership at all."

Those folks traditionally did not vote, he said, whearas 80 percent or more of Presbyterians and Anglicans[†] went to the polls. "If it were a graph, on one end you'd have the Church of God and then I would say Baptist, Methodist and [the other end] would be Presbyterian and Anglican."

Those trends changed due to efforts like Golden's campaign, which reflected larger, national trends of religious, political involvement sparked by the pro-life movement and groups like the Christian Coalition. These groups helped move Chattanooga and Hamilton County from being majority Democrat to majority Re-publican in a ten-year period. The key year was 1994, when Republicans challenged every countywide Democrat incumbent and elected stalwart Republican conserva-tives like Senator David Fowler and Congressman Zach Wamp, who scored 100 with the American Conservative Union.

"There's no doubt that the people of East Tennessee, Democrats and Re-publicans, trend more conservative and have a biblical worldview as opposed to a humanistic worldview," Wamp told me. "We always say that in East Tennessee the three issues that matter most are Bibles, babies, and guns."[10]

He believes the Chattanooga area is more conservative than the rest of East Tennessee. "Mountain Republicans are a more populist bunch. They're not as evangelical, and they're not as socially conservative as people from Southeast Ten-nessee. This area is still very socially conservative."

The Nation's Largest City With No Abortion Clinic

The pro-life movement in Chattanooga not only solidified the conservative Republicans and provided new elected officials, it won a major, tangible local

---

[†] Anglican and Episcopal are treated as interchangeable terms in this book.

victory for its cause by shutting down all abortion clinics in the area. Chatta-nooga is now considered the largest city in America without an abortion clinic.[11]

Simple picketing in the late '80s persuaded Erlanger Hospital to end its abortion services. Eventually, the lone abortion option was the Chattanooga Women's Clinic on Vance Road behind Sam's on Lee Highway. Eighteen years of activism ensued across the street from the clinic in the form of marches, prayer vigils, preaching, sidewalk counseling, communion services "to atone for the shedding of innocent blood," 10,000-person demonstrations, and medical malpractice lawsuits. Activists like Daugherty's wife, Sally, blocked the clinic's doors and were dragged away by police and thrown in jail.

Still, as in all other cities, the abortion clinic remained. One day the bankrupt owner of the building told his realtor, Chet DeVaney, he wanted to sell. DeVaney reviewed the lease and immediately informed pro-life attorneys that the property could be purchased at auction. The new owners could name new tenants. The pro-lifers raised $280,000 in seven days, and the abortionists were shown the door.

AAA Women's Services moved in. It had been the crisis pregnancy center across the street formed years before by Daugherty, Dr. Dennis Bizzoco, Charles Wysong, and their wives. As the movement grew, PROMACC was formed, the Pro-Life Majority Coalition of Chattanooga. This was the entity that bought the clinic. One-half of the building, the part where the abortions were performed, was bulldozed to the ground and replaced with the National Memorial for the Unborn.[12]

"People come mostly at night to this place," wrote the *Washington Times* in 1997, "walking past an unlocked gate to a 50-foot wall to lay bouquets and baby dolls on a small ledge."

"[The memorial] includes a wall bearing 600 plaques with the names of the aborted. One woman . . . leaves a card to 'Abigail.'"

"God gave me your name last summer. [He] has given me a wonderful husband who would've loved you as his own. Please forgive me."[13]

Women from forty-eight states have sent in plaques to hang on the memorial's wall:

Baby Jones. Spring 1978: "We Loved You Too Late."

Jesse Banks. 1975: "Someday . . . Love, Grandma."

Elizabeth April. August 1984: "I'll Hold You in Heaven."

Thirty-five thousand abortions took place on the site that is now a memorial. "What was once a place of immeasurable sadness and despair is now a place of hope and healing," said Pat Lindley, a spokeswoman for PROMMAC. "A lot of people have drawn parallels between the Vietnam Veterans Wall and this, saying these children are a victim of a culture war," she told the *Washington Times*.

Jane Roe Reverses History in Chattanooga

Another plaque on the wall is from the most famous of all women associated with abortion, Norma McCorvey, better known as Jane Roe of *Roe v. Wade*, who visited the site in March 1997.

"Today, I publicly recant my involvement in the tragedy of abortion," the plaque says. "I humbly ask forgiveness of the millions of women and unborn babies who have experienced the violence of an abortion. In this place of healing, the National Memorial for the Unborn, I stand with those who honor the worth of every unborn child . . ."

During her visit to Chattanooga, McCorvey (Jane Roe) joined with Sandra Cano, (Mary Doe), whose case making abortion legal to the ninth month was argued the same day by the Supreme Court. The two women publicly recanted for the first time their roles in the landmark case and explained their knowledge of the legal and factual inaccuracies in the record.

Asked why they chose Chattanooga to make their statements, McCorvey said, "They were the first to think of it."

Cano responded, "What better place to do this than the National Memorial for the Unborn?"

The event, entitled "Setting the Record Straight," involved a drama troop reenacting the Supreme Court arguments followed by the two women correcting the record.

McCorvey, who never had an abortion, said her stated reason for needing one, that she was gang-raped on a pool table, was a complete lie. "My little lie grew and grew and became more horrible with each telling," she said. "So the entire abortion industry is based on a lie."

Sandra Cano also never had an abortion. She visited Atlanta attorney Margie Pitt Hames to regain her foster children from an abusive husband. "I signed papers I never looked at," she said.

She did not know of her role in the landmark case until the day it was announced. During the arguments, Hames pointed to an affidavit Cano allegedly signed requesting an abortion. After years of being stonewalled, Cano said she was able to have the affidavit unsealed in 1989. In a stunning announcement at the Chat-

"Jane Roe" of *Roe v. Wade* (Norma McCorvey) interviewed in 1997 by author Dean Arnold, then-publisher of *Chattanooga Fax.*

KENT KRESSENBERG

tanooga event, Mary Doe said she "is 98 percent sure it's not my signature on the affidavit."

"It's just pure fraud on the United States," she said.

Dr. Dennis Bizzoco, who sat on the bulldozer that razed the clinic, wrote the script for the reenactment. "A decision resting upon a nonexisting incident is no law," he told the audience. "It is the antithesis of law. It is lawlessness."[14]

The Pro-Family Issue of the 21st Century

Chattanooga also has strong conservative views on the bigger pro-family issue of the 21st century: homosexuality and same-sex marriages. "I'm supporting an outfit now called Alliance for Marriage, [which is] trying to put an amendment in the Constitution with a definition of marriage as the union between a man and a woman," said Scotty Probasco. "You've got the broader minded people that get into all the arguments, you know . . . but the definition of marriage is the union between a man and a woman."

"I sure don't want to see us get like Canada or France or some of those places," he said. "I mean, I'm going to tell you something. That pretty much screws up the underlying strength of a country. . . . It's scary."

The president of the Lyndhurst Foundation, Jack Murrah, has a number of reasons for disagreeing with Probasco. "Being gay—some people have a certain picture of what that means, and it's a hot button issue for them. [They] think that no person who admits to that part of who they are can be someone who cares about spiritual life or virtue in the community. And I—I just disagree."

Murrah made brief headlines in 2001 after opposing funding by the United Way for the Boy Scouts. Murrah criticized their refusal to hire gay Scout leaders and their discrimination against homosexuals "such as myself." The roundabout outing of the high-profile community leader who purposefully chose to come out of the closet did not cause the stir or uprising one might expect from such a strong, Bible Belt community.

As for the Lyndhurst directors, they quickly issued a statement denouncing prejudice against sexual orientation. They called Murrah's actions "courageous."[15]

Murrah thinks homosexuals should find acceptance in the Christian community in the same way a person of another religion may be accepted. "You may belong to a faith tradition that says, 'I can accept the Buddhist and I can accept the Catholic, but I can't accept a queer.' It's just fundamentally contrary . . ."

"Jack didn't have to do that," said Lyndhurst Chairman Allen McCallie. "We are a small, Southern Bible Belt town. [His] decision to take that out as a public discussion was remarkable, strong, brave—and a lot of that has now disappeared."

"I was very pleased that it didn't remain a large point of public outcry. The optimistic side of me would say that's because we've grown up and we've taken a step forward. The pessimistic side of me would say . . . people are moving on because it's not reaching them on a daily basis."

Perhaps the only public statement of criticism against Murrah and Lyndhurst came from Pat Horne, pastor of Church of Living Faith, who voiced his concerns to *Chattanooga Fax*: "If the Lyndhurst Foundation is here to build our community for the good of people, they need to stop trying to force people to accept aberrant behavior for young people." He said the revelation leaves "a pretty large blemish on the Lyndhurst Foundation" and "does not represent the mainstream Chattanooga community."[16]

If that is true, then mainstream Chattanooga remains a silent majority on the major moral issue of the 21st century. "I think it has to do with the privacy of most people's faith," said Doug Daugherty. "Whether you think that's negative or positive, I just think that's the truth. I just think that enormous numbers of people around here really do believe [in] Jesus . . . as their Lord and God and as the Savior of the world. But I don't think it has necessarily affected all of the behaviors in the same way it has affected some of the behaviors."

The Godfather of Chattanooga Churches

Daugherty's Chattanooga Resource Foundation continues to promote their vision, "Chattanooga: A City for God." Since Daugherty became the first staff member in 1990, the interdenominational group has initiated citywide crusades, prayer rallies, and racial reconciliation events. A youth network and women's network have been launched, conservative pro-family voter guides have been distributed to 40,000 churchgoers each election, and nearly all of the churches and local ministries have been loosely networked through newsletters, lunches, retreats, and regular leadership development seminars.

Daugherty plays an informal role of overseeing the churches in this zealous, Bible Belt community. Ironically, when he took the helm of the Resource Foundation, he was not aware that his great-great-great-grandfather was called the "godfather of Chattanooga churches."[17]

Daugherty's ancestor is James Whiteside, the same Whiteside who purchased Cameron Hill and Lookout Mountain after the Cherokee removal, and the same man credited as having "singlehandedly made Chattanooga a railroad center."[18] The town's first lawyer and first banker, he also built the first brick house after moving across the river in 1839. He was involved in the formation of the First Presbyterian Church, and though Episcopalian, he was a trustee for the Presbyterian Church for many years. St. Paul's Episcopal was started in his home beneath Cameron Hill.

Daugherty's earliest memory is watching a house burn down in St. Elmo when he was four years old. It belonged to Whiteside's daughter, Thankful, and her husband, Abraham Malone Johnson. The foundation and front wall still remain on Alabama Avenue across from Thankful Episcopal Church, which was named after Whiteside's daughter.

Thankful Whiteside attended elementary school with T. H. McCallie a few years before the Civil War. When she became of age, she fell in love with A. M. Johnson, who was in the tinning business. The wealthy Colonel Whiteside disapproved. When Johnson would arrive at their home on Cameron Hill, a sister would shout from the staircase, "Sister Thank, 'Tinner' Johnson is here."

Colonel Whiteside brought a young man to Chattanooga to read law with hopes of marrying him off to Thankful. Instead, she and Johnson eloped. Her enraged father did not speak to them for a year.

Eventually, A. M. Johnson became quite a prominent citizen, helping Whiteside with various railroad ventures and playing an early role with Chattanooga Medicine Company and Coca-Cola Bottling. This great-great-grandfather of Doug Daugherty was in the congregation when shells hit the Presbyterian Church while the pastor kept praying. He was also in attendance when William Crutchfield confronted Jefferson Davis at the Crutchfield House.

Johnson founded Forest Hills Cemetery, and his prominent monument on a hill can be seen clearly from the St. Elmo post office. Daugherty sometimes visits with his six children. The oldest is named Thankful.

"I had a great aunt named Thankful," Daugherty told me. "And I have a lot of memories of Aunt Thank. She played the organ at Thankful Episcopal . . .a real cultured kind of lady."

Daugherty grew up knowing he was directly descended from A. M. Johnson but did not catch until later that he is also a direct descendent of Whiteside. "The kinds of things that would be said was stuff like, 'Oh, well, you know, we used to own Lookout Mountain'—which, it turns out, was actually true."

"I have a peculiar idea that life is full of callings, that God makes people, and that he makes them with a purpose—that not only our immediate past, but even our past from generations we don't know anything about may have something to do with that calling. So I really think that there probably is a good reason to think I have an interest in Chattanooga as a community. I have a deep and abiding love for this community and a desire to see it prosper in every way. And I find that that is somewhat legitimized, at least in my own mind, by Colonel Whiteside's legacy."

Daugherty pronounced *Chattanooga* with a short "oo," like *nook* rather than *nuke*. I recalled other multigenerational Chattanoogans saying it the same way.

Whiteside passed legislation for the city's first railroad and owned the first deed to Lookout Mountain. Called "Old Man Chattanooga" and "Old Man Lookout Mountain" Whiteside was also known as the godfather of Chattanooga churches.

JAMES WHITESIDE
1803–1861

✸

THANKFUL WHITESIDE
1838–1890
= **ABRAHAM MALONE JOHNSON**

✸

DOUGLAS EVERETT = **FANNY AMANDA JOHNSON**

✸

MALONE JOHNSON EVERETT

✸

THANKFUL EVERETT = **HARRY DAUGHERTY**

✸

DOUG DAUGHERTY
b. 1952

(Charts are partial, not exhaustive, highlighting key links or characters in the book.)

The Spiritual DNA of Chattanooga

The building Doug Daugherty watched burn to the ground as a child, the home of his great-grandparents, was apparently the site of the oldest known resident of the area. According to historian Henry Wiltse, the spot which became 4215 Alabama Avenue was the home of a Cherokee chief named "Parnassee." The man Wiltse interviewed saw it in 1828. "Not in all the area covered by this city and its suburbs now, was there a human habitat, white, black, or red, with probably one exception . . . [Chief Parnassee] had a fine wigwam in the territory covered at present by St. Elmo. . . . All about was a dense wilderness."[19]

Perhaps because of his connection to that home, Daugherty has some self-described "strange" ideas regarding the Cherokees, the missionaries, and the destiny of Chattanooga.

"This could all sound strange to someone who is not familiar with it, but I think that the Cherokees—their culture, in terms of its institutions—were fairly sophisticated," he said. "They had roads and a post office and printing presses and schools. . . . And an integral part of that story is the presence of the Presbyterian missionaries."

"People who were contemporaries went from looking at the Indians as being subhuman to embracing them and saying that they were children of God in a democratic sense. . . . I've read one person who said this was the greatest move of God with Native Americans in history. . . . So, to me, that was part of the DNA of the community. Someone might argue, 'Well, yeah, but we ran all those people off.' But there was something left of that here in the community."

"I think God was doing something here and it was stopped. I think that God still wants to do something here. It's similar to what he did then, which was a cultural thing—a conversion and cultural thing. . . . I think there is a purpose on this place of taking that which may have been wild and away from God, bringing it to himself, and so working in it that it affects not only the individual but the community around them and then, ostensibly, the whole world. I think all through our history you can see that idea has come in and out of this community."

"That's pretty strange in itself and may get more strange. [But] why are we like we are? Why is there something that's made us different? There are historical reasons that happened, at least I think. That's due to that spiritual DNA kind of idea."

I asked him to reiterate the theory. "So you're saying there's a "spiritual DNA" from what happened 160 years ago that is still with us today?"

"In terms of God's purposes for this area, yes. Yeah, I think so."

Saints, Fools, and "Holy Fools"

Strange-sounding ideas are not incompatible with Christianity. The Apostle Paul himself says in the New Testament that God chose "the foolish things of this world to shame the wise." And Daugherty's theories are tame compared to the antics of some great saintly folks in history. In fact, one of the categories used to designate saints, historically, is what the Russian Orthodox call *yurodivi*, which means "holy fools."

The patron saint of Holy Fools, Saint Simeon Silos, retreated to the Syrian desert in the sixth century to devote his life to prayer. At times, he would return to town to throw nuts at the priests during the worship service. He publicly ate sausage on Good Friday, a holy fast day, but no one doubted that he was holy, even the priests he pelted with nuts. Simeon simply poked fun at the self-righteous.

Another holy fool, Basil the Blessed, eventually had a cathedral in Moscow named in his honor. Basil threw rocks at wealthy people's houses and stole from dishonest traders in Red Square. He once demanded that Czar Ivan (the Terrible) eat raw meat during the fast, saying, "Why abstain from eating meat when you murder men?" Countless Russians died for much less, but Ivan was afraid to let any harm come to the saintly Basil.

Saint Francis of Assisi is a well-known holy fool who stripped naked in the marketplace, leaving behind all his possessions.

In a city with as rich and pervasive a Christian presence as Chattanooga, unusual characters are certain to emerge. Chattanooga undoubtedly has had its fair share. Some are extraordinary, some saintly, some are holy fools, and some are just plain fools. A description of many of these colorful characters are listed below in generally chronological order. The author believes all the categories are represented: saints, holy fools, fools, and several hybrids.

Hernando De Soto and the Casqui Indians, c. 1540

A giant painting in the U.S. Capitol depicts a member of the entourage of Spanish explorer Hernando De Soto carrying a crucifix during their journey, which passed near the Chattanooga area on the way to discovering the Mississippi. It was the inner continent's first experience with Christianity.

When De Soto presented the cross to the conquered Casqui Indians, they adopted the new religion and wore crosses on their headdresses as they fought alongside the Spaniards. When De Soto felt he had been double-crossed by the chief of Casqui, he threatened to destroy the tribe.

"Casqui groveled before De Soto while verbally needling him," writes historian Charles Hudson. "Why, after the men, women, and children of Casqui had devoted themselves to the cross and the Christian God, did De Soto intend to treat them so cruelly?"

"Some of the Spaniards . . . were moved to tears by Casqui's seeming simplicity and faith. Even De Soto may have had a tear in his eye. Both the Indians and the Spaniards were amazed at the force of Casqui's words." The Casquis were spared.

"That's better. Thank you."

In another town, an Indian youth who, according to a De Soto chronicler, was used for a guide and interpreter, "began to froth at the mouth, and threw himself on the ground as if he were possessed of a Devil. An exorcism being said over him, the fit went off," and the youth continued to guide the Spaniards.[20]

And then the French, c. 1672

Father Jacques Marquette, a French Jesuit priest and explorer, followed the Spaniards in exploring similar areas a century later. He gave this reason for his journeys: "The Father had long premeditated this Undertaking, influenced by a most ardent desire to extend the Kingdom of Jesus Christ, and to make him Known and adored by all the peoples of that country."[21]

Gun-Toting, Whiskey-Selling Preacher to the Cherokees, 1806

The first Christian presence in Hamilton County arrived in Sale Creek in 1806 upon the building of a mission and school by Rev. Gideon Blackburn. Known for carrying a gun in one hand and a Bible in the other, the Presbyterian chaplain during the wars with the Indians resolved to reach the natives for the gospel after peace treaties were signed. With his long white mane of hair and tremendous enthusiasm, Blackburn in a short time educated hundreds of Cherokee students and raised a substantial amount of money from donors, which included the federal government.

Blackburn felt that adult, warlike Cherokees could not be civilized, but he saw hope in the bright eyes of their children. The chiefs agreed to let him teach them. The curriculum included biblical teaching along with the three *R* s, personal hygiene, and the use of cutlery at table. When Governor John Sevier, a well-known Indian fighter, saw the children perform at an assembly, he was moved. The little children, arrayed in Western clothing, read out loud, demonstrated skills in spelling and arithmetic, and sang from *Watt's Hymnal*. The teary-eyed general shook Blackburn's hand. "I see civilization taking the ground of barbarism, and the praises of Jesus succeeding the war whoop of the savage."[22]

Abruptly, Blackburn ended his initiatives in 1810 under a cloud of secrecy and suspicion. According to Sevier's journal, the missionary had some side activities in progress: a group of Creek Indians intercepted two fully loaded flatboats on the Tennessee River several miles below Chattanooga. They "seized upon and took Parson Blackburn's whiskey."

Blackburn was a distiller of liquor, a practice not necessarily frowned upon for clergy in the early 1800s, but selling liquor to Indians was against the law. Those who knew but little of the scandal may have concluded that Blackburn left for that legal violation; however, documents translated over a century later show that

Gideon Blackburn

Blackburn, always a patriot, had agreed to help the federal government in a secret mission to identify a waterway through hostile Indian territory that could reach all the way to the Gulf. This espionage was done in the name of protecting the frontier and under the auspices of transporting whiskey.[23]

The few chiefs who understood the real reasons for Blackburn's departure kept the matter silent. Otherwise, a tainted name for missionaries would have prevented the Brainerd Mission from starting their school a few years later. In her 1940 history, Zella Armstrong says Blackburn shut down his mission for "financial reasons." Later, she decided Blackburn's problem was declining health.[24]

Wolves at Chickamauga Creek, 1819

Brainerd missionary Daniel Butrick was unable to cross the flooded Chickamauga Creek after arriving late the night of March 24. He was returning from a journey that was typical of Brainerd missionaries in their duties to pastor souls and care for the mission, traveling 40 miles and crossing two other creeks before reaching the Brainerd Mission complex. It was extremely cold, and he had eaten nothing since that morning. The floods had washed all boats and canoes downriver. The current was too strong for him to swim across, so he was forced to spend the night in the woods at the edge of the water. His clothes were wet. The ground was filled with water, and he had no blanket except the cloth under his saddle.

The other missionaries feared he might die from the elements with no fire to warm him. According to the *Brainerd Journal*, "Various attempts were made by the strongest men, to throw a brand of fire to him, but without success. In this dilemma, an Indian boy proposed to fasten a piece of lighted spunk to an arrow and shoot it over. This plan was immediately adopted, and fire very readily sent over to him. Our joy on this success was but transient, for no fuel could be found except green trees and bushes and what had been soaked in the water, so that all his attempts to kindle a fire failed. We built a fire on our side of the creek, which, though it could afford him no heat, served to render the darkness of the night less gloomy, and to keep off the wolves, which were howling in numbers near him."

"Some of us kept watch to keep him from sleeping too long at a time, and hands were dispatched down the creek to get a canoe to bring him over. . . . By occasionally taking a little rest in sleep, and walking the remainder of the time, he kept the use of his limbs. . . . About sunrise, we succeeded in getting him over."[25]

Chattanooga's Mysterious Holy Grail, 1822

The whereabouts of a communion set that has been with Chattanooga since its founding are not known. It still exists, but the owners are unknown to the public.

This pewter communion utensil set was sent from a Congregationalist church in Amherst, New Hampshire, to the Brainerd Mission. The platter bears the name "Edgar & Son, London," and the Presbyterian history says the set is from the 11th century. According to information at the Brainerd cemetery, it was made during the reign of William Rufus, King of England from 1087 to 1100 A.D. He was the son of William the Conqueror.

The communion set was acquired by missionary Ainsworth Blunt in 1822. It was used during the last service at the mission in 1838 before it was closed and Blunt joined the Cherokees on the Trail of Tears. When he returned to Chattanooga to start First Presbyterian in 1840, the communion set was also used until Blunt took it with him to the Dalton Presbyterian Church in 1847. Blunt's descendents loaned the set to First Presbyterian for their 90th anniversary in 1930.

According to a bulletin board at the Brainerd Mission cemetery, the current owners recently agreed to let pictures be taken of the communion service as long as the location of Chattanooga's holy grail is kept secret.[26]*

Area's First Author Left Behind, 1833

Hamilton County's first author was Abel Pearson, pastor of the Presbyterian Church in Soddy. His book, *An Analysis of the Principles of Divine Government*, was published in Athens, Tennessee, in 1833.

His book shared content similar to the popular *Left Behind* series of today but without the success. Few were printed and sold. The contents page of Pearson's work includes a section promising the following: "A Calculation showing the exact time and Death of Christ, And Also calculations showing the Precise Time of the Rise and Fall of the Beast."[27]

A "Pauper" Leaves Church a Fortune, c. 1910.

The majestic Catholic Church in downtown Chattanooga was built through a gift left by a miserly hermit who lived in a small hut. Columnist Sam Divine tells the story:

"Dan Hogan was a rock mason by trade and a miser by nature. . . . He lived alone in a shanty not much bigger than a good-sized dog kennel. He worked at his trade alone and hoarded his earnings, which he invested in real estate. At his death, he owned much of the Stone Fort area, land that is today worth a million dollars.† The Hotel Patten, post office, city hall, *News* building, and Patten block on Market Street mark the site of Dan Hogan's rock quarry."

Communion set for Brainerd Mission

"He paved the sidewalks in front of these lots with flagstones quarried on Stone Fort and carried them in his wheelbarrow to their places and laid them with his own hands. He went shabbily dressed and unkempt in his person, and would have been taken by strangers as a pauper. . . . He was one of Chattanooga's wealthiest citizens at his death, and the Catholic church was his sole heir."

"The only personal property Dan Hogan, the miser, was known to possess was his wheelbarrow, hammer, and chisel, with which he chiseled out and rolled up a fortune in real estate."[28]*

"And they shall pick up serpents . . ." 1947

A popular name for a denomination in the area is the "Church of God." Historian Charles Govan reminds us that there is "the Church of God (Tomlinson), Church of God, and the (Original) Church of God." The "Original" version was started in Chattanooga, but Govan says the oldest is the one without parentheses.

In 1909, the "Church of God with Signs Following After" was started in Hamilton County. Several members were arrested following a 1947 law prohibiting snake handling. "Just you wait. *Now* its handling serpents [but soon] they'll go after the Bible itself," said one leader. Another denounced a judge who "was a-feared to let the serpents come in the courtroom. But *I've* handled 'em all my life—been bit four hundred times . . . but the judge wouldn't look at 'em! And he was a *learnt* man."[29]

Future Politician Cites Miraculous Healing, 1977

Long considered the most conservative legislator in the entire Georgia House of Representatives, Republican Brian Joyce of Lookout Mountain received an atypical

---

† $87 million (2006)

standing ovation from the Democrat-controlled body after his final speech in 2004. He was not always so loved by the establishment.

Three decades earlier, he lived alone in a hut with no electricity overlooking the Pacific Ocean. He dabbled in Eastern philosophy, took a boat to British Columbia, grew hair to his waist, and wore no clothing in the summertime. He was a vegetarian for twelve years and ate only fruit for a year.

During a trip to Guatemaula, he says he was miraculously healed of epileptic seizures and became a born-again Christian. He started a family and moved to the Chattanooga area to avoid strict laws against homeschooling. Pro-life activism and Pat Roberston's presidential bid drew him into politics. When he was elected to the state house, Republicans were outnumbered nearly four to one. The GOP gained the majority in 2005, but Joyce retired at age 51, just as he was about to be named to a top leadership post. "I'd be down there all the time," he said. "I'd lose my life."[30]

The Backwoods, Born-Again, Bible-Belt Buddhist, c. 1980–present

He is arguably the most popular elected official in a Fundamentalist stronghold, but that does not stop Dalton Roberts from proclaiming the wonders of meditation and certain untraditional religious practices, including a form of time travel.

He was an agnostic for 20 years. "When I was 45, I invited God into my life, and, to my amazement, God came."

"My basic fundamental faith is very Jesus-oriented because I grew up in a Christian home. I developed a profound love and appreciation for Jesus and for what he said and for the spirit he brought to this planet. But that doesn't mean I can't appreciate the Buddha."

"The two places you can learn about meditation from religious thought leaders are the Catholic and Orthodox Church and the Buddhists. There's a form of walking meditation where you walk mindfully. . . . Transcendental meditation has been one of the most successful forms. . . . Bird-watching does the same thing for me. I've got a goldfinch feeder, a hummingbird feeder, a woodpecker feeder, and then I've got the regular sunflower seed disposals for cardinals, tufted titmice, chickadees, you name it."

"I really believe that everything has a spiritual atmosphere that is affected by everybody who comes in contact with that. I don't believe that, I know that."

"The Indians were here so long. There's a lot of the Indian, Cherokee spirit still here. I believe you can commune with that. In fact, I do."

"I find it to be a very sacred thing to feel this oneness with other cultures and with other people of other times and places. Because, really, we're all one. Life is just one, big ol' colorful quilt, and every little time and place is just one little piece of it."

Prayer Turns Burning Bush into Miracle, November 2000

Dan Rather announced it. Al Gore had won Florida, and that meant George W. Bush would lose the 2000 presidential election. A packed audience of Republicans at the Chattanooga Trade Center stood in disbelief, but GOP Chairman Robin Smith took the stage to announce that it was time to pray.

Smith told those who might be offended by prayer that they may want to leave the room. She then asked the crowd of nearly 1,000 to join hands "in agreement" because "the future of this nation is at risk."

"I pray in the name of Jesus for you to send a man who will be a man of character and integrity to the White House," Ms. Smith said in her prayer. According to reports, the scene was visibly awkward for some there in attendance, the intensity of the moment palpable.

About ten minutes later, Dan Rather announced that Florida had been moved back to undecided status. It was later awarded to Bush.[31]

Cherokee Prayer Initiative: Spiritual "Mapping"

Bettye Lundquist of Missionary Ridge believes the sins of our ancestors still haunt us today. As the Regional Coordinator for the Cherokee Prayer Initiative launched in October 2000, she joined many others in praying at a number of sites related to the Trail of Tears, including the Brainerd Mission cemetery.

"I was there to repent for myself, my region, and our Scot-Irish forefathers who have defiled this land by committing the four iniquities that God says defile the land: idolatry, broken covenants, immorality, and innocent bloodshed."

Representatives from a number of Native American tribes attended the prayer session at the cemetery along with "intercessors" from several countries. They believe that the Brainerd Covenant, a vow taken by blacks, whites, and Indians, is the only covenant or treaty by the whites that was never broken since the missionaries joined their brethren on the Trail of Tears. The movement also believes that modern issues like abortion are inherently related to past injustices. "We believe that if we deal with the 'roots' of injustices toward the First Nations People and the African Americans, God will deal with the modern 'fruit' of abortion," said Lundquist.

"We had a microcosm of all the world at the cemetery," she said. "We all entered into the covenant together, sealing it by signing our names to the back and taking communion." She said the leader, Lou Engle, head of The Cause in Washington D.C., renamed the Church of Chickamauga, the name of the church that made the original covenant, "The Church of All Nations." The signed Brainerd Covenant hangs in a frame on Lundquist's wall.

Her journey into strategic prayer began two decades ago when she taught a spiritual warfare class at the Chattanooga Bible Institute founded by Dr. James

Fowle. She later earned a master's degree in spiritual warfare and prophecy from the Wagner Leadership Institute in Colorado Springs and is now working on a doctorate.

In 1999, the *Christian Science Monitor* tried to get a grasp of this movement, asking, "Can the "spiritual DNA" of a community be altered?" The prominent D.C. publication said "a global movement of evangelicals has developed over the past decade that seeks to free cities and neighborhoods from social scourges even as it 'takes them for God.' Through 'spiritual warfare' and an in-depth research effort called 'spiritual mapping,' they aim to bring people to Christ and, in their words, 'break spiritual strongholds' holding communities in their grip."

The *Monitor* cited Wagner's institute as the vanguard of the movement. While "ground-level" spiritual warfare involves casting demons out of individuals, "strategic-level" warfare directly confronts "territorial spirits assigned by Satan to coordinate activities over a geographical area."

The article says a video called *Transformations* tells the story of five cities changed by strategic prayer initiatives. The Chattanooga Resource Foundation and other local ministries have showcased the video. Inspired by those five cities, a number of pastors have for nearly two years joined over thirty intercessors each week at various churches to pray strategically for Chattanooga. Once a month, they meet at the Forrest Avenue Methodist Church in North Chattanooga.

Lundquist said the first efforts she is aware of to identify strongholds and pray on-site in Chattanooga started in the late 1980s. Strategic places included the Brainerd Mission, Orchard Knob, Moccasin Bend, Missionary Ridge, and the Confederate Cemetery. They also prayed at Lookout Point. Team members concluded that on a three-dimensional map, the mountain looks uncannily similar to a serpent. Its mouth is poised to swallow the city, and its tongue (Missionary Ridge) divides it. When the foot of Moccasin Bend was seen from Point Park, the prayer time that day focused on Genesis 3:15.[32]

The Mayor's Impromptu Theology

When the Chattanooga City Council announced its plan to outlaw sound trucks, rolling amplified pulpits, in 1937, Howard Cook protested.

"The Bible tells us to go into the highways and hedges and preach the gospel to the people," he said, "and that is what we are trying to do."

Ed Bass, Chattanooga's longest serving mayor (four terms), replied, "God did not tell you to take a sound truck with you, did he? I do not believe God inspired the sound truck."

Based on the law passed the following week, God inspires one block's worth of amplification.[33]

The City that Launches National Street Preachers

Chattanooga seems to have more than its fair share of street preachers. Some of this can be attributed to the Highland Park/Tennessee Temple phenomenon, but Chattanooga also has an inordinate number of street preachers who have gone national. Only one of the several mentioned below was associated with Highland Park.

Carrying the Cross for the Country. Chattanoogan Mike Seimer has traveled the country for years with his long hair, beard, and giant cross nearly twice his size while preaching and dramatizing Jesus. He also takes his family along in a bus.[34]

Preaching Damnation, then Salvation. Jim Rudd worked at the American Rights Coalition in Chattanooga before leaving in 1993 to preach in the streets of Washington, D.C., but then he focused on abortion clinics. "Open-air preaching makes it hard to nail the sinner in their sin," he said. "Instead, I like to preach to those entering abortion clinics, sodomite clubs, or pornography shops." Rudd, the editor of *covenantnews.com*, said he likes "to preach that they are damned in their sins, then preach Jesus to them."[35]

Old Testament Al. A man who calls himself "Al Bishop—Prophet" has been known to make downtown Chattanooga his regular place to act as a walking bill-board. The sloppy handwriting on his T-shirt says, "The savior of Israel was never a baby," "My God and savior never wore diapers," and, more to the point: "Jesus was a liar."

The beggarly looking prophet apparently has enough money for a several-thou-sand-dollar half-page ad in the paper. "Christians worship only the words of Paul," he tells readers. "Jah-Wah recommends conservative Judaism! For: the entire world." He also notes that "The churches of the World preach from President Jefferson's Bible."[36]

Baylor's Prep School Preacher. Chattanoogan Bill Adams, a graduate of Baylor School, is a good-looking, clean-cut street preacher. Always wearing a jacket, tie, and occasional cowboy hat, the smiling all-American guy urges passersby to "pray for revival," or he might simply pass out tracts about forgiveness. Other times, he reads the Bible out loud or prays.

At age 43, he has displayed these more positive antics at Riverbend and other places in Chattanooga for eight years but is now seen more regularly in the Buck-head area of Atlanta. He has also preached at the Super Bowl, the Final Four, the Masters, the Olympics in Atlanta and in Greece, the Oscars (including exclusive private parties beforehand), and at various other noteworthy events.

He could have done many other things. Previously, he served as finance director for Congressman Zach Wamp and then Bob Barr in Georgia, raising over $3 million for Republican politicians. Nevertheless, he was considered nothing less than a security risk when he walked around the White House five times in 1999 holding a sign that said, "Forgiveness: Please help our nation heal. Let's love and forgive each other as we love and forgive ourselves." Five Secret Service officers frisked him, he said. "They told me, 'The White House has seen your sign,' and implied they didn't like it." Nevertheless, he shook Bill Clinton's hand on another occasion and encouraged him to "heal our nation."

Adams says he feels compelled by the Lord to publicly preach, pray, or read Scripture. Personally, he would rather do something else. "Before, I could just chill out on the couch, but now, it's like someone is inside of me, pushing me to go. I used to resist it."

In New Orleans, a man poured a beer on his head. Another man told him he was going to travel to Atlanta "and preach about Satan." At the Capitol one woman shouted, "Why don't you just shut up!"[37]

The Most Legendary of All: Dan Martino. Dan Martino spent the entire 1980s on Chattanooga's streets holding signs and preaching against abortion, pornography, and homosexuality. He held a sign at the 1988 Republican Convention in Atlanta that said, "God is a Republican." Thus, he landed his first fifteen minutes of fame, but there would be many more.

No street preacher was more famous in Chattanooga than the late Dan Martino. In fact, no *person* was more well known or at least more widely recognized, admired and/or hated. He left Chattanooga in the 1990s to become the self-appointed "Missionary to the Supreme Court." Ten years later, he was still the hands-down winner on a talk radio poll for the most colorful character in Chattanooga.

A few weeks after that GOP convention, he held a sign at the Democrat convention in New Orleans: "AIDS is a Cure, Not a Disease." He was quoted in the national media saying, "Like capital punishment, it is 100 percent effective."

He lost all credibility in 1992 when he admitted to forty-five homosexual encounters the previous two years. So, the legend was an enigma. While partly sincere, he was mostly hypocritical. While capable of the greatest sensitivities, he was generally rude, obnoxious, self-centered, cruel, ungrateful, and a first class jerk. He was also my friend.

I have the advantage of providing a particularly personal glimpse of Chattanooga's most colorful character since I had the occasion to get to know the street preacher quite well for a period of time. Martino got his start preaching and singing hymns every day in front of Scotty Probasco's American National Bank while

BASEBALL's BEST HITTERS

PADRES' GWYNN WINS NL TITLE: .336

TWINS' PUCKETT TOPS IN AL: .339 1C

▶ LAST-DAY RESULTS, 1,4,5C
▶ TUESDAY: PLAYOFF GUIDE

RAMS EDGE 49ers IN FINAL SECONDS 1C

▶ WEEK 4 GAMES, 1,6,8,9,11C
▶ EAGLES' 'TOUGH' RYAN vs. BEARS' DITKA TONIGHT, 1C

By Krik Schlea, Allsport

TONY GWYNN: Goes 3-for-4 to win 4th title, 1C

USA TODAY

NO. 1 IN THE USA...6.3 MILLION READERS EVERY

MONDAY, OCTOBER 2, 1989

NEWSLINE

A QUICK READ ON THE NEWS

WEATHER: Snow, light rain in Rockies; warm in South Central; rain in Northeast, Southeast; showers on West Coast, Midwest, North Central. Full color page. 14A.
▶ 24-hour weather hot line: 1-900-370-USAT; details. 14A.

WALL STREET AHEAD: Third quarter markets report: Proceed with caution on stocks. 1B. They're still good investment. Surprise rules bond market. 3B.

CHINA CELEBRATES: China marks 40 years of communist rule with public fete at Tiananmen Square. Beijing University students under tight reins. 4A.

...on, left, ...term as ... Predic-...oral run-...pset. 3A.

... Seven ...n USA's ...are traf-...e. 3A.

House ...sday on ...law. 4A.

...Top-paid ...n in '88.

...terbury, ...r talk of

...eeg, 100, ...r. 2A.

...ud trial; ...NE. 3A.

...claims ...4A

...divided

In USA ...woman

...islation

SPECIAL REPO
YOUR GUID

NEW

Tomorrow: Wh

The Supreme Court returns
Abortion issue
tops the docket

**The three case
before the cou**

▶ A 1981 Minnesota law ba... abortions under age 18 u... least 48 hours after both b... cal parents have been notifi...

▶ A 1985 Ohio law requiring ...tors to notify at least one p... 24 hours before performi... abortion on a minor.

▶ Illinois regulations requ... abortion clinics to meet ... dards similar to those of fu... vice hospitals.

PREME COURT U.S. SUPREME

By Martin H...

PREACHING AGAINST ABORTION: Dan Martino, a street preacher from Chattan... Tenn., is back in Washington. He spends nights in a youth hostel and days picketing o... the Supreme Court. **(What states are working on, 6A; Today's Debate, 12A.)**

The early **Dan Martino** (left) preached a gospel message on the streets of Chattanooga. Later, his moral crusading led him to the Supreme Court and to national exposure (above).

businesspeople awkwardly hurried past. A graduate of Tennessee Temple, his message grew from salvation to controversial moral issues. He became an activist and government gadfly, speaking at every City Council meeting and causing local legislators to introduce the three-minute-only rule.

Early on, Martino was admired by many. Eventually he was loathed by most people, including the Christian and pro-family community. He ignored them and shamed them long before his outing. For some reason, I had a place in my heart for the guy. There was something of the genius in him (the close relative of insanity). His deep acumen with words and ideas emerged through the bitterness once in a while in the form of a very sharp wit. He may be the most complex person I've ever known as well as the most confused.

Every town does not have a guy like Dan Martino. He had a knack for visual antics in front of the Supreme Court, often using dolls and baby carriages. His image made the *AP Wire* several times, the front page of *USA Today* (twice, above the fold), and all the major networks. Andy Rooney even featured him on *60 Minutes.*

After confronting Justice Harry Blackman in the Court cafeteria ("A woman's exclusive right to an abortion ends where the placenta begins," he instructed the author of *Roe v. Wade),* a guard told him, "You're the talk of the Supreme Court." In fact, a spokesman for the Supreme Court said Dan was a fixture there. When *The West Wing* came to tape an episode about a new justice, he kept meddling with their background view. "He ended up being amenable," the spokesman said, "and he ended up posing with Martin Sheen for a picture."

When the nude stage play *Oh! Calcutta* came to Chattanooga, Martino was carried off by police as he walked down the aisle announcing a citizen's arrest. After purchasing a Coke that felt odd, he called in the bomb squad, paranoid that he was an enemy's target. When the experts opened the can, a $10 bill tumbled out, part of a national promotion. Claiming distress, Dan filed a lawsuit.

During the holidays, he had paint sprayed on him while holding a sign that said, "Santa is Satan's Helper." Then, he left for Washington, D.C., with bitterness toward the city. "I have been good for Chattanooga, but Chattanooga has not been good to Dan Martino," he told the media.

Though it can be argued that he did more harm than good, he did accomplish a few things. When the district attorney would not prosecute adult bookstores in Chattanooga, Martino visited the grand jury and presented evidence for them to indict the D.A. for failing to carry out his constitutional duties. He had a certain genius for such schemes. Under the grand jury's pressure and a growing citywide anti-porn campaign, the D.A. shut down eleven bookstores.

Dan was also instrumental in the boycott that caused Erlanger Hospital to stop performing abortions. Regarding the Supreme Court, he sensed the need for someone, somewhere to confront the justices, admitting that he himself was hardly the best candidate and was only "partially healed" of his sexual struggles. "Do you realize there's no one in front of the Court? There's no one else doing this!" he said passionately. Sincerity seemed to be at least part of his motive.

Dan Martino had physical challenges. He was very short, with a limp and sizable humpback. He was deeply ashamed of his rotten, crooked teeth. He was writing his autobiography, he said. He entitled it *Sentenced to Live,* once again revealing that biting wit hidden by anger and rage.

Dalton Roberts felt sorry for him. "I have a hard time seeing that his activism has been healthy to the city, the county, or himself," the former county executive said. "I hope people won't be too severe on him. It's hard not to be so empathetic with someone so disturbed. I'd like to see him find peace. I hurt for him. I really do."

Dan was jealous of men who were attracted to women. At one point, when he was desperate for help, he asked a group to come to his apartment and pray for him. It was not your usual gathering. Evil spirits were identified, including one associated with suicide, and what I believe to be an exorcism took place. He shrieked and convulsed and exhibited other behaviors appropriate for the moment.

When he came to, he looked better and felt better. Knowing that he was likely to have a relapse, he told me to remove the stuff from his top dresser drawer. I opened it and found three loaded guns. He called me two weeks later, and then he had an attorney send a letter demanding I return his "property." I had already thrown them off the Market Street Bridge into the river. A few days later, he was heavenly minded again, so I seized the moment to have him sign a letter absolving me of stealing the guns. We both laughed, knowing he would be demanding them again in a few days. He did, but I had the letter.

One of the reasons I cared for Dan was that part of him truly wanted help. In certain moments, he knew the wretchedness of his problems and the level of his hypocrisy. At the end of his life, he started to heed that easy-to-forget teaching, "Blessed are the merciful, for they shall obtain mercy." In 1996, he returned to Chattanooga after a few years of therapy in Kentucky and presented each City Councilman with a plaque that read, "Life is all about living mercy to everyone without exception." It was an awkward moment.

He was never completely consistent with his new mantra. He later roamed the halls of Congress preaching from "Sinners in the Hands of an Angry God." He also held a sign in his final years saying, "Lord Jesus, please heal all people with HIV."

His October 2003 obituary said he died at age 55 "after a long illness." I called the coroner but was unable to learn the cause of death. Whatever the cause, it was not by gunshot. For that, I am very grateful.[38]

LYNDHURST

Artist: Gordon Wetmore

CHAPTER EIGHT

The Spirit of the Luptons

The Last Vestiges of Aristocracy

In the spring of 1966, a great chunk of plaster crashed down from the ceiling of the First Presbyterian Church onto the pew of the Lupton family. The building was empty; nevertheless, it may have been Chattanooga's most significant event of the 20th century.[1]

The significance is in the metaphor, of course. Around the same time, the multigenerational tradition of Luptons and Presbyterianism suddenly changed and with it a major change in philosophy for the community of Chattanooga.

To understand this transition, however, one must first understand the post-bellum tradition of very strong leadership in Chattanooga by the prominent families, particularly the Luptons.

A 1997 *Chattanooga Free Press* article referred to this phenomenon as the city's "aristocracy." It quoted Dr. Ronald Foresta, a professor of geography at the University of Tennessee (Knoxville) who had researched Chattanooga's renaissance. He told the *National Journal* the city "had a powerful and coherent elite with a sense that this is their community."[2]

"Chattanooga is run by old money families," Foresta told me. "They beat the populists. Knoxville is a populist town. The populist scoundrels won. Knoxville's elite is still here, but they're not active. They quietly count their money."[3]

This elite group in Chattanooga who beat the populists in the early 20th century was a rather unique distillation of the Northern elite manufacturers who moved here after the Civil War and the few remaining prominent Southern families. Kathryn McCallie Johnson, after editing T. H. McCallie's 1837–1912 journal 40 years later, saw in it "a new vision of the character that marked the aristocracy of the Old South." She said a new age then formed in which "the loyal Southerner admits the faults of the Southern character and praises fine characteristics in the rougher, less courteous invaders from the North."[4]

A *Saturday Evening Post* columnist in 1949 agreed with Mrs. McCallie Johnson on the merging of Confederates and carpetbaggers. "Most of the old families, instead of ostracizing the eager newcomers, married them. Today, Chattanooga society is so mixed up that it is hard to tell who is bona fide Old South and who is bona fide Old-South-by-North."[5]

Chapel Hill historian James Leyburn gives the following recipe for a lasting upper class: "Stable social classes flourish...when upper classes are fairly exclusive in their marriages; when sons are indoctrinated with the idea that they have not only rights but also obligations of leadership and responsibility; and when tradition guides institutions into conservative channels."[6]

On the last point, the scholar on the Scotch-Irish was referring specifically to the Presbyterian Church. The second-to-last component is summed up in the phrase *noblesse oblige* (French for the "obligation of the nobility"), and a prestigious prep school is an excellent place to inculcate such values. Lyndhurst Foundation director Jack Murrah speculates that the unusual prep school phenomenon in Chattanooga may be related to aristocratic notions.

"I wonder if, in Chattanooga...the ownership class felt a greater cultural gap with the indigenous population," he said. "And so, in addition to their private golf clubs, which wealthy classes created everywhere, and moving into separate neighborhoods like Lookout Mountain or Riverview as people have done in all sorts of places, they created a separate set of schools for their children, removed from the influences of local culture. They didn't believe that the local culture would provide an adequate education for their kids."

Partying with a Purpose

Professor Foresta places just as much emphasis on the golf and other social traditions. "I put a lot of weight on their clubs, their institutions," he said. "They were talking to each other all the time. They worked together all day, and at night they're at the symphony together. They were tight."

He gave a positive example he had heard where a more racist member of the group was confronted and told to get on board with more tolerant policies in the community. "There was elite cohesion. Once they made a decision, it stuck."

Chattanooga has a number of these private, elite clubs and institutions including the Mountain City Club, the Fairyland Club, the Cotton Ball, and golf courses like Chattanooga Golf & Country Club, Lookout Mountain Golf Club, and more recently, the Honors Course. A few of these will be discussed in more detail, but possibly the most influential elite group this century has been the Rotary Club.

Rotary, like few other institutions, advances the concept of noblesse oblige. The civic club meets weekly downtown for lunch to hear speakers. Only heads of companies or specified leaders in the community are invited to join. The first Rotary Club, with the motto "Service above Self," was founded in 1905 in Chicago. Chattanooga's Rotary was the 103rd group when it was granted a chapter in 1914. Today, there are 30,000 clubs in 163 countries.

Past Rotary presidents in Chattanooga include names like Patten, McCallie, Ochs, Guerry, Smartt, Chapin, and McDonald. Last year's president, Frank Brock, says Chattanooga has an unusually strong Rotary Club compared to other cities. He calls Rotary "intentionally elitist," but he says it plays a crucial role. "There really is something to sitting down and having lunch with people you don't know. I would not know half the people in that room if it were not for Rotary. I would be a lot less interested in Chattanooga. Just simple. Rotary has created an interest and love for the community. Where are you going to learn that? I think United Way, and to a certain extent Allied Arts, all have a similar sort of communitywide perspective. But nobody cultivates that like Rotary."

The 1922 president, Thomas Spencer McCallie, took it upon himself to more clearly define Rotary. The document oozes noblesse oblige. "Rotary is a training school in unselfishness, where personal gain is subordinate to public good.... Rotary views service as a privilege to be sought, not as a burden to be avoided." Such talk has been backed by action. In their first year, 1914, the Rotarians raised the entire budget for Associated Charities, the forerunner of the United Way. Since 1970, they have raised over $170 million.[7]

One of the most significant social happenings of the early 20th century was the Cotton Ball and its precursor, the Spring Festival. A group of businessmen in 1898 decided such an event would promote business, so plans were made to elect a queen of the festival and find a man to dress up as the symbol of the festival, "Baldur," the God of Spring. Arriving on the river landing by float on May 3, Baldur was greeted by eight men and four fair young ladies to commence a flower parade. A gigantic crowd estimated at 75,000 people lined Market Street. It was called "the most magnificent sight ever seen in the city or this section of the South."[8] The event included bike races, art exhibits, manufacturer's displays, huge bonfires and the coronation of the "Queen of the May." Queens from other towns and cities attended, and hundreds of floats were entered in the parade.

To supplement festival events, the Clover Leaf Club was formed. At the Clover Leaf Ball, "Titania, Queen of the Fairies," was elected along with "Oberon, the King." Myra Smartt was an early queen, and Oberon, the King, was John T. Lupton in 1900.[9]

PATTEN ~ LUPTON

Founder of Chattanooga Medicine Co. (Chattem), which produced Black Draught and Wine of Cardui (forerunners of Coca-Cola). Patten was the city's first millionaire and built the Ashland Farm mansion in Flintstone.

ZEBOIM CARTTER PATTEN
1840–1925

=

ELIZABETH PATTEN
1871–1941

JOHN T. LUPTON
1862–1933

Ashland Farm

A decade previous, Lupton's marriage to Liz Patten was the biggest society event in years. The attorney from Virginia, 26, had fallen for the 17-year-old daughter of Chattanooga's richest man, millionaire Zeboim Patten, founder of the Chattanooga Medicine Company. Lupton came through Chattanooga on his way to Texas but was caught up in the real estate boom of the 1880s. He met Patten and was then engaged to his daughter.

"Few social events in the history of Chattanooga have so completely absorbed the attention of society as the wedding yesterday of John T. Lupton to Miss Lizzie Olive Patten," wrote the *Daily Times*. "Society has been on the tiptoe of expectancy ever since the cards were issued announcing the event." "A surging mass of femininity" swarmed the steps of the First Presbyterian Church for the occasion.[10]

The crowds "danced a German" that lasted past midnight and then accompanied the newlyweds to the train station where they departed for New Orleans to take a steamer to various South American islands. They most certainly rode in a "Pullman Palace Sleeping Car," as did other wealthy elites on their honeymoons such as the Ochses a few years before and Anne Lupton a generation later.

———————◆———————

Before the Pullman sleeping cars, train passengers were forced to spend the night on hard benches. The Pullman car, through nifty fold-out benches, plush interior, fine paint, curtains, and fixtures, allowed the nation's elite to ride in "rolling palaces." This revolution in rail travel first affected Chattanooga in 1867.[11]

The subject is of particular interest to me. My 3rd-great-grandfather, Theodore Tuttle Woodruff, invented the sleeping car. He held forty-four patents but never enjoyed the fruit of his innovations. It was my one big chance at enjoying a bit of aristocracy myself. Instead, the honors went to the descendents of George Pullman and Andrew Carnegie.

I have an original receipt in my file, a confirmation of stock ownership in T. T. Woodruff's company signed by Andrew Carnegie, the Bill Gates of the 1800s, who became the richest man in America through the steel and rail industries. Carnegie called the investment in Woodruff's sleeping car "the first considerable sum I ever made." A biographer called it "the start of the Carnegie fortune."

According to another biographer, George Pullman "openly copied Woodruff's designs...without permission—or shame" after taking many rides in Woodruff sleeping cars as a youngster. Carnegie found a way to garner control of the stock in Woodruff's company and then chose to join up with Pullman rather than sue him for stealing the patent. The actual inventor was left behind.

When Carnegie wrote his autobiography a few years later, he described his happenstance meeting with Woodruff one day on a train.

"A tall, spare, farmer looking kind of man...drew from a green bag a small model of a sleeping berth for railway cars. He had not spoken a minute, before, like a flash, the whole range of discovery burst upon me."

In fact, Woodruff had built dozens of railcars before meeting Carnegie, and they were already running on several railroads. They were "a little too big for the said green bag," Woodruff commented wryly in a letter to the multimillionaire. Litigation ensued. The sleeping car inventor, who had spent his life maneuvering in and around train yards, was able to get one long letter printed in the Philadelphia paper before being suddenly struck and killed by an express train in New Jersey. "For Carnegie, who liked tidy endings, there were now no loose ends left," wrote biographer Joseph Wall, "and his venture in sleeping cars could finally be closed."[12]

Many Mansions

Several years after John and Lizzie Lupton's ride in the Pullman car, father-in-law Zeboim Patten held a grand housewarming party in 1906 for his "Ashland Farm" mansion at the foot of Lookout Mountain in Flintstone, Georgia. He had become a millionaire many times over.

"Ashland has been the scene of many lovely parties," writes Helen Exum beside her entry for Ashland Farm Sweet Potatoes. "[They include] informal tennis gatherings, formal teas in the winter, morning coffees in the spring [and] lunches for the Colonial Dames."

"Ashland Farm [is] a brick colonial home with Corinthian columns on the porch, a winding stairway inside [that] reminds you of a gracious Virginia plantation.... Hundreds of Chattanoogans love Ashland Farm as one of the still beautiful homes here, as the scene of daffodils in the spring, as a symbol of the gracious living that took place in less hurried years."

Ashland boasted the South's largest private ballroom. According to the *Atlanta Journal,* "Probably no more artistic and beautiful place can be found in the South."[13]

The mansion still stands today. It was Chattanooga's premiere home of the early 20th century. The premier social happening of that era was the Spring Festival, later the Cotton Ball, and the key social figure of the period was Zella Armstrong.

"Miss Zella," as she was known, spent a lifetime promoting social events, weddings, and debutante balls and extolling the beauties of Chattanooga belles. A daughter of a Confederate officer and descendent of Revolutionary War heroes, she completed a two-volume history of Chattanooga and Hamilton County in 1940. She also published a society magazine, *The Lookout,* for 50 years.

Zella Armstrong

The first issue of *The Lookout,* published in 1908, promised to do "all that is within our power to relate the social happenings in Chattanooga." Zella promised that advertisers "will represent the cream of fashions" and the articles will "chronicle all of the events week by week that will be of interest to the smart set."

"There will appear from time to time in *The Lookout* pictures of Chattanooga's most beautiful matrons and young girls," Zella writes. "Few cities have such a reputation for the beauty of its women as Chattanooga. [Several] are noted nationally for their looks, while no list of southern beauties is complete without Chattanooga girls."

Zella made perhaps her biggest mark on Chattanooga when she founded an event to reinvigorate the dying Spring Festival tradition. The 1933 "Cotton Ball" introduced debutantes from Chattanooga and other Southern cities and elected a King and Queen. She chose the theme of the Old South for the event. Thousands attended. Anne Elizabeth Patten, the daughter of Zeboim's nephew, was the first Queen. Other kings and queens that decade included Montagues, Caldwells, Ochses, and J. T. Lupton's future daughter-in-law, Katherine Rawlings, according to a chapter in Zella's history on the 1930s. After this list, Zella names the mayors of that decade.[14]

Zella Armstrong died in 1965 after a lingering illness and was eulogized by both papers. A flat stone in the Forest Hills Cemetery marks her grave. She never married.

Zella's Big Bash

Zella's two volumes on Chattanooga "isn't the greatest history in the world, but it's got stuff in it that you can't get anywhere else," said Lee Anderson, another local historian. "When I knew her, she was an elderly spinster who started the Cotton Ball."

"It was a big thing. It was in the Memorial Auditorium. As a boy, I used to go, and everybody in town went to dance," he said. "The stage was decorated with columns like a Southern mansion. They would have two bands alternate playing and then have a grand march led by the governor. All these belles would be presented in identical dresses. They'd be called by their name, and they'd have an escort to take them up on stage, [some] in Confederate uniforms."

"There would be several thousand people in attendance," he said. "Only in later years has it become smaller....I was king a few years ago and I think there were maybe six or seven hundred or something like that."

"Other cities will have a ball but nothing quite like this. And, of course, they invite belles from all the cities around. They would have to get dates for all the belles

(Above) The **Cotton Ball** with a Southern mansion set. (Below) A collage of Cotton Ball Queens.

who came from out of town. You would date these new girls that you'd never seen before from Nashville or Birmingham or something. As college boys, we thought it was great. They thought Chattanooga was the greatest place in the world socially because all this activity was going on here. There was a party every night and a key dance at the country club, and all leading up to the grand march and the Cotton Ball."

The Cotton Ball tradition continues to this day, and still has an aura of empowering the aristocracy. In his 1997 column "Bubba Misses Cotton Ball," the iconoclast Bob Barnes says this prestigious event for "local elites" is where "rich folk get together to decide who will and won't be running the city the next 20 years."

Arch Willingham responded to Barnes's column, calling his charges ridiculous. Willingham's four cousins were in the ball, including cousin Shelly Haney, the Queen. "I can assure Bob that everyone there put his pants on the same way he does. There were no discussions about who would or would not be running the city," he wrote. "Most of the discussion centered around, 'The food is really good....That's a pretty dress....How 'bout them Braves?'"

"Nothing sinister," he said. "While some might think the idea of the party is goofy...it is just a party. Remind ol' Bob that snobbery works both ways."[15]

This Guy Knows How to Party

While Zella was the key social figure during the first part of the century, looming large during the second part of the century was Paul Carter, who never met a party, idea, girl, or venture he didn't like. The buddies he names, before they headed out for World War I, were George Hunter and Frank Harrison, the Coke millionaires, along with Scott Probasco, Burkett Miller, and many others. After crashing a fighter airplane and walking away, this early version of Forrest Gump returned to Chattanooga and led his group of friends in diligent partying.

"Many social events had been and were still being held in honor of the returned soldier," Carter writes in his memoirs. Clubs throwing regular parties included the Calumet Club, the Commercial Club, the Cotillion Club, and the Little Club, a group of twelve where each member was commissioned a certain month "to give the nicest, and most original party—each member, of course, taking the girl of his choice. These parties were really good."[16]

The members and chaperones of the Cotillion Club read like a Who's Who of Chattanooga. "In thinking back over the past 50 years and the wonderful times we were having at these various parties, I think how conditions have changed since that time," said Carter, "for, believe it or not, the members of the Cotillion Club never thought of taking a drink while at these parties. We would take our ladies home and possibly after that some of us would end up at Mr. Freeman's chili parlor on the ground floor of the Read House," he said. "Life was enjoyable in those days, and we kept our lady friends on a pedestal."

For Carter's big party of the month one year, he rounded up all his friends and drove them to the copper mines he and his father had bought a few years earlier in Copperhill, Tennessee, counting on a big demand because of the war. After the war, however, demand dropped and so did copper stocks. They had already poured a half million into the venture, but Paul Carter kept talking up the great opportunity with his rich friends. At Rotary, he received much applause after being introduced as "Paul Carter, the copper king of the South."

"We were rather desperate, as our indebtedness started to increase," he writes in his memoirs. His last gasp of hope was his old buddy, Frank Harrison, the Coca-Cola Bottling millionaire who married Anne Lupton. Only a few weeks before, Paul and Frank had finally decided to get to work after all the partying. "I decided we owed it to ourselves to have one last fling . . . to get away from it all for a period of two weeks. And a visit to Havana, Cuba, would be just what we needed."

Upon returning, Paul pitched Frank for the $100,000[†] he needed to dig out of the hole. Frank consented before mentioning that he had an old sweetheart in New York he wanted to visit. "He suggested we take her and her friend out to dinner, which we did. They were both very attractive girls." Unfortunately, while at dinner at Mory's in New York, some Ivy League boys got in a fight with the waiters. "The bouncer of the place, evidently thinking Frank was with the students, hit him with a pair of knucks. In return, Frank gave him a kick that will never be forgotten by him."

His face swelled up. "The doctor diagnosed a broken jaw. The next day we had a luncheon engagement with the two young ladies, but Frank wasn't a very presentable sight and had to eat through a straw."

The mining venture went belly-up, so Carter turned his focus to their earlier idea of a 200-room hotel on Lookout Mountain. "The majority of those interviewed thought it would be a good idea, should be a grand success, and would be wonderful for Chattanooga," he reported with continued optimism. "We had broadened our plans considerably to build an air field, polo grounds, dam up Rock City above Lula Falls, and make this entire section of the mountain into one great playground."

When *New York Times* publisher Adolph Ochs happened back to town, Carter took him up to his hotel site, driving him to the back of the mountain and using all sorts of dirt roads but avoiding the giant holes. Adolph told Paul it would be a miracle if he could build the giant hotel on the back of the mountain. "If you do succeed, it would at the end of the road, so to speak. You would go 'busted' sooner or later."

[†] $1.1 million (2006)

Ochs was hesitant to invest. He did congratulate Carter for his excellent driving skills around the mountain. "If the hotel is built and you do go broke, come to New York. Being the good driver you are, I will give you a job as my chauffeur."

Crash Goes the Hotel

Carter did get the hotel built. In 1928, Adolph Ochs returned again to celebrate his 50th anniversary of publishing the *Chattanooga Times.* He and his friends from New York were some of Paul Carter's first guests at the hotel on Lookout Mountain.

Carter then traveled to New York to sell stock in the Lookout Mountain Holding Company, and Ochs wrote several letters of introduction for him. Not too long after, the great stock market crash of 1929 occurred, and Chattanooga's Forrest Gump was in New York on that historic day. "After the morning of the crash, it was requested that all citizens of New York stay away from the financial district, as all offices would be closed," said Carter. "Of course, that just made me more anxious to go down on Wall Street, which I did, and there hundreds and hundreds of people were milling around looking up at buildings, trying to see what the situation in general was. About that time, a big policeman came over, nudged me and said, 'Big Boy, move along. There's no need for looking at the upper stories today because people won't start jumping out until tomorrow.'"

Because of the crash, Carter could not sell any more stock and the hotel eventually went bankrupt. He called Adolph Ochs. "How about giving me the job as your chauffeur?"

But he decided to return to Chattanooga instead. He packed up his battered Lincoln hoping against hope that he had enough gas money. "I surely was not the proverbial returning hero," he said. "Instead of Carter arriving in Chattanooga in a rip-roaring, glorious manner, he arrived not only completely broke, but owing...over a million dollars."[†]

He quickly devised a plan, however. He became an insurance salesman. He told his wealthy friends that if they bought his insurance plan he would put half of his commission into paying back what he owed them from the mining and hotel boondoggles. "However, some of the insurance companies here were very unhappy," he said. "And lo and behold, one day I got a call from Nashville—State insurance commissioner's office....I was informed that what I was doing was against the law....I told the commissioner I owed considerable money to Chattanoogans, and it was the only way I knew of paying my debts, and if he could suggest a better way, I would like to hear about it. He stated he didn't care how I paid them, but that I couldn't continue as I was doing. So, again my balloon busted."

[†] $10 million (2006)

Paul Carter's **Lookout Mountain Hotel**, later the "Castle in the Clouds," and finally Carter Hall on the **Covenant College** campus.

"Dinner at Eight" at Anne Haven. (From left) Rody Davenport, Scotty Probasco, Bobby Jones, Elizabeth Lupton Davenport, Tommy Lupton, Betty Probasco, Frank Harrison, Paul Carter, Jack Lupton, Alice Probasco Lupton, Betty Duff, Peggy Jones, Frank Duff, Beth Lupton.

Carter Hits the Lupton Jackpot

Eventually, however, Carter found a way to reach his fortune—a traditional Chattanooga strategy: he married someone wealthy. His best buddy Frank Harrison had died a few years before. "Needless to say, Anne knew I was broke 'as flat as a flounder.'" Paul then describes their wedding in Dr. Fowle's office and how the two took a Pullman car to New York for their honeymoon.

Carter offers no specifics on how he and Ann Lupton Harrison came to be married. "I could bring this to a conclusion right here by simply saying that we fell in love and were married on October 7, 1935, and we spent thirty-two happy years together in our home at 1649 Minnekahda Road."

It is an address to remember, because this home is also important to Chattanooga's history. For the purposes of this chapter, it serves as the key house of the second part of the century. The gigantic brick mansion became a central social spot for Chattanooga's elites thanks to Paul Carter's insatiable appetite for partying. Even after Anne died, Carter kept up the socializing and perhaps even increased it. In January of 1969, he held a grand dinner at the mansion and printed a French menu for "le Restaurant Anne Haven." A picture of the fourteen members of Chattanooga's top aristocrats, which appears in a number of the local history books, captures the scene. The stately dining room is graced with silver, china, and chandeliers. The long table shows Paul Carter standing at the end, flanked on each side by Coke magnates Frank Harrison, Jr. and Jack Lupton. All the men wear tuxes. The others around the table are Jack's wife (Alice), Scotty and Betty Probasco, Rody and Elizabeth Lupton Davenport, Tommy and Beth Lupton, Frank and Betty Duff, and Bobby and Peggy Jones. The caption says, "Dinner at Eight."

That was the core of Chattanooga's elite in 1969. Of those that remain today, their presence is still strong. The transition to a new generation of leaders is, amazingly, still a work in progress after 36 years.

Mountain City's Guineas

The elite club of this period was the Mountain City Club. Helen, who lets us in on the secret to Mountain City Club Bean Soup, says that "for many years the most prominent men in town have had breakfast or lunch or dinner with privacy, dignity, and convenience." Harry Probasco was a founding director in 1889, and Ben Thomas served as president in his days as a bottling magnate. But the Mountain City Club reached its heyday when the likes of Paul Carter and other luminaries sat at the Guinea Table, described by Frank Brock as the place for the "rich-rich" and those who personified the idea of a small power structure. Originally, it was simply Carter and his war buddies. "This group being young and vociferous," he writes, "was nicknamed the Guineas' table by the older members, due to our chattering; and by many this table still goes by that name. I kinda think the reason for our racket was that we had been honored so much for 'saving the Country for Democracy,' we probably thought we were privileged characters." Paul Carter was the last survivor of the original Guineas.

Later in life, Paul got one last chance to enjoy his boondoggle of a hotel that went belly-up. He and some friends were at the Fairyland Club and heard the hotel was under new management and offered new games. "Someone said, 'Why don't we go up there and see what it is all about.' This we did, and [it] was operating wide open, with dice and all alcoholic drinks."

"I was particularly lucky, and left the game ahead. After our visit to the hotel, we decided to visit the Stardust Club," he said, "and they were running wide open also. I was quite lucky there also. [But] the next morning 'old man remorse' caught up with me. I thought the best thing I could do would be to listen to Dr. Fowle's sermon on the radio. During the course of the sermon—with Dr. Fowle seemingly looking me right in the face—he stated, 'I am happy to announce that the following members of the church have been elected deacons,' and this list included my name!"

Feeling the hypocrite, Paul told Dr. Fowle what he had been doing the night before and asked to be excused from the deacon board. Paul reports that Dr. Fowle told him certain deacons had done far worse. "This might be just the thing you need to make a man of you—especially if you will give to the church one-half of what you won."

A few months before he died, a declining Paul Carter got a visit at his Lookout Mountain home from Scotty Probasco. "He offered me a cigar," said Scotty. "He was just chipper and cheerful, and I said, 'Doggone, Paul, you never cease to amaze me. Here you are not in real good health, but you just have more fun, and just entertain the hell out of your guests.' And he said, 'Well, I have to. If I wouldn't, nobody would come see me.'"

One of those regular visitors was Allen Duble, a fundraiser for Covenant College. He would give Carter updates on the college, but one day Paul told him the visits were unpleasant. "Don't you know it's a terrible memory for me? I went bankrupt. I had a dream for that place, that people from all over the country would stay in Chattanooga for a weekend."

Stunned, Duble told Carter that students now come to his hotel from all over the country and the world (today, forty-seven states and thirty countries). "Not just for a weekend," he said, "but for four years." And hundreds have married and stayed in Chattanooga, he said.

"Tears were pouring down his face," said Duble. "He'd gotten his dream back."[17]

The Mansion of the Century

While Ashland Farms and Carter's Minnekahda mansion represent the first two parts of the century, undoubtedly the most important house of the 20th century is the Lyndhurst mansion. It certainly was the largest. At 34,000 square feet, the Riverview home provided visual evidence for John T. Lupton's gigantic fortune in Coca-Cola bottling. He became many times richer than his very wealthy father-in-law.

Reputed to be the largest home in the South, the Lyndhurst showplace overlooking the river boasted ten bedrooms, twelve baths, an indoor swimming pool, a bowling alley, and a ballroom with a pipe organ. "Its hospitality is traditional and many notable entertainments have been given within its walls," wrote Zella Armstrong. "Its stately charm and beauty as well as its generous welcome are reminiscent of famous old Virginia places."[18]

The Lyndhurst mansion suffered a tragic fate when it was razed in the 1960s. This might have ended its legacy and memory had not Jack Lupton chosen to name the most important foundation in Chattanooga's history the "Lyndhurst Foundation." Before Jack Lupton became chairman, the foundation of the Lupton fortune was headed by First Presbyterian pastor James L. Fowle. Contrasting these two major figures and their agendas provides a key to understanding the major shifts in Chattanooga during the 20th century.

I was eagerly looking forward to an interview with Jack Lupton on this subject. While awaiting a response to my letter, I had the opportunity to interview Tommy Lupton—a cousin of some type to Jack.

The office of Thomas Allen Lupton II sits on the twelfth floor atop the Tallan Building, which Tommy built 30 years ago along with the Krystal Building beside it. A great many members of Chattanooga's power structure operate from these two buildings. Lupton was also the developer of Heritage Landing, the Dupont warehouses, and many other major landmarks.

I was a little edgy before the interview began. I had written many articles about the Lupton family in my news publication, such as "Jack Lupton Obtained Prime Spot by Aquarium Without a Bid."[19] I figured it best not to mention the *Chattanooga Fax* to Tommy Lupton, and he did not mention it to me. I guess I had sailed under the radar screen once again.

Tommy on the Luptons

T. A. Lupton motored into the boardroom in a wheelchair. His delivery was quiet and gentle. I found him to be rather helpful and not at all intimidating.

"Tell me, did you know John T. Lupton?" I asked. "You probably didn't know J. T. Lupton did you?

"Oh yeah," he said. "I was a young fellow. I was four years old when he died."

LUPTON ~ HARRISON

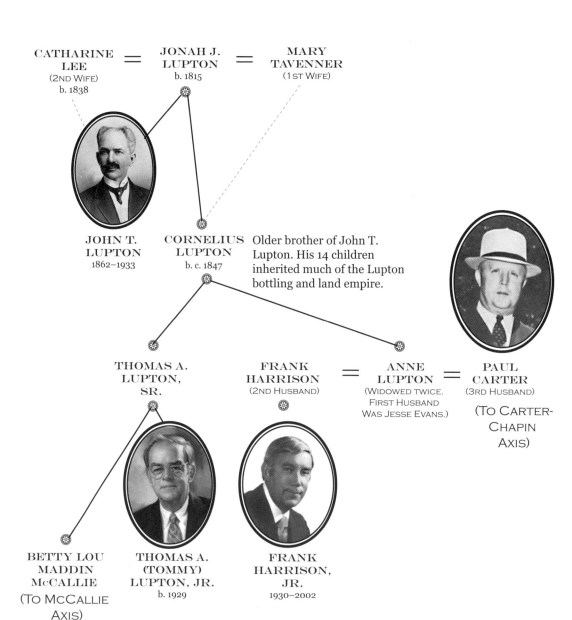

CATHARINE LEE (2ND WIFE) b. 1838 = **JONAH J. LUPTON** b. 1815 = **MARY TAVENNER** (1ST WIFE)

JOHN T. LUPTON 1862–1933

CORNELIUS LUPTON b. c. 1847 — Older brother of John T. Lupton. His 14 children inherited much of the Lupton bottling and land empire.

THOMAS A. LUPTON, SR.

FRANK HARRISON (2ND HUSBAND) = **ANNE LUPTON** (WIDOWED TWICE. FIRST HUSBAND WAS JESSE EVANS.) = **PAUL CARTER** (3RD HUSBAND) (TO CARTER-CHAPIN AXIS)

BETTY LOU MADDIN McCALLIE (TO McCALLIE AXIS)

THOMAS A. (TOMMY) LUPTON, JR. b. 1929

FRANK HARRISON, JR. 1930–2002

(Charts are partial, not exhaustive, highlighting key links or characters in the book.)

"So you did know him?

"I knew him. Yes, sir, I did. He scared me to death. He had a mustache, and I wasn't accustomed to that, being a four-year-old boy. I was terribly upset. I remember crying when he died. They brought him back on a train. I remember his funeral. I remember going to his house with my daddy."

I was trying to remember exactly how they were related. "J. T. Lupton is your grandfather?"

"No, he's my half-uncle to tell you the truth. But, anyway, that's a long story."

Actually, that long story was precisely why I was there. I kept probing until I got a better understanding. He explained to me that his father died when he was 17.

"Who was your father?"

"Allen Lupton."

"How are you related to the other Luptons?"

"J. T. Lupton was a half brother to my daddy's daddy, or my grandfather. I never knew a grandparent on either side of my family. All of them were dead from my birth. Frank Harrison and I were first cousins. His mother was my daddy's sister. My grandfather died way before I was born."

"What was his name?"

"I can't—I don't know."

After two years of research, it's still been difficult for me to decipher the Lupton family tree. (Part of the confusion is that Frank Harrison and Anne Lupton may have been first cousins when they married.) We do know that Tommy Lupton's grandfather was Cornelius Lupton, the half brother of J. T. Lupton (see chart). Tommy Lupton grew up knowing Jack Lupton's father and grandfather, not his own, and he was proud to be a part of that extended family.

"You know, once you're a Lupton, you're kind of always a Lupton. I was proud of what my family did and felt a commitment to live up to what they represented themselves to be."

"What's it like to grow up in Chattanooga and be a Lupton?"

"It's kind of tough in a way. J. T. Lupton was so very wealthy. For instance, when I went to Baylor I would be called 'Tommy Baylor of Lupton School.' But, I mean, you always live under the awning that someone in your family had some money, so that kind of rubs on you because you've got the same name. I told Jack one time, if I'm going to live up to his name, he better help me out a little bit."

Jack means "favored son." *Thomas* means "the twin."

"But, anyway, it was not hard," said Tommy. "I came in with some prestige and a good name, and I was always conscious of the responsibility to live up to that name. I was proud of it."

"Did you know Cartter Lupton?"

"Oh yeah. I knew Uncle Cartter. He was tough—tough as hell. He had a fear of doing business with his family because he didn't want to have to fire them. But, at the same time, his daddy—there were fourteen kids in my daddy's family—and J. T. hired almost every one of them or their husbands and then gave them Coca-Cola territories to run. For example, Uncle Charlie took over Texas…Uncle Fred was New Orleans, and Frank Harrison's daddy was North Carolina and things of that sort."

J. T. Lupton brought T. A. Lupton, Sr. to Chattanooga to run the Stone Fort Land Company in 1932. When he died in 1947, Tommy's mother ran the company until Tommy later took the reigns.

"The Coca-Cola side was where all the money was," said Tommy. "The real estate side was work like hell."

Tommy tells the story about the Krystal Building, the first speculative downtown construction venture by anyone in decades. "Rody Davenport, who ran Krystal, and I were great friends. He asked me to build a building for Krystal. He's the one who married Elizabeth Lupton."

"Incidentally, she is an unsung hero," said Tommy, who took a brief diversion to give tribute to the recently deceased sister of Jack Lupton. "She gave money right alongside Jack. You don't see her name on buildings or anything. She didn't want any credit for it. For instance, in the Aquarium she matched Jack dollar for dollar."

"She followed more of her daddy. She was a churchgoer, just like her daddy was," said Tommy. "Jack separated from his daddy—I mean that in a figurative sense. He wanted to go on with his life, and he was in his daddy's shadow. I don't mean to be critical of that."

"Anyway, Rody Davenport asked me to build a building for Krystal after their plans to buy the Double Cola building fell through." Tommy says he persuaded his friend Summerfield Johnston to rent some space, as well as his cousin Jack. When he built the Tallan Building a few years later, he constructed a special skywalk for Jack that connects the seventh floor of both buildings.

When Stone Fort Land Company decided to build the Krystal Building, Tommy Lupton's buddies, fellow directors at American National Bank, "wished me luck and kind of shook their heads and said, 'You're not gonna make it, but gear yourself up for the next thing.' Well, I did make it, and I built many more buildings."

J. T. Lupton's Hard and Soft Legacies

Stone Fort Land Company was started in 1886 "by a gang of carpetbaggers from the Midwest," said Tommy. They named the land company after a rock quarry located by today's City Hall that was used as a munitions depot by both the North and South during the Civil War. "Along the way, Zeboim Patten bought an interest in it, and, in 1912, J. T. Lupton got interested in it. And the two of them built all those warehouses that constitute Warehouse Row."

While Jack Lupton has continued J. T. Lupton's legacy of an international soft drink business and strategic foundation giving, Tommy has continued a more tangible J. T. Lupton legacy that affects the very warp and woof of the city. From his twelfth floor office in the Tallan Building, Tommy pointed to a stone wall across Highway 27 made of large blocks. He said these thirty-pound blocks of limestone from the Stone Fort quarry can be found at the University of Chattanooga, Warehouse Row, and all over the city.

"I always felt like the Stone Fort Company tied things together in Chattanooga, supplying bricks and mortar and land where it was needed," he said.

He pronounced it *Chattanooga* (as in *nook*, not *nuke*), just like Doug Daugherty.

Lupton Legend #2: Cartter

Cartter Lupton was 11 years old when he moved into the Lyndhurst mansion. When he was thirty-four, his father, J. T. Lupton, died and left a five-sentence will. Everything was passed to his only child, Cartter. His wife, Elizabeth Patten Lupton, was allotted $100,000 a year. When Cartter died in 1977, the will was twenty-eight pages, and his $200 million estate was the largest ever probated in the South. By comparison, Howard Hughes's estate the same year was $168 million.[20]

Like Hughes, Cartter Lupton was considered by many to be a recluse. "He was very shy, very shy," Scotty Probasco told me. "I mean, you'd never see him at the Mountain City Club or anything like that. But he was a devout, strong Christian. Very conservative. Very generous. I really loved him. He was a whale of a guy."

Lee Anderson knew Cartter Lupton from church. "You would think somebody with money like that would be dominant in church. He wasn't. He would sit on the back row. He was a good friend of Dr. Fowle's. He contributed heavily to things for the church."

Anderson taught Sunday School, and Cartter would often call him the next day and offer to send him a book on the subject he spoke about. "I'll send it over to you." I said, "Yes, sir, Mr. Lupton." "We got to be friends that way. I never asked him for anything. I never collected any money from him."

"Mr. Roy was chairman of Erlanger Hospital," said Lee, "and so Mr. Lupton would call Mr. Roy at Christmas and say, 'Roy, you got anything over there you need?' And Mr. Roy would say, 'Yeah, we need so and so.' And he'd say, 'Okay, I'll send you a check.'"

Cartter Lupton

One time Lee Anderson was speaking at church and mentioned offhand how the guy at his gas station had a family and was studying at Tennessee Temple to be a preacher. He told Lee, "I haven't gotten enough money to pay tuition. But the Lord will provide."

"The next morning my phone rang. 'Lee, this is Cartter Lupton.'" He had Lee send a check to the man for his tuition, but only if the donor remained anonymous. "That was my relationship with Cartter Lupton," said Lee.

I asked Tommy Lupton to compare Cartter Lupton and his son Jack. "Oh, much different styles. Jack is more outgoing. You wouldn't ever see Cartter's name on anything," he said. "He always gave anonymously. Jack lets his name go along with it. That's a big difference between them. They both have been very generous. They have built things and done things in this town you would never know about."

Scotty Probasco talks religion when comparing father and son. "Well, in the first place, Cartter Lupton was, I would have to say, a devout, strong Christian," said Scotty. "[Jack's] got a great heart, he really does. Surprisingly, he's not swell-headed or cocky. But he's never had to work for a board or anything. He owned all their businesses, so he has never reported to anybody, including God. I mean, I have a little problem there."

"People are scared of him, but he's always been moody. So you catch him in a bad mood, and he's a terror. Catch him in a good mood and he can charm the eyeballs off a rattlesnake. I mean, literally."

During the interview, Probasco referred to his brother-in-law as "Leopard Head."

"Leopard Head?" I asked.

"Old Leopard Head. Yeah. I've always called him Leopard Head."

"What is that?"

"Oh, that goes way back." He explained that in high school the sports page editor listed Jack Lupton's name in the paper in a golf box score as "Jack (Leopard Head) Lupton."

"Back then, I was still in the championship flight, and Leopard was listed way on down there in the third flight. But his father came into his office and his dad said, 'Son, where did this name Leopard Head come from?' That's where it came from, 50-some years ago."

"And you don't know why he called him that?" I asked Scotty.

"The only reason I can tell you is, it really does fit him well. I tell him he kind of looks like a leopard and he walks and stalks like a leopard, so he's been my Leopard Head ever since."

You might say Jack stalked the Lupton bottling enterprise for many years before pouncing. "I made a bad mistake in not challenging my father earlier in my career,"

Jack told *Beverage World.* "He was incapable of doing some of the things I knew needed to be done. That's a pretty big statement to make about a guy that most people didn't think made any mistakes. But he was too conservative. He became a caretaker and stopped being an entrepreneur early in his career."

Rick Montague made similar but more cautious statements. "[Jack] wanted the business to be more vibrant, to be more aggressive, to be better managed. What Cartter Lupton had done with the business was much more taking damn good care of what he had. Both are responsible positions."

"Anybody with any sense who had known those two personalities and said, 'What's going to happen now that Cartter Lupton is dead?' the answer would have been a 180-degree change, guaranteed."

The Lyndhurst Survives in Spirit Only

Cartter Lupton did make one decision that his son could not undo. He chose to raze the Lyndhurst mansion.

"It was built to last a thousand years," said Tommy. "I'll tell you what happened to it. Uncle Cartter went off to war and. . . . squirrels got into [the roof] and all the water downspouts came through the walls. . . . The gutters got stopped up, squirrels stopped them up, and that roof rotted out...All the water poured into it for four or five years and just took all the plaster off of it. All the paneling that was in there was warped and ruined, and it was a mess."

"Uncle Cartter called me one day and said, 'I want to sell this place. It's a wreck, and it's too big a house to ever do anything with, so I want to sell it.' I said, 'Uncle Cartter, I'd just have to tear it down.' He said, 'That's what I want.' So I set about tearing it down [and] made the Lyndhurst subdivision over in Riverview."

Elizabeth Patten Lupton had lived at Lyndhurst until she died in 1941. It was shuttered for two decades until it was razed. It was said that Lyndhurst "was born with Elizabeth Patten Lupton and it died with her."

Tommy Lupton found himself in a controversy over another historic building in Chattanooga, the Union Depot station. Chattanooga's railroad heritage was founded on the site, but the Tallan Building eventually replaced it. "I'm always a believer in saving a building if it really has true economic value," said Tommy. "That building had very limited economic value."

"It needed to be torn down?" I asked.

"Yes. Absolutely."

"It couldn't have been saved?"

Tommy Lupton explained to me that a shed connected to the back of the building needed to be torn down, and he hired a man to pull out just one piece of it to see how bad it was. "He tied a rope to a pickup truck and pulled down the whole damn building. He was just going to pull out one piece of it. The whole thing fell down."

That was over the weekend. Monday morning he got a call. "Dr. Fowle, who was my preacher, asked if he could come talk to me about tearing Union Station down. A group of women went to see him to ask him to ask me not to tear that building down. Well, he came by my office and I said, 'Dr. Fowle, the building's already—most of the building is already down.' He said, 'Well, there's no sense in us wasting words then.' So we talked and prayed, and then he went back."

Man of the Century

While the Lyndhurst mansion is Chattanooga's home of the century, Dr. James L. Fowle is the best choice for the social character of the century. His role was of a more serious nature than that of Zella Armstrong or Paul Carter, but in terms of brokering relationships on a communitywide scale, there may have never been an individual so prolific and so capable. Understanding Dr. Fowle is crucial to understanding the significance of that plaster on the ceiling of First Presbyterian that landed on the Lupton pew.

"He was chaplain of the City Commission. He wrote newspaper columns. He was a teacher at the University," said UTC professor Larry Ingle. "He was the grand ol' man when it came to religion in the community. I mean, that's just the way it was."

Lyndhurst Mansion

He also raised $18 million for the university and chaired the United Way for ten years. He campaigned for the Cancer Society, Goodwill, Hunter Museum, YMCA, GPS, Bright School, Princeton Theological Seminary, and a multitude of other charities. He even spearheaded the war-bond campaigns. He is considered by many to be the greatest fundraiser in the entire history of the city. "His niche was raising money for everybody," said Tommy Lupton. "He helped the United Way get off the ground. He helped everybody raise money. He'd look at you and say, 'Now Tommy, all the money is in this room.' You've probably heard Scotty Probasco say that. And, sure enough, it would be in that room, and all of us had to kick in."

Dr. Fowle once told a friend, "I love to preach, but in heaven, I don't think they'll let me preach. I love to sing, but in heaven, I don't think they'll let me sing during the worship service. But they will need someone to pass the collection plate. I think I may get to pass the collection plate in heaven."

Dr. Fowle wore only two outfits all year long. Through fall and winter he wore a gray, pinstripe suit with a long, swallowtail coat. On Easter, he switched to an all-white linen suit, which he wore faithfully through the summer. He kept the original Latin and Greek text of the Bible on his desk. When asked his favorite Bible translation, he once said, "The Fowle translation." A gifted speaker, he gave sermons without notes, but he always wrote the pastoral prayer word for word. "He thought the intercessory pastoral prayer was the most important part of the worship service," said Tom McCallie.

Fowle was famous for saying, "You can't outgive God," said Pete Cooper, head of the Chattanooga Community Foundation. "He said that to Scotty dozens of times. He said that to Cartter Lupton and everybody else in town." Formerly with the American National Bank charitable trust department, Cooper said Fowle's obsession with money had its quirks. Every year without fail, Dr. Fowle would show up on January 2 to physically examine the stock certificates given to the charities he promoted, insisting on verifying each by number. Cooper said he is the only person to ever do so. "You're talking about the biggest, most prestigious trust department in town, overseen by members of his church," said Cooper, "But he felt this stewardship responsibility so strongly. He [wanted] to be able to go to Cartter Lupton or somebody else and say, 'I know they're there. I've seen them.'"

He was a large, imposing man. One day he was in the Hamilton National Bank when the bank got held up. Dr. Fowle grabbed the robber from behind and held him in a bear hug until the police arrived.[21]

"A powerful personality. And a great speaker," said Rick Montague. "I would say, as many people would, that Dr. Fowle was felt in your heart to be God. This is the way God talks. This is the way God looks. You know, seeing God would be a disappointment after seeing Dr. Fowle."

The Junket to Replace Dr. Fowle

"I felt like Dr. Fowle could never be replaced," said Tommy Lupton. "He was a wonderful, genuine man. But, sure enough, we did replace him with a vibrant preacher that wanted an outreach to the world, and he had it."

The search for a replacement included Lupton, Probasco and Lee Anderson. One of the candidates was in Key Biscayne, Florida. "Scotty and I flew down there in a little Piper Cherokee," said Lee Anderson. "We went in and Scotty said, 'Look, see who's over there.' And here was Billy Graham, sitting in the next pew." Anderson said Richard Nixon was also a frequent attender. "They had a helicopter pad there for him."

When the pulpit committee met to decide on Rev. Ben Haden from Florida, eight of the nine were in favor. The decision became unanimous when Tommy Lupton walked in late and said, "He's the man."

When Rev. Haden replaced Dr. Fowle as pastor of First Presbyterian Church, many changes took place. The two differed greatly in both style and focus.

"Dr. Fowle was behind the pulpit," said Lee. "Ben moved the pulpit back, and he'd walk back and forth. He would often have a Flair pen in his hand, and that was just a prop. He'd have a mike on, and he would be walking back and forth across, which was new to us and a different style."

"Dr. Fowle was a more, I think, dignified personality," said Tommy Lupton. "Ben was dignified but—Ben was more gung ho and wanted to do things. And Dr. Fowle did too—Dr. Fowle got more done than probably anybody else in the history of Chattanooga."

While Fowle's strength was a focus on the community, Haden's focus was more national and international. "It boomed," said Lee. "Attendance went up. The budget went up. The outreach went up. He preached to more people in one Sunday than the church had in its whole history because of TV and radio."

The First Presbyterian history captures the differences in the dedication page devoted to the two men. On Dr. Fowle: "In modern Chattanooga history, probably no individual—preacher or otherwise—has had the widespread influence of civic good and for the advancement of the things of Christ." On Ben Haden: "In all of Chattanooga history, probably no individual has shared the Good News of Christ with more people."

Haden himself recognized the differences, expressing thanks to the church for "the love and acceptance our family has received, despite the fact I probably didn't fit into the mold of the church."

There was also a difference in theological perspective. "Ben's emphasis was on evangelism," said Doug Daugherty.

Dr. James Fowle

294

"This whole thing about culture and community was not something he really even thought about. It didn't even come into his thinking. When he looked at the human condition, he thought of everyone making a decision to follow Christ, which in my mind is sort of what an evangelist does."

"Whereas, I think someone who is more steeped in theology—or at least Reformed theology, when they look at creation, they think in terms of God's purposes for the whole thing. The Calvinists [Presbyterians] and the Thomisists [Anglicans and Catholics] are the only ones that engage the culture. The other faith traditions don't even enter into the debate. That's why Highland Park with 42,000 people did not have the effect on leadership that you would have expected."

Tom McCallie called Fowle a typical Presbyterian Calvinist. "Everything was God's and it was all appropriate. . . . he was involved in most every aspect of life in Chattanooga."

Chattanooga Mega-Shifts

Other shifts were taking place simultaneously in the community. A few months before Ben Haden's arrival at First Presbyterian Church, the plaster from the church ceiling dropped onto the Lupton pew. Around that same time, Jack Lupton left the Presbyterian Church, and so did his son-in-law at the time, Rick Montague.

"Our departure from the church coincided with the arrival of Ben Haden," said Rick. "The Luptons, Jack and Alice, were moving their family. Ben Haden's style was very different. The church was very different."

Up until that time, the major fortunes of Chattanooga had been under one roof and one ideological umbrella since the city's inception. When Jack Lupton and Rick Montague left the conservative Presbyterian church, they commissioned the Lyndhurst Foundation to chart a different vision for the community. It was less religious, more secular, and more "progressive." Few doubt that the new mission, on its own terms, has been wildly successful.

But it wasn't just the difference in the preacher's style that caused the change. Conservative, fundamental Christianity was also in question.

"Well, golly heck fire. You know, religion does wonderful things for people," said Rick Montague, when asked about the big questions of life. "Sometimes it can be a little frightening."

He went on to explain his Fundamentalist pedigree. For eight years, he scored perfect in attendance and Scripture memory as president of the Sunday School department at First Presbyterian. He was very active in the church youth group and won the first-ever J. P. McCallie Memorial Award for Christian Leadership at McCallie school. "I took all this stuff very seriously, very seriously," he said. "Whatever

I'm getting at First Pres, I'm getting a double dose at McCallie and am programmed to take all these things very seriously."

He had some generational pressure. A hundred years before, Rev. T. H. McCallie praised Rick's great-grandfather for "the promptness and regularity with which he came to our services." Theodore Giles Montague was "honorable and upright, kind and genial, gentle and modest. He left an ineffaceable record."[22]

"My family's relationship with Dr. Fowle was in the ethos of the First Presbyterian Church," said Rick. "As I picked it up, you have a responsibility to this city," he said. "If you're in this church, part of what you do, if you believe these things, you act on them. So it was very strong."

But when Rick headed to the University of Virginia, his views began to change. He also began attending the Episcopal church. "Over time, you're talking to people from equally sincere religious backgrounds ... you know, your mind broadens a bit. You begin to ask a number of questions for yourself. I took courses in history and literature, and when you read a lot of literature, you begin to understand [about] words and myths and symbolism, and how truth can exist and be powerfully true without being literally true. It changes the way you think about the Scriptures."

Montague tells a story that occurred one summer after returning from college that clearly shows his issues with First Presbyterian were larger than who was the preacher. Rick invited a speaker named Ron Osborne he had heard at Boy's Club to address the church youth group. "He talked about Albert Schweitzer, and he talked about living your beliefs. And at the end of the thing, while he was still up there this woman says, 'Mr. Osborne, Albert Schweitzer didn't go to heaven.' And he said, 'What?' She said, 'Young people, Albert Schweitzer didn't go to heaven. He didn't believe Jesus Christ was his Lord and Savior.'"

"Well, Ron's brother and father and grandfather were all in social work that they had been introduced to through the Salvation Army. It was this sense of, 'Let me tell what your life has been dedicated to and what it means.' . . . you know, this cut-and-dried thing. And that was not unusual."

"So, anyway, [the Presbyterian Church] is an institution, and it has got its followers. But I'm happy not to have continued to be one of them."

Lupton Legend #3 Changes the Whole Foundation

Neither is Montague surprised that Jack Lupton broke tradition with his father. "I mean, you know, Jack's a rebel. He wasn't interested in the same things his dad was interested in. He didn't have the same fears, the same guilts. Jack loved money and what money could do for people. His dad, in my opinion, didn't love money. It was a burden. It was a responsibility. He was not a public man. Jack loved the—loves—you know what I mean. They were completely different kinds of people, so it was only natural that the foundation would be completely different."

Jack Lupton's colleagues witnessed the difference. "He changed the agenda," said Tommy Lupton. "The Memorial Foundation was primarily for the benefit of schools and [charities]. I'm not sure I agree with what he's done, but he's changed it.... He finances things like the Indian Dancers of the Great Smoky Mountains or some such thing like that.... He changed the name from Memorial to Lyndhurst, and he changed the direction."

Lee Anderson said Jack "moved back towards a kind of secular, hands-on, community vision."

"Mr. Lupton was a very strong Christian," said Scotty Probasco. "Old Leopard Head shifted the whole thing."

No More Checks—Unless It's Strategic

Chattanooga's most significant event was not, literally, plaster on a pew. The big change took place in the mind of Jack Lupton. According to Rick Montague, the first sign of such change in relation to the Lupton fortune took place in the conference room of the recently deceased Cartter Lupton at his offices in the Volunteer Building.

A few days earlier, Rick Montague had mentioned to his father-in-law that he was leaving his teaching position at Baylor School and was available to help him. Jack decided to hire him as executive director of the Lyndhurst Foundation. He made the announcement at the next meeting of the full board of directors. "When he introduced me to them, in his opening remarks he said, 'I'm not sure what we're going to do, but we're not going to do what we've done in the past.'"

At that moment, Jack Lupton put everyone on notice that big changes were in store for Chattanooga.

The first thing Lyndhurst did was send a letter to everyone that got an annual check and told them not to expect another one after that year. That included a number of schools like Baylor, Tennessee Wesleyan College, King College, and others, and local charities such as the United Way, Hunter Museum, and Allied Arts.

Rick told them, "We're not going to do traditional kinds of giving. We're going to look at professional philanthropy. We're going to set some targets. In the meantime, there are things that individuals ought to do. Sometimes it was pretty pointed conversation."

Rick ran into one of the organization's directors. "I saw him socially, and I'm telling you, he was ready to chew my ass out. I'm on the record, aren't I?"

"Yes."

"He was irritated."

"Okay."

"And he took it personally." Montague continued. "Jack Lupton was able to impossibly, perversely enjoy cutting against the grain. People would say, 'That's just Jack. He's just that way, He's going to run hot. He's going to run cold, and that's the way it is.'"

Within a few months, Rick hired another Baylor teacher, Jack Murrah. "Jack Lupton had almost an irrational love for this town and the city," said Murrah. "And he would never let Rick and me get off the hook. If we would say, 'Well, things are not really popping in Chattanooga... that's why the proposals you see are not all that exciting,' he would say, 'I didn't hire you to tell me that.' I'm improvising on the words, but basically he said, 'Either you or your successor will find out how to use this foundation.'"

Through the Southeastern Council on Foundations, Rick became familiar with the Mary Reynolds Babcock Foundation in North Carolina. It was known to be a small, progressive foundation, and its executive director, Bill Bondurant, was particularly insightful.

Rick called Bondurant for advice. It was a big moment. "That changed the Lyndhurst Foundation," he said. When Rick visited them in North Carolina, he wanted to copy their grant request form. "Forget the form," Bondurant told him. "What's this foundation going to do?"

"What?"

"Are you going to have any priorities, any guidelines, any goals?"

"Why, we really haven't thought about that," replied Rick.

"Forget all this other stuff. You go back to your board, and if you'd like me to come over there, I'll talk to them. . . . You may not want to do the same things we do, but this is how you will do the best job for philanthropy."

"He was right," Rick told me. "That was really a groundbreaking event for us because it put us on a track of trying to figure out what we were going to do, rather than always be reactive. . . . He was the one that put that bee in the bonnet that said, 'Reactive philanthropy is a waste of a foundation's time.'"

In their search for goals and priorities, the Lyndhurst Foundation sent Rick Montague to a conference for foundations in Seattle. There, on his plate, was a booklet written by Gianni Longo, the guru of the visioning process.

———◆———

Montague means "pointed hill," from the Old French *mont* and the Latin *acutus*. The name first appears in Northern France as "Monte-acuto," where there are many sharp eminences. In 1066, William the Conqueror crossed the channel to fight the

Battle of Hastings and was joined by Drogo de Monte-acuto. In return, William, the Duke of Normandy, gave Monte-acuto vast properties. The Montague coat of arms bears the kite-shaped shield of the Norman invader and the full-length figure of a winged griffin.

Lupton Tower at Eton College in London

The meaning of *Lupton* is not known. There is a town in Midwestern England, thirty miles from Liverpool, named Lupton, and a nearby manor is called "Lupeton." Scholars suggest this means the dwelling place (*tun*) of *Hllupa*. No one knows the meaning of that Old English first name. The town of Lupton was part of the holdings of a noble named Torsin who was granted property by Charlemagne in 778.

A Lupton tower was built on the bank of the Thames River about 1520, during the reign of Henry VIII, for Eton College, which was founded by Henry VI in 1440. Approximately 1.6 million bricks were used to build Lupton Tower. When you enter England's most prestigious school, whose students have included Prince William and Prince Harry most recently, you can see a statue of Henry VI in front of Lupton Tower. Both are also clearly in view from the terrace of Windsor Castle.[23]

A Lupton Tower can also be seen at Baylor School in Chattanooga. The first known ancestor of the Chattanooga Luptons is Thomas Lupton, born around 1570. His son, Martin, was born in Leeds, a few miles from Lupton, England. The migrating ancestor, Joseph Lupton, a weaver, settled in Bucks County, Pennsylvania as a young man and married Mercy Twining in 1713. They were Quakers, members of the "Society of Friends," and were cleared by the "clearness committee" for marriage. But when their first child came too early, the clearness committee determined they had committed "unchaste actions before marriage." The couple then presented a written confession, which was accepted and read aloud at the next worship meeting.

Their fifth child, John Lupton, was born in 1725 and settled near Winchester, Virginia. Possibly due to hearing old family stories about clearness committees, this son was known as "the Presbyterian Lupton," and his family became known as the Presbyterian branch of the Luptons. The Presbyterian Lupton's grandson, Jonah Lupton, had a son, Cornelius, from his first wife. (This was Tommy Lupton's grandfather. Cornelius had fourteen children.) Jonah's second wife, Rebecca Catherine Lee, was a distant relative of Robert E. Lee and the second cousin of Light Horse Harry Lee. Jonah was 45 and Catherine was 23 when their were married. Their son, John T. Lupton, Jack Lupton's grandfather, was born in Winchester, Virginia, in 1862.[24]

Woodruff versus Lupton

The story of J. T. Lupton and his success with Coca-Cola bottling has already been told at length. Suffice it to say that the triumvirate of J. T. Lupton, his son, Cartter Lupton, and grandson, Jack Lupton, controlled for a century the greatest Coca-Cola bottling dynasty in the world.

Their antagonist was the CEO of Coke in Atlanta, Robert Woodruff. Starting in 1922, he spent 60 years attempting to buy out the bottlers and place them under one roof in Atlanta. He was extremely competitive as an outdoorsman and a golfer, constantly upping his handicap to compete with his friend, Bobby Jones. Woodruff never lost at poker, keeping the game going until all hours of the night if necessary. On one occasion, he told the company pilot to keep circling the airfield until he finally won at gin rummy.

He also demanded total control of Coca-Cola and lost patience with J. T. Lupton, who called Woodruff's officers "the kindergarten." Woodruff tired of hearing Lupton brag about his successful efforts marketing Black Draught in 1893, as if that mattered decades later. He also noted that Lupton had disapproved of the wildly successful "Pause that refreshes" slogan.[25]

Unable to buy the Luptons out, Woodruff spent six decades chipping away at other bottling efforts. First he bought New England interests, then the Southeastern region, followed by the Western areas and Texas by 1940. It took thirty more years to buy Ben Thomas's bottling concerns. Finally, in 1986, the largest Coke bottler in the world, John T. Lupton II (Jack), elected to sell his JTL Corporation to Atlanta Coke for $1.4 billion.[26]

Today's Elite Club: The Honors

While he was selling a legendary company, Jack Lupton was creating a legend in golf, the Honors Course. It lies beyond a small, unmarked gate off the Ooltewah exit, about fifteen minutes from downtown Chattanooga. The little driveway actually leads to one of the most celebrated golf courses in the world, the site for the 1991 U.S. Amateur and the 1996 NCAA Championship won by Tiger Woods in 1996.

Lupton had long been a prominent member of the world's most prestigious and exclusive golf club, Augusta National. Seven small cabins grace the center of the world's most exclusive golf course. One of them, the "Butler Cabin," is

Robert Woodruff

famous as the spot where winners of the Masters are interviewed after the tournament. Another of the cabins is the "Lupton Cabin."

Jack Lupton determined to bring the excellence of Augusta to his course in Chattanooga. In the process, he created the city's premier club for the last part of the 20th century. It is regularly listed by various golf magazines as one of the best courses in the world. Designed by Pete Dye, the by-invitation-only membership fee cost $20,000 in 1983. In that year, there were 128 local members and 75 national members. "At the present time, the national membership is closed for reevaluation," Lupton told the paper. He also has made clear that a mere PGA tournament will not be allowed at the Honors Course. He did allow the U.S. Amateur to be played there and is also willing to host a U.S. Open.

The architecture is deliberately understated in the motif of a turn-of-the-century Appalachian farmhouse. Antique Scottish golf clubs dating back to the beginning of golf decorate the clubhouse along with 100-year-old books and brass light fixtures. An all-black waiting staff serves the lounge and the quiet restaurant, which cannot be entered without a sport coat.

A framed, cartoon-like poster on the wall is titled simply "The Committee." Nine men are shown sitting around the boardroom table of the Honors Course. Every face on the nine men, including the chairman, is the face of Jack Lupton.

The high standards and exclusive nature of the club are legendary. According to one regularly repeated account, a member was urinating on the side of the fairway near the woods when Lupton drove up in a cart, handed him a $20,000 check, and told him to never come back. Members say it is complete myth, but the story makes its point.

Mayor Gene Roberts considered himself rather lucky when he got to play this course in a community where he was the highest ranking official. (Chattanooga's

GOLF HOUSE TENNESSEE

Jack Lupton plans the Honors Course

aristocracy is hardly starstruck by politicians.) On the tee, the mayor told the member who invited him, "I believe I can drive that green."

"That's isn't the green," the member replied. "It's the fairway." [27]

New Man, Same Mansion

Who guides Chattanooga's aristocracy today? Who plays that role of social connector in the community, the position of party host played by Zella Armstrong and Paul Carter or the more serious social role conducted by Dr. James Fowle? Jack Lupton has been a great man in the century but generally avoids the public view. Scotty Probasco, the best fundraiser of the past quarter century, is also a top nominee. But Chattanooga has launched into another level, the age where private meets public.

The man who best embodies these qualities today is not a multigenerational Chattanoogan. Nor did he inherit wealth. He did buy the Volunteer Building and Cartter Lupton's old offices from Tommy Lupton, along with the rest of his Stone Fort properties. He is also a member of the elite Honors Course. Ironically, this same man also purchased Paul Carter and Ann Lupton's Minnekahda mansion—former Chattanooga mayor Bob Corker.

The grand Riverview home that once hosted the elite of Chattanooga society continues to do so today. But, as mayor of Chattanooga and as a fundraiser for President Bush, and now for his own campaign for U.S. Senate, Bob Corker has allowed that mansion to be visited and viewed now by thousands of Chattanooga citizens and voters. The dining room where fourteen Chattanooga aristocrats had "Dinner at Eight" is now enjoyed by countless locals who do not have the slightest connection to the Coca-Cola bottling fortune.

"Anne Haven" mansion of Anne Lupton and Frank Harrison, now owned by Bob Corker.

Modern Americans do not know how to throw parties like they did in Paul Carter's day, but they do seem to show up for political fundraisers, especially at a mansion, and no one has thrown more than Bob Corker.

Today, the mansion—actually the complex—that best reflects the next era for Chattanooga is not Corker's Riverview home. Instead, the Hunter Museum of American Art serves as an icon for the challenge Chattanooga now faces to connect its aristocratic past to its more public future.

With its most recent addition, the Hunter Museum perfectly depicts the three eras of the 20th century discussed in this chapter. The classic columned mansion represents the aristocratic wealth of Chattanooga's beginnings. It was donated by Coca-Cola bottler George Hunter, Ben Thomas's heir. The modern, cubish, less exciting addition of the 1960s represents the era of Cartter Lupton and his cronies at the Guinea table who capably maintained the city but did not effectively develop it. And this most recent contemporary addition, connected by the Holmberg pedestrian bridge, represents the very progressive age of the Lyndhurst Foundation with all its risks and hopes.

Appropriately, the new addition is still under critical examination by the public and the architectural connoisseurs. It is undeniable that the new, risky addition takes a small slice of grandeur from the majestic mansion beside it. This may be unavoidable, and the positive results from the new addition will hopefully prove to be a risk worth taking. Similarly, the city's leadership today must find a way to build on the great traditions of Chattanooga without abandoning her crucial and critical values.

Will There be a Future Elite?

A healthy elite can help guide that transition, but even the Rotarians are concerned that basic values, such as community and relationships, will not be passed down. Neither will the value of noblese oblige, which is critical to the leadership class. "I was talking with Bob Corker about how Rotary could help him to help the city move forward in economic development," said Frank Brock. "He was like, 'Really?'"

"Rotary can no longer take for granted that it will have the influence it had in the past if we cannot sell the idea of community first of all. The younger generation, they don't know what community is. They grew up in an impersonal neighborhood. They went to big public schools. They were not in strong churches, often. The places where community is learned, they never learned it. They're latchkey kids. They're eat-and-run kids. When you're talking about a cohesive community, they will say, 'Well, I'm really into jogging' and 'I really like the club' and 'I really like to go to the beach—what has Chattanooga got to offer me?' They've not got a strong sense of the welfare of the community. The generation that is coming along, unless we cultivate that, I think we're going to lose it."

The Last of the Lupton Legacy

What about the next generation of Luptons? As is stands today, Chattanooga's most legendary family will not survive by name beyond Jack and Tommy Lupton, who are both well past age 70.

"Jack Lupton has a son, but he lives in South Carolina," said Tommy.

"Does your son live here?" I asked.

"No. He lives in Athens, Georgia."

"So it may be that 20 years from now we may not have the Luptons in Chattanooga. How do you feel about that?"

"I'm sad about it," said Tommy. "But there's nothing I can do about it now. I did the best I could when I was capable of doing something."

I was ready to ask Jack Lupton some similar questions, but a letter arrived in the mail after I had interviewed Tommy that ended my long awaited hopes to chat with Chattanooga's most intriguing character. The letter was actually from Joel Richardson on letterhead for "The Lupton Company, LLC":

"Dear Mr. Arnold:

Jack Lupton has asked me to let you know that he is not willing to be interviewed by you for the book you are writing on Chattanooga.

Jack is a private person, and he has no interest in discussing a number of the matters you desire to discuss.

Moreover, in view of his current physical condition, Jack grants few, if any, interviews.

Sorry."

Out of nearly fifty of Chattanooga's leading citizens, Jack Lupton was the only one who decided not to grant an interview. It may have been the scope of my questions. It may have been his private nature, or it may have been his physical challenges after a stroke two years ago. He may have read the *Chattanooga Fax*. The answer is ambiguous, like the unknown meaning of *Lupton*, like the mysterious man himself.

I may never meet this man who is a central character in my book. For what it's worth, I can take some consolation in a discovery I made during my two years of research: Jack and I are connected through our ancestors. As it turns out, Robert Woodruff and I are cousins. The longtime rival of the Lupton family whose company finally bought Jack's bottling enterprise is related to me through my 3rd-great-grandfather, T. T. Woodruff, the sleeping car inventor. (My full name is Dean Woodruff Arnold—*Woodruff* means "ruler of the forest" and *Arnold* means "eagle power.") Robert Woodruff and I have the same direct migrating ancestor, Matthew Woodruff, who sailed from England to Connecticut in the early 1600s.[28]*

For whatever reason, Jack Lupton seems to like keeping himself at arm's length. "Makes me more interesting, doesn't it?" he told the *Chattanooga Times*.

I must say, I agree. But at least I got my interview with Tommy Lupton. He gave me all that good information apparently unaware of all my past reporting.

"I wish you a lot of luck on your book," he told me.

"Thank you."

"And let me say one thing to you," he added. "You published the *Chattanooga Fax?*"

"Uh. . . . Yes, sir."

"You've had some controversial articles in there. I'm aware of some of those."

"Yes, sir."

"Make this book positive. It's too important. This book is going to be something good for the history of this city, and you can be an integral part of it."

"Yes, sir," I repeated.

I hope I successfully followed his admonition. I certainly tried to.

Artist: Brent Sanders

CHAPTER NINE

The Spirit of Ninth Street

African Americans and the Bell of Freedom

On August 28, 1963, in Washington D.C., Dr. Martin Luther King, Jr. delivered one of the greatest speeches in American history. Just before its climax, "Thank God, Almighty, I'm free at last!" Dr. King challenged Chattanooga to find true racial harmony.

"I have a dream that one day, down in Alabama with its vicious racists . . . little black boys and black girls will be able to join hands with little white boys and white girls as sisters and brothers. I have a dream today!" he said.

"But not only that," he continued. "Let freedom ring from Stone Mountain of Georgia. Let freedom ring from Lookout Mountain of Tennessee. Let freedom ring from every hill and molehill of Mississippi, from every mountainside. Let freedom ring!"

Unlike most of her neighboring cities, Chattanooga did not see massive racial uprisings during the civil rights movement. There is a real sense in which Chattanooga avoided the turmoil of the '60s. There is also a shared sense by Chattanooga's black community that true harmony is still a faraway dream and that Chattanooga's peaceful exterior is more surface than substance. A decade after King's assassination, Chattanooga continued to show the ability to quickly ignite into racial conflict. The particular incident ironically involved changing the name of Ninth Street to Martin Luther King Boulevard. Once again, the Lupton family played a crucial role in a key aspect of Chattanooga history.

Other major Chattanooga families and leaders also got involved in preventing the possibility of major riots during the turbulent '60s. Once again, the "Spirit of Chattanooga" prevailed, that longtime tradition of seeking peace over conflict, prevention over confrontation, and compromise rather than controversy, but the tradition can sometimes be a two-edged sword.

"We had more communication. You'd like to think that," said Mai Bell Hurley, a white member of the first City Council that allowed primarily black districts and led, therefore, to black elected officials. "But there is a theory, you know, that we would have been better off [in the civil rights movement] if we'd had the catharsis that took place then. I don't really know. . . . I've thought a lot about this. I don't know."

"I would like to say that some of our lack of unrest has been because we've had people like Senator Brock and other people . . . making an honest effort over a long period of time."

I interviewed Senator Bill Brock III in his office in Annapolis, Maryland, and asked him about Chattanooga race relations. He told me how his grandfather, Bill Brock, Sr., opened his candy manufacturing plant every morning at 5:00 a.m. until the day he died. "When every worker came in, he knew their name. He knew when their little girl had a broken finger or little boy had a broken arm in a football game." So did Senator Brock's father, Bill Brock II, who chaired a committee of civic leaders for "the Peaceful Desegregation of Chattanooga."

"Dad got the national award of the National Association of Christians and Jews for his leadership in that effort. He was nationally recognized," said Bill III. "One of the suggestions I made to him that I think made a difference is that we put a note in every paycheck of every employee of every manufacturing firm in the town saying how much economic interest we had in having black and white, rich and poor, male and female, all a part of the community and economically participating. And we were successful."

"Some didn't want to do it. They said, 'Well, I don't want to make our workers mad.' But most did, and it was a pretty good sign that Chattanooga was not going to play the racist game."

Brock noted that Chattanooga still had a number of "inexcusable" things such as separate water fountains at the airport and other facilities. "But, by and large, Chattanooga was recognized nationally for being the most successful and the most peaceful in its efforts to get rid of the vestiges of the old way."

Perhaps because of such acclaim, the Anti-Defamation League in Atlanta informed Chattanooga elected officials of the top Klan leader in their area, information privy to the FBI but not typically shared with state and local leaders.

"He ran a little gas station in East Chattanooga," said former Mayor Gene Roberts. "The leaders summoned that gentleman to the mayor's office." In the room were Mayor Rudi Olgiatti, Sheriff Bookie Turner, the County Judge, the Police Chief, and Congressman Bill Brock. "I was standing at the door," said Gene, a staffer for the mayor. "And they put the fear of God into that gentleman. They told him that they were going to be watching him twenty-four hours a day and seven days a week. There would be a police unit parked next to his station and next to his house."

"They would be with him everywhere he went, and if he did one thing to frustrate the peaceful segregation of those schools, they'd have him under the jail so quick he wouldn't know what hit him. After that engaging meeting, he caused no problems."

"On more than one occasion, we would have meetings like that," said Brock. "We had some people who were true racists and there isn't any other way to put it. Gene and I and others would say, 'Go somewhere else. Don't live here. Don't stir things up.'"

Brock did get one notable reward for his efforts. "In the old days, if somebody was—I can't use the expression anymore—if he was 'pro-black,' the ultimate insult was to give him a bag of chitlins. And I came into my headquarters on one occasion and [my secretary] said I missed Mr. So-and-so."

"He wanted to see you, and he gave me this really wonderful bag of chitlins."

"And what did you say?" Brock asked.

"'I'm so grateful to you. That's probably the nicest thing that's happened to Mr. Brock all day.' The guy got so mad he stormed out."

"We had a street"

"We really never had any large skirmishes from a racial point of view," said Walter Williams, the area's first black judge to be elected citywide. "I mean, we've had one or two, but I don't call them mega-skirmishes—like Birmingham had, like Atlanta had, like Memphis had."

"These cities that had these problems dealt with them. And I think it was good to deal with them, put the real issues on the table, deal with them, and move on."

"To some extent, one would argue that maybe that's Chattanooga's problem: we never had that. It's always been a more accommodating city. . . . You know, if there's a problem let's just push it to the side. Let's just try not to think about it. So . . . more accommodating."

For some, the perception in Chattanooga is not reality. It's an "illusion of camaraderie," according to Pete Drew, a former state legislator and county commissioner from Knoxville. "This illusion takes place that there is a respect for each other that exists here, when in fact, it is not a respect for each other. It is a willingness to go along and get along."

Nonpolitical members of the black community echo the politicians. "We were complacent. We didn't want to fight," said Lee McWhirter, a barber in East

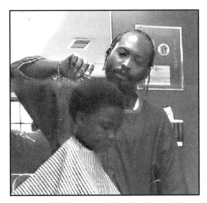

Lee McWhirter at his barber shop.

Chattanooga. "We just thought things were good like they were. It's okay to go up on the mountain and wash clothes and iron them, cut grass."

"We were scared. It was beneficial to take what we could get, and that's what we did. We didn't see nothing else."

"We were scared to put our foot down. In the other places, the people didn't like how they were being treated, and their mentality was different because they were more hungry than we were. We just accepted what happened. Chattanooga is still that way today. Everybody else has grown—Birmingham, Atlanta. . . . Nothing has changed here. We just laid down. We still do the same. We still lay down."

McWhirter is simply a barber. The shop on Glass Street is called Progress, but being a barber in the black community is not so simple. It can be one of the central communication spots for the African American culture. McWhirter is rather plugged in to the voice of the community, as is his father who has operated the Renewal Barbershop on MLK Boulevard for many decades.

Being a barber also means you own your own business, a rarity in America today. McWhirter says the black leaders in Chattanooga are CEOs. "Not a lot of businessmen. They are businessmen in a corporate sense where they are workers. CEO, the Vice CEO, whatever. You really can't say much. You have to keep your mouth shut—that's if you want to keep that job. You want to feed your family? Be quiet and accept things for what they are."

"We didn't have a Rosa Parks here. When we got on the bus, shit, we didn't give up an argument. We just walked to the back of the bus."

"We had a street. We didn't even have a side of town. We had a street. MLK was our street."

Actually, it was called Ninth Street until the '70s when two Luptons disagreed on whether to change the name. At the time, the black community was concerned about names. McWhirter believes the bigger issue is ownership.

"I saw the street go from thousands of people enjoying this place to walking outside and nobody is on the sidewalk, because we get to go to Brainerd Road now! We can go out here to Dairy Gold now and get us one of them big hamburgers. We never been able to walk in that place."

Pete Drew

"So we let what we built—we had drugstores, grocery stores, movie theaters—we gave it up. Why couldn't we go to our own movie theater, and you come to the movie theater and enjoy the movie with us, you understand? Keep it in the family; then, everybody is growing."

McWhirter wonders if the days of being poorer were better in light of empowerment issues. "We were living. There was food on the table. We had a little raggedy house to stay in. Black people had homes. Maybe we didn't have money to get groceries and things of that sort. But some had chickens running around in the yard. You wanted something to eat, you go out there and get that chicken and you bring it in the house, pluck some feathers off. The family ate."

"Now, you can record this. This is what pisses me off with my race of people. We had this, and we gave it away to take supplement that somebody was giving us, because we never got nothing before. So, you going to get some food stamps? Yeah, let's get in line, because nobody ever gave us nothing."

"It ruined us as a race of people. It killed us. That's wrong. I wish we could have just stayed like we were."

"Parents instilled in us . . . to be that doctor or that lawyer or that dentist. How about plumbing? It's hard work, sure. Maybe your daddy was a plumber, and you stood there and watched him—nasty hands, clothes dirty. But he gets paid, and he pays himself. It's not Erlanger. It's not Memorial Hospital, okay? One man working a job at his own pace, at his own time. That makes him a role model."

"That's our biggest problem. Maybe we need to stay in Glenwood. Don't take that $100,000 equity to buy a $300,000 house—now you try to pay a house note. And you're still getting up and going to work. You can't walk into the office and say, 'You mistreat me. I'm sick of this.'"

McWhirter, who owns the building where he works and owns his home outright, laments the demise of the Ninth Street community. "We lost our stuff and gave it away. We wanted what everyone else wanted: move out to East Brainerd and buy a new house. Our community died. Wasn't enough people in the community that was strong, that wanted to form a coalition to keep that place."

Doing Fine on the Big Nine

There was a time when Ninth Street was a bastion for black-owned businesses. Known as the "Big Nine," musicians, actors, politicians, and celebrities from across the nation regularly frequented the hot spot that rivaled Harlem for activity and entertainment. The black-owned Martin Hotel enjoyed regular visits from the likes of Duke Ellington, Count Basie, Louie Armstrong, Cab Calloway, and politicians like Booker T. Washington and W.E.B. Dubois. (The Martin Hotel was featured in a book Dubois published in France.)[1]

Jimmy Blanton

These jazz legends would perform to mostly black audiences at Memorial Auditorium (whites sat in the balcony) and would spend the rest of their evenings hitting clubs along the Big Nine. Chattanooga bass player Jimmy Blanton is credited with the original ideas behind bebop jazz. Blanton was a "creative genius who helped inspire the Ellington band's distinctive, rhythmic 'swing,'" said historian Doug Day.

Another famous bass player from Chattanooga, Wilfred Middlebrooks, played with Ellington, Basie, and Armstrong. He toured with Ella Fitzgerald for ten years and played at Kennedy's inauguration. Middlebrooks considered Blanton a role model, and he remembers Ninth Street vividly. "It was the place to be," he said. In later years, he worked the Southside Jazz Junction in Chattanooga before it closed in 2004. During one gig at the Jazz Junction, the younger players asked him if he knew "Summerwind," the jazz standard. "Yes," he said. "I recorded the original with Sinatra."[2]

The most famous musician spawned on the Big Nine was Bessie Smith, "Empress of the Blues," who starred with Louie Armstrong in the movie *St. Louis Blues* and preceded him in worldwide fame. Born in 1912 in "Blue Goose Hollow," the west end of Ninth Street, she was considered "the most successful black recording artist of her time" by 1928. She died in a tragic car accident in 1937. White hospitals in Mississippi refused to treat her, and she bled to death before reaching Memphis. Today, the Bessie Smith Hall stands on the former site of the Martin Hotel.[3]

Ninth Street's early builder and promoter was John Lovell. Like Lee McWhirter, he earned his initial capital as a barber; however, Lovell saved enough money to buy a tent, which he pitched on Ninth Street for selling whiskey and women. The 1870 census lists three pages of prostitutes, all employed by Lovell. Over time, Lovell built a block of buildings on Ninth Street, each three stories tall, which became Mahogany Hall, the biggest bar and dance club in the city.

Lovell also ran gambling tables and built a racetrack and farm for his racehorses in the Brainerd area. Later in life, he became one of Chattanooga's richest citizens and donated his farm to the city. Lovell Field at the airport is named after this colorful philanthropist. "They found a white aviator to name it after, but it's really named after John Lovell," I was told by Ray Evans, the editor of *Chattanooga's African American Legacy*.

Lovell was the nephew of Uncle Bill Lewis, an extraordinary free black man who bought the freedom of his sister,

Bessie Smith

Lovell's mother, and many other relatives. Born a slave to Cherokees, he married an Indian, worked as a blacksmith, and moved to Ross's Landing in 1837. One of his early jobs was forging the mortar and pestle used in the "Little Log Cabin" on Fifth and Lookout Streets, a sort of makeshift bell to call community meetings. On one occasion, city fathers rang Lewis's bell to call a meeting to choose the town's name.

Another of Uncle Bill Lewis's notable jobs was forging the chains for Andrews' Raiders, the Union prisoners who stole the train "The General" before participating in the famous locomotive chase. One of those prisoners, W. R. Pittenger, met Lewis and left a glowing report: "Being an expert blacksmith, he purchased his time for $350 a year. He was soon able to buy his wife and himself for $1000[†] each; then, he set up a shop, hiring other hands, and bought his six-year-old son for $400; his mother and aunt for $150 each," two brothers for $1000 each, and $400 for his sister. "Then, he paid his house and laid up a large amount of money besides. Such a man is a genuine hero. He was not able to do business in his own name under the black laws and was obliged to pay a white man largely to legalize his transactions."[4]

By 1870, William Lewis's net worth through real estate and other properties reached $7,000, a millionaire by today's standards. The bell that Lewis forged for Chattanooga was making early and successful attempts to "let freedom ring." This trend grew rapidly for a half-century. Then the sound of that bell was abruptly silenced.

"Good for Government," Bad for Blacks

There were 457 blacks in Chattanooga in 1860 out of a population of 2,500. Ten years later, the black population alone was 8,000 and soon comprised over 40 percent of the town's residents. They came as Union soldiers. Lincoln initially balked at using black soldiers, and the sentiment up north was that it was a "white man's war." However, that decision changed as casualties mounted.

Five U.S. Colored Regiments served in Chattanooga, four infantry regiments and one artillery. Besides fighting in the battles, they also comprised much of the Federal army's workforce, building the city's first bridge, the water works, massive fortifications, mills, foundries, the National Cemetery, and miles of roads and railroad tracks. After the major conflicts of Chickamauga and Chattanooga, they remained in the city keeping peace during difficult times. When they were mustered out, most of these black soldiers chose to remain in the city they had built.

General John Wilder provided them with jobs. "He was the only Union hero in the battle of Chickamauga," said Raymond Evans, who referred to Wilder as ruthless, business-minded, and highly successful. "He felt that was his contribution to combat, got out, and became a quartermaster and started making plans for after the war."

[†] $160,000 (2006)

Artist's rendition of the **Martin Hotel**, adapted from picture in *Small Nation of People: W.E.B. DuBois and African American Portraits of Progress.* Amistad, 2003. (Sketch by Andrew Wilkie.)

The only known photograph of either **John Lovell** (bottom row, second from left) or **"Uncle Bill"** Lewis (middle row, far right) comes from this 19th century family photo on the porch of Lewis's home in Chattanooga.

"He organized a consortium of seventy-three officers, and he meticulously planned to retain control of Chattanooga and did. Various facilities were sold as military surplus. Grant protested that the government was getting defrauded out of millions of dollars, and they were. But Wilder had contacts in D.C., and no problems came from it. They were the only element of the army that personally profited from the war."

"Wilder had the city captured. He saw the iron reserves in the area, and he had a workforce. The foundries, railroads, and industrialization offered employment opportunities for blacks that weren't available in any other place in the country."

The first African American community where these ex-soldiers resided was in today's North Chattanooga and was called Camp Contraband. One Federal soldier called it "damp, unhealthy, without good water and filthy in the extreme." Laws forbid them to cross the river without permission. The sickness and high mortality rate was appalling, causing the soldier to wonder if "their condition is improved by obtaining their freedom."

Over time, through hard labor and diligent education, a black professional class emerged. By 1903, hundreds of black Chattanoogans were quite wealthy, a number of them amassing fortunes in real estate. Randolph Miller, publisher of *The Blade*, the only newspaper in the country owned by a former slave, had the power to organize a bus boycott and provide an alternative taxi line for getting blacks to and from work.

Political power also increased. Republicans and blacks ruled the day through a strategic coalition. Local African Americans held major posts in the community, were elected to many city offices, and were appointed to a significant part, sometimes the majority, of the police force.

One particular black leader, Hiram Tyree, was a major burr in the saddle that motivated Chattanooga's powerful leadership to take action. An ex-slave who lost his leg in a railroad accident, Tyree became a successful shoe salesman and real estate speculator. He held several offices, including justice of the peace, school commissioner, alderman in city government, and chairman of the Republican Party.[5]

White leaders and citizens began to tire of the significant influence of blacks such as Tyree. According to one editorial statement in the *Chattanooga Times*, "We have no prejudice against the Negroes, but dislike to be ruled and ruined by them." Another man lobbying the legislature said, "If any of you gentlemen will come over to Chattanooga . . . we will furnish a nigger to arrest you, a nigger to lock you up, and a nigger to take care of you after you get into jail."[6]

Over time, local leaders and editorialists at the *Chattanooga Times* began decrying the tactics of "machine politics" and other corruptions deemed irreparable. Ballots were allegedly removed from the polls, and some ballots were given creatively

Randolph Miller

colored covers to help illiterate voters know which candidate to choose. The Citizens Civic League, a forerunner to the Good Government League, was formed in 1909. The list of names included Pattens, Probascos, Chamblisses, Mc-Callies, Brocks, and many others. This elite group called for nondescript ballots that required literate voters. They also called for a more permanent solution, changing the form of government from individual districts (called "wards" at that time) to five at-large commissioners, all chosen by the entire voting population. Ochs's *Chattanooga Times* framed the choice as either "good government" or "machine politics."

The effort was successful. *The Times* reported on Tyree's demise: "... his glory has dimmed considerably of late, and if the movement for commission government succeeds, his light promises to go out forever."[7]

UTC history professor Larry Ingle sharply criticized the 1911 change in government. "They went up to Nashville [and] botched the wards," said Ingle. "And when they did, there wasn't another black man to serve on the city commission until 1971. They did their work very well in 1911."

"It destroyed equality in Chattanooga," said Raymond Evans. "It was intended to."

For a period of time in the late 1800s, Chattanooga "was the greatest place for equality for blacks anywhere in the country," said Evans. The process to change black representation began two decades before 1911. Foreseeing the inevitable, half the black population left the city, along with a good part of the professional class. "It was a tremendous setback."

The establishment argued that they were cleaning up corruption in government. Evans sees it differently. "They were trying to take over the government themselves, pure and simple. And, of course, they couched it in terms of cleaning it up. And in 1991, the people who filed the lawsuit that got the situation turned back around said they were cleaning up government also."

While businessmen like Randolph Miller and John Lovell, who began as a barber in Camp Contraband, tried to change the community through investment and politics, another early black leader focused on religion and education. E. O. Tade arrived at Camp Contraband in 1866 and started a church in the community later called Hill City, then North Chattanooga. A graduate of Chicago Theological Seminary, Tade denounced slavery but was also passionate against alcohol and the "abominable use of tobacco." He used what he called a "tripartite" strategy, providing religious, economic,

John Wilder

and educational instruction. He founded Howard School, the first public school in Chattanooga, and later built the First Congregational Church on Ninth Street, which still stands next to the Bessie Smith Hall.

Tade also formed a bank. His efforts were so successful, both for himself and the larger black community, that he donated his entire salary as school commissioner to the American Missionary Association. One journal entry captures his tireless labors: "Up at 3:30 a.m., traveled 15 miles on the RR; walked six miles; made up Civil District Clerk's report; visited three schools; examined one teacher; traveled nine miles further; and reached home by [street] cars at 8 p.m., eating one meal."

Tade faced resistance from both sides. Many in the black community opposed his stance on alcohol and tobacco and refused to participate in his church and educational efforts. In the white community, Tade's relationship to the powers-that-be was excellent early on as he was elated to gain public funding after starting Howard School. A few years later, he denounced the healthy funding of white schools as a "sham and a disgrace" while his scholars shivered as they studied. "Here I must live a sort of dog's life—hated, shunned, and despised because I am a 'nigger preacher,'" he wrote bitterly.

After ten years of work in Chattanooga, E. O. Tade left for mission work with Indians and Chinese in Los Angeles. As he departed in 1875, he gave a more hopeful parting comment. "I feel that my ten years in the South has not been in vain," he said.

Howard School was likely Tade's greatest legacy. Recent Howard High School Principal Lurone Jennings, like Tade, is one of many on a long list who faced challenges from both whites and blacks while attempting to reform the African American community through religious efforts.

As the executive director of the Miriam A. Brock Bethlehem Community Center in Alton Park, Jennings first darkened the doors of "The Beth" as a first grader in 1960, the year it began. An inner-city mission of the United Methodist Church, it was founded by Senator Brock's grandmother. "The whites had the Wesley Center," said Jennings, "and she had a heart for Christ and wanted blacks to have a mission like this."

Jennings said his focus is on sharing the gospel and teaching kids to read. He also runs a summer sports program that he started when he was principal at Howard. That program caused the rise and fall of Lurone Jenning's tenure at the school founded by E. O. Tade.

"I believe juvenile crime increases in the summer because of lack of activities and involvement," Jennings told me from his office at The Beth. "In June, crime increased." His summer camp had a tripartite strategy as well: sports, academic training (reading and math), and character development through Bible studies and prayer groups. "We had 450 students involved," he said. According to court records, "juvenile crime in this area decreased."

Lurone Jennings

The funding for the program came through high-profile Christian leaders on Lookout Mountain. He named Hugh O. Maclellan, Jr., Frank Brock, Sam Smartt, and Bob Huffaker, who sought out Jennings a few years before when he made front-page news for his public Christian faith as Brainerd High's football coach. "I took the football team to the E. V. Hill Crusade, and many of them either gave their lives to the Lord or rededicated their lives. That captured the attention of some key leaders in this city," said Lurone. The ACLU started pressuring Jennings after players posted flyers all over school inviting friends to watch their baptisms. Lurone did not back down.

When Superintendent Harry Reynolds later asked him to become principal at Howard, Jennings used the relationships on the mountain to fund his highly successful summer sports camp, but Jennings believes others in the system were jealous of the new source of revenue. Eventually, Jennings was fired.

"I didn't realize being a high school principal was so political. I was too naive," said Lurone. "I was focusing on folks getting excited about helping our children. I think there was a lot of jealousy or a lot of questions [with] my alliances with these shakers and movers in Chattanooga. I had too much connection or contact with people who had resources that they couldn't control, you know. People always like to control things."

"I can't understand, even to this day, why black folk have a problem with you garnering resources from others to help your own—feel like you're an Uncle Tom or like you have sold out. But there's a mentality in the black community sometimes that says if you take that money and you build those relationships, something is wrong with that. I don't understand that."

After hundreds of parents protested and picketed Howard School, Lurone Jennings was reinstated as principal by Superintendent Reynolds. A few months later, Jennings resigned. "I'm going back to the classroom," he told Dr. Reynolds. "I don't like it up here at this level. It doesn't feel right. It doesn't smell right."

Demonstrations over M.L. King Boulevard

Another former Howard High principal used his position to change the community through a political strategy. For 60 years, Chattanooga had seen no black elected officials thanks to the removal of political districts by the elite leaders in 1911. Funeral Director John Franklin, whose parents buried Booker T. Washington, ran for the office of City Commissioner in 1971.

Judge Walter Williams worked in Franklin's 1971 campaign. He had just graduated from Howard High. "There was a group of blacks and a few whites who decided it was time to have a black on the commission. John Franklin was not one of the first names. He surfaced because he was a school principal, obviously, and his father had the oldest funeral home at one time, so he was well known in the community. Several whites knew him. They thought that of all the persons who could possibly run, he was more likely to be elected."

They chose to target the seat of Dean Peterson, Commissioner of Health and Education. "I don't think Dean Peterson had even finished high school. So there were some legitimate issues," said Williams. "How are you having this person be commissioner of health and education? He ain't finished high school!"

"I was here when the victory celebrations took place," said Williams. "It was an exciting time because it gave promise that maybe we had now moved to another era in Chattanooga."

The new commissioner held only one of five votes. On a key piece of legislation, he could not even get a second to force a vote. The motion was to change the name of Ninth Street. The year was 1976, and the black community wanted to honor Dr. Martin Luther King, Jr. They wanted Ninth Street to become M. L. King Boulevard. Tommy Lupton, who had recently built the Krystal Building and the Tallan Building, strongly opposed the name change with concerns of how it would affect business. Soon, crowds were protesting outside his buildings.

"I didn't have anything against Martin Luther King. I couldn't have cared less," Tommy Lupton told me. "But I didn't know at that time if people would want an MLK address. This was one of the first ones. I said this all the way through: I don't want the street name to change because I've got six million invested in the building. I've got another eight million to put into it, and I don't want it to stand empty as a memorial to the fact that the street name was changed right in the middle of the construction. Now, had they done it earlier or done it later, it would have been an entirely different story, but I was in the mode of having to rent that building. I had only eight percent of it rented when I started."

Walter Williams remembers it well. "Tommy Lupton was opposing it because his building would have an M.L. King address. John Franklin didn't even get a second at the City Commission to have the name changed. People were marching and complaining, going down to City Commission meetings, and raising cane. I remember incidents. There were a couple of ministers who got up on ladders on poles and took a sticker and [pasted] it over Ninth Street and put M. L. King Boulevard."

Lupton was doubly frustrated since he was an honorary member of four different black churches and had received plaques from a number of them for helping build their facilities. In one instance, New Zion Church was burned down. "I went to see

John Franklin

Rev. Brooks," said Tommy. "I had known him, and I said, 'Reverend, we'll build your church back.' I raised $200,000 for him and arranged a loan for him, and we built the church back."

That did not help him in the name-change controversy. "I tried to stop the name change right in this area alone and do it from Georgia Avenue, and that wasn't acceptable. I tried to suggest other alternatives—Third Street and different areas. The arguments got kind of heated. We were threatened. My family was threatened. They had a demonstration right out in front of the Krystal Building. Two police-men, both of them black officers, were looking out the window. They said, 'That fellow over there, in the blue shirt. He's a murderer. That fellow over there in the overalls. He's a convicted arsonist.' These black men were telling me this, and there was a sea of black people out there."

"Well, to make a long story short, I stuck to my guns. The City Commission was scared to death to do anything."

Another sea of humanity showed up for the next City Commission meeting, including Tommy Lupton, to see what would happen next. Walter Williams got the rest of the story from Jack Lupton. "It just got all mixed up and Tommy was really fighting it," said Williams who explained that Jack Lupton was on the West Coast when he picked up a newspaper and read the story, "Lupton In Chattanooga Fights Renaming of Street in Honor of M.L. King."

"It didn't say which Lupton," said Williams. "It just said 'Lupton.' Jack had a major bottling concern, and he didn't want his name associated with it. In any event, Jack apparently got tired of this and made one call. One call. He didn't go to any meetings. He made one call to city hall and said, 'I'm tired of this. Do it. Get it done, and I don't want to hear anything about it.'"

The next morning at the packed commissioners meeting, Commissioner Paul Clark, who according to Williams had previously said he would never approve the name change, seconded John Franklin's motion. "The gentlemen almost fell out of their seats," said Williams. "The motion was made. It was seconded, and it was done."

"It was a shock, but that's the kind of environment we live in. One call. Here are all these ministers and all the other public people—a lot of blacks, some whites—wanting this to be done and marching, protesting and trying to get government to do it. They couldn't get it done. One call. That is a true story. If you ask Jack, he'll tell you."

Tommy Lupton tells the same story. "Jack called him and said, 'Paul, this has got to end. You and Tommy are in a bind and the City Commission is in a bind. Go ahead and name the street after Martin Luther King.' Paul made the motion. I was there. I didn't fuss about it. Well, I was mad about it . . . but it turned out that I changed the name to Union Square and gave [tenants] the option of calling it Two Union Square or 200 MLK Boulevard. Most took Two Union Square. Some of them took MLK."

Tommy wasn't mad at his cousin. "Hell, I could understand. Out of respect for me and the fact that I had half a building built, the commissioners were not going to pull the rug out from under me. And Jack didn't pull it out from under me, per se. I think he saw a situation developing, and he wanted to stop it before it ruined both of us. He did that, and it was a good thing."

Once again, Chattanooga headed off a major conflict through private negotiation rather than public confrontation. The black community gained confidence. In 1988, a decade after this major victory, black leaders filed suit against the city for violation of the Voting Rights Act claiming the at-large system "dilutes the voting strength of blacks." After an eleven-day trial, the judge ruled against the city. In 1991, a new City Council was established, comprised of nine separate districts similar to the ward system before 1911.[8]

The first recorded African American in this general region was a member of Spanish explorer Hernando De Soto's expedition in the 1540s. These adventurers spent a number of weeks with the Indians of Coosa, just east of today's Dalton, Georgia. A "negro" and a "Levantine," possibly a Turk, were left behind. When more Spaniards returned two decades later, they learned that both men had died after living with the Coosas for twelve years. A Spanish chronicler tells us that this negro's name was "Robles."[9]

Since the Coosas had been at war with another tribe sixty miles north, at what is today the city of Chattanooga, it is quite possible that at some point Robles found himself in the area. Twenty years later, however, another Spanish expedition came through Coosa before heading up to fight this village. The Chief of Coosa, taking his first thrilling but frightening horseback ride, was provided with a negro by the Spaniards to guide his horse into battle. This unnamed servant was the first black man known with certainty to have stepped on Chattanooga soil, preceding the British by at least a century.[10]

In 1777, British troops exploring this same area of wilderness came across a settlement of blacks thirty miles south of the future Chattanooga at Battle Creek. They apparently escaped slavery before creating their own clearing of land and planting crops. Major John Norton was stunned. "How insurmountable slavery must be!" he wrote. "To escape from it, [they] were content to purchase liberty at the expense of being sequestered from all mankind."[11]

(Above) Tommy Lupton built a special corridor for his cousin, Jack, connecting the **Krystal and Tallan buildings**.

(Right) The two buildings sit at the corner of Carter Street and **M.L. King Blvd** (formerly Ninth Street).

Ten years later, American militia attacked a Chickamauga force at the foot of Lookout Mountain near today's St. Elmo and Alton Park. American soldiers reported that one of the Indians they killed "proved to be a mulatto but in every other respect a savage."

An early flatboat of settlers was saved by an African American as they approached Moccasin Bend and were suddenly attacked by Indians. They would have all died "but for the strategy and bravery of a Negro boy. He upset the boat of the Indians and threw them into the river, just as they were about to board the boat of the white people." Another boat of quarantined smallpox victims was captured instead. The suffering Indians took relief in Citico Creek near the old Gardenhire farm. An old settler said the bodies of those killed by the epidemic were thrown in the nearby Gardenhire Cave where General John Wilder later found 200 skeletons. "Citico means death, and it was thus that the creek took its name," reports the settler.[12]

The father of Judge Lewis Shepherd organized an early version of the traveling minstrel show. In 1844, he came to town promoting James K. Polk's presidential campaign "with a drove of Negroes. . . . He bought each of them a new hat . . . and they all began to sing their political song. No circus street show ever excited the boys of Chattanooga more than this." Columnist Sam Divine reports an abundance of food dumped onto Ross's Landing in the early days. "Chicken and ham was the daily diet of the 'colored brother.'" The abundance of food at the river was "an inspiring scene and made lively by the queer songs and antics of the negro boat hands."[13]

Cherokees began acquiring African American slaves in the 1700s. By 1825, the Cherokees owned over 1,200 slaves. John Ross owned dozens of slaves for his plantations, and his grandfather, John McDonald, owned ten when the missionaries bought his little cabin on Chickamauga Creek in 1817. McDonald left behind for the newly arriving missionary Cyrus Kingsbury "a negro boy and girl to keep house and do my little affairs until I can get assistance." They were quickly dismissed when Cherokee help arrived.

The missionaries, theologically opposed to slavery, eventually abandoned the practice of hiring nearby slaves. They helped some of the area slaves buy their freedom and brought a number of blacks, slave and free, into their congregation. An ordained black minister once preached to their congregation. They ate together, worshipped together, and were buried together.

The missionaries told the mission board back in Boston that the "Cherokee and African converts" are "your treasure . . . your crown of rejoicing in the day of the Lord Jesus."

The missionaries did cite instances of negro laziness, where they tended toward "diversions, of which they are very fond." But the Brainerd missionaries' relationship to African Americans was truly exceptional compared to the nearby mission in

Spring Place (Dalton, Georgia). The Moravians never admitted a black into their congregation. If they did, the mission board in Salem instructed them to make sure "the cup is given them last of all."[14]

Most of the African slaves belonging to Cherokees joined them on the Trail of Tears in 1838, as did some of the free blacks. Those who stayed behind worshipped with the rest of the community in the "Little Log House" or "Community Log Cabin" where all denominations gathered each Sunday until separate facilities could be built a few years later. According to some accounts, the blacks sat in the front, but others say a separate section was reserved in the back.

Chattanooga's first black church was located immediately beside the Little Log House. Called the "Pepperbox Church,' and sporting an odd cupola-like steeple for unknown reasons, it was actually built in Soddy Daisy in 1847 and floated down the Tennessee River before being placed on the Fifth and Lookout site. The building was later used for a Civil War hospital and prison. In 1887, it was destroyed by arson, and a new building was built on the lot next door where the Little Log Cabin had once stood. This Wiley Methodist Church structure still stands today on the site where Chattanooga was founded and named.

Rise and Fall of Chattanooga Black Power

Since its founding, Chattanooga has seen a rise and fall of the black community. After 1911, various boycotts and demonstrations were ultimately unsuccessful. A bus boycott following Randolph Miller's original attempt was squelched by the use of fire hoses decades before the same tactic was used during the civil rights movement.

The case of the Scottsboro Boys gained national attention in the 1930s when nine young black men, four from Chattanooga, were falsely accused of raping two white prostitutes on a train to North Alabama. They were all cleared. The Communist Party organized the defense of the young men from their headquarters on South Broad Street. The Communist Party held its national convention at Memorial Auditorium a few years later, and Chattanooga was considered a center for Communism until federal law made membership a crime in the 1950s.

Chattanoogan Willie "Papa" Ricks is credited with originating the slogan "Black Power" during the civil rights movement. According to Raymond Evans, a security guard at Loveman's Department store shot and killed a demonstrator at an early lunch counter sit-in. Otherwise, Chattanooga was relatively quiet during those years except for a sit-in by Howard High students at the lunch counter at Woolworth's downtown. It created a "near riot," according to one history. Current City Councilman Leamon Pierce was one of those students who had fire hoses turned on them, the first time this happened during the civil rights era.

"No other demonstrations in the country were conducted exclusively by high school students," said Brian Cagle, who produced a 30-minute documentary on the incident for the Chattanooga Regional History Museum. "I think this alone makes it worthy of historical record."[15]

Successive gains for the black community after those years included the election of John Franklin, the renaming of Ninth Street to M. L. King Boulevard, and the change of city government to its pre-1911 structure of district representation.

Despite these gains, a majority of blacks have never controlled the City Council. Chattanooga has never elected a black mayor, unlike most of her neighbors. However, current Mayor Ron Littlefield, with a majority of the black support, won the mayoral election in 2005 although no black candidate was fielded by the African American leaders. Councilman Yusuf Hakeem called this fact "a little alarming," but longtime County Commissioner Paul McDaniel pointed to financing challenges. "Certainly, money is a reality," he said.[16]

Pete Drew thinks 1996 was the crucial year. "The greatest opportunity that the city of Chattanooga had to move forward was the opportunity to elect Howard Roddy when he ran for mayor against Jon Kinsey. If he couldn't get elected, there ain't nobody going to get elected to mayor in my estimation," he said. "He had all the attributes, and he couldn't get elected."

"This whole concept that we all get along here is on the surface. When you get with black people one-on-one, away from the general public, they will tell how they hate the position they're in. These relationships with the white leadership—it's overwhelmingly surface. It's 'you leave me alone and I'll leave you alone and we'll get along.'"

"In what I call the real South—Georgia, Alabama, Mississippi—there was no illusionary theory that we get along. . . . 'We believe we're superior to you and if you try to get out of your place, I'll put you back in your place.' In Chattanooga, you didn't have that confrontation. Mainly because there was no challenge to the position of authority that was held by white people because when black people came to town the leadership got involved in what was taking place. They brought them into the mix, gave them a certain portion of the pie, and then sent them back on their way."

Lee McWhirter is no longer interested in government assistance. "That's part of our problem—waiting on someone to give us something. Work it. You can get it yourself. There's a constant struggle for everybody. Color doesn't have anything to do with it."

"There's something that a white man wants that he's struggling for, too. And then you've got friends, I'm sure, that's got parents that are well-to-do. The kids stay at home, or they stay in the little house in the back waiting on Mom and Dad

"The Big Nine" in earlier decades

to die because when they die we're gonna get all this money. Kind of crazy ain't it? Why don't you just go out there and work your own?"

Money, the Mountain, and Maids

Lee McWhirter's view of inherited wealth from down in the valley is not too different from Sam Smartt's up on the mountain. "I grew up with a lot of rich kids and was good friends with a lot of them," Smartt said. "I remember very well in 1974 when Cartter Lupton died and all those kids had to come home and sign all kinds of documents. I mean, it was kind of like that was the day that things changed hands in some respect."

"We never talked about it or anything like that. You always knew. If a kid is from a wealthy family and drives a nice car that does not mean the kid is rich. A lot of these families don't pass all the money on to these kids, and that's a good thing. A lot of them do pass it on early, and it ruins the kids. Some kids get access to their money when they're thirty, some then they're thirty-five. Some hardly ever get it."

"I've got a number of friends that are very wealthy people and very unhappy people. They've had tough lives, difficult relationships, divorces, tremendous strife with their parents. The amount of money people have is not in direct relationship or correlation to the happiness in their life by any stretch of the imagination. In fact, it works just the opposite oftentimes."

"If the way you are judging your success is by what you've got, you're never going to be there, because somebody else is going to have more and you're going to want it," he said. "[People] need to develop an eternal perspective. They need to develop a perspective that Orrie Zackery had on life."

The late Orrie Zachery was an elderly black woman that Smartt says raised him. On one occasion, he broke down and wept uncontrollably for several minutes in attempting to honor her memory while emceeing a racial reconciliation event for the Chattanooga Resource Foundation in the early 1990s.

"I feel like I was raised by a godly black woman," Smartt later told me. Orrie was the Smartt family's African American live-in maid from before Sam was born to well after he left for college. His father died when he was nine, and his mother was not around nearly as much as Orrie.

"She was a very, very godly woman. This is a woman who had one son, who was divorced, and who was crippled. She stepped in a manhole when she was younger and messed up her legs. She always walked with a limp. She never had a driver's license, never owned a home, never made more than $35 a week, plus room and board, living in our home. So she had nothing, but she loved Jesus Christ. And my little sister and I can remember vividly going down to her apartment in the bottom of our home in the evenings and sitting down with her, rocking in her lap, and she's reading Bible stories to us out of a children's Bible book and telling us about the Lord and praying for us and on and on. She died an awful death with cancer, suffered a lot, but she left this earth with a smile on her face and Jesus on her lips."

"Orrie Zackery was a woman that from the world's perspective had nothing. That's one image that I have in my life. The other one is my grandfather Kennedy: brilliant man, respected in the community because he was a self-made millionaire, retired in his early fifties. So, from the world's perspective, he was a great success. But I also heard him brag about the fact that he never entered a church except for weddings of his children and grandchildren. He was never sick. Everything was completely in opposition to Orrie, but I realize that at the end of their lives, she had contentment and he did not. It's been a wonderful contrast for me."

Near-billionaire Frank Harrison, one of several local Coke bottling magnates, chose not to be buried at the elite Forest Hills Cemetery below Lookout Mountain but instead was laid to rest in 2002 next to his white housekeeper, Virginia Smith, at Chattanooga Memorial Park in Red Bank. "She was the only person who truly loved me," Harrison told his friend Larry Wells.[17]

Smartt says nearly all the families on the mountain had live-in nannies. He named the Luptons, Fontaines, Davenports, Brocks, and others. "Am I a racist? I was having this conversation with Al Chapman the other day [a local African American leader in the Christian community]. Yeah, probably I'm a racist. You can't help it growing up in the South. Even though I loved and revered this woman, as a mother, because my mom was three times widowed and was really not very involved in our upbringing at all. Orrie was a 'servant' in the house. Everybody 'had one.' So am I a racist? Yes. But hopefully I see through all that. Certainly, I saw God's hand in it."

"I feel like I was raised by a godly black woman just like Al Chapman was. Callie raised him, but Orrie raised me. That sounds weird, but that's how I feel about it."

Letting Freedom Ring, Someway, Somehow

While Smartt's story is extraordinary, it is not an unusual one in Chattanooga history. For generations, blacks and whites have lived together and found a way to somehow peacefully coexist. Rev. T. H. McCallie, whose mother taught slaves to read in the basement of First Presbyterian Church in violation of Tennessee law, provided a similar eulogy for a black woman who lived in the their household. She died just as the Union army was approaching Chattanooga.

"Aunt Phyllis, an old Negro woman that had been a slave in the family for over 30 years, died," McCallie wrote. "She died, I humbly believe, in the faith of our Lord Jesus Christ. When my father bought her, she was a terror. She was capable, could cook, wash, iron, milk and do most anything. She was industrious and had her good qualities, but she had a temper that was well nigh ungovernable. She would get angry with a fellow servant, seize a hatchet, knife, or ax, and chase him all over the yard, and if they had not been more fleet of foot, it would have fared ill with them."

"But the patience with which my mother trained and instructed her in the knowledge of God in Christ at length brought forth fruit. She became a member and faithful attendant of the Methodist Church. In those days, there was no colored church. The colored people belonged to the same church with the white people, went to the same services, and sat at the same communion table. A few pews in the rear of the church were always left for the colored people, and they were kindly received and treated."

"It has to be a very dark and stormy night that kept Aunt Phyllis from going to church on the hill of Fifth and Lookout Streets where now stands the colored Methodist Church. But dear old soul, just as freedom was coming to herself and her people, she was taken on angels' wings to a fairer and better land where there is no slavery, no war, no sin, no sorrow, pain, or death. Farewell Aunt Phyllis, till . . . we meet again in the presence of our Lord."

Dr. Martin Luther King, Jr. also preached about a time with no slavery, war, hatred, or prejudice. He was challenging us to bring it to Chattanooga on this side of heaven. Today, Chattanooga's African American community is still in pursuit of that dream.

Uncle Bill Lewis, the wealthy blacksmith, achieved economic freedom in Chattanooga's early years. The makeshift bell he forged for the Little Log Cabin no longer exists, but the church on Fifth and Lookout Street still stands. Wiley Methodist Church, now called Bethlehem Wiley, is pastored by Rev. Lurone Jennings.

"It was supposed to close down because of the declining congregation," said Lurone. "God has allowed us to be part of the resurrection of that congregation. When we come together, we make it a point to pray for the City of Chattanooga— our mayor and the City Council, county commissioners, [asking] what this city could possibly be for God."

Rev. Jennings is well aware of the significance of the spot.

"Nothing happens accidentally," he said. "There's always an orchestrated plan."

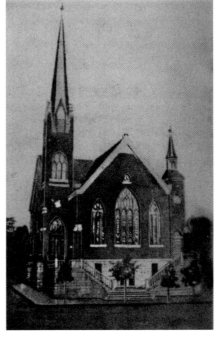

These churches all stood on Fifth and Lookout Streets, the site where Chattanooga was named and founded: (Clockwise from above) The Little Log Cabin, the "Pepper Box" Church, and Wiley Methodist. Bethlehem Wiley (right), minus the steeple, still stands today.

Artist: Andrew Wilkie

CHAPTER TEN

The Spirit of T. H. McCallie

Schools and Other Legacies

Three grown men weeping in public.

This would be an unusual site anywhere but especially when the men are prominent leaders in the community. In attendance were T. Hooke McCallie, his son, Tom McCallie, and nephew, Allen McCallie—the latter two serving as executive director and chairman, respectively, of the Maclellan and Lyndhurst Foundations, arguably the two most influential institutions in Chattanooga.

On that day 25 years ago, the three McCallies were asked by the Daughters of the American Revolution to speak to their group at Shoney's restaurant downtown. Excerpts of Dr. Thomas Hooke McCallie's journal had been printed in the paper, and the DAR wanted to hear from the legendary Civil War pastor's progeny, grandson T. Hooke and great-grandkids Tom and Allen. As the three stood and read the journal aloud, they could not keep back the tears.

"Neither T. Hooke, nor Tom, nor I could keep from weeping," said Allen McCallie. "His Christian faith and his incredible relationship with the Lord . . . it's such a personal and phenomenal story. Here we are reading a story from T. Hooke's grandfather, and he might as well have been in the room with us."

This extraordinary man creates such emotions a century after his death and inspires awe and respect generations later from leaders of institutions across the ideological spectrum. Earlier chapters detailed portions of T. H. McCallie's story:

T. H. McCallie

how he remained as the sole pastor of Chattanooga after threats of being arrested, how he ministered to the infected without fear, how he preached to soldiers in Grey one Sunday and soldiers in Blue the next, refusing to bless either side but asking, "Who is on the Lord's side?" How he shaped the Spirit of Chattanooga by preaching reconciliation after the war and by finding joy in doing good to his enemies.

Further research into his journals helps to portray this man's character as does an explanation of the many legacies he left for Chattanooga through churches, charities, schools, relationships, progeny, and prayers.

A Crisis in Chattanooga

This saintlike man at first glance seems incapable of inspiring an emergency meeting full of intense rivalry and partisanship held in 1940 by local scions Cartter Lupton, Summerfield K. Johnston, and Ed Finlay. History shows that T. H. McCallie can indeed take credit for it.

These three men, members of Baylor School's executive committee, met for two consecutive days. According to a Baylor historian, no other issue had engaged them so intensely. Their decision would affect the community for decades to come. The crisis at hand was straightforward: the McCallie School wanted to temporarily discontinue the most talked-about event of the year, the annual Baylor-McCallie football game. And they wanted Baylor to agree to it.

The rivalry was indeed intense, and Baylor was usually the beneficiary. McCallie won the first few informal meetings, but from 1919 to 1924, Baylor won five of six games and skunked the Blue Tornados in the years 1922–1924. Some students from McCallie got so fed up they vandalized the Baylor campus with graffiti. Baylor professor Alexander Guerry threatened to expel any Baylor student who tried to retaliate. Nevertheless, the next year their halfback led a band of vandals in painting the McCallie campus.

Spencer McCallie   **J. Park McCallie**

Both administrations were upset by the developments. Park McCallie, school cofounder with brother Spencer McCallie, proposed an end of the annual football game in 1925, fifteen years before this 1940 crisis, and tried to convince founder Roy Baylor that the two schools "were making too much of football." The McCallie School had already discontinued their games with Central High School, also located at the time near the foot of Missionary Ridge. "We were right next to each other," said Park, "and the boys could throw rocks at each other and have regular fights and get to hating each other, and we didn't want to do that, and I said, 'Now we're two prep schools here, so let's just cut this thing out.' [But] when Mr. Baylor heard of it, he just hit the ceiling, and Guerry had to call me up and say, 'The whole thing's off. We can't do it. He simply will not stand for it.'"

By 1940, Baylor was continuing in its dominance. They were led by star running back Eddie Prokop, called by one sports writer the greatest high school player he had ever seen. Thanks to "Handsome Eddie," the Raiders outscored their opponents 280 to 32 that year. Eddie later ran for 199 yards in the 1944 Sugar Bowl, a record unbroken until Tony Dorsett eclipsed the mark in 1977.

Baylor was enjoying an undefeated season in 1940 up to the final game against McCallie on November 22. A few days before, the McCallie brothers sent their letter to Lupton and Johnston of Baylor's executive committee calling for an end to "over-emphasis on football" and asking Baylor to agree to a "temporary" discontinuing of the rivalry, "so that any publicity (which must inevitably follow) may be given out as from both schools, and not unfavorably reflect on either school."[1]

If either school stopped the competition, "that school would be seen as a 'quitter,' a 'weak sister,' by many potential patrons in the community," wrote Baylor historian John Longwith. It would also affect enrollment during a difficult time at the tail end of the depression. Another Baylor historian said the football rivalry was already steering students toward Baylor. "They will choose the school that wins its games," wrote James Hitt. "The basic competition between Baylor and McCallie, therefore, has always been economic in nature from the beginning, not athletic, not academic."[2]

So Cartter Lupton and Summerfield Johnston took the decision to the larger board, which deliberated carefully. Their response led to a late-night meeting of McCallie's board of directors on the eve of the big game. The results were rather unexpected.

The Private School Phenomenon

"Where did you go to school?" When two Chattanooga businessmen ask the question, no one is thinking about college. The appropriate answer is still either "McCallie," a hundred years after its founding, or "Baylor," founded twelve years earlier.

By the early part of the 20th century, students from prominent families across the Southeast were attending Baylor, McCallie, and the Girls Preparatory School (GPS).

Today, a boarding student attending one of the "Big Three," as they are termed, can expect to pay $30,000 a year, a non-boarding local around $15,000. McCallie recently launched a $125 million capital campaign for their 882-student school. Baylor, with over 900 students, recently completed a $45 million campaign after a $24 million effort ten years before. GPS, with an enrollment near 800, has conducted similar campaigns and has an endowment of $22 million. Baylor and McCallie each have endowments of approximately $70 million. The Big Three are reported to have assets of nearly $300 million, possibly the greatest concentration of private school financial support per capita in the nation.[3]

Baylor boasts an 8 to 1 student-to-faculty ratio and was the first school in the South to offer advanced placement courses. In 2004, McCallie had more National Merit finalists than Baylor, but private schools in Chattanooga together had 22 National Merit finalists compared to only one from the public schools. The Big Three regularly send graduates to the most prestigious colleges, including all the Ivy League schools.[4]

With such a strong tradition of prestigious schools, it is not surprising that reunions are well attended, such as the one where Scotty Probasco, Ward Crutchfield, and Mai Bell Hurley caught up on old times. They all graduated together in the same class. It is indeed rather surprising that the reunion was for their private *elementary* school.

"We had a reunion recently, the Bright School graduating class of 1940," said Ward. "Mai Bell was there. Scotty was there. The Luptons went there too. I think Jack was a year ahead of me. Tommy was a year behind me. Mai Bell accused me of dying my hair, which I've never dyed."

"In Charlotte, everybody sends their kids to public schools, or most everybody does," said UTC professor Larry Ingle, a North Carolina native. "In Greensboro, there was one struggling Catholic high school in the town, and that was it. Everybody else went to public schools. Everybody. No private education, period."

Over 12,000 students in Chattanooga are educated privately compared to 40,000 in the public school system. At 23 percent, this private student ratio is twice the national average and triple the rate in Tennessee. Three-fourths of those privately educated students in Chattanooga do not attend the Big Three, but instead, they are educated by nearly fifty religious and parochial schools scattered throughout Hamilton County. A healthy and growing homeschooling community has also emerged. Gary Hargraves, who runs the local home education association, estimates the number at somewhere between 1,600 and 2,400 students. Two Chattanooga homeschoolers, Matt and Josh Downer, attended Harvard during the past two years.[5]

The Spirit of Competition

To what can Chattanooga attribute these extraordinary numbers? Most of those interviewed offered a one-word answer for the cause of Chattanooga's unique educational soil: competition.

The competition started "when McCallie really began to give Baylor a run for their money," said Frank Brock. "Competition was good." Then Frank fueled the fire during our interview with his offhand comment that his alma mater "left Baylor in the dust, frankly, in recent years."

"Both schools by that time had people who graduated there to give out money. GPS got caught up in the whole thing, and it was just a case where competition grew at all the schools." He credits those early McCallies for creating the competitive environment. "I'm a big fan of the McCallie family here. A remarkable family, really a remarkable family."

—◆—

I interviewed four McCallies for this book. Three of them, Tom, Allen, and Spencer III, are the great-grandsons of T. H. McCallie.[†] Dr. David McCallie is a grandson but was born after the legendary pastor of Chattanooga died. David McCallie lives in Riverview in an impressive Tudor home. It appears to be somewhere between a house and a mansion, just what you might expect when combining a McCallie with a Lupton.

David McCallie married Maddin Lupton, Tommy Lupton's sister, connecting the McCallie family to the Lupton-Probasco axis. However, the McCallies had intermarried into Chattanooga's elite several generations before when Julia McCallie, T. H.'s daughter, married Sam Divine. The Divine axis connects to the Keys and Johnstons and the Sharps and Gillespies, both of which eventually make their way to the Luptons from different angles (see chart on next page).

During our interview in his Riverview home, I asked Dr. McCallie why his father, Spencer McCallie, Sr., and his uncle, Park McCallie, founded McCallie School when Baylor already existed. He did not take the bait.

"The better question is, 'Why not?'" he replied.

He was the first McCallie I interviewed. He is a medical doctor, Erlanger's first chairman when it reorganized as a state authority, and, as you might expect from

---

[†] Tom McCallie is actually Thomas Hooke McCallie III. (T. H. McCallie, Sr. did not name any of his eleven sons after himself.) To help with clarity in this book, the three are always referred to as T. H McCallie, T. Hooke McCallie, and Tom McCallie.

⇥═ McCALLIE ═⇤

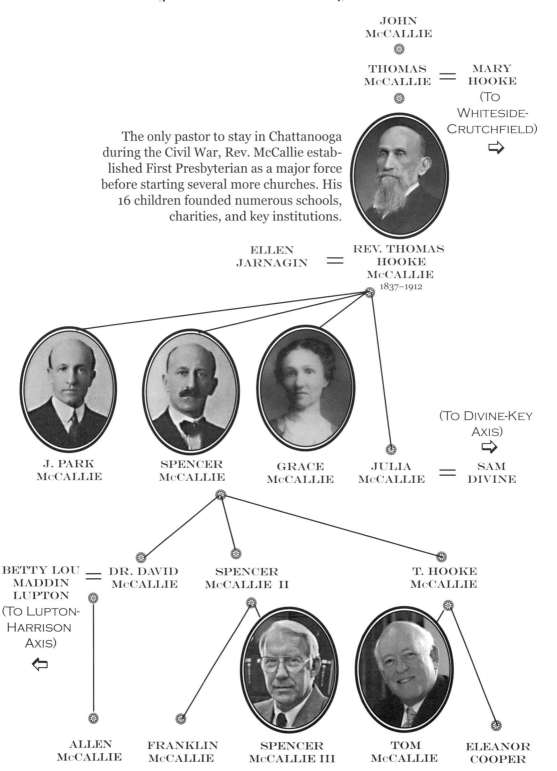

JOHN
McCALLIE

THOMAS
McCALLIE ═ MARY
HOOKE
(TO
WHITESIDE-
CRUTCHFIELD)
⇨

The only pastor to stay in Chattanooga during the Civil War, Rev. McCallie established First Presbyterian as a major force before starting several more churches. His 16 children founded numerous schools, charities, and key institutions.

ELLEN
JARNAGIN ═ REV. THOMAS
HOOKE
McCALLIE
1837–1912

J. PARK
McCALLIE

SPENCER
McCALLIE

GRACE
McCALLIE

(TO DIVINE-KEY
AXIS)
⇨

JULIA
McCALLIE ═ SAM
DIVINE

BETTY LOU
MADDIN
LUPTON
(TO LUPTON-
HARRISON
AXIS)
⇦

DR. DAVID
McCALLIE ═

SPENCER
McCALLIE II

T. HOOKE
McCALLIE

ALLEN
McCALLIE

FRANKLIN
McCALLIE

SPENCER
McCALLIE III

TOM
McCALLIE

ELEANOR
COOPER

(Charts are partial, not exhaustive, highlighting key links or characters in the book.)

the scientist type, he gave me precise answers. He also provided some excellent sources on the McCallies and on the Scotch-Irish. But he pointed me to his nephew, Spencer McCallie III, to get the good quotes.

"He's a storyteller," Dr. McCallie said. "And like all storytellers, you'd better double-check him."

I drove out to Chickamauga Lake to interview Spencer, whose one-story, A-frame house has more of that austere McCallie look, similar to Tom's decades-old Volvo. The home was decorated with African art. A modern translation of the Bible, *The Message*, sat on the coffee table. His wife offered me a Coke or a Diet Coke even though all the bottling magnates attended Baylor.

Spencer McCallie III is one of the very few third-generation headmasters this country has ever seen. Recently retired to his home on the lake, he lived his entire life on the McCallie campus where he was born.

"When I was ten, they still had mules," he told me. "There wasn't a lot of money. There were no servants. The place wasn't fancy."

"There were a lot of kids around. It was fun to watch boys practice athletics. I'd slip into the games. Nobody really cared. They didn't take tickets."

"What's it like to carry the McCallie name in Chattanooga?" I asked.

"I don't know that I've ever gotten a cup of coffee off of it," he said. "I'm sure it makes some difference, and it's a nice name to have. But the family is large. I think the schools respect it."

I asked him why he didn't give his son, Douglas, the name Spencer McCallie IV.

"At the time, I was teaching at McCallie and my grandmother, Ms. Spencer McCallie, Sr. was alive. Spencer McCallie II was the head of the school. I was Spencer McCallie III. Having this other one, he's got to be named something else. It was confusing, goodness. It confused people and bank statements."

Spencer comes from the Middle English "spense," a cool pantry where hunks of raw meat were stored for a great house or monastery until they were ready for use. I asked Spencer about his ancestors.

"I may not know. You may be horrified about how little I know," he said.

I'd heard that one before from other longtime Chattanoogans.

"Tell me how far back the McCallies go in Chattanooga."

"Gosh, I think to the 1830s. I think when my great-great-grandfather moved into Old Washington. You know where that is?"

Old Washington, now under water, was the closest town up the river when Ross's Landing opened up for occupancy in 1838. Spencer also told me how his great-great-grandfather, Thomas McCallie, commissioned his brother Looney to build him a very large frame house at the site of the current Memorial Auditorium and First-Centenary Church. When it was done, Thomas floated his family down the river to Ross's Landing. Little T. H. McCallie vividly remembered the experience at age four.

As I suspected, Spencer McCallie III knew a great deal about his heritage. His facts and dates for Thomas McCallie were on the mark and did not need double-checking. In fact, he and David had even conducted research at the library scouring old newspaper advertisements to ascertain the names of Thomas McCallie's various business enterprises. Chattanooga's first McCallie dealt in sashes, doors, blinds, furniture, lumber, and hats from the latest fashions in Paris.

Spencer III, perhaps like his grandfather, always had a lingering grin when he talked with me, unlike the other three McCallies I interviewed whose senses of humor were apparent but hidden just beneath more stolid faces inherited from generations of Presbyterian Calvinists.

T. H. McCallie was "my childish idea of what God must look like," said Eleanor McCallie Cooper in her book *Grace in China*. "Tall and grave, with stern, deep-set eyes and a full gray beard." She said T. H.'s son, Park McCallie, was also stern. "[But] Uncle Spence was given to sarcasm, which he mistook as humor. He offended me mightily when he referred to my legs as toothpicks and my arms as pipe stems."[6]

Uncle Park, however, was all business. "He was nobody's chum," said Spencer III. One graduate said Park would tell the boys that procreation was the only reason he engaged in marital relations.[7] When Park, a Baylor grad who later earned a doctorate in astronomy from the University of Virginia, contacted his brother Spencer about the idea of starting a school, his brother was single and less settled.

"Spencer went to college in Memphis. He got kicked out," said Spencer III.

"Kicked out for what?"

"Oh, I don't know. I think somebody said he put a dead skunk on an unpopular professor's porch. Pranks, whatever. He got his master's in Chicago and that's where he was when Uncle Park wrote him a letter and said, 'Let's talk about this possibility of a school.' My impression is that my grandfather wanted to go out to the frontier. He was thinking about becoming a university teacher in Oregon. He thought that would be great fun."

A little double-checking showed that Spencer Sr. was actually headed to Washington State University.[8]

It was Park McCallie who had the burning vision for a new school. Spencer admitted he was on the fence and could go either way. He suggested to Park that the question of their destiny, and ultimately much of Chattanooga's destiny, be decided by T. H. McCallie. "Let's leave it up to Father," he wrote back to Park. "He knows how to talk to the Lord and

Spencer McCallie III   is a wise man."

Scotty Probasco's desk. He uses the nameplate of his father, Scott L. Probasco Sr. The two pictures behind his desk—the board of directors for American National Bank—are the best images available of the largest number of "power structure" figures standing together. These photos from two generations appear on the next page.

American National Bank board of directors, 1941. Left to right: Hewitt Wood, Sam Campbell, J.H. Davenport, R.B. Davenport, Jr., Scott Probasco, Sr., Cartter Lupton, Hardwick Caldwell, R.C. Jones, Jr., Jo Conn Guild, Summerfield Johnston, Sr., Charles Hardie, George Hunter, Ed Finlay, E.Y. Chapin, Sr., Morris Temple, Clarence Avery, Z.C. Patten, Sam Hutcheson, Burton Frierson, C.S. Steward, Burkett Miller, T.O. Duff, D. H. Griswold, Gaston Raoul, R. J. Maclellan.

American National Bank board of directors, 1962. Left to right: Percy Wood, Robert Jones Jr., Don Overmyer, Burkett Miller, Harold Almond, Jo Conn Guild, Hardwick Caldwell, Richard Moore Jr., Walter Temple, Rodolph Davenport III, E.Y. Chapin, Jr., Scott Probasco, Jr. (center back), Scott Probasco, Sr. (center front), Sam Yarnell, Robert L. Maclellan, Cecil Woods, Hugh O Maclellan, Sr., Thomas Duff, Jr., Paul Carter, Alex Guerry, DeSales Harrison, Mertland Hedges, Burton Frierson, James Hedges, Joseph Davenport.

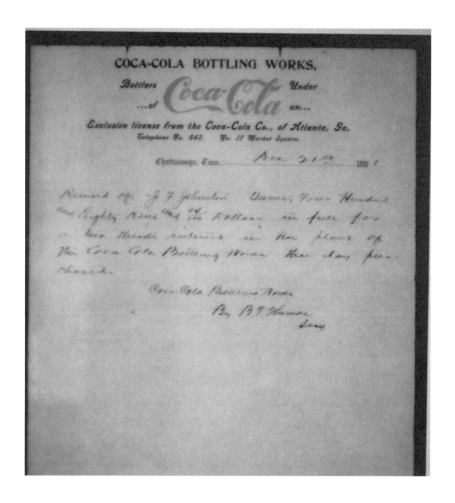

DRINK

A BOTTLE OF

Coca-Cola

5 CENTS

The most refreshing drink. Used summer and winter.

Sold at all stands, Grocer's and Saloons.

(Above) The **original contract for the first Coca-Cola bottling plant** between James F. Johnston and his best friend Ben Thomas. It hangs in the office of Summerfield K. Johnston, Jr.

(Left) The **first advertisement** for bottles of Coca-Cola appeared in the *Chattanooga Times* in 1899.

The **Bright School graduating class of 1940**. Their 60th class reunion included **Ward Crutchfield** (top row, second from left), **Mai Bell Hurley** (next row, second from right), and **Scotty Probasco** (Bottom row, second from left).

Helen McDonald Exum poses in the *Chattanooga Cook Book*. "At Christmas we make a simple tree of apples for the centerpiece, bake cheese cookies, a chocolate log, and various confections and pies, and ask the neighbors in for coffee."

Missy Crutchfield, formerly an actress and model, now serves as Administrator of Arts, Education, and Culture for Chattanooga Mayor Ron Littlefield.

David Andrews, Chattanooga, TN

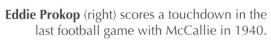

Eddie Prokop (right) scores a touchdown in the last football game with McCallie in 1940.

Painting of the **James Whiteside family** from his mansion at the point of Lookout Mountain. The depiction of Moccasin Bend in the background is the first known image of the famous view. The painting now hangs in the Hunter Museum of American Art.

Adolph Ochs's home on Cameron Hill was razed during the urban renewal project.

The **Chattanooga Spring Festival** was a precursor to the Cotton Ball.

The Lyndhurst Mansion

Theodore Tuttle Woodruff, the author's 3rd great grandfather. The patent for his sleeping car invention was copied illegally by Geoge Pullman, who merged with Andrew Carnegie. In his autobiography, Carnegie credits this venture as the beginning of his fortune.

The letter was sent to their father in Chattanooga. Park was in Indiana and Spencer in Chicago. Rev. McCallie gathered together his mother and his wife, both of whom had weathered with him through the battles of Chattanooga, his son, Thomas, and daughter, Grace. At 8 p.m., May 31, 1905, in Rev. McCallie's study, the five McCallies prayed about the matter before them. Then, they discussed it.[9]

—————◆—————

In 1893, Professor Roy Baylor was recruited by a handful of Chattanooga's most prominent leaders to move to the city and start a private school. The University of Virginia graduate, who entered the college at age 15, was actually John Roy Baylor VII, descended from Virginia aristocracy. One ancestor attended Oxford and another, Cambridge.[10] The first class he taught in Chattanooga at what was then called the "University School" contained thirty-one students including his star pupil, Park McCallie.

"There wasn't anything J. Roy Baylor couldn't teach," Park later said, naming such subjects as physics, chemistry, Greek, French, Latin, and history. "Mathematics was his first love. It turned out to be my first love."

Though it would be several years before Baylor became a military school, discipline was emphasized from the beginning. "Mr. Baylor had a big voice and was a big, burly man," said Park. On their first day he marched them up to the front porch of the facility.

"Place your hands down by your sides with your fingernails out, and raise your hands so that I can see them," Baylor ordered. "I want to see if your shoes are shined, your fingernails are clean, your hands are clean, your face is clean, your hair is brushed and properly cut and you are properly dressed."

When Baylor gave the command, "Fall in!," the boys lined up immediately according to height, the tallest next to the door. After inspecting every detail of their appearance, notebook in hand, he recorded any demerits. "Then [came] his orders, in the crisp, stern voice of the traditional army sergeant," explains Park McCallie. "'Right face! Forward march!' and we would file into the schoolroom to our desks."

Professor Baylor named his dog Theodorus. When students said, "Teddy sit!" the dog stood still. When Baylor said, "Theodorus, sedite!" the dog sat down immediately.

Upon graduation, Park McCallie received the school's highest grade average from Professor Baylor: 97.83. At the ceremony, Rev. Bachman from First Presbyterian prayed while Mayor George Ochs, Adolph's brother, handed out the awards and gave Park a gold medal.

Professor Baylor's insistence on the University of Virginia caused great stress for Park. "He didn't say 'The University of Virginia,'" said Park, "just 'The University,' as if there weren't any other in the world." The other great figure in Park's life did not agree.

Spencer McCallie III knows the story well, generations later. "My Uncle Park, who was the first honor graduate of Baylor, went to John Roy Baylor's school. Great-grandfather wanted Uncle Park to go to the University of Tennessee. Uncle Park got sick. I think he really got sick. He was so honest, I don't think he'd be pulling a trick. But he got sick for several weeks and then announced to his father: "I will have missed two weeks at the University of Tennessee, but Professor Baylor informs me that the University of Virginia starts in two days, and I'll be in time."

"So he went. And when he went off to school, John Roy Baylor was at the train." Baylor showed up at 6:30 a.m. and brought his prize student six different books on various academic subjects to help with a test given for scholarships. "I got the scholarship," said Park. "Mr. Baylor was so tickled."[11]

Upon graduating, Park headed to Culver Military Academy in Indiana. "Culver is more of the traditional prep school," said Spencer III. "Culver has dormitories. Culver has athletic fields. Culver teaches boys to swim. Culver has horses. That was the first time Uncle Park had seen that kind of school."

"Dr. Baylor didn't believe in sports. He didn't believe in athletics. Baylor was a traditional academy where you would get an outstanding man, who would hire three or four young teachers, and he was really the center of the school. There were

Baylor's first students in 1893. Park McCallie is at far right wearing a straw hat.

hundreds in the United States, actually several hundred in Tennessee over a 30- or 40-year period. If the old professor left town, the academy was gone. If he died, that was probably the end of it."

"My grandfather used to talk about old Professor Duncan. Old Nashville guys still remember Duncan's school. Duncan died, and that was the end of that. That was the kind of school Baylor was."

"So Uncle Park wanted to talk to his brother about starting this other kind of school with the full program. My impression is that Uncle Park didn't even see himself being in competition with Dr. Baylor. It was like, gosh, Baylor is just a little academy. Dr. Baylor is always going to have his forty students and now there's room in town for a hundred and fifty boys to be in schools like this. We'll start one, too, to take care of the growth."

Roy Baylor did not see it that way. Park clearly remembered their conversation before the school opened. "He said that it was strange to him that one of his own students would set up a school in competition to his, that he didn't think he deserved that kind of treatment from one of his own students."[12]

Five McCallies Debate Their Destiny

Roy Baylor's likely resentment was certainly one of the prime concerns that Rev. T. H. McCallie must have relayed to his four other family members as they weighed the decision that evening in 1905 whether to advise Park and Spencer to start a McCallie school for boys.

"My Dear Son," the father wrote to Park. "Your and Spencer's letter rec'd yesterday morning. I at once called Thomas up over the phone. At 8 p.m. we assembled in the study. Mother, Grace, Thomas and I. After prayer for divine guidance, we took up the matter and debated it."

All five of them reached a consensus. As might be expected, the venerable pastor's first point (out of eleven separate points) provided a sweeping mission statement: "1. Our aim is not wealth, or even having the family together, as desirable as this is, but the glory of God in Christ."

He then noted that Baylor did not provide what they were proposing. Also, the city was growing. And though he had never said so, he did not like Park's situation at Culver. "You have no . . . serviceable future in the Kingdom of God there," he said.

He added that the venture would be quite a struggle for a while, but that would be good. "Spencer especially needs it," he noted.

The next part of the letter captured the essence of Dr. T. H. McCallie's wisdom. He knew human nature. He knew competition would make every man involved become far better.

"You should not be droning your life out as professors, well-fed, well-salaried, stupid, sleepy and just half-alive," he said, "but you should be masters of your own business, feeling the tremendous weight of responsibility that weighs upon you for Christ and precious souls."

Certainly Dr. McCallie knew that competition would also be good for Roy Baylor. Not only did he approve of his two sons' proposed rival school, he also offered them $2,500[†] to get started. As a helpful bonus, he provided forty acres at the foot of Missionary Ridge. A nice house near the property served as the school's first facility.[13]

The letter was dated June 1. School started in September, and the two McCallie headmasters hoped they could recruit twenty-five students by then. On the first day, twice that number arrived, causing one student to shout from the window, "All of Chattanooga is coming to school!"[14]

Enrollment grew each year. According to Baylor historian James Hitt, "while McCallie was thriving with 125 pupils that enrolled in 1912, Baylor's University School was watching its student body of fifty-one dwindle away to a handful. . . . All the symptoms indicated that Baylor [was] a very sick school. McCallie School—with its elbow room, country setting, youthful enthusiasm, and full program of athletics—was simply too much competition for the strictly academic, cramped little school on Palmetto Street. Baylor [was] just about dead."

Park tried to explain the higher purposes, but to no avail. "Yes, he was grievously hurt. I hated awfully bad that he should be hurt because I loved Professor Baylor," Park insisted. "I said then, and I still say now, that one school is good for the other. I told him that both schools being here, the very competition would make them better. They would vie with each other. They would see what the other did that was worthwhile and then would follow suit."

Baylor Becomes the Real Thing

Those platitudes did not appease Roy Baylor. They would have remained simply platitudes until Baylor's school shut down had it not been for another visionary in Chattanooga: John T. Lupton.

According to a student sitting at lunch with Baylor and Lupton on graduation day in 1914, the owner of the Coca-Cola bottling empire pulled Baylor aside. He told him some friends of the school were interested in building a nice big campus, like McCallie's, on the outskirts of town.

The eavesdropping student, J. C. Pitner (who later claimed this moment as one of the proudest of his life), reported that Professor Baylor was unable to speak at first. Then, with tears in his eyes, he cried, "Oh, wonderful, wonderful, wonderful, wonderful!"

[†] $240,000 (2006)

Spencer III said Dr. Baylor "realized he needed to do something, and he had seen a beautiful farm out on the river, and he got off of a trolley at Signal Mountain and slogged across some farmer's field. By Sunday afternoon he was back with Mr. Lupton who, with a group or either by himself, bought the farm and presented it to the school. I'm not real good on the history of Baylor."

Roy Baylor

Well, that story did sound a bit apocryphal, slogging across a farm and all. I double-checked the facts, and that is exactly how the account goes. Roy Baylor came across the farm called "Locust Hill" on the river next to Williams Island, and John T. Lupton provided at least $30,000[†] toward the funds needed to buy the land and build a building on it. Today, the property serves as Baylor's breathtaking 400-acre campus.

Athletics were also needed at Baylor, but the old professor adamantly opposed the idea. According to Spencer III, the heavyweights at Baylor in time realized that the venerable professor "did not quite have the vision it was going to take to move forward. So they hired a young man who had experience in this broader vision of a prep school. They hired away Alex Guerry, who was one of the young men on the staff at McCallie. He goes over to Baylor and begins to change Baylor." Even so, Roy Baylor retained the title of President for several more years.

"So now you have two schools with campuses and two schools with the vision of the boys prep school with sports and all the other stuff," said Spencer III. "And that kind of competition was just a very unusual situation. You don't get too sleepy when you've got somebody that's pretty good going after the same crowd of students. That keeps you sharp."

"So Baylor is the older school. It's an academy. McCallie is really the older prep school. Then Baylor went co-ed, which changes things but in a very interesting way. It gives Chattanooga this choice. You have a girls' school, a boys' school, and a co-ed school."

Middle-Class McCallie Needs a Baylor-Class Board

Despite the fact that McCallie is currently involved in a $125 million capital campaign, Spencer hinted on several occasions that he feels McCallie has more of a middle-class feel than its crosstown rival. "The McCallie founders were seen as kind of entrepreneurial folks at that time. They didn't have the backing of any wealthy families. They were doing this all on their own hook. I think Dr. Baylor is getting help from fairly wealthy guys, which was pretty normal. I mean, in the early 1900s,

---

[†] $2.5 million (2006)

the Robber Barons started Groton and a lot of the great New England schools with millions of dollars. The Mellons have always been big on Choate."

Early Baylor board member Jo Conn Guild, Jr. described the generosity of the Baylor backers. "When there was an annual deficit in the 1920s, Mr. Lupton would say, 'All right, I'll pay half of it. Jimmy [Johnston], you and Scott [Probasco] and Jo got to pay the rest of it.' Uncle Jimmy would pay half of what was left and I used to argue with Scott how much he owed and how much I owed."[15]

Baylor was moving forward quickly under this new regime, headed not by one high-profile headmaster but by that old Presbyterian secret weapon: the board. The McCallie School, feeling the financial strains of the depression, also decided it was time to turn ownership over to a board.

"To have a really quality school they had to turn it over to a board," said David McCallie. "In short, that's what happened to all the other academies that cranked up at the time McCallie started. They tried to do it on their own, and when the founding genius was gone, the schools were gone. I think GPS followed somewhat the same pattern [of acquiring a board], and Baylor probably was that way from the beginning. Why that happened here and didn't happen elsewhere, I don't know."

For their first board chairman, the McCallies turned to 28-year-old Robert L. Maclellan, one of a long line of devout Presbyterian Covenanters. The school's board of directors, anywhere from fifteen to twenty-five people, is still limited to only three McCallies at any one time.

"The trustees really do control it," said Spencer III. "I mean, they set my salary. They evaluate me. They told me what they wanted me to emphasize. That's just a fact."

"R. L. Maclellan was on that board until his death. I think he had a heart attack in a New York hotel room [while there] for a big insurance meeting. And his younger brother, Hugh, was on the McCallie board for a long time, and they were fairly generous."

Spencer quickly clarifies their situation compared to Baylor. "I don't think anybody was really giving much money to McCallie. Things were kind of austere. I don't know that the Maclellan stock was all that valuable at the time."

Trampled you today, Spence!

The restructuring did move the McCallie School to the next level of excellence. Athletics helped do the same for Baylor, and even Roy Baylor, steeped in the classics, started enjoying the lopsided victories over the school founded by his own personal Brutus. He reversed his previous position on

Robert L. Maclellan

football. Perhaps it was too difficult for him to talk to Park, but Roy Baylor always made a point to telephone Spencer McCallie after each year's win. "How about it, Spencer? How about it?" he'd say. "Trampled you today. Oh, my, sho."[16]

Dr. Baylor passed away by the time the new football crisis of 1940 arrived. Ironically, the McCallie brothers, who had extolled the virtues of competition, were now planning to quit the growing football rivalry. They wanted Baylor's board to help them save face by agreeing publicly to temporarily discontinue the games. They certainly did not look forward to playing against star running back "Handsome Eddie" Prokop.

Baylor, under the watchful eye of Cartter Lupton and Summerfield Johnston, sent a letter to McCallie refusing their request.

"[Professor Baylor] felt, and we feel now, that the friendly rivalry between the two schools should be continued," they wrote. "We believe . . . this tradition of more than 30 years should not be broken."

"We do not share your views that the rivalry between McCallie and Baylor is detrimental to either school, at least it does not apply here."

"Feeling as we do, we cannot acquiesce in your views and must necessarily decline to issue a joint statement to the press. If it becomes necessary, you may publish this exchange of letters. We will feel at liberty to do the same."

"This entire organization [wishes] continued success to The McCallie School."

The letter led to the McCallie board's late-night meeting on the eve of the game, producing the following response:

"We regret your inability to acquiesce. . . . McCallie's relationship with Baylor is so good and has been for so many years that we do not want anything so relatively unimportant as a football game to interfere with it in the future. . . . We are sorry that you cannot agree to a joint statement to the press."

"All at McCallie School [send] best wishes for the continued success and prosperity of Baylor School."

McCallie then issued a statement to the press: "You can watch a baseball game and come home and eat a good dinner. But losing a football game does something to you that you don't get over for weeks. We want to keep our main stress on scholastic work."

How would the deceased T. H. McCallie have viewed this retreat from the competition at hand? That question can never be answered, but Spencer and Park McCallie were adamant that their motives contained no malice. "There is no bitterness between the two schools," the press release insisted. "Just an effort to lessen the importance on one game, unfortunately a game in the same city."

A few hours later, Baylor met McCallie in their last football game before the "temporary" discontinuance. The two rivals would not meet again for 31 years.

Today's Baylor board members still talk about it. "McCallie quit playing us in football," said Tommy Lupton. "Now that we have girls and don't have enough boys to compete, we ought to quit playing them. But we're not even thinking about it. If we happen to get beat, we get beat."

As expected and feared in that final game of 1940, Eddie Prokop scored two touchdowns in the first half. In the second half, McCallie scored a touchdown and then had the ball on the one-yard-line with a minute to go. However, on fourth down, Baylor's defense stopped them from scoring. On the last play of the game, Handsome Eddie called a play that had not been used all year and ran ninety-three yards for a touchdown as the clock expired. "At that moment he entered the mythic dimension," wrote John Longwith in his Baylor history. "Time froze and Eddie Prokop, like a figure on a Grecian urn, kept running in the minds of Baylor loyalists—their single most powerful memory of the competition between the two schools."

———————————

Very little education has taken place in Chattanooga since its founding that was not somehow influenced by, associated with, or started by a McCallie.

In ages past, the First Peoples here taught their young boys to hunt, to walk without noise, and to mimic the cry of the fawn to attract the deer. Early missionaries like Gideon Blackburn brought literacy to the area, and for a time, Blackburn taught the children of Daniel Ross at his home below Lookout Mountain. The missionaries at Brainerd continued Blackburn's efforts and from 1817 to 1838 faithfully taught reading, writing, practical skills, agriculture, and Christian principles to red, black, and white children alike.

One of those missionaries, John Vail, continued teaching after the Cherokee removal and, along with colleague Ainsworth Blunt, served as the first public school commissioner for Hamilton County. They also were the founding elders of First Presbyterian Church, which T. H. McCallie later brought to prominence. "They were not ministers, but laymen, sent out . . . not to preach but to train the Indians in agriculture and handicraft," Rev. McCallie later said of these Chattanooga founding fathers whom he knew personally. "They were good and consecrated men."[17]

By 1840, five common schools were supported by Hamilton County tax dollars, one of them meeting in a McCallie home. Young T. H. McCallie learned how to read and write in the early 1840s while being homeschooled by his father, Thomas McCallie.

By age 15, T. H. McCallie was leading an underground school for slaves. His mother was the instigator, setting up a classroom in the basement of the First Presbyterian Church on Market Street. "I was, at that time, not only teacher but superintendent of the school," McCallie writes in his journal. "At that time the laws of Tennessee did not allow anyone to teach the negro slaves to read, lest they should get hold of abolition papers from the North and become incorrigible. This wicked law my mother taught me to disregard."[18]

When McCallie later moved from the basement to the pulpit of First Presbyterian, he saw the need to start a school in his home after the devastation of war had left him in a town where he was the only pastor and no schools were available. "There was no education system in 1865," Dr. David McCallie told me during our interview. "He was a preacher. He had the time. He had the education, he had the resources, so he figured it was his job to . . . run a small school for a while."

T. H. McCallie was the sole survivor of four children. One boy died in infancy, another at age eleven, and his sister at age 19. Determined to not let the family name perish, he prayed for a son after having three daughters. He ended up with eleven. He and his wife, Ellen Jarnagin McCallie, had sixteen children in all, eight of whom reached adulthood.

"The history of the church, county, and city is closely bound with this interesting couple," writes Zella Armstrong. "Mrs. McCallie was the greatest woman Chattanooga has ever produced. Besides being the mother of sixteen children, she taught a Sunday School class, helped to organize the Vine Street Orphans Home (and was president for several years), the WCTU, the Frances Willard Home, the YWCA, the Home and Foreign Missionary Societies, [etc.]."[19]

Young T. H. McCallie met Ellen when several ministers were invited to a tea. He heard her voice and turned to admire "her fine intellectual face and her neat figure." He was struck, he said. "I said to myself, 'Here she is at last.' . . . I lifted up my head in prayer to God and said, 'Father, if this is she, do guide me and lead me and give her to me in due time.'"

He did not see her for months and thought that was the end of it. Then he began to see her regularly as she taught school near his church. For two years, nothing happened except McCallie's new concern "that Miss Jarnagin may have too much temper." He wrote her pastor, who explained her temper was "like the blade of Damascus, of highest polish and finest finish, but uniformly kept well in hand."

Persuaded, McCallie wrote her a letter of proposal. "You are the first woman to whom my pen or lips ever uttered a word of affection," he said in conclusion. "I expect you to be the only one. If you can approve my affection for you and return me a favorable answer accepting my offer of heart and hand I will be happy to style myself: Yours ever, T. H. McCallie."

T. H. McCallie and wife, Ellen, with their five sons.
(From left) Douglas, Edward, Thomas, Spencer, and Park.

T. H. and Ellen McCallie and their progeny at their 50th wedding anniversary.
Rev. McCallie is in the center with Rev. Bachman to his right.

She replied four days later. "I respect and esteem you very highly and am willing to trust my future happiness to your keeping. Yet, I do so with some fear that you may have deceived yourself with regard to my character. . . . A mistake in this respect might render the lives of both miserable."

"I will state that your suit meets with the approbation of my mother. Truly, Ellen Jarnagin."[20]

On Christmas Eve two years later, T. H. McCallie's church had become a hospital and amputation facility. The floor of his home was covered with soldiers and other refugees for Ellen to care for. There was hardly any food anywhere. The landscape was nothing but barren hills, felled trees, and thousands of mules dead from starvation.

"I've always hung my stocking Christmas Eve night since I was a child," Ellen told her husband. She hung it by the fireplace and went to bed. "Too bad that the dear woman should be cheated out of the joy of waking up on Christmas morning and finding that Santa Claus had been here," Rev. McCallie thought. He waited until she was definitely asleep. "I put on my overcoat and sallied out into the winter night." He found one Union supply tent still open. Despite his being a Southerner—or perhaps because he ministered to Federals as well as Confederates—he found favor with the Union officer. The next morning his wife arose to a stuffed stocking: some candy, cove oysters, and a can of tomatoes. "The woman was a child again. She could hardly believe her eyes. She wondered where on earth these things could have come from."

"Mr. McCallie, where and when did you get them?" she cried.

Within a short time after the war, new schools opened and T. H. McCallie was free to focus solely on his thriving church in a booming town. Besides his own services each week, he traveled around the region, averaging forty or more sermons in other towns each year. He took no vacations for eight years despite esophageal problems that only grew worse.

"I realized that my health was gone," he wrote in 1873, "that Chattanooga was growing, my church increasing and that it was my duty to resign my work. This was one of the most painful events of my entire life. I came to the conclusion slowly, I struggled against it. [But I realized] as important a pulpit as the one I occupied demanded a stronger man, and that I must give way."

"I resigned, not knowing the future or what was in store for me, whether life or death, whether work or a paralyzed condition of my man." He was replaced by Dr. Jonathan Bachman, a former chaplain for Robert E. Lee and Stonewall Jackson. McCallie, age 36, made himself available for mission work, new church starts, and itinerant preaching. "During that entire year, I preached fourteen times and was really not able to preach once," he said.[21]

The congregation, who had watched their pastor heroically stand with them through a horrible seige and the worst two days of battle the nation had ever seen, was devastated when he announced his retirement. "The idea that he was going to such a scattered, unpromising field for a man of his years appeared to his people a sacrifice of a dear life," the *Chattanooga Times* later wrote.[22]

Legacy's Narrow Road

It was T. H. McCallie's personal test to live out the challenge he gave to his two sons a half-century later—to choose the best course, the road less traveled, rather than becoming fat, lazy, and well-salaried. As it turned out, his feeble frame brought forth perhaps the most productive and extraordinary life in the city's history.

As he gained his strength, he began a 50-year effort of starting churches, charities, and schools all across the area. Through his efforts in large part, the First Presbyterian Church started new churches including Central Presbyterian, Lookout Mountain Presbyterian, and Mission Ridge Presbyterian (later called Westminster Presbyterian, now a mixed-race Presbyterian church called New City Fellowship). One of T. H. McCallie's sons, T. S. McCallie, founded Signal Mountain Presbyterian. This son was later named Chaplain to the City by the Chattanooga City Council.

Dr. Bachman, the former Confederate officer, was the first to be named Chaplain to the City, and it was McCallie's relationship to Bachman that allowed the city's flagship church to so successfully prosper during that era. T. H. McCallie did not resent his successor and never tried to upstage him. Instead, the two were best friends, working side by side in the ministry for 50 years. Zella Armstrong seems to indicate they were both on the staff of First Presbyterian during this half decade. She opined in her history of the city that Chattanooga "is the only community in the world where two ministers each served 50 years."

Dr. McCallie offered the dedicatory prayer for the landmark building erected by First Presbyterian in 1910 on McCallie Avenue. His lifelong friend, Dr. Bachman, worked closely with the architects. "No detail escaped him," his daughter said, "but he never could understand why they added the small cupola on the top."[23]

The McCallie-Bachman legacy was followed by the Fowle legacy at First Presbyterian Church.

Spencer III told me about Dr. Fowle's love for people. The pastor was devastated when his friend Henry Bibb died, Park McCallie's brother-in-law. "I just remember going to the funeral and Dr. Fowle sobbing as he tried to go out of the church. He was so upset."

Jonathan Bachman

Spencer shed some tears while telling the story. "It touches me even now, as you can see."

Grace McCallie

T. H. McCallie's daughter, Margaret Ellen McCallie, co-founded the Bright School along with Mary Gardner Bright. This private Riverview elementary institution is still known as Chattanooga's most prominent grade school.

Another daughter, Grace McCallie, determined to find a way to help girls in Chattanooga go to college. While a teacher at City High, she petitioned the school board to create a preparatory program for girls, but her request was denied. During that fateful evening at her father's home when the five McCallies agreed to starting a boys school, Grace advocated letting girls attend as well. Her father liked the idea, but her two brothers declined.

Finally, with the help of her first cousin, Eula Jarnagin, and another City High teacher, Tommie Duffy, Grace Eliza McCallie established the Girls Preparatory School. Having studied advanced mathematics at Cornell, Grace started the school in her home on Oak Street, converting one of the bedrooms into a chemistry lab.

These GPS founders noted that the community was more interested in three women living alone upstairs, considered improper at the time, than they were in the academic venture. They also offered sports for the girls, even though this was also deemed inappropriate, and insisted that daily exercise was important "to prevent that nervous breakdown so common among girls."[24]

"Those three women were real feminists, but they didn't know it," said Mai Bell Hurley, a GPS graduate and board member. "They created it because they really thought people needed to think about preparing their daughters for college."

"It was the antithesis of finishing schools. After all, we wore those sort of sacks," she said. "I mean, they were just straight with a string tied around them with a grosgrain ribbon. And they are still wearing them."

The story has already been told of the two McCallie boys who left another great legacy for T. H. McCallie by founding a school a few years after Baylor School was established. Ironically, T. H. McCallie can also be given a portion of the credit for the founding of Baylor. His best friend and colleague, Dr. Bachman, was one of the handful of men who recruited Roy Baylor to Chattanooga. The meeting at which they persuaded Baylor to take the job was held in Bachman's study at First Presbyterian.

After Baylor agreed, the next key decision was where to conduct the school. The professor chose to lease the old McCallie homestead as his first schoolhouse. T. H. McCallie had moved to the Ridge by then. Roy Baylor paid $100[†] per year

---

[†] $11,000 (2006)

to T. H. McCallie along with providing free tuition for three of McCallie's sons, including Park. Baylor leased the McCallie home for twelve years, a facility described by students as a windy barn and "one hell of an old house."

Dr. Baylor felt the need early on to make improvements and additions to the facility, and there is some speculation that words in the second edition of Baylor's annual catalog reveal the beginnings of a Baylor-McCallie rivalry. The professor noted that "the principal was compelled to build an addition, at his own expense, to accommodate the pupils for the second year." It seems Dr. Baylor was upset that Dr. McCallie would not help with the expenses of a new addition. It is curious that this seemingly unimportant phrase remained in the catalog for over 20 years. It is equally curious that the phrase *"at his own expense"* was highlighted in italics starting in 1905–1906, the very year Park McCallie started his competing school.[25]

The Dilemma for Public Education

For decades, area leaders have been debating whether Chattanooga's extraordinary private and prep school phenomenon is, in fact, a double-edged sword.

"The halo that surrounds private education in our community is a noose around the neck of its future," said Lyndhurst Foundation Director Jack Murrah. "The future belongs not to those nations and communities that do a superb job at an exalted price of educating the top 10 percent of its children. It belongs to those that can do an excellent job at a moderate price of educating the other 90 percent."[26]

Murrah says these schools that cost three times more per student than public schools "demonstrate the most expensive, least cost-effective path to excellence in

The McCallie homestead served as Baylor's first facility for several years.

education that I know of." He also says there is no research showing that lower teacher-student ratios improve education.

Murrah, a former teacher at Baylor and the man who oversees the gifts of the fortune of Baylor's greatest supporting family, is an ironic critic of the Big Three. "I don't think Jack Lupton would be sitting here saying the same things to you," Murrah admits. "[But] he decided that it is important for the future of this city that our public school system be better. He accepted my [suggestion] that Baylor, McCallie, and GPS had legions of wealthy loyal alumni, and they would be healthier institutions if their financial support came from those people . . . that they would not be healthy if they had sort of a sugar daddy who took care of them. He bought the idea that the Lyndhurst Foundation ought to at least try its hand at trying to improve the public schools."

A key vehicle for accomplishing this goal has been the Public Education Foundation, founded in 1988. It has been chaired by Ruth Holmberg for years and has been healthily funded by Lyndhurst for "creating outstanding schools by applying resources to bold ideas." Founding director Steve Prigohzy pushed early childhood development, professional development, and higher standards during his ten years at PEF, which included a merger of city and county schools for which PEF provided the blueprint. However, the merger was bitterly contested in the public arena—the black community wanting to keep its city system, and some in the white community protesting potential tax increases or potentially too-liberal ideas in the blueprint. The merger was pushed to a second vote thanks to the largest petition drive in Chattanooga's history. Although the pro-merger party won the election, the school system continues to struggle with an electorate that avoids tax increases and is skeptical regarding the idea that there has been improvement in the schools.

Murrah thinks the performance in public schools in Chattanooga is typical of what you find across the country. "I think our achievements, our scores, are not wildly out of line with what you will find in a lot of other towns," he said. He does believe the attitude in the community needs to improve. "As long as we believe that those children cannot be taught successfully because of their home circumstances, then we won't do it." Instead of working toward such self-fulfilled prophecies, he calls for recruiting more talented teachers.

"It is a harder job to teach children with less support than it is to teach children who have lots of support from home. There are many people who do this better than others. You've got to have more tricks up your sleeve to enable those children to get into the game." He says the "union culture" in public education has a hard time accepting this notion. "They would say, pay a person according to the degree they have, the number of years experience they have, but never according to whether they're teaching a more challenging set of circumstances or are doing better."

Murrah also does not believe the Big Three are evaluated in terms of "value added," that is, the amount of improvement made based on the students abilities. "Saying the hardest school to get into is the best school in the country—that's a little bit like saying the best hospital in America is the one that admits the healthiest people," he said. "Well, okay, [these schools] have to be pretty good to attract those kids to come there. There must be something about the school that's probably not a completely fraudulent place, but it's not held up to a rigorous standard of assessment. Who knows whether Harvard adds more value to a person's intellectual development than Ohio State? They may, they may not. Who's got the evidence? No one has asked them."

If the Big Three are not being measured for effectiveness, Murrah sees it as little wonder that such standards have not come yet to public schools. "There are influential people in this town who feel as though they really don't have to think much about the public schools because their kids aren't going there, and their major management people won't go there. That probably reduces the number of resources available to try to push the public schools to a higher standard of performance."

Scotty Probasco agrees that the city's elite, historically, were wrapped up in the Big Three. "This could be a fault of what we call the power structure. Then your school boards didn't get the leadership, which was in the private schools. So that's a downer. That's a minus, there's no question."

"But in the last 15 years or so this 'power structure,' I'd have to say, really recognized the importance of public education. And I've said so to many people because I've solicited money and given some pretty dang big money to public education."

The Public Education Foundation continues to push toward improvement of local schools, but founding director Steve Prigohzy left in 1998, after ten years of struggle. It was not because of the personal persecution from a suspicious populace, which he was able to withstand—rocks were thrown through his windows at home, and he received threatening and obscene phone calls. Rather, he cited the power structure as his reason for resigning, not the elite citizens themselves, whom he extolled for their involvement, but the lethargy such activism may cause in the electorate. "Most of our citizens are prideful [of the city's efforts], but in reality, they are not a part of it," Prigohzy said, noting that despite "powerful arguments" to the contrary, a "power structure" runs the city.

"Influence exerted by a few—that's not helpful," he said. "It makes the rest of us powerless. Whether those few are working for the good is almost irrelevant." Prigohzy also noted that the disparity between public and private education in Chattanooga reached its way into the central office. He said a number of administrators in the public school system were not sending their kids to the system where they worked.[27]

The chasm became even more evident when the Maclellan Foundation gave $800,000 in 1999 toward partial scholarships to help hundreds of students attend private schools, part of over three million dollars worth of funding for the Children's Educational Opportunity Foundation (CEO). Private school proponents saw it as a way to use the strength of private schooling to the community's advantage, but school board members like Janice Boydston disagreed. "I resent that implication that you can't get as good an education in public schools. It's untrue. It just makes me so mad."

Nearly 600 mostly minority students received scholarships though the CEO Foundation, about the same number of students added to private school rosters in 1998. Public school enrollment declined the same year by 700. Over 3,300 students were on the CEO program's waiting list. School board member Debbie Colburn called the private scholarship program underhanded. "There has been a movement for quite a while toward undermining the public school systems," she said.

CEO President Rodger Piersant said private schools provide a better scholastic foundation for nearly half the price of public schools. "What is wrong with this picture," he said. "I'm so sick that the only discourse is that public schools just need more money. It's not about money. It's about innovation."[28]

Public Ed's Golden Age of the Creed

The perception of Chattanooga's public schools has not always been such a struggle. In fact, there have been moments of greatness. "It's a sad story," said Frank Brock. "When I grew up, City and Central were very good, strong public schools. Creed Bates and Hobart Millsaps were the two principals. Both were known as wonderful educators, wonderful men of character, wonderful in every sense—the kind of people every community wants and needs."

"When desegregation came, it really just fundamentally upset those two schools. All of the sudden you had busing, and you had people being taken out of their local neighborhood. . . . The idea of the local school was replaced by the county school board, and state and local regulation became the way they tried to run the schools. It was bureaucratic. It was heavy-handed. It was detail-oriented, and it basically disenfranchised the local parents from the local schools."

He said people just threw their hands up in frustration. "And so they started private schools and nobody, including the people who send their kids to private schools, really liked it."

People thought Creed Bates "walked on water." Scotty Probasco said Bates ran a great school and that many of his senior vice presidents graduated from City High. "Hell, the president of the University of Georgia went to City High," he said.

"City High was awesome," said Bob Corker, who was student body president. "Colonel Bates had retired. We would go visit him. He had an apple orchard and lived in this log cabin on the back of Signal. I was able to meet him. He was such an outstanding person."

"Creed Bates was a great man," said Lee Anderson. "He was an old bachelor, and he had two sisters. One of them was my homeroom teacher, and he was the principal. He was dedicated thoroughly to that school. He wouldn't let you say City High School. It was Chattanooga High School. He'd say it all together like that: 'Chattanooga High School.' He wanted it to be the best school anywhere there was, and it was."

"He told us, 'You all have to win more scholarships than Baylor, McCallie, and GPS put together.' He had the clout to bring in the best teachers when they were not paid anything. He had a faculty that was second to none. Academics were everything. Honor code, the ROTC. We were always lousy in football, but everything else was [great]. I was captain of the band. We won a state band championship, and our ROTC always had the red star."

"And he knew everybody in school. He'd know what you were thinking before you would think of it. He went into the Army as a captain during World War II and came out a colonel. He could have been the superintendent of city schools, but he didn't want to be."

"Now, if you graduated at the bottom of the class, you might not have as much as somebody at Baylor, McCallie, or GPS. But if you graduated at the top of the class, you got as good an education as you could get. I could not have gotten a better education anywhere else."

At that time, excellent public and private education may not have been mutually exclusive. Bill Brock III, a McCallie graduate, believes the same is true today. "To think that we would have better schools if we didn't have Baylor and McCallie and GPS is insane. We have better leaders because of [the Big Three], and those leaders make for better public schools," he said.

"Being able to send your kid to McCallie, Baylor, or GPS does mean you don't have to pay attention to the public schools in direct, personal terms. Absolutely true," he conceded. "And I think that some people in Chattanooga did that. Not all."

Creed Bates

Brock believes the Big Three create a sense of civic involvement that should cause graduates to take a leadership role in improving public schools. "It is insane to do otherwise," he said. "Of course, it doesn't always work that way."

It did for Bill Brock, the former U.S. Senator and then secretary of labor under Ronald Reagan. Now in his early '70s, he is dedicating the rest of his life to the initative he started, Bridges Learning Systems, headquartered in Annapolis, Maryland. When I visited him there for our interview, he was dressed in casual clothes and worked in a rather small, cramped office on a floor that reminded me of middle-management cubicles in a school systems' central office. There was barely room for the large portraits of Winston Churchill and Teddy Roosevelt, his two heroes.

He told me his center focuses on the research of scientists like J. P. Guilford, who identified ninety different intellectual abilities. Brock says students need to be assessed and profiled before being prescribed an educational strategy. "That's my life's passion. That's all I do," he said. "We need to treat students like individuals instead of like products on an assembly line. We must begin to address their learning needs diagnostically instead of as if they were boots into which we pour knowledge."

The former U.S. trade representative believes, based on developments in China and the rest of the world, that the country's future is in jeopardy if we don't "rethink our entire education system." When Brock accepted his appointment to Reagan's cabinet, 12 percent of Americans worked on an assembly line. "I said by the end of the century it will probably be close to 5 percent. I was right."

Brock told me that when he got his big call from the White House, he was knee deep in the mud planting flowers. He loved being U.S. trade representative and told Reagan's chief of staff the day before that he was not interested in a cabinet post.

"Tell him not to call," Brock told the chief of staff. He told his wife, Muffet, to tell anyone who calls he is not there since he would be in the garden. "I really was up to my knees in mud in my rose garden trying to hide and she came out and said, 'The President's calling.'"

"Muffet, the President is not calling."

"It's the White House, calling for the President."

He was terrified that Reagan was on the line, and that he would not get there in time because of all the mud. When he brushed himself off and answered the phone, it was the chief of staff. He told him the President was announcing Brock's appointment as secretary of labor in two hours. He needed to come right away if he wanted to join the party. Bill dashed into the shower and headed to D.C.

"When I went into the Oval Office, the President said, 'Bill, you're so good to do this.' And I said, 'Mr. President, I have one final request.' The chief of staff looked at me like I had shot him in the heart. 'Well, of course. What is it? the President asked."

Brock told him he wanted to call AFL-CIO President Lane Kirkland first before he heard it on the news. Reagan consented, and the man whose family's candy company never went union chatted briefly with Lane Kirkland, the nation's biggest union leader.

"You know me," he told Kirkland. "You know I'll never lie to you and I'll never surprise you. We won't agree on a lot of stuff, but I will tell you what I'm going to do, and I will work with you to the extent that we can. And I need your help."

"This is the nicest call I ever got," he told Brock. "You will have my support."

McCallie and Christianity; Baylor and the Bible

Brock says he got much of his "spiritual rootstock" during his years at McCallie. "You were expected to be students of the Bible," he said. "You understood the importance of faith in your life, family, community, and formation of the country. That's important stuff," he said. "That's very important stuff."

Upon entering the McCallie School campus, the stone gates greet the driver with an inscription: "Man's Chief End is to Glorify God and to Enjoy Him Forever." This is the first answer to the catechism accompanying the Westminster Confession of Faith, Presbyterian's founding charter. Both documents were written with the help of Scotty Probasco's ancestor. The hard evidence on the stone gate helps to fuel an ongoing debate this past century as to whether McCallie is a more Christian school than Baylor.

"It was very much motivated by Christian principles," said McCallie grad Frank Brock. "I think it was true for GPS and Baylor to a lesser extent. But the motto for McCallie was 'Man's chief end is to glorify God.'"

In his historic letter to his two sons, T. H. McCallie made the point clear. "You would expect to make it a Christian school," he wrote. The seeds of McCallie School's stronger articulation of a Christian emphasis started years before the school was founded when Park McCallie found himself disillusioned with Thomas Jefferson's University of Virginia, the college recommended by his mentor, Roy Baylor. Park later explained how, as a student, he "just happened" to open his Bible to the verse in I Corinthians that says "the wisdom of this world is foolishness." By 1926, the McCallies were still making it clear in their catalog that "there is no true education that does not lead directly to God."

Baylor School was always less specific in giving any particular religious stance. Early headmaster Alex Guerry made it a point to say that the educated man "knows there are such things as beauty and truth, not because someone has declared this to be so, but because he has read the story time and again—in history, in literature, in philosophy . . ."[29]

Today, the official websites for the two schools offer an explanation of their current Christian emphasis. Baylor's website acknowledges that while "the majority of Baylor's students and faculty are Christian, all major world religions are represented in the school." The website also notes that the school's chaplain "is an ordained Christian minister who is conversant with all faith traditions." McCallie's website says, "McCallie believes that its ongoing Christian tradition builds a strong moral foundation and a sense of civic and social duty" and instills "a respect for, and understanding of, other religions and faiths."

During our interview, Spencer McCallie told me that, regarding the leadership providing a Christian emphasis, "I think probably most people would say they were stronger at McCallie. I think most people would."

Scotty Probasco is not one of those who thinks McCallie is more Christian. "I am so sick of that I want to puke," he told me. "Baylor is a very Christian-dominated school. We have the greatest FCA program (Fellowship of Christian Athletes). We have a great Young Life program. It's 90 percent Christian kids, and they still have Christian chapel programs and what not."

"McCallie tries to wave the flag that they're a great Christian school. I'm going to tell you something: when I'm really under the sheets, I think we're a much stronger Christian school than McCallie. Baylor ain't hypocritical. We were the first of all the private schools that accepted Jews. Humphy Heywood was a Catholic. He was our business manager. He was a great football coach, too. McCallie quit playing football with us for a bunch of years because we were whipping their ass all the time."

"I mean, Baylor and McCallie are not 'Christian schools,' which the Chattanooga Christian School 'is.' And the Chattanooga Christian School is prospering. It's doing a great job, and it has a role to play."

Enter the "Christian School"

In fact, Chattanooga Christian School (CCS) is now the largest private school in Chattanooga. At just over 1,000 students, CCS states on its website that their official purpose is "to provide a quality educational program from a Biblical perspective, for children of Christian families, designed to prepare students to influence cultures and society for Christ."

"Chattanooga folks, particularly in the Bible Belt, are very concerned about morals and values," said CCS Headmaster Don Holwerda, "and they are looking for ways to teach those things to their children."

CCS has the added benefit of costing less than half of the Big Three. At $6,000 per year, they charge $1,000 less than public schools cost the taxpayer, while still providing more National Merit Finalists last year than Baylor and all the public schools combined. Notre Dame, the local Catholic school started in 1879 (and actually the oldest private school), has a tuition rate similar to that of CCS. Other private schools such as Tennessee Temple, Grace Academy, and Silverdale Baptist Academy cost even less, with Calvary Christian charging as little as $2,950.[30]

A number of multigenerational families associated with the Big Three now send their children to CCS. "It was very difficult for me and my family," said Sam Smartt, the CCS board chairman for many years. "My mom and my sisters would see us put our children in the Christian School downtown when they would have been third generation up here at Lookout Mountain. They would have been third generation at McCallie or Baylor because our family went to both schools, actually. But if you ask my mom and sisters, they would say there is no question CCS has been a wonderful thing for my kids."

Smartt, a Baylor graduate, felt like McCallie had a stronger Christian emphasis when he was in school. He also explained that McCallie is willing to teach evolution, and other difficult topics, "lay both out there, and maybe let the kids decide, rather than lay both out there and then look at it from a Christian perspective. I guess the premise would be that our Christian faith encompasses all aspects of life."

A generational shift occurred in the community when Hugh O. Maclellan, Jr. began sending his children to CCS. "I think Hugh O. Jr. is the one that has the vision for Christian education," said Smartt. Indeed, it was Hugh Maclellan, Jr., whose uncle chaired McCallie for decades, who began sending his daughter to CCS soon after it was founded in 1970 and then helped the school purchase their current property on Broad Street below Lookout Mountain. Started by Covenant College board member Joel Belz, Chattanooga Christian School began in association with Lookout Mountain Presbyterian, a church founded by T. H. McCallie, giving that great minister something else to add to his quiver of educational legacies in Chattanooga.

"Joel Belz came to me and said, 'I wish you would pray for ten acres we need to start a school,'" Hugh O. Maclellan said. "The Covenant professors didn't have anything for their children. I thought to myself: Man, that would be a miracle to be able to get a school like that going for ten acres. But the Lord blessed that. The Maclellan

Foundation was a major player by helping buy the campus and renovating all the buildings."

Balaak Billy Graham

Frank Brock sits on the Maclellan Foundation but sent all his children to McCallie and GPS. "I would say Spencer McCallie III is one of the top educators in the country," Brock said. "He was very concerned about a reactionary Fundamentalism. I think he would probably say that the school his father ran and certainly the school his grandfather ran, was far more religiously conservative than the school he wanted to be associated with. We talked very specifically about this. He said, 'It's hard to say that all the good teachers are Christians. It's hard to say that being a Christian is what makes a person a good teacher.'"

"I think a lot of parents who have Christian children feel that McCallie has been at worst a neutral environment and at best a nurturing environment for Christian kids. It's kind of an interesting contrast with a school that is more explicitly Christian. I think there are arguments for what Spencer did—that it worked well."

For his part, Spencer McCallie III seemed to make a point in our interview of shying away from the idea that McCallie was more Christian than Baylor. But he did enjoy the subject for its comic value.

"I told Rotary the story about Billy Graham and the Baylor chapel—how Frank Harrison wanted to find the most famous minister in all of Christendom, and flew him over here in a jet. And I said that Frank Harrison had helped build this chapel in an effort to bring Christianity to Baylor."

"And people just laughed. They knew I was teasing. I saw Baylor people laughing. They knew I was kidding. But afterwards, one of the Guerrys came up to me and said, 'Now, you do know that my grandfather became Chancellor of the Episcopal University and was a bishop,' going through all that. So, yeah, it gets too personal. It's not fair to go on some of the perceptions. They get overblown."

However, the McCallie folks certainly got the last laugh on the day Billy Graham was flown in to dedicate the new multimillion dollar Baylor Chapel. Graham may have recalled the many summer meetings he and Park McCallie enjoyed back at Graham's Montreat facility in North Carolina, because during his long-awaited prayer to dedicate the Baylor chapel, the world's greatest evangelist asked the Lord to make this chapel a blessing "for the McCallie boys."[31]

McCallie's Howard Legacy

Judge Walter Williams sends his African American kids to Baylor, but it has nothing to do with religion. "I do believe in God. Of course, Baylor does not push that necessarily, but they do have chapel programs and all that," he said. A graduate of Howard High, Morehouse College, and Howard Law School, Williams understands that most kids cannot afford private schools, and he says he has tried to help public schools as much as possible.

"The biggest problem is discipline," he said. "When you don't have any discipline, you're going to have chaos. I don't know of one educational program where discipline is part of the curriculum. It's just not there. There are good teachers of English and math and all, but they have no training in dealing with discipline. Even in my court, I believe in discipline. Whether people liked me or not, people knew when they came into the court that it was very orderly. No talking. No carrying on. It was very structured. There was discipline. And so that's part of the problem with public schools."

"There's not proper funding. . . . The teacher's responsibility is to teach students. Now if these students bring in all these other things for which these teachers are not equipped to deal with, then there ought to be resources provided."

Williams is old-school regarding academics as well. "Every time you turn around, the public schools are trying something new. What's wrong with reading, writing and arithmetic? You don't find Baylor, McCallie, and GPS trying all these things."

When Williams was in high school, he was greatly influenced by one of Howard's first white teachers, who later became a principal. This was Spencer McCallie III's brother, Franklin McCallie. "He taught me English," said Judge Williams. "He was very comfortable teaching black students and just excited us and was a very good teacher."

Williams explained how Franklin McCallie was instrumental in electing John Franklin, the city's first black elected official in 60 years. "He was very involved in Johnny's initial campaign and worked hard. As one of his former students, he gathered us together. I put up campaign signs and did all kinds of other things with Franklin McCallie. He did a lot of speech writing and what have you. He was a close friend. I was one of his first students, I guess, and he just was a nice guy. Still is a nice guy. Lives in St. Louis now. I see him when he comes home. We get together."

Former Howard principal Lurone Jennings has similar feelings for this great-grandson of T. H. McCallie. "This guy was a jewel," said Lurone. "Franklin McCallie was like a daddy to us. We didn't even look at him like he was white. He was that cool."

While Lurone and others were marching in the civil rights movement, "he was teaching us how to protest and how to do it with sense and with dignity. He was a godsend for us, and that helped us have a different mind-set about white people. You can imagine—I never had a white friend, never went to school with white kids."

When Franklin McCallie returned to Chattanooga to speak to the Rotarians on September 20, 2001, his brother introduced him and said he was "proud to present him . . . and a little nervous." Franklin is more liberal than your average McCallie. But at the Rotary Club, he focused his remarks on improving public education and also reflected a bit on his days at Howard High.

"I had one kid: feisty, argumentative, asked questions, a gadfly. Always pushing, never left me alone. I said, 'Son, what are you gonna be?' He said, 'A lawyer.' I said, 'I think you should.'

That student was Walter Williams.

"One day I was walking down the street in Chattanooga," Franklin said. "An old McCallie grad saw me.

"What are you doing?" he asked.

"I'm teaching."

"You're back at McCallie? Way to go!'

"No, I'm at Howard High School," I said.

"You're at the nigger school?"

"No, I'm at the all-black school."

"That's what I said."

"No, that's not what you said," Franklin replied. "I'm at the all-black school, Howard High School."

"He said, 'Oh,' and walked off."

Franklin McCallie told the Rotarians that he learned after writing a research paper in 1963 that 90 percent of kids go to public schools. "I didn't know that. I thought it was 50 percent."

That helped push him into public education. He then talked about one of his black assistant principals in St. Louis who was very difficult. "She wasn't racist. She just didn't like anybody. She was too tough, too mean. I don't think that's how my father ran McCallie. There was a love . . ."

Franklin teared up a moment and then continued. "My dad saw us twice a day—fifteen minutes in the morning, a half-hour at lunch. He started two assemblies a day and spoke for four minutes. I use the McCallie model of caring, loving and building community. I talk to them. I started to have a little love. I started hiring teachers who love kids as much as they love their subjects."

He has been at Kirkwood High in St. Louis, a minority school like Howard, for 22 years. He reported that test scores began to soar and the number of students taking advanced placement courses rose from 68 to 600. "We didn't have a school where there was love and affection and touching, and that's what we had to do. I hug my kids. I hug 100 kids a day."

"One day I said to Spencer, 'How can you afford to build this $12 million athletic center and you're sending kids to Harvard, Stanford, and Princeton?' And he said, 'Franklin, at McCallie School they want the best in music, the best in science,

Three generations of Spencer McCallies, c. 1960

the best in art, the best in athletics. They want the best. We say at McCallie: why not the best?'"

"And, by gosh, I went back to my faculty and said, 'At Kirkwood High School, why not the best? Why not the best?'"

Franklin teared up before saying again, "Why not the best?"

———◆———

One of the reasons Spencer may have been a bit nervous when he introduced his brother was that Franklin had recently won an award in Atlanta from the Parents, Families, and Friends of Lesbians and Gays. At Kirkwood, the man who stood up for the rights of blacks in Chattanooga continued to do so for gay students in Missouri. He also lobbied Missouri legislators to approve gay marriage unions. Needling conservatives from another angle, he is known at times to escort young women to Kirkwood's abortion clinic, and to respond to pro-life protesters with the verse from John chapter eight, "The truth shall set you free."[32]

How does the extended McCallie family handle such divergent views on such controversial subjects? "It's not an agenda item that we have for family meetings to discuss," said Allen McCallie. Inevitably, such discussions do occur from time to time and are "wonderful and sometimes bruising discussions," he said. Some McCallies believe the more modern views are in conflict with their heritage handed down from T. H. McCallie and some do not. "I don't see a conflict between that and my Christian principles," said Allen.

"We have great differences in the family," said Tom McCallie. "Yet, at the end of the day, those differences are not what control it. It's what you're related to—another individual who is important," he said. "We've always been brought up that relationships are important, that kinfolk mean something, that family is part of God's design for you."

When Allen McCallie's brother, Freddy, died early from cancer, it caused the McCallies to remember the importance of family. In his will, Freddy directed that his insurance money go to efforts to promote the McCallie heritage. One project was a trip to a church cemetery near Old Washington where T. H. McCallie's grandfather was buried.

"We all went up about five years ago," said Spencer III. "A whole bunch of family—maybe two small busloads of us, twenty-five or thirty of us. And, gosh, I can't even think of the name of this little ancient church, but the cemetery is the original. We just went up there for the heck of it on Saturday and had a picnic. Our direct relative they didn't have. They had one of his brothers. Somebody thought our direct relative was buried up on a hill in the woods that you couldn't get to anymore."

McCallie comes from the clan MacAulay, meaning "Son of Olaf," a name immortalized by a Viking baptized in Norway in A.D. 1014. As a fiery youth, he traveled to England and fought many battles, was converted to Christianity, became King of Norway, and then made it his object to extinguish heathenism from the land and make Christianity the basis of his kingdom. Like his predecessor, Olaf Tryggvesson, he demolished temples and built Christian churches in their place. In 1030, he was wounded in battle, and his final words were "God help me." Norway's Coat of Arms display a lion with the battle-axe of St. Olaf in its forepaws. Others suggest *McCallie* may derive from *Ollamh*, a term applied to a learned person or a doctor.[33]

Although the Chattanooga McCallie clan could not find the grave of John McCallie during their trip to the cemetery, John's prayers for his future progeny still resounded. Thomas McCallie tells us in his brief journal that his father John "kept family worship up twice a day." His grandson, T. H. McCallie, recounts conducting similar daily prayer times with the family.

The importance of those journal entries were apparently not lost on the 94-year-old senior statesman of the McCallie clan—T. Hooke McCallie, the grandson of the Civil War pastor. He offered the following as part of his prayer over the extended McCallie family on Christmas Day, 2004, before passing away a few months later:

"We thank you also for Thomas Hooke McCallie, that humble Presbyterian preacher who prayed for us here. He tells us in his memoirs how he prayed often and fervently for future children, including generations yet unborn, in his great zeal that none of his progeny would be denied the joys and pleasures of your eternal kingdom, which knows no end."[34]

Artist: Tabitha Arnold

CHAPTER ELEVEN

The Spirit of the Ancients

Earliest Peoples and the word "Chattanooga"

As the Cherokees were being removed to the West, Chattanooga's early citizens were moving across the river to Ross's Landing.

One of the first stores on the river landing was operated by Thomas McCallie and his partner, John P. Long. No early citizen sat in a better position to determine the meaning of *Chattanooga* than Long, the man who proposed the word for the new town in 1838.

Described as large and well built with an earnest, benevolent countenance, Long said the village in 1836 was "only a few squatters" and said it was "pretentious to call it a city while still in the woods." However, he and McCallie both strongly believed the northern terminus for the Georgia railroad would eventually locate at Ross's Landing, so John Long built himself a log house in the thick forest "and settled down for life."

He also traveled to Washington, D.C., to petition the federal government for a post office in his newly adopted hometown. Authorities said Ross's Landing was too small but relented when McCallie and Long offered free space in their store. Long agreed to serve as postmaster at no cost.

When he proposed *Chattanooga* for the town's name, Long reminded his listeners that "it was the name of a valley and creek in the neighborhood and was said to be the original name of Lookout Mountain."

As one might expect from someone as enterprising as Long, he conducted a lengthy investigation into the meaning of the name he had championed. "In regard to the word *Chattanooga*, I have made diligent inquiry of the intelligent Cherokees," he wrote, "and they were unable to give me the meaning of it in the English language.

They said it was not a Cherokee word. [They say] that there was a race inhabiting the country before them that left certain names of places that they adopted, and that this was one of them."[1]

Long could gain no further information to identify the people who preceded the Cherokees. This remains the great conundrum for those interested in the prehistory of the area and the etymology of this modern city's name: Who were the Chattanooga peoples that preceded the Cherokees? Long concluded that the meaning of *Chattanooga* was "lost in antiquity." Has new evidence come to light to help answer the question?

"Chatanuga"

In 1816, the area at and around Ross's Landing was only sparsely populated by Cherokees—almost entirely mixed-bloods—when Chief John Ross established his ferry and trading post where the Tennessee Aquarium now stands. A decade before, John and his brother, Lewis Ross, operated a ferry three miles downriver at their father's property called Ross's Towhead at the foot of Lookout Mountain. This landing near the mouth of Chattanooga Creek was next to a small village called "Chatunuga." The names of its residents included Chestnut, Big Dollar, and Black George. The first known mention of this village comes from a list of towns protesting a treaty in 1789. Around that time, it is also listed as *Chattanugy* and *Chattonogee.*[2*]

A missionary visiting in 1817 said the mountain received its name for obvious reasons. It served as a lookout to the surrounding area. Similarly, other legends say the unmistakable summit provided a warning to watch out for the upcoming whirlpool, or pioneers should "look out" for robbers who regularly attacked boats spending the night anchored at the foot of the mountain in preparation for a daytime navigation of the Suck. The missionary said there was also a Cherokee word for the mountain that meant "Mountains looking at each other."[3]

The *Tennessee Encyclopedia of History and Culture* tells us the Cherokees "dubbed the spot 'Chado-na-ugsa,' meaning 'rock that comes to a point,' a reference to nearby Lookout Mountain." Nearly all present-day scholars discount this most prevalent definition including UTC anthropologist Nick Honerkamp and Lawrence Alexander, another highly credentialed archeologist in the area. The alleged definition is derived from a literal translation of the syllables in the language of the Creeks, the neighbors of the Cherokees in the early 19th century. Zella Armstrong once corresponded with Joshua Ross, Chief John Ross's nephew, who told her, "My own impression is that Chattanooga is derived from a Creek Indian word, as 'Creek Path' is not many miles distant." However, whereas ancient relatives of the Creeks may have lived in modern-day Chattanooga, those particular Creek neighbors of the Cherokees did not, and the different languages of these two tribes were indecipherable to each other's members. The theory is "utter nonsense," said one expert.[4]

Of course, we know from John Long that the Cherokees of his day, including John Ross himself, clearly stated they did not know the meaning of *Chattanooga* but only adopted it from the people before them.

Dragging Canoe and the Chickamaugas

A people called the "Chickamaugas" inhabited the area in the days before Chief John Ross. Their great leader was Dragging Canoe, who led thousands of his people in bloody combat against colonial forces before and during the Revolutionary War. Dragging Canoe was son of the famed Chief Atta-culla-culla, who once appeared before the King of England. Dragging Canoe's father forbade him to join a war party, but the determined young boy hid in one of the canoes. When discovered, his father said he could remain with the men if he could carry the boat. Unable to lift it, he pulled it along instead and earned the name Dragging Canoe.

Later described as muscular and pockmarked, he planted his headquarters on the north side of Chickamauga Creek, across from the future mission. Dragging Canoe continually refused to join other tribes in making treaties and land cessions, and he soon gained the reputation as the greatest Indian war chief on the frontier. "Finally, the whole country . . . will be demanded," he warned, and we "will be compelled to seek refuge in some distant wilderness."

Dragging Canoe recruited for his chief advisor, Scotsman John McDonald, who ran the trading post on the other side of the stream before selling it decades later to the missionaries. The Chickamaugas' ability to make alliances with both Britain and Spain forced colonial militias to eliminate the threat since they believed there was no possibility "of a lasting peace with them at Chuckemogo." Colonel Evan Shelby floated his nearly 1,000 men up the "Chickamoggy" Creek and conducted a scorched-earth campaign on eleven of Dragging Canoe's villages and McDonald's trading post, but the Chickamaugas themselves were able to escape to the foot of Lookout Mountain. On his northward journey home, Shelby sold his war booty at auction by a stream now known as "Sale Creek."[5]

Mrs. Jackson's Bloody Trek Around the Bend

Dragging Canoe was able to successfully impede river traffic on the Tennessee River around Moccasin Bend for another decade. One of the few exceptions was a flotilla of forty ships headed by Colonel John Donelson, who was on his way to establishing the future city of Nashville. His daughter, Rachel, later married Andrew Jackson. To prepare for the dangerous journey

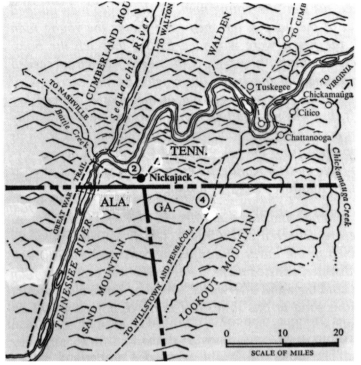

An early map shows villages of Chattanooga, Citico, and Chickamauga, as well as a village named **"Tuskegee"** at or near Williams Island.

power in their behalf. I am unacquainted with Mr. Ballew, but I think I owe it to him to inform you, that he is strongly recommended to me by the honorable William Fleming, as an honest, upright, intelligent man.
            I have the honor to be, with the highest respect,
                                                    Your obedient servant,
                                                                        BEVERLY RANDOLPH.
    To the PRESIDENT *of the United States.*

___

                    To the President of the United States of America.

The memorial of Bennet Ballew, agent plenipotentiary from the chiefs and head warriors of the Cherokee nation, resident and living in the towns of Chota, Toquoh, Cotties, Little Telliquo, Timotly, Nioh or the Tassel's town, Coettee, Chilhowah, Tallassee, Big Tilliquo, Big Highwassa, Cheestowa, Eastanolee, Chatanuga, Chickamaugah, Stickoee, Ottilletaraconohah, Catatogah, Nicogachee, Tuskeegah, and Cheesohetha, lying on and being on the great rivers Tenasee, Telliquo, Highwassa, Ammoah, &c. respectfully sheweth:
    That your memorialist, sensible of your past exertions, and pleased with the thoughts of your continued efforts, for the welfare and happiness of the United States in particular, and of mankind in general, and that nothing which concerns them will be thought beneath your attention; your memorialist is encouraged to lay before you a brief account of the present unhappy and distressed situation of the Cherokee Indians, notwithstanding his want of abilities to do justice to a cause of such difficulty and importance. From his long residence among them, and other Indian nations, on the southwestern frontiers of the United States, he hath in some measure become acquainted with their language, manners, and politics; and more particularly, with their hardships and sufferings, from the unrighteous and cruel war lately waged against them. Your memorialist, being importuned by the distressed chiefs of the nation, to lay their grievances before the beloved President of the United States, and solicit redress, being deeply impressed with compassion for their sufferings, and impelled by the apparent advantages that must accrue to the United States, should a firm and lasting peace and union be effected, he was, from these considerations, induced to undertake the arduous though pleasing task, relying chiefly on the providential influence of the Supreme Ruler of the Universe; on the justice and energy of the Federal Government; and on the magnanimity and benevolence of its first magistrate, for success in his feeble, though earnest endeavors, to rescue a nation from the deepest imaginable distress, and to make them a prosperous and a happy people.
    They thought that they had a well grounded hope, that they might quietly and peaceably have enjoyed all their

The **first known mention of "Chatanuga"** included in a list of Cherokee towns on a petition in 1789 protesting the treaty of Hopewell (American State Papers, Indian Affairs).

the next day, the boats stopped for the night just above Lookout Mountain, where Mrs. Ephraim Peyton gave birth to the first white baby in the area.

As they approached the foot of the mountain, warriors painted in red and black approached the flotilla in canoes from the rear, making gestures of friendship. Then, a Chickamauga sniper shot a young man from the bank of Moccasin Bend. The rest of the warriors then attacked while more Indians shot at them from the cliffs of Lookout Mountain. Four whites were wounded, and one of the ships capsized near the Suck. Several jumped for the shore. A black man was shot, two escaped, and another was captured and burned at the stake. The newborn also died in the confusion.

When the Donelson party finally arrived in Nashville, Dragging Canoe's forces attacked him there, conducting various massacres and livestock raids. Three years later, Colonel John Sevier, who later became Tennessee's first Governor, attacked Dragging Canoe's forces again at Lookout Mountain. As Sevier torched "Tuskegee Village" next to Williams Island, the Chickamaugas taunted Sevier's men from the cliffs. A spirited fight took place on the bluffs of Lookout Mountain in the exact spot later immortalized by Union and Confederate soldiers. This battle between Dragging Canoe and Sevier, with no clear victor, occurred eleven months after the surrender of Yorktown, but since the Continental Congress funded it, the conflict is sometimes referred to as the "Last Battle of the American Revolution."

Dragging Canoe continued to defy American forces for yet another decade. On February 28, 1792, a celebration was held in his honor after another great victory against the new United States government. The next day, the famous chief died. Within months, the Chickamaugas lost several battles and submitted to a peace treaty with President Washington. Ultimately, this treaty was violated by the United States in a maneuver called "fraudulent" and "an eternal disgrace upon the country" by John Quincy Adams. Dragging Canoe's instincts had been accurate.[6]

The great chief's people were dubbed *Chickamaugas* because they joined John McDonald on Chickamauga Creek. Dragging Canoe left the Smoky Mountains and the upper Cherokee people of his father who had grown weary of fighting the white man. Since the Chickamaugas were actually Cherokees, they provide us no clues to the question of Chattanooga's former people or to the language that gave us the word *Chattanooga*.

Names in an Old Manuscript

In my quest to answer these questions, I perused an early history of Chattanooga that was never published. The manuscript of Henry Wiltse, housed in the special collections at the Hamilton County Library, offers a number of theories on the name of the city. Wiltse cites several early citizens who offer "hawk's nest" or "crow's nest" or "eagle's nest" but with no convincing reasons. Rev. McCallie told Wiltse he also thought it meant "bird's nest," but "recalled hearing years before that it stood for "look out." McCallie also gave no explanations, but by now I had learned to carefully consider his words.

"Fish Bringer" is offered by Wiltse as the literal Cherokee meaning for the syllables *chatta* (a fish) and *nooga* (to bring). However, we already know that *Chattanooga* is not a Cherokee word. This fact is confirmed by renowned ethnologist James Mooney, who interviewed hundreds of Cherokee elders in North Carolina in the late 1800s to better understand the tribe's legends and language. "The name originally belonged to some location along the creek," wrote Mooney. "The Cherokees pronounced it 'Tsatanugi,' but say that it is not a Cherokee word and has no meaning in their language."[7]

After many months of searching, I began to grow frustrated with the attempt to discover the peoples here before the Cherokees. With so little written information on the subject, I wished some little fairy or elf would pop into my life and provide an answer to the mystery. But life never works that way.

Tuskegees?

Actually, Mooney did write about another group that could possibly shed light on the question. The "Tuskegee Village," mentioned previously as a battle site for Dragging Canoe on today's Williams Island, is apparently named after a group called the Tuskegees who lived there. We are told by John Swanton, the preeminent early 20th century ethnologist, that they also had villages at Citico Creek (near Erlanger today), on Moccasin Bend, and at Audubon Acres in East Brainerd.[8]

Mooney called them Taskigis. "Who or what the Taskigi were is uncertain, and can probably never be known. But they were neither Cherokee nor Muskogee proper[†] . . . The name may be derived from *taska* or *taska yi* meaning 'warrior' in several of the Muskogee dialects. It is not a Cherokee word," Mooney insisted, "and Cherokee informants state positively that the Taskigi were a foreign people, with distinct language and customs."

We learn nothing else about these predecessors on Chattanooga soil except Mooney's one interesting anecdote: "They had an upright pole from the top of which hung their protecting 'medicine,' the image of a human figure cut from a cedar log."[9]

Archeologists provide one related and interesting clue

Swimmer, a medicine man, was a key source for ethnologist Mooney.

[†] "Muskogee" was an early grouping of tribes in the Southeast. Some of these tribes became members of the later "Creek" confederation.

from Williams Island and Moccasin Bend. Buried in the dirt they found Spanish weapons and necklaces with tusks from Spanish pigs.[10] However, modern research strongly confirms older notions that the army of Hernando De Soto, the first European to step foot into this section of America, did not come near Chattanooga or Moccasin Bend (despite Zella's great attempts to steer him this way). So where did these artifacts come from?

Yuchis?

Mooney again makes clear that the Tuskegees (or Taskigis) were not Creeks, and they were not "Uchee." The Yuchis (Uchee, Euchee, etc.) are another tribe identified by ethnologists and archeologists. They had their own language and moved often from place to place. They are known by several other names, including *Hogohegee.* This name is significant because an early European map refers to the Tennessee River by this name. Rivers were usually named by the peoples who lived near them, but there is no evidence to date that the Yuchis lived on the section of the Tennessee River near Chattanooga.

Another group associated with the Tennessee River is named by a great number of early maps in abundant forms. The "Caskinampo" peoples and the river near them are named by the Spanish, French, and English as *Kasquinampo, Kakinonba, Karkinonpols, Caskemampo, Kasin8ba* [sic] and several other inventive transliterations.[11] Who were these people, and did they ever live in Chattanooga?

Theories on word origins in Southeast America can go from confusing to difficult to outright bizarre. Words like *Alabama, Cherokee, Kentucky, Tennessee,* and *Seminole* may have Turkish roots according to one theory provided in the *Tennessee Encyclopedia of History & Culture.* This stems from DNA tests conducted on the Melungeons, an anomalous dark-skinned, European-featured group in the Appalachians near the Tennessee-Virginia border. The Melungeons themselves always claimed Portuguese or Turkish ancestry despite the patent absurdity. But the encyclopedia tells us that DNA samples from 177 Melungeons indicate no differences from people living in regions near Spain, Morocco, Greece, and Turkey, and also notes that Cherokees like Swimmer and Sequoyah may have worn turbans because of this Middle Eastern influence.

Theories on how Mediterranean folks arrived in Appalachia now focus on a failed Iberian (Portuguese and Spanish) colony in South Carolina in 1587 whose slaves included a number of Turks. Could *Chattanooga* have Middle Eastern origins?[12]

Welsh? (Yes, I said Welsh.)

Zella Armstrong tells us the early predecessors of the Cherokees were white. In fact, she insists they were Welsh. "This is clearly indicated by tradition and supported by documentary evidence," she tells us. First, she points to ruins of ancient forts around present-day Chattanooga and upriver near Hiwassee. Governor John Sevier developed a fascination with these old ruins. In an 1810 letter, Sevier says he asked an ancient Indian chief named Oconostoto, "if he could inform me what people it had been which left such signs of fortifications. . . . The old chief immediately informed me: 'It was handed down by the forefathers that the works had been made by the white people who had formerly inhabited the country.'"

Oconostota

Oconostoto, identified by some as the the great chief "Oconostota" whose portrait has survived, then described to Sevier how the Cherokees and these people fought a war and the whites were driven out. "They are no more a white people," the chief said. "They are now all become Indians and look like other red people of the country."

Sevier then asked if the chief ever heard to what nation these whites belonged. "He answered: He had heard his Grandfather and father say they were a people called Welsh: that they had crossed the Great Water and landed first near the mouth of the Alabama River near Mobile and had been drove up to the heads of the waters until they arrived at Highwassee River . . ."[13*]

An account in 1797 speaks of Cherokees describing their predecessors as a "certain 'moon-eyed' people who could not see in the daytime. "These wretches they expelled." Mooney, years later, strengthens the myth. "There is a dim but persistent tradition of a strange white race preceding the Cherokee, some of the stories even going so far as to locate their former settlements and to identify them as the authors of the ancient works found in the country."[14]

Zella points to a Roman coin found in 1818 near one of the forts as further evidence. "The probable date of the coin is 140 A.D, which was after the Roman invasion of Wales," she writes. "According to recitals of the Welsh bards which appeared in print as early as 1584, Prince Madoc [and] his followers sailed from Wales westward and discovered a new land. Hakluyt in his *Principal Navigations* (1589) . . . based Great Britain's claim to America, in part, upon the discovery and settlement of the Welsh people shortly after 1170."[15]

Nuh-Who?

Welsh, Melungeons, Turks, moon-eyed people. Tuskegees and Yuchis. The more I researched the subject, the more confusing it became. In a feeble attempt to work a theory based on the Spanish artifacts on Williams Island, I headed to the downtown library to read more on the expedition of Hernando De Soto in 1540. While making copies from a book, I came across a small, elderly gentleman. He stooped slightly and sported an elfish looking white goatee.

"What are you reading there?" he asked.

"It's a book about De Soto by Charles Hudson," I told him. I explained to him my quest to find the group who preceded the Cherokees.

"It was the Napoochies," he said.

"The Nuh-who?"

"The Napoochies. You need to read Hudson's book about the Juan Pardo expedition. That one talks about Chattanooga and the Napoochies. De Soto didn't reach Chattanooga," he said.

My serendipitous new acquaintance was E. Raymond Evans. He was in the library helping an African American woman with research for a legal problem. Evans is the man quoted in Chapter Nine as a consultant for the African American museum. He is also a respected archeologist and longtime area historian who has written a number of scholarly but little-known pieces housed in the local library.

Raymond pointed me to sources and connections on early Chattanooga that I never knew existed. In fact, he may be the only one who did.

—◆—

Although modern Chattanooga has developed three miles upriver, the great visual landmark of our area has always been the point where the river turns around Moccasin Bend under the immediate shadow of Lookout Mountain.

This famous ancient scene has been called "Mockasin Gap" and the "Great Bent."[16] Surely it has known many other names as early peoples have dwelled on this wide foot below the mountain for at least 12,000 years.

The archeological significance of Moccasin Bend was first recognized by two officers in the Union Army who noticed the burial mounds there while engaging their foe on the summit. They came back to excavate the area. After taking their discoveries on a nationwide tour, the valuable ancient artifacts eventually found their way to the Smithsonian Institute in Washington, D.C.

All of the archeologists I interviewed agreed that this area, especially Moccasin Bend, boasts some of the best if not the very richest archeological remains in North America.

"For the most part, they are unexplored," said Lawrence Alexander, whose firm Alexander & Associates has provided ongoing professional archeological services in this region the past two decades.[17]

Alexander actually references four famous sites in Chattanooga: Moccasin Bend, Williams Island, Citico (the UTC practice field behind Chattanooga School for the Arts & Sciences), and Audubon Acres (East Brainerd). The artifacts found include

(Above) **Williams Island** with Lookout Mountain in the background, as seen from Signal Point.

(Left) **Pottery excavated on Williams Island** in 1929 and later placed in a collection in Biltmore, North Carolina.

shells, earrings, bone instruments, flint knives, arrowheads, pipes, necklaces, pots, bowls, and child rattles. The many burial sites include one of a child that was discovered holding his dog. Both skeletons crumbled upon discovery, and only the dog's skull remained.[18]

"We need to find out how deep these sites are," said Alexander, who noted that no digging is currently being conducted. "They have been looked at, but it is so miniscule compared to what is there."

The Citico site was almost entirely destroyed in 1914 when Amnicola Highway was built. However, this is not uncommon according to Alexander. Hundreds of sites are destroyed each year for roads and developments. "Of the sixty or so villages in East Tennessee, there are only fifteen or sixteen left." The fact that Chattanooga has saved three of its four sites is actually quite an accomplishment, he said.

Though he lived out west and then in Alabama, Alexander's people hail from nearby areas around the Smoky Mountains, and those places helped inspire his career in archeology. "Most rural Tennessee boys have artifact collections in one form or another," he said. "They would pick up arrowheads while they were plowing."

Early Wampum Artifacts

My best interview for this subject was with one of those locals who collected hundreds of arrowheads as a young man. "The Hudson brothers grew up farming the Bend long before the hospital was built," said Louie Wamp, the brother of Congressman Zach Wamp. "'Well, I saw their plowed fields right off of Pineville Road. They generally would chase everyone off their fields that were looking for arrowheads, but I just talked to them about it." He promised to be sensitive to their situation and was allowed to continue.

"You know, you would find one whole arrowhead for 300 pieces because the plows would slice everything up. [Eventually], I realized that everything I was finding was 7,000 to 12,000 years old."

"When I was seven or eight, I told my parents I wanted to be an archeologist. They said I should be an architect. 'You draw and dad's an architect.' But I could have used all that in archeology."

Wamp is a bit of a renaissance man. An architect by trade, he is also an artist, a poet and a professional musician who plays basically any stringed instrument that is handed to him. There seems to be a bit of genius in the family, as Zach can talk nonstop about public policy and Louie can go on continually about all his various interests. Their other brother, Trent, can outtalk them both, says Louie. They are all part Cherokee.

"I call Louie *Cochise*, after the great chief," said Zach. "He's got that Indian nose."

Mammoths, Tigers, and Bears (& Giant Sloths)

While Louie is not an official expert on local archeology, he does have an unusual knack for explaining it. That is why I asked him to show us laymen how the stuff in the ground can tell us what the peoples here were like 12,000 years ago.

First, he talked about Paleo man, the earliest in the area.

"What do we know about the Paleos?" I asked.

"You've got one people group. It appears they were nomadic, following herds. Really, about all we've got is the stone because everything else perished, except there's a few caves out west where it's real dry. They found actual bone pieces and stuff that did not rot, but here in the East all you've got are the flint and stone tools. You'll see the same point types, the same kind of flaking.

"How do you know how old they are?"

"It's buried, you know, so many feet deep," he said. "When excavating on those sites, the Mississippian stuff (A.D. 1000 to 1600) is in the top foot or two. You go three or four feet down and you're into Woodland (2000 B.C. to A.D. 1000). You go eight or ten feet down, you're in Archaic (2000 to 7000 B.C.), and eighteen to twenty feet deep we found Paleo relics—7,000 to 10,000 or 15,000 B.C. It's disputed. You can date them. You know where you are by the layers, by how deep you are."

He said the reason he found early arrowheads in the topsoil at Moccasin Bend was because they were on high ground near Stringer's Ridge, where the ground erodes instead of where silt from the river builds up the land, creating the helpful dating layers. "It was exciting to find Clovis at Moccasin Bend and the early Paleo pieces right at the mouth of the canyon."

"Clovis?" I asked.

"Clovis is the very first arrowhead, oldest point type. It is a lance shape. Fluted." He showed me a few in his office and said he had 200 more Paleo artifacts in the other room. "Paleo and Archaic Man are completely hunter-gatherer and nomadic. Meat is the big thing. There's no weaving. No fabrics, no pottery. Just all knives and projectile points."

"What did they kill?"

"Mastodon, mammoth, bear, bison. We're talking extinct varieties that were very big."

"What's a mastodon?"

"An elephant—you know, like the wooly mammoth? You had the wooly mammoth, and then you had the mastodon, which is not quite as big and hairy. And the sloth. Actually, we had a giant sloth here in North America that was, like, up to twenty feet long. Obviously, he was an easy kill because he was not a

Louie Wamp

382

predator like a saber-toothed tiger. I mean, they were around—the big cats and giant bison and the elephants."

"So they were all hunter-gatherers?"

"Right. And pre-tribal. Essentially, we don't have any evidence that they were split into tribes because we see the same type points like this way across the country, from California to New England."

Progress Hits in 2000 B.C.

"So we move from Paleo and Archaic to . . . ?"

"To Woodland. There's a big change there. Suddenly you have pottery. You've got clay, and the tempering of the clay goes through three phases. It starts with sand and then goes to lime and then shell. You can date the pottery. . . . You have baskets, and the weaving patterns are embossed into the clay. We don't have any remnants of their fabrics because they rotted, but we have those impressions pressed into the clay."

"So, we know the Woodlands are stopping and making pots and baskets to store water and food. They're farming, and they're not roaming as much. By the Woodland period, there are several burial mounds, burial sites. They actually used slabs of limestone to create a box underground with walls and a lid—you know, burying somebody with their effects. So you have a little more of a social thing where they care about the dead and preserve them and put them all together in a plot. The first mounds appear in late Woodland along the Mississippi River, the Ohio River. Tennessee has Woodland mounds: the Bend, Amnicola, and Citico."

"Mississippian is the beginning of towns. You had thousands of people. I think those twin towns there on Moccasin Bend had as many as 4,000 residences. Well, that's a lot of people. There were actually two towns. It's kind of like the Baptists splitting up into two churches. They actually split the town. It had two walled fortresses, so they weren't getting along."

"It's only the Mississippians where you see them actually building down on the river basin where they got flooded annually, which they liked because it washed off all the feces and all the trash and gave them a new layer of top soil. It might wipe out all the huts, but they would just rebuild. They are building a city on low ground. It's rich to farm. They could have picked higher elevations. Archaic and Palco sites are all elevated out of flood plains."

"The mound is the center of the town, the big central chapel if you will, the priest's house. He lived on top. They had a social hierarchy. A mound is something that grows over a period of several hundred years. The very base of it might be Woodland, but the final ten or twenty feet is Mississippian. Those mounds on Moccasin Bend were Mississippian mounds built before the Cherokee. The Cherokee

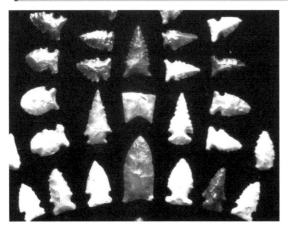

(Top) Early artist's rendition of the ancient landmark of **Lookout Mountain and Moccasin Bend**.

(Left) A portion of Louie Wamp's collection of prehistoric **spear points,** gathered in places like the old roads and fields on Moccasin Bend (above).

did not build them. The Cherokee were recent. They were as recent as Europeans in my mind. The Cherokees barely beat the Spanish into the Tennessee Valley."

Discovery of Document Changes Chattanooga History

Actually, my further research showed, thanks to the sources provided by Raymond Evans, that the Cherokees may not, in fact, have beaten the Spanish into the Chattanooga area of the Tennessee Valley. Newly uncovered documents related to the Spanish expeditions show that the Spanish fought a battle with the Napochies,[†] the ones mentioned by Evans, in 1560, almost two centuries before the Cherokees began moving into the area. That battle between Spaniards and Napochies was fought in today's downtown Chattanooga on the Citico site. The fighting of these first-known veterans of war continued at Maclellan Island (formerly Chattanooga Island), now connected to both shores by the Veterans Bridge.

While information is miniscule on the other historically referenced pre-Cherokee tribe, the Tuskegees, this account of the Chattanooga Napochies is very detailed and several pages in length. For me, it was an historical gold mine.

The most recent Chattanooga histories, published in 1979 and 1980, did not have access to later discoveries. For decades, scholars were familiar with the lengthy account of the Napochies provided by eminent ethnologist John Swanton in the 1920s. What they did not know was where this well-described battle between Spaniards and Napochies took place. No one was able to determine that it was on Chattanooga soil until the University of Georgia's Dr. Charles Hudson taught a class for only two graduate students, Marvin T. Smith and Chester DePratter, solely for the purpose of conducting a scientific effort to determine exactly where the Spaniards traveled during their journeys.

The great breakthrough occurred when DePratter located a little-known but very specific account of the 16th century Juan Pardo expedition, handwritten in Spanish by Juan de la Bandera. Through this discovery, along with the use of U.S. Geological survey maps and other modern mapping technologies, the three scholars pinpointed with a high level of accuracy the travels of the Spanish explorers. "The description of the river of the Napochies could fit only the Tennessee River," writes Marvin T. Smith in his book *Coosa*, published by the University Press of Florida in 2000. He says Chattanooga's big four archeological sites fit "precisely" the positions identified by Spanish chroniclers. "Thus, the sites clustered near Chattanooga are likely the Napochie towns of the Luna accounts."[19]

God, Gold, and Glory

The Napochie account is provided to us by a Spanish priest, Father Avila Padilla,

---

[†] Usually pronounced "Napoochies" but spelled Napochies in most texts.

who describes this expedition in 1560. At the time, the Chattanooga area as well as the rest of the Southeast was known as *La Florida*, the land of the flowers. Ironically, Chattanooga is one of the greatest flora-collecting sites in all America; 551 species of wildflowers were counted in one local reserve. But the flowery moniker was actually the result of Spanish explorer Ponce de Leon looking out from the Dominican Republic on April 2, 1513, and naming the land across the water. It was the feast of Pascua Florida, Easter of the Flowers, and the Spanish were known to order their lives, language, and events around the Christian calendar.[20]

Hernando De Soto

In search of fortunes, whether through gold or conquest or land—and always in the name of God—the Spanish embarked on a number of expeditions along the coast of La Florida. But the first great adventure into the interior was led by Hernando De Soto in 1540. De Soto was a blood brother of Ponce de Leon. The two rich explorers had agreed to co-own all their property, and De Soto was a high governing official during and after the conquests in Central America and Peru. Already one of the richest men in the New World, his great ambition became obtaining the title of Marquis, which could only be granted from Emperor Charles V if De Soto conquered a vast amount of territory. The great explorer's efforts are immortalized by four men who chronicled the first journey by white men across the American Southeast. At the end of his epic journey, De Soto discovered the great Mississippi River and died there.[21]

Of the many Indian tribes visited by De Soto's army, the chroniclers tell us that none was greater than the paramount chiefdom of Coosa, located today an hour's drive south in Georgia, about thirty miles southeast of Dalton at the edge of the Smoky Mountains. The Coosa empire resulted from conquering many vassal tribes, including the Napochies. When De Soto arrived in Coosa, he immediately killed a number of warriors, enslaved several more, including the chief's sister, and took the chief himself captive until he promised to meet the soldiers' demand for food. A previous tribe ran from the Spaniards when the soldiers demanded thirty Indian women. After De Soto's troops were amply supplied and refreshed, they left Coosa and traveled through Alabama toward the west.[22]

First Spaniards Reach Chattanooga

On their way to Coosa, they traveled through Bradley County, thirty miles east of Chattanooga, but never made it to the land of the Napochies. However, a second expedition in 1559 also traveled to the Coosa region. Tristan de Luna, whose ships were destroyed by a hurricane as they landed in the gulf near Mobile, oversaw this venture. As the soldiers grew hungry and faced the threat of starvation, a few De Soto veterans remembered the abundance of food they had seen in the great Coosa chiefdom. Desperate, Luna dispatched 100 infantry and 40 cavalrymen to Coosa to obtain more provisions.

This entourage, led by Mateo del Sauz, numbered 300 men when including all the soldiers and slaves, along with two friars. When they arrived at Coosa in July 1560, they found the remains of a devastated empire. Through war and Old World diseases passed along by De Soto's men, the Coosas were reduced to a few hundred people. They provided the Spaniards what they could—about six bushels of corn each day along with some beans and pumpkins—but not enough food to take back to the gulf.[23]

The Spaniards then asked about gold. The Coosas told them there was gold in the land of the Napochies about a day's trip north. This may have only been a ruse for the Coosas; their ulterior motive was to induce the mighty ironclad soldiers to help them defeat their enemies, the Napochies, who 20 years before had been one of their many vassal nations. The Napochies broke away after Coosa's decline and no longer delivered their annual tribute of game, nuts, and fruit. Rather, they regularly attacked the Coosas and killed many of their warriors.

After much discussion, the Spanish captain, Sauz, agreed to dispatch twenty-five soldiers and twenty-five horsemen. They would join 300 Coosa warriors in battle against the Napochies.

"All the deeds in this life are done for some interested reason," writes Father Avila Padilla, who provides the primary account of the battle.[24*] He notes the Spanish had their motives—wanting both gold and provisions—and the Indians were "hoping that with their aid they could take full vengeance on their enemies." The priests also had their motives, "hoping that a greater population might be discovered to convert and maintain the Christian creed."

Preparing for War with the Relatives of the Gods

As they all marched toward the land of the Napochies, the Spaniards observed the practices of the Coosa warriors. "Every Indian uses a bow as tall as his body," wrote Padilla. "They also use three or four feathers tied on their arrows to insure straight flying, and are so skilled in shooting them that they can hit a flying bird. The force of the flint arrowheads is such that at a moderate distance they can pierce a coat of mail."

The Coosa warriors were awed by the Spanish soldiers who carried mighty swords made of the hardest metal they had ever seen. They also carried metal shields and wore metal armor. Their primary weapon was a crossbow, but a few of them carried early matchlock guns called "harquebuses." Their most intimidating feature was the great horses they rode into battle, creatures never before seen by the Indians of the Southeast except by those few who interacted with De Soto 20 years before.

The Native Americans believed themselves to be the center of the world. Tribes often referred to themselves as "the Principal People." Encountering these light-skinned mighty men from a land far away in the East most certainly disrupted their ancient cosmology.

At one point, the entourage stopped to watch the Coosa leader climb a mound while holding a stick object richly decorated with feathers. "He pointed it toward the land of the Napochies in the same fashion as would an astrologer the alidade . . . or the pilot a sextant in order to take the altitude of the sea." The chief then chewed up some seeds and spit them out of his mouth, saying, "Console yourselves, my friends. Our journey will have a prosperous outcome; our enemies will be conquered and their strength broken, like those seeds which I ground between my teeth." In a similar ritual, he again encouraged his fellow warriors: "If we came alone, we might be obliged to see the loss of life, [but now] we have in our company the brave and vigorous Spaniards, sons of the sun and relatives of the gods."

Many of the soldiers laughed while watching the strange rituals. "But the blessed father, Fray Domingo de la Anunciacion, mourned over it, for it seemed a sacrilege to him and a pact with the demon."

Surprise Attack in East Brainerd

They then approached a Napochie village but spent the night a distance away with plans to attack in the morning. This town was called "Olitifar," and scholars agree that it is the Audubon Acres archeology site in East Brainerd just across the Georgia border in Tennessee, a mile or two from Hamilton Place Mall today.[25]

The Coosas said the Napochies were great spies and pleaded with the Spaniards to stay quiet that evening. "They begged of the captain not to have the trumpet sounded that evening, which was the signal to all for prayer, greeting the queen of the Angels with the Ave Maria, which is the custom in all Christendom at nightfall,"

Padilla's description of **Coosan warriors** resembles this drawing by Englishman John White in the late 1500s, one of the first eyewitness depictions of Native Americans.

wrote Padilla. But Father Anunciacion "with his pious devotion, went around to all the soldiers telling them to say the Ave Maria, and he who was the bugler of the evangile now had become the bugler of war in the service of the Holy Virgin Mary."

When they attacked the next morning, the Napochies had apparently lived up to their reputation as excellent spies and evacuated just in time. "They even left their food, and in several houses they found it cooking on the fire. [They found] maize, beans, and many pots filled with bear fat—bears abounding in that country and their fat being greatly prized. The highest priced riches which they could carry off as spoils were skins of deer and bear, which those Indians tanned in a diligent manner very nicely and with which they covered themselves or which they used as beds."

"In the center of the village they found a pole of about [15 feet] in height which served as a gallows or pillory . . . that was full of scalps of people from Coosa," wrote Padilla. The Coosas immediately tore down the pole and buried the scalps. Seeking vengeance, "they went from house to house looking for someone like infuriated lions, and they found only a poor strange Indian [from another tribe] who was ill and very innocent of those things. . . . They tortured the poor Indian till they left him dying. Before he expired though, the good father [told him] that if he wished to enjoy the eternal blessings of heaven, he should receive the blessed water of baptism and thereby become a Christian. [But] the unfortunate Indian, with inherent idolatry and suffering from his fresh wounds, did not pay any attention to such good council, but delivered his soul to the demon as his ancestors before him had done. This greatly pained the blessed Father Domingo, because, as his greatest desire was to save souls, their loss was his greatest sorrow."

"When the Indians were all quieted, the chief took possession of the village in company with his principal men, and with much singing and dancing, accompanied by the music of badly tuned flutes, they celebrated their victories."

On to Chattanooga, the Holy River, and Maclellan Island

Where had the Napochies gone? They had fled to "the great water," the Coosas said. "When the Spaniards heard the name of the great water, they thought it might be the sea, but it was only a great river, which we call the River of the Holy Spirit, the source of which is in some big forests of the country called La Florida. It is very deep and of the width of two harquebuse-shots. In a certain place which the Indians knew, it became very wide, losing its depth, so that it could be forded."

Hudson, DePratter, and Smith identify this as the Tennessee River and the village next to the ford as Citico. The ford itself was later known as Ross's Shoal, then Ross's ferry—the shallows that connected to Maclellan Island and then to the north bank of the Tennessee River.[26] "Before the Spaniards arrived at this little hamlet,

Citico mound, an ancient town and burial site, was leveled to build Amnicola Highway.

Maclellan Island (bottom left of picture), formerly called Chattanooga Island, was the sight of the 1560 battle between Spaniards and Napochies. It is now spanned by Veterans Bridge. At right are the Walnut Street and Market Street Bridges with the Olgiati Bridge at far right.

however, they saw on the flat roof of an Indian house, two Indians who were on the lookout. . . . When the horsemen spurred their horses, and when the Indians on guard saw them, they were so surprised by their monstrosity [on horseback] that they threw themselves down the embankment towards the river, without the Spaniards being able to reach them, because the bank was very steep and the Indians very swift. One of them was in such a hurry that he left a great number of arrows behind which he had tied up in a skin, in the fashion of a quiver."

The attackers found the village abandoned. The Napochies had fled across the river to Maclellan Island, "quite confident that the Spaniards would not be able to ford it. They ridiculed and made angry vociferations against the people of Coosa. Their mirth was short lived, however."

The Coosas knew the location of the ford, and the Spaniards crossed the chest-high waters, some on horseback. "When our soldiers had reached about the middle of the river, one of them fired his flint lock which he had charged with two balls, and he felled one of the Napochies who was on the other side. When the others saw him on the ground dead, they were greatly astonished at the kind of Spanish weapon, which at such a distance could at one shot kill men. They put him on their shoulders and carried him off, afraid that other shots might follow."

The Napochies then left Maclellan Island for the north shore of the river. But when the Coosas began to cross as well, "the Napochies called out to them and said that they would fight no longer, but that they would be friends, because the Coosas brought with them the power of the Spaniards." When the Napochies returned to the Citico village and humbled themselves before the Spanish and Coosa authorities, the Coosa chief "received them with severity, reproaching them harshly for their past rebellion and justifying any death he might choose to give them." But the Spaniards intervened and the Chief of Coosa agreed to spare their lives and restore them to their former state as vassals.

"The Napochies pledged themselves to pay as tributes, thrice a year, game, or fruits, chestnuts, and nuts, in confirmation of the Coosas' superiority, which had been recognized by their forefathers." After the peace was negotiated, the Spanish and Coosa armies returned to Olitifar (East Brainerd) for three days and then traveled back to Coosa. Other than this detailed account of fighting in 1560, no other historical documents provide any information or even any other mention of the Napochies of Chattanooga.[27]

And while De Soto's armies had been unpopular with many Native American tribes, this particular expedition of Spaniards headed back to the gulf "to the great grief of the Indians who accompanied them two or three days journey weeping, with great demonstrations of love. But not for their religion, since only one dying Indian asked for baptism, which Father Salazar administered to him."[28]

Answers in Elvish

This newly discovered knowledge of the presence of the Napochies in Chattanooga provides a better understanding of what happened in this area between the end of the Mississippian period and the arrival of the Cherokees. It also provides major clues to the meaning of *Chattanooga.*

Raymond Evans is the man who has done the best job so far of connecting the dots to all the various ethnological and archeological pieces. He sent me his paper, "The Napochin Chiefdom of the 16th century," which led to my understanding of Hudson, DePratter, and Smith's discoveries and answered many other questions. I sat down with Raymond for an interview at the African American Museum, where he serves as an ethnic historical consultant.

I asked him about the Napochies. He said the correct pronunciation is actually "Nap-ooch-in," based on the actual spelling obtained from other newly discovered, 16th century handwritten documents.[29]

According to Raymond, the Napochin fought in another famous battle two decades previous to the Maclellan Island incident. After De Soto's first hostile interaction with the Coosas in 1540, the head of that great chiefdom recruited warriors from various tribes and from all of his vassals, including the Napochin, for an attack on De Soto. The battle took place at "Mabila," which some scholars believe is in central Alabama near Selma. The Spaniards suffered heavy casualties but survived. However, the Indians returned home in triumph.

"The Napochins thought they had killed De Soto," said Raymond, "and brought back much Spanish plunder with them as proof of their winning. At least one man had a Spanish lance, and the head of this weapon was found at the site of the town of Tuskegee on Moccasin Bend. [Another] brought back an unusual trophy in the form of tusks from one of the Spanish pigs. . . . Napochin artists painted pictures of horses and Spanish lancers on the walls to commemorate their victory that proved the appropriateness of the Napochin being called *Tuskegees*, or 'warriors.'"[30]

Connecting the Tuskegee Dot

As it turns out, the mysterious Tuskegees indentified by Mooney are the same as the Napochin. This may explain the similarity between the pole described by Mooney where the Tuskegees hung an image of a man cut out of cedar and the pole built by the Napochin where they hung the scalps of their Coosan enemies.

It was not uncommon for Native Americans to call themselves one name and be called something else by other tribes. For example, the Cherokees called themselves the "Ani-yun-wiya," or Principal People.

"The Muskogee speakers called these people *Cilo-kkita*, meaning 'People who speak a different language,'" said Raymond. "The Spaniards called them *Chalaque* while the French corrupted the Muskogee word to *Cheraquis*, and the English Anglicized it to *Cherake, Cheerake,* or *Cherokee.*"

Raymond commonly referred to this now solidly identified precursor to the Cherokees in Chattanooga as the "Tuskegee-Napochin." He said they occupied all the four ancient sites—Moccasin Bend, Williams Island, Citico, and Olitifar. He also noted that the 1567 Juan Pardo expedition referred to a town called "Casquiqui" that was only a few miles from East Brainerd's Olitifar.[†] "Casquiqui was the Spanish for Tuskegee," he said. "Just the *C* and *T* substitute does it . . . and we assume that they called themselves Napochin because that's what the Coosa people called them."

Evans also believes the Caskinampo people who gave the Tennessee River so many different names on maps are likely the same as our Tuskegee-Napochins. One of the many forms of Caskinampo was "Tasquinapous." Another map identifies a village called "Caskighi" on the "Isles de Caskinampo" in the middle of the "Kaskinampo" river.[31]

Since Tuskegee comes from *taska*, meaning "warriors," the next obvious question was what *Napochin* means. Raymond had some good answers for me. First, however, it was helpful to understand how the Napochin may have arrived in the Chattanooga area and what the circumstances were that caused them to leave.

Who Preceded the Napochin?

Louie Wamp told us about the era of the Woodland Indians (2000 B.C. to 1000 A.D.), who pioneered in pots, baskets, and stone box burials. They were followed by the Mississippians, who built towns closer to the rivers in flood-prone areas. Two tribes of the Mississippian era are likely to have preceded the Napochin (who were also Mississippian) into Chattanooga. These tribes are the Koasatis and the Yuchis.

While the Yuchis had their own separate language group, the Koasatis and Napochin were part of the Muskogee confederacy, with similar languages. They would have required interpreters to understand each other in the same way the romance languages of French and Italian are different but both derive from Latin. The Cherokees utilized a completely different language grouping called Iroquoian.

The Koasatis and Napochin likely migrated to the Chattanooga area from the south and west. The Yuchis, however, may have been there all along.

"On the basis of available data, a good argument could be made for the Yuchis being the earliest known people in the Southeastern United States," said Raymond. "Unlike most other people, they did not have migration legends about coming from

---

[†] This same expedition identified another town between today's Chattanooga and Knoxville called "Tanasqui," which many scholars believe to be the origin of "Tennessee." (Charles Hudson, *The Juan Pardo Expeditions*, p. 103)

Raymond Evans

somewhere else. . . . They also worked native copper, and we know that the Middle Woodland people in this area had a very advanced metal industry."

Evans has his own theory on how the Napochin migrated from the Mississippi area, then into the Cumberland area (Nashville) for a time, and then drove out the Yuchis in East Tennessee. "It's just a hypothesis," he said. "You might learn something tomorrow that will totally invalidate it." He bases his theory on the existence of large numbers of stone burial boxes in the Cumberland area that are discontinued around the same time that they appear suddenly on Williams Island in the 1300s and 1400s. As an added bonus, the Cumberland River (instead of the Tennessee) is for a short time called the Caskinampo River. If the Tuskegee-Napochin drove the Yuchis out, it may also explain why the Tennessee River is named after the Yuchis for a brief time before it again is named after the Tuskegee-Napochin.

"If the Yuchis were the former Woodland period inhabitants of the Tennessee Valley, it is easy to understand their resentment at being pushed out by the Muskogee-speaking Mississippian peoples," said Raymond.

The Fate of the Tuskegee-Napochin

If this is how the Tuskegee-Napochin arrived in Chattanooga, what caused them to leave? We know they were a strong tribe in 1560 thanks to the chronicle of the battle on Maclellan Island, but, like most tribes in the New World, they suffered plagues after being exposed to European and African diseases. Famine, war, and slavery also caused destruction.

"There was one documented three-year period where there was no rain at all," said Raymond. "For a people who depended on corn that was devastating. It is estimated that only one out of twenty people survived from that time period." Then there was the slave trade. "The early English were slavers, and Indians were their product. They were much easier to get than Africans."

"Had the Napochin stayed here, they would have been weakened from the drought and from serious population drops from the diseases. And they would probably have ended up being totally exterminated by the slave traders. So it was in their best interest to merge. That's how the people that survived did so. They formed different alliances and relocated over considerable distances."

"The people of Coosa migrated down the river into Alabama. Some of the Tuskegee-Napochin went with them and later became part of the Creek federation." He said the other Napochin reached an agreement with the Cherokees up the river, who permitted them to live with them as refugees.[32]

So the Tuskegee-Napochin split—some went north, some went south. For a time, there was a town named Tuskegee near Tellico just below Knoxville. There still exists today a Tuskegee in Alabama, home to a well-known black college.

Debunking Those Whites from Wales

Evans believes the withdrawal of the Napochin may have led to both Cherokees and Yuchis vying for the available land. This may provide an explanation for the strange myths about white people preceding the Cherokees and the wretched "moon-eyed people" they expelled.

"These most likely were Yuchis. The Indians used the term *white* to indicate 'powerful,' not necessarily meaning skin color," said Raymond. "So when Chief Oconostota told Governor Sevier about an early war between the Cherokees and white people, he may have been talking about Yuchis. . . . It is almost certain that the ruins Sevier called 'forts,' were, in fact, remains of 16th or 17th century Indian towns, [possibly] fortified Yuchi towns that were occupied after the Napochin left the area."

If the Cherokee drove the Yuchis out, the Cherokees did not remain in the area. We know this, says Evans, because of "negative evidence." No remains have been found during that time period. Also, a Frenchman in the early 1700s traveled through the area and reported it being totally uninhabited. It remained in that state until Dragging Canoe moved his forces to Chickamauga Creek in the 1770s, precisely because it was uninhabited. At that time, legends existed that the area was diseased. An early missionary, who rejected the site for a location, called it "malarial."[33] Cherokees and others may have traveled through the area and perhaps set up temporary camps or hunting parties, but, by and large, the Chattanooga area served simply as a wilderness and frontier for a century. The arrival of the Cherokees to an abandoned wilderness contrasts sharply with the arrival of the whites, who forcibly removed the occupants of the land.

Actually, a small number of Napochin did remain in the area during this century of desolation, Raymond said. "They may have distrusted the Cherokees, or they may have simply been so attached to their familiar river and mountains that they could not bring themselves to leave. For safety, they lived in some small caves on the side of Raccoon Mountain, overlooking Williams Island and Moccasin Bend." They were finally buried in those caves. "This was a small number, possibly no more than one or two families."

Few as they were, there would have been enough of the Napochin tribe remaining to keep alive the memory of the area, its former peoples, and the name they had given it. They passed the name along to their successors—this place in the Cherokee language called *Chattanooga*.

The Difficulty with Definitions

Raymond was a little skeptical of my attempts to define *Chattanooga.* "You can hypothesize and offer a few syllables and make it anything you want it to be," he said. "Just like some of the Melungeon bands have made *Alabama* a Muslim word."

"I've heard that."

"Yeah. And you can do that," he said. "Most of what I know about the 16th century comes from Spanish sources, and they were not the best ethnographers. I mean, they wrote down what they heard. And language changes through time. *Chattanooga* is an English version of what Cherokees called it, with them trying to pronounce earlier Muskogean names, which may have derived from even earlier words."

Scholar Charles Hudson echoed some of Raymond's frustrations after examining the seventy-one-page Juan Pardo document by Juan de la Bandera. "Like many documents from Bandera's hand, this document is a mixture of carefully written and hastily, not to say sloppily, written text," said Hudson, who couldn't distinguish between the Spaniard's *u* and *v.* And if the letters *n* or *i* or *m* were next to each other, that also created problems. Although Spanish words could be deciphered from other documents, Native American words written by Bandera were often uncorroborated and left to Hudson's best guess.[34]

Archeologist Lawrence Alexander seems to prefer the evidence in the dirt to the more elusive handwriting. "The joke is that these Spaniards were sitting around the bar 20 years later, reminiscing on what they did."

What did the Napochin look like? No drawings are known to exist, but archeologist Raymond Evans identified from a collection in North Carolina this Napochin-era pot (right) found on Williams Island with a face carved on the side (left).

First, The Meaning of the Mountain

Determining the roots of *Chattanooga* was proving to be difficult. However, Raymond was more hopeful on obtaining the meaning of *Napochin* and the etymology of *Lookout Mountain*. "I think the original name of Lookout Mountain—or the 16th century name—was *Napochin Mountain*," he said.

Evans bases this theory on Swanton's dictionary of Indian names that says *Napochin* is "perhaps from a dialect variant of Napissa, 'those who see or look out.'" Earlier scholar Frederick Hodge had defined *ni pissa* as "spy" or "sentinal," and Swanton also said it could mean scouts or an outpost.[35]

"Since they were on the western edge of the paramount chiefdom of Coosa, near the mouth of the Tennessee Gorge, the name *Lookout* would be appropriate," said Evans.

The Napissa were first identified by the founder of Biloxi, Mississippi, Pierre Iberville, who was called "the most dashing military figure in New France." He spelled it Napyssas.[36]

Again, Raymond connected the dots. "The Cherokees knew *Napochin* meant "look out," so they simply named it *Lookout Mountain*," he said. He also noted this may explain the early reports of the Cherokee word for Lookout Mountain meaning, "Mountains looking at each other."

"There is apparently in the language the concept of 'look,'" said Raymond. "The Cherokee who gave it the most thought told me it just means, 'There. Lookie!'"

———————

I now had enough ammunition to close in on my own definition of the word *Chattanooga*. First, I asked Raymond a few more questions.

"The Cherokees didn't pronounce *p*'s, correct?"

"Right. The Cherokees don't make sounds where your lips have to come together," he said. "No *m* or *p*."

He agreed that when the Cherokees tried to say "Napochin," it would have sounded something like "Nuh-chin" or "Noochin."

I asked one more question. "Could the term *taska*, which means 'warrior' and is the root word of *Tuskegee*—have a relationship to *Chatta*?"

"You could hypothesize that it did. But this is beyond the scope of what I do," he answered. "But that doesn't prevent anybody from doing it."

That was all the encouragement I needed.

The Most Definitive Definition?

My sense is that *Chattanooga* resulted from many tribes and several European groups simply trying to identify the land of the "Tuskegee-Napochin." These two different names for the same people group that ended up on Moccasin Bend and nearby villages were apparently lumped together often, as we can see from the many names of the Tennessee River on old maps (Caskinampo, Tasquinapous, etc.).

Taska, the root word of Tuskegee, has some interesting forms, including *Casqui*, *Casquin*, and *Cattougi*. The most intriguing version is one that appears on a 1755 map as *Jaskegee*.[37] This form emerges just a few years previous to the earliest known form of our city's name, *Chatanuga*, which appeared in 1789.

Combining the "Jaskegee" form of Tuskegee with the Cherokee pronunciation of "Noochin" (they dropped the *p* in Napochin), forms the word *Jaske-Noochin*. Although it takes a while to get there (which is to be expected with so many languages and races involved in the journey), this theory provides us with a word that calls the area of Lookout Mountain and Moccasin Bend "the land of the Tuskegee-Napochin." Thus, Chattanoogans are "warrior-lookouts."[†]

This interesting theory provides a few bonuses. Firstly, it sheds light on the confusion over the years as to whether the mountain was ever called *Chattanooga*. Some say it only referred to the creek and valley, but Governor William Blount referred to it as "Chatanuga Mountain" in 1792.[38] If, in fact, the word *Napochin* applied to both the mountain and the village of Chattanooga, then that helps explain the matter.

Secondly, why do multigenerational Chattanoogans like Doug Daugherty and Tommy Lupton still pronounce the city as *Chattanooga*, with a short "oo" (like *nook* rather than *nuke*)? This could be explained from the Cherokee pronunciation of *Napochin*. If, in fact, the Cherokees said "Nuh-chin" rather than "Nooh-chin," then "Chatta-nuhga" would have indeed been passed down through the generations. This also explains early spellings (*Chatanuga*, *Chattonogee*) which seem to avoid an "ooh" sound. Otherwise, the earliest spellers would have used a double "o."

Thirdly, *Roget's Thesaurus* provides some interesting alternatives to the word *lookout* (the noun). Among them are "citadel," "cupola," "eagle eye," "hawk," and "crow's nest." Several of these allude to Wiltse's reports of early definitions like "eagle's nest" and "hawk's nest" and "crow's nest." Also intriguing is that Rev. T. H. McCallie may have come closer than all his peers in passing along the definition of *Chattanooga* when he said he thought it meant "bird's nest," but then "recalled hearing years before that it stood for 'look out.'"[39]

Towards an Authentic Chattanooga

Roget's Thesaurus also provides some interesting words for the verb version of *look out*. They include "watch out, "be alert," "listen," and "pay attention." *Look out* is also used as a synonym for "guard" and "warn."

[†] *Jaske-Noochin* comes closer to the goal if the *k* is substituted for *t*, not unlike the Spanish "Casquiqui" becoming "Taskigi." The final solution to the riddle is accomplished by dropping the final *n*—a common practice—and exchanging *ch* with *g*. Those two sounds are similar, both originating in the back of the throat, according to John Walker, classical languages instructor at Notre Dame.

The overall connotation is one who defends or protects in their duties as a sentinel. In many ways, the land of the Tuskegee-Napochin continues to house two types of people who must work together in harmony to survive as a culture. In ancient days, the lookouts on the mountain were trusted to warn and protect the warriors in the valley. In later days of manufacturing power, those on the mountain, the owners of the factories, were charged with protecting and watching out for the workers in the valley.

Today, the symbiotic relationship continues. By and large, those in the valley no longer work in factories, and those above do not own them. But Chattanoogans still need wisdom and direction from those on the mountain—or perhaps from today's version of those who are in a position to be far-sighted—in order to overcome new threats and to prosper. And, like before, those watching out from above have no real significance apart from the strength of the many below. And they have no purpose apart from serving them.

As always, some of those below resent the lookouts and hope to deconstruct this ancient paradigm. And some of those above follow their own agendas and forsake their sacred duty to the community. But where and when these two entities work together—with the other's best interests in mind—at that point Chattanooga is true to its name.

The Spirit of the Ancients

There are many things we can learn from the ancient members of our community. When possible, we should build on their wisdom, just as each generation built on the same mound. But, as in everything, a balance is required.

"We romanticize the Native American. I did it when I was younger," said Louie Wamp. "But I've read and studied. They weren't so in tune with everything. They overhunted and wiped out species. Some were very kind and sweet, and others were mean, vicious, and warring."

"It's like any heritage, I guess. You want the kids to understand the rudiments of the simpler life. I mean, our technology is mushrooming at such an incredible rate. Europeans called them savages, but they were in touch with the earth, the weather, the trees, the animal life. Finding those artifacts when I was hunting those fields was just incidental to the experience of being out in the fields of those river bottoms—you know, with the hawks circling overhead and the wind blowing and the river and the dirt and the earth—retracing your steps into that ancestral world where everything was tied to the earth."

"We've left the earth. What we do, and what I do as an architect, is we pretty much desecrate it. We grate it. We cut it. We trim it. We reshape it. We make it into concrete and paving and subterranean piping. Everything is managed. Everything is controlled. If you subscribe to the Garden of Eden, then we are here to tend the garden and care for it. Well, we don't do that. We just try to eliminate the garden as fast as we can."

"Some people are very scientific about archeology, and that's it. For me, it's real spiritual. I'm not a believer in reincarnation as such. But, in fact, we are the next generation of the same seed. We're all from one man—just the latest propagation of the same seed. You know, I just had beans and corn for lunch. That's still related to the first corn ever, right? It can't not be. For me, that's where you find out the rest of your story. You know, I might not have done it in this life, but my ancestors did. I'm the sum of all those previous lives, and it's all dwelling in me."

"To me, those arrowheads are just like treasures. I don't feel like I've acquired any of it. I'm just a curator. They belong to some other guy from thousands of years ago. Plus, every artifact, every little arrowhead or spear point or knife is unique. When you've hunted them for a long time, you can recognize the subtle differences in every one. They are like the very people themselves, each one unique and each one an individual."

"Every time I'm out there, every little piece I find is like finding a piece of myself."

Artist: Brent Sanders

CHAPTER TWELVE

The Spirit of the Bridge

Passing the Power to the Next Generation

For many in the valley, wealth is a distant dream.

However, Judge Walter Williams, a prominent member of Chattanooga's black community, makes enough to send his kids to Baylor. He also makes it clear that he does not have anywhere near the money of his friends on the mountain. He is "dealing with rent payment and all that" for his office.

George Elder, the real estate broker, does have a mountain named after his family, but he will also tell you he is not like the Lookout Mountain folks. He still has to work for a living.

Then there is Frank Brock, one of those on Lookout Mountain. He says he and his family are not part of the big money crowd either. "My dad always felt that the rich-rich banked at the American bank. We banked at the Hamilton bank, and right there, you're in a different category."

What about Scotty Probasco, the longtime director at SunTrust, formerly the American National Bank, whose family has chaired and directed the bank for generations? Is he rich?

"Well, I've run with Jack Lupton. He's a brother-in-law. I grew up with Frank Harrison. He was really rich! And people think, 'Well, he owns the bank.' It would have been nice if I did."

"But I'll tell you something. They're going to put my greatest quote on my tombstone: 'It's a curse to be reputedly wealthy.'"

Lands or Lineage?

While Chattanoogans today have the class or savvy—or both—not to brag about who is the wealthiest, such was not the case 500 years ago. When Hernando De Soto and two chiefs sat down for dinner, the leader of the earliest known Chattanoogans argued about who should sit at the great explorer's right hand. Like today, the two issues discussed were wealth and ancestry.

De Soto had conquered the Pacahas and the Tuskegees (the Spaniards called them Casquins[†]). To earn De Soto's favor, Casqui had given a daughter to the Spaniard. Pacaha was not to be outdone, giving him a sister and one of his wives.

Pacaha argued that he deserved the position of honor because he had more lands than Casqui. He was the richer of the two. But Casqui countered that the preeminence of his ancestors was superior to Pacaha's wealth. "Finally, De Soto intervened," writes Hudson, "and set Pacaha on his right side on the grounds that he was the greater chief, and his genealogy was the more illustrious."[1]

Today, in Chattanooga, there is still an interest in whose family goes back the furthest. However, like deferring over who is the wealthiest, few, if any, would rush to publicly claim the title. As Helen Exum reminded us in the beginning of this book, "It is not considered good taste to brag about one's ancestors."

Which family actually is the oldest? Those multigenerational citizens who good-naturedly describe themselves as "carpetbaggers" have been here now for five or six generations, yet a handful of families preceded the Civil War. The two discussed the most in this book are the McCallies and the Crutchfields. The Crutchfields' arrival is not exactly known, but they probably preceded the 1841 arrival of the McCallies by about two years. And the Gardenhires moved across the river in the early 1830s, before Ross's Landing was even established.

Albert Waterhouse can trace an ancestor back to 1820, not as a resident but as the owner of the twenty miles of riverfront on the north shore, today's spot for Coolidge Park and Heritage Landing. It is the first deed of property in the records of Hamilton County.

The secular Richard G. Waterhouse had a very religious wife. She brought several ministers to his deathbed. Asked for his last request, he said, "Bury me in a poplar casket so I can go a poppin' and a crackin' through Hell."[2]

Albert Waterhouse did not know the story when I shared it with him. "Maybe that's where my sense of humor comes from," he said.

[†] The Casquins are are likely the same as the Caskinampo tribe, according to leading ethnologist John Swanton, who also identifies the Caskinampos as the likely forerunner of the "Tuskegee-Napochin" of Moccasin Bend and Maclellan Island. This scene between the two chiefs occurred near Memphis, from which the Casquin/ Tuskegees are believed to have migrated to Chattanooga. (John Swanton, *Indians of the Southeastern United States*, p. 143, and Swanton, *Early History of the Creek Indians*, p. 213)

McCallie, Crutchfield, Waterhouse. That was as far back as I could trace a family name. Then, one day I was having lunch at Schlotzsky's Deli on Brainerd Road, and I ran into an old acquaintance. I told him and his friend about my book and my quest to find the oldest family.

"My family's been here since the early 1800s," said the friend.

"And who are you?" I asked.

"Ron Vail. My ancestor is buried over there." He pointed to the Brainerd Mission Cemetery about 100 yards from where we were eating.

"The missionary?" I asked.

"Yeah."

The Oldest Name in Chattanooga

It turns out that the family name of Vail precedes all of the earliest families of Chattanooga by more than a decade. Missionary John Vail and his wife Julia moved to Chattanooga from New Jersey in 1819. Ron Vail actually knew nothing about his own heritage until an article by John Wilson appeared in the paper in 1998. Much of Wilson's information came from the research of David Vail, a navy captain and Chattanooga native. He was unaware of his relative Ron Vail, and vice versa.

Captain Vail says he also knew nothing about his heritage as a child. Later, he learned he was related to people in the cemetery and that one was a missionary, so he examined the original documents in the Harvard Library. Donning special white gloves and reading a plastic-wrapped 1821 letter by John Vail, he began to put together the pieces of the family heritage.

"He ran the farm. He ran the mill. He ended up acquiring the mill," said David Vail. However, John Vail lost the mission property to Thomas Crutchfield because Vail's New Jersey residence did not allow him to acquire property left by the Cherokees. "He bitterly contested this until he lost every dollar that he possessed," wrote Zella Armstrong. Vail was urged to ask the mission board in Boston for money, but he replied, "Every dollar that they send to me takes from poor heathen that I have to meet at the great days."[3]

The *Brainerd Journal* tells us that Vail oversaw the farm at the mission along with the orchard of fruit trees. Most of his activities were more practical, but there is one mention of him preaching at a camp meeting on Missionary Ridge where the Indians "got happy" and "would shout and clap their hands as well as anybody."[4]

Vail also cut a trail in the wilderness all the way to the river. (The path is known today as Highway 153.) The purpose was to provide access to a small corncrib by the edge of the river for their supplier a few miles to the north. This was none other than George Gillespie III, the great-great-great-grandfather of Scotty Probasco.[5]

(Top right) **The Brainerd Cemetery** sits in the middle of the Eastgate Mall and office park.

(Top left) **John Vail's stone**, broken in half, has no markings. (Bottom right) The marker for **Mary Ann Vail**, one of John and Julia Vail's many children who died at Brainerd Mission. Harriet Blunt's stone stands in the background.

Memories Lost in a Generation

I asked David Vail why none of John Vail's children became missionaries.

"They all died," he said.

Indeed. Vail's wife, Julia, was sick the first day they arrived after the six-week trip from New Jersey. Soon, their daughter Carolyn fell critically ill while their youngest child contracted the measles. Julia was too fatigued from vomiting to care for them. Little Carolyn died a few days later. Another daughter, Mary Ann, died in 1831. She was described as "remarkably affectionate and dutiful." Their son Noah died a month afterward. A younger son, Elizar, drowned the following April in the Chickamauga Creek.

Julia was buried in the mission cemetery in 1843. Vail's second wife was buried there in 1850. In fact, more Vails are buried in the cemetery than any other family, and John was laid to rest there in 1871 at the age of 84.[6]

He did have one surviving son, John Vail, Jr., who was born to a third wife when John Sr. was 71. The current Vails have little memory of John Vail, Jr.

"He had a store on Long Street," said Alfred Vail, 78, who now lives in East Ridge. Alfred has a vague memory as a young boy of meeting his grandfather, who sat in front of the store and talked with another adult. "That was the first time I seen him and the last time," he said.

During our interview, Alfred pulled out his giant-print Bible, which he faithfully reads. He did not know his great-grandfather was a missionary. "No one took an interest until David got into this," he said, noting that his own father was not a religious man. "The Vail family, really, has kind of been scattered. They never was close."

Neither David nor Albert's son, Fred Vail, has an answer for the lost heritage. "I really don't know what happened during those generations," said Fred, who lives on the side of Lookout Mountain below Ruby Falls. He has taken several mission trips himself into the deep interior of Guiana, South America, traveling 250 miles by boat to minister to the Arawok Indians. He said they have no water or power, cook over a fire, and sleep on the floors of their huts.

"I've been back in the bush three times," he said. Renewed knowledge of his missionary ancestor was a big motivator. "That's why John Vail came to Chattanooga to begin with," said Fred.[7]

David Vail, who now lives in North Carolina, feels the same way. "How can it not have an effect on me?" he said. "I sometimes measure time in terms of what John was doing at that time [in history]. I'm very proud of the sacrifice they made, of the impact they made on the Cherokees."

Early drawing of **military bridge** built during the Civil War and lost to the 1867 flood.

Opening of the **Market Street Bridge** in 1917.

Vail comes from the Gaelic "Mac Phail" or "son of Paul," the first missionary. John Vail joined co-laborer Ainsworth Blunt and the rest of the missionaries on the Trail of Tears in 1838. Vail and Blunt both contracted illnesses during the journey and were forced to return. These two remaining members of the mission founded the First Presbyterian Church in 1840. Blunt moved to Dalton a few years later, but Vail remained as the one single fiber linking Chattanooga's prehistory to its future as a great city.

Appropriately, there was no bridge in Chattanooga at the time, only a rope for the ferry system that guided flat vessels across the river. The first bridge was built across the Tennessee River during the Civil War but was destroyed by a flood in 1867. This is also an appropriate symbol of the almost total disconnect between antebellum and postbellum Chattanooga.

In 1891, a permanent bridge was finally constructed across the mighty Tennessee. The Walnut Street bridge was dedicated with much fanfare by thousands of citizens like Adolph Ochs, E. Y. Chapin, and Harry Scott Probasco, who had all been caught up in the city's latest booms and busts. This bridge was built during the golden age of Chattanooga when new empires were emerging. The Spirit of Chattanooga, that complex mix of principle and tolerance, had just been forged from the elements of diversity, forgiveness, and an ancient faith.

As Coca-Cola Bottling Company, Provident Insurance, and other dynamic companies revitalized the city's prospects, another bridge was appropriately scheduled for construction in 1917. Adolph Ochs, now a wealthy New York publisher, was involved in its financing.

Current U.S. Congressman Zach Wamp tells the story. "It was supposed to cost $1 million, which was a ton of money in 1917. It went over budget. County Judge Will Cummings [the forerunner of county mayor] was distraught and grabbed Adolph Ochs and said, 'I'm in a pinch. Where are we going to get another $500,000?' And Ochs said, 'We're going to Wall Street.' So he took Judge Will Cummings to New York City and went around Wall Street and got people to issue $500,000 in long-term bonds to finish the Market Street Bridge."

Zach Gets the DNA Chills

I interviewed Zach Wamp at his downtown office in the Federal Building across from Miller Park. Ironically, it was more than double the size of any of the offices of the several near-billionaires I had interviewed. Wamp's assistant, a sharp fellow who, every now and again, clicked his pen repeatedly, joined us during the session.

Zach has been reading a book about Cummings because he feels a special connection to this famous Chattanooga politician of the early 20th century. "I'm living on the very property in Lookout Valley where he farmed. His mother's house was literally on the same property. When I bought it, the foundation was still there."

Wamp's house by the Black Creek golf course in Cummings Cove is a stone's throw from the original Will Cummings mansion where Franklin Delano Roosevelt stayed a number of times while visiting Chattanooga. Wamp also gets inspired by FDR's appointment of Hayden Aldridge, a Southern politician connected to Wamp's own Aldridge relatives in Alabama.

"My parents told us when we were young that they were distant cousins. Both of my grandmother's maiden names were Aldridge. Nathan Aldridge lived in Knox County in 1792. [Then] they went down to Northeast Alabama where Enoch Aldridge, my father's great-great-grandfather, served 40 years in the Alabama General Assembly. I mean, these things kind of send chills up and down your spine. . . . Maybe through their DNA, and my blood, and God's divine providence, I get to do the same thing at a later generation."

I asked Zach how this family history might relate to Todd Gardenhire, the opponent in Zach's first Republican primary. Wamp's assistant clicked his pen.

"What's so ironic, you know, is I ran for Congress in '92, and I didn't know any of this," said Zach. "And Todd Gardenhire rightly comes out and claims all of his heritage in this region, and all of this was right in front of me. I mean, can you imagine if I had said, 'Well, that's nice. Now let me tell you about this person and that person.' Because he didn't have anybody born in Pikeville in 1807."

When I mentioned these Wamp discoveries to Todd Gardenhire, he told me Jacob Gardenhire bought property in East Tennessee in 1795. But Zach's Aldridge kin were already in East Tennessee by 1792. Zach does concede, however, that the Gardenhires easily win the oldest-name contest for the Chattanooga area.

Will Cummings and FDR

Zach Wamp and George W. Bush

TVA and International Ideology

Cummings was a "big, great Democrat," said Wamp. "He thought FDR hung the moon. Cummings really pushed FDR. 'We've got to have a dam. We've got to have a dam,' he said. 'We've got to have the dam hydro power.'"

"I would suggest that hydro power had a big influence in Chattanooga maintaining our progress in the post–industrial revolution," Wamp said. "Because we could have had a bottoming-out if we would have had higher costs of electricity."

The Tennessee Valley Authority also provided solutions to the age-old flood problems in Chattanooga. Stories are legendary, and pictures show several floors of downtown buildings submerged during major deluges. A pregnant Mrs. William Crutchfield had to be taken by boat to Cameron Hill to give birth to her child in 1867. Another citizen watched his house get swept away, but a better one came to rest on the same spot as did a houseful of better furniture.[8]

When the new TVA dams were completed, the progressive waters finally tamed the legendary and dangerous whirlpool known as the Suck. They also covered many ancient landmarks, including Hamilton County's oldest cemetery and the town Spaniards called Tanasqui, the namesake of "Tennessee."

President Roosevelt spoke to a crowd of 80,000 at the 1940 dedication of the new Chickamauga Dam. His speech was part of a visit that included an evening at the Cotton Ball. President Roosevelt and the others danced and honored Mrs. John L. Hutcheson, "The Lady of the Lake."[9]

A new bridge was built above the dam. The TVA era had begun.

The battle leading to the Tennessee Valley Authority was actually a great ideological war on a national and international level between those promoting more government ownership, particularly in the power industry, and those with more conservative views of private property. Englishman Julius Huxley described TVA as "efficiency . . . without totalitarian regimentation." A French notable called it an effort to "adjust capitalism to present realities."

Historian Clarence B. Carson said Roosevelt's push for TVA in 1932 "secured support for him in several western states where Progressives had made public power a popular issue. [However, Tennessee] was remote from the area where there had been much agitation for activity."[10]

Like the Cherokee Removal and the Civil War battles, the massive TVA changes were yet another federal imprint on this place of destiny in which locals had little power in the origin or operation of epic events.

"Chattanooga was regarded to be the poorest area in the South," said Dr. James Livingood during our interview at Alexian Village. He has since passed away. "Believe it or not, there were labor disputes around here as to whether labor—that's pick-and-shovel labor—should earn more than 19.5 cents an hour. This is what caused

Franklin Roosevelt to choose this area for the Tennessee Valley Authority. Of course it was not anything that a lot of people approved of at the time. For what reason?" he asked.

"He was a Democrat?" I offered.

"Because it was federal."

Taking Sides on TVA

Many of those who got jobs from the New Deal initiative did appreciate the federal intervention. One often-sung mountain ballad included the following lyrics:

"My name is William Edwards, I live down Cove Creek way.

I'm working on the project they call the TVA . . .

Oh, see the boys a-comin'—their government they trust.

Just hear their hammers singin'—they'll build that dam or bust."[11]

Modern scholars, such as William Chandler (*The Myth of TVA*, Harper & Row), question the importance of creating a waterway from the sea to Knoxville, where an average of only one barge a day arrives. He also suggests that the economic benefits of the multibillion dollar program would have offered better results by simply mailing checks to the poor Tennesseans. It would have been much easier to solve Chattanooga's flooding problems, he writes, "by relocating the existing structures out of the floodplain." Compared to TVA's eventual outlays, "the cost would have been miniscule."[12]

President Eisenhower later referred to TVA as "creeping socialism," and privately commented, "I'd like to sell the whole thing." Nevertheless, the agency grew under his administration and remains a powerful entity in Chattanooga and the South today.[13]

"TVA played a great role in steady economic development in this region," said Wamp. "We wouldn't have had the Brock Candys and the McKee Foods—not just U.S. Pipe and Wheland in the traditional sense, but we wouldn't have had all this modern manufacturing without low costs of electricity."

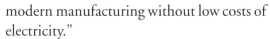

In 1959, the city built another bridge across the river. Stark, practical, and efficient, the plain, undecorated strip reflected an age when function triumphed over form.

The Olgiati Bridge is named after Mayor Rudy P. Olgiati, a man who dominated city politics while a few titans on the mountain

Mayor Rudy Olgiati poses beside the Olgiati Bridge.

dominated local industry. "Chattanooga had a commission form of government," wrote longtime *Free Press* reporter J. B. Collins. "But it was run by one man: Olgiati. . . . Virtually nobody opposed him."

Olgiati was all about progress. He positioned Chattanooga as the first city in Tennessee to get the freeway. He built sewers, the airport, and the new bridge. He also expedited traffic into one-way streets and did away with the myriad of obstacles caused by the railroad companies.

"He got their attention in pure Olgiati fashion," said Collins. "He had several of their engineers arrested for blocking traffic. They were hauled off the engines and taken to jail by police acting under Olgiati's directions."

In his waning years, Olgiati made clear in a 1987 article his disapproval of the power structure's influence on city government and the "Chattanooga Process."

"Remember what they tried to do when I was mayor?" he said. "Well, it's worse now," he chuckled, adding that he "hadn't let 'em run me."

Unexcited about talks of developing twenty miles of riverfront or building a new aquarium, the longtime mayor complained about the decline of unions and high-paying manufacturing jobs. "The city can't thrive on fast food places and tourists," Olgiati said. "I know things are different now, but if I was a little younger . . . in six months I'd show 'em."[14]

However, he may have done well to listen better to the power structure. Or perhaps they weren't speaking loud enough. Consequently, Mayor Olgiati is best remembered today for razing the historic mansions on Cameron Hill and removing a major portion of the hill itself. What used to look like a miniature Lookout Mountain now resembles a giant flat-topped mound akin to what the Woodland Indians built. The dirt was used to lay a foundation for the new freeway, and the mansions were replaced with cube-shaped apartments designed for the Age of Aquarius. The nearby Golden Gateway strip mall and low-income high-rises, once claimed as a model of technological progress, sit empty or static today. They exude a spirit similar to the nearby apartments, which, like the mansions before them, are scheduled to be bulldozed soon to accommodate modern office buildings.

Women like Zella Armstrong tried to warn both the power structure and the mayor, but without success. Ruth Holmberg mentioned another, Mrs. Sims Perry Long. "She tried hard to save Cameron Hill," said Ruth, "and she wore everybody out, and nobody would listen to her. She was right."

The Five White Guys

Chattanooga has many such stories that seem to conflict—Olgiati's complaints of an overbearing power structure versus Holmberg's description of a weak, ill-informed leadership on a major issue. The contradicting views are one of many examples that communicate the mystical nature of Chattanooga's famed power structure. After two years of research and study, I have clearly discerned a strange ambiguity. What is the precise nature of this power structure? Who are the specific members? What are its limits and capacity? How, exactly, does the position, wealth, faith, and heritage of these families affect the city? No one knows for sure, including the power structure.

The power structure cannot be quantified. Like the fascinating web of their interrelated ancestors, this group is mysterious, almost spiritual. Nonetheless, it is very real.

Community Foundation President Pete Cooper may have enjoyed the best view of Chattanooga's ethereal power structure. He talks about serving Cokes decades ago in the American National Bank boardroom to "the five white guys who ran Chattanooga."

As the 26-year-old head of the bank's Charitable Trust Department, Cooper managed the assets of a number of key nonprofits, including Baylor, First Presbyterian, and the Hunter Museum. In those days, the board members of these organizations were largely overlapped, as were the boards of the Big Three, the United Way, the University of Chattanooga, the bank, and other key institutions.

Cooper erased some of the mystique. "You could always count a Lupton," he said. "You could count a Probasco. You could count a Davenport, probably a Frierson, maybe a Guerry or Patten. In some cases it was also a Whittaker or an Overmyer."[15]

He then reverted back to the mystique. "There really weren't five white guys. It's just a euphemism, but with the exception of Ruth Holmberg, they were all guys and they were all white."

Indeed, these symbolic five "were making a lot of the decisions in the city at that time," said Cooper. "They were wonderful, wonderful citizens. They weren't always particularly well informed on grassroots issues, but they were doing the best they could. It wasn't about lining pockets. I never heard the discussion, 'What will Provident or SunTrust or some other bank get out of this?' I never heard that discussion. It was always, 'What's best for the community?'"

"The question now becomes: how are those decisions going to be made in the future and where are those leaders going to come from? I don't think it's going to be five white guys. I don't think it's going to be five. I don't think they're going to be white. I don't think they're going to be guys. I think it is going to look a lot more like a Chattanooga Venture process where lots of people weigh in with lots of communication. You can't leave the low-income out of it. You can't leave other races out of it. Everybody's got to be at the table."

Pete Cooper

"You actually must start talking to politicians," said Cooper, who noted that some of the Five had such massive concentrations of wealth they were never forced to do so. "Most of the things that were done in this city were done, literally, without the help of any political structures. We didn't even ask permission. Now, we need public-private partnerships."

On Zach and Jack

I asked Zach Wamp about Jack Lupton. His assistant clicked his pen. The story of Wamp's relationship with Lupton confirms Cooper's account of the need for more private and political interaction despite the myth of an historical alliance between the two.

"I spoke to Mr. Lupton a few times when I ran in 1992, but I don't think he knew who I was," said Zach. The two had interacted one time years before when Wamp, age 26, attended a meeting at Miller-Reid Advertising to promote metro government. "I was intimidated," said Zach. "I knew who he was. I'm sure he didn't know who I was."

On the day after Wamp was barely defeated in the '92 election for Congress, he passed Lupton who was entering the Mountain City Club for lunch. "In a routine sort of way I said, 'Hello, Mr. Lupton.' He stopped me and complimented me on the race I ran, and he encouraged me to run again. I'll tell you, it had a huge impact on me, not because I knew him but because I knew how much influence he had."

"After that, of course, I got to know him much better. He said, 'Don't call me Mr. Lupton. Call me Jack.' I would go out to the Honors and would see him playing golf. He had such a strong presence about him, carried himself so well. Everybody knew what a tremendous contribution his life had been to this area, and so I would always speak to him in those terms. Every time I was with him, I would say Mr. Lupton, and he would say, 'Quit calling me Mr. Lupton! Call me Jack.'"

"And then he had a stroke. I went to see him and he was in a wheelchair. He still looked great. He still had all his faculties, but I could tell that, physically, he wasn't where he wanted to be."

"I was very candid with him. 'It's got to be awfully hard on you,' I said. "Having basically conquered the world, given so much, and been so virile, and then to be in this condition."

"He told me point blank: 'It sure does change your perspective on life. You sure do focus on things that are important, and not other things as much. It not only gets your attention, it just consumes you.'"

Zach and Jack connected. "For the first time, right there, I felt like he and I were on the same wavelength," said Wamp. "We really connected. I sent him a couple of notes to encourage him and told him I was praying for him."

"While he's been known to cuss and be a rough, tough guy where you don't want to get in his way and all these things that you always hear, what you see is a man who's got a heart of gold that is willing to do whatever he can for the place he loves. I would say, until somebody has walked in his shoes, people shouldn't criticize. And that's true with anybody."

I asked Zach about the legend of a power structure. "So it wasn't like you and Jack Lupton and a few of his other rich friends got in a room and decided that you were to become the next congressman?"

"My experience was exactly the opposite of that," Zach said. "I had to work really hard even to get their attention. I gain my calling from the books I read, the stories I hear, and the people I meet, not from any group of people. I think a whole lot of that is blown out of proportion. It's probably based on a few stories that are more isolated than general. Now Will Cummings, when he got in a pinch with the Market Street Bridge and needed money, he did go to Adolph Ochs, Ruth Holmberg's grandfather."

"[But] whether it's Bob Corker or Zach Wamp or people in this region working together, it wasn't concocted by any power structure. As a matter of fact, what we're doing in this region today is concocted by our generation saying, 'This is our destiny. This is the hand we were dealt. These are the assets we have. These are the liabilities we have. Let's carry forward.'"

———◆———

Chattanooga's most striking bridge—a fresh version of the original— provides several symbols for Chattanooga: the emerging of this New South city as it recovers from industrial decay, the realities of a more individualized economy, and the changing color of its citizenry.

VENCE RIZZO

The restored Walnut Street Bridge represents, most importantly, the transfer of leadership to the next generation, which Wamp cites as the city's next vanguard.

Restoration began in 1991, one hundred years after the bridge first opened. According to the *Atlanta Journal-Constitution,* "Most of the money came from a fundraising campaign called 'Bridging the Generations,' which solicited donations from individuals who paid $100 to $300 for bridge planks with brass plates inscribed with the names of children, grandchildren and grandparents."

Like Chattanooga's trend toward a more diverse leadership, the bridge's donors represented a broader mix of the populace. However, the influence of the old families still remained. The committee to save the bridge was chaired by Ben Probasco. Ellen McCallie Cooper was cited as a key promoter at the opening ceremony, and E. Y. Chapin's great-grandson served as architect. (Garnet Chapin previously served as project director for the restoration of the Statue of Liberty.)

"Bridges always connect things, that's the beautiful thing about them," Chapin told the *Constitution.*[16]

The neglected Walnut Street Bridge was shut down in 1978, a time when Chattanooga's economy was at its nadir. Officials felt pressure to demolish the growing safety hazard. But in 1980, an unknown soul flew a banner from the bridge with the words "Save the Walnut!" Around the same time, Jack Lupton charged the Lyndhurst Foundation staff with finding some way to save the city.

Thanks to the banner and thousands of letters and phone calls, officials delayed demolition. Chattanooga Venture appointed a task force headed by Ben Probasco to study ways to save the bridge. In 1987, the Walnut Street Bridge Resolution Committee announced that the bridge could be saved as a pedestrian walkway for $4 million. The city donated $1.5 million, the cost of demolition, and President Reagan signed a bill in 1988 adding $2 million. The remainder was raised primarily by the individuals in the "Bridging the Generations" campaign.

However, just as the generational transfer in Chattanooga should build upon the past rather than forget it, funding also came from historically familiar names and agencies. Benwood, Lyndhurst, and the Community Foundation were listed together. The city's two great fortunes were listed side by side, Coca-Cola and Provident, as were business rivals Ruth Holmberg and Roy McDonald. Jack Lupton, Tommy Lupton, and Scotty Probasco were also among the list of twenty-seven top sponsors. The last sponsor listed was "1,690 Plaque Contributors."

The Walnut Street Bridge was converted to a linear park and is now the largest pedestrian bridge in the world. The asphalt roadway on the camelback truss span was replaced with 2,370 feet of planks and stays brightly lit at night. This symbol connecting the generations has become wildly popular with Chattanoogans.

Chapin is quite pleased. "People are running on the bridge before six in the morning and after midnight—just a wide variety of folks on bicycles, tricycles, baby carriages, roller blades, and wheelchairs."

George Edwards, director of the Atlanta Preservation Center, thinks Atlanta can learn from Chattanooga. "Preservationists say Chattanooga, unlike Atlanta, has become a national example for cities that want to salvage their pasts," writes the *Constitution.* John Gallager, chairman of the bridge's opening festivities, agreed. "What it says to other cities and future generations is: You can preserve a piece of your history and make it useful for the future."[17]

The Next Generation of Leaders

Can Chattanooga be as successful with transforming its leadership? "The transition is underway," says Pete Cooper. "I deal with a number of the prominent families, and we have done a fairly good job of teaching philanthropy to the next generation. They are charitable within their means. But their means are not their parents' means. They may have a name where somebody thinks they have as much money as their parents. In reality, they probably don't. Not that they're poor, but they can't give the significant big gifts their parents were capable of. They're out working every day to make a living. While they do serve on some boards, they don't have the same flexibility."

"When money goes through two or three generations, it gets a lot thinner. I remember several years ago there was a gathering of Vanderbilt heirs at Vanderbilt University. There were like 700 of them. There was not a single person in the room that was a millionaire. Do the math: you start with $100 million, and after a few generations, especially when people don't work and they consume the assets, they have three or four kids, and you keep dividing it. You take out some estate taxes. Nobody has any money left."

"I'm not saying these folks are broke, but it's clearly diluted, and their focus is not as much on a community leadership role as it had been in the past."

"The good news in this whole conversation is that those folks who may have been shut out in previous generations because they did not have the right name—didn't live on the right street—now have an opportunity to come forward with leadership regardless of demographics, economics, gender, etc. The opportunity for leadership in this community is unlike any time in its history."

"Yeah, you will see the Lupton and Probasco names, but you will also see the names of people who did not grow up with money, who have the skills, abilities, and willingness to step up to the plate and lead."

Cooper was right about the Probasco name. Scott Probasco III and his brother Ben Probasco have a handful of sons that should keep that family legacy alive into future generations. But the Lupton name will disappear in Chattanooga when Jack and Tommy's generation passes on. The Patten name is also barely alive, with golf instructor Zeb Patten the only one of his generation who remains in the city. When Jack Kruesi, the last Kruesi descendent, leaves us, that famous Chattanooga name will leave with him.

Summerfield Johnston's name continues for now through his son Robert, who runs RiverCity Bicycles in North Chattanooga. Will Johnston took on his maternal grandfather's last name. The Crutchfield last name no longer mixes with the blood of the famous owners of the Crutchfield House, but the name will survive the next generation thanks to Neal Crutchfield's two adopted sons. Sam Read Smartt III, recently graduated from Chattanooga Christian, is now the lone carrier of that family name into the next generation. Even the once prolific McCallies are reduced to only two or three name-bearers in Chattanooga. One lone McCallie teaches at the school, and the headmaster has a new last name after three generations of Spencer McCallies.

Many great names are gone: the Keys, Reads, Gillespies, Williamses, Carters, and Whitesides to name a few. Others are numerous. The Chapins have several children here, thanks to E. Y. Chapin III's five children. A few Davenports remain, and Burton Frierson has a handful of name-bearers in town. T. G. Montague's remaining progeny include Rick's son and two grandsons, but several more Montagues descend from T. G.'s brother. Thomas Maclellan has over ten progeny in town under 40, and the candy maker Bill Brock is the proud great-great-grandfather of over twenty-five Brocks on Lookout Mountain who are still too young to drive.

Cotton is King Again

The Cotton Ball is also ripe for new blood. This year's queen, Kathryn Smith, 21, does not hail from a prominent family but earned her stripes as a trainbearer at age 12. She had always dreamed of being the queen of the traditional event, so she memorized the entire ceremony.

"It's an honor to be asked," said Smith, a senior at the University of Alabama. "Since I was a trainbearer, I've been addicted to the Cotton Ball."

Her dance partner was Frank McDonald, Jr., 53, the king for the 71st annual Cotton Ball. Seventy belles from several states were presented.

McDonald is the son of Frank McDonald, Sr., the 1998 king, and is the grandson of publishing legend Roy McDonald. Frank Jr. first attended at age ten. "I was dressed as a soldier to go along with a cannon," he said. "Many other balls have gone away or [are] considered out of fashion," he said. "The tradition of honoring our next generation . . . weaves a thread of heritage through our young and old people to remember the rest of their lives."

The queen mother agrees. "The tradition is not dying at all," said Gloria Smith. "I guess that may surprise some people, but the girls who participate in it today do it because they want to."[18]

Just like the Cotton Ball, Wamp believes Chattanooga's power structure desires new leaders. "My experience was, not only will they accept you, but if you are determined, and if you persevere, and if you are willing to get in there and scrap and scrape, you will become one of them, so to speak. But the theory that there is a stiff arm or that there is no way to do it—I would discount those theories and tell you that there's a lot of stability that comes from multigenerational family commitments."

King and Queen of 2005 Cotton Ball: Kathryn Smith and Frank McDonald, Jr.

"Every single major family has several tentacles of people. Sure, some spend too much time at the club and don't do things. But, for the most part, every single major family has people that continue the legacy of giving more than they take, doing for others, investing in philanthropic and political activities, and moving the city forward. That's why we've had steady, stable growth throughout our history."

"There's beauty in that, frankly, because we've been able to avoid bottoming out at any time. As a result, we've been very stable throughout our history. Now we are really poised for some great years."

Innovation May Be the Answer

Wamp's positive forecast will be a challenge. International megatrends suggest Chattanooga's economy of the future will no longer look like a four-lane bridge accommodating manufactured vehicles. Rather, it will resemble a great crowd of entrepreneurs and niche industries, each individually marching across a pedestrian walkway.

Local officials, however, still hold high hopes for a major manufacturer to locate at the city's Enterprise South Industrial Park, a 1,200-acre tract uniquely located only eight miles from the downtown of a major metro area.

Chattanooga "has it all" in terms of attracting a major auto manufacturer, said Bill Ford, the great-grandson of Henry Ford. He traveled to Chattanooga to address an audience of 1,200 in July 2005 at the Kruesi Spirit of Innovation Awards breakfast. It didn't hurt that Jack Lupton and Bill's dad were close friends. Bill Ford, Sr., Jack, and Scotty played the Honors Course on a regular basis.[19]

Speaking of innovation, Ford gave high marks to Chattanooga for its cutting-edge work in clean fuel research (hydrogen cells, hybrid fuels, and electricity). He also commended the efforts to connect to Oak Ridge Laboratory's supercomputer through the Sim Center and plugged the Advanced Transportation Technology Institute, both housed at the University of Tennessee at Chattanooga.

Bill Brock also believes that innovation is our only chance to compete globally. "If we want Chattanooga, or the United States writ large, to be productive in the future, we need to rethink our entire education system," the former secretary of labor told me during our interview in Annapolis. "China is preeminent in the world in manufacturing They are paying more attention to education right now than we are. It's incredible. India is doing the same thing in the service field."

Brock, of course, is the great-grandson of John Kruesi, whose name graces the innovation event. After Thomas Edison scratched out a drawing of the first phonograph, he sent it to his right-hand man and scrawled below the blueprint, "Kruesi, Make this. Edison."[20]

Chattanooga manufacturer Robert Kwasnik witnessed firsthand Brock's concerns regarding China during a recent visit to the Far East. He saw entire cities in China purposely created for industry—large, new, and high-tech facilities with highly educated manufacturing teams. "They had clean streets and nicely landscaped buildings," said Kwasnik. "I realized it wasn't just the low-tech, labor-intensive industries that will be challenged."

Kwasnik's company sells $15–$20 million in textiles each year. They make zippers. There were 255 such manufacturers in America when his father founded the company in 1966. Today, there are three. "We had to either find international partners at significantly lower costs or slowly go out of business," he said. Headquartered in Chattanooga, they now have plants in China, India, Taiwan, Jordan, and their original site at Dunlap, Tennessee. Many of their products now bypass the United States and are shipped directly to foreign customers. "We're very optimistic, but the face of our company is going to change dramatically," he said.

However, it is not just manufacturing. Kwasnik says the Chattanooga economy, which has depended for decades on the service industry, needs to prepare for similar trends. Local industries such as calling centers, medical information, and insurance analysis are all being done offshore.

"I think it has just begun, as frustrating as that might be," he said.[21]

The Chattanooga Chamber of Commerce, while continuing to promote Enterprise South as a "Certified Automotive Megasite," is also aware of the need for more innovation. "Entrepreneurs Wanted!" proclaims a link on their website, which lists a multitude of reasons to locate to the New South city.

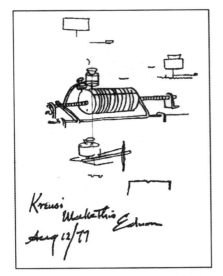

Original 1877 sketch of the phonograph with notation: "Kruesi, Make this. Edison."

Another Kruesi descendent echoes his cousin's call for more entrepreneurs. "You've got to look for areas where you can be the very best," said Dan Frierson, president of the Dixie Group. "Invest in those. Innovate in those."

Frierson's company was founded by J. T. Lupton. Formerly known as Dixie Yarns, it is one of Chattanooga's oldest manufacturers. They left the yarn business ten years ago and switched to carpet, one of the few products exported to China. Global competition forced their hand.

"It's not as easy as it used to be," he said.[22]

And the Schools Saga Marches On

One of Chattanooga's greatest challenges for economic success, by nearly all accounts, is the improvement of its education system. "The Chattanooga school system is not nearly as good as it could be. But that's true for every public school system in America," said Bill Brock. "So we need to have a much more sophisticated and aggressive education system. We need lifetime learning. The education system doesn't do that."

Brock says Chattanooga's extraordinary private school phenomenon should act as an asset to improve public schools. Zach Wamp agrees. "I will say that these schools are an incredible asset," he said. "When *The Hill* wrote a 20-year summary of my sobriety last week, they talked about my McCallie experience, that I went to one of these great prep schools." (Before his first campaign, Wamp confessed to an early cocaine addiction followed by a born-again conversion and successful recovery.) "They listed the alumni—the likes of Howard Baker, Bill Brock, Ted Turner, Pat Robertson, and on and on. It's an impressive list," he said. "People in leadership—business, philosophical, political—come right out of these schools."

"Chattanooga Christian offers a very credible alternative to those schools in terms of centering in on a Christian education," said the congressman.

"Is that why your kids are there?" I asked him.

"No, my children went to CCS by choice, not by my choice. My son went to McCallie for three years. They were three very good years, but one of the problems that families face when you have generations upon generations in a community . . . sometimes the expectations aren't fair."

Zach said his son, Weston, was viewed as the congressman's kid. "My son, frankly, said, 'At McCallie, I was your son. At Chattanooga Christian, I get to be Weston.' Well, you know, I want my son to be himself. God created him very different from me. He may one day be a congressman himself, but that's a path he needs to walk of his own volition."

"Wouldn't he be Zach Wamp's son at Chattanooga Christian?" I asked.

"Well, I've got to tell you. It's different. There's not that family lineage thing at Chattanooga Christian like there is at McCallie. If you're a Davenport at McCallie, the gym's named after you. If you're a Maclellan, the office is named after you. If you're a Wamp at McCallie, you're dad's a congressman. At Chattanooga Christian, you've got a lot of kids from Georgia, a lot of kids from Covenant College. Actually, the thing to be at Chattanooga Christian is a Presbyterian."

Wamp Speaks Boldly on Every Topic

The Wamps go to Red Bank Baptist. Zach is quite vocal about his faith. As Chattanooga struggles to redefine its economic identity, the city's strong spiritual tradition is also up for reinterpretation by the next generation.

I asked Wamp if his colleagues think Chattanooga is a Bible Belt kind of town.

"Oh, yes," he said. "As a matter of fact, the perceptions are even more intense than the reality. In Washington, we are perceived to be so fundamental that people have difficulty believing [we have] moderate Republicans."

I asked him about the hottest religious–family value issue of the day: homosexuality and gay marriage. The pen clicked with a fury.

No wonder. Wamp made headlines in October 2003, after telling a reporter that homosexuality is a "sin" and a "sickness." The quote was picked up by *USA Today*, the *Washington Post*, and the entire *Associated Press*. Then James Carville and Tucker Carlson debated Wamp's stance on *CNN's* "Crossfire."

The pen clicking was futile. As I suspected, Wamp spoke at great length on this subject. Like his two brothers, he is an indomitable talker and a rather fearless one.

"The reporter took part of what I said and then created a story around it," said Wamp. "It was unfortunate."

"Well, let me just tell you," he continued. "Last week I went over and spent a couple of hours at Chattanooga Cares with people who have AIDS. We had a roundtable meeting, and we touched and hugged and got to know each other, and I listened to their plight and the challenges they face. The people followed me out to the parking lot, and we were overjoyed. They were an inspiration to me that they are living life and loving life even in the midst of going through the difficulties they have with medications, pain, rejection, and discrimination."

(Left) Opening of the restored **Walnut Street Bridge**.

(Below) Walnut Street Bridge lit up at night with Market Street Bridge in the background.

Wamp called for Chattanoogans to show "the true love of Jesus Christ" in this area. "I just honestly believe that if this city is after God's own heart, [then] we need to love everybody. You know, we don't have to love what they do. . . . I try and I fail sometimes, but I try to put it in a context of Jesus' love, and that's my motive, too—it's to have his love for others. But sometimes it doesn't come across that way or doesn't get reported that way or printed that way. But that's my heart."

"So, while I believe by statute . . . marriage ought to be defined [as between] a man and a woman, that doesn't in any way say that we shouldn't as believers or as people love each other, and love the people who are engaged in homosexual behaviors. As Billy Graham said when they asked him, 'If you found out your son was homosexual, would you love your son?' He said, 'I'd love that son even more.'"

Bridging the Races

Chattanooga today faces new challenges of growth and diversity. Appropriately, the restored bridge is a different color. Bright blue—or turquoise blue, to be exact. Chattanooga's historic people of color, African Americans, encountered difficulties as the opening festivities were announced for the Walnut Street Bridge. Many black leaders approved, but others protested after being apprised of plans during the ceremony to commemorate five deaths on the bridge, four during its construction and restoration and one by a lynching party in 1906 when a black man was tragically hanged.

Ed Johnson, accused of raping a white woman, proved to be innocent. The sheriff who allowed a lynch mob to conduct a lawless execution was convicted for the travesty, the only time in history that the U.S. Supreme Court, which traditionally only hears appealed cases, conducted its own criminal trial.

Before he was hung, Johnson spoke to the crowd: "I am going to tell the truth. I am not guilty," he said. "I was not there. I know I am going to die, and I have no fear to die. . . . God bless you all. I am innocent."[23]

Members of the NAACP protested the commemoration at the opening of the restored bridge. A man unjustly lynched should be placed in a different category than men who died by accident, they said. A special committee, however, was able to reach a compromise and settle the activists' concerns. Johnson was honored in a separate ceremony. The committee called for the dedication to be a "disavowal" of the tragic event. "We want it to be a bridge between the black and white community," said committee chairman Jeff Boehm, a local attorney and preservationist.[24]

As previous chapters explained, the African American community in Chattanooga flourished for decades before seeing their right to district representation stripped away at the turn of the century. The city had no black representation again until the 1970s. In 1976, officials announced the construction of a bridge next to the Dupont plant in Hixson. It was named after C. B. Robinson, a longtime black educator and state legislator from Chattanooga. The construction, however, took five long years. As the project was nearly finished, the bridge collapsed. It was finally completed in 1981.

Killing Pathkiller's People

Similar racial concerns regarding injuries to Native Americans led to UTC getting rid of their longtime mascot, "Chief Moccanooga." Todd Gardenhire was at the meeting discussing the concern.

"The chancellor said the Indian descendents were upset that the chief was running around the sidelines with feathers and a stick, and they didn't want to offend anyone," said Todd. "And I remember raising my hand and saying to the chancellor,

"Well, if you don't mind offending them, why do you mind offending me?"

"What do you mean?" he said.

"Well, I'm part Cherokee, and I'm proud that we've got something. You're offending me by taking that away. You're doing away with the Cherokees. You're offending a Cherokee descendent now by taking it away."

A Gardenhire married the daughter of Principal Chief Pathkiller, the famous Indian who preceded John Ross as the Principal Chief of the entire Cherokee Nation. The actual injustices to the Cherokees, substantive abuses in contrast to today's problems with symbols, were eerily foreshadowed by Pathkiller in an 1821 *Brainerd Journal* account.

"This afternoon the old king, Path killer, came to make us another visit," writes a missionary. "After supper the king related with apparent reserve some of the decisions of the late council against disposing of their land. But in a little while he became quite open and told us plainly that he was afraid of the white people."

"President Washington agreed where the line should be and [said] this should always be the line between the Cherokees and the white people. Soon after there must be another treaty and another line—again another treaty and another line—and so on—always telling them this is the last line."

"He then gave in long detail a long list of murders which had been commited in the nation by the whites, and the murderers not brought to justice. He said that four members of his own family had been murdered [and] that just in that part of the nation where he lived, twelve persons had been murdered by whites since the Creek war, and no murderers killed for it."

"It was not so among Red people," said Pathkiller. "If a person of one nation killed one of another, they always gave up the murderer. And if a Cherokee killed a white man they always gave him up. He knew there were good people among the

426

whites, but knowing all these things as he did, he could not but be afraid of white people."[25]

What Will Be Our Legacy?

The Market Street Bridge is officially named the Chief John Ross Bridge. Congressman Zach Wamp used this bridge as a metaphor for the kind of legacy each individual, each politician, and each generation leaves with the city.

"I draw a lot of energy from their lives and the legacy they believed," he said. "I feel a sense of carrying it forward, and I want to be a part of it. I don't want to get eerie with you, but when I go for an early morning run—as I was reading about Judge Will Cummings' life and I ran by his home—I could feel life. I was experiencing some of what he experienced. I was on the same road. Some of the same trees are there. You feel a real sense of purpose. You feel like your roots are deep in the ground," he said. *Zach* means "one who remembers."

"I'm fascinated by the legacy they left. What will my legacy be? What will our legacy be? When you talk about Cummings building the Market Street Bridge—what is our Market Street Bridge?"

For Wamp, the first thing he names for his own legacy is Moccasin Bend. Since the turn of the century, leaders like Adolph Ochs have worked to preserve this archeological and historical treasure. In 1950, the Bend almost became a national park. However, Governor Frank Clement blocked the initiative in its final stages.

Wamp said he pled with House and Senate leaders to include funding for Moccasin Bend in the 2003 Omnibus Spending Bill. "Senator Frist actually called down on the Senate floor and told them it was okay," said Wamp, who described the victory as "an incredible step forward for our community, for history, and for Native Americans."

The Bend is now a part of the Chickamauga and Chattanooga National Military Park, and, according to Wamp, the only such archeological district in the country. Plans are in place to build a $30 million interpretive center about the Trail of Tears, which crossed over Moccasin Bend, and for water taxis to travel back and forth from downtown Chattanooga.

"Getting an 880-acre national park added right near downtown doesn't happen very often," said Bobby Davenport of Trust for Public Land, who helped with the strategic purchase. "You certainly won't find it in Atlanta."

Davenport, from a prominent Chattanooga family, senses the destiny of the moment. "What is going to happen here will just blow you away."

Wamp agrees. "It's a thrill of a lifetime to be involved in something that will leave a generational legacy and is bigger than us," he said. "I have this vision, ultimately, [of] this amphitheater at the river as it comes underneath Lookout Mountain, and the people will gather there again like they did for literally hundreds and thousands of years—where the mountains and the plains and rivers all come together."

Littlefield's Legacy

Newly elected Mayor Ron Littlefield has also marked out Chattanooga's relationship with the Cherokees as a key part of his legacy. He plans to introduce to the Chattanooga City Council a "Resolution of Repentance" for the city's role in the Trail of Tears. Some have said they are unsure about the word "repentance." Littlefield says the discomfort may be the reason it is just the right word.

"Wrongs have been done," said Littlefield. "I don't think anyone questions that. And somehow there has to be a way to get beyond the breaking of the covenants, the breaking of the treaties. There has to be some sort of forgiveness for that."

The mayor gained much of his inspiration for this need for spiritual reconciliation after attending an event in his Brainerd district while he was chairman of the City Council two years ago.

It was called the "Chattanooga Area Concert of Prayer/Brainerd Concert of Covenant." Littlefield was told a number of Native Americans and out-of-town guests would be in attendance, and there would be prayers, drums, and dancing. He felt he should go since it was an event in his district.

"I was expecting, based on what they had hurriedly explained to me on the phone, that it would be some kind of New Age sort of gathering. . . . I was somewhat cautious about it. My wife and I are religious people. We're Christians, so I didn't tell her where I was going. I took some gifts like we give to visitors—you know, some city pens, a couple of our plates with the city seal on it."

"When I got there, the Native Americans were all carrying Bibles and speaking in very familiar evangelical Christian ways. Growing up and going to movies and watching Roy Rogers and cowboys and Indians, I had kind of a mental disconnect—forgive me, I grew up watching Native Americans badly depicted. But to have them speaking from their Bibles and talking about their Christian testimony, . . . it was a wonderful new experience for me."

Littlefield was also surprised to see pastors of Chattanooga's largest churches—including Woodland Park Baptist's John Meador, City Church of Chattanooga's Pastor Mike Chapman, and Pastor Sean Teal, whose Friendship Community Church hosted the event. Native American attendees included Dr. Nigel

Mayor Ron Littlefield (right) with press secretary Todd Womack.

Bigpond of Tulsa (Yuchi), Jay Swallow of Oklahoma City (Cheyenne Tribe), and Chief Walker Dan Davis of the North Georgia Cherokee Tribe.[26]

Chapman opened in prayer. Music was led by an Indian drum and dance team. "I spoke," said Littlefield. "I didn't pray. The pastors prayed. They gave me an amulet and Nigel Bigpond gave me a name, 'Man with a Friendly Face' or something like that."

"I pointed out that the seal of the city, which was on the pens and the plates I gave them, has a cannon overlooking a drawing depicting Moccasin Bend, which played an important part in the Trail of Tears. I told them I really have no position to issue any kind of official apology, except personally. Personally, I feel like a wrong was done, and they understood that. I forgot exactly what my words were, but I invited them to return, and some of them said they would."

"I stayed much longer than I intended to. I went home and told my wife about it. She was not upset that I went. She was upset that she didn't get to go."

Geronimo Meets Braveheart

The event was organized by Daphne Swilling, who works closely with Bettye Lundquist and other spiritual warfare intercessors mentioned in the earlier chapter on the Bible Belt. "She lives in East Ridge," said Ron. "She's not here all the time. She's either in Ireland or out in Oklahoma or sometimes up in Canada working with tribes. I tell her she's a leprechaun, because she's a missionary of sorts between the Native American tribes and Ireland."

Huh?

"I can assure you its very mainline," Ron said. "Daphne works between Ireland and Native Americans, particularly the Cherokees. The Scotch-Irish were the first to move into this area. Andrew Jackson was Scotch-Irish. They married into Native American families, and then they were the leaders in removing them to a great extent. It's very difficult to understand. Daphne can explain it. Anyway, there are interesting connections and parallels."

It did not sound real mainstream to me. Ron downplayed his role at the prayer ceremony in Brainerd, but, according to Daphne, when Chairman Littlefield welcomed Native American leaders back into the city, "a spiritual dam burst that had been binding up our region for 165 years."

A little research showed that Littlefield is not the only mayor with an interest in the Cherokee–Ireland connection. Irish Mayor Gearoid O'heara of Londonderry welcomed a delegation of Native Americans in November 2004. The event was organized by Daphne Swilling.

"The Mayor said he was honored at being conferred with warrior status by Creek Indian peace chief Nigel Big Pond," reported the *Belfast Telegraph*. "In a speech, [the mayor] compared the annihilation of the Native American culture in the U.S. with the erosion of the Gaelige culture."[27]

Two months later, Daphne and her friends welcomed an Irish statesman to Cherokee country. "The Irish and Cherokee nations celebrated their friendship Monday night with a celebration of their respective cultural traditions," reported the *Asheville Citizen-Times.* "John, The Lord Alderdice, who sits in London's House of Lords and is a former speaker for the Irish Assembly, was guest of honor at the event." Lord Alderdice told the crowd of 450 he was "hugely impressed." The evening included "traditional drumming and bagpipes, kilts and loincloths, and war cries and jigs."[28]

In Ireland, Mr. Bigpond told the *Telegraph* that the Indians were extending a hand of friendship after two centuries of hurt from the Trail of Tears. Swilling and others say the Scotch-Irish were themselves victims of oppression and of land theft by England during their days in Scotland and Ireland, and, like abused children, they found themselves abusing others later.

Bettye Lundquist says the name of Andrew Jackson, whose parents lived near the town visited in Ireland, raises as much rage for Native Americans as any leader of a genocidal movement. "Just as the Holocaust is the ultimate symbol of persecution to all Jews, the Trail of Tears is the symbol of all First Nations' persecution around the world," Lundquist said. Praying in Ireland, they "began to understand how the iniquities behind the Trail of Tears developed through hurting people hurting people in the same way they had been hurt. This made forgiveness, even of Andrew Jackson, much easier."

Daphne said it has been a long and eventful history. "We have come on a journey of goodwill to renew friendships and to build a bridge between the native Indian Americans and the Irish."[29]

(Far left) **Chad "Corn Tassel" Smith**, Principal Chief of the Cherokee Nation, talks with Congressman **Zach Wamp**.

From Silly to Solemn

Such spiritual subtleties were not as front and center when all of Chattanooga's major elected officials met with the two leaders of the Cherokee Nation in May of 2005. In an historic homecoming, these officials dedicated the Passage, an ornate walkway underneath Riverfront Parkway allowing pedestrians to access the river directly.

Chattanooga officials, sensing the spirit of the age, determined to devote the design of this key portion of the 21st Century Waterfront Project to the First Peoples and the Trail of Tears. Seven waterfalls representing the seven Cherokee clans now begin a flowing stream down hundreds of steps to a pool by the river. Artists from the Cherokee Nation in Oklahoma created a visual display, and seven brightly colored six-by-six-foot ancient shell art reproductions now decorate the walls of the celebrated passageway.

During the morning ceremony to dedicate the Passage, the art team director said "a lot of spirits were with us" to help them finish the project in time. In attendance were the city and county mayors, former mayor Bob Corker, and Congressman Wamp. Representing the Cherokees were Oklahoma Chief Chad "Corn Tassel" Smith and Eastern Band Chief Michel Hicks. When I interviewed Smith a year before while conducting research for *America's Trail of Tears*, I learned that some Indians still refuse to use a twenty-dollar bill, the one with Andrew Jackson's picture.

The ceremony at the top of The Passage steps drew a sizable audience. Providentially, a natural amphitheatre formed as many spectators watched from the Market Street Bridge. A hushed, respectful crowd remained quiet for the solemn event.

Unfortunately, the masters of ceremony did not seem to share the sense of solemnity. The emcee was Wes Studi, the famous actor from *Geronimo* and *Last of the Mohicans*. Wearing dark sunglasses, a trendy white suit, and sporting long, jet-black hair, the Hollywood figure peppered the ends of each serious speech with bits from a stand-up comic routine.

"Chattanoogie. What does that mean? Is it like a noogie?" he asked, pulling up his underwear to demonstrate.

Returning to normalcy, Chief Hicks told the children to stand while a prayer was offered. "We are proud to always start with a prayer," he said. This chief wore a brightly colored, long striped shirt, slacks, and Bass Weejuns with tassels. "Take a moment to listen and feel the Cherokee essence," Hicks charged the crowd.

When he was done, Wes Studi, who looked very Indian, explained that he was actually 3/16th Scotch-Irish. "That's why I can save money," he said.

Perhaps Studi was providing satire in response to comments by some of the elected officials regarding their Cherokee blood. It was obvious that the Chattanooga elected officials were not happy with Studi's tone during the ceremony. It did seem unfortunate. Maybe all those prayers for Ireland should have been redirected to Chattanooga.

Next, Chief Smith stepped up to address the crowd. The lawyer and MBA graduate wore a suit, and his tie had letters from the Cherokee alphabet. He held up a facscimile of an 1836 petition with 17,000 signatures, the very petition where nearly the entire Cherokee nation protested the "treaty" which allegedly gave their consent to removal. It was a powerful document.

Wes Studi cracked more Scotch–Irish jokes. "I used to be able to put away a lot of beer," he said. "And Irish whiskey."

A few more comments were made about the tragic events of the Trail of Tears and the terrible actions of Andrew Jackson. Then, just as the event came to a close, Mr. Studi suddenly became very serious.

"I have come to the place where I will forgive," Studi said.

He paused, and the crowd, surprised, listened in rapt attention.

"I won't forget," he said. "But I also won't carry this hatred for a man who did me harm."

Never was a man more serious.

"I'm going to throw it in the river," he said, pointing to the great stream to his left, "and invite others to join me."[30]

Spirit of Removal: 21st Century

While it is appropriate to choose to forgive, history seems to have its own ironic sense of justice. The spirit of removal continues in Chattanooga today, and the people group making the most headway, Latinos, are also Native Americans.

The Walnut Bridge's new color deftly symbolizes the sudden influx of Hispanic peoples into Chattanooga the past decade. Hispanics are now the fastest growing segment of America's population. They were 6.4 percent in 1980, 9 percent by 1990, and in 2000 over 12 percent. Chattanooga's Latino population more than doubled the past decade.[31]

Because of declining birth rates, Western nations will suffer population losses and economic challenges. United Nations projections show a world population increasing to nine billion by 2050, according to Maclellan Foundation executive Dr. Stephen Steele. "The vast majority of that growth takes place in nine nations," he said. "One of those happens to be the United States, but it's the only one that doesn't go through biological growth—they'll be coming from India, Pakistan, Bangladesh, Indonesia, Latin America."[32]

The U.S. Census Bureau reported 5,500 Hispanics in Chattanooga in 2001. But, because of non-reporting, a director of a Chattanooga nonprofit for Latinos estimated the population at closer to 15,000. Based on the rapid rate of growth, the number may have now doubled. More than 11 percent of East Ridge Middle School's children are immigrants or first-generation Americans. According to the principal, the largest number are from Mexico and Guatemala. Seventy-five percent of the membership is Hispanic at the Catholic Church in nearby Dalton, Georgia.[33]

While the Southwest has been the traditional destination for Mexicans, Chattanooga has now become a particular spot of interest. Hispanics now outnumber African Americans as the largest minority in America. Pete Drew, a seasoned black politician, understands the ramifications. "They are coming straight here from Mexico and putting a stake down in Chattanooga," he said. "They're saying, 'This is the center of the universe.'"

Bill Brock likes the megatrend. "The first thing we ought to say to them is, 'Thank you for coming. Hallelujah. Glad to have you.' The second thing we ought to do is require Spanish to be taught in our schools. We are going to be a bilingual country. Let's just admit it and start dealing with it."

"They want a piece of the American dream. They want to grow and prosper and work. They are very, very hard workers, and they are good, good family-oriented people. We ought to be saying, 'Boy, this is a great thing.'"

"We take in more immigrants in the United States every year than all the other nations in the world put together. Isn't that an extraordinary statement? Doesn't that make us at least wonder if that constant infusion of new blood, new vitality, new enthusiasm, new patriotism, new love of family, new love of country is what makes the United States so unique and so very special?"

"Now, if we've got Latinos coming into the country, into Chattanooga, that to me says, 'How quick can we get them into our schools? How quick can we start teaching our kids Spanish so that we respect their language and their culture? How quick can we get them into leadership so that they can make the contribution they are capable of making?' That would be the Chattanooga of my dream."

———◆———

Brock's heart is still in Chattanooga. "I love it. I miss it," he said. But his work in education reform requires him to be near the nation's capital. "That's the world we live in."

He said there really are no words to describe the uniqueness of Chattanooga. "There is a substance about the spirit of Chattanooga. There is a depth and an integrity and a character that is different. It's not that we're better people. But there is a soul there that encourages people to do those things that make a difference for others. And that, I think, is really what life is all about."

Zach Wamp gives a similar assessment. "This is a city that gives more than it takes, a city that has turned the corner from the heavy manufacturing past to a clean, technology-driven manufacturing and distribution center with an incredible future."

"But, in large part, it's because of the commitments, the dedication over the years, the perseverance over the years of these families. It's had a huge impact."

Thanks to my early interview with Scotty Probasco, I was able to glean quite a bit of insight about those old Chattanooga families and then get the others to grant interviews following his lead. Probasco and I chatted for over three hours that day.

"I've really enjoyed this interview, and I really appreciate your work," I told him.

"You haven't learned a damn thing."

I assured him otherwise.

"Well, I'll tell you something," he said. "I just came back from a seven-day cruise in the Baltic with my wife. This is our fiftieth anniversary year, and she conned me into going on that cruise. I didn't really want to go."

"But, you know, it was the most interesting thing. We were in five different countries. We'd get off the boat and go ashore. They had the old city and it was over 900 years old with walls and all the history."

"And then we went into St. Petersburg in Russia. They built those palaces. And then we were in Sweden, a clean country, and Denmark is beautiful, and then we were in Finland."

"But it really made me think. I found myself sitting out on that boat praying and saying, 'Thank you, Lord, for letting me live in Chattanooga and in the good old USA.' . . . We are so blessed to be here. We're the microcosm, I think, of everything good and everything bad in the United States—right here in Chattanooga."

"I see my kids coming and my grandkids coming now. They're growing up. [And] I go back 90 years ago—a hundred years ago—and my grandfather was hauling up my father in a little cart up Signal Mountain. Think of the changes in that time. I mean, you wonder. What's the next hundred years going to produce? Boy, it's a great question. And that's when I say, 'Thank you, Lord. Because it's in your hands.'"

ACKNOWLEDGMENTS

Twenty years of key relationships, high idealism, vision, and risk taking (thanks to the help of many supportive friends) provided the soil from which this book emerged. My mother is at the top of this list, and I want to thank her and all the other mothers who have labored for hours to create wonderful meals that are thanklessly devoured in a few minutes. This book takes a few hours to read but took an entire year to write, along with two more years of research.

The effort was funded by scores of financial supporters. The first check was written in 2001 and provided the springboard for future success. This donor, a descendent of John Kruesi, is not a figure in the book, but several interviewees did contribute to the project.

Excellent content from important books can be credited to those who recommended them. Larry Wells suggested *For God, Country and Coca-Cola*, Betty Lundquist, *The Brainerd Journal*, and Stephanie Shankles, the *Chattanooga Cook Book*. Bill Schultz has served Chattanooga for decades as an extraordinary private librarian, and the clippings and books he provided were invaluable. Thanks also to the staff at the local history department of the Chattanooga-Hamilton County Bicentennial Library—Jim, Karen, Suzette, April and Mary—and to Bill and Gail at the Chattanooga Regional History Museum.

John Wilson deserves special mention as the indomitable researcher of Chattanooga history. For years, I used his content on *Chattanoogan.com* to write stories for the *Chattanooga Fax*. It seemed almost unfair that I could take his reams of hard work and piece together short articles that captured the public's imagination. This book is a repeat of that phenomenon; several of his books provided the foundation for the story of *Old Money, New South*. John has a pesky habit of not citing his sources, but I have never found a single fact to be unreliable. He is quite low-key in person, but behind that deadpan delivery is a great sense of humor for those experienced at reading his material. Ultimately, only paper will outlive us, and the soft-spoken John Wilson will roar in our city's history.

My favorite Chattanooga historian, however, is Zella Armstrong. Students of local history often roll their eyes at the mention of "Miss Zella," but I have always been enchanted with her work. She has a knack for choosing the most interesting material, and she always discusses the question you most want to ask. She died about the time I was born, and I truly regret that that our destinies did not cross.

It would be impossible to thank all of those who helped in some way. Many of those are mentioned in the text itself and will not be named here. Carolyn Talley faithfully typed nearly fifty interview transcripts. Karen Zylstra provided a great deal of supporting research. Jason Luther helped with currency equivalents. Todd Bickerstaff inspired the idea of enhancing the storyline through making the author/interviewer a character. Early readers with excellent suggestions included Andrea, Sember, and Stephanie. Buck Roebuck and Jim Gilliland provided significant encouragement with logistics.

Jared Brewer served as an editor of sorts, and his differing ideology and literary acumen were most helpful. He also did me the favor of striking a number redundant lines and obvious connections so I might appear less like the guy who repeats his bad jokes. For nearly twenty years, Dan Bockert has added professionalism, style, and accuracy to my writing and did so again as my typesetter and proofreader. His many hours of labor as the deadline approached were offered up because of his friendship to me and his love for excellence in publishing, and I am truly grateful. Thanks also to Eric, Perk, and Roger, my Macintosh mentors, and to Rob Tipton, a childhood mate, whose cover and design work added masterful touches to the text.

The manuscript was written in its entirety from the foot of Lookout Mountain, at the edge of the woods, with an excellent view of the Point. This location can be credited to Kevin Whitmore, a friend since we were nine.

A host of supportive friends are responsible for the author being sane enough to write today. I will provide a few monikers with the unfortunate certainty that some have been unwittingly omitted: Mick, Tracy, Phil, Tony, Bennett, Robert and Bobbie, Frank, Krue, Ham, Marshall, Paul, Pete, Brian, Father Stephen, Larry and Jane, Mark, Brian, Arny, Lubelski, Travis and Kimberly, Bryant and Ashley, Cheryl, Hattie, Todd and Sara, Cliff and Debbie, Lindsay and Christine, Tom and Becky, Barry and Becky, Bill Nelson, and Dorothy.

Several others were key in shaping or empowering my early career in politics, activism, and the *Chattanooga Fax*, including Charlie Wysong, Ole Hansen, Chris Clem, Bob Bibee, Jonathan Rummel, Garry Mac, and Mike Mahn. The art of writing can only be accomplished after years of unacknowledged labor by teachers such as Ray Clark, Ralph Knight, Carol Yosafat, and Richard Poindexter.

The earliest seeds of this book were planted two decades before when several close friends met regularly on High Street to pray for this unusual city. I will be forever grateful to Hal and Susanne, Gayle, Gussie and Paulie Chan, and Patrick.

Andy Mendonsa, who has been a similar visionary and also an encourager of my writing, lost a beautiful daughter the year this book was written. Hadrienne was 19.

My father died the same year. While preaching in Orlando on his favorite verse, "For to me, to live is Christ and to die is gain," he talked about being ready to go. "And when I go to heaven . . ." were his last words before he died instantly of a heart attack and fell to the ground. The story made the *AP Wire*, *CNN,* and even Paul Harvey. Like the rest of us, he was flawed and human—a complex mixture of failure and idealism. But his strong finish was one for the ages.

This book is dedicated to him.

Dean W. Arnold

PICTURE CREDITS

The large majority of photos in this book were acquired from the Local History and Genealogy section of the Chattanooga–Hamilton County Bicentennial Library and from several books published by Roy McDonald of the *Chattanooga Free Press* (and provided for use by *Chattanooga Times Free Press* Publisher Tom Griscom).

Pictures by current photographers such as Doug Barnette and Vincent Rizzo are generally credited beside the photos themselves. The publisher has attempted to acknowledge every photo where appropriate and regrets any unforeseen omissions.

Some photos are not credited, such as those provided by the family or those owned and/or taken by the author. Unless credited in the book next to the picture itself, the remaining photos are credited below:

7 Chattanooga–Hamilton County Bicentennial Library (CHCBL)

12 J. T. Lupton: CHCBL

  H. S. Probasco: CHCBL

  Jack Lupton: Golf House of Tennessee

  Scotty Probasco: Doug Barnette, Chattanooga, TN

14 Walter Williams: *Chattanooga Times Free Press*

16 Antique collection of Dorothy Farmer

18 River City Company

20 RiverCity Company

28 Cooper, David, *Catalyst for Christ.* Chattanooga News-Free Press, 1990.

34 E. Y. Chapin: CHCBL

38 Exum, Helen, *Chattanooga Cook Book.* Chattanooga News-Free Press, 1970.

44 Divine, Sam, *Wit and Wisdom of Sam Divine.* Chattanooga News-Free Press, 1986.

  James Whiteside: CHCBL

48 Thomas Crutchfield: CHCBL

  Tom Crutchfield: CHCBL

  William Crutchfield: Wilson, John, *Chattanooga's Story. Chatt. News-Free Press*, 1980.

50 Crutchfield House: CHCBL

52 Samuel Williams: CHCBL

57 David Key: CHCBL

69 Hiram Tyree: "Biography and Acheivements of the Colored Citizens of Chattanooga," 1904.

72 Cartter Lupton: Wilson, John, *The Patten Chronicle. Chattanooga News-Free Press.*

82 T. H. McCallie: CHCBL

84 Two soldiers: CHCBL

  Moc Bend and NY Monument: CHCBL

98 Summerfield and Mary Key: CHCBL

Inserted picture pages:

BIBLIOGRPHY

The key sources for this book are the many interviews conducted over a three year period. Each interview was recorded and a transcription of the interview remains in the possession of the Chattanooga Historical Foundation. Several conversations by phone and in-person were also used as sources and are cited in the endnotes.

Interviews

Anderson, Lee

Barnes, Marion

Brock, Frank

Brock III, William E. (Bill)

Chambliss, Jac

Chapin, Bill

Cooper, Pete

Corker, Bob

Crutchfield, Ward

Daugherty, Doug

Decosimo, Fred

Descosimo, Tom

Drew, Charles (Pete)

Elder, George

Evans, Raymond

Fowler, David

Holmberg, Ruth

Hurley, Mai Bell

Ingle, Larry

Jennings, Lurone

Johnston, Summerfield K. Jr.

Littlefield, Ron

Livingood, James

Lundquist, Bettye

Lupton, Thomas A. Jr. (Tommy)

Maclellan, Hugh O. Jr.

McCallie, Allen

McCallie, David

McCallie, Spencer III

McCallie, Thomas Hooke III (Tom)

McWhirter, Lee

Montague, Rick

Murrah, Jack

Probasco, Scott L. Jr. (Scotty)

Roberson, Lee

Roberts, Dalton

Roberts, Gene

Smartt, Sam

Smith, Chad "Corn Tassel"

Vail, Ron

Wamp, Louie

Wamp, Zach

Waterhouse, Albert

Watson, Stroud

Williams, Walter

Primary Sources, Special Collections

Although the author consulted various special collections, including some in other states, a large portion of the primary sources examined are housed in the manuscript collections of the Chattanooga–Hamilton County Bicentennial Library on the Third Floor: Genealogy and Local History. This department also collects a vast number of clipping files on many subjects. These files were a major source for the book and are cited in the endnotes by specific newspaper article. The following is only a partial listing of primary sources consulted:

Allen, Penelope Johnson. *Genealogy of a Branch of the Johnson Family and Connections*, Helen Betts Miller, pub, 1967.

Allen, Penelope Johnson. *History of the Cherokees*. Chattanooga: Unpublished manuscript, 1935, Manuscript collections, Local History Department, Chattanooga–Hamilton County Bicentennial Library.

Allen, Penelope Johnson. *Leaves from the Family Tree*. Southern Historical Press c/o The Rev. S. Emmett Lucas Jr, Easley, SC.

Ballew, Bennet. "To the President of the United States of America; the memorial of Bennet Ballew," American State Papers. Vol. IV.

Divine, Mary. "Mary Divine's Story of Wartimes." Neil Family Papers, Blythewood Farm, Cleveland, TN.

Elder, George S II. Speech to Elder Mountain Garden Club. April 30, 1995.

Fiftieth Confederate Anniversary Scrapbook. Manuscript Collection, Local History Department, Chattanooga–Hamilton County Bicentennial Library.

First Presbyterian Church of Chattanooga, Minutes. Microfilm, Local History Department, Chattanooga–Hamilton County Bicentennial Library.

Gardenhire Family Papers. Todd Gardenhire's office. Chattanooga, TN.

Hyde, Anne Bachman. Scrapbook. Manuscript Collections, Local History Department, Chattanooga–Hamilton County Bicentennial Library.

Layman, Elizabeth Waterhouse. *Richard Green Waterhouse*. Missouri City, TX, 1996.

Johnston-Key Family Scrapbook, Bendabout Farms, McDonald, TN.

John Ross Papers, Special Collections, Gilcrease Museum of History and Art, Tulsa, OK.

Neil, Elizabeth Mayfield. Private Papers. Blythewood Farms, Cleveland, TN.

Maclellan, Thomas. *Thomas Maclellan's Covenant with God.* Maclellan Foundation, Chattanooga, TN.

McCallie, Rev. T.H., 1837-1912. *An Early Family Record: The McCallie Family in Tennessee. An Autobiographical Sketch.* Catherine McCallie Johnson and James Park McCallie, eds., 1958-59, Corrections and additions made Aug. 30, 1965,. Manuscript Collections, Local History Department, Chattanooga–Hamilton County Bicentennial Library.

Pearson, Abel. *An Analysis of the Principles of Divine Government.* Athens, TN, 1833, Manuscript Collections, Local History Department, Chattanooga–Hamilton County Bicentennial Library.

"Rotary Defined," by Thomas Spencer McCallie, 1922-23, Chattanooga Rotary office.

Smartt family papers. Family summary by Kennedy Smartt.

Schultz, W. C. Personal library and archives of Chattanooga history. 103 South Moore Rd, Chattanooga, TN.

Summerfield Key Johnston Sr., Interview, Oral History Project,. Manuscript Collection, Local History Department, Chattanooga–Hamilton County Bicentennial Library.

Wiltse, Henry M. *History of Chattanooga.* Unpublished manuscript, 1916. Manuscript Collections, Local History Department, Chattanooga–Hamilton County Bicentennial Library.

Woodruff File. Personal papers of Dean Woodruff Arnold.

Worcester-Robertson Family Papers, Manuscript Division, University of Tulsa Library.

Newspapers, Periodicals, News Programs

Asheville Citizen-Times

Atlanta Journal-Constitution

Belfast Telegraph

Catholic-Forum.org

Chattanooga Fax

Chattanooga Free Press

Chattanooga News

Chattanooga News-Free Press

Chattanooga Pulse

Chattanooga Times

Chattanooga Times Free Press

<Chattanoogan.com>

Christian Science Monitor

Cityscope

Civil War Times

Crisis Magazine

Forbes

Hamilton Gazette

Intercessors for Chattanooga

The Lookout

Los Angeles Times

Lookout Mountain Mirror

Metrovoice.net

National Public Radio

New York Times

Newsweek

Online Encyclopedia

Parade

Philanthropy Roundtable

Reason Magazine

Time

U.S. News & World Report

Vision Chattanooga

Washington Times

Books, Articles, Documentaries

12 Days in Dayton: The Scopes Monkey Trial. WTCI, Channel 45, Video Documentary, 2001.

Allem, Warren. "Backgrounds of the Scopes Trial at Dayton. Tennessee." Thesis. University of Tennessee, 1959.

Armstrong, Zella. *History of the First Presbyterian Church of Chattanooga,* Lookout Publishing Co., 1945.

——*The History of Hamilton County and Chattanooga, Tennessee.* (Two volumes.) Chattanooga: Lookout Publishing Co., 1940.

Arnold, Dean W. *America's Trail of Tears: a story of love and betrayal.* Chattanooga Historical Foundation, 2005.

——*Fighting Scots: A History of the American Spirit.* Unpublished manuscript: PO Box 2053; Chattanooga, TN 37409, 1997.

Baird, James. *Thunder Over Scotland.* Campbell, CA, Greenleaf, 1982.

Bass, Dorothy C. "Gideon Blackburn's Mission to the Cherokees: Christianization and Civilization," *Journal of Presbyterian History*, Fall 1974.

The Bible. New International Version.

Bolton, Herbert. *The Spanish Borderlands: a chronicle of old Florida and the Southwest.* New Haven: Yale University Press, 1921.

Bourne, Edward Gaylord, ed. *Narratives of the career of Hernando De Soto in the Conquest of Florida as told by a Knight of Elvas.* New York: A.S. Barnes and Co., 1904.

Brown, Lloyd Arnold. *Early Maps of the Ohio Valley.* University of Pittsburgh Press, 1959.

Fite, Emerson D, ed. *A book of old maps dileneating American History from the earliest days to the close of the Revolutionary War.* New York: Dover Publications, 1969.

Bradley, Norman and Frances, eds. *Lookout Mountain: A Place and Its People.* Chattanooga: Lookout Mountain Committee, 1986.

Buchanan, Patrick J. *The Death of the West: How Dying Populations and Immigration Invasions Imperil our Country and Civilization.* New York: St. Martin's Press, 2002.

Bunnell, Gene. *Making Places Special.* American Planning Association, 2003.

Butrick, Daniel S. *The Journal of Rev. Daniel S. Butrick*. Park Hill, OK: Trail of Tears Association, Oklahoma Chapter, 1998.

Carson, Clarence B. *A Basic History of the United States: The Welfare State, 1929-1985*. Wadlee, AL: American Textbook Committee, 1986.

Chandler, William U. *The Myth of TVA: Conservation and Development in the Tennessee Valley, 1933-1983*. Cambridge, MA: Ballinger, 1984.

"Chattanooga Rotary in the 1990s." Channel 3 WRCB, Dec 30, 1999.

Cooper, David. *Catalyst for Christ: 150 Years. First Presbyterian Church, Chattanooga, Tennessee*. Chattanooga: Chattanooga News-Free Press, 1990.

Council, R. Bruce: Principal investigator, Nick Honerkamp. *Ross's Landing at Chattanooga: a cultural resource*. Jeffery L. Brown Institute of Archeology, University of Tennessee at Chattanooga, 1989.

Curriden, Mark and Leroy Phillips, Jr. *Contempt of court: the turn-of-the-century lynching that launched 100 years of federalism*. New York: Faber & Faber, 1999.

Davies, Mervyn. *Presbyterian Heritage*. Richmond: John Knox Press, 1965.

Douglas, J.D. *Light in the North: The Story of the Scottish Covenanters*. Grand Rapids: Eerdmans, 1964.

Davis, William C. *Jefferson Davis: The Man and His Hour*. New York: HarperCollins, 1991.

Divine, Sam. *The Wit and Wisdom of Sam Divine*. Thomas McCallie Divine, ed. Chattanooga: Chattanooga News-Free Press, 1986.

Evans, Raymond, ed. *Chattanooga's African American Legacy*. Chattanooga African American Museum, 2003.

——"The Napochin Chiefdom of the 16th Century." Unpublished paper.

Exum, Helen McDonald. *The Chattanooga Cook Book*. Chattanooga: Chattanooga News-Free Press, 1970.

Falwell, Jerry, ed., The Fundamentalist Phenomenon. Garden City: Doubleday, 1981.

Frierson, Cartter. "History of Lookout Mt. Presbyterian Church." <www. lmpc>org.

Frist William H. and Shirley Baldwin. *Good People Beget Good People: A Genealogy of the Frist Family*. Rowman & Littlefield Publishers, Nov. 1, 2003.

Gaston, Kay Barker. "The Remarkable Harriet Whiteside." Tennessee Historical Quarterly, Winter 1981.

"George Gillespie: 1613-1648: Biographical Sketch," A Puritan's Mind, <www.apuritansmind.com>

Govan, Gilbert E. and James W. Livingood. *The Chattanooga Country 1540-1951: From Tomahawks to TVA*. New York: E.P. Dutton & Company, Inc., 1952.

Hanks, Patrick, ed. *Dictionary of American Family Names*. New York and Oxford: Oxford University Press, 2003.

Hazard, George Jr. *When We Came to the Ridge: part one of the history of the McCallie School, 1905-1937*. Chattanooga: The McCallie School, 1991.

Hitt, James E. *It Never Rains After Three O'Clock: A History of the Baylor School*. Chattanooga: Baylor School Press, 1971.

Hudson, Charles. *The Juan Pardo Expeditions: explorations of the Carolinas and Tennessee, 1566-1568*. Washington: Smithsonian Institution Press, 1990.

——*Knights of Spain, Warriors of the Sun: Hernando de Soto and the South's Ancient Chiefdoms*. Athens: University of Georgia Press, 1997.

——"A Spanish-Coosa Alliance in Sixteenth Century North Georgia," *Georgia Historical Quarterly*. Vol. 72, 1988.

Hodge, Frederick Webb. *Handbook of American Indians North of Mexico*, Bureau of American Ethnology, Bulletin 30, parts 1 and 2, Government Printing Office, Washington, 1907 & 1912.

Howie, John. *Lives of the Scottish Covenanters*. Greenville, SC: A Press, 1981.

Hulbert, Archer Butler. *Historic Highways of America*. Vol. 1. Cleveland, OH: Arthur Clark Co., 1902.

Irwin, Ned, "Bottling Gold." *Tennessee Historical Quarterly*, Winter 1992.

Johnson, Paul. *A History of the American People*. New York: HarperPerennial, 1998.

Kernfield, Barry, ed. *New Grove Dictionary of Jazz*. Oxford University Press, 1994.

Kirk, Russell. *The Roots of American Order*. Washington, D.C.: Regnery, 1999.

Knox, John. *John Knox's History of the Reformation in Scotland*. William Croft Dickenson, ed., New York: Philosophical Library, 1950.

Leyburn, James G. *The Scotch-Irish: a social history*. Chapel Hill: University of North Carolina Press, 1962.

Livesay, Harold. *Andrew Carnegie and the Rise of Big Business*. Boston: Little, Brown & Co., 1975.

Livingood, James W., Norman O. Burns and Patrice H. Glass. *Chattanooga: An Illustrated History*. Sun Valley Press: American Historical Press, 2001.

Livingood, James W. "Chattanooga's Crutchfields and the Famous Crutchfield House." *Civil War Times*, November 1981.

——*A History of Hamilton County, Tennessee*. Memphis State University Press, 1981.

Longwith, John. *Castle on a Cliff: A History of Baylor School*. Chattanooga: Baylor School, 1994.

——*Provident: A Centennial History*. Chattanooga: Provident Life & Accident Insurance Company, 1986.

Martin, Martha Gaither. *The Chattanooga News-Free Press*. Chattanooga: Published by Roy McDonald, 1981.

Martine, Roderick. *Scottish clan and family names: their arms, origins, and tartans*. Edinburgh: J. Bartholomew & Son, 1987.

McCallie, Eleanor Cooper. *Grace in China: An American Woman Beyond the Great Wall. 1934-1974*. Black Belt Press, Montgomery, 1999.

McCallie, Eleanor Grace. *Don't Say "You," Say "We:" The Founding of Girl's Preparatory School*. Chattanooga, TN, 1982.

McCrumb, Sharyn, "The First Appalachian Journey," *Appalachian Voice*, Late Winter, 2005.

McLoughlin, William. *Cherokees and Missionaries, 1789-1839*. New Haven and London: Yale University Press, 1984.

——*Cherokee Renascence in the New Republic*. Princeton, NJ: Princeton University Press, 1986.

——"The Mystery Behind Parson Blackburn's Whiskey," *Cherokee Ghost Dance: Essays on the Southeastern Indians*. Macon, GA: Mercer, 1984.

Mooney, James, "The Cherokee River Cult," *The Journal of American Folk-Lore*. Vol. XIII, Jan-March, 1900.

——*Myths of the Cherokee*. Bureau of American Ethnology 19th Annual Report, Government Printing Office, Washngton, 1900.

Moulton, Gary, *John Ross: Cherokee Chief*. Athens, GA, 1978.

Pendergrast, Mark. *For God, Country and Coca-Cola: The Unauthorized History of the Great American Drink and the Company that Makes It*. New York: Charles Scribner's Sons, 1993.

Phillips, Joyce B. and Paul Gary Phillips, eds. *The Brainerd Journal: A Mission to the Cherokees, 1817-1823*. Lincoln: University of Nebraska Press, 1998.

Potts, Nancy J., " Unfilled Expectations: The Erosion of Black Political Power in Chattanooga, 1865-1911." *Tennessee Historical Quarterly*, Summer 1990.

Roberts, Dalton. *Kickstarts: Common Sense and Uncommon Wisdom on Life, Loving, Friendship, Faith, Health, Politics, and Paying the Bills*. Chattanooga: Phase II: Publications, 1997.

Smith, Marvin T. *Coosa: The Rise and Fall of a Southeastern Mississippian Chiefdom*. Gainesville: University Press of Florida, 2000.

Stone, Irving. *Clarence Darrow for the Defense: A Biography*. New York: Doubleday, 1941.

Swanton, John. *Early History of the Creek Indians and their Neighbors*. Smithsonian Institution, Bureau of American Ethnology, Bulletin 73. Washington: Government Printing Office, 1922.

——*The Indians of the Southeastern United States*. Bureau of American Ethnology, Bulletin 137, Government Printing Office, Washington, 1946.

Thomas, Lewis. *The Prehistory of the Chickamauga Basin in Tennessee*. Knoxville: University of Tennessee Press, 1995.

Tifft, Susan E. and Alex S. Jones. *The Trust: The Private and Powerful Family Behind the New York Times*. Boston, New York and London: Little and Brown Company, 1999.

Van West, Carroll, ed. *The Tennessee Encyclopedia of History & Culture*. Nashville: Rutledge Hill Press, 1998.

Walker, Robert Sparks. *Torchlights to the Cherokees*, Johnson City, TN: The Overmountain Press, 1931.

Wall, Joseph Frazier. *Andrew Carnegie*. University of Pittsburgh Press, 1970.

Wilkins, Thurman. *Cherokee Tragedy: The Ridge Family and the Decimation of a People*. Norman and London: University of Oklahoma Press, 1970.

Wilson, John, *Chattanooga's Story*. Chattanooga: Chattanooga News-Free Press, 1980.

—— *Early Hamilton Settlers*. Chattanooga: Sheridan Books, 2001.

—— *The Kruesi-Smartt Legacy*. Adams Lithographic Company, Chattanooga, 1996.

—— *Hamilton County Pioneers*. Michigan: BookCrafters, 1998.

——*The Patten Chronicle*. Chattanooga: Published by Roy McDonald, Undated.

ENDNOTES

CHAPTER ONE ENDNOTES - THE SPIRIT OF THE FATHERS

[1] For detailed commentary on the meaning of Chattanooga, see Chapter 11; "Mountains looking at each other" originally cited by Missionary Elias Cornelius, "Tour in Virginia, etc., etc., etc.," in Phillips, *New Voyages and Travels* III, 103; Henry M. Wiltse, *History of Chattanooga*, Unpublished manuscript, 1916, (Manuscript Collections, Local History Department, Chattanooga–Hamilton County Bicentennial Library), p. 3–6. Regarding "Experts generally discount the theory": Author's conversations with Nick Honerkamp, UTC Professor of Anthropology and taped interview with Raymond Evans, anthropologist. Dec. 2004. On Cherokees unaware of Chattanooga's meaning, see Wiltse, *History of Chattanooga*, p. 4.

[2] Helen McDonald Exum, *Chattanooga Cook Book* (Chattanooga: *Chattanooga News-Free Press,* 1970), p. 17, 22 (hereafter cited as *Cook Book*).

[3] "Coke Sold—$1.4 Billion," *Chattanooga News-Free Press*, July 1, 1986; Paul Neely, "Man behind The Honors," *Chattanooga Times*, Aug. 20, 1991; "Lupton Challenges City On Its Future," *Chattanooga Times*, Aug. 28, 1988; "Jack Lupton talks about a city and its destiny," *Chattanooga Times*, Jan. 27, 1986.

[4] "Powerful People," *Chattanooga News-Free Press*, May 15, 1988.

[5] *Chattanooga Fax*, Feb. 22, 1999.

[6] Ironically, both words are basically misleading. Coca-Cola no longer has any coca and "OK" stood for "All Correct," a facetious marking, purposely misspelled, by Boston newspaper editors to approve a piece of writing <Dictionary.com>. Ned Irwin, "Bottling Gold," *Tennessee Historical Quarterly*, Winter 1992, p. 226–228; Mark Pendergrast, *For God, Country and Coca-Cola: The Unauthorized History of the Great American Drink and the Company that Makes It* (New York: Charles Scribner's Sons, 1993), p. 10, 75 (hereafter cited as *For God, Country and Coca-Cola*); John Wilson, *Chattanooga's Story* (Chattanooga: *Chattanooga News-Free Press,* 1980), p. 284.

[7] Irwin, "Bottling Gold," p, 228, 236; "Building for the Future for 75 Years," American National Bank special publication, 1986, American National Bank Clipping File (Local History Department, Chattanooga–Hamilton County Bicentennial Library).

[8] *Chattanooga Times*, Oct. 22, 1962; Author's taped interview with Scott L. Probasco, Jr.; "In Work and Play, Scott Probasco Jr. is Right Up Front Leading the Cheers," *Chattanooga Times*, July 8, 1982.

[9] These comments taken from author's recorded interview with Scott L. Probasco, Jr. All quotes from persons interviewed for this book (see list in Bibliography) should be assumed as part of the recorded interview unless otherwise noted.

[10] David Cooper, *Catalyst for Christ: 150 Years. First Presbyterian Church, Chattanooga, Tennessee* (Chattanooga: Chattanooga *News-Free* Press, 1990), p. 313, 315 (hereafter cited as *Catalyst for Christ*).

[11] Zella Armstrong, *The History of Hamilton County and Chattanooga, Tennessee* (Chattanooga: Lookout Publishing Co., 1940), Vol. I, p. 354 (hereafter cited as *Hamilton County*); Cooper, *Catalyst for Christ*, p. 317; *An Early Family Record: The McCallie Family in Tennessee. An Autobiographical Sketch*, by Rev. T. H. McCallie, D.D. (1837–1912), Catherine McCallie Johnson and James Park McCallie, eds., 1958–59 (Manuscript Collections, Local History Department, Chattanooga–Hamilton County Bicentennial Library), p. 2 (hereafter cited as *Early Family Record*).

[12] Wilson, *Chattanooga's Story*, p. 342; John Wilson, *The Patten Chronicle* (Chattanooga: Published by Roy McDonald, Undated), p. 82–83, 87-89 (hereafter cited as *Patten*); Irwin, p. 235.

[13] Wilson, *Patten*, p. 91–92; Wilson, *Chattanooga's Story*, p. 416.

[14] Exum, *Cook Book*, p. 115–116.

[15] James L. Livingood, Norman O. Burns, and Patrice H. Glass, *Chattanooga: An Illustrated History* (Sun Valley Press: American Historical Press, 2001), p. 153; "The Reborn American City—A Place You Might Want to Live," *Parade Magazine*, April 1999.

[16] Armstrong, *Hamilton County*, Vol. II, p. 182.

[17] *Cityscope* magazine, May 1999.

[18] Livingood, Burns, and Glass, *Chattanooga: An Illustrated History*, p. 155, 157, 163; *U.S. News & World Report*, June 8, 1998.

[19] "Morning Edition," National Public Radio, Feb. 20, 2001.

[20] "Jack Lupton talks about a city and its destiny," *Chattanooga Times*, Jan. 27, 1986; *Cityscope* magazine, May 1999; Livingood, Burns, and Glass, *Chattanooga: An Illustrated History*, p. 175.

[21] *The Tennessee Encyclopedia of History & Culture*, Carroll Van West, ed. (Nashville: Rutledge Hill Press, 1998), p. 141.

[22] "A foundation for city's renewal," *Chattanooga Times Free Press*, Dec. 24, 2000; "Top Ten Foundations in Chattanooga," *Chattanooga Fax*, Nov. 22, 1999.

[23] Quote from *Philanthropy*, July/August, 2005. Other facts on Maclellan Foundation taken from transcribed interview with Hugh O. Maclellan, Jr. and staff on July 25, 2005.

[24] Author's conversation with Chris Maclellan.

[25] The author interviewed Maclellan, but all these quotes actually come from an interview in *Philanthropy Roundtable*, July 2001, and a speech by Maclellan, posted on the Maclellan Foundation website, given March 1–3, 2001, at the annual Generous Giving Conference in Phoenix. <http://www.maclellan.net>

[26] "Thomas Maclellan's Lifetime Covenant With God," June 7, 1857. Document acquired from Maclellan Foundation, Chattanooga, TN.

[27] All name meanings in this book, unless otherwise noted, from *Dictionary of American Family Names*, Patrick Hanks, ed. (New York and Oxford: Oxford University Press, 2003); <http://Catholic-Forum.com>

[28] "Closing the Marriage Gap," *Crisis Magazine*, June 9, 2002.

[29] Anecdote on returned $20,000 check from author's conversation with Henry Henegar, Chattanooga Christian Community Foundation; Cooper, *Catalyst for Christ*, p. 48.

[30] "George Gillespie," *LoveToKnow 1911 Online Encyclopedia*. 2003, 2004.

[31] *Laws of the Cherokee Nation* (Tahlequah: Cherokee Nation, 1952), p. 18–125, cited in William McLoughlin, *Cherokee Renascence in the New Republic* (Princeton, NJ: Princeton University Press, 1986), p. 396.

[32] John Wilson, *Early Hamilton Settlers* (Chattanooga: Sheridan Books, 2001), p. 313–314; *The Brainerd Journal: A Mission to the Cherokees, 1817–1823*, Joyce B. Phillips and Paul Gary Phillips, eds. (Lincoln: University of Nebraska Press, 1998), p. xix, 39, 133, 138–39, 181, 300–301, 461 (hereafter cited as Phillips, *Brainerd Journal*).

[33] "City grounded in faith," *Chattanooga Times*, Oct. 15, 1998.

[34] "A Civic Vignette: The Chattanooga Story—From Troubled Raw River Town to Global Model," The Academy of Leadership, University of Maryland, 1998–2003; "Chattanooga's Economic History," <chattanoogafun. com>, Chattanooga Area Convention and Visitors Bureau, Aug. 4, 2003; Lupton Wants to Make City Stadium Reality," *Chattanooga Free Press*, Feb. 5, 1995.

[35] "Chattanooga Pay Below U.S. Average," *Chattanooga Times Free Press*, Feb. 16, 2002; "Suburban growth ourstrips city," *Chattanooga Times*, Oct. 28, 1998; "City Strives to Balance "Smart Growth" w/ Market Growth," *Chattanooga Fax*, April 28, 2003; "Rutherford Takes on Power Structure," *Chattanooga Times*, April 18, 2000.

[36] "Local Leaders Got A Big Fish But It Slipped Off the Hook," *Chattanooga Fax*, Dec. 2, 2003. The author learned from other sources that the big fish was Toyota.

[37] "City Strives…"

[38] Irwin, p. 224; Wilson, *Chattanooga's Story*, p. 229; Wilson, *Chattanooga's Story*, p. 231.

[39] Irwin, op. cit.

[40] Ibid.

[41] "Probasco, Chapin Recount Benwood History," <Chattanoogan.com>, May 20, 2004.

[42] According to a history of the Patten family, Lupton was able to invest in Coke because he "made substantial earnings at the medicine company" and his wife "gained an early share of her father's medicine company fortune." Wilson, *Patten*, p. 82.

[43] James W. Livingood, *A History of Hamilton County, Tennessee* (Memphis State University Press, 1981), p. 472 (hereafter cited as *Hamilton County*).

[44] Armstrong, *Hamilton County*, p. 247; Wilson, *Chattanooga's Story* p. 168.

[45] Gilbert E. and James W. Livingood, *The Chattanooga Country 1540–1951: From Tomahawks to TVA* (New York: E. P. Dutton & Company, Inc., 1952), p. 287 (hereafter cited as *Chattanooga Country*).

[46] Govan, p. 329, 349; Armstrong, op cit., Vol. II, p. 93; Author's conversation with Michael Golden, New York, May 5, 2003; Govan, p. 318.

[47] Govan, *Chattanooga Country*, p. 171; James W. Livingood, "Chattanooga's Crutchfields and the Famous Crutchfield House," *Civil War Times*, November 1981 (hereafter cited as "Crutchfield House").

[48] Govan, *Chattanooga Country*, p. 172, 287.

[49] Livingood, *Hamilton County*, p. 245–6.

[50] Ibid., p. 213.

[51] Exum, *Cook Book,* p. 51–52.

[52] Wiltse, *History of Chattanooga*, p. 29; "Proposals," p. 2, *Hamilton Gazette*, Volume 1, Number Two, July, 26, 1838 (Manuscript Collections, Local History Department, Chattanooga–Hamilton County Bicentennial Library).

[53] Livingood, op. cit., p. 103; Paul Johnson, *A History of the American People* (New York: HarperPerennial, 1998), p. 290.

[54] Armstrong, op. cit., p. 288–291; Daniel S. Butrick, *The Journal of Rev. Daniel S. Butrick* (Park Hill, OK: Trail of Tears Association, Oklahoma Chapter, 1998), p. 6, 10, 26. Camp Cherokee was located on the current site of Chattanooga School for the Arts and Sciences, near Erlanger and the UTC McKenzie Arena.

[55] William H. Frist and Shirley Baldwin, *Good People Beget Good People: A Genealogy of the Frist Family* (Rowman & Littlefield Publishers, 2003).

[56] Wiltse, *History of Chattanooga*, p. 29, 37–38; Wilson, op. cit., p. 7.

[57] Wiltse, p. 31, 37.

[58] Wilson, *Chattanooga's Story*, p. 120.

[59] Wilson, op. cit., p. 30; Rev. T. H. McCallie, *Early Family Record*, p. 4.

[60] Undated, unnamed news clipping in Johnston-Key Family Scrapbook, Bendabout Farms, McDonald, TN.

[61] Ibid.

[62] Author's conversation with attorney Robert Divine, Chattanooga, TN.

[63] Wilson, op. cit., p. 31; Govan, *Chattanooga Country*, p. 155; Kay Barker Gaston, "The Remarkable Harriet Whiteside," *Tennessee Historical Quarterly*, Winter, 1981, p. 334; Armstrong, op. cit., p. 119.

[64] Gaston, p. 334; Wilson, op. cit., p. 65.

[65] Armstrong, op. cit., p. 482; Wiltse, *History of Chattanooga*, p. 59.

[66] "Missy Crutchfield Told Movie Was 'R,'" *Chattanooga Fax*, Sept. 2, 2002; "Catanzaro," *Chattanooga Fax*, July 12, 2002.

[67] Author's conversation with Linda Johnson, Chattanooga, TN; Author's interview with Ward Crutchfield.

[68] John Wilson, "The Chattanooga Crutchfields," *Chattanooga News-Free Press*, Sept. 21, 1980; Livingood, "Crutchfield House," p. 20.

[69] "Ward Crutchfield, Chris Newton Arrested in Nashville," <Chattanoogan.com>, May 26, 2005; "Charles Love Set to Enter Guilty Pleas in Tennessee Waltz Case," <Chattanoogan.com>, Aug. 10, 2005; *The Pulse*, June 1–7, 2005.

[70] Wilson, op. cit.

[71] Armstrong, op. cit., p. 124–5; Govan, *Chattanooga Country*, p. 175.

[72] Johnson, p. 457. There are various versions of the confrontation. The words "despot" and "traitor" show up in several accounts. The meaty verbage used in the text comes from Johnson is hard to trace. He names William C. Davis as the source, who cites the Jan. 24, 1885 *Chattanooga Press*. However, the downtown library's records show the short life of the *Chattanooga Press* did not begin until well after 1885. Emails to Mr. Davis on the matter were not returned.

[73] Armstrong, op.cit.; Govan, op.cit..; William C. Davis, *Jefferson Davis: The Man and His Hour* (New York: HarperCollins, 1991), p. 296–7.

[74] Livingood, *Hamilton County*, p. 226, 472; Govan, *Chattanooga Country*, p. 160; Wilson, op. cit., p. 60, 62.

[75] Govan, *Chattanooga Country*, p. 201, 239.

[76] McCallie, *Early Family Record*, p. 14, 22–3, 30.

[77] McCallie, *Early Family Record*, p. 22; Livingood, *Hamilton County*, p. 161–2, 164–5.

[78] McCallie, *Early Family Record*, p. 19, 22; Wilson, op. cit., p. 83.

[79] Wilson, op.cit, p. 87.

[80] Livingood, "Crutchfield House," p. 23.

[81] Livingood, *Hamilton County*, p. 164; Wilson, op. cit., p. 66–70.

[82] McCallie, *Early Family Record*, p. 25–28; Livingood, *Hamilton County*, p. 161–2, 187.

[83] Gaston, p. 340.

[84] Wilson, op. cit., p. 99; Wilson, *Early Hamilton Settlers*, p. 326.

[85] Wilson, *Chattanooga's Story*, p. 92.

[86] Wilson, op. cit., p. 113; Armstrong, op.cit., p. 26.

[87] Armstrong, op.cit, Vol. II, p. 36–7; Govan, *Chattanooga Country*, p. 234, 244–5.

[88] Govan, *Chattanooga Country*, p. 207.

[89] Sam Divine, *The Wit and Wisdom of Sam Divine*, Thomas McCallie Divine, ed. (Chattanooga: Chattanooga News-Free Press, 1986), p. 2.

[90] Wilson, op. cit., p. 109; Wilson, op. cit., p. 108; Exum, *Cook Book,* p. 187.

[91] Govan, *Chattanooga Country,* p. 251; Wilson, op. cit., p. 120, 122.

[92] Johnson, p. 296.

[93] Govan, *Chattanooga Country,* p. 273–4, 287.

[94] Wilson, op. cit., p. 206, 120.

[95] Armstrong, p. 247; Govan, *Chattanooga Country,* p. 286; Wilson, op. cit., p. 179.

[96] McCallie, *Early Family Record,* p. 32, 24, 36, 41; Armstrong, op. cit., p. 249.

[97] "Next to the News," *Chattanooga Times,* Oct. 10, 1952.

[98] Wilson, op. cit., p. 160.

[99] Govan, *Chattanooga Country,* p. 365, 368–71.

[100] Livingood, *Hamilton County,* p. 260, 285, 289–90; Wiltse, *History of Chattanooga,* p. 87.

[101] Gary Moulton, *John Ross: Cherokee Chief* (Athens, GA, 1978), p. 204.

[102] Nancy J. Potts, "Unfilled Expectations: The Erosion of Black Political Power in Chattanooga," 1865–1911, *Tennessee Historical Quarterly,* Summer 1990, p. 116.

[103] Livingood, *Hamilton County,* p. 247.

[104] All facts and quotes from Potts, p. 113–123.

[105] Livingood, Burns and Glass, *Chattanooga: An Illustrated History,* p. 170–171.

[106] All quotes from Jack Lupton appeared in previously cited newspaper articles, but primarily in "Jack Lupton talks about a city and its destiny," *Chattanooga Times,* Jan. 27, 1986.

[107] Dave Flessner, "Local Residents Split Over Power Structure," *Chattanooga Times Free Press,* May 30, 1999.

[108] *Chattanooga Times,* Feb. 5, 1988; "Crowe Cites Evidence Aquarium Not Mentioned in Public Meets," *Chattanooga News-Free Press,* June 18, 1986.

[109] "Aquarium Issue Sparks War of Words," *Chattanooga News-Free Press,* Feb. 24, 1987.

[110] *Chattanooga News-Free Press,* May 17, 1988.

[111] "Lupton Wants to Make City Stadium a Reality," *Chattanooga News-Free Press,* Feb. 5, 1995.

[112] *Chattanooga Fax,* Feb. 15, 1999; "Businessmen Assured Stadium to Pay Its Way," *Chattanooga Free Press,* Oct. 26, 1995.

[113] *Chattanooga Fax,* May 8, 2000.

[114] Paul Neely, "Man behind The Honors," *Chattanooga Times,* Aug. 20, 1991;

[115] Anderson's quotes cited in "Another Take on Power Structure," *Chattanooga Fax,* Aug. 9, 1999.

[116] "Laying a new foundation," *Chattanooga Times Free Press,* Sept. 4, 2002.

[117] Wiltse, *History of Chattanooga,* p. 22.

[118] *Knoxville Dispatch,* Dec. 15, 1880, cited in Govan, *Chattanooga Country,* p. 314.

[119] "Great Work!" *Cityscope* magazine, Spring, 2003.

CHAPTER TWO ENDNOTES - THE SPIRIT OF THE MOUNTAIN

[1] Exum, *Cook Book,* Introduction, and p. 405.

[2] Armstrong, op. cit., Vol. II, p. 121.

[3] Ibid., p. 1.

[4] Exum, *Cook Book,* p. 155; Armstrong, op. cit., p. 123.

[5] Author's conversation with Andrew Wilkie, Chattanooga, TN, March 2005.

[6] Govan, *Chattanooga Country,* p. 348; Speech by George S. Elder II to Elder Mountain Garden Club, April 30, 1995.

[7] Wiltse, *History of Chattanooga,* p. 3.

[8] Wiltse, p. 3–5.

[9] Author's taped interview with Summerfield K. Johnston, Jr.

[10] "Forbes Faces," April 12, 2001.

[11] Wilson, *Chattanooga's Story,* p. 371.

[12] Livingood, *Hamilton County,* p. 244.

[13] Govan, *Chattanooga Country,* p. 309–11.

[14] Exum, *Cook Book,* p. 113–115.

[15] *The Lookout Mountain Mirror,* Oct. 2004.

[16] Conversation with Elizabeth Mayfield Neil, Cleveland, TN, 2004.

[17] "Mary Divine's Story of Wartimes," Neil Family Papers, Blythewood Farm, Cleveland, TN.

[18] Unnamed news clipping dated Nov. 13, 1927, Neil Family Papers.

[19] Interview with Summerfield Key Johnston Sr., Oral History Project, Chattanooga–Hamilton County Bicentennial Library, July 6, 1984.

[20] See <www.cokebottles4sale.com/2001SummerfieldJohnsonJr.html>

[21] Pendergrast, *For God, Country and Coca-Cola*, p. 9. Much of this chapter is taken from Pendergrast's book and the author is indebted to his superb research and investigative reporting, all extremely well-documented.

[22] Wilbur Kurtz, Jr., "Papers and Speeches," p. 172–173. (Coca Cola archives), cited in Pendergrast, *For God, Country and Coca-Cola*, p. 9.

[23] Robert Chistison, "Observations on the effects of Cuca, Or Coca, the Leaves of Erythroxylon Coca," *The British Medical Journal*, April 29, 1876, p. 530, cited in Pendergrast, *For God, Country and Coca-Cola*, p. 23.

[24] *American Druggist*, Nov. 1886, p. 214; Sigmund Freud to Martha Bernays, June 2, 1884, as quoted in Freud's *Cocaine Papers*, p. 10; both cited in Pendergrast, *For God, Country and Coca-Cola*, p. 23, 24.

[25] *Atlanta Constitution*, March 10, 1885, cited in Pendergrast, *For God, Country and Coca-Cola*, p. 27.

[26] Pendergrast, *For God, Country and Coca-Cola*, p. 24, who quotes O'Reilly, *Life of Leo XIII*, p. 566–575.

[27] Lewis Newman letter and scribbled note, 1886, (Sherman Collection), cited in Pendergrast, *For God, Country and Coca-Cola*, p. 30. See also p. 25, 26, 29.

[28] Minutes of the Eleventh Annual Meeting held in Savannah, GA, April 1886, p. 17–21 (Sherman Collection); Coca-Cola label patented June 28, 1887 (CC Archives); both cited in Pendergrast, *For God, Country and Coca-Cola*, p. 31, 33.

[29] Meeting discussion reconstructed by Pendergrast from quotes in 1899 report issued Jan. 11, 1900, Pendergrast, *For God, Country and Coca-Cola*, p. 70–71. See also Pendergrast, p. 56, 60.

[30] Pendergrast, *For God, Country and Coca-Cola*, p. 72. Irwin's account says the drink in Cuba that inspired Thomas was "champagne cola" (p. 224).

[31] Irwin, "Bottling Gold," p. 224.

[32] J. J. Willard, *CC Bottler*, April 1959, p. 89, 189; Asa Candler, "Confidence in Your Product," 1916 Bottlers Convention Booklet, *Equip Yourselves With Knowledge*, p. 74 (CC Archives); both cited in Pendergrast, *For God, Country and Coca-Cola*, p. 440 (page 73 endnote).

[33] Candler, "Confidence in Your Product," p. 74; Pendergrast, *For God, Country and Coca-Cola*, p. 75; Irwin, op. cit., p. 224.

[34] Fred Hixson, "Fear of Investing Years Ago Cost Him Million, Sam Erwin Reveals," *Chattanooga Times*, July 27, 1941, cited in Irwin, op. cit, p. 226.

[35] Pendergrast, *For God, Country and Coca-Cola*, p. 76–77.

[36] Irwin, p. 228.

[37] Pendergrast, *For God, Country and Coca-Cola*, p. 74, 78. "It was also among the first franchises in the world," he adds in a footnote on p. 440, citing Vaughn, *Franchising*, p. 19–21.

[38] Govan, *Chattanooga Country*, p. 388; Pendergrast, *For God, Country and Coca-Cola*, p. 76.

[39] Cocaine: Use of the Drug Increasing Among Negroes of the South," June 21, 1903, *New York Daily Tribune*, p. 11; "Cocaine is Sold Illegally," *Atlanta Constitution*, Nov. 20, 1901; both cited in Pendergrast, *For God, Country and Coca-Cola*, p. 90.

[40] Sam Willard and Sam Dobbs Affidavits, July 13, 1907; *Acts and Resolutions of the General Assembly of the State of Georgia*, 1902, p. 100; both cited in Pendergrast, *For God, Country and Coca-Cola*, p. 90–91.

[41] Pendergrast, *For God, Country and Coca-Cola*, p. 109–119; Wiley, *History of a Crime*, p. 378.

[42] Pendergrast, *For God, Country and Coca-Cola*, p. 119–121; Sizer faints, p. 141.

[43] All facts and quotes regarding Paul Carter from *Paul B. Carter: His Family, Friends, and Great Adventures* (Chattanooga Published by Roy McDonald, 1977). Specific page citations are given only for particularly notable facts and quotes or if necessary to clarify the source.

[44] *Chattanooga Times*, May 17, 1913, from *Fiftieth Anniversary Scrapbook*, Manuscript Collection, Chattanooga–Hamilton County Bicentennial Library.

[45] Govan, *Chattanooga Country*, p. 374; Gaston, "The Remarkable Harriet Whiteside," p. 335, 343–345.

[46] Exum, *Cook Book*, p. 322–325.

[47] "Chattanooga in History," *Vision Chattanooga*, Spring 1993, (Chattanooga Resource Foundation), p. 8.

[48] This story is a hybrid of Bill Chapin and Paul Carter's versions.

CHAPTER THREE ENDNOTES - THE SPIRIT OF THE RIVER

[1] Clint Cooper, "Bringing in the New Year," *Chattanooga Times Free Press*, Jan. 8, 2005, F1.

[2] John Swanton, *Early History of the Creek Indians and their Neighbors* (Smithsonian Institution, Bureau of American Ethnology, Bulletin 73, Washington: Government Printing Office, 1922), p. 238.

[3] Phillips, *Brainerd Journal*, p. 522,

[4] James Mooney, "The Cherokee River Cult," *The Journal of American Folk-Lore*, Vol. XIII, Jan–March, 1900, p. 1–2;

[5] Livingood, Burns, and Glass, *Chattanooga: An Illustrated History*, p. 153.

[6] *Cityscope* magazine, May 1999.

[7] Taped conversation with Lamar Alexander, Washington, D.C, May, 2004.

[8] Gene Bunnell, *Making Places Special* (American Planning Association, 2003), p. 70-84, 112–113. A great deal of the facts and quotes for this chapter come from this excellent source. Not all the quotes from interviews by Bunnell are cited with specific page numbers.

[9] Livingood, *Hamilton County*, p. 257.

[10] Bunnell, *Making Places Special,* p. 82.

[11] This is a contrived scenario. These quotes are taken from author's interview with Watson, who used the word "mantras" to describe his pithy sayings. Documents on his meetings in the early eighties suggest he was repeating the same mantras then as he did during the interview.

[12] Livingood, op. cit., p. 107.

[13] This fascinating map (see p. 152) is on page 131 of Armstrong's history, Vol. I. She identifies the Public Road as what today would be Cherry Street. However, the map shows the road starting at the Market Street area as identified by Armstrong, moving northeast (closer to Cherry Street) toward "Mrs. Henderson's Residence," and then back to the Market Street area. Also, a letter from an early citizen describing the area in 1840 placed the widow Henderson's Inn at "the corner of Market and East Second Streets." (*Chattanooga News-Free Press*, July 12, 1955.) But since this was likely the only road in use at the time, it seems it would be the same as the Rossville Road, "The Road," or, Market Street.

[14] Bunnell, op. cit.

[15] Bunnell, op. cit., p. 81.

[16] When this was quoted earlier, the task force portion was left out to avoid confusion until that part of the story was explained.

[17] Bunnell, op. cit., p. 84. McDonald, a former Republican nominee for Congress, is not directly related to the publishing McDonalds.

[18] Wilson, *Chattanooga's Story*, p. 132-133, 264; Sam Divine, *The Wit and Wisdom of Sam Divine,* p. 28–29.

[19] Wiltse, *History of Chattanooga*, p. 81.

[20] *The Writings of Thomas Jefferson*, II, p. 14, cited in Govan, *Chattanooga Country*, p. 15, fn 6.

[21] Ibid., p. 79.

CHAPTER FOUR ENDNOTES - THE SPIRIT OF THE VALLEY

[1] "Lupton Challenges City on its Future," *Chattanooga News-Free Press*, July, 28, 1988; William U. Chandler, *The Myth of TVA: Conservation and Development in the Tennessee Valley, 1933–1983* (Cambridge, MA: Ballinger, 1984), p. 16.

[2] *Lookout Mountain: A Place and Its People*, Norman and Frances Bradley, eds. (Chattanooga: Lookout Mountain Committee, 1986), p. 1.

[3] Archer Butler Hulbert, *Historic Highways of America* (Cleveland, OH: Arthur Clark Co., 1902), Vol. I, p. 20.

[4] Lloyd Arnold Brown, *Early Maps of the Ohio Valley* (University of Pittsburgh Press, 1959).

[5] Armstrong, op. cit., Vol. 1, p. 121, 517.

[6] William McLoughlin, *Cherokee Renascence in the New Republic*, p. 77-82,

[7] Wiltse, *History of Chattanooga*, p. 67; Govan, *Chattanooga Country*, p. 102; Armstrong, op cit, Vol. 1, p. 49; Exum, *Cook Book,* p. 126–127.

[8] Thurman Wilkins, *Cherokee Tragedy: The Ridge Family and the Decimation of a People* (Norman and London: University of Oklahoma Press, 1970), p. 36, 43, 50.

[9] William McLoughlin, *Cherokees and Missionaries, 1789–1839* (New Haven and London: Yale University Press, 1984), p. 46, 70, 77.

[10] Wilkins, op. cit.; McLoughlin, *Cherokee Renascence*, p.124.

[11] Wiltse, *History of Chattanooga*, p. 18.

[12] Ibid., p. 21.

[13] Ibid., p. 63.

[14] The Montgomery quotes are from Wilson, *Chattanooga's Story*, p. 28. However, Wilson uses the word "world" at the end, which was replaced with the more interesting "universe" as quoted by Govan, *Chattanooga Country*, p. 99. Montgomery probably used both words at various times.

15 "Grave of Postmaster Discovered by Walker," *Chattanooga Times*, Nov. 15, 1946, p.5.

16 Govan, *Chattanooga Country*, p. 100 fn; Wilson, op. cit., p. 28, Armstrong, Vol II, p. 177.

17 "Grave of Postmaster Discovered by Walker," *Chattanooga Times*, Nov. 15, 1946, p.5.

18 Govan, *Chattanooga Country*, p. 126–127.

19 Wiltse, *History of Chattanooga*, p. 84.

20 Wiltse, *History of Chattanooga*, p. 7.

21 Paul Johnson, *History of the American People*, p. 307-310.

22 Govan, *Chattanooga Country*, p. 130.

23 *Tennessee Encyclopedia of History & Culture*, p. 139; Johnson, p. 64.

24 Wilson, p. 35; Govan, *Chattanooga Country*, p. 133, 298.

25 Dalton Roberts, *Kickstarts: Common Sense and Uncommon Wisdom on Life, Loving, Friendship, Faith, Health, Politics, and Paying the Bills* (Chattanooga: Phase II: Publications, 1997), p. 1.

26 This quote was passed along to the author by a local businessman who wished to remain anonymous.

27 Livingood, *Hamilton County*, p. 130; Wiltse, *History of Chattanooga*, Vol 2, p. 8.

28 Livingood, *Hamilton County*, p. 35, 91; Wilson, p. 84, 86; Govan, *Chattanooga Country*, p. 129.

29 *Paul B. Carter: His Family, Friends, and Great Adventures*, p. 27–29.

30 "City Called Lego Set for Elite Families," *Chattanooga Times Free Press*, Feb. 5, 2005, p. B3.

31 "Get off the Can and Get on the Stick," by Wilt Chamberlain, *Chattanooga Fax*, Oct. 6, 2003.

32 "Designing Off: Littlefield takes city planning from the Planning studio," *Chattanooga Pulse*, Aug. 3-9, 2005; "Ripples from RiverCity," *Chattanooga Times Free Press*, March 13, 2005.

33 *Reason Magazine*, Sept. 9, 1998 cited in *Chattanooga Fax*, Jan. 4, 1999.

34 "New Group Opposes State Aquarium Plan," *Chattanooga News-Free Press*, Jan. 28, 1986; June 18, 1986.

35 *Chattanooga Fax*, May 8, 2000; July 17, 1999.

36 "Dalton Roberts: Redneck Elitist," *Chattanooga Fax*, July 21, 1997.

37 "The Mayor & Jeff's Modern Relationship," *Chattanooga Fax*, March 2003.

38 "Bones of the Mountain," by William G. Raoul in *Lookout Mountain: A Place and Its People*, p. 1.

CHAPTER FIVE ENDNOTES - THE SPIRIT OF SCOTLAND

1 Phillips, *Brainerd Journal*, p. 27–29.

2 Paul Carter, p. 187.

3 James G. Leyburn, *The Scotch-Irish: A Social History* (Chapel Hill: University of North Carolina Press, 1962), p. xvi-xvii.

4 Wilson, *Chattanooga's Story*, p. 343.

5 "Great Work," *Cityscope* magazine.

6 Wilson, *Patten*, p. 90.

7 Johnson, p. 71.

8 Sharon McCrumb, "The First Appalachian Journey." *Appalachian Voice*, Late Winter, 2005;

9 Ibid.; Los Angeles Times Notable Book, <SharynMcCrumb.com>.

10 *Dictionary of American Family Names*.

11 Armstrong, Vol 1, p. 57–58; Wilson, op. cit., p. 6; Moulton, *John Ross*, p. 5.

12 Moulton, p. 4–5.

13 Phillips, *Brainerd Journal*, p. 30, 439.

14 A marker on Broad Street in front of Chattem (the former Double Cola building) provides the yardage and direction to the spot in the middle of the CCS track.

15 Livingood, *Hamilton County*, p 60; Moulton, p. 6.

16 The notable exception is the home, tavern and ferry of Chief John Brown, another mixed blood whose individual activities did not particularly affect larger community developments. But the 1803 tavern remains standing as the oldest structure in Chattanooga's city limits.

17 Phillips, *Brainerd Journal*, p. 4.

18 The Chief John Ross House in Rossville, Georgia is approximately 300 feet from its original spot on the Federal Road. For more details and commentary on the interesting story of the Chief John Ross House, see *America's Trail of Tears* by Dean Arnold, p. 241–242.

19 Phillips, *Brainerd Journal*, p 4, 27.

20 The historian calls Ross's Landing an "afterthought," as Daniel Ross's earlier landing was the more natural spot. (Interview with Penelope Johnson Allen, Oral History Project, Manuscript Collection, Local History Department, Chattanooga–Hamilton County Bicentennial Library. p. 18.

[21] Wiltse, *History of Chattanooga*, p. 2, and Volume II, p. 2. See also Bruce Council, *Ross's Landing at Chattanooga*.

[22] Govan, *Chattanooga Country*, p. 80.

[23] Phillips, *Brainerd Journal*, p. 476.

[24] Ibid., p. 27–32, 260.

[25] Ibid., p. 28.

[26] Ibid. These facts compiled from a number of scattered pages in the journal.

[27] Zella Armstrong, *History of the First Presbyterian Church of Chattanooga* (Lookout Publishing Co., 1945), p. 38 (hereafter cited as *First Presbyterian*).

[28] Phillips, *Brainerd Journal*, p. 274.

[29] The Brainerd Covenant printed in the church bulletin sources Robert Sparks Walker, *Torchlights to the Cherokees*, p. 121–122.

[30] Author's conversation with Joe Novenson, Sept. 2004.

[31] Armstrong, p. 230; Phillips, *Brainerd Journal*, p. 517–518.

[32] *Chattanooga: An Illustrated History*, op. cit.; *Chattanooga Fax*, May 8, 2000.

[33] "Ripples from RiverCity," *Chattanooga Times Free Press*, March 13, 2005; "Morning Edition," National Public Radio, Feb. 20, 2001.

[34] "Bored with Boards," Bob Barnes, *Chattanooga Fax*, July 9, 1997.

[35] Johnson, *History of the American People*, p. 173.

[36] Program brochure for Kruesi Spirit of Innovation—Award Breakfast, May 9, 2003, Author's papers.

[37] Armstrong, Vol. 1, p. 465; Cartter Frierson, "History of Lookout Mt. Presbyterian Church." <www.lmpc.org>

[38] From *Logistics Today*, cited in *Chattanooga Times Free Press*, March 9, 2004.

[39] *Fiftieth Confederate Reunion Scrapbook*, May 26 and May 28, 1913, Manuscript Collection, Local History Department, Chattanooga–Hamilton County Bicentennial Library; Smartt family papers. Family summary by Kennedy Smartt.

[40] Smartt actually uses the phrase "Reformed, Christian heritage" instead of Presbyterian. "Reformed" is generally a synonym for "Calvinististic" in Presbyterian circles, although the term is not always clearly defined. It usually refers to issues broader than merely church polity such as the Calvinistic beliefs of cultural transformation, predestination and election, and "Covenant Theology," which emphasizes a closer tie between the Old and New Testaments than does "Dispensational Theology."

[41] Microfilm copy of handwritten minutes, Local History Department, Chattanooga–Hamilton County Bicentennial Library.

[42] "Capt. John Long," by Anne Bachman Hyde cited in "Next to the News" by Aldred Mynders, *Chattanooga Times*, Nov. 21, 1947, from Anne Bachman Hyde Scrapbook, Manuscript Collections, Local History Department, Chattanooga–Hamilton County Bicentennial Library.

[43] Wilson, *Early Hamilton Settlers*, p. 187–188.

[44] Livingood, *Hamilton County*, p. 105; Wilson, op. cit.

[45] Govan, *Chattanooga Country*, p. 102; Livingood, op. cit., p 103–106; Armstrong, *Hamilton County*, p. 246.

[46] Govan, *Chattanooga Country*, p. 107–108; Wiltse, *History of Chattanooga*, p. 65.

[47] Wiltse, *History of Chattanooga*, p. 26.

[48] Govan, *Chattanooga Country*, p. 77.

[49] Wiltse, *History of Chattanooga*, p. 50, 53; Armstrong, op. cit., p. 153.

[50] To date, none are known to the author, who has made sincere attempts and has published announcements to find them. Also, the family of Robert Doak, current head of the Chattanooga Convention and Visitors Bureau, cites Dr. S.S.M. Doak on the marker as a great uncle.

[51] Armstrong, op cit, p. 250–253; Wiltse, *History of Chattanooga*, p. 10.

[52] Armstrong, op. cit., p. 246.

[53] John Long Clipping File, Local History Department, Chattanooga–Hamilton County Bicentennial Library. Chattanooga Library.

[54] Armstrong, *First Presbyterian*, p. 21–22.

[55] Frierson, "History of Lookout Mt. Presbyterian Church."

[56] In fact, the first wedding recorded at Ross's Landing involves a Kennedy and a Smartt—cousins but not direct descendents of Sam Smartt. (Armstrong, *Hamilton County*, Vol. I, p. 142–143 [picture caption]).

[57] Wilson, *Early Hamilton County Settlers*, p. 187–188.

[58] Ibid., p. 250.

[59] James Baird, *Thunder Over Scotland*. Campbell, CA, Greenleaf, 1982, p. 131–133; John Howie, *Lives of the Scottish Covenanters* (Greenville, SC: A Press, 1981), p. 31–37.

[60] John Knox says of Wishart: "He was so clearly illumined with the spirit of prophecy, that he saw not only things pertaining to himself, but also such things as some towns and the whole realm afterward felt, which he forspake not in secret, but in the audience of many, as in their own places shall be declared." (*John Knox's History of the Reformation in Scotland*, Ed. William Croft Dickenson, New York, Philosophical Library, Inc, 1950, p. 60.)

[61] Howie, op. cit.

[62] It is difficult to cite every source for this section on the Scottish Reformation. Much of it is taken from the author's 1997 unpublished manuscript, *Fighting Scots: A History of the American Spirit* by Dean W. Arnold (PO Box 2053; Chattanooga, TN 37409).

[63] Mervyn Davies, *Presbyterian Heritage* (Richmond: John Knox Press, 1965), p. 56.

[64] J.D. Douglas, *Light in the North: The Story of the Scottish Covenanters* (Grand Rapids: Eerdmans, 1964), p.13, 17, 28.

[65] Russell Kirk, *The Roots of American Order* (Washington, D.C.: Regnery, 1999), p. 256.

[66] According to Provident's official history, Thomas Maclellan was a "devout Covenanter who followed to the letter the teachings of that zealous Presbyterian sect." John Longwith, *Provident: A Centennial History* (Chattanooga, TN, 1986), p, 12.

[67] Alexander Whyte, "George Gillespie: 1613–1648: Biographical Sketch," A Puritan's Mind, <www.apuritans-mind.com>

[68] "Great Work!" *Cityscope* magazine, Spring, 2003.

CHAPTER SIX ENDNOTES - THE SPIRIT OF THE NEW YORK TIMES

[1] Susan E. Tifft and Alex S. Jones, *The Trust: The Private and Powerful Family Behind the New York Times* (Boston, New York and London: Little and Brown Company, 1999), p. xiv. Unless noted otherwise, the facts and quotes from Chapter Six are taken from this book by Tifft and Jones. The author is greatly indebted to their work and research. Most but not all of the facts and quotes related to the following areas come from these pages: life and work of Adolph Ochs pp.1–45; Ruth Sulzberger's early life pp. 133–138; life in Chattanooga pp. 405–414; battle with Roy McDonald pp. 204–205, 275–276, 458–459, 577–581. Isolated facts or quotes are sometimes cited, as well as particularly interesting or unusual items.

[2] Ibid., p. 81.

[3] Armstrong, *Hamilton County*, Vol. 1, p. 154.

[4] *Hamilton Gazette*, Vol. 1, Number Two, July 26, 1938.

[5] Govan, *Chattanooga Country*, p. 202; Livingood, *Hamilton County*, p. 180.

[6] Armstrong, op cit, Vol II, p. 138.

[7] Author's interview with Ruth Holmberg, Chattanooga, Tennessee. Quotes by Mrs. Holmberg not taken from this interview are cited.

[8] Govan, *Chattanooga Country*, p. 318.

[9] *Tennessee Enclcyopedia of History and Culture,* p. 143.

[10] Govan, *Chattanooga Country*, p. 320–321.

[11] Ibid., p. 299.

[12] Wilson, op cit, p. 220.

[13] Govan, *Chattanooga Country*, p. 327–328.

[14] Ibid., p. 336.

[15] Sam Divine, *The Wit and Wisdom of Sam Divine*, p. 31.

[16] Author's conversation with Michael Golden, New York, May 2004.

[17] "Dome Building Approaching 100th Birthday," *Chattanooga News-Free Press*, Nov. 24, 1991.

[18] Tifft and Jones, p. 29, 33.

[19] Ibid., p. 34.

[20] Ibid., p. 35.

[21] Ibid., p. 39–40.

[22] Ibid., p. 43.

[23] Ibid., p. 405.

[24] The specifics of the problems and divorce are detailed in *The Trust*, but are not necessary for this treatment.

[25] Tifft and Jones, p. 414.

[26] *Newsweek*, Sept. 5, 1966.

[27] Ibid.

[28] Tifft and Jones, p. 204–205, 275.

[29] *Time*, Sept. 9, 1970.

[30] *Newsweek*, Sept. 5, 1966.

[31] This fact and all subsequent quotes taken from author's interview with Lee Anderson.

[32] "one cent" from conversation with Lee Anderson. Facts of commerce case from "New–Free Press Found Guilty in "Trust" Suit, Seeks New Trial, *Chattanooga Times*, Dec. 12, 1940.

[33] Tifft and Jones, p. 407.

[34] John Meacham, "Chattanooga Times," *Tennessee Encyclopedia of History & Culture*, p. 144.

[35] Exum, *Cook Book*, p. 256–257.

[36] Martha Gaither Martin, *The Chattanooga News-Free Press* (Chattanooga: Published by Roy McDonald, 1981).

[37] Tifft and Jones, p. 579.

[38] Tifft and Jones, p. 12.

[39] Ibid., p. 151.

[40] Ibid., p. 7.

[41] According to a top executive at Chattanooga City Hall, who requested no attribution.

[42] Both quotes from dedication ceremony for Hunter Museum, Chattanooga, April 23, 2005.

[43] Hebrews 11:10, New International Version of the Bible.

CHAPTER SEVEN ENDNOTES - THE SPIRIT OF THE BIBLE BELT

[1] Jerry Falwell, ed., *The Fundamentalist Phenomenon* (Garden City: Doubleday, 1981); "The World's Largest Church," Tennessee Temple Library, p. 120.

[2] Ibid., p. 134.

[3] Statistics taken from the following: *Chattanooga Times Free Press*, Oct. 7, 2002. p. A6; Barna Research Group polling results, March 1997, cited in *Intercessors for Chattanooga*, July, 1999, Chattanooga Resource Foundation; "City Grounded in Faith," by Dave Flessner, *Chattanooga Times*, Oct. 15, 1998.

[4] Author's taped interview with Senator David Fowler, Nashville, TN.

[5] This quote and surrounding facts from *12 Days in Dayton: The Scopes Monkey Trial*, WTCI, Channel 45, Video Documentary, 2001. Many of the more interesting facts in this chapter come from this source.

[6] Three decades earlier, President Wilson's father served as stated clerk for the General Assembly of the Presbyterian Church in the United States that met at First Presbyterian Church in Chattanooga. In a curious forerunner to the Scopes Trial, Woodrow Wilson's maternal uncle, Dr. James Woodrow, was placed on trial for stating that evolution applied to the body of Adam, but not to his soul. He was forbidden by the Presbyterian leaders to continue teaching his views (Armstrong, *First Presbyterian*, p. 27).

[7] Allem, Warren. "Backgrounds of the Scopes Trial at Dayton. Tennessee." Thesis. University of Tennessee, 1959.

[8] Irving Stone, *Clarence Darrow for the Defense: A Biography* (New York: Doubleday, 1941), p. 315, 323.

[9] "Chattanooga Leads the U.S. in Charitable Giving," *Vision Chattanooga*, Chattanooga Resource Foundation, Summer 1991.

[10] Author's taped interview with Zach Wamp.

[11] Named the largest city by NARAL (National Abortion Rights Action League) according to Dr. Robert O'Bannon with University Faculty for Life <www.uffl.org>

[12] Summary of this history from author's own recollections and from *Chattanooga Fax*, Dec. 6, 1999, and HISTORY by AAA Women's Services, Inc.

[13] *Washington Times*, Sept. 10, 1997.

[14] "Roe & Doe Recant Abortion Case," *Chattanooga Fax*, March 24, 1997.

[15] Murrah's memo and the official Lyndhurst response reported in *Chattanooga Fax*, May 29, 2001.

[16] *Chattanooga Fax*, May 7, 2001.

[17] Armstrong, *Hamilton County*, p. 482.

[18] Wilson, *Chattanooga's Story*, p. 65.

[19] Wiltse, *History of Chattanooga*, p. 2.

[20] Charles Hudson, *Knights of Spain, Warriors of the Sun: Hernando de Soto and the South's Ancient Chiefdoms* (Athens: University of Georgia Press, 1997), p. 302; *Narratives of the career of Hernando De Soto in the Conquest of Florida as told by a Knight of Elvas*, ed., Edward Gaylord Bourne (New York: A. S. Barnes and Co., 1904), p. 59.

[21] *A book of old maps dilineating American History from the earliest days to the close of the Revolutionary War*, Emerson D. Fite, ed. (New York: Dover Publications, 1969), p. 161.

[22] Govan, *Chattanooga Country*, p. 60.

[23] Dorothy C. Bass, "Gideon Blackburn's Mission to the Cherokees: Christianization and Civilization," *Journal of Presbyterian History*, Fall 1974, p. 203–226; William McLoughlin, "The Mystery Behind Parson Blackburn's Whiskey," *Cherokee Ghost Dance: Essays on the Southeastern Indians* (Macon, GA: Mercer, 1984), p. 369ff.

[24] Armstrong, *Hamilton County*, Vol II, p. 158; Armstrong, *First Presbyterian*, p. 87.

[25] Phillips, *Brainerd Journal*, March 24, 1819, p. 111–112.

[26] This information was obtained by the author from the outdoor bulletin board at the Brainerd cemetery in August, 2003. A website with the same information no longer exists. Armstrong, in 1940, said the communion set was owned by Blunt's grandson in Dalton, Dr. A. W. Blunt, and by his daughter, Mrs. Thomas M. Kirby. (Armstrong, *Hamilton County*, p. 78–80; See also Cooper, *Catalyst for Christ*, p. 224; Armstrong, *First Presbyterian*, 32.)

[27] "Book a Hundred Years Old Published in Athens Tenn." *Chattanooga News*, July 12, 1938. This clipping is attached to the inside of the actual book in the manuscript collections at Chattanooga–Hamilton County Bicentennial Library.

[28] *Wit and Wisdom of Sam Divine*, p. 27. Tommy Lupton questions whether Hogan ever owned the land belonging to the Stone Fort Land Company, proper. He may have owned much of the land surrounding it.

[29] Govan, *Chattanooga Country*, p. 428–429.

[30] *Chattanooga Fax*, April 20, 2004.

[31] *Chattanooga Fax*, Nov. 13, 2000.

[32] Interview with Bettye Lundquist, Chattanooga, July, 2005. "Prayer Intiatives Relative to Chattanooga's Role in Native American Issues and Trail of Tears," by Bettye Lundquist, Private Paper; "Targeting Cities with 'Spiritual Mapping,'" *Christian Science Monitor*, Sept. 23, 1999;

[33] George Hazard, Jr., *When We Came to the Ridge: Part One of the History of the McCallie School, 1905–1937* (Chattanooga: The McCallie School, 1991), Chapter 23.

[34] *Chattanooga Fax*, May 15, 2001.

[35] Ibid.

[36] *Chattanooga Fax*, Oct. 8, 2000.

[37] *Chattanooga Fax*, May 15, 2001; May 31, 1999.

[38] *Chattanooga Fax*, Oct. 11, 1999; Nov. 3, 2003.

CHAPTER EIGHT ENDNOTES - THE SPIRIT OF THE LUPTONS

[1] David Cooper, *Catalyst for Christ*, p. 338.

[2] *Chattanooga Free Press,* March 20, 1997.

[3] This and subsequent quotes by Foresta from phone conversation with the author, May 25, 2005.

[4] McCallie, *Early Family Record*, p. 1.

[5] Wilson, *Chattanooga's Story,* p. 132.

[6] James Leyburn, *The Scotch-Irish*, p. 266–267.

[7] "Rotary Defined," by Thomas Spencer McCallie, 1922–23. From Rotary office; "Chattanooga Rotary in the 1990s," Channel 3 WRCB, Dec 30, 1999.

[8] Wilson, op. cit., p. 282.

[9] Armstrong, *Hamilton County,* p. 100–102.

[10] Wilson, op. cit., p. 342; John Wilson, *Patten,* p. 82.

[11] Livingood, *Hamilton County,* p. 208.

[12] Joseph Frazier Wall, *Andrew Carnegie* (University of Pittsburgh Press, 1970), p. 138, 202, 212. See also Harold Livesay, *Andrew Carnegie and the Rise of Big Business* (Little, Brown & Co., Boston, 1975); Woodruff File, Personal papers of Dean W. Arnold.

[13] Exum, *Cook Book,* p. 136; Wilson*, Patten,* p. 27.

[14] *The Lookout*, May 2, 1908; Armstrong, *Hamilton County,* Vol. II, p. 112.

[15] Arch Willingham, Letter to the Editor, *Chattanooga Fax,* July 13, 1997.

[16] All quotes by Carter from *Paul B. Carter, His Friends, Family, and Great Adventures.*

[17] Duble's quotes are taken from his words during Covenant College's 50th Anniversary celebration, Aug. 19, 2005.

[18] Wilson, op. cit.; Armstrong, op. cit., Vol. 1, p. 354.

[19] *Chattanooga Fax,* Sept. 10, 2001.

[20] Irwin, p. 235.

[21] Cooper, *Catalyst for Christ*, p. 41–58.

[22] Armstrong, op. cit.. Vol. I, p. 439.

[23] *Dictionary of American Family Names,* Patrick Hanks, ed., Oxford University Press, 2003; The Montague Millennium, Inc. 1996–2003 (<www.montaguemillennium.com>); MJP Grundy, Lupton, 2002, <freepages.genealogy.rootsweb.com>; <UKStudentLife.com>; <bradfordgenealogy. org>; Kirkby–Lonsdale Parish, Images of Cumbria, <www.stevebulman. f9.co.uk.cumbria/kirkbylongsdale.html>.

[24] John Wilson, Untitled article on Lupton Family History, e-mailed to author on Dec. 6, 2004.

[25] Frederick Allen, *Secret Formula,* p. 217.

[26] Pendergrast, *For God, Country and Coca-Cola,* p. 186, 377.

[27] "Man Behind the Honors," *Chattanooga Times,* July 20, 1991; "Group Buys Ooltewah Tract for Golf Course," *Chattanooga News-Free Press,* Sept. 10, 1981; "Honorable Clubhouse," by Susan Pierce, *Chattanooga News-Free Press,* Nov. 20, 1983.

[28] Allen, p. 135. On an unrelated ironic note, Robert Woodruff spent the entire year of 1929 living on a Pullman car. A wealthy penny-pincher to the extreme, he cited as his reason his "serious and critical financial condition" (Pendergrast, *For God, Country and Coca-Cola,* p. 175).

CHAPTER NINE ENDNOTES - THE SPIRIT OF NINTH STREET

[1] Author's interview with Raymond Evans, June 3, 2005.

[2] *Chattanooga Fax*, Feb. 24, 2003.

[3] *New Grove Dictionary of Jazz*, Barry Kernfield, ed., Oxford University Press; 1994; *Chattanooga's African American Legacy*, Raymond Evans, ed. (Chattanooga African American Museum, 2003), p. 54.

[4] Govan, *Chattanooga Country,* p. 108, 161; Livingood, *Hamilton County*, p. 140.

[5] Nancy J. Potts, " Unfilled Expectations: The Erosion of Black Political Power in Chattanooga, 1865–1911," *Tennessee Historical Quarterly*, Summer 1990, p. 116.

[6] Livingood, op. cit., p. 247.

[7] All facts and quotes from Potts, p. 113–123.

[8] Livingood, Burns, and Glass, *Chattanooga: An Illustrated History*, p. 170–1.

[9] John Swanton, *The Indians of the Southeastern United States*, Smithsonian Institute, Washington, D.C, 1946, p. 60.

[10] John Swanton, *Early History of the Creek Indians*, p. 233, 239.

[11] *Chattanooga's African American Legacy*, p. 13–14.

[12] Andy Williams, quoted in Wiltse, *History of Chattanooga*, p. 23, 65.

[13] Wiltse, *History of Chattanooga*, p. 24, 74; Sam Divine, op. cit., p. 35.

[14] Phillips, *Brainerd Journal*, p. 28, 62, 209; McLoughlin, *Cherokees and Missionaries*, p. 49.

[15] *Chattanooga's African American Legacy*, p. 38–39; "Film Records Significant Events of Chattanooga Sit-ins," *Chattanooga Times Free Press*, Feb. 21, 2004.

[16] *Chattanooga Times Free Press*, Nov. 3, 2004

[17] Author's conversation with Larry Wells, Wireless Properties LLC, Chattanooga, May, 2004.

CHAPTER TEN ENDNOTES - THE SPIRIT OF T.H. MCCALLIE

[1] John Longwith, *Castle on a Cliff: A History of Baylor School* (Chattanooga, TN, 1994), p. 56–59, 86–93; James E. Hitt, *It Never Rains After Three O'Clock: A History of the Baylor School* (Baylor School Press, Chattanooga, TN, 1971), p. 67–70.

[2] Longwith, *Castle on a Cliff,* p. 88; Hitt, *History of the Baylor School,* p. 58.

[3] "School Choices and Challenges," *Chattanooga Times Free Press*, April 24, 2005; "Philanthropy Reshapes Chattanooga," *Chattanooga Times Free Press*, Nov. 1, 2000.

[4] "Chattanooga Choices and Challenges"; See also the websites for the Big Three.

[5] "Chattanooga Choices and Challenges"; "County parents, teachers contact private schools," *Chattanooga Times Free Press*, July 11, 2004; "Private Schools' tuition, enrollment growing," *Chattanooga Times Free Press*, Aug. 29, 2002; "Education Enterprise: Private School Boom Here Triples State Average," *Chattanooga Free Press*, March 17, 1996; "Beyond Homeschool," *Chattanooga Times Free Press*, July, 12, 2003.

[6] Eleanor Cooper McCallie, *Grace in China: An American Woman Beyond the Great Wall. 1934–1974* (Black Belt Press: Montgomery), 1999, p. 84–85.

[7] Interview with George Elder.

[8] George Hazard, Jr, *When We Came to the Ridge: Part One of the History of the McCallie School 1905–1937* (Chattanooga: The McCallie School, 1991) p. 8–10.

⁹ Ibid.

¹⁰ Hitt, p. 7; Johnston family papers, Bendabout Farms, McDonald, TN.

¹¹ Hitt, p. 10–11, 14–15, 24–25.

¹² Hitt, p. 64.

¹³ Hazard, p. 8–10.

¹⁴ Hitt, p. 61.

¹⁵ Longwith, *Castle on a Cliff*, picture page caption.

¹⁶ Ibid., p. 58.

¹⁷ Govan, *Chattanooga Country*, p. 76; Armstrong, *Hamilton County*, Vol II, p. 160; "History of First Presbyterian Church," *Chattanooga Times* (or *News?*—clipping unclear), Dec. 27, 1909.

¹⁸ McCallie, *Early Family Record*, p. 94;

¹⁹ Hitt, *History of the Baylor School*, p. 59; Armstrong, *First Presbyterian*, p. 39, 60.

²⁰ McCallie, *Early Family Record*, p. 15–17.

²¹ McCallie, *Early Family Record*, p. 41–48.

²² "Dr. McCallie Passes Away," *Chattanooga Times*, May 1, 1912.

²³ Cooper, *Catalyst for Christ*, p. 311.

²⁴ Eleanor Grace McCallie, *Don't Say "You," Say "We": The Founding of Girl's Preparatory School* (Chattanooga, TN, 1982), Part 1 and 2; Wilson, *Chattanooga's Story*, p. 299–300.

²⁵ Hitt, *History of the Baylor School*, p. 4, 6, 21, 58.

²⁶ "School Choices and Challenges."

²⁷ "Steve Prigohzy to Exit Post As PEF Head," *Chattanooga Free Press*, June 14, 1998.

²⁸ "Public vs. Private School Debate Heats Up," *Chattanooga Times Free Press*, Nov. 18, 1999.

²⁹ Hitt, op. cit., p. 111.

³⁰ "School Choices and Challenges."

³¹ The story of Billy Graham's famous mistake was shared by Spencer McCallie III, and the author remembers "the buzz" being discussed around town. But efforts to find any press coverage of the slip-up on Sept. 24, 1991, have been, to date, unsuccessful.

³² "Face of families likely to change, not the Struggles," *St. Louis Post–Dispatch*, May 20, 2004; "Missouri Lawmakers Push for More Gay Rights," Metrovoice.net <www. metrovoice.net/0401stlweb/0401Articles/MoLawmakers.html>; Small Victories Ministries, "Street Report: Aug. 2–7, 2004. <http://www. smallvictoriesusa.com/StreetReports/2004/Augw1_04.html>

³³ *Dictionary of American Family Names*; <catholic.org>; Roderick Martine, *Scottish clan and family names: their arms, origins, and tartans* (Edinburgh: J. Bartholomew & Son, 1987), p. 80.

³⁴ Email from Tom McCallie (T. H. III) with transcription of prayer by T. Hooke McCallie.

CHAPTER ELEVEN ENDNOTES - THE SPIRIT OF THE ANCIENTS

¹ Article on John P. Long by Gilbert Govan, John P. Long clipping file; "Ross's Landing: Brief Sketch of Chattanooga's Early History," by John P. Long, John P. Long Clipping file, Local History Department, Chattanooga–Hamilton County Bicentennial Library; Wilson, *Chattanooga's Story*, p. 14; Wiltse, *History of Chattanooga*, p. 3.

² Black George is written "Blk. George."; "To the President of the United States of America; the memorial of Bennet Ballew," *American State Papers*. Vol. IV, p. 56, 1832, Library of Congress; Wilson, *Chattanooga's Story*, p. 10; Penelope Johnson Allen, *History of the Cherokees*, Unpublished manuscript, 1935 (Manuscript collections, Local History Department, Chattanooga–Hamilton County Bicentennial Library).

³ This long Cherokee word was, "O-tulee-ton-tanna-ta-kunna-ee." Govan, *Chattanooga Country*, p. 12.

⁴ *Tennessee Encyclopedia of Culture & History*, p. 138; Wiltse, *History of Chattanooga*, p. 5; Author's conversation with Nick Honerkamp; Taped interview with Lawrence Alexander; Taped interview with Raymond Evans.

⁵ Livingood, *Hamilton County*, p. 44–48.

⁶ Livingood, op. cit., p. 49–56; Thurman Wilkins, *Cherokee Tragedy*, p. 292.

⁷ Wiltse, *History of Chattanooga*, p. 3–6.

⁸ John Swanton, *Early History of the Creek Indians and their Neighbors* (Smithsonian Institution, Bureau of American Ethnology, Bulletin 73, Washington: Government Printing Office, 1922), p. 207–211; Swanton, *The Indians of the Southeastern United States* (Bureau of American Ethnology, Bulletin 137, Government Printing Office, Washington, 1946), p. 27–29, 219.

⁹ James Mooney, *Myths of the Cherokee* (Bureau of American Ethnology 19th Annual Report, Government Printing Office, Washington, D.C., 1900), p. 389.

¹⁰ Charles Hudson, *Knights of Spain, Warriors of the Sun* (University of Georgia Press, Athens and London, 1997).

[11] Lewis Thomas, *The Prehistory of the Chickamauga Basin in Tennessee* (Knoxville: University of Tennessee Press, 1995), p. 598–602.

[12] *Tennessee Encyclopedia of History & Culture*, p. 604.

[13] Armstrong, *Hamilton County*, Vol. 2, p. 279–280. The letter by Sevier is quoted from Judge Samuel Cole Williams, *Dawn of Tennessee Valley and Tennessee History*. The letter itself is housed in Ayers Collection, Newberry Library, Chicago.

[14] Mooney, p. 22, 319–320.

[15] Armstrong, op. cit.

[16] Armstrong, *Hamilton County*, Vol. 2, p. 115, 286.

[17] All quotes unless otherwise noted from author's taped interview with Lawrence Alexander, Chattanooga, TN, July, 2005.

[18] Armstrong, *Hamilton County*, Vol. 1, p. 14.

[19] Marvin T. Smith, *Coosa: The Rise and Fall of a Southeastern Mississippian Chiefdom* (Gainesville: University Press of Florida, 2000), p. xvii, 85.

[20] Govan, *Chattanooga Country*, p. 13; World Book online, "Ponce de Leon."

[21] Charles Hudson, *Knights of Spain, Warriors of the Sun*, p. 1–61.

[22] Smith, p. 60–62; Hudson, p. 202.

[23] E. Raymond Evans, "The Napochin Chiefdom of the 16th Century." Unpublished paper, p. 5–7. All subsequent information taken from the primary account by Padilla cited in note 27 below.

[24] Padilla served as an editor for the final account, which is likely a compilation of the accounts of the two friars who were eyewitnesses—Father Domingo de la Anunciacion and Father Domingo de Salazar.

[25] On location of Olitifar, see Evans, p. 10.

[26] Charles Hudson, "A Spanish-Coosa Alliance in Sixteenth Century North Georgia," *Georgia Historical Quarterly*. Vol. 72, 1988, p. 599–626.

[27] All quotes on this account of the Napochies from Father Avila Padilla in John Swanton, *Early History of the Creek Indians and their Neighbors*, p. 230–239.

[28] This last quote from a chronicler named Barcia. "Barcia, La Florida," p. 35, cited in Swanton, op. cit., p. 239.

[29] Evans obtained this information from linguistic scholar John Worth, associated with the Randall Research Center at the Florida Museum of Natural History.

[30] This "interview" with Evans is actually a compilation of the actual interview, quotes from his 15-page paper on the Napochin, and another phone interview on Oct. 25, 2004.

[31] "Louvigny, Louis de la Parte; Carte du Fleuve Misisipi," 1700?; "de l'Isle, Guillaume, Carte du Canada et du Mississipi." *The Prehistory of the Chickamauga Basin in Tennessee*, p. 598–599.

[32] Evans, p. 14; Mooney, p. 389.

[33] McLoughlin, *Cherokees and Missionaries*, p. 47.

[34] Introduction to "The 'Long' Bandera Relation," in Charles Hudson, *The Juan Pardo Expeditions: explorations of the Carolinas and Tennessee, 1566–1568* (Washington: Smithsonian Institution Press, 1990).

[35] Frederick Webb Hodge, *Handbook of American Indians North of Mexico* (Bureau of American Ethnology, Bulletin 30, parts 1 and 2, Government Printing Office, Washington, 1907 & 1912), p. 28; Swanton, *Indians of the Southeastern United States*, p. 158, 218.

[36] Herbert Bolton, *The Spanish Borderlands: a chronicle of old Florida and the Southwest* (New Haven: Yale University Press, 1921), p. 218; Mars 1699, *D'Iberville Reconnait le Mississipi* (UTC Library microfiche), p. 181.

[37] Swanton, *Early History of the Creek Indians*, p. 208; Smith, *Coosa*, p. 79.

[38] Wilson, *Chattanooga's Story*, p. 10.

[39] Wiltse, *History of Chattanooga*, p. 3.

CHAPTER TWELVE ENDNOTES - THE SPIRIT OF THE BRIDGE

[1] Hudson, *Knights of Spain*, p. 303.

[2] Layman, Elizabeth Waterhouse. *Richard Green Waterhouse*. Missouri City, TX, 1996, p. 9.

[3] John Wilson, "Vail Forbear Was Missionary to Tribe Before Trail of Tears, *Chattanooga Free Press*, May 3, 1998; Interview with Ron Vail, Jr.; Author's conversation with David Vail, June 12, 2005; Armstrong, op cit., p. 77; Wilson, op. cit.

[4] Wiltse, *History of Chattanooga*, p. 16.

[5] Phillips, *Brainerd Journal*, p. 146, 148.

[6] John Wilson, *Early Hamilton Settlers* (Sheridan Books: Chattanooga, 2001), p. 313–314; Phillips, *Brainerd Journal*, p. 138–9,181,30–301.

[7] Author's conversation with Alfred Vail, June 30, 2005; Author's conversation with Alfred Vail, Jr (Fred), July, 2005.

[8] Wilson, *Chattanooga's Story*, p. 136–137.

[9] Livingood, *Hamilton County*, p. 401.

[10] Govan, *Chattanooga Country*, p. 452; Clarence B. Carson, *A Basic History of the United States: The Welfare State, 1929–1985* (Wadlee, AL: American Textbook Committee, 1986), p. 45.

[11] Govan, *Chattanooga Country*, p. 455.

[12] William U. Chandler, *The Myth of TVA: Conservation and Development in the Tennessee Valley, 1933–1983* (Cambridge, MA: Ballinger [Harper & Row], 1984), p. 16, 80.

[13] *Tennessee Encyclopedia of History & Culture*, p. 961.

[14] "Veteran Official Says City Moving Too Slowly," *Chattanooga News-Free Press*, June 6, 1987.

[15] All quotes unless otherwise indicated from author's taped interview with Pete Cooper, July 2005.

[16] "Bridging the Past," *Atlanta Journal-Constitution*, April 25, 1993; "Walnut Bridge Begins 2nd Life," by John Shearer, *Chattanooga News-Free Press*, May 5, 1993.

[17] "Chattanooga Has a New, Blue Friend," *Chattanooga News-Free Press*, May 1, 1994; "Bridge Chronology," *Chattanooga News-Free Press*, April 25, 1993; Gallagher quote from *Chattanooga Times*, May 3, 1993; "Historical Overview" and "In Gratitude" in program leaflet for opening ceremonies program, Walnut Street Bridge Clipping File, Local History Department, Chattanooga–Hamilton County Bicentennial Library.

[18] "Cotton Ball queen's dream comes true," by Karen Nazor Hill, *Chattanooga Times Free Press*, July 30, 2005.

[19] "Bill Ford sincerely impressed by city," by David Magee, *Chattanooga Times Free Press*, B1, July 27, 2005.

[20] John Wilson, *The Kruesi–Smartt Legacy* (Adams Lithographic Company, Chattanooga, 1996), p. 9.

[21] "Local Manufacturers Warn Other Industries of Globalism," *Chattanooga Fax*, May 3, 2004.

[22] *Chattanooga Fax*, ibid.

[23] Mark Curriden and Leroy Phillips, Jr. tell the unprecedented story of Ed Johnson in their nationally acclaimed title *Contempt of Court: The Turn-of-the-Century Lynching that Launched 100 Years of Federalism* (New York: Faber & Faber, 1999).

[24] "Bridging the Past," *Atlanta Journal-Constitution*, April 25, 1993.

[25] Phillips, *Brainerd Journal*, p. 355–356.

[26] "Reconciliation service Friday will honor American Indians," *Chattanooga Times Free Press*, F4, May 17, 2003.

[27] "Indians give warrior status to city mayor," *Belfast Telegraph*, Nov. 11, 2004.

[28] "Irish, Cherokee work to build cultural ties through song, dance," *Asheville Citizen-Times* (NC), Jan. 25, 2005.

[29] Typed statement by Daphne Swilling. Author's papers.

[30] This is a first-hand account. The author attended the event.

[31] Patrick J. Buchanan, *The Death of the West: How Dying Populations and Immigration Invasions Imperil our Country and Civilization* (New York: St. Martin's Press, 2002), p. 136.

[32] Transcribed interview at Maclellan Foundation, Chattanooga, July, 2005.

[33] "Immigrant amnesty not likely, experts say," *Chattanooga Times Free Press*, Jan. 6, 2002; "East Ridge handles influx of immigrants," *Chattanooga Times Free Press*, (date?); "Hispanics are largest minority in the U.S." *Chattanooga Times Free Press*, Jan. 22, 2003; "Keeping the Faith," *Chattanooga Times Free Press*, July 22, 2003.

INDEX OF NAMES

M

ABOUT THE AUTHOR

STUDY of DEAN ARNOLD WRITING OLD MONEY/NEW SOUTH

Dean W. Arnold is a journalist and publisher in Chattanooga, Tennessee, and the author of *America's Trail of Tears: A Story of Love and Betrayal.*

He graduated from Covenant College on Lookout Mountain with an emphasis in history and philosophy but has learned a good bit of late from John Chrysostom.

His avocations include jazz, genealogy, golf, and good cigars.

Arnold is a fifth-generation Californian on both sides. His great-grandfather Dr. Perceval T. Gerson practiced in a small suburb called Hollywood at the turn of the century. After watching several stages built and torn down for outdoor dramas, he called together the town's leaders to build a permanent amphitheater—the Hollywood Bowl.

Arnold's 7th great-grandfather, Stephen Arnold, settled the furthest edge of the frontier in southwest Virginia just before Thomas Jefferson bought the Natural Bridge property next door.

Contact the author at dean@deanarnold.org

ABOUT THE ARTISTS

Gordon Wetmore (Chapter 1, 8) is one of the country's leading portrait artists, has produced bestselling large-format artbooks, and for eight years has been chairman of the Portrait Society of America, the nation's largest.

gordonwetmore.com

Cessna Decosimo (Chapter 2) is one of the nation's top sculptors and an alumnus of the Florence Academy of Art.

cessna.coptix.com

Brent Sanders (Chapter 3, 9, 12) is a self-taught acrylic and ink artist now in great demand as Chattanooga's most celebrated painter of local landscapes and icons

brentsanders.com

Andrew Wilkie (Chapter 4,6,10) is a traveling caricature artist in Minneapolis, Chattanooga, San Francisco, New Orleans, and Universal Studios. He enjoys various artistic mediums and entertains as a street character, puppeteer, acro-balancer, and guy playing with fire.

andrewlandstudios.com

Shaun LaRose (Chapter 5) is an accomplished muralist with commissions in Minneapolis, Houston, Austin, and locally at Covenant College and Greyfriar's Coffee Shop.
shaun.larose@gmail.com

Tabitha Arnold, age ten, was nine when she drew her picture for Chapter 11. She won first place in an art contest this year for the *Lookout Mountain Post*. Her favorite subject to draw is horses. She is also an aspiring writer.
tabitha.deanarnold.org

Justin Cox (Chapter 7) is an up and coming artist with eclectic interests in painting, cartooning, graffiti-inspired sketching, poetry, and modern writing.
librason73@yahoo.com

487

ORDER FORM

www.OldMoneyNewSouth.com

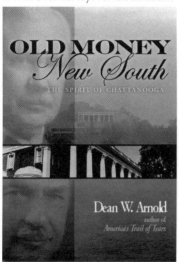

$24.95

www.TrailofTearsBook.com

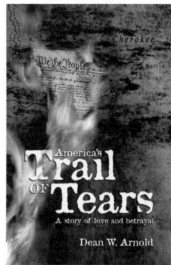

$19.95

• •

Please send me

_____ Copies of "Old Money, New South" ($24.95 each)

_____ Copies of "America's Trail of Tears" ($19.95 each)

*** Add $3 shipping to any size order***

Make check payable to Chattanooga Historical Foundation and send to:

Chattanooga Historical Foundation
P.O. Box 2053
Chattanooga, TN 37409

Orders can also be placed online through:
www.OldMoneyNewSouth.com
www.TrailofTearsBook.com

For more information, or to inquire about large orders:
info@historyofchattanooga.com
phone: 423-595-3621

To contact the author: dean@deanarnold.org